To Nancy,

With best wishes,
Glenn Altschuler

Isaac Kramnick

CORNELL

We have not invited you to see a university finished, but to see one begun.

Ezra Cornell

CORNELL

A History, 1940–2015

GLENN C. ALTSCHULER AND ISAAC KRAMNICK

Cornell University Press   ITHACA AND LONDON

First published 2014 by Cornell University Press

Printed in the United States of America

Library of Congress Cataloging-in-Publication Data

Altschuler, Glenn C., author.
   Cornell : a history, 1940–2015 / Glenn C. Altschuler and Isaac Kramnick.
      pages cm
   Includes bibliographical references and index.
   ISBN 978-0-8014-4425-8 (cloth : alk. paper)
   1. Cornell University—History.   I. Kramnick, Isaac, author.   II. Title.
   LD1370.A57 2014
   379.747'71—dc23   2014018297

Cornell University Press strives to use environmentally responsible suppliers and materials to the fullest extent possible in the publishing of its books. Such materials include vegetable-based, low-VOC inks and acid-free papers that are recycled, totally chlorine-free, or partly composed of nonwood fibers. For further information, visit our website at www.cornellpress.cornell.edu.

Cloth printing   10 9 8 7 6 5 4 3 2 1

*To our families,
extended and ceremonial*

Contents

Preface:
The "Cornell Idea"

Institutions, like individuals, develop narratives about themselves. Cornell constructed its sense of self, its sense of how it was special and different, in the middle twentieth century, on the eve of World War II, when America defended democratic freedom from fascist dictatorship. Cornell's fifth president, Edmund Ezra Day, and Carl Becker, its preeminent historian, discerned what they called a Cornell "soul," a Cornell "character," a Cornell "personality," a Cornell "tradition"—and they called it "freedom."

"From its beginnings," President Day declared on April 27, 1940, at Cornell's celebration of the seventy-fifth anniversary of its founding charter, "the special quality of the tradition of freedom . . . has always prevailed upon its campus."[1] Other universities encouraged free inquiry, but Cornell's historical traditions, Day insisted, and its daily practices, embodied rebelliousness and liberation. Among America's great universities, Cornell alone, Day told the celebrants, could claim to embody the spirit of freedom, which was the legacy of Andrew Dickson White, its first president, who had "released the forces that transformed higher education in this country. It was he who made men see the narrow restriction of the old academic schooling with its concentration on the classics and mathematics. It was he who pointed out the hampering effects of once sacred collegiate customs. It was he, in short, who brought into the field a totally unprecedented freedom of action."[2] Professor Becker followed the president to the podium and agreed that "Cornell has a character, a corporate personality, an intellectual tradition by which it can be identified. The word which best symbolizes that tradition is freedom," he concluded.[3] A plain-speaking midwesterner, and a universally esteemed scholar and stylist, Becker praised his university as characteristically "impudent," "a little wild at times," and "a rebel against convention." Like Day, Becker saw Andrew Dickson White as the source of Cornell's rebelliousness: "Mr. White wished to found a center of learning where mature scholars and men of the world, emancipated from the clerical tradition and inspired by the scientific idea could pursue their studies uninhibited by the cluttered routine of the petty preoccupations of the conventional cloistered academic life."[4]

In this seventy-fifth anniversary talk—which would itself become a Cornell tradition, recommended as reading to generations of undergraduates, alumni, and newly hired professors—Becker imagined what he named "The Cornell Tradition: Freedom and Responsibility." He linked Cornell's unique historic vision—and version—of collegiate freedom to the worldwide struggle in 1940 between liberty and dictatorship, in which the United States, to Becker's regret, still sat on the sidelines. Cornell's glorious trademark, its emancipatory and uninhibited character, its rational and humane ideals, its embrace of the freedom of learning and teaching, embodied the values of Western democracies, Becker argued, in stark contrast to the fascists who worshipped naked, brute force, and believed, as he put it, that "might makes right, that justice is the interest of the stronger." This historic confrontation between "half the world now controlled by self-inspired autocratic leaders" and "the champions of freedom," Becker suggested, had guided him in his search for "the historic personality" of Cornell. This great war of values "makes it seem to me appropriate, on this memorial occasion, to recall the salient qualities which have given Cornell University its peculiar character and its high distinction."[5]

Cornell's sense of itself as a feisty unconventional champion of freedom would be codified some years later by Morris Bishop, '13, PhD '26, professor of Romance studies, limerick writer, and university marshal, whose magisterial book, *Cornell: A History,* has amused and instructed generations of Cornellians. Bishop's Cornell is the *enfant terrible* of academia, always rebellious, courageous, and innovative. What he imagines as the "Cornell Idea" welcomes nay-saying skeptics to the university; "many of its guiding principles were negative," he recounts, with Cornell rejecting many of the dominant assumptions and practices of nineteenth- and twentieth-century university educators. Ezra Cornell and Andrew Dickson White founded an institution, Bishop wrote, that "thumbed its nose at old-fashioned required curricula and the recitation system, against the hierarchy of studies, against clerical domination, against theological and social obstructionism, against imposed discipline, against social distinctions based on wealth."[6]

Bishop added the second crucial part of Cornell's narrative about itself, about what makes it special—its egalitarianism. At Cornell University, he wrote, students of all races, women and men, were welcome from its founding. Cornell was a "people's university," he quotes President Jacob Gould Schurman announcing in 1888, open to all talented and industrious young adults, as it realized Ezra Cornell's vision of a college "where any person could find instruction in any study." Bishop describes nineteenth-century Cornell as "a non-pretentious college, enrolling ambitious and talented students from poor families, as well as the children of the privileged."[7] Cornell was defiantly non-sectarian, free from creedal connections, shrugging off early attacks on it as a "godless university," and deftly deflecting the efforts of trustee Henry Sage to "make it a Christian university."[8]

In its early history, according to Bishop, Cornell celebrated an equality among disciplines, with no hierarchy of subjects of study. The practical "mechanical" arts were valued as highly as the "liberal" arts; agriculture and engineering were as prestigious as classics and economics. Early Cornellians wore as a badge of pride the mockery heaped upon them by the English nineteenth-century writer and cultural arbiter Matthew Arnold, who wrote in his influential *Culture and Anarchy*: "The university of Mr. Cornell, a really noble monument of his munificence, yet seems to rest on a misconception of what culture truly is, and to be calculated to produce miners, or engineers, or architects, not sweetness and light."[9] Cornell's egalitarian response to Arnold was articulated by President Schurman, who wrote: "The analysis of soils is as important as the analysis of literature."[10] And it breathes through Cornell's persistent self-image as the Ivy League school with a Big Ten soul.

In Morris Bishop's rendition of freedom as what he called the "Cornell Idea," even the everyday practices of academic life revealed Cornell as the radical pioneer of educational freedom. Cornell, he notes, introduced electives into American universities. The "Cornell Idea" had students choosing their own classes, not following a prescribed curriculum, and often attending classes voluntarily. Inevitably, some aspects of this freedom would disappear over the years or vary by college, but the principle of free choice would persist. The life of male students at Cornell was relatively unregimented, as well. No dean of students appeared until 1929. Men could live where they chose, in town, in fraternities, or in university dorms. Women students were much less free. They had to live in college dorms, under the watchful eyes of house matrons. On this issue, Henry Sage had put his foot down, vetoing the more liberal suggestions of Andrew Dickson White.

Faculty, too, experienced a headier, livelier freedom at Cornell than elsewhere. The president, deans, and chairs of departments had little authority over them. In his 1940 speech, Becker compared his life as a professor at Cornell since 1917 with his previous teaching positions at the University of Kansas and Penn State. The dean of Cornell's College of Arts and Sciences, he had discovered, "was scarcely more than a bookkeeper." There were not many rules or regulations, and those that were enforced were not "very oppressive." No one, "no authority," decided what subjects a faculty member would teach. To Becker's surprise and delight, Cornell fostered "a refreshing sense of liberation from the prescribed and insistent." It was "an easy going, loose-jointed institution."[11] And since 1916, the faculty even sent three of its own to Cornell's board of trustees, a first in American higher education.

That freedom, of course, shaped another part of Cornell's enduring sense of self: "responsibility." As Becker realized that he alone "had to decide what was right and worthwhile" to do as a professor, he began to feel bound, not to directives from superiors, but "bound by some inner sense of responsibility" and an "elemental sense of decency and fair play." Becker felt connected in a moral yet very practical way to students and fellow faculty members, to the dean, to the president, to the trustees, even though they had imposed no obligations on him, or ever "employed the imperative mood." Indeed, because they didn't, or couldn't, constrain him, Becker felt "bound to justify myself by doing . . . the best I was capable of doing." Becker then named what would become the definitive Cornell self-understanding: "The Cornell tradition which allows a maximum of freedom and relies so confidently upon the sense of personal responsibility for making a good use of it."[12] Nor should it be forgotten that Becker ended his remarks with a clarion call to Cornell's responsibility—and America's—to preserve freedom and the democratic way of life against the dictatorial regimes that threatened their most precious values.

As Becker acknowledged, Cornell's sense of its "responsibility" alongside its prized "freedom" was part of the founders' legacy, as well. Ezra Cornell had insisted on the university's responsibility to train the industrious poor and instill in them a work ethic by requiring all students to do some form of manual labor, mechanical or agricultural. The university also recognized its land grant responsibilities to the citizens of New York State, setting aside each year scholarships from every legislative district and then developing outreach extension programs in every county. A sense of responsibility to the nation was enshrined in Cornell's commitment to military drill for male students, as required by the Morrill Land Grant Act.

Ezra Cornell's most enduring legacy was his Quaker-based insistence on the university's obligation to produce "useful" graduates, educated men and women who would serve others by improving and ameliorating the human condition. This essential, elemental Cornell quality, responsibility, was in 1898 inscribed on the Eddy Street gate:

> So enter that daily thou mayest become more learned
> And thoughtful
> So depart that daily thou mayest become more useful
> To thy country and to mankind.

The "Cornell Idea," as Day, Becker, and Bishop would name it, would be tested and contested in Cornell's second seventy-five years. Cornellians would use the ideals of freedom and responsibility as weapons for change—and justifications for retaining the status quo. To protect academic freedom—and to rein in radical professors. To end *in loco parentis* and parietal rules, to preempt panty raids, pornography, and pot parties, and to reintroduce regulations to protect and promote the physical and emotional well-being of students. To add nano-fabrication, entrepreneurship, and genomics to the curriculum—and to require language courses, freshmen writing, and physical education. In the name of freedom (and responsibility), black students would occupy Willard Straight Hall, the anti–Vietnam War SDS would take over the Engineering Library, proponents of divestment from South Africa would build campus shantytowns, and Latinos would seize Day Hall. In the name of responsibility (and freedom), the university would reclaim them.

The history of Cornell since World War II, we believe, is in large part a set of variations on the narrative of "freedom," the removal of restriction and regulation, and its partner, "responsibility," the obligation to others and to one's self to do what is right and useful, with a principled commitment to the Cornell community—and to the world outside the Eddy Street gate.

Acknowledgments

We are grateful for the assistance of many Cornellians. Elaine Engst, university archivist, guided us through the massive Presidential Papers. Robert Barker, director of university photography, Laura Linke '73 (Arts and Sciences), '80 (Human Ecology), senior reference specialist at Rare Books and Manuscript Collections, and Don Lebow, graphic designer for the School of Continuing Education and Summer Sessions, helped us identify the illustrations that appear in this book. Eisha Neely, reproductions, permissions, and exhibitions coordinator at Rare and Manuscript Collections, was masterly in managing the transfer of those photos to the finished book. The editors of the *Cornell Daily Sun* allowed us to keep bound volumes of the newspaper in our offices as we completed our research. Jim Roberts, editor and publisher of the *Cornell Alumni Magazine*, tracked down articles and "tidbits" of information we had overlooked. Former vice president Tommy Bruce and several colleagues in University Communications, especially Claudia Wheatley, assisted us in searches through the *Cornell Chronicle*. J. Robert Cooke, emeritus professor of Engineering and former dean of the faculty, has spent an enormous amount of his time, energy, and resources digitizing documents about Cornell's history, including memorial statements for deceased faculty and minutes of university faculty meetings. We are among many Cornellians who are in his debt. Our friend Keith Johnson '56 shared his immense knowledge of the history of Cornell with us and provided encouragement just when we needed it. John Ackerman, the former director of Cornell University Press, has been unfailingly patient, persistent, and professional. We are grateful as well to Ange Romeo-Hall, who went well beyond her responsibilities as managing editor of Cornell University Press to copyedit our manuscript. Michael Busch, executive staff assistant, Office of the Vice Provost, was once again indispensably helpful.

ACKNOWLEDGMENTS

Several talented Cornell undergraduates helped us identify relevant articles in the *Cornell Daily Sun*, the *Cornell Chronicle*, and the *Cornell Alumni Magazine*. Our thanks to Nicole Antonuccio '11, David Gura '06, Steven Jacob Lewis '09, Lindsey MacKay '06, Cam Marchant '06, Michael Sharp '00, and Rebecca Weiss '09. And a special shout-out to Brandon Schumacher '11 and Jonathan Jaffe '15. No expression of gratitude seems adequate to the contributions to this book made by Beth Beach, assistant to the deans, School of Continuing Education and Summer Sessions. Beth prepared the manuscript, made revisions, deciphered difficult-to-read handwriting, checked dates of graduation for individuals referred to in the text, searched the web for shards of information that one of us needed "right away," and made more revisions. She did it all, almost every workday for years, along with many other assignments, with an awe-inspiring speed, competence, and good grace.

Authors' Note

The history of Cornell since World War II is divided into four parts, organized around its presidents: Edmund Ezra Day and Deane Waldo Malott from 1945 to 1963; James Perkins and Dale Corson from 1963 to 1977; Frank H.T. Rhodes from 1977 to 1995; and Hunter R. Rawlings III, Jeffrey S. Lehman, and David J. Skorton from 1995 to 2015. The three chapters in each of the four parts trace, in turn, academic and bureaucratic developments in the undergraduate colleges, the professional schools, and the central administration; student life; and Cornell's relationship with the world outside the campus in that era. Although this approach may occasionally violate the overarching chronology of those years, it allows us to provide more coherent narratives focused on specific themes and to examine the emergence of Cornell as a modern American research university, with myriad components, ranging from "big science" to the professionalization of fund-raising. We have not included here a history of the Medical College, by this period removed from Stimson Hall and located entirely in New York City. It deserves its own history.

Our writing has been truly collaborative. While one of us took the lead in drafting various chapters, the other vigorously revised. We used as our principal sources the *Cornell Daily Sun*, the *Cornell Alumni News*, the *Cornell Chronicle*, the *Ithaca Journal*, the *Proceedings of the Board of Trustees*, the minutes of meetings of the university faculty, and, most important, the papers of Cornell's presidents, from Day to Rawlings. Jeffrey Lehman and David Skorton have not yet given their papers to the Cornell Library. We have supplied the year of graduation for every individual referred to in the book who completed a degree at Cornell (the first time he or she is mentioned in each chapter). Finally, to avoid clutter, we have restricted our footnotes to direct quotations.

PART I
1945–1963

1 | Building a Research University

The news of Japan's surrender August 14, 1945, burst from loudspeakers and swept over Cornell students assembled in front of Willard Straight Hall, who answered the announcement, which effectively signaled the end of World War II, with vigorous chants: "We want liberty!"[1] The university had itself made an extraordinary contribution to the war effort: 4,500 of its undergraduates had left campus for the armed services; 3,758 army and 13,577 navy personnel, and 30,144 workers in twenty-three New York State industrial centers, received training in various Cornell programs, and the university was remunerated $10.6 million for training and research from the United States government. A substantial number of professors did war-related research on campus even as scores of others left Ithaca to do war work in this country and around the world. In important and intangible ways, Cornell would be forever reshaped and redefined by World War II.

At the end of the war, Cornell confronted a changed world with profound implications for its physical campus, its culture, academic and student affairs, and the university's engagement with American political, economic, and social life. In the 1930s, research had played a relatively minor role at Cornell and other American universities. Publication was often not a requirement for tenure. Faculty members who did conduct research, including those in the sciences, relied almost entirely on financial support from corporations and foundations. At the end of the decade, the federal government allocated less than $100 million to all universities for research and development, most of it directed at agriculture and public health. During World War II, however, Washington enlisted academics to work on radar, atomic bombs, and other weapons, and after the war, the Cold War generated substantial increases in federal funding, distributed by the Department of Defense and the National Science Foundation, often for research related to "national security." Committed, as well, to eradicating diseases, the federal government established the

3

National Institutes of Health in 1947. In 1954, the NIH disbursed $74 million for research; by 2010, its budget had risen to more than $30 billion. By the twenty-first century, through these agencies and others, the federal government supplied almost 60 percent of the support for research at universities.

Cornell would become a premiere "research university," an institution that privileged research over teaching, research "sponsored" principally by the state and federal governments, foundations, and private corporations. This transformation, which had implications for all academic disciplines, would occur under the leadership of two presidents, Edmund Ezra Day and Deane Waldo Malott.

In an era when presidents still administered the internal affairs of the university and occasionally claimed the mantle of national spokesman for intellectual and cultural life, the new Cornell was being shaped by two leaders whose characters mirrored in many ways those of Cornell's legendary founders, Andrew Dickson White and Ezra Cornell, the one the scholar, the other the businessman. When Day became Cornell's fifth president in 1937, he had been an academic for over three decades. A Phi Beta Kappa graduate from Dartmouth in 1905, he received a PhD in economics from Harvard in 1909. After teaching economics, first at Dartmouth, then Harvard, where he became chair of the department, Day moved in 1923 to the University of Michigan to become dean of the business school and subsequently dean of the university. He left Michigan for the Rockefeller Foundation, where until 1936 he directed its activities in the social sciences, while also serving as director of the National Bureau of Economic Research.

The author of four books, and holder of fifteen honorary degrees, Day brought to Cornell a deep commitment to linking academic excellence to public service, the sense of responsibility that Carl Becker paired with rights and freedom. Most of the new programs and colleges established at Cornell during his years, Nutrition, Industrial and Labor Relations, Business and Public Administration, even Nuclear Studies, were principally schools of public service. During his tenure, Day pressed the need for heightened social consciousness throughout the university, as he had in his president's inaugural address in 1937: "The time has passed when it can be assumed that social well-being will flow automatically from self-interested individual enterprise. If democratic institutions are to be preserved and individual liberty remain our proud possession, the citizen must recognize his obligation to make his life add to the commonweal."[2]

So, too, after the war, Day called on Cornell to demonstrate "the ways of democracy in a combination of individual and collective freedom and responsibility; it stands for strengthening the forces of good will among men, makes a constant effort to establish and maintain common justice among men."[3]

Day was a Socratic gadfly, who, according to his friend Morris Bishop '13, MA '14, PhD '26, "liked to shock, unsettle and disturb. He disliked complacency

Edmund Ezra Day, president of
Cornell from 1937 to 1949.
(Division of Rare and Manuscript
Collections of the Cornell University
Library)

and satisfaction with routine."[4] Day could be sharp, abrupt, and even tactless with
those he considered fuzzy thinkers. He enjoyed confronting faculty with provocative questions. Although he made it a priority to restore the humanities to its
"proper importance" after the war, he still challenged an English professor with,
"What are you trying to do? What are the educational outcomes of studying literature?"[5] He delighted in moving faculty to think about the purposes and aims
of their calling.

Toward the end of his presidency, Day articulated what he took to be the
unique and distinguishing characteristics of Cornell. There was Cornell's extraordinary physical setting, its diverse student body, "a cross section of American life," and its unusual combination of public and private support. Finally,
there was its most significant attribute, "the spirit of educational adventure,
which at its founding was the first revolt from the accustomed ways of higher
education in America and whose innovations have swept the field and become
traditional."[6]

Many members of the faculty respected Day's seriousness and fairness, his
zeal for social betterment, and his devotion to Cornell. They were impressed
when he turned down a request in 1946 from the State and War Departments
to head the program of reeducation in postwar Germany, a position subsequently accepted by Harvard's president, James Bryant Conant. Robert Cushman, a professor of government, remembered at Day's retirement the president's

courage in the face of claims that Cornell leaned too far left. "With tact and good temper, but with force and tenacity, he defended the principle of freedom of thought and freedom of speech on the campus and elsewhere," Cushman wrote.[7] Day's provost, the historian Cornelis de Kiewiet, wrote that Day "is looked upon as one of the half dozen foremost college presidents in the United States, whose influence upon national educational statesmanship has been profound."[8]

Suffering from heart troubles, Day retired at the end of June 1949. The board of trustees appointed him to be the university's first-ever chancellor, with responsibilities for fund-raising, relations with New York State, and activities of the medical school. Provost de Kiewiet was appointed acting president, while a search for a new president was mounted. Eight and a half months later, Day died at the age of sixty-eight.

A historian, born in the Netherlands and educated in South Africa, who had served as dean of Arts and Sciences before becoming provost, de Kiewiet expected the board of trustees to offer him the presidency. In fact, members of the board had another candidate in mind—their chairman, Arthur Dean. Raised in Ithaca (his father, William C. Dean, was Cornell's superintendent of steam heating and water service from 1894 to 1910), Dean '19, JD '23, was a senior partner in the prestigious law firm of Sullivan and Cromwell, had been a trustee since 1935, and was one of the few non-industrialists on the board.

In early January 1950, Dean agreed to have his name put forward for final approval, with the understanding that he would assume the presidency in 1951, allowing him ample time to finish an antitrust suit in which he was chief counsel for the United States government. Before he could inform his partners and clients, however, the news of his choice was leaked to the *Ithaca Journal*, and the next day, the headline "Arthur Dean Slated to Head Cornell" appeared in the *New York Times*. Under intense pressure from clients as well as partners, Dean withdrew his name, citing "obligations and commitments which cannot be put asunder."[9]

Once again de Kiewiet assumed the trustees would turn to him, but it was not to be. He was passed over again, perhaps in part because of an arrogant manner and penny-pinching memos complaining of faculty wasting heat and light or ordering too many mimeograph machines. When he learned that the new president was to be Deane Malott, the chancellor of the University of Kansas, de Kiewiet abruptly resigned as acting president in December 1950 to become the president of the University of Rochester. For six months preceding Malott's arrival, Theodore P. Wright, the vice president for research, served as acting president.

The *Cornell Sun* celebrated the selection of a president who was "not a scholar . . . but a CEO of a vast educational institution . . . a businessman."[10] Malott was from

Deane Waldo Malott, president of
Cornell from 1951 to 1963. (Division
of Rare and Manuscript Collections
of the Cornell University Library)

Abilene, Kansas, where his banker father, known as the "dean of Kansas bankers,"
was a friend of the Eisenhowers. He had served in World War I as a navy seaman,
majored in economics at the University of Kansas, and then earned an MBA at
Harvard in 1923. After six years as a faculty member and administrator at the
Harvard Business School, he became a vice president of the Hawaiian (later Dole)
Pineapple Company. An expert on agricultural economics, he returned briefly to
the Harvard Business School before becoming chancellor of his alma mater, the
University of Kansas, in 1939. His business connections, forged at Harvard and
enhanced by memberships on numerous corporate boards, brought him to the
attention of Cornell industrialists on the board of trustees: John Collyer '17 of
B. F. Goodrich, Walter Teagle '99 of Standard Oil, Myron Taylor, JD '94, of U.S.
Steel, Spencer Olin '21 and John Olin '13 of Olin Mathieson Chemical Corporation, Nicholas Noyes '06 of Eli Lilly, Walter Carpenter '10 of DuPont, and Victor
Emmanuel '19, owner of Avco, a manufacturer of agricultural tools and machines.

Malott had been on campus only three months when he became the center of an academic firestorm. Under the heading "Funny Coincidence Dept.,"
the *New Yorker* magazine published side by side three paragraphs of President
Malott's inaugural speech of September 19, 1951, with the almost identical

three paragraphs from an article written by the president of Sarah Lawrence College, Harold Taylor, in the *Harvard Educational Review* in the spring of 1949. After initially declining to respond to inquiries, Malott told the *Sun* on November 30 that the quotes, an application of a line from Ralph Waldo Emerson to issues then dividing traditionalists and innovators on college campuses, had come from "random notes in his speech file, having appeared in some educational handout or filler paragraphs in a weekly paper which was printed with no reference to source or authority. He had never seen Dr. Taylor's speech, so he had no way of crediting Dr. Taylor with the authorship of these particular thoughts, which he would, of course, have gladly done, if he had known the source."[11]

Even though, according to the alumni office, "talk concerning the '*New Yorker* incident' has been negligible," perhaps because "the story broke just prior to the Cornell-Michigan football game," Malott offered his resignation to the board of trustees.[12] It was refused. Malott would guide Cornell for twelve years, retiring in 1963, ten days short of his sixty-fifth birthday. He was one of Cornell's greatest builders. Under his stewardship, Cornell doubled the university budget, trebled the volume of research, and increased the physical plant by more than two-thirds. The university expanded to the east with the new College of Veterinary Medicine buildings, south with the new engineering quad, and north with the purchase of land from the Ithaca Country Club, to be used for dormitories. Malott was delighted that Cornell became a major research university, driven by "big science," but also, presciently, worried that faculty priorities were changing. A year before he retired he reported to the board of trustees that "the professor now has developed a loyalty to his profession through membership in national professorial societies. Likewise in the natural and applied sciences, the faculty member has developed a sort of loyalty to physical facilities in that he has developed a tendency to join that institution having the finest equipment with which to work."[13]

Two principal issues dominated Malott's presidency: navigating Cold War passions on campus, which he did well, and responding to the new undergraduate culture, with students' demands for greater control over their private lives, which he did less well. Malott had a contentious relationship with the faculty, into whose domains he often intruded himself, presiding, for example, at faculty meetings in every college and interviewing nearly every faculty member being considered for tenure. His determination to reject Day's more decentralized management style brought him into conflict with powerful deans. And for most of his presidency, Malott was seriously at odds with Cornell students, whom he felt "evidenced more freedom than responsibility."[14]

Malott was a handsome man, with a direct speaking style, a contagious laugh, and keen sense of humor. He had, as one Cornell professor put it, "a vivid zest for life."[15] A fierce proponent of free enterprise, deeply traditional in his moral and religious views (he read scriptures at Sage Chapel every Sunday he was in town), he boasted in public that he was a conservative Republican.

After his retirement in 1963, Malott continued to live in Ithaca and served on the boards of B. F. Goodrich, Owens-Corning, and General Mills. He was for many years a striking presence at Cornell ceremonial occasions. In 1996, at the age of ninety-eight, he died in Cayuga Heights, close to the university he had so indelibly transformed four decades earlier.

———

"BIG SCIENCE" DEFINED the postwar "research university"—and Cornell was already a major player in 1950 when the *New York Times* anointed it as "one of the major centers of science in the world."[16] But a great research university in the middle of the twentieth century, even one rooted in big science, needed a great research library, and Cornell did not have one. President Day had made the case as early as 1946. "A modern university library," he declared, "becomes more than a book storage plant with study halls attached—it becomes in fact what it should be, namely a place in which the materials for research are made readily and conveniently available under appropriate conditions for their most efficient use by students and research workers at all levels."[17]

When built in 1890, Cornell's library was one of the best, its collection of books ranking fourth largest in the nation. It had 426 seats for a college population of 1,500. In 1949 it had about the same number of seats for a university community of more than 10,000. In 1900 nearly 6 percent of the university budget went to the library; by 1946 only 2 percent did. In 1949 Cornell's expenditures on its library ranked twenty-second ($325,000, compared with $1.2 million at Columbia and Illinois and $1 million at Harvard). The building had eight hundred thousand volumes jammed onto shelves intended to hold one hundred thousand books. Often misshelved, books filled every available corner, wall, and aisle space in the stack area. According to Day, "many are so tightly wedged on the shelves that the bindings are loosened and seriously damaged."[18] The library could not use carts to bring books from the stacks, had no elevator, and no tube system. The *Cornell Sun* picturesquely captured what students thought of their library:

> The Cornell library occupies a curious position in Cornell hearts. Alumni remember the majestic tower and its celestial chimes; undergraduates shudder and think of creaking chairs, missing books, and thudding feet. Alumni fondly remember the ivy which has been creeping up the walls nigh unto sixty years now; most students regard confinements in the structure as torture and will do almost anything not to be forced "to study" in the noble landmark.[19]

President Day centralized the administration of all Cornell's libraries in 1946 by appointing a new director of university libraries, Stephen McCarthy, who had been assistant director of libraries at Columbia. McCarthy became a tireless champion for new facilities. In 1947 he proposed an addition to the central library extending down the library slope, which would provide seats for no fewer than two thousand readers and space for approximately three million volumes. The trustees rejected his plan as too expensive and "an inappropriately large structure for the slope."[20]

Two years later Acting President de Kiewiet appointed an "Ad Hoc Committee on the Building Problem of the University Library," with McCarthy as chair. It proposed the construction of a new library, at a cost of $6.5 million, to be built across from the 1890 library, in a space cleared by razing Boardman Hall. In his opinion, de Kiewiet wrote to John Parke, chair of the trustees' Buildings and Grounds Committee, the "matter of cost is quite academic since $6,500,000 is an inaccessible figure for us anyhow." He had brought McCarthy "closer to realism," he reported, but the director was still "trying to push the University into impossible projects. . . . McCarthy is quite a fellow, and it may be some time before we have him straightened out."[21]

De Kiewiet was soon gone, and President Malott (who shortly after his arrival told the trustees that "if you go into the library . . . you have the impression that you are in an ill-lit, ill-ventilated monkey house") became an avid sponsor of McCarthy's vision, undaunted by the difficulty of fund-raising.[22] Nonetheless, it would still take another ten years for McCarthy's "impossible project" to be built. Part of the problem was the state's construction in the early 1950s of a new library for the College of Agriculture and the College of Home Economics. Planning for this library, named after Alfred R. Mann '04, dean of Agriculture from 1917 to 1931, dean of Home Economics, and first provost of the university, absorbed the time and attention of the university's administrators. The next problem, raising the money, would not be solved until December 1956, when Malott announced at a dinner honoring the 150th anniversary of Ezra Cornell's birth that trustee John M. Olin would give $3 million to fund the library that would ultimately bear his name.

Further delay resulted from the totally unexpected "battle over Boardman Hall," the home of the History and Government Departments, which stood on the projected site of the new library. Led by Frederick Marcham, PhD '26, the Goldwin Smith Professor of English History and university boxing coach, and Gilmore D. Clarke '13, former dean of the College of Architecture, faculty members launched a "Save Boardman" campaign, which for several years successfully resisted razing Boardman, using claims like Marcham's that Boardman Hall was "an academic building as near perfection as one can hope to find . . . the best equipped building on the campus, indeed one of the best in the country for this kind of teaching in the liberal arts."[23]

The professorial troops surrendered in February 1959. Two years later, the seven-story Olin Library, then one of the world's largest library buildings, opened with three stone gargoyle-like heroic heads of men, removed from old

Boardman Hall, the Arts quad building, razed to make way for Olin Library, c. 1950. (Division of Rare and Manuscript Collections of the Cornell University Library)

Boardman, placed along its interior lobby wall, and five others on the outside walls separating the Arts quad from the library. Clarke called the new library "a vulgar modernization"; students, citing its four parallel rows of tall, narrow window openings, dubbed it an "IBM punch card"; but on its opening day, the *Sun* labeled it "one of the three finest college libraries in the United States."[24] Sensitive to the library's significance to the new Cornell, Malott observed, "We have built many other buildings on this campus and we shall build more, but none is or will be so important to the University's capabilities or so descriptive of its character as this one is." Most important, perhaps, the *Sun* reported late that February that "between 7 and 10 p.m. Olin is so crowded students cannot find room to study."[25]

THE WORLD-CLASS LIBRARY added momentum to the transformation of Cornell into a major research university, with financial support from the federal government, private foundations, and business corporations. In 1946, externally funded research at Cornell—"sponsored research," in "university speak"—was $4.5 million. When Day resigned in 1949 it was $9 million. Ten years later, the total reached $39.4 million.

An important architect of this transformation was Theodore Wright, who spent twenty years at the Curtiss-Wright Corporation and served as head of the Civil Aeronautics Administration before coming to Cornell as a professor of engineering in 1948. He served for the next twelve years as Cornell's first-ever vice president for research, also filling in for six months in 1951 as acting president of the university. When he retired in 1960, he had presided over a more than fourfold increase of sponsored research, which ranged from livestock-insect control to nuclear energy projects. By 1952, Wright calculated that research funds accounted for 26 percent of the budget in endowed schools, 42 percent in state schools, and 52 percent at the medical school. Underwriting much of this was Washington, the source of more than 75 percent of all Cornell research.

The doors were wide open between the university and the federal government, with ideas and money flowing back and forth. In 1945, in testimony before the Senate Military Subcommittee, President Day called for the creation of a National Research Foundation and asked that 30 percent of its funds be allocated to state land grant institutions. Several years later he served as chairman of the Committee for a National Science Foundation, which was created by Congress in 1950.

At the same time, the Office of Naval Research asked universities, including Cornell, to identify research "suitable for support." Of the twenty-eight projects submitted by Cornell faculty in 1946, ranging from basic research on jet propulsion to methods of teaching spatial perception to the blind, twelve were supported. Cornell's only obligation, in what was described as a "new departure for the Navy," was "to report from time to time."[26] No wonder, then, that in this period Cornell would hire a half-time lobbyist in Washington.

To find "points of energy, never previously located or known to exist," Cornell astronomers used a grant from the Office of Naval Research to set up a large radar antenna in a converted pasture near campus.[27] And a group of Cornell oceanographers under contract with the Office of Naval Research studied the circulation of coastal waters off New Jersey, New York, Connecticut, and Rhode Island. Equally generous to Cornell was the National Science Foundation. An NSF grant of $50,000 in 1957 for a Cornell computing center brought Cornell out of the punch-card era into the modern electronic digital computer age. That same year six Cornell faculty received nearly $200,000 for polymer research.

But nothing came near the sums that flowed to Cornell from the Defense Department, especially after the spectacular Soviet *Sputnik* exploration of 1957. In 1959, the Advanced Projects Agency of the Department of Defense paid Cornell $4.5 million to build a giant radar observatory in Puerto Rico with an antenna one thousand feet in diameter, with Professor Thomas Gold as director of the new Radiophysics and Space Research Center. The same Defense Department agency gave Cornell $6.1 million for a Materials Research Center, to house a laboratory for atomic and solid-state physics research on nuclear reactors, rocket engines, and transistors. Cornell used the bulk of the money to construct a Physical and Material Science Center between

Rockefeller Hall and Baker Laboratory. Completed in 1964, Clark Hall, named after W. Van Alan Clark '09, whose wife's family founded Avon products, became the largest building on campus, covering almost two acres, with more floor area than the Olin Library.

Although its grants tended to be much smaller, the National Defense Education Act, passed by Congress in 1958 to help colleges increase offerings in mathematics, science, and foreign languages, was another funding source to grow out of the post-Sputnik Cold War anxiety. Cornell got its fair share of the $1 billion set aside by Congress during the act's initial four years and in the decades that followed its renewal, especially in support of Cornell's foreign language instruction.

The major government grants to Cornell in space science, physics, and engineering physics highlight the centrality of physics in the creation of Cornell, the research university. Here, too, the federal government played a crucial role with a $500,000 research contract from the navy in 1947, leading to the creation of a Laboratory of Nuclear Studies at Cornell and a bit later to the construction of a synchrotron to investigate the atomic nucleus and nuclear forces. The navy chose Cornell because of the unusually talented set of young professors teaching physics there, led by Hans Bethe.

Bethe had begun to teach at Cornell in 1935. Born in Strasbourg in 1906, he fled Germany after the Nazis removed him from his academic position because he had two Jewish grandparents. At Cornell, Bethe carried out the groundbreaking work on the theory of energy production in stars that would earn him the Nobel Prize in Physics in 1967. During the war, as chief of the Los Alamos National Laboratory's Theoretical Division, he helped develop the first atomic bomb. After the war Bethe brought a cohort of outstanding young physicists—Richard Feynman, Robert Wilson, Lloyd Smith (PhD '30), Philip Morrison, and Dale Corson—from Los Alamos to Cornell to do cutting-edge work in high-energy elementary particle physics. During the Cold War, Bethe took public stands against nuclear proliferation and for nuclear disarmament, urging President Kennedy to sign the Limited Test Ban Treaty in 1963. Although he retired in 1975, Bethe wrote seminal scientific papers well into his nineties, nearly to 2005, when he died.

In 1946, Bethe was offered a position at Berkeley to replace J. Robert Oppenheimer. Cornell matched Berkeley's offer, raising Bethe's salary to $12,000 (plus $3,000 for a research associate) after Vannevar Bush, the architect of Washington's postwar partnership between science and government, told President Day that "the departure of Bethe would be a real loss."[28]

Bethe decided to remain at Cornell—but only after Day made a commitment to nuclear studies. Day had told the trustees that in order to retain physics faculty engaged in "important work connected with the development of the atomic bomb," many of whom were being tempted by offers from industry and

The Physics professor and Nobel Laureate Hans Bethe and professor Boyce McDaniel bicycling in the Cornell Synchrotron, 1968. (Division of Rare and Manuscript Collections of the Cornell University Library)

other educational institutions, Cornell needed between $1.5 and $2 million to build facilities and purchase scientific equipment. Day would describe the decision to raise "special funds" for nuclear studies as "perhaps the most momentous decision made in the University during my term of administration."[29]

> We had to accept one of two alternatives. If we did not create a laboratory of Nuclear Studies, we would lose most of our key physicists, jeopardize not only our position of leadership in the physical sciences but also, in consequence, the strength of our programs in engineering and other areas of applied science. If we did not create such a laboratory without first securing special funds for the purpose [above current budget allocations] we ran the risk of throwing our academic structure out of balance and so weakening the entire University. The Trustees, with great courage, adopted the latter course.[30]

Private foundations also helped underwrite Cornell's new research orientation, and not just in the natural sciences. Cornell was already renowned for its wartime officer-training program for foreign languages, using intensive, high-pressure immersion in speaking and conversation through drills with native speakers. Offering a grant of $125,000 in 1945 to create a Department of

Modern Languages, the Rockefeller Foundation played a crucial role in making the university a world-class center for language instruction and area studies.

The Rockefeller Foundation saw language instruction as the centerpiece of creating "language area programs" where mastery of a language would lead to historical and cultural study of a particular geographical area. Rockefeller wanted Cornell to focus on China studies, so in November 1945, President Day sent cablegrams to the historian Knight Biggerstaff and the anthropologist R. Lauriston Sharp, both of whom were still involved with war work in China: "Your advice and cooperation indispensable. Your leadership needed. Can you hasten return."[31] They did, and Biggerstaff became head of the Far Eastern Studies Department, where students, including State Department officers, took courses in colloquial Chinese from Charles Hockett, coauthor of the Army Manual of Spoken Chinese, and in contemporary China and the Far East from Biggerstaff and Sharp.

The Rockefeller Foundation also helped make Cornell the world center for Southeast Asian Studies. The foundation's director, Charles Fahs, wrote to Acting President de Kiewiet in August 1950, suggesting that, since the center at Yale was "inadequate to meet national needs," Cornell should consider "refocusing your oriental interests on Southeast Asian Studies." A month later Biggerstaff and Sharp submitted a laundry list memo of resources such a center would need and concluded by invoking Cold War imperatives: "Today our government and international agencies are trying to keep the region from falling under Russian control; yet we do not know enough about the region to formulate policy intelligently. Our Southeast Asia Program at Cornell is and would continue to be directed toward securing the information that is necessary for intelligent formulation of policy."[32] In January 1951 the Rockefeller Foundation gave Cornell's Southeast Asia Program $325,000 and in December 1954 another $500,000.

. The architect of Cornell's preeminence in Southeast Asia studies was George McTurnan Kahin, who arrived to direct the program in July 1951. An expert on Indonesia, who had grown up in Seattle, Kahin had graduated from Harvard, received his PhD from Johns Hopkins, and would spend his entire career at Cornell, mentoring most of the world's Southeast Asia specialists. Like Bethe, Kahin became a political activist during the Cold War. An advocate of a more progressive American posture to the newly independent nations of Asia and a vocal critic of the Indonesian dictator Sukarno, Kahin became a victim of McCarthyite Washington. The State Department deprived him of his passport, but President Malott and the Rockefeller Foundation continued to support him. In May 1965 Kahin would lead one of America's first "teach ins" against the Vietnam War.

Using the Rockefeller Foundation's "area approach," Kahin's SEA Program cut across disciplinary boundaries, training specialists in the region's economics, government, history, anthropology, and culture, and made extensive use of Cornell's Wason Collection of research materials on the Far East. The program also had a research center in Bangkok, Thailand, where Cornell had strong links. More Thai had attended Cornell than any other American college or university. The program's graduates became leading academic and governmental specialists on Southeast Asia, just as Cornell became the place where U.S. Foreign Service officers and personnel from other government agencies came to learn about the region's languages, politics, cultures, and economics. But it was not just Asia. Cornell's new research agenda was global. In 1961, the university created a Center for International Studies, with Mario Einaudi, Cornell professor of government and the son of a recent president of Italy, as its first director.

The Ford Foundation got into the act as well, providing $300,000 for a Social Science Research Center at Cornell, which would have the sociologist Robin Williams at its head. Ford would also be the principal patron of the revitalization and relocation of the Engineering College in the late 1950s. Yet another beneficiary of foundation support was the Graduate School of Business and Public Administration, which in 1957 received a grant of $750,000 from the Alfred P. Sloan Foundation to develop a research and teaching program in hospital administration.

Wright was an advocate of corporate research sponsorships as well, the third leg in financing the research university. He worked hard to raise more money from corporations than the 7 percent of its total research funds that Cornell received from them in the early 1950s. Wright was proud that much of the university's research for the Defense Department was being done at the Cornell Aeronautical Laboratory in Buffalo; the laboratory had been a gift to the university at the end of the war from Wright's former employer, the Curtiss-Wright Corporation, and in the middle 1950s it did an annual volume of around $12 million in research. Acknowledging that federal and state government–funded research at Cornell "has not led to government control," Wright nevertheless hoped "for corporate support to prevent too much government encroachment." The "free enterprise system depends on universities," he told a group of alumni businessmen, insisting that their increased sponsorship of research would check and balance the influence of government.[33]

Malott believed that "tapping corporations for research funds" would be best confined "to soliciting funds for the physical sciences, engineering and mathematics."[34] General Electric helped fund an electronic research laboratory on Cornell property near Ithaca's East Hill Airport in 1951, and several corporations funded the polymer research of Chemistry Department professors Peter Debye and Franklin Long. What would help, of course, were Cornell business connections, so Cornell's new vice president for university development conducted a survey, which revealed that there were "approximately 400 corporations of which Cornell alumni are senior officers or directors."[35]

The strategy succeeded. The Chemistry Department received a substantial sum of money for the improvement of undergraduate teaching from the DuPont Company in 1953, and the *Alumni Magazine* noted that Walter Carpenter, Cornell trustee and DuPont CEO, along with five other Cornellian "executives in the far-flung DuPont organization," made it happen.[36] The same year, the Department of Biological Chemistry received an impressive grant from Eli Lilly and Company, the pharmaceutical company presided over by trustee Nicholas Noyes.

What about the humanities? It was no surprise, with the important role the natural and social sciences played in the new research-oriented Cornell, that the humanities wanted in. They had an ally in President Day, who had worried that wartime science research had eclipsed the liberal arts. And, in the frenzied wake of *Sputnik*, Malott had also warned against "the tendency to overemphasize science and engineering training to the neglect of the great fields of the humanities."[37]

And so a Society for the Humanities was proposed. The concept originated in a 1956 memorandum from the philosophy professor Max Black, proposing "a Society of Fellows in the Humanities," consisting of visiting retired scholars, visiting postdoctoral fellows, and resident Cornell faculty. Based on the "Council of the Humanities" created at Princeton in 1953, Black's vision attracted the support of Theodor Mommsen of the History Department and M. H. Abrams of English. A committee of the three, with Abrams as chair, was appointed to explore creating a center "that would invigorate teaching and research, and enlarge the role of the humanities both in the Arts College and in the University community."[38] Its report, calling for a Cornell Humanities Center, wended its way for two years through the Arts College, the university administration, and finally the board of trustees. In an October 1959 editorial, "An Appeal to the Trustees," the *Cornell Daily Sun* pointed to the problem:

> The Society of Fellows is far different from the type of projects which the University has undertaken in the recent past. Consequently, the difficulty in raising funds for the Society has been magnified. There is little glamour—for an individual or a foundation—in contributing towards the establishment of a Society of Fellows. The Society will bear no famous alumnus' name. It will not receive a federal grant, as in the case of the nuclear reactor. And it will not attract the spontaneous enthusiasm of Cornell's alumni, as in the case of the engineering quadrangle.[39]

The *Sun* got it right: efforts to obtain support from alumni and foundations were unsuccessful. University support for a Society for the Humanities would not come until Max Black and M. H. Abrams tied their proposal to planning the university's centennial for 1965 and an endowment of $2.5 million was included in the centennial fund-raising campaign. The Society for the Humanities opened in 1966, with Black as its first director.

17

Of course, a research university needed an expanding faculty on the frontiers of emerging scholarly inquiry in all disciplines, and so the numbers of professors at Cornell grew dramatically, from a prewar total of six hundred to nearly fifteen hundred when Malott retired in 1963. And it needed a new breed of professor, who, like Hans Bethe and George Kahin, deemed scholarly research as important as teaching, if not more so. Clinton Rossiter '39 exemplified well the postwar professor. Rossiter produced seminal books on the American presidency and the politics of the American founding. He understood the new Cornell, as he made clear in a "fan letter" he wrote to President Day when he received an appointment to the Government Department in 1946. "I have never been as proud of my alma mater as I am today upon my return from three and a half years of war. . . . The war time courses on Russia, the new School of Industrial and Labor Relations, and the revolutionary steps being taken in the teaching of modern languages are concrete examples of what I mean."[40]

An eminent scholar, Rossiter was also a popular teacher with "genial good humor and ingratiating lecturing manners . . . besides a voice that could be heard bellowing forth at Madison Square Garden even if the microphones went dead."[41] No less eminent and no less a revered teacher, if more soft-spoken and less flamboyant, Vladimir Nabokov, professor of Russian literature, would give postwar Cornell international literary renown beyond its wildest imagining with the publication of his novel *Lolita* in 1956.

A significant number of the new breed of postwar faculty were Jewish. There had been a handful of Jewish professors before the war. Harry Caplan '16, MA '17, PhD '21, who joined Cornell's Classics Department in 1924, was one of Cornell's most beloved professors until his retirement in 1980; Wallie Abraham Hurwitz came to Cornell in 1910 and taught mathematics until his retirement in 1954. But, just as the GI Bill transformed the composition of the student body, so, too, did the change in postwar American attitudes to bias and discrimination lead to a dramatic increase in the number of Jewish faculty at Cornell, and at all elite research schools.

This new Jewish presence knew no disciplinary boundaries. In the humanities there was the philosopher Max Black, born in Baku, Azerbaijan, and schooled in England, who came to Cornell in 1946 and taught until his retirement in 1977. For his book *Critical Thinking*, one of the most widely used philosophy texts, and eight other books, Black became the first American to be president of the Paris-based Institut International de Philosophie. M. H. (Meyer "Mike" Howard) Abrams, born in Long Branch, New Jersey, the son of a house painter and first in his family to go to college (Harvard), came to teach in the Cornell English Department in 1945. His 1952 book, *The Mirror and the Lamp: Romantic Theory and the Critical Tradition*, was selected by the Modern Library in 1999 as number twenty-five on its list of the "100 Best Non-Fiction Books Written in English during the Last Hundred Years."

Equally noteworthy, there was hardly ever a Cornell football or basketball game in Ithaca over six decades that "Mike" didn't attend.

In the social sciences there was Urie Bronfenbrenner, who was born in Moscow, grew up in New York, and graduated from Cornell in 1938. He became a pioneer in the study of childhood and human development after returning to Cornell in the 1950s to teach at the College of Home Economics. Milton Konvitz, PhD '33, the son of a rabbi, and born in Safed, Palestine, left the practice of law in New York to come to Cornell in 1933 to get a PhD in philosophy with Professor George Sabine '31, PhD '36. After a stint at NYU, Konvitz became one of the original faculty members of the new College of Industrial and Labor Relations in 1945. His course "The Development of American Ideals" would be taken by over eight thousand undergraduates from colleges throughout the campus, including a future Supreme Court justice, Ruth Bader Ginsburg '54. Over his long career, Konvitz wrote important books on civil rights, the First Amendment, and religious liberty. Like Rossiter, he was moved to write President Day of his joy at being appointed a Cornell professor. "For years, like Odysseus, I have been dreaming of home in Ithaca. And now the dream will become a reality. For this sublime fortune I am grateful to you. My sense of obligation to you will never waver or change."[42]

The new postwar Jewish presence was just as evident in the sciences. Born in Brooklyn and educated at New York's City College, Harold Scheraga joined the Chemistry Department in 1947, where for the next fifty-five years he conducted research in the structure and function of proteins, nucleic acids, and carbohydrates. Benjamin Siegel from Superior, Wisconsin, joined the Engineering Physics Department in 1949 and became an expert in electron microscopy. New Yorker Howard Evans (born Epstein) '44, PhD '50, a faculty member in the College of Veterinary Medicine for four decades, taught thousands of students, including three future deans of the college. His *Anatomy of the Dog* (1964) and *Guide to the Dissection of the Dog* (1969) are the standard references in the field.

Students were well aware of the research inclinations of the new faculty at Cornell. One hears their misgivings about Cornell the research university, even as it was being created. A columnist for the *Sun* wrote in 1950: "In recent years Cornell has made extraordinary progress in research: the synchrotron, the aeronautical labs at Buffalo, and all the rest. But one way or another, the faculty has been convinced that teaching doesn't matter."[43] Nearly ten years later another declared, "Faculty devotion to research at Cornell University has become immoderate to the extent that the prime function of the faculty to teach is being neglected."[44] But what cannot be denied is that virtually all the great researchers hired during Cornell's transformation in this era were legendary teachers whose classroom presentations were grounded in and nourished by their scholarship.

Nonetheless, in his last report to the trustees in June 1963, President Malott also warned of possible unintended consequences of Cornell's otherwise remarkably successful transformation into a world-class research university:

> Large research grants add considerable distinction to the institution. But there is slow erosion of the University's ability to determine its own direction of development and even to retain budgetary control over expenditures. In addition there is an erosion of the faculty member's dedication and willingness to teach—due to the opportunities under such grants for travel, concentration on research, and other off-campus commitments. . . . It would take skillful cooperation and diplomacy on the part of all concerned to stem the tide toward control of the University's program from the outside and to restore some measure of institutional control at a time when the University receives some 53% of its financial support from governmental sources.[45]

SHORTLY AFTER COMING to Cornell in 1937, President Day sought to create a business and public administration school and a school in industrial and labor relations. Both new ventures reflected his commitment to social service and social improvement, as well as his belief that future leaders of business, government, and unions should be trained in academically focused social science research. These two initiatives were shelved with the financial and manpower constraints of World War II but were realized at the end of the war—one with, as academic innovations go, an easy birth, and one with a rocky and contentious beginning.

The opening in September 1946 of the School of Business and Public Administration was the culmination of an idea that had been raised often in Cornell's past. At the university's founding, President White had hoped to create a "Department of Trade and Commerce" to train the merchants of post–Civil War America. President Jacob Gould Schurman advocated what he called a "College of Commerce" in the late 1890s and again in 1915. It went nowhere as well. Pushed more vigorously by President Day, the idea was finally approved by a faculty committee in 1940 and by the trustees two years later. When it opened, Cornell's graduate business school was one of only nine in the country, and the only one that offered education for business and public administration. Not only was Cornell's combination unique—it was potentially divisive, given the distrust at the time between the business community and the intrusive government of the New Deal. The blending of the two fields worked at Cornell in no small measure because the committee that Day had assembled to plan the college had a strong public-sector orientation, provided by William Myers and Martin Catherwood, PhD '30, both from the College of Agriculture.

In addition to Day, the school's first dean was a driving force. Professor of economics Paul M. O'Leary, PhD '29 earned his doctorate in economics and remained in the College of Arts and Sciences. So keen was Day to appoint O'Leary that he violated his own ethic of public service by pleading with General Lucius Clay in April 1945 not to extend O'Leary's war service (as supervisor of rationing and price controls in Germany) since "there is absolutely no one on the University staff who can substitute for him in the work" of heading the new college.[46] O'Leary presided over the school for seven years, hiring all its faculty, and managing its move from Goldwin Smith to McGraw Hall. By 1949 the Business School had 118 students, a majority of whom were Cornell undergraduates. O'Leary demanded that the college be academically rigorous and "seek to provide a type of training that can be found only in a large university rather than the type of specialized training that a large corporation might want to develop for its own personnel."[47]

Moved by Malott to the deanship of Arts and Sciences, O'Leary was succeeded by Edward Litchfield. Convinced that one of the main functions of the school was to "develop people who are able to step from business into government and from government into business," Litchfield emphasized the public administration side of the school. During his two-year tenure, the college took its place in the new research university as well, creating an influential academic journal, the *Administrative Science Quarterly*. In 1955, B&PA, as it was called, became an exclusively graduate institution.

Initially, finances were precarious, to the point that O'Leary informed Acting President de Kiewiet in 1949 that the new college "must have more money, or it must be abandoned";[48] the permanence of the school was only guaranteed in the middle 1950s when the Sloan Foundation funded the Sloan Program in Hospital and Health Services Administration.

B&PA expanded to parts of Rand Hall in 1958, and five years later left McGraw and Rand for a new building on the northwest corner of the intersection of Tower Road and Garden Avenue, across from the Agriculture School. Fittingly it was named Malott Hall, after Cornell's recently retired businessman president, who had predicted that with Sloan's patronage "the Business School will be one of the best."[49]

The School of Industrial and Labor Relations (ILR) was the brainchild in 1938 of Irving M. Ives, a liberal Republican who was the majority leader in the New York State Assembly and chair of the Joint Legislative Committee on Industrial and Labor Conditions. In a 1940 report his committee noted that "though we may legislate to the end of time, there never will be industrial peace and harmony without good faith, integrity, a high degree of responsibility, and a real desire to cooperate on the part of all parties concerned."[50] By 1942, Ives's committee recommended the establishment of a School of Industrial and Labor Relations at Cornell. Although Syracuse University and Union College lobbied to be home to the school, the State Legislature established it at Cornell, with Governor Thomas Dewey signing the bill in May 1944.

The school epitomized Day's belief that understanding, education, and goodwill could solve social problems. But there was concern from some trustees. Walter Teagle, chairman of the Standard Oil Company, warned the president that "the new School is going to take a lot of careful handling and will doubtless bring us some headaches." And Willis Carrier '01, chairman of the Carrier Corporation, worried that the contemplated school would force Cornell to "verge on politics."[51]

Unfazed by the fact that "the subject is hot politically," Day relished an opportunity for Cornell to help develop a "better understanding by industry and labor of each other's problems"—and perhaps even end the "continuing warfare between the contending parties."[52] The trustees went along, but their suspicions that the place would be a school for labor agitators promoting collective bargaining and unionization did not go away. Some nicknamed ILR "the little red schoolhouse." Others regarded it "with horror as an incubator of radicalism." They noticed when several years later, at the height of the Cold War, the *Chicago Tribune* described the ILR School as "an institutionalized hot bed of left-wing activity."[53]

Nonetheless, December 1, 1945, was a time for celebration. As he dedicated the new college in a speech carried nationally by NBC radio, Governor Dewey, the once and future Republican nominee for president of the United States, proclaimed,

> This is no labor school where dogma will be taught, from which trained zealots will go forth. This is no management school where students will learn only to think of working men and women as items on a balance sheet. . . . It is a school which denies the alien theory that there are classes in our society and that they must wage war against each other. This is a school dedicated to the common interest of employer and employee and of the whole of the American people.[54]

The ILR School's first homes were seven single-story wooden barracks and a Quonset hut, built as temporary quarters for troops in training during the war, on Sage Green, where the Engineering quad is now located. Its first dean was Irving Ives. Unperturbed by the rough setting of the college, Ives told the provost that the huts "will serve his purpose very satisfactorily for the present."[55] Elected in 1946 to the United States Senate, Ives gave way as dean to Martin Catherwood, a professor of public administration in the College of Agriculture, who remained in office until 1958. Catherwood was no stranger to Albany, having served as state commerce commissioner and state industrial commissioner.

The builder of the ILR School, Catherwood recruited distinguished faculty, including Milton Konvitz, Morris Neufeld, Vernon Jensen, and William Whyte (the sociologist and author of *Street Corner Society*). He hired Frances

School of Industrial and Labor Relations, 1946. (Division of Rare and Manuscript Collections of the Cornell University Library)

Perkins, Franklin Roosevelt's secretary of labor, and the first woman cabinet member. Perkins, who never went hatless and frequently wore white gloves and pearls while lecturing, taught at the college from 1957 until her death in 1966. Catherwood also brought Alice Cook to ILR. An expert in labor history and union administration, Cook became a legend when she singlehandedly opened the Statler Faculty Club to women.

Catherwood integrated his new college into the research university. In 1947 he helped create a quarterly professional journal, the *Industrial and Labor Relations Review*, which became the leading publication in its field. *ILR Review* joined the ILR Press, established by Ives in 1945, which published faculty work in hundreds of bulletins, books, and "occasional papers." While the focus of the school was teaching and research, Catherwood also introduced ILR into extension work throughout the state. By the end of his deanship, the school offered nearly three hundred courses to approximately seven thousand persons. To be sure, as Catherwood noted in 1949, "The most interest and the most aggressive demand for the extension work has come from the union groups."[56]

Catherwood assumed that the school would quickly move out of the barracks and Quonset hut into new state-financed quarters. In 1946 the state agreed to construct buildings on Campus Road, which would sit on a portion of Hoy baseball field, where Lou Gehrig had once hit a home run for Columbia University. For a year and a half there was no notable opposition to the plan, and during this time negotiations for transferring the land to the state had been undertaken, and plans for the new buildings were completed at a cost to the state of some $100,000. Serious and orchestrated agitation against the plan emerged, however, in the spring of 1948. It was bad enough that detractors of the school referred to it and its barracks home as the "cardboard Kremlin."[57] Now, ILR faced the anger of Cornell students, the athletic community, and its large network of alumni supporters.

A trustees' committee affirmed the earlier decision by a narrow margin and concluded that, given its strategic location, all of Hoy Field would ultimately have to give way to academic buildings. Even as Day stood by the agreement with the state, the Association of Cornell Class Secretaries responded with a resolution opposing the new site, and a front page "Open Letter to the President and Board of Trustees of Cornell," endorsed by fifty-three undergraduate organizations, appeared in the *Cornell Sun* "deploring the impact on intercollegiate and intramural sports of touching Hoy Field, one of the best baseball diamonds in the East."[58] Robert Kane '34, Cornell's director of physical education and athletics since 1943, entered the fray, "putting on the record his opposition to 'the invasion of Hoy Field' for an ILR building."[59] Despite Day's sense that opponents used the Hoy Field controversy "as a means of expressing disapproval of the School," he surrendered, writing in February 1949 to trustee Robert Treman '09, "I was driven to the conclusion that emotional resistance to the encroachment on Hoy Field had risen to a point at which completely rational handling of the whole matter was no longer possible, and hence my decision to retreat from my earlier position."[60]

The ILR School again became a target during the eleven-day strike against the university in November and December 1950 by members of Local 296 of the Building Service Employees Union, American Federation of Labor, which sought recognition as the bargaining agent for between five hundred and eight hundred university employees. Acting President de Kiewiet refused formal recognition of the union, claiming that nonprofit educational institutions were exempt from collective bargaining. The university was not opposed to the trade union movement, de Kiewiet told the *Sun*; "The ILR School of which it is rather proud proves otherwise . . . but the proper area for a trade union is in industry, not in a university." The strike was settled with both sides saving face. Local 296 accepted the university's maintenance of its formal nonrecognition policy, and the university agreed to allow union officials "to appear" with union employees at grievance proceedings and agreed "to confer" with representatives of the local union on "matters involving wages, hours, and working conditions."[61]

In the fallout after the strike, however, the trustees lashed out at the ILR School. Linking the strike to the presence of a "labor school" at Cornell, Robert Treman asked for a meeting to discuss "communism on the campus." Acting President de Kiewiet shared these concerns: "It is, of course, unfortunate," he wrote trustee Mary Donlon, "that there are three or four active communists in the student body. These played a noticeable role in the strike agitation." To Maxwell Upson '99, he noted "the mistakes Catherwood and the School have made . . . their very damaging and impolitic activities of the past weeks," and the appointment of faculty "with a restricted and militant commitment."[62]

Because the ILR School had, in fact, taken no formal position on the strike, though some of its faculty and students openly supported the union, de Kiewiet was loath, he wrote Donlon, to have any action taken against it by trustees. "On the other hand," he added, there was without doubt a cloud hanging over ILR: "No matter what the explanation may be, its position is jeopardized and somebody is going to have to have the wisdom and courage to do something about it. My own formula is a very simple one. It is that the Dean or the faculty of the School should adopt the simple formula that students of the School will not become active officials in any union that may come into collision with the University."[63]

Even when the dust settled from the strike, ILR's problems continued. Angered by the Hoy Field reversal, New York State officials dragged their feet on authorizing a new home for the school. ILR finally left its "temporary" World War II barracks and Quonset hut in the early 1960s. Nestled between Tower Road and Barton Hall, the new ILR quadrangle consisted of a large classroom, library, and office building, Ives Hall, constructed at a cost of $3 million, and four smaller remodeled buildings formerly used by the Veterinary College (which had moved to the east end of Tower Road). The formal dedication took place during the weekend of October 1, 1962, presided over by Governor Nelson Rockefeller, with hundreds of guests from education, government, labor, and management.

The third new college created at Cornell in the postwar years was the School of Hotel Administration. In reality it had been around for a long time. In 1922 a Department of Hotel Administration had been created by Martha Van Rensselaer and Flora Rose in the New York State School of Home Economics, the first four-year degree program of its sort offered anywhere. Its first and much beloved chair for nearly forty years and "father of the Hotel School" was Howard Meek, a graduate of Boston University, with a graduate degree in mathematics from the University of Maine, who would ten years later receive a

PhD in economics from Yale. In 1922 Meek was a twenty-nine-year-old one-man faculty for a program that included twenty-one students and four courses.

Meek developed the department into the leading academic hospitality program in the world. He established a research program in 1947, seeking grants from the hotel and restaurant industries for the nearly twenty faculty by then teaching hundreds of students. Meek encouraged faculty publications like Professor John Sherry's seminal text on hospitality law, *The Laws of Innkeepers*. In the late 1950s he oversaw the founding of the *Cornell Hotel and Restaurant Administration Quarterly*, a journal signifying a serious faculty research commitment. He also enhanced the department's national and international visibility by instituting short courses for industry employees as early as 1928 and executive educational seminars in 1955. During World War II, Hotel School graduates were highly sought after to run the housing and feeding operations in the nation's military bases.

In the 1920s the department had already come to the attention of America's then most famous hotelier, Ellsworth Statler. In the 1930s the Statler Foundation offered to provide $1 million for a departmental home, including an inn, to be built on the shore of Beebe Lake. The initiative was interrupted, as so many were, by World War II. After the war a grander building, the Statler Inn, was built, not on the lake, but in the heart of the campus on East Avenue, displacing four faculty houses. The building included classrooms, laboratories, kitchens, lounges and club rooms, faculty offices, and an operational "practice" inn of thirty-six rooms, to be run by Hotel Administration students. Memorable for several generations of Cornellians would be the basement Rathskeller restaurant with its oak-paneled walls.

At the building's dedication on May 6, 1950, Arthur Dean announced that the board had officially changed the name of the program from "Department of Hotel Administration" to the "School of Hotel Administration" in the College of Home Economics and that Professor Meek would be appointed director. The physical independence of the new school from Home Economics, and its increasing reputation off campus, led some to advocate that it become an autonomous college. The issue was resolved by the state, which in 1954, as the trustees' minutes tersely report, requested "that the Hotel School be made either a State contract college or be separated entirely from Home Economics. Since a contract college cannot charge tuition to New York State students the only practical alternative appears to be an independent school among the endowed divisions of the University."[64]

Cornell's final college was born. Meek, now dean, stayed on another seven years. He was succeeded by Robert Beck '42, M Ed '52, PhD '54, a professor of hospitality financial management in the new college's Department of Real Estate since 1954. Beck presided over the college for the next twenty years, his by-the-rules, occasionally autocratic style tempered by his wife, Jan, who for years opened up their home, "The Slaterville Hilton," to students. During Beck's tenure the school doubled in size, a master's of professional studies was introduced, and "Hotel" became de facto the most popular source of business-oriented courses for Cornell undergraduates. During the campus upheavals of the Vietnam era, Beck insisted on proper dress and decorum from the "Hotelies," and proudly claimed that "the Hotel School was a capitalist island in the socialist sea of Cornell."[65]

IN POSTWAR CORNELL several of the older colleges experienced something of an identity crisis. The College of Arts and Sciences, President Malott noted on his arrival, had a puzzling tradition of being led by deans "with backgrounds in the humanities, which placed some limitation upon their acquaintance with the special problems of the physical sciences."[66] Moreover, the culture of the Arts College self-consciously cultivated departmental autonomy. Its deans came and went, exercising little power, and after the war it never had a visionary dean to mobilize or inspire the college. The dean, Carl Becker had noted with approval in 1940, was "scarcely more than a bookkeeper."[67] Until 1945, in fact, the Arts College dean had no secretary.

Malott's director of public relations wrote him in 1953 of the need "to give the Arts College new identity and esprit de corps."[68] Part of the problem was its service role in teaching over half the total undergraduate credit hours in the university. This essential teaching mission, principally in chemistry, math, physics, and biology, was being presided over by deans from the humanities. Nothing epitomized this disconnect more than Dean Francis E. Mineka, an authority on English Victorian literature, lecturing alumni assembled in Ithaca in 1958 in their new "University Council" on "what is necessary to keep Cornell in the forefront of scientific leadership."[69]

Articulate Arts College students' complaints to the *Daily Sun* underscored the malaise about the college's lack of direction. Since courses were open to all, was the lament, why not "a lecture series specifically for Arts students?" Why not a better advising system for the many students undecided about a major? Why not a more serious "intellectual atmosphere" in the college? On the other hand, students complained that there ought to be more discussion classes in the college and fewer large lectures. And there were concerns that the Arts College was getting short shrift from university administrators. In 1958, for example, a student pointed out that "not a single new building has been provided for the College in over 30 years."[70]

The malaise could not have been helped by Malott's misgivings about the college. In 1952 he told the trustees that "Arts and Science is not as distinguished a College as it should be." Instruction in English, math, and economics, he added, "is not up to standard in some courses." Six years later, Malott was still suggesting that "the No. 1 problem of the University is the improvement of the College of Arts and Sciences."[71] Unfortunately, the president showed little interest in doing something about it. The faculty did take a few steps to improve things. A literary review, *EPOCH*, was launched in 1947, with Baxter Hathaway of the English Department as editor. Recruited from the University of Michigan, Hathaway began a Creative Writing Program that, under his leadership and that of his colleagues Jim McConkey and Walter Slatoff, would become nationally eminent, producing in Goldwin Smith an overly large share of America's future literary giants, such as Toni Morrison, MA '55, Thomas Pynchon '59, Richard Price '71, Lorrie Moore, MFA '82, Junot Diaz, MFA '95, and Alice Fulton, MFA '82.

The faculty also designed a more focused curriculum, introduced an honors program in 1954 to allow the best students to do advanced work in small seminars, and designed a "plan of common studies" requiring all Arts students to study a foreign language and complete a sequence of courses in the natural sciences, social studies, the humanities, and history. Still, the tensions between humanities and sciences, as well as students' concerns over lacking the focused identity of their peers in the other colleges, remained a feature of Arts College culture.

The College of Agriculture went through an even more serious identity crisis. Like other states, New York experienced a dramatic (almost 50 percent) postwar decline in the number of farms and in the amount of land in agricultural production. By the late 1940s only 40 percent of Cornell Agricultural students came from farms; 30 percent had some farm experience but were not farm reared, and 30 percent had no farm experience at all, a figure that would climb steadily in the 1950s. Even more disturbing, only 14 percent of first-year students indicated a vocational preference for farming.

These demographic changes manifested themselves vividly in agitation to eliminate the "farm practice" requirement. In the '50s Cornell was the only agricultural school in the nation to oblige all male and some women students to do a prescribed minimum of farmwork each week. Recognizing the need to adjust to new realities, the college in 1960 reduced dramatically the units required for "farm practice," admitting that as it stood "it is a major deterrent to attracting academically well qualified male students into the fields of biological science, social science, science teaching, and agri-business."[72] As students found creative ways to get around the requirement, it would die slowly, just as Ezra Cornell's insistence on student manual labor had been abandoned by the university after his death in 1874.

At the same time, Farm and Home Week lost its central place in the state's agricultural calendar and in university life. Since 1911, farmers from all over New York State had flocked to Cornell's campus to celebrate farm life with state fair–like agricultural and animal displays, workshops, symposia, lectures, demonstrations, and traditional rural fun: greased pigs, crosscut sawing, roping, tractor towing, pie baking, potato throwing, and milking contests. A queen of Farm and Home Week was crowned at the huge square dance that ended the festivities. Farm and Home Week, the *Cornell Alumni News* boasted in 1948, was "the greatest single public relations event the University puts on."[73] Attendance at the week peaked at eighteen thousand in 1954, when the U.S. secretary of agriculture, Ezra Taft Benson, spoke at Bailey Hall. By 1956 it was twelve thousand, and in 1958, after the smallest turnout ever, a *Daily Sun* editorial predicted that "Farm and Home Week may become nothing more than a monument to the past." The College of Agriculture itself, the paper suggested, "is devoted to a way of life slowly disappearing in this country."[74]

Unlike the Arts College, however, the College of Agriculture had a long-serving dean, who enabled his college to resolve its identity crisis. Born and raised on his family's farm near Elmira, New York, William I. Myers '14, PhD '18, was a professor in the Department of Farm Management, specializing in farming finances, from 1918 to 1932, and then served in Washington, drafting the New Deal legislation that created the Farm Credit Administration and provided financial assistance to farmers. Myers served as that new agency's executive director until 1938, when he returned to Cornell, first as chair of the Department of Agricultural Economics and from 1943 to 1959 as dean of the

Farm and Home Week exhibit demonstrating the digestive processes of a sheep and a pig, 1952. *Cornell Daily Sun*, March 19, 1952. (Courtesy *Cornell Daily Sun*)

college. Under his leadership the college came to view "farming as a business rather than a way of life."[75] Modern agriculture, Myers believed, relied upon research into greater efficiency, better marketing, and skillful management. By the late 1950s, Myers's college was devoting more than 40 percent of its annual budget to 750 research projects.

Myers also took his college into the politics of agriculture, as he himself moved to the political Right. He forged close relationships with agribusiness, serving, for example, on the boards of several farm and food corporations. He was an adviser to the Grange League Federation (GLF), the largest farmers cooperative in the world, which would become the Agway Corporation. Also involved with the GLF was Myers's colleague and friend Howard Babcock, professor of marketing, who as president of the State Grange was an ex officio member of Cornell's board of trustees for decades, and from 1940 to 1947 its chairman. In 1946, Savage Hall, named for Elmer Savage, PhD '11, a professor of animal husbandry, home for the new departments of biochemistry and nutrition, was built with funds provided by the GLF, the first building on the agricultural campus constructed with private capital. Babcock and Myers were also central figures in the development of the School of Nutrition. After efforts led by them to have Nutrition become a free-standing contract college were rebuffed by the state, they reinvented it as a school straddling the Colleges of Agriculture, Arts and Sciences, Engineering, and Home Economics.

In the 1950s Myers was a close adviser to Ezra Taft Benson, Eisenhower's secretary of agriculture, drafting memos for him on the need to cut back government involvement in agriculture, return to free-market principles, and provide, as he put it, "greater freedom and individual responsibility."[76] Myers saw no conflict of interest when he joined the corporate board of Avco Corporation, manufacturer of agricultural equipment, owned by Cornell trustee Victor Emmanuel. Myers shared Emmanuel's conviction that businessmen–farmers were the nation's best hope against "regimentation" and "socialism."[77] In 1953, on Emmanuel's suggestion, Myers invited George Sokolsky, a conservative columnist for the Hearst newspapers, to be the principal speaker at Farm and Home Week. Speaking to a full house at Bailey Hall and to thousands listening on the radio, Sokolsky defended congressional investigations "of communist infiltration into the nation's universities," insisting that faculty lack "the perspicacity to grasp the nature or significance of the communist menace." A few Cornell faculty, most noticeably the historian Henry Guerlac, protested Sokolsky's appearance, while the audience of farmers and friends of Emmanuel were pleased. For Myers's critics on the left, the Sokolsky invitation was yet more evidence that Myers was "a spokesman for big business."[78]

Myers's relationship with the Rockefeller Foundation—he became a trustee of the foundation in 1943—left an indelible stamp on the College of Agriculture and its involvement in the spread worldwide of "the green revolution."

Myers traveled extensively in Latin America and Asia for Rockefeller and for Cornell, culminating in the close collaboration of Cornell with the Philippine College of Agriculture at Los Baños begun in 1952. By the time he retired in 1959, Myers had greatly enhanced the reputation of his college as a center for international agriculture.

Engineering would be the most transformed college in the postwar era, intellectually and physically. Like Agriculture, Engineering had a long-serving, visionary dean, Solomon Cady Hollister. Born in Michigan, raised in the Pacific Northwest, and schooled only with a BS from Wisconsin, Hollister had been a nationally recognized expert in reinforced concrete, who played an important role in the construction of the Hoover Dam. He came to Cornell in 1934 as professor and director of the School of Civil Engineering and was appointed dean of the college three years later. When Hollister took charge, Engineering was dispersed in Franklin, Sibley, and Lincoln Halls, cramped buildings at the north end of campus, and was mired in a long-term decline, which saw its enrollment drop from a high in 1909–10 of 1,755 students to a Depression low in 1935–36 of 812. Much of the college's equipment was antiquated. Once a source of pride for the university, the college had been eclipsed by Illinois, Wisconsin, and Purdue.

The renaissance of Engineering began when Hollister persuaded Day and the trustees to relocate the college to the south end of the campus. In 1941 Olin Hall for Chemical and Metallurgical Engineering opened on the corner of Campus Road and Central Avenue, a gift of Franklin Olin '86, as a memorial to his son, Franklin Olin Jr. '12. After Hollister declined to be considered for the presidency of Lehigh in 1945, he designed the first five-year engineering curriculum in the nation. Cornell engineers were required to take courses in economics, English, psychology, and history to broaden their management skills, their training in humane subjects, and to enhance their social awareness. "Holly" (his nickname since college) was particularly interested in history, and in the new curriculum all engineering students had to complete Henry Guerlac's course "The History of Science in Western Civilization."

Hollister brought a School of Chemical Engineering into the college, a School of Engineering Physics, and a program in Aeronautical Engineering. By the 1950s the enrollment in the college had returned to the robust numbers of the early twentieth century, stabilizing at between seventeen hundred and nineteen hundred students. Hollister was full of new ideas. He introduced double registration in the fifth year for his Engineering students with the Law School, ILR, and the School of Business and Public Administration. He advocated a six-year combined BA and BS in answer "to the problem of liberal education in professional school curricula," an idea that never took hold.[79] One that did was his encouragement of scholarship support to Engineering students from the engineering industry itself. But Hollister's most lasting achievement would be the creation of the new Engineering quad.

31

Holly masterminded the placement of the new buildings on the south side of the campus and helped finance their construction, serving for a time as the vice president in charge of raising capital funds as well as dean. Clustered just south of Olin Hall, where the last faculty homes had stood, were Kimball-Thurston Hall, named for two early Engineering deans; a Center for Materials and Material Processing, built in 1952 at a cost of $1.7 million (contributed by two hundred alums); Phillips Hall, the home of Electrical Engineering, constructed in 1955 with a $1.75 million gift from Ellis Phillips '95; Carpenter Hall, the site of the college administrative offices and the college library, built in 1957 with a $1 million gift from the trustee Walter Carpenter; and Upson Hall, for Mechanical and Aeronautical Engineering, constructed in 1958 from a $2 million gift from trustee Maxwell Upson, president of the Raymond Concrete Pile Company. The twenty-year process ended in 1960 with the new home of Civil Engineering, paid for by a donation of $2 million from Spencer T. Olin '21, who asked it be named for Hollister, who had retired the previous June.

The principal beneficiary of Engineering's exodus from the north end of campus was the College of Architecture. Created as a branch of the College of Civil Engineering in 1871, the College of Architecture had occupied the top floors of White Hall since 1906, as well as some rooms in Franklin and the basement of Morse Hall, the part left standing after a fire in 1916 (and present site of the Johnson Museum of Art). Gilmore Clarke, the dean of the college from 1938 to 1950, had used Carnegie Foundation money to develop a regional planning program within the college. Although he continued his private practice in New York City, spending only three days a week in Ithaca, Clarke was still an active participant in campus controversy. When President Day wanted to split Fine Arts off from the college in 1945 and put it into the Arts College in a building with Music, Clarke resisted. "Music and visual Arts have little in common," he wrote; "the philosopher only may demonstrate their kinship."[80] Clarke won. He lost, as noted above, in the battle over Boardman Hall.

Clarke was succeeded as dean in 1951 by Thomas Mackesey, and as leader of the college's Planning Program by John Reps, the first chair in 1952 of the college's Department of City and Regional Planning. Under Mackesey, the college retained its five-year architecture degree, instituted in 1945, and restricted the number of first-year architects to around sixty, even though more than seven hundred usually sought admission. Mackesey oversaw the move by most of the college in 1958 and 1959 from White Hall into Sibley (vacated by Mechanical Engineering), a space it would share for much of the next decade with History and Government, exiles from Boardman. Parts of the college remained in Franklin, and with the final destruction of Morse some took up residence in Rand Hall. In 1961 Mackesey changed life at Cornell—night life, that is: he allowed the architectural drafting room to stay open twenty-four hours a day.

Cornell Law School also had a peripatetic history. From its beginning in 1887 on the fourth floor of Morrill Hall, it had moved to Boardman Hall in 1892, and then to its permanent home, Myron Taylor Hall, on Central Avenue near Cascadilla Creek, in 1932. Chairman of the board of U.S. Steel and trustee of Cornell, Myron Taylor, JD '94, was the principal benefactor of the college in the postwar years as well. In 1952 his gift of Anabel Taylor Hall, to honor his wife, filled out the Law School quad. In the early 1960s he gave $1 million for a Law School residence center named Hughes Hall after his teacher, the great jurist Charles Evans Hughes.

The preeminent postwar Law School dean was Robert Stevens. Born in Attica in upstate New York, Stevens had earned his BA and LLB from Harvard and had come to the Law School in 1919. An expert on corporate law, he became dean in 1937 and spent the war as assistant general counsel for the Lend Lease Administration. Upon his return, Stevens revived the school, whose former enrollment of two hundred had plummeted to thirty-three in 1943 and forty in 1944. By 1950 the school had over four hundred students, leveling off slightly in the remainder of the decade.

In 1948 Stevens's faculty shored up student quality by requiring satisfactory performance on the new Law School Admission Test (LSAT). The Law School made cooperative degree arrangements with ILR and Business and Public Administration. Stevens worked hard to obtain endowed professorships for the first time in the college's history, creating four between 1949 and 1951. He also realized the fervent hope of the internationalist Myron Taylor, who had been ambassador to the Vatican, that the college develop a program in international law. Comparative law became a strength of the Law School in these years, with Taylor providing funds for visiting lecturers and the Ford Foundation making a $400,000 grant in 1956 to support seminars and summer conferences. No longer a provincial training ground for preparing New York residents for the New York bar, Cornell Law School had been transformed into an institution with a national and international reputation.

The College of Home Economics retained its New York State focus in the postwar years, though it, too, would fundamentally redefine itself as part of the research university. The school had begun in a basement room in Morrill Hall in 1900 as a department within the state-funded College of Agriculture, with Martha Van Rensselaer, soon joined by Flora Rose, teaching courses on "home and family life." In 1919 it became a school, and six years later it was made an autonomous college, making it the first state-funded college of home economics in the country. Its home at Martha Van Rensselaer Hall, built in 1933, was presided over by Flora Rose until 1940. Rose was succeeded by Sarah Blanding, a professor of political science at Kentucky, who was dean through the war, a period when the faculty were in great demand for their expertise as dietitians and apparel designers. When Blanding left in 1946 to become president of Vassar, she was succeeded by Elizabeth Lee Vincent, a social psychologist with a PhD from Columbia.

Vincent and her successor, Helen Gertrude Canoyer, a professor of economics from the University of Minnesota and Cornell dean from 1954 until 1968, had to deal with the consensus on campus that Home Economics was Cornell's college for women. The figures are striking. For most of this period, women were about one-third of Arts College students, 688 women to 1,001 men in 1946, and 1,090 women to 1,938 men in 1963. No class in Engineering had more than twenty women. Agriculture in 1948 had 173 women to 1,341 men, and in 1963, 288 to 1,611. With class-year sizes in Home Economics hovering between six hundred and seven hundred, however, not one male student registered in the college over the entire seventeen-year period—though, of course, men from other colleges took courses in home economics. The faculty figures were equally dramatic: in 1951 there were eighty-four women and eight men serving as professor, associate professor, or assistant professor; in 1957 ninety-seven women and fifteen men taught in the college's main departments, Economics of the Household and Household Management; Textile and Apparel; and Child Development and Family Relationships.

The curriculum had changed little from the original mission of teaching women how to be accomplished mothers and home managers. A core offering in the late 1940s was Homemaking Apartments 300, a course in which two instructors, five students, and a baby (recruited from an adoption agency) lived in a college-provided apartment for seven weeks. The "students did laundry, planned menus, cooked, cleaned, had much needed experience in the care of a small child." Instructors in child development supervised the babies' bathing and feeding, and faculty from Nutrition "discussed the babies' food as well as the students' diets."[81]

Vincent was generally comfortable with the college's role, as she put it, in providing "an education for homemaking" and for "skillful and economic management of homes." So was Edmund Ezra Day. At a Home Economics Council Meeting in 1950 the recently retired president said, "Women as homemakers in their own homes need a different set of education than men do and should perhaps have some home and family life education as part of their general education," since "their professional lives are not competitive in the same sense as men's lives are."[82]

Under Canoyer, the college curriculum would become more professional, more scientific, research-based, and policy oriented, focusing on family, public health, and social and consumer issues. Canoyer was a recognized authority in these areas. Coauthor of two books on income and consumption, she became the first woman faculty member of Cornell's Graduate School of Business and Public Administration, where she taught in the Marketing program. In 1962 she was chosen by President Kennedy to be chair of his Consumer Advisory

Council. "This College is looked to for leadership in research by other educational institutions," she wrote in 1957, "and is consulted for home economics information by public and private agencies concerned with the well-being of families and by various fields of industry involved in the production of food, clothing, household textiles and furnishings."[83] In 1962, the college faculty voted unanimously to change the mission statement of the college, affirming in gender-free language its place in the new pre-professional Cornell, where research-informed instruction provided "preparation for professional careers in which the interests and well-being of the individual, the consumer and the family are paramount. . . . The specialized studies in the College relate basic knowledge to an understanding of the needs of people with regard to food, shelter, clothing, management of resources, and interpersonal and family relationships."[84]

The College of Veterinary Medicine was demographically the mirror opposite of Home Economics. Of its annual student body of around two hundred in this period, there were never more than five women students, proportions that did not trouble Dean W. A. Hagan, who served from 1932 to 1959. In 1953 he informed an angry mother that her daughter's "application had sufficient merit to have gained her admission, probably in the first group of those accepted, had she been a boy." Women lacked the physical strength to deal with large animals, Hagan wrote. "They can't ride over rough country roads in the middle of the night." Furthermore, the few recent women graduates of the school had had professional careers that were "disappointing." Women would be admitted only when there were "not enough boys who could meet the admission requirements." Too much prejudice existed against women vets in upstate rural areas, Hagan added, and when asked whether similar prejudice against a Negro or a Jew meant rejecting their applications, he replied, "Certainly not, because there is an anti-discrimination law in New York State."[85] Nonetheless, the Veterinary College Council agreed that spring that the college should "occasionally admit a competent girl to prove there is no consistent policy of discrimination."[86] How ironic that when the Veterinary College celebrated its centennial in 1994, over 90 percent of its students were women.

Under Hagan's leadership, the Vet School, one of only three in the Northeast and twenty-eight in the country, flourished. The author of a widely used textbook, *The Infectious Diseases of Domestic Animals*, who also taught that subject each year, Hagan presided over the college's reincarnation in 1957 and 1958 as perhaps the best-equipped, most scientifically advanced Vet School in the country, with nineteen new buildings on twenty acres at the east end of Tower Road. For most of its life the school had sat at the other end of Tower Road, between Garden Avenue and East Avenue. Its proximity to the president's house, across Tower Road, had led Malott to move off campus, the first Cornell president to do so, in order, as he put it, to avoid the nighttime noises of barking dogs and other animals. The college's migration eastward set off the complicated domino effect in which the ILR and Engineering Colleges found their permanent homes.

An earlier proposed move of the Veterinary College, over much greater distance, had been firmly rejected. In 1949 the state of New York suggested that the college move to Syracuse to be part of the new Upstate Medical Center. Howard Babcock, the most politically connected trustee, scotched the idea with a letter to Governor Dewey. A Vet School, he wrote, "must be closely associated with agriculture and near a College with agronomy, animal husbandry, and nutrition."[87]

CORNELL'S RELATIONSHIP TO the state of New York underwent a dramatic change in the immediate postwar period, at least on paper. Anticipating a shortage of college places for returning veterans and concerned about discrimination in admissions to private colleges, the Legislature created in 1948 the State University of New York (SUNY), an entity designed to include the existing state teachers colleges, technical and agricultural institutes, a new community college system, new four-year liberal arts colleges, graduate centers, as well as Cornell's four "state" colleges. Cornell was gravely concerned that the heretofore relatively autonomous Agriculture, Veterinary, Home Economics, and ILR schools, "by contract" under the jurisdiction of the State Education Department, which provided construction funds and operating budget support, would now be run, operated, or constrained by the trustees of SUNY.

President Day and the four "contract" deans—Myers, Hagan, Vincent, and Catherwood—vigorously lobbied the legislature, the trustees of SUNY, and Governor Dewey, then preoccupied with his presidential race against Harry Truman. Day telegrammed Dewey: "Cannot believe that public interest will be served by impairment of the highly successful relationship which has long existed between New York State and Cornell University in the administration of the State Colleges at Ithaca." He wrote to the SUNY trustees that Cornell's four "primarily State supported" Colleges "are generally acknowledged to be the leaders in their respective fields in the United States" precisely because of "a minimum of regulation by the State authorities." He added that Cornell was "very loath to see its existing relations with the State and the State Colleges disturbed" and hoped the "actual administration of the four State Colleges at Cornell will be left in the hands of the Board of Trustees of Cornell University."[88]

Cornell's fears were misplaced. As a result, perhaps, of the expression of concerns by Day and the appointment of Arthur Dean as the vice chairman of the SUNY board of trustees, SUNY would prove no more interested in closely overseeing the operations of Cornell's four "contract" colleges than the State Board of Education had been before 1948.

Still, some friction became the norm between SUNY, the state government, and Cornell. Malott complained to Governor Rockefeller in 1960, for example, about the state's foot-dragging on Cornell's recommendations for increased pay to keep contract college faculty from being raided by peer institutions and to bring them closer to parity with endowed faculty. A year later, after a decade of squabbling over the meaning of Cornell's authority "to set tuition after prior consultation with the State University Board of Trustees," an agreement was reached allowing Cornell to charge New York State residents tuition in the contract colleges and to set tuition in them "at a rate not less than the tuition charged at other SUNY units."[89] The state also agreed to fund twenty-five new faculty positions for the four contract colleges and to provide an across-the-board 7.5 percent pay increase for the faculty, as part of its $15 million allocation to Cornell that year.

Financial negotiations with Albany became an annual ritual for Cornell administrators after the creation of SUNY. The complications of its financial relationship with Albany would be mirrored in Ithaca in the postwar period by the demands of a more assertive city. Cornell wanted more money from the state—and Ithaca wanted more money from Cornell. In March 1948 Mayor Baker asked President Day to increase Cornell's annual contribution to the city for sewage disposal from $5,500 to $8,000 a year. Day's counsel, Robert Meigs, LLB '27, informed the president "that an additional contribution to the City was justified."[90] The following year, the local Ithaca trustee, Robert Treman, passed on to Day "the gripes of Ithaca businessmen with respect to the commercial activities of Cornell."[91] The list of grievances was long, from Law faculty giving free legal advice and Architecture faculty doing work in town to the College of Agriculture selling meat at retail venues.

A "Resolution of East Hill Merchants" (Collegetown) asked in 1950 that the Cornell Co-op sell only "class-room necessities," not "jewelry, greeting cards, athletic equipment, magazines, etc." If the university competes with local shops, "we believe that taxes should be assessed by the City of Ithaca on their college stores."[92] In 1954 the Tompkins County Board of Supervisors complained that the College of Agriculture sold milk in "destructive competition" with county producers. Dean Myers aggressively defended the practice as "actually a by-product of our research and teaching."[93] The town "gripes" and requests for larger contributions from tax-exempt Cornell would never go away. So, too, the less confrontational, more conciliatory, "gown" response was forged in this period, to be trumpeted in each future confrontation with the "bustling town" on which Cornell "looks proudly down." President Day was advised in 1949 that "we should undertake as a part of our public relations program to engender among Ithacans a greater understanding and appreciation of the advantages they enjoy from Cornell University . . . we should undertake a planned program to get this story across and to convert criticism to approval and support."[94]

As they transformed Cornell into a research university, President Day, and especially President Malott, presided over a "construction boom, aptly characterized by the *Daily Sun* as "the most significant expansion and physical growth in Cornell's history."[95] The *Sun* estimated that university construction from 1947 to 1957 cost $38.6 million. A new office building at the intersection of Tower Road and East Avenue was built in 1947 for officers of the central administration, equipped "with new IBM machines and time-saving devices." Into it the university president, vice president, and provost came from overcrowded Morrill Hall, along with 230 administrators and offices including the dean of the faculty, dean of the graduate school, the registrar, the Buildings and Grounds Office, the Campus Patrol, the Placement Office, Purchasing, residence halls departments, Admissions, counselors of students, the treasurer, and Alumni Affairs, who had been, as the *Sun* put it, "spread out all over the campus in little nooks and cubby-holes."[96] One month after Day's death in 1951, the trustees voted unanimously to name the "Administration Building" Edmund Ezra Day Hall.

In addition to the building destined to bear his name, the postwar Day years saw the construction of Clara Dickson Hall (1947), a women's dormitory named after Andrew Dickson White's mother; Savage Hall (1947); the Nuclear Studies Lab (1948); and Statler Hall (1950). Malott then became Cornell's "master builder." In his twelve-year presidency, the university's two great libraries, Mann (1953) and Olin (1961), were built, as were Anabel Taylor Hall (1952) and the Gannett Medical Clinic (1957) on Campus Road south of Willard Straight Hall. The new clinic, a gift of the Gannett Newspaper Foundation created by trustee Frank Gannett '98, moved the university's health clinic out of the first floor of Cascadilla Hall. Most monumental in Malott's tenure were all the buildings in the Engineering quad (1956–59), the buildings for the College of Veterinary Medicine (1957–58), and ILR Ives Hall (1962). But there was also Morrison Hall (1961), which was the new home of Animal Husbandry in the Agriculture College, and Clark Hall (1963) in the Arts College.

As early as 1946, Gilmore Clarke, the Architecture dean, had proposed an art museum in the south end of Goldwin Smith's basement, adjacent to "the Museum of casts," an idea that was rejected by Day because of its cost. Once the Malotts eschewed living in the A. D. White House in 1951, that house became the obvious site for an art museum. In November 1953, the University Art Museum opened there with eight galleries and two major traveling exhibits—the Lessing Rosenwald Collection from the National Gallery in Washington and works by French photographer Eugène Atget, on loan from New York's Museum of Modern Art. The university's permanent collection of artwork, collecting dust in the lofts of the Law School, was moved to the President's Mansion for all to see, and one gallery room was set aside for Cornelliana, documents and exhibits relating to the history of the university. In its first year, ten thousand people visited the University Art Museum.

Malott built dormitories as well. Women students at postwar Cornell were required to live in either Sage, Balch, Risley, or Clara Dickson Hall, while men were free to reside as "independents" in Ithaca rooming houses and apartments, or in university housing, such as the nineteenth-century Cascadilla Hall in Collegetown, and the World War I "Gothics" on West Campus: Baker Court, Founders Hall, and Boldt Hall, and Mennen, Lyon, and McFaddin Halls. Each year since 1945 between five and eight hundred male students also lived in "temporary" wooden barracks on West Campus, below the "Gothics," built to house some of the military trainees stationed at Cornell. Flimsy and drafty, the barracks were potential fire traps. The students voted with their feet; in 1951 more men students lived off campus than lived in all the dormitories, barracks, and fraternities on campus.

Shortly after his arrival on campus, Malott named student housing and a central library his two top priorities. He told the trustees that "Cornell is losing students to institutions which are building dormitory quadrangles in anticipation of an era of education in which the University cares for its students 24 hours every day seven days a week." His concern was wrapped up in an evocation of the ideal of *in loco parentis*, of moving students from apartments to dorms, as revealed by his announcement in his first talk to the trustees that his administration's job "was to keep Cornell a wholesome place."[97] Arthur Dean agreed that "the need for more decent living space for male students is urgent, pressing and immediate. It is here now. Every day that it is not solved is a disgrace."[98]

The board approved a plan for new housing for six hundred to eight hundred students five weeks later. There were deep divisions within the board, however, on how to finance the buildings. Since no donor emerged to fund them, the issue was whether, like Rensselaer Polytechnic Institute and Syracuse University, Cornell should borrow money from the federal government's Housing and Home Finance Agency. Myron Taylor objected "in principle to any borrowing from the Federal Government." Nicholas Noyes railed that such "borrowing only encourages government growth." Both claimed that government support meant "government control."[99] The principal advocate for taking the forty-year loan at 2.75 percent was Arthur Dean. The university, he noted, received millions in research funds from the federal government and "12,000,000 per annum from New York State to operate four-state supported colleges and schools. . . . Is that humiliating?" As he understood the terms of the proposed federal loan, "the government would have absolutely no control over the operations of the dormitories, its position being only that of a lender." Using Cornell's own endowment funds to pay for the dorms, Dean concluded, would make it impossible for the university "to maintain our academic standards as a first-class institution."[100] After weeks of debate, nineteen of twenty-two trustees voted to finance the construction entirely out of an internal loan from the university's endowment, to be repaid over time from housing fees.

While the financing debate raged, Malott informed the *Daily Sun* about plans to build new student residences for men, "designed to further a new way of life on campus, not as mere dormitories."[101] This approach had circulated around Cornell since 1945 when the dean of men, Harold Speight, had suggested Harvard-like "houses" on campus instead of "dormitories," with graduate students, or young faculty, living in them, dining halls as part of the "house," and "frequent visits at the dinner meal of faculty members and their wives."[102] Malott borrowed from this plan by announcing that each new residence "hall" would include dining and recreational facilities, along with graduate student couples in residence. In the fall of 1952 architectural plans were released for six new residence halls to be built on north-south horizontal plateaus, breaking up the east-west sloping hill between the "Gothic" dorms on West Avenue and Stewart Avenue, where the World War II barrack dorms still sat. Because of the expense, the idea of placing a dining hall in each of the six 225-men units was dropped, and a large student center where all West Campus students could eat was contemplated, ultimately to be funded by Nicholas Noyes. Soon after the plans were made public, the Architecture College class of 1953 published a full-page critique of them in the *Sun*, assailing the design, with the five stories dwarfing the nearby Baker group, the cramped sizes of the rooms, the absence of sound insulation, and the "four showers for every 55 students." Using Cold War rhetoric, perhaps ironically, the critique concluded, "These buildings do not reflect our American way of life in that there is a striking similarity to brick barracks." Malott told the students, as they recounted it, that "all this design quality was very subjective. He was glad we were interested, but said the University had four architects, all of them Cornellians, who believed these plans to be good."[103]

Built at a cost of $4.2 million, the six University Halls opened in September 1954. Although the presence of married-couple chaperones permitted weekend entertaining of women in the lounges, the students didn't like the new dorms. They called the U-Halls "The Stables" and complained about the quality of the construction. The green and yellow cinderblock walls soon cracked, and the plywood doors were vulnerable "to strong fists" and "ambitious knocking." "The long, uniform corridors gave rise to shaving cream fights and other sorts of rumbles." The *Daily Sun* editorialized that instead of Malott's new style of campus living, "living arrangements like these promote either frolic and conformity or escape, or both."[104] When no donors came forth to name the University Halls, numbered one through six, and an ad hoc committee of the trustees considered naming them after distinguished Cornellians like Charles Kendall Adams or "Teefy" Crane, the *Sun* wrote in an editorial: "This seems to be merely an attempt to cloak the dreary uniformity of these dormitories with fancy names, which will perhaps lend an air of distinction where none is, in fact, present. A spade should be called a spade: the dorms should be allowed to stand for what they are . . . The Stables. . . . The University should not waste such good names on such undeserving buildings."[105] Reluctant to foreclose a fund-raising opportunity, the trustees' committee declined to give the U-Halls names, and so they would remain, reviled or beloved, as the U-Halls, by generations of Cornellians.

Malott also built housing for married students and for women. Apartments for ninety-six married student families were constructed in 1956 on Pleasant Grove Road at the far northern end of campus; more were added in 1961, and a large dorm for 480 women, who were still required to live on campus, was built in 1961 on North Campus near Dickson and Balch Halls. Named for Judge Mary H. Donlon of the U.S. Customs Court in New York City, a graduate of Cornell Law School in 1920, when women lawyers were almost nonexistent, and the only female member of the university's board of trustees, Donlon Hall was the first Cornell residence to have any form of freshman-upperclass integration. It had lounges on the main level, first-year women on the first three upstairs floors, and upperclass women on the fifth and sixth floors. The ideological battles of ten years earlier had waned, or perhaps there was less suspicion of government, because Donlon was the first dormitory on campus financed by a low-interest $4.1 million loan from the New York State Dormitory Authority.

And, finally, Malott built athletic facilities. In 1954 trustee Walter Teagle, who had been assistant manager of football as an undergraduate, funded a men's gymnasium, to be named for him, with two swimming pools and two basketball courts. That same year trustee Leroy Grumman '16, chairman of Grumman Aviation, told the president that he was troubled that his son, then at Deerfield Academy, might go to Harvard or Yale because Cornell had no squash courts. With Malott's encouragement, Grumman donated the courts; and David Grumman '57 came to Cornell, becoming captain of the 1956–57 squash team. A hockey rink with seating for nearly four thousand spectators, named for James Lynah '05, university athletic director from 1935 to 1943, was built in 1957 with money from Walter Carpenter. Making it possible for the university to resume ice hockey as a varsity sport, after a ten-year hiatus, the rink was inaugurated with an exhibition game pitting the New York Rangers against a Rochester minor league team. That same year the Collyer Boat House was built, a gift of John Lyon Collyer, a member of the Cornell crew as an undergraduate, who was then Cornell's chairman of the board of trustees and the CEO of B. F. Goodrich Company. In Malott's last year as president in 1963, Helen Newman Hall, the first athletic facility for women students, was begun on North Campus, overlooking Beebe Lake and near the cluster of women's dorms, Balch, Dickson, and Donlon, the gift of trustee Floyd Roy Newman '12, cofounder of the Allied Oil Company of Cleveland, in honor of his wife.

INTERESTED IN PROVIDING enhanced opportunities for physical exercise, Malott, who swam almost daily in the Teagle Hall pool, was relatively unenthusiastic about intercollegiate sports (with the exception of basketball, which he had followed at Kansas). Early in his presidency he indulged in some "idle dreaming," in which athletic budgets were cut so that "coaches would be paid salaries commensurate with professors, thus making college athletics merely another intramural activity of little interest to sports writers, and, as with baseball, the public's ardor would be transferred to the professional teams." It was only a dream, he wrote, because "it is impossible to put into effect."[106] Still, Malott built on the efforts of President Day to reconceptualize intercollegiate athletics.

In 1937, the presidents of Harvard, Yale, and Princeton, worried about the professionalization of football and the recruitment of star athletes in midwestern and southern schools, had agreed on more stringent rules for eligibility. James Lynah, Cornell's athletic director, made similar commitments to the principle of collegiate amateurism. The formal creation of the "Ivy Group" (the term "Ivy League" was invented in the 1930s by *New York Herald Tribune* writer Caswell Adams), agreed to by the presidents of Cornell, Harvard, Yale, Princeton, Columbia, Penn, Dartmouth, and Brown, took place in the fall of 1945, with the pledge to continue

> intercollegiate football in such a way as to maintain the value of the game while keeping it in fitting proportion to the main purposes of academic life. Under proper conditions, intercollegiate competition in football offers desirable recreation for players and a healthy focus of collegiate loyalty. These conditions require that the players themselves shall be truly representative of the student body and not composed of a group of special recruited and trained athletes . . . and that they be permitted to enjoy the game as participants in a form of recreational competition rather than as performers in a type of public spectacle.[107]

President Day, a devoted fan who attended every home football game and many away games as well, was deeply committed to what he called "football in the Ivy Way." He wrote in 1942 to the vice president of Princeton that "the football squad should reproduce in miniature the profile of the entire student body. Standards of admission ought not to be any lower for football players than for any members of the student body." During the following year he informed a Yale dean of his concern that the Eli were "going all out to produce winning teams," which would force others in the league to follow suit and "defeat the fundamental purposes for which the League was constituted." And in 1944 he told New York's Francis Cardinal Spellman that "after careful consideration it would be unwise for Cornell to commit itself to football contests with Notre Dame as you have suggested," since it would repudiate the principles of the new "so-called Ivy League."[108]

Robert J. Kane, who had succeeded Lynah as director of athletics in 1943, was, not surprisingly, skeptical of the new rules. He saw the hands of Harvard, Yale, and Princeton behind its "restrictive measures, which tend in every respect to deemphasize the game of football . . . to depress and to cast suspicion on intercollegiate athletics and to bring the others (the five other signatories) in line." Kane opposed the elimination of spring practice, because it "would prove to be a great handicap at Cornell." He had no problems with the prohibition of athletic scholarships or the ineligibility of freshmen, but he worried about the supervision of athletics by academic officers, the limitations imposed on athletic budgets, and "the confinement of team personnel to those only in the upper three quarters of the class." The new rules, he concluded, would "take the color from football and attach restrictions until the game becomes entirely devoid of interest to the collegiate world and to the general public."[109]

Day forwarded Kane's concerns to the president of Yale, Charles Seymour, the driving force behind the new "Ivy Group," noting that "there are many institutions over the country in which the sport has assumed an importance which, in our opinion, does violence to the fundamental purposes of the institutions in which it is conducted."[110] Seymour stood firm on the rules Kane had questioned, and Day signed the eight-college agreement in October 1945.

President Malott also did not share Kane's concern that the "Ivy Group is in effect now advertising to the public that it is not playing first rate football and in fact is telling the world it does not wholly approve of intercollegiate football."[111] In 1952, he signed a protocol that prohibited spring practice and postseason games. A final iteration of the football pact was agreed to by the eight university presidents in December 1953, creating an "Ivy League" in which the schools agreed to play an annual "round robin schedule in football and in as many sports as practicable."[112] From 1956 on, the football season comprised nine games, allowing each Ivy school to play the seven others in the league and two outside rivals. Gone forever were the glory days of Cornell football on the national stage, playing powerhouses such as Ohio State, Michigan, and Navy. Gone were invitations to play in the Rose Bowl, which the 1939 team, number one in the country, had turned down because, as Kane later described it, "our boys had had enough football and had to get down to the books."[113] Malott's "wholesome" decision in 1956 to ban alcohol at Schoellkopf Stadium meant that gone as well were the large crowds—like the 35,500 at Schoellkopf in 1947 who saw Navy clobber Cornell 38–19—which provided the revenue to support the rest of the university's varsity teams.

ONE OF THE most important administrative changes at Cornell in the postwar period was the professionalization of fund-raising, which was triggered, fittingly enough, by the need to finance the new research university. In January 1946, trustees chairman Howard Babcock lamented that Cornell fund-raising was "inadequate and ineffective. . . . Every day fundraising activities remain in the present fuzzy state, Cornell's future is jeopardized."[114] He knew that Cornell had a unique problem in calling on alumni for gifts. He had recently heard from trustee Neal Dow Becker '06 that few trustees were "prepared to make Cornell their principal avocation in life . . . this is a hell of a big order. . . . Cornell being a first generation college, we rarely have men of wealth and leisure who can sacrifice other interests."[115] Babcock was also concerned about the designation of the university provost as chief fund-raiser. Provost George Sabine and his successors, Arthur Adams in 1946 and de Kiewiet in 1948, in fact had their offices adjoining the Alumni Fund to facilitate collaboration. Meanwhile, the board of trustees had hired a consultant on fund-raising, whose recommendation that the university create a new vice president in charge of "raising capital funds" was implemented in 1946. Their choice for that position was Solomon Hollister, "upon the understanding that he will retain the Deanship of the College of Engineering."[116] Fund-raising was thus the part-time responsibility of two already busy university officers. Babcock explained why this approach didn't last:

> At the end of the war the University had picked up reserves and it had on hand a good many hundreds of thousands of dollars of unrestricted gifts. The University then embarked on a construction program for buildings which were badly needed. These buildings were put up and there would have been hundreds of thousands of dollars left of free money had we not run right into "the atomic age," i.e. the Laboratory of Nuclear Studies.[117]

The need for the university to raise at least $1 million, and perhaps $2 million, in 1947 and 1948 to pay for the nuclear lab to house a high-energy electron accelerator brought rapid and permanent professionalization of fund-raising. Day announced that the provost would henceforth "be largely concerned with academic and educational matters, certain governmental agencies, and the operation of the great foundations."[118] Hollister shed his vice presidency, which became a full-time position: vice president for university development, "responsible for all fundraising activities of the University."[119] Day appointed

Asa Knowles, a nonacademic, career college administrator with no Cornell background, to the position. He would be succeeded in 1951 by Willard I. Emerson '19, a partner in a New York investment bank.

Day and the trustees had had to respond quickly, to retain Hans Bethe and his cohort of young physicists. They now scrambled to raise the money they had committed but did not have. Even as fund-raising responsibilities were being changed, the Laboratory of Nuclear Studies was built, overlooking Beebe Lake between Baker Chemistry Labs and Martha Van Rensselaer Hall, and dedicated on October 8, 1948, with an address by the Columbia University physicist Isidor Rabi '19, a future Nobel laureate.

By then, the new fund-raising operation was in place. A "Greater Cornell Committee" composed of some four hundred alumni leaders of business, industry, and the professions "enlisted to aid in furthering the development of the University" was formed by Knowles in 1948, with John Collyer as chair. Cornell announced an unprecedented "campaign" to raise $12.5 million over two years "to meet the most urgent needs of the University."[120] A year later, administrators celebrated a contribution of $1,434,000 for the Laboratory of Nuclear Studies from Floyd R. Newman, whose Allied Oil Company had that year merged with Ashland Oil Company. On October 21, 1949, the lab was rededicated as the Newman Laboratory of Nuclear Studies, with Newman noting, "I believe in scientific research as a basis of our industrial strength and our economy."[121]

John Collyer announced completion of the Greater Cornell Fund "campaign" in March 1951. With gifts from more than twenty-three thousand alumni totaling $12,649,000, Collyer described the thirty-month campaign "as one of the largest to be undertaken by an institution of higher learning . . . an outstanding achievement in the fundraising history of colleges and universities." The cost of the campaign, he boasted, was around $900,000, or 7 percent of the gross amount of gifts received, much less than the percentage in similar campaigns. Some seventy thousand Cornellians had learned of the university's financial needs during the campaign, he noted, a testimony to the university's new approach. "During the campaign, the organization of the Office of University Development has been improved greatly. The campaign has resulted in establishing a permanent fundraising organization, for the first time," Collyer told the *Cornell Alumni News*.[122]

Fund-raising at Cornell was permanently professionalized. The vice president for development transformed the large and unwieldy ad hoc Greater Cornell Committee into a leaner permanent Cornell University Council, with Francis Sheetz '16 as chairman. The 150 alumni, serving three-year terms, made "alumni assistance more effective and more readily available to the Trustees and the University."[123] Vice President Emerson centralized annual giving, gifts for special projects, bequests, and life income agreements in the Development office. On the fourth floor of Day Hall, a staff of twelve kept files on eighty thousand Cornell alumni, filled with the details gleaned from newspaper clippings, wedding and birth announcements, and professional publications. In 1951 Emerson created a Parents Committee, soliciting gifts from non-Cornellian parents of students in the endowed colleges. The following year, eleven business firms became charter members of the new "University Associates," industries providing "unrestricted financial support" to Cornell. Among the founding associates, paying an annual membership fee of $1,000, were some "usual suspects": Avco Manufacturing, B. F. Goodrich, and the Raymond Concrete Pile Company.

The "fuzzy state" of Cornell fund-raising was but a distant memory in 1962, Malott's last full year as president, when the Development office established the "Tower Club" for donors of $1,000 or more in a given year, "to raise the sights of other alumni capable of making larger gifts."[124] That fund-raising for Cornell was a permanent, professional operation was clear to all Cornellians that fall when Arthur Dean took time out from his duties as President Kennedy's ambassador to the disarmament negotiation at Geneva to announce in Ithaca the beginning of a $73.2 million, three-year "Centennial Campaign." One-fifth of the funds had already been subscribed, Dean announced, and, not surprisingly, bringing us full circle, the $13,692,000 already pledged included a Ford Foundation grant of $3.7 million for the College of Engineering and a $4 million commitment from the Advanced Research Project Administration of the U.S. Department of Defense.

The pieces were in place to support and sustain Cornell, the research university. As he prepared to leave office, President Malott advanced an interesting rationale to justify his confidence about the future. At a meeting with members of the university's Traffic Board, the body charged with adjudicating disputes over parking and making recommendations about the location of additional lots, Professor John Reps, MRP '47, one of the nation's leading authorities on city and regional planning, suggested that Cornell needed a permanent Campus Planning Committee composed of faculty and administrators. Three or four sentences into Reps's prepared presentation, the president raised his hand and demurred. "Now, now, Professor Reps," he said, confidently, "do you not recognize that the campus is essentially complete?"[125] To the dismay of some alumni, Malott's successors and the vast majority of faculty and administrators did not agree.

2 | The Death of *In Loco Parentis*

The wartime students who had chanted "We want liberty!" in front of Willard Straight the day Japan surrendered continued their celebrations when classes were cancelled. They left, according to one account, "State Street strewn with beer bottles." They could not know then that their numbers, relatively small because of wartime, would grow dramatically with the postwar "GI invasion" of East Hill.[1] Six months after the end of hostilities, President Day, along with eighty-five other presidents of institutions of higher education in New York State, was summoned to a meeting in Albany to help Governor Thomas E. Dewey develop a strategy for educating and housing the vast number of veterans whose tuition, room, and board would be paid by the GI Bill of Rights. Dewey proposed that each institution increase the number of its enrolled students "by 26 percent or more."[2]

Cornell was already on board. President Day's sense of public responsibility, displayed so clearly in 1943 when he warmly welcomed the thousands of servicemen and women sent by the federal government for wartime training on the Ithaca campus, had led him to form a committee in 1945 to plan for the return of thousands of former Cornell students who had left campus to enter the armed services, as well as new veteran applicants. Day's committee agreed that Cornell's enrollment in 1946–47 would be over 9,000 students, an increase of nearly 40 percent over the largest enrollment of the prewar years. Of the students who appeared on campus in 1947, 7,400 were men, 1,900 were women—and 5,200 of them were GIs. "Cornell is ready for the veterans," university officials told Dewey in September 1946.[3] To prove it, the institution mailed a brochure, *Cornell Is Ready*, to 54,000 alumni, 1,300 new students, 900 faculty, and 400 newspapers and national magazines.

The university's handling of the GI invasion was not without its problems. In 1946 the director of admissions told Day that "we shall send out about 2,000 refusals to veterans in the next month, and not less than 4,000 during the spring and summer."[4] Recognizing that many of those who had been turned down would be bitter, he worried about an adverse reaction from the public. This concern, however, paled next to the truly monumental challenge of housing over five thousand veterans along with their thirteen hundred wives and nearly one thousand babies. After identifying and rejecting a wide range of possible locations for temporary housing—George Jr. Republic, a residential community for teenage boys in nearby Freeville, the Auburn Theological Seminary, even the top floor of the new administration building—Cornell took over the abandoned Glen Springs Hotel in Watkins Glen; purchased some barracks from the Sampson Naval Station and moved them to Ithaca; and leased hundreds of prefabricated two-family houses, transporting them from a war plant in Massena and reassembling them on a plot of land beyond the East Ithaca Railway Station, which was quickly christened Vetsburg. More apartments were built nearby in what was soon called East Vetsburg, with others to follow, on land at the end of Tower Road used for the dairy herds, despite concern that bulls might endanger the safety of the children. New apartments were constructed on Kline Road in leafy Cayuga Heights, as well.

Student housing in Vetsburg. (Division of Rare and Manuscript Collections of the Cornell University Library)

Even with this new housing and the repurposing of barracks that had housed the troops who had trained on campus during the war, there was still an acute shortage, especially for married veterans. Some lived in a trailer camp on Route 13 in Varna, which was featured in a November 1947 *Life* magazine article on GIs on college campuses. More enterprising types tried the Ithaca rental market, as indicated by the entry in the *Ithaca Journal*'s "Wanted to Rent" section in November 1945: "Young lady, two years old, wants furnished or unfurnished apartment or house. No crying at night, scribbling on walls, smashing windows. No pets, two parents, father is veteran. Mother is nervous wreck, but a house will remedy that."[5]

Yet another problem created by what Day labeled "the battle of the G.I. bulge" was the dire need for new faculty to teach so many new students. In 1946 and 1947 two hundred faculty were hired. They, too, needed housing, and the university in 1946 put prefabricated buildings on South Hill for fifty faculty families. Cornell was indeed ready, or, more precisely, rough and ready. This readiness, however, entailed a reduction in the education of women. Unhappy with the university's rapid response to the veterans' invasion, women students and alumnae complained that as veterans' numbers soared, the number of women students tumbled; their letters piled up on Day's desk.

Once housed, the veterans found a university committed to helping them. Headed by Emeritus Professor Bristow Adams '00, the Cornell Veterans Education Office was well staffed with counselors, ready to dispense advice about courses and address personal concerns. Prenatal clinics were created for vet wives, a cooperative nursery school for vet children, and career counseling for the vets themselves. The bookstore gave veterans priority, first in line, in course book purchasing, extending them temporary credit if their benefits checks were late. A special university coordinator of faculty affairs helped veterans plan how to make do with their spartan $65 per month stipend, or $90 if married. This service was particularly important, since the GI Bill was bringing to colleges like Cornell qualified students from less privileged backgrounds who had difficulty making ends meet.

The presence of so many veterans on campus until the early 1950s had a profound and sometimes paradoxical impact on student life and culture at Cornell. University officials repeatedly described the veterans as "mature," "serious," and "worldly-wise," with more "assurance," "poise," and "better manners" than their prewar predecessors. "We have never had a more diligent, intelligent, and generally satisfactory body of students," Day noted.[6] The returning engineer Wilbur Gundlach '45 was typical. Gundlach knew the campus and felt at home on East Hill, but "many items are different. My social life is first on the list here, as I now have a beautiful wife and seven month old son. There's a great incentive to study and 'hit' the books."[7] The married veterans were indeed serious and scholarly. In the fall 1947 term, their average grade of

77 was higher than sorority, frat, and independent student average grades; only tiny, selective Telluride did better. Single veterans were high academic achievers as well, but they seemed to play and party more conspicuously than prewar Cornellians, exhibiting a greater willingness to experiment with sexuality, drugs, and alcohol.

The veterans' presence on campus challenged the perhaps illusory notion of undergraduate innocence. Three novels written by Cornellians in the 1950s and set in Ithaca provided illustrative details. In *On a Darkling Plain*, Clifford Irving '51 (who decades later would write a fraudulent memoir of Howard Hughes and land in jail) portrayed returning veterans flouting convention through mindless and never-ending bouts of drinking and sex in an apartment on Linden Avenue. Similarly, in *After Long Silence*, Robert Gutwillig '53 filled wild Collegetown parties with GIs. The most popular of these Cornell postwar novels, *Halfway Down the Stairs*, by Charles Thompson '51, MA '52, set in stone this reading of veterans on campus. In the book's preface and in the *Cornell Sun*, Thompson claimed, quite presciently, that after veterans from World War II came back to university campuses, those campuses would never be the same again. Sexual life, in particular, would be forever altered. The ad copy for Thompson's book read: "*Halfway Down the Stairs* is a dramatic and rewarding novel about an extraordinary group of undergraduates at an eastern university during the late 1940s and early 1950s. They were a group in pursuit of kicks, which they found in liquor, marijuana, and intense, but loveless sexuality."

This is, of course, literary exaggeration, but the "worldly-wise" veterans with their sense of personal freedom and independence and their new moral codes shook Cornell and much of student life at Cornell in the 1950s. The student riots of 1958 in part reflected the confrontation between this aspect of the veterans' legacy and the restrictive social codes, especially for women students, demanded by a university still committed to being *in loco parentis* and presided over by the rather puritanical Deane Malott. They would be an utterly unintended consequence of Cornell's "battle of the G.I. bulge," which Day solemnly declared over, in 1949, when he announced that more freshmen accepted for the class of 1953 came directly from secondary schools than from the armed services.

THE SOLDIER STUDENTS had fought a war against the racist ideology of the Nazis. They brought to America and to Cornell a new sensitivity to discrimination against racial, religious, and ethnic groups. Laura Z. Hobson '21 contributed to that awareness with her successful 1947 novel about anti-Semitism, *Gentleman's Agreement*. It would take time, however, to abandon old ways of thinking, as indicated by an exchange in July 1945 between Day and Newton Burnett '24, a Boston businessman who had been president of the Cornell Club of New

England and an alumni trustee. After a visit to campus with his son, a senior at Deerfield Academy, Burnett wrote to Day about his misgivings of sending the young man to Cornell. It was not the Cornell of his father, class of 1890, he opined, or his own Cornell of the early 1920s. "Cannot something be done to restrict the Jewish element to the former small percentage? I certainly do believe that unless the present trend is promptly stopped that they will soon take the university over."[8] In his reply, Day struggled to accommodate old expectations and new realities:

> After the war we shall have a reasonable representation of Jewish elements on the campus, but not so large a representation as to make it unpleasant for first class gentile students to continue coming to Cornell. . . . Cornell ought to take a considerable proportion of Jewish students, given the section of the country in which it is located, in fact as large a proportion of Jewish students as can be taken without running into the sort of repercussions you have in mind crowding out legacies. In other words, I do not think we can wisely go as "pure" as certain other Eastern institutions.[9]

Young Newton Burnett Jr., it is worth noting, matriculated at Cornell, in the fall of 1946, but did not complete a degree. That same year trustee Nicholas Noyes '06 wrote to Day with similar, if not so explicit, misgivings. "I do hope that next fall we can get in more boys who have established Cornell connections."[10]

In the postwar years, according to a Cornell United Religious Work survey, Jews made up 12 percent of the undergraduate student body and 22 percent of the students in Arts and Sciences. Despite their numbers on campus, Jews were seen by many administrators, faculty, and fellow students as different. When the then dean of Arts and Sciences, Cornelis de Kiewiet, wrote to Provost George Sabine '31, PhD '36, about hiring a Harvard zoologist, Marcus Singer, later to make his mark on Cornell history, he noted, "He is Jewish which does not bother me, even though I do not like racialists or Zionists."[11] Sabine himself wrote to Day that same year, 1945, about hiring Milton Konvitz, PhD '33. "He is a Jew. His appearance is such you can't mistake it."[12] And when the dean of students, Harold Speight, wanted to allay concerns over the Marxist Discussion Group in 1946, he described its membership as tiny; moreover, "most of its members are Jewish," who "attract almost entirely their own type."[13]

The Jewish presence at Cornell, then, did not go unnoticed. A memorandum to Day in July 1945 from the director of the School of Education, Howard Anderson, offered "an analysis of the racial composition of the summer school population." Using as its criteria "(1) surname, e.g. Cohen, (2) middle name, which is often the mother's name, and (3) given name . . . and the student's home address, e.g. in the Bronx, and his college, e.g. Brooklyn," Anderson listed 173 names from Anne Adalman to Rhoda Weiskopf, which constituted 56 percent of the summer students. The director recommended a "quota" on students from "such institutions as New York University and Hunter." If this were done, he concluded, "it should be possible to make a selection which would materially reduce the proportion of Jewish students admitted."[14]

Students, too, seemed concerned about "the Jewish problem." A *Cornell Sun* poll found in 1947 that 43 percent of Cornell students would "not like to have a Jewish roommate."[15] One student in these years recalls that when she introduced herself at a Willard Straight Hall "mixer" as "Sheila Epstein, a freshman at ILR," a fellow student responded, "Are you a kike, a commie or both?" Other students tell of two worlds at Cornell in these years, with, for example, the Ivy Room at Willard Straight having a "Jewish and a white side." Fraternity and sorority "rushees" were often asked "What holidays do you celebrate?"[16] No surprise, then, that two Jewish students wrote a piece in the *Sun*, "God and Man at Cornell," using William F. Buckley Jr.'s recent best-selling exposé of what he saw as Yale's rejection of Christian values to make the opposite case for Cornell. The university, they argued, had abandoned its historic nonsectarianism and was forcing "its students to accept one religious belief, Christianity."[17]

That same *Sun* poll found 33 percent of students preferring not to have a Negro roommate, the lower percentage perhaps a reflection of how unlikely it was that an undergraduate would be matched with one of the ten black undergraduates attending Cornell in 1952. Minute numbers, however, did not mute the bias directed against blacks. An Ithaca restaurant's refusal in 1946 to serve dinner to two black students led to the formation of a small but active Ithaca chapter of the NAACP. Its members protested the racial stereotyping rampant in Cornell's humor magazine, the *Widow*, and the refusal of Ithaca barbers to cut blacks' hair. The Ithaca NAACP disclosed, and alone opposed, the minstrel show held at the College of Agriculture's annual Farm and Home Week in 1951. And in 1947 the local chapter's survey of department chairs found that 29 percent of them had "hesitations about employing a qualified Negro" on the staff.[18]

The chapter's major grievance in these years, however, was housing discrimination in Ithaca. When a *Sun* survey found that three hundred of six hundred Ithaca landlords would not rent to a "colored student," a petition signed by 650 students and endorsed by the Student Council proposed in 1952 that the university require providers of off-campus housing to sign a nondiscrimination pledge. Malott rejected the proposal, claiming that university intrusion into the local real estate market would impinge on the "freedom of individual initiative." He also noted that he was somewhat "suspicious that leftist students were behind the petition."[19]

The university was slow to recognize changing attitudes about bias. In 1947 the New York State Department of Education sought legislation eliminating discrimination in college admissions. A Fair Education Practices bill prohibited colleges and universities from requiring applicants to provide photographs of themselves or asking questions about family background and character references, and recommended reliance on objective evaluations of academic performance. Enlisting the argument traditionally used to exclude Jews and blacks from elite universities, Day opposed the bill. "Questions of character and personality, and emotional stability, of leadership qualities, are important and not seen on objective scales," he wrote the State Department of Education.[20] Cornell's director of admissions, Herbert Williams '25, told Albany officials that the university would agree to stop asking applicants their place of birth and their mother's maiden name, but would continue to ask for a photograph: "I feel very sure that photographs are not used for discriminatory purposes. . . . I have the disturbing feeling that the less personal background information we are able to request of applicants, the less able we will be to give full and sympathetic attention to those, who because of foreign parentage and consequent language handicap, or because of color or race, most need full understanding on our part."[21]

Albany was less than persuaded about Cornell's "sympathetic attention" to those most needing the university's "full understanding." In 1950 Frederick Hoeing, the administrator of the Fair Educational Practices Act signed into law by Governor Dewey in 1948, and the man to whom Williams had written about photographs, sent a chart to Cornell, detailing the percentage of Jewish and non-Jewish applicants who had been rejected by selected New York colleges in 1949. Cornell did not look good.[22]

College	% of Jews Rejected	% of "Non-Jews" Rejected
Brooklyn	6.6	10.7
Syracuse	8.5	5.7
Vassar	9.5	11.1
Hamilton	10.0	18.2
Univ. of Rochester	16.2	13.8
Skidmore	25.0	21.1
Barnard	33.3	11.1
Columbia	35.1	13.6
Colgate	46.2	15.2
Cornell	51.7	35.8
Sarah Lawrence	53.8	66.7

Herbert Williams stood his ground. There "is no discrimination in Cornell Admissions," he insisted; and the university would continue to require that photos accompany applications. "People who are refused by Cornell because they are not qualified frequently fish around for a reason. If they are members of a minority group, they may say it was discrimination that kept them out."[23]

Members of the Hillel Council, the Council of Independent Students, the Young Democrats, the Young Progressives, the NAACP, and the *Cornell Daily Sun* advocated ending the practice of admissions photography. In the 1950s Cornell finally complied with Albany's legislation. Other students took positive steps to combat bigotry and encourage racial and religious tolerance on campus. Two sophomores, Samuel Sachman and Jack Shenkman, established an interracial, interreligious co-op, Watermargin, on 103 McGraw Place, with the credo "All men are brothers." Still flourishing, Watermargin, the name of a Chinese classic translated by Pearl Buck '25, MA '38, opened in 1949 with an initial membership of sixty, half of whom lived in the co-op. Among its initial sponsors were three distinguished Cornell graduates, the novelist Laura Z. Hobson, the judge Samuel Leibowitz, LLB '15, and the black athlete Jerome Holland '39, MS '41. A year after it opened, Watermargin brought Eleanor Roosevelt to a packed Bailey Hall, where the former First Lady praised her hosts for "doing at home what must be done in the world at large."[24] In its early years, Marian Anderson, James Farmer, Malcolm X, and Langston Hughes would also be guests of Watermargin.

Postwar issues of bias and discrimination were most contested in Cornell's fraternity and sorority culture. Ever since Andrew Dickson White had declared that he would like to see "the whole body of students . . . divided into fraternities, each living upon the university grounds in its own house, with full responsibility for its keeping and character, and never to be interfered with," fraternities had flourished at Cornell.[25] Although fraternities were labeled "anti-intellectual" and "dissipation societies" by some in the years after the war, nearly 50 percent of undergraduate men were members of some fifty-seven fraternities in 1950, most of which had restrictive "clauses" excluding Jews and Negroes from membership.

In 1949, two Jewish Cornellians spoke out against these fraternity practices. Edward L. Bernays '12, nephew of Sigmund Freud and founder of the field of public relations in the United States, sent a telegram to the *Daily Sun* criticizing the university and Provost Cornelis de Kiewiet for "pussyfooting" about the restrictive clauses, and thus "endorsing . . . [and] encouraging . . . the principle and practice of prejudice." Robert Fogel '48, leader of the small Cornell Marxist Discussion Group and future Nobel laureate in economics, chimed in a month later, blasting Cornell administrators for "buttressing anti-Semitism and Jim Crow in fraternities."[26]

True to White's vision of self-governance, the university let the fraternities handle the issue themselves, and they did. The Cornell Intrafraternity Council (IFC) announced in the spring of 1949 that "restrictive clauses in any shape or form that discriminate along racial or religious lines create a paradox and also tend to be undemocratic as we understand the institutions of this country"— even though in 1947 the IFC had defeated a resolution "decrying racial discrimination in fraternities" with only one affirmative vote cast.[27] So began a more than decade-long battle over bias between the Cornell fraternity leadership and individual chapters. A *Sun* survey in 1949 supported the IFC's new stance, finding that 72 percent of all students (78 percent of independents, 64 percent of fraternity men) disapproved of restrictive clauses. A "Discrimination Committee" was created by the IFC in 1950, which issued a report in 1952 claiming that twenty-one Cornell fraternities had "restrictive clauses." The committee reiterated its conviction that such discrimination is "wrong and should be eliminated," but urged that "the elimination should come from within."[28] To compel fraternities to abolish discrimination was a violation of fraternity rights. The leadership pledged, however, that it would persuade the twenty-one chapters to drop their restrictive clauses. The university remained uninvolved, ratifying, in effect, the IFC's strategy, while the Student Council supported a more activist administration role.

A committee of faculty, IFC leaders, and Student Council members found in 1954 that only eight of the twenty-one offending chapters had dropped their bias clauses. By 1955 a less passive President Malott had appointed a joint student-faculty committee on discrimination in fraternities, and its student chair, Stephen H. Weiss '57, of Beta Sigma Rho (a future chair of Cornell's board of trustees), announced that December that eight fraternities still had formal restrictions on membership. Since some offending Cornell fraternities were obligated to abide by the discriminatory rules of their national organizations, Weiss noted, his committee was advising local chapters on how to change them at their national conventions. On the other hand, Weiss, using the phrase the novelist Laura Hobson had made famous, admitted that some Cornell houses had successfully immunized themselves against possible university sanctions by retaining unwritten "gentlemen's agreements" as to who could be a member.[29]

The university's involvement in the issue intensified that year when the local chapter of Sigma Kappa, one of the thirteen sororities then at Cornell, all of which had agreed in 1952 to have no restrictive clauses, was suspended by the sorority's national council for pledging a black woman. Malott and Dorothy Brooks, dean of women students, condemned this interference with "our students seeking a way of life which meets their needs and justifies their own sense of justice."[30] When the national council refused to lift the suspension, the sorority members, with encouragement from university administrators, voted unanimously to go it alone as an unaffiliated local chapter.

And it was Cornell students who effectively ended official bias at the university. In April 1961, the executive board of the Student Council voted 5–3 to end "categorical discrimination" in all undergraduate organizations, sending the resolution to Malott with the request that he present it to the board of trustees for their approval as official university policy.[31] The university announced that fall that any fraternity with restrictive clauses still in place by 1965 would

not be allowed to remain on campus. The next year, 1962, the university instituted random selection in rooming assignments to reduce the possibility of racial or religious discrimination. Administrators hoped as well that "this policy
will make it more likely that predominantly Christian fraternities will rush and
pledge Jews, since roommates often rush the same house."[32]

THE POSTWAR TENSION between maintaining old ways and adapting to changing times was also evident in the demise of some fabled Cornell traditions.
For decades freshmen had been subject to "frosh rules": they had to wear
little red beanie caps until the Cornell-Penn football game at Thanksgiving, and they could not walk on campus grassy lawns, only on paths. Some
saw such traditions as symbols of upperclass snobbery, while others endorsed them as mechanisms for the freshmen to bond with one another and
promote class spirit.

Freshmen were required to wear beanies until 1958. (Division of Rare and Manuscript Collections
of the Cornell University Library)

The hallowed tradition that these "rules" were enforced by sophomores, however, did them in. Claiming the "ancient" right of their class to shave the heads of freshmen "rule" violators, a mob of sophomores in 1949 cut the hair of three "offending" first-years.[33] In response, the Student Council ended all special freshmen rules. Traditions such as the freshman caps were allowed as long as there was no coercive enforcement. By the fall of 1958 the freshman beanie was gone, replaced by name tags.

Less easily removed were dogs. Cornell's campus, its quadrangles, lecture hall, libraries, and cafeterias had long been an open and hospitable haven to current students' dogs and the abandoned mutts of students past. Here, too, Cornell tradition was whittled away. President Day banned them from the Willard Straight cafeteria in 1948. A year later, the *Cornell Sun* began a campaign to keep them out of libraries, and in 1953 President Malott excluded them from graduation ceremonies. By 1959 dogs were personae non gratae in all university buildings, with the explanation that "dogs in the library are destroying books and disturbing study conditions; dog fights in classrooms have occurred, and students and staff alike have been bitten." Some were unconvinced. One professor wryly noted that "dogs don't make nearly as much noise and commotion as these radiators, or some students." Another critic of this "end of a Cornell era" suggested that if the dogs destroyed books, "the Library just shouldn't let them take out any more."[34]

Other Cornell traditions were laid to rest as well. Historically a twenty-four-hour holiday, Christmas was made a full-blown ten-day recess by the faculty in 1945. Live bears as team mascots were banned from football games in 1948. Tobogganing down Libe Slope was proscribed in 1956, although "sliding" was still allowed. In 1958 the thirty-three-year-old practice of large numbers of freshman spending four days of orientation off campus at camps run by Cornell United Religious Work ended. Of course, new customs appeared. A physical education requirement, introduced during the war, became obligatory for freshman and sophomores in 1945. "Study music" was piped into dorms during exam periods for several years, beginning in the early 1950s. Freshmen men were given preference for dormitory rooms in 1950, with most of them living in Cascadilla Hall. In 1958, as a result of the rising cost of tuition, the increasing number of students needing scholarships, loans, and part-time employment could visit, as so many generations have since, the university's new Financial Aid Office.

Some things didn't change: students still pulled pranks. A group of them took over WVBR's studio at the Straight in 1952. Jarring frayed Cold War nerves, they announced, in a Cornell version of Orson Welles's famous radio broadcast of *War of the Worlds*, that Russian planes were attacking France. Students cheated. In 1949, after three students were suspended for stealing final exams, the *Sun* staff had no trouble getting copies ahead of time for tests in six courses and were promised "any Math or Hotel School exam you want." After interviewing several students, the *Sun* reporter noted, "few had qualms about using the exams." Two years later a Student Council poll showed that "47% of students admit cheating."[35]

The school year was still punctuated with student rituals. The fall had Agriculture–Home Economics Day with its greased pig, handless pie-eating and apple-dunking contests, its crosscut sawing, and tractor-driving events. Commenting on Ag-HEC day one year, a *Sun* columnist observed "no wonder Harvardites [*sic*] refer to Cornell as 'the frontier of the Ivy League.'" January had its "Junior Week" with tray races, ice sculptures, and entertainers such as singer Vaughn Monroe. On St. Patrick's Day in March, there was Willard Straight's annual battle, begun in 1902, between the architects and "the snakes," soon to be called "Green Dragon Day." Every late May there was "spring weekend," with float parades that went from Thurston Avenue's Risley women's

A fraternity-sponsored float at the Spring Weekend parade, 1954. (Division of Rare and Manuscript Collections of the Cornell University Library)

dormitory through campus, down the tunnel of boughs created by budding American elms lining Central Avenue in front of the Straight, finally to Collegetown and State Street downtown. There were gaudy bedecked boats on Beebe Lake, fireworks, sideshows, and variety show performance competitions with the mayor of Ithaca as judge. Coeds from other colleges, "imports," arrived by bus and train summoned by fraternities to augment the insufficient number of Cornell women. And there was lots of drinking.

The spring weekend of 1951 was described in the *Cornell Alumni News* as "a gruesome picture of excessive drinking at 52 fraternity house parties that go on [*sic*] night and day."[36] In a lead editorial, "Cornell's Own Lost Weekends," the *Sun* agreed that the "excessive drinking is too widespread and obvious to go unnoticed or unquestioned by even the most casual observer or visitor." The editors lamented the inability of Cornellians to stop "escaping from themselves and their personalities by scurrying off through a whiskey bottle to the screwball, nuthouse, clobbered, and too often vulgar world of continuous and sustained alcoholic partying."[37] Out of a sense that the events of that spring revealed "a decline in responsible social conduct and an increase in irresponsible drinking," administration, faculty, and student leaders urged the Student Council to form a "conduct committee" to study the issue. The committee released its report in March 1952, concluding that neither the Student Council nor the administration "could improve the situation. . . . The solution requires realization on the part of students of their individual and group responsibilities and problems."[38]

This was not an isolated example, alas, and the university was itself somewhat complicit in alcohol abuse. With the New York State legal drinking age at eighteen, Cornell recognized a number of "drinking societies" as official campus organizations. Two of them were struck from the list by Acting President de Kiewiet in 1949, after the near death of a hazed initiate who had to consume a quart of martinis. In 1950 the prizes for the tray race winners in Junior Week were bottles of champagne, scotch, and rye whiskey. Malott was struck by Cornell's culture of drinking as soon as he arrived as president. He told the board of trustees in January 1952 that "weekends were becoming longer and more frequent [*sic*] and that drinking is playing too prominent a role in social events." Students and faculty were "having difficulty handling these issues."[39] He would, he said, see what he could do about giving student life a higher moral tone.

Nor could the new president have been pleased with the recurring incidents of another student tradition, the panty raid, which was almost an annual rite of spring. In May 1952, 850 men, summoned by a bugle call, marched on Balch and Dickson, the women's dorms, "doing damage to electrical fixtures, railings, drain pipes and doorways. Campus patrolmen followed them," according to the *Sun* account, "but did not intervene."[40] Two years later, three hundred "souvenir-seeking" men raided Dickson with shouts of "we want sex" and "Hey! Hey! All the Way." Unable to get into the dorm, which was quickly locked down, "the raid fizzled," and, on their way back to the main campus, the men "sang the alma mater on the suspension bridge."[41] Looming over the panty-raid tradition at Cornell in the postwar years was a pervasive misogyny that objectified women as sexual playthings even as it denigrated and dismissed their presence on campus, an attitude that on any given day could find the *Daily Sun* describing women students as not "pre-meds, but pre-weds," or the Cornell humor magazine, the *Widow*, repeatedly extolling the superior quality of "imports" to locals.[42]

<hr>

THE STEREOTYPING OF women was, of course, writ large across the tapestry of American life in this period. The central narrative of student life in the 1950s was the story of Cornell women and the beginning of the end of their status as second-class citizens. Having been founded with no barriers to the admission of women, the university had long taken pride in its visionary role in women's education in America. But when female students began arriving in sufficient numbers in the late 1870s they were, as one of them wrote, "tolerated and ignored," segregated in classrooms, a gymnasium, and an infirmary in Sage Hall.[43] In the university's early years male students were nearly unanimously opposed to coeducation, convinced that the presence of women on campus prevented Cornell from achieving the social status of all-male institutions like Harvard, Yale, and Princeton. An early university announcement about the admission of women made clear its assumptions about gender roles. A Cornell education was "for young ladies who have a real taste for study and desire for knowledge so that in case of adversity they may be sure of a good self-support."[44]

Constricted by Cornell's 1884 decision "that all lady students be required to room and board at Sage College" and the paucity of designated women's dorms in the following decades, women's numbers were never that high at Cornell, reaching a peak of 23 percent in 1940 when the national average of women receiving undergraduate degrees was 40 percent.[45] To be sure, with most men off at war in the fall of 1944, women outnumbered men by two-to-one on campus. While the navy had taken over Sage Hall, women had moved into a half-dozen of the virtually deserted fraternities. After the war and the arrival of the veterans, women's numbers dwindled dramatically, with, for example, places set aside for only fifty women (out of two thousand who applied) in the 1946 entering Arts College class of 350.

By the 1950s, after veterans left Sage, the percentage of women on campus was back to prewar levels, fueled by the School of Home Economics, which was all female, and the Arts College, where by 1959 women constituted 38 percent of freshmen. Still, old attitudes died slowly. An initiative that year to increase the numbers of Arts women was rejected by Herbert Williams. It would, the director of admissions wrote in a memorandum to the president, require a reduction in the number of male students, which would "cut off the alumni potential of the Arts College. . . . The fewer seeds we plant, the smaller will be the crop of dollars which we can harvest." Even more significant, Williams added,

> As the absolute number of or the ratio of men goes down, the college tends to become less and less of a "men's" college with women students and more a "women's" college with men students. The prestige of attending liberal arts at Cornell for the type of students we have applying (who also apply to strictly men's institutions, Harvard, Yale, Princeton, and Dartmouth) will be less because of the large enrollment of girls.[46]

Curiously absent from serious weight in these deliberations was a concern whether "girls" were themselves "the type of student" Cornell sought, when, in fact, among the freshmen in the academic year 1957–58, the average grade of the "boys" was 74.1, while that of the "girls" was 78.39.

Despite the women's superior academic performance, there was a university-wide consensus on women's secondary and less-serious role on campus. In an orientation address in 1947, Lucille Allen, counselor of women, urged the vastly outnumbered freshman women not to "take the first man you see." Not because marriage was not—or should not—be uppermost in their minds, but because "you can afford to be choosey now."[47] Later in the 1950s, the dean of the School of Home Economics told the freshman class that their school sought to produce "thinking homemakers."[48] Cornell women were assumed to be preoccupied with clothes or marriage. Each September the university held "a fashion show" at the Straight to show new women students "how to dress for appropriate occasions," and in 1951 the women were told that "a minimum wardrobe for an entering freshman is 2 formals, 3 date dresses, 2 suits, 4 skirts, 5 sweaters, 5 blouses."[49] The *Widow* joked in October 1953:

"Daddy, the girl who sits next to me in class has a dress just like mine."

"So you want a new dress?"

"Well it would be cheaper than changing colleges."[50]

The *Widow* joked stereotypically about sexuality, as well. In October 1951, it quoted two women students: "I caught my boyfriend necking." "I caught mine the same way." The next year it described a mother-daughter conversation:

Mother: "Now remember, dear, if you neck, smoke, and drink, men will call you 'fast.'"

Daughter: "Yeah; just as fast as they can get to the phone."[51]

Some faculty embraced and perpetuated demeaning stereotypes of Cornell women. When "coeds in pants" invaded Zinck's, the "favorite drinking place of all Cornellians," which reopened on South Aurora Street in 1947, Clinton Rossiter '39, the John L. Senior Professor of American Civilization, told the *Sun* that "women should be excluded in the old tradition, leaving Zinck's a haven for the men." Some years later, when the university banned dogs from classrooms, Rossiter used the occasion to condescend to women students again. As quoted by the *Sun*, he "surveys the situation before each class and throws out any wild puppies. Dogs are like co-eds knitting. I'm willing to put up with them if they stay quiet. Who knows? Like the co-eds, they might learn something."[52]

No wonder then, given these views, that women students were treated as second-class citizens. Until 1946, for example, they could compete only for "women's editor" of the *Sun*, responsible for the weekly "women's page," offering a "detailed report of women's activities."[53] Though women ran for the news board after 1946, very few women were selected through the 1950s. Until Helen Newman Hall was opened in 1962, women had no space of their own for physical education activities. Women could not at first attend the popular lecture series "Preparation for Marriage: The Anatomy and Physiology of Sex," inaugurated at the Straight in 1949 by Dr. N. S. Moore '23, MD '26. But following complaints that the series sent the message "that marriage is not, in effect, a contract between two persons with mutual and co-equal responsibilities," the ban was lifted.[54] Male students' dorm rooms were cleaned daily and females' weekly. More serious, when "early decision for exceptional new students" was introduced in 1959, it was for men only.[55]

Despite their success as students, the differential attitude toward and treatment of Cornell "co-eds" was represented most grievously in the "spirit" that pervaded their years on campus, the ideal of "gracious living." Gracious living meant that when fraternity men put in a Saturday of community service at a downtown community center, sorority women were on hand to serve them food and refreshments. "Gracious living" meant not wearing slacks or "Bermuda" shorts, and wearing stockings on Saturday night. And it was an ideal shared by many women students themselves. In 1962, the Women Students Government Association defeated by a vote of 15–5 a proposal to let women wear slacks and shorts at breakfast and lunch in dining halls (not classes or libraries). Five months later a second vote allowed slacks at breakfast. A decade later everyone wore jeans.

"Gracious living" assumed female students needed special protection. Unlike men with their long tradition of living off-campus as "independents," women under twenty-two were required to live in university dormitories or sororities, even if their parents gave them permission to live off-campus. "Gracious living" also required women students to take all meals by term contract in the dining room of their dorm or sorority, and, indeed, to rise and stand at the house head resident's arrival at and departure from meals. Unlike the case with male students, for women there was no ability to "pay as you go," to purchase your own individual meal, until 1962, when Donlon, the first women's dorm with no dining hall, was completed. Absorbing the cultural ideal of middle-class womanly graces in dining halls included domestic rituals that would one day extend to the homes they presided over, the proper etiquette for pouring tea, the tablecloths, the polite conversation.

"Gracious living" involved not being out and about at night, a code of curfews, which of course did not govern male students. A complex, often changing, set of rules regulating signing out, signing in, lateness points, and special "late nights" persisted. From 1946 to 1951 the norm on weekday nights was "in" by 10:30. It was extended to 11:00 for sophomores and midnight for juniors and seniors. Freshmen women still had a 10:30 curfew, preventing them from taking out overnight reserve books, which became available at libraries exactly at 10:30. Here, too, most women students accepted this as part of a life of "gracious living," with three out of four Cornell women, in one survey, finding the rules "not too strict." Only a minority insisted that "the rules were a nuisance and an insult. In an adult community, they should be unnecessary."[56] But, change, albeit incremental, was in the wind. By 1962, although opponents

"Gracious Living": teatime at Delta Gamma Sorority, 1949. *Cornellian*, 1949, Vol. 81. (Courtesy *Cornellian*)

still worried about "parents' disapproval and deterioration of the University's reputation," an overwhelming majority, 22–2, of the Women's Self-Government Association voted to end curfews for seniors.[57]

———

As with its response to discrimination and bias, so, too, Cornell was slow to sense the new mood of postwar students with respect to sexuality, which was shaped, in part, by the returning veterans, who felt themselves quite capable of regulating their own personal and social conduct. This would lead to a dramatic confrontation between students and President Malott in 1958 over the university's claim *in loco parentis* to regulate student social and sexual actions and even attitudes. There was a foreshadowing of this cultural lag in late 1953, when Malott took offense at the presence of what he labeled "filthy words" in a short story published in the student literary journal, the *Cornell Writer.* The president complained in a letter to Baxter Hathaway, the English professor who was the faculty adviser to the publication, that because "Cornell" appeared on the masthead, "a public relations problem" loomed.[58] He urged Hathaway to remove obscenities from future published student pieces. The president's anger reveals much about him and the ensuing confrontation between him and the students. The story "Indian Love Call," by Ronald Sukenick '55 (who became an English professor at the University of Colorado and author of five novels), contained, in fact, no obscene phrases, no four-letter Anglo-Saxon words, no anatomical or even erotically charged passages. The filth Malott objects to is clearly the general "immorality" in the story's portrait of college life, which is a narrative about drunken, dissolute college students, disaffected intellectuals, whose friendships include casual sex, never described.

Hathaway responded to Malott's letter with the claim "that I have no business to act as censor." Not all students write as their predecessors in the "Genteel Tradition" did, he added in a mini-lecture, describing the new "realist school" in contemporary fiction, concerned with "real-life behavior." Hathaway concluded by noting that "there is a point somewhere within which the educational process must be protected against the demands of good public relations."[59] An infuriated Malott replied, "I cannot believe there is literary or educational value in filthy words. I suppose as an administrator it is scarcely appropriate for me to have opinions on education, but certainly to publish filth seems even to a layman scarcely a part of the educational process, regardless of how educational may be either the reading or the writing of it."[60]

Malott immediately referred the matter to the Faculty Committee on Student Activities and Student Conduct, which that spring had done his bidding by "reprimanding" editors of the *Cornell Daily Sun* and the *Widow* for "obscene and profane material appearing within their pages." The president urged a similar rebuke to the editor of the *Cornell Writer* and the author of the offensive story.[61] With the *Daily Sun* editorializing against "the forces of righteousness, virtue and purity on the Cornell campus" and English professors opposing what they labeled the "clear-cut trend to bring open expression of student thought under tight control," the Faculty Committee declined to act on the president's request that the two students be "reprimanded." The story was "a bona fide effort in the field of modern realistic writing," the committee held, even if, as committee members acknowledged, it "went beyond the limits of the standards of good taste."[62] Around campus, jokes were told of faculty responding to an angry Malott asking if there was nothing professors found unacceptable, with "Yes, Mr. President, plagiarism."

The faculty would soon have its authority in such matters undermined. When the same Faculty Committee in late 1953 allowed male students to entertain women "guests" in unchaperoned apartments with two or more rooms, if at least two non-freshman women students were present, and permitted the women to remain in the apartment until midnight, or 1 a.m. on Sunday, the president had had enough. Ignoring a poll that revealed that half of women students thought they should be allowed to visit men's apartments "under any circumstances," he decided in May 1955 to move responsibility for supervising and disciplining student conduct and extracurricular activities from the faculty, where it had resided since 1901, to the university president.[63] Despite almost unanimous faculty disapproval and the resignation of the dean of the faculty, William H. Farnham '18, LLB '22, the board of trustees changed the university's bylaws so that the formerly autonomous Faculty Committee would henceforth be appointed by and report to the president. Whereas usually seventy-five to one hundred professors showed up at faculty meetings, three hundred came to the one responding to the Malott-inspired board action. A resolution condemning the bylaws change as "contrary to sound educational policy" was passed by acclamation.[64] So began the multiyear Malott "morals crusade."

Skirmishes saw Malott's own dean of women, Dorothy Brooks, recommend in the spring of 1957 that, except for a ban on freshmen women, all regulations on apartment parties be abolished. Brooks pointed out that 62 percent of parents gave "blanket permission" for their sophomore daughters to attend parties.[65] Malott would not budge, writing to the chair of the Faculty Committee—a committee that now reported to him—that allowing male students an unrestricted right to entertain female students in their apartments at night would be "in complete disregard of conventional mores and morals."[66]

The conflict escalated after a particularly alcohol-besodden Spring Weekend, which saw a student, Frederick J. Nowicki, die in the university infirmary from a fractured skull suffered in a fifteen-foot fall from a second-floor porch at Phi Kappa Tau fraternity house at 5:30 a.m. on Saturday, May 11, 1957. On Sunday, Malott called a group of student leaders to his office. He demanded that they take action to prevent any recurrence of "rowdiness, vandalism, and public displays of drunkenness." Agreeing that "wild and drunkard parties" had to be prevented, the students promised to establish new social standards for parties.[67] In the fall, they proposed earlier closing hours, along with limitations on "party-hopping" and "public" drinking. The President's Committee on Student Activities, which had recently imposed an unpopular alcohol ban in Schoellkopf Stadium, found the student-authored social code inadequate, especially in controlling sexual activity, and in December announced much more stringent rules. The committee specified, for example, that for four hours, from 3 to 7 a.m. Saturday and 4 to 8 a.m. Sunday, at overnight parties, there could be no one of the opposite sex present in any room or house on or off campus.

In January 1958, the Student Council by a vote of 16–0 rejected the Faculty Committee's "university social standards," as did the Intrafraternity Council and the Women's Self-Government Association. Malott replied by informing an open meeting of 350 students, faculty, and administrators in the Memorial Room of Willard Straight Hall, with another 175 students listening to a broadcast of the session in nearby rooms, that neither students nor faculty had jurisdiction over matters in the social code; the board of trustees gave authority to him alone over such issues. When asked about the appropriate role of the university in setting up a "standard morality" for students, Malott shot back that "students should conform to the mores of the society in which we live. Most students have acceptable habits of conduct. Some do not, and have to be controlled."[68]

A tense truce persisted through most of the remaining spring term. Invoking Carl Becker's already canonical words, Malott repeatedly insisted on the need for student responsibility to temper their excessive freedom. The *Daily Sun* in its editorials, letters, and columns responded that "the imposition and codification of responsibility is a dangerous precedent to set. It is not a question of Freedom with Responsibility, but of the insult given to the students by the imposition of rules, which if followed make the student moral and responsible, which if broken make the student immoral and irresponsible."[69] The chair of the president's Faculty Committee, Theresa R. Humphreyville, who taught in Home Economics, defended the code in terms of the university's role "as a parent, providing a place to live, and an atmosphere to meet and get together, both normally the functions of a family, a role which parents put the University in. The University feels responsible for what happens to students while they are here."[70] She told a Student Council meeting that "there was just too much social activity at the University. Anything which limits partying provides an opportunity to pursue academics."[71] In response, Cornell erupted in the first broadly based "student power" protest of the kind that swept American campuses during the 1960s.

Open warfare broke out in mid-May, when Humphreyville and Lloyd Elliott, the executive assistant to Malott, informed the Student Council that the president's Faculty Committee was seriously considering restoring the ban on unchaperoned parties in off-campus apartments. Apartment entertaining, Elliott told the council, "was not in the best interests of an educational environment leading to co-educational achievements." The university "should lead in the ethics and moral development of students." Humphreyville added that "since the apartment situation is conducive to petting and intercourse it is an area with which the University should be properly concerned."[72]

Students countered first with a flurry of letters and opinion pieces in the *Sun*. "No amount of legislation is ever going to prevent society—much less students from 'necking,'" an editorial proclaimed. "The administration is operating under the magnificently false assumption that our parents do not trust us unchaperoned in a room with the opposite sex," wrote Stephanie Green '59. "The main rationale for the Committee's contemplated action is a Victorian belief in the fundamental immorality of sex; the Administration plans to change bad old Cornell into a Bible Sect Seminary," claimed another student, "name withheld." "It is time for the University to abandon its ill-conceived and non-purposeful attempt to impose moral 'standards' on its student body," declared Stephen A. Schuker '59. And Jay Cunningham '58 asserted that "what really hurts is seeing the university set itself up as a molly-coddling goddess, a sort of Johnny-come-lately Mom in the form of a new and all powerful pseudo-parent."[73]

On Friday and Saturday, May 23 and 24, the students took to the streets in anti–Malott rioting, in an unprecedented protest against their own administration. The leaders were John Kirkpatrick Sale '58 and Richard Fariña, who shared an apartment at 109 College Avenue. Sale, the son of Cornell English professor William Sale, had grown up in Ithaca and in 1958 was editor of the *Cornell Sun*. He was a student radical, who a year and a half earlier had written a *Sun* opinion piece that decried student apathy and acceptance of the 1950s status quo. "Cannot Cornell take its place with other people across the country in refuting the abominable notion of The Silent Generation?" he asked.[74] Sale's editorials relentlessly criticized Malott for treating students as if they were children and encouraged students to take direct action. On May 13, he had written "Let Cornell students not sit passively by once more while the President's Committee takes away privileges and attempts to define morality for the undergraduate. If there is resistance to the elimination of apartment parties, let it be formulated now."[75]

We know from Fariña's critically acclaimed 1966 novel, *Been Down So Long It Looks Like Up to Me*, that "resistance" was in fact being planned. Fariña, whose first writings appeared in the tainted *Cornell Writer*, and who would also become a respected folk singer and composer (and husband of Mimi Baez), would die in a motorcycle accident two days after his novel's publication. The novel describes endless drug- and drink-filled planning sessions in the spring of 1958 with campus anarchists and the editor of the *Sun*. They designed protests against "Sylvia Pankhurst" (Fariña's fictional Cornell vice president, a composite of Humphreyville and Elliott), who, the novel relates, "actually said that male apartments, if you follow me, are conducive to petting and intercourse."[76]

One thousand students gathered in front of Willard Straight Hall at ten o'clock on Friday morning, unsure of what was going to happen until Sale stood up and addressed the group. "We're here to protest the social code, and the crushing of the faculty. Today is a day for action. We don't need people who are going to chicken out." The group then marched to Day Hall, chanting such slogans as "We want Malott shot" and "No ban." Malott, "tall, tanned, greying and tending toward natty blue suits and red neckties," according to *Newsweek*'s account, had already "made a fortunate escape." Eventually the crowd circled the Arts quad and returned to Day Hall. Sale announced that the women at Sage Hall would stay out late that night to protest the proposed ban and the existing curfew rules. The group then sang the alma mater, but before breaking up at 10:50 to go to classes, a few students threw eggs at Day Hall, some of which splattered the dean of men, Frank Baldwin '22, who had been speaking to them from the steps of the building, and whose daughter Polly was one of the protesters. Despite this incident, a faculty observer deemed the protest "orderly and good-natured," commending the organizers for stationing students in front of the doors of Boardman and Goldwin Smith to prevent anyone from interfering with classes.[77]

That night, over three thousand students gathered in front of Sage to urge women students to stay out after the 12:30 a.m. curfew. Some of them carried flares and torches, and from time to time firecrackers were set off. Officers of the Student Council and the Women's Self-Government Association tried to calm the crowd. P. K. Kellogg '59, president of the council, said he had met with university officials that afternoon and saw some evidence that administrators might not impose the ban.

They were shouted down as "puppets" with cries of "we want Sale." And they got him. Proclaiming "what we need now is less Student Council and more student body," Sale asked the group if they wanted the new tighter rules governing house and apartment parties, and a chant went up "we want a new President."[78] When over a hundred women did not return to their dorms after 12:30, the protest turned nastier, with a burning effigy of Malott hanged from an elm tree in front of Sage. Sale and others took down the effigy, put out the flames, and tried to convince the crowd that, having accomplished its purpose of encouraging women students to break their curfew, it should disperse. When a few students cried out that the protesters should march to the president's home in Cayuga Heights, Sale tried—and failed—to dissuade them.

Deane Malott was the first president of Cornell not to live in Andrew Dickson White's house on central campus. He resided about half a mile away, on Oak Hill Road in a university-purchased home. On this particular weekend, he and his wife, Eleanor, had as houseguests John Collyer '17, chairman of the

Effigy comment during anti-Malott riots on May 23, 1958. (Division of Rare and Manuscript Collections of the Cornell University Library)

board of trustees, and his wife. On Friday afternoon the Collyers had presented the university the new Collyer Boathouse. On Saturday morning at about one o'clock, a leaderless throng of almost one thousand students arrived at Malott's house, trampling the lawn and landscaping, setting off a smoke bomb, and throwing eggs and stones, all the while chanting "Go back to Kansas." Appearing on his front steps, Malott told them, "This University will never be swayed by mob rule." Obscenities were shouted at him, and some windows were smashed. On seeing the demonstrators, Mrs. Collyer reportedly said to her husband, "Are these the boys you are giving the boathouse to, John?" The next morning, Sale, who had not gone to Cayuga Heights, said that "he regretted the violence against President Malott, and expressed the hope that there would be no further violence on campus."[79]

It was too late for regrets. Sale, Fariña, and two other students were suspended by the dean of men on Sunday night for "inciting fellow students to riot." They were not permitted to attend classes or otherwise appear on campus until the Men's Judiciary Board considered the charges against them. Sale repeated his criticism of the violence at Oak Hill Road but condemned the president and "the entire attitude of the Cornell administration over the last eight years to limit the student voice, to limit faculty powers, and to impose standards of morality and social behavior on the students."[80]

As the Men's Judiciary Board, composed of eight undergraduates appointed by the Student Council, considered its verdict, there was a flurry of activity on campus. A petition supporting the four students was signed by 1,860 Cornellians, and a sit-down strike at Day Hall to end the "reign of error" was called off at the urging of friends of the suspended students. Lloyd Elliott, an architect of the social code, resigned, to become president of the University of Maine. He was replaced by John Summerskill, one of the directors of the new Gannett Health Clinic, associate professor of clinical and preventative medicine, and an authority on student psychology. With a new title, vice president for student affairs, Summerskill quickly orchestrated a meeting of the four suspended students with Malott to apologize for the violence. A bit chastened, perhaps, the president asked Summerskill to create an advisory committee of students "to assure a constant and free flow of opinion and understanding between the administration and the students." Speaking on WVBR, Theresa Humphreyville backed away from a ban on unchaperoned parties, claiming to favor "spot checks" to assess "their effect on the general social atmosphere at Cornell." Off campus, the protest was front-page news in the national press, with the *New York Journal-American* story displaying the headline "Four Suspended by Cornell after 2-Day Riot over Girls." The *San Francisco Chronicle*'s story was headed "Students Stone Head of Cornell."[81]

In a meeting that began at 7:30 p.m. on Tuesday and lasted until 6:30 a.m. Wednesday, the Men's Judiciary Board decided to put Sale and Fariña on "parole" and to give "reprimands" to the other two miscreants. The board rejected suspension, it reported, because none of the four "had participated in the acts of violence which marred the demonstrations." Because "they had in large part contributed to the atmosphere out of which the violence arose," Fariña and Sale were required by the parole to be under the direct supervision of a faculty member or university administrator to whom they had to report periodically.[82]

Sale had the last word in a full-page editorial in the *Sun* a month later on graduation day. Anticipating the general mood of 1960s student radicalism, he offered a blistering attack on "the lack of a sound intellectual atmosphere at this campus," where there is no longer any chance "for a student talking and thinking with his professors." He was convinced that "as long as the fraternity social atmosphere at Cornell is dominant, the intellectual life of the students is irreparably damaged." The Malott administration, Sale added, "seems to have had very little regard for the magnificent tradition of Cornell." Day Hall was "far too impressed with efficiency . . . too [much] big business and not enough Cornell," and all too willing to trample on "student rights and student freedom."[83] Sale would become a founding member of the national Students for a Democratic Society, the history of which he would write in his long career as a public intellectual and author of books on Columbus, Robert Fulton, and the Luddites.

During the board of trustees meeting on that very weekend, Collyer presented a telegram from Humphreyville suggesting that the board should annul the parole of Sale and Fariña, suspend them, and thereby prevent Sale, a senior, from graduating. The trustees declined, voting 18–7 to uphold the decision of the Men's Judiciary Board. The trustees also voted, however, "that John Kirkpatrick Sale be not admitted for further study in any division of the University without approval of this committee."[84] Meanwhile, graduating Hotel School students gave Malott a two-layer marble cake with the note "whenever you receive eggs from students in the future, they will be in this form."[85]

Malott remained ambivalent in the wake of the riots. Sobered by the intensity of student anger, he seemed content to turn over student issues to Summerskill and the newly created Student Advisory Committee. He would accept dramatic policy innovations brought by Summerskill that fall. But a part of him resented the catastrophic ending of his morals war. "My attempts to bring the University within a framework of decent standards is primarily the cause of their rebellion," he insisted. Three days later, however, he wrote to the president of Ohio University that the mob was "not vicious or malicious" but simply "trying to make a point—which I don't think was valid, to be sure, that they were getting too many rules and regulations inhibiting their social activities."[86]

Malott was particularly hurt by a trustee revolt over the affair, led by Arthur Dean '19, JD '23, and Maxwell Upson '99. In the midst of the May crisis, Dean had urged privately "that the President has to be relieved of his central, untenable position in the handling of these social disciplinary cases." Upson went even further, becoming the ringleader of a veritable coup, unsuccessful to be sure, but the nature of which he ultimately shared with the president in an unusually candid letter. He had, he wrote, been "under great pressure from many of my co-Trustees, the alumni and professors" to do something about "the marked and severe criticism of some of your methods, during the past three or four years." Upson assured Malott that he had defended him in the past, "always hoping and expecting a betterment of the situation." But the events of the spring "reached a degree of seriousness that caused me to feel it was my duty to take steps to rectify the situation," in which the "reputation of Cornell was being seriously menaced." One possibility involved "putting you in as Chancellor and finding an understudy who would have charge of relationships with the faculty, the students and the alumni. The areas of most serious discord." Happily, Upson wrote, with the installation of Summerskill, and the realization "that you were leaving him completely alone, permitting him to handle the whole matter," such an intervention proved unnecessary. Reassured, Upson "deeply regretted succumbing to the Trustee pressure" and felt that there was no longer any justification for board interference, since it was evident that "[you had decided to] delegate responsibilities and . . . discarded your offensive operational methods." He concluded with "a sincere hope my confidence is going to be justified."[87]

Malott replied with an unapologetic defense of his morals crusade. He knew little about "the charges which you and apparently others whose names are unknown to me have made"—and was astonished that "some of you have become so frightened about my ability and fitness." Malott assumed the trustees shared his determination "to cut down on the drinking, licentiousness and wanton sexual misbehavior—the extent of which I do not believe you realize and which was out of hand when I came in and if you think this can be done without some upheaval, you are in my opinion expecting the impossible." He had ended the traditional faculty role in supervising student conduct, the president noted, because "the faculty here has long had a wide reputation for an almost libertine sense of freedom; I am frequently kidded about it by other university presidents." Reminding Upson of the many "letters of backing from alumni and parents over my stand, and Cornell's objectives, at the time of the deplorable demonstrations," Malott expressed regret that "I displease those whom I look to for wise council [*sic*]."[88]

The headline in the *Daily Sun* greeting second-semester students in January 1959 was "Big Change . . . Fall 1958: A New Era Opens." The hero was John Summerskill, "who, like David, is out to slay Goliath. What he seeks to destroy is the atmosphere of distrust between students, administration and faculty which has characterized relations among these groups for the past few years." If the students, faculty, and administration supported this David while "he stoned the creature of their own making to death, it would be the happiest thing to have happened at Cornell in years."[89]

Summerskill restored the faculty, which had been alienated by the 1955 trustees action, to the process of making policy in extracurricular affairs. In the miracle fall of 1958, the deans of the seven undergraduate colleges produced a fifteen-page report on student activities and conduct. They urged that jurisdiction over student activities and conduct be put back in the hands of committees composed of elected faculty and student representatives, concluding that "the University cannot undertake to act *in loco parentis*, if this means maintaining concern for and supervision over all aspects of the student's life—social, moral, and religious as well as intellectual. The University should not attempt to spell out rules, regulations, and codes governing student behavior beyond the bare minimum necessary in any society."[90]

In a rare display of unanimity, the faculty accepted the deans' recommendations, which had already been endorsed by various student groups. At the end of their meeting on December 17, 1958, faculty members broke into loud applause to commend the report, which brought back a supervisory faculty committee over student conduct, appointed by and reporting to the faculty, but giving students substantial control over their own affairs. The restored Faculty Committee delegated actual power over student affairs to a central student government body with responsibility for writing actual codes to govern student conduct. In the *Sun*'s coverage of the faculty vote, passing reference was made to the effect that "President Deane W. Malott has already announced his support of the measures." According to the *Sun*,

> Eight months have seen a virtual miracle. Salvaging the wreckage of an out-moded and disastrous policy, John Summerskill—and it does not seem unfair to give so much credit to one man—has led the Cornell Administration forward to the point where it is on the verge of becoming one of the most progressive in the country. . . . And it cannot be doubted that it was the demonstrations which signified the end of the old era and the beginning of the revolution.[91]

The Cornell "miracle" fall of 1958 was the beginning of the end of the university *in loco parentis*. Dwarfed in subsequent accounts of the Cornell story by the events of the spring of 1969, and its relationship to national racial issues on college campuses, the "apartment" riot of 1958 deserves to be accorded its true historical significance. From East Hill a wave of student anger at being told when, where, and how they could personally interact with other students would sweep through American universities and lead to the end of parietal hours, curfews, and most university restrictions on social conduct. It would be an important part of the general student unrest of the 1960s over other aspects and attitudes of American life that students also repudiated as what they considered the misguided follies produced by the insensitivity and arrogance of their parents and their universities.

Summerskill was given the honor of welcoming the new midyear freshmen class of 1962 in January 1959. He could not resist marking the moment. Cornell, he announced, was "gradually and quietly taking the University out of an overly extended *in loco parentis* position. At the same time, we are strengthening the various student self-government agencies." Good social psychologist that he was, Summerskill began his list of the many forces of social change that led to the demise of the university-as-parent with the observation that "after World War II the many veterans on campus had assumed considerable responsibility for their own personal and social conduct."[92]

3 | The Cold War at Cornell

"Cornell goes Bolshevist," proclaimed the *New York World-Telegram* on October 19, 1943. The university's Russian courses, the newspaper declared, were being taught by communists, making Cornell a breeding ground for "Muscovites." For the next several days the paper repeated its accusation in articles and editorials carried in other Scripps Howard and Hearst papers across the country.

The attack was focused on two Russian émigrés, Joshua Kunitz and Vladimir Kazakevich, who had been hired to teach in the Intensive Russian Language and Culture Program, which the university had designed for the United States Army in the summers of 1943 and 1944. The army chose Cornell because since 1939 it had offered an innovative Slavic language and area studies program funded by the Rockefeller Foundation. For twelve weeks, hundreds of U.S. Army trainees, in what was called the Army Specialized Training Program (ASTP), were brought to Ithaca and immersed in conversational Russian language training. The students also took courses in Cornell's Institute of Contemporary Russian Civilization.[1]

President Day had been delighted that the army asked his university to play an important role in the war effort. "Because of Cornell's well-known reputation as a pioneering institution," he wrote, after the Soviet Union had become an ally of the United States, "strong representations were made that it take a lead in the development of modern Russian studies."[2] Answering this call was what Day had in mind when he insisted in his 1937 inaugural address that universities as well as citizens had an "obligation" to "add to the common weal."[3] Not that Day didn't foresee problems in such activities. "We knew," he later noted, "that we were taking a calculated risk in agreeing to run the Army program," given the lack of "authentic and validated information" about Soviet Russia and by "an even worse lack of critically trained teachers."[4] And, of course, given the potentially controversial nature of the subject matter.

Several weeks before the first *World-Telegram* attack appeared, Day asked Cornelis W. de Kiewiet—then a professor of history and the director of the army program that sponsored the language and culture courses in German, Italian, Czech, and Chinese, as well as Russian—to inform all the members of Cornell's faculty about the initiative. Controversial material would be taught in these courses, de Kiewiet conceded, but this was the intention of the army authorities responsible for the program. If instructors had "burning convictions" about their subjects, they should lay out their views and "provide the opportunity for free discussion." De Kiewiet was as concerned with courses about our enemies, Germany and Italy, as he was about Russia, a "friendly and associated power." In a surprisingly capacious vision of academic free inquiry, he wrote:

> There is no objection whatever to handling controversial material if the purpose is to improve the understanding or promote the efficiency of army trainees. Marxism and communism, the genuine achievements of Hitler or Mussolini, attractive characteristics of enemy peoples—these can and should be freely handled. The ASTP wishes its trainees to have a mature and sympathetic comprehension of other areas and peoples.[5]

Day responded to the *World-Telegram*'s charge that the students were being indoctrinated by "communist" faculty. Day's letter to the members of Cornell's board of trustees on January 7, 1944, reflected his reputation for candor, honesty, and idealism:

> For reasons which are relatively easy to understand, the only available instructors who have an intrinsic knowledge of contemporary Russian conditions are individuals who had been repeatedly in Russia during the period since the revolution. Perforce, most, if not all of those individuals have exhibited "Russian sympathies"; otherwise they would not have had opportunities for close observation of developments under the present Soviet regime.

The university, he added, could have picked instructors "above suspicion" who had little firsthand experience with Soviet Russia or those who "are bound to be in some quarters suspect." Since the army had a practical objective in the program, "we have thought it was due the men in training to have access to the latter type of instructor." He assured the board, however, that "the university would not, any more than the army, tolerate any program of indoctrination. This was made clear to all members of the participating staff."

Day then reviewed the careers of Kunitz and Kazakevich, their study in America, their travels in and writings about Soviet Russia. "As far as we can see," he concluded in his letter to the trustees, "there is nothing in [the] entire record that suggests 'un-American activities.'" Having talked with the Russians, Day was prepared to vouch for their loyalty and their "thorough" commitment "to the American way of life." Moreover, he added, the army was constantly monitoring the program and "has been thoroughly satisfied with the character and quality of the instruction being provided." Day ended the letter with an optimism about postwar "realities" that may not have been shared by all the trustees. The fears of the *World-Telegram* about cooperation between the Soviet Union and the United States, he suggested, were unwarranted.

> But how, under all the circumstances, this cooperation can be wisely challenged at this time I, for one, cannot imagine. Let me be perfectly clear; I am not suggesting that the USA yield to communism. I am urging, however, that it is of the utmost importance that we learn how to get along amicably with Russia, and that this necessitates a much larger understanding of contemporary Russian life than we have thus far had. I am not myself fearful of the consequences of such improved understanding. Those who think that there are grave risks about closer contacts with Russia seem to me to evidence a fundamental lack of faith in America. It is a distrust which I do not share. If the USA is all that I am convinced it is, we need not be fearful of the impact of alien ideologies. The men in army training appear to have the same idea.[6]

Having reassured the trustees, Day turned next to calming fears in the general public about "Red Cornell." In March 1944 he stated the university's position in the prestigious *Saturday Review*. Written in an age before professional speechwriters, "So Cornell's Going Bolshevist! The Strange Case of the Russian Courses" is a beautifully crafted, at times moving, essay, interwoven with a history of Cornell and an almost lyrical paean to freedom of inquiry.

It was an "unpleasant experience," Day began, with wry understatement, and a touch of intellectual disdain, to find the "good name" of his institution "aspersed in the columns of a metropolitan daily." Day felt particularly sad for anxious alumni, fearing that their alma mater "is pulled down from the serene heights on which their adolescent imaginations had placed her." He then addressed head-on what he referred to, in terms not yet part of common American political parlance, as the *World-Telegram*'s "witch-hunting." It wasn't the first time his institution had been so publicly attacked, he pointed out, recalling the accusation in the nineteenth century of "Godless Cornell." Having its "faith tested" could be salutary, he proclaimed, if it forced Cornellians to realize that "a principal obligation of any university is a certain fearlessness about the knowledge which it professes and the end which it pursues."

Day then described what he saw as the "two functions of all education" in terms that captured the university's purpose, framing his exposition in, of all things, Christ's enjoining Peter "to bind and to loose." Universities, he contended, "bind men together" in a common historical and cultural bond, preserving and passing on the wisdom and tradition of the past. But the authority of the past could become ossified and stifling, so education had the opposite function as well: it must loosen the tyranny of the past, "emancipate the mind of its people, young and old, from decayed concepts, misleading principles, and narrow loyalties," to allow them to "live and work realistically in their changing world." University education has thus two contradictory obligations: "to perpetuate and to create."

Only at this point, more than three-quarters through his short essay, did Day turn to the facts at issue. He offered Russian Studies as an example of educational experimentation, embraced by the U.S. Army, that would help create "a new understanding of the post-war world." Although "for its pains" the university had been accused of "indoctrinating its students," Cornell would continue to teach them about Russia, and about communism. Given the general neglect of "what we now recognize to be one of the greatest moments of modern history—the political and industrial organization of Soviet Russia," Day conceded that the teachers with the best knowledge of Russia may well have been at some point in their careers "attracted to the communist experiment." Nonetheless, universities were right to choose them rather than "exiles for whom Russia has become all but a foreign country." America's youth, he concluded, should not be denied "knowledge that will enable it to bear . . . in the enduring tradition of freedom, the weight of the world that is descending upon its shoulders."[7]

In his 1944 commencement address Day once again defended Cornell's Program in Russian Civilization by insisting it to be "of the utmost importance that Americans understood its ally Russia more clearly and accurately" and to realize that the world could "accommodate in peace a great Russia and a great USA." But he was prudent enough, as well, in April 1945 to send for army scrutiny a list of the staff in the Russia program "to satisfy ourselves of [their] reliability and integrity."[8]

Little could Day know in 1944 that Cornell's encounter with "a metropolitan daily" was a minor prelude to the full-blown drama of postwar anticommunist hysteria—the phenomenon we now know as McCarthyism—that would engulf the university for the next twenty years, requiring Day and his successor, Waldo Deane Malott, to walk a fine line, balancing their commitments to academic values with demands of loyalty and Americanism. In meeting these challenges, Cornell's presidents, administrators, and faculty would sometimes falter and stumble as the weight of the political world outside East Hill fell upon their shoulders. For the most part, however, in the face of pressure from trustees, politicians, and the popular press, they bent but did not break. To be sure, as the historian Ellen Schrecker has reminded us, Cornell, like other institutions of higher education, did not often provide a sanctuary for dissenters and, at times, lent legitimacy to rabid red-baiters. But the institution did not purge left-wing faculty members. And it refused to exclude unpopular ideas from Cornell's definition of academic freedom.

ROBERT FOGEL '48, who would win the Nobel Prize in Economics in 1993, was Cornell's leading student radical in the 1940s, when Soviet-American friendship was replaced by the bitter suspicions of the Cold War. The son of Russian immigrants and a graduate of New York City's prestigious Stuyvesant High School, where he concentrated on physics and chemistry, Fogel switched to economics and history at Cornell, as well as political agitation—as head of the Marxist Discussion Group and the campus chapter of American Youth for Democracy (AYD), the successor to the Young Communist League and an organization Attorney General Tom Clark placed on his 1947 subversive list. The *Cornell Alumni News* estimated in Fogel's last years on campus that the AYD had "about a dozen members," with most radical students preferring instead either the Henry Wallace politics of the Progressive Citizens of America or the Students for Democratic Action, linked to its anti-Stalinist parent organization, Americans for Democratic Action, founded by Arthur Schlesinger Jr. and Reinhold Niebuhr.[9]

Although his followers were few, Fogel put Marxism on the postwar campus map. In speeches, public debates, and letters to the *Cornell Sun*, Fogel proclaimed that communists "fight for anything that will help the majority of the people."[10] Fogel's views infuriated trustees, but they seldom shocked the

The student radical Robert Fogel '48, future Nobel Laureate in Economics, led the Marxist Discussion Group at Cornell. (Photo: Howard Sochurek / Time & Life Pictures / Getty Images)

student body, a majority of whom were World War II veterans. A 1948 *Cornell Sun* poll of five hundred students indicated that 70 percent of respondents believed that "we should continue to try to cooperate with Russia." While 27 percent felt the work of the House Un-American Activities Committee (HUAC) was "valuable," 35 percent thought "it actually does harm"; the rest had no opinion. The *Sun* also noted that non–fraternity students were nearly twice as likely to be liberal as those in fraternities, and that 55 percent of students with academic averages over 85 were liberal, compared with only 20 percent with averages under 75.[11]

Unlike most Cornell students, the mayor of Ithaca was shocked by Fogel's Marxism. In May 1946, citing an ordinance prohibiting littering, he banned AYD from leafleting downtown.[12] More important, Cornell trustees, including Nicholas Noyes '06, Franklin Olin '86, John Collyer '17, and Horace Flanigan '12, were convinced that, as Olin put it, Cornell was "riddled with communism."[13] Day, who once remarked that Olin "saw a communist under every bed," had by now certainly shed his wartime hopes for the Soviet Union. He reassured alumni and trustees that Fogel's American Youth for Democracy was "a small, highly vocal and virtually impotent" organization.[14] As if to minimize any need for concern, Cornell's dean of students noted that, like Fogel, "most of its members are Jewish" and that they are "attracting almost entirely their own type."[15]

The trustees had more than Fogel to fret about. Adolphe Menjou, the film star, who had attended Cornell without completing a degree, told the House Un-American Activities Committee that there was "a group of communists functioning in Ithaca."[16] *Collier's* magazine photographed a Willard Straight Hall meeting of the Marxist Discussion Group for an article it was preparing on campus reds, and in 1947 Eugene Lyons, author of *The Red Decade*, singled out Cornell in a pamphlet, *The Enemy in Our Schools*, published by the Catholic Information Society. Some colleges may have been as "deeply infiltrated" by communists, but "few others," he claimed, "have been as frivolous in defending the infiltration or as stubborn in persisting in the error after it has been exposed." Lyons recycled the charges against the wartime Russian program, "honeycombed with notorious pro-Soviet propagandists," and accused the university of using the same faculty, "seasoned mouthpieces of Red propaganda," when it revived the program in 1946.[17]

In the immediate postwar years trustees worried a lot about the tone of campus politics. In a 1947 speech at Barnes Hall, the NAACP leader Roy Wilkins described the new American campaign against communism as "stupid, foolish, and at times hysterical. . . . Anyone who challenges the status quo seems to be branded as communistic."[18] Along with the Ithaca chapter of the American Veterans Committee and the *Cornell Sun*, Fogel urged that ROTC training, a requirement for all male students in Cornell's land grant colleges, be made voluntary. After voting twice to retain compulsory ROTC, the Student Council endorsed the reform in December 1947. The faculty and the administration, however, would not be moved.[19]

To the trustees, moreover, too many professors seemed to be radicals or fellow travelers. The History professors Paul Gates and Curtis Nettles opposed Truman's 1947 proposal for aid to Greece and Turkey as the two countries battled against communism.[20] Most scientists on campus refused to work on government grants, if the research was "classified" and therefore secret. Concerned about the arbitrary dismissal of faculty from American universities, Robert Wilson, director of the Laboratory of Nuclear Studies, the Nobel laureates Hans Bethe and Peter Debye, the chemist Simon Bauer, and the physicist Philip Morrison formed a committee in 1948, affiliated with the Federation of American Scientists, "to investigate the spy investigators."[21] Nettles, Harrop Freeman of Law, and Morrison told two hundred students at Barnes Hall in November 1949 that the New York City trial of eleven communist leaders was "a blot on civil liberties . . . one phase of an anti-American revolution under the direction of Mr. Truman."

The trustees took note, as well, of the position of the faculty on the sensitive issue of student organization membership lists. Concerned that students on academic probation might participate in student organizations, the faculty, with the support of the Student Council and the *Cornell Sun*, had required for years that all registered student groups submit lists of their members to the administration. In January 1948, Fogel's Marxist Discussion Group and the Cornell chapter of the Young Progressive Citizens of America refused to comply, fearing that the students named would then be under "suspicion of disloyalty." Breaking what the *Sun* described as "an all-time attendance record," the university faculty met in February and by a vote of 155–149 repealed the policy about membership lists.[22] With considerable justification, President Day feared that the trustees would read the vote "as a victory of the campus reds"[23] and for Fogel. Three months later his assistant, Whitman Daniels, wrote to Day that "these queries in regards to communism and kindred activities at Cornell seem to be coming in with such frequency that I am almost inclined to believe that we should adopt a form letter by way of reply!"[24]

Of course, Fogel didn't always win. In early 1949, a year after his graduation, Fogel, still on campus, invited Eugene Dennis, secretary of the American Communist Party, then under indictment in Federal District Court for advocating the overthrow of the U.S. government, to speak at Cornell at an event sponsored by the Marxist Discussion Group. The Faculty Committee on the Scheduling of Public Events, however, unanimously turned thumbs down, declaring: "No person under indictment should be permitted to substitute the campus of Cornell University for the legally constituted courtroom as a forum

CORNELL BARS TEACHER

Withdraws Offer to Professor Who Balked at Red Inquiry

ITHACA, N. Y., May 21 (*P*)— Cornell University announced to-day it had withdrawn its offer of a summer teaching job to Harry C. Steinmetz, who was dismissed by San Diego State College after he had refused to tell a Congressional committee whether he was or had been a Communist.

Dr. Steinmetz, a professor of psychology, said in San Diego Tuesday that Cornell had hired him for the summer and that this represente...
cation." ...
that he wa...

DILLINGS SAY CORNELL HARRIES ANTI-RED SON

Professor Denies Charges of the Author of 'Red Network'

Special to THE NEW YORK TIMES.

ITHACA, N. Y., May 6—Disci-plinary action of the faculty commit-tee on student conduct imposed on Kirk Dilling of Kenilworth, Ill., a Cornell sophomore, on charges of ...urbances in the uni-them publicly. ...tial halls, led to a to have denied m...ay by his father, party but to ha...ing, that the student operation with ...ecuted because of his tions to Commu...t activities.

Assistant Fe... Professor George E. William Hitz sa...rman of the commit-of two other wi...g, a Chicago lawyer, the committee w...ssor Peabody and "a ed to the grand...st" of his committee volved Wilbur L...st-influenced. a suspended Ph... teacher, and Fra... ley of New Yor...

¶Mrs. Goldie ... er in an eleme... Philadelphia. S... in five counts ... tell whether she... nist or active ...

U. S. JURY INDICTS 8 FOR CONTEMPT

Professors at M.I.T., Cornell and Temple Are Accused of Silence at House Inquiry

Special to The New York Times.

WASHINGTON, Nov. 22 — In-dictments charging contempt of Congress were returned by a Fed-eral grand jury today against

Newspaper headlines highlight allegations that Cornell harbored communists. (*Cornell Alumni Magazine*)

to plead his case."[25] At a rally that April, Fogel charged that the faculty caved in because it was "unrepresentative, lacking professors who believed in Marxist doctrine."[26]

The trustees saw a different faculty. In a series of long letters in 1949, Nicho-las Noyes complained that Cornell was "unwittingly providing a sounding-board for a lot of Reds, Pinks and crack pots." With "fuzzy ideologies and beliefs," he suggested, "rattle-brained" faculty seemed to share "the fuzzy moral beliefs of Bertrand Russell." Noyes endorsed Day's commitment to fire self-professed com-munist professors, but he also wanted to regulate "borderline teaching," which "stops just short of communism," by faculty who "under an apparent cloak of academic freedom . . . undermine the American government and the Ameri-can way of life, and those morals which are generally believed in." Noyes sin-gled out the physicist Philip Morrison, "who spoke a week or so ago to a communist front organization," the National Council of American-Soviet Friendship. "This morning," Noyes told Day, "I am besieged by several of our Eli Lilly executives as to why we have such men at Cornell," and "it is hardly necessary for me to mention that this sort of thing is going to hurt us tremendously in getting financial support for the university."

Businessmen might boycott the university, Noyes suggested, if Cornell didn't stop "encouraging . . . this fuzzy, un-American thinking and teaching." Noyes said that "one of our very great American businessmen" told him that "he was not going to give a dollar to any American educational institution until he could be absolutely certain they were not encouraging the sort of fuzzy thinking referred to above. He is currently resigning from the boards of trustees of two great universities because of this tendency."[27]

Trustees also complained about "pinko" textbooks. When Frank Gannett '98, J. Howard Pew, John Collyer, and W. C. Teagle '99 objected to the classroom use of Lorie Tarshis's "subversive, wicked, and vicious" textbook, *Elements of Economics*, Day and Provost Arthur Adams felt the heat—and asked C. C. Murdock '13, dean of the faculty, to investigate. *Elements of Economics*, Murdock reported, "adopts the approach of [John Maynard] Keynes . . . it is admittedly modern and somewhat to the left."

Deciding to take no action, Adams also sought to placate the trustees, assuring them, a bit disingenuously, that "no member of the Economics Department shares Tarshis' viewpoint," but allowing himself to add that "the young men and women who are now studying economics will some day be confronted with versions of this doctrine [Keynesianism]. . . . It would be doing them a disservice to withhold ideas which are a part of current economic thought and to fail to train them in the ability to form and defend their own judgments."[28]

The trustees tried a different tack as well, pushing for pro-American courses. Endorsing John Collyer's proposal for a required course on "the American way of life," Frank Gannett claimed it "would impress on our students the great benefits that we have derived from our system of government and the opportunities it has made possible."[29] President Day agreed, writing to Devereux Josephs, president of the Carnegie Foundation, "that we need such a program of indoctrination seems to me incontrovertible. . . . We are faced with an enemy who is engaged in an all-out mass indoctrination by authoritarian means. . . . I doubt very much whether we can relax and assume that in a free society no counter propaganda need be undertaken."[30]

Day also sent the proposal to Dean Murdock, who appointed a faculty committee, which deemed the initiative "a program of indoctrination"—and refused to make the course an undergraduate requirement. Scrambling, perhaps to save face, the university sponsored a series of lectures and conferences entitled, suitably enough, "America's Freedom and Responsibility in the

Contemporary Crisis," funded with a $10,000 grant from Carnegie for speakers, and tried, without success, to recruit former president Herbert Hoover as the first speaker.

Clearly, then, Day worked hard—and repeatedly—to respond to the trustees without compromising academic freedom. An especially thorny challenge came when Nicholas Noyes informed him that Marshall Stearns, who had just been hired by Cornell's English Department, had been engaged in "subversive activities" at his former institution, Indiana University.[31] After checking with Indiana's president, Herman Wells, who verified that the allegations were true, Day (for the first and only time, as far as we know) applied a political test for the retention of a faculty member. "Fortunately he is on a limited term appointment for 3 years," Day wrote to Noyes. "He was already hooked up with us before I had my first report from you . . . and I do not see that anything more can be done at the present time." But he wanted Noyes to know that as president he had "put the dean of the college and the chairman of the department on notice with respect to the record the man made at Indiana . . . if and when the question of Dr. Stearns' retention or possible promotion comes up for forward action."[32] Stearns soon left Cornell for what became a distinguished career as an expert on American jazz.

As the Cold War shattered Day's hopes for Soviet-American cooperation and intensified attacks on academic freedom, the president told the board of trustees that "a member of the Communist Party cannot be free or honest, and therefore has no place on the university faculty." Communist faculty were "traitors to the American academic tradition," he insisted, a view endorsed in 1951 by three hundred faculty members who voted that an advocate of forceful overthrow of the government "is guilty of such malfeasance as makes him unfit to teach." Because "students should see all points of view," communists, Day conceded, should be allowed to speak on campus. But only if questions were allowed after the lecture. After the Marxist Discussion Group brought a speaker to campus who spoke about the latest trends in Soviet genetics, he pointed out, "a competent group of animal and plant majors matched minds with him after his lecture and were able to win out very substantially."[33]

Day went along with a federal mandate that applicants for Atomic Energy Commission fellowships sign a loyalty affidavit. But he opposed congressional investigations of the curriculum. When Congressman John S. Wood of the House Un-American Activities Committee asked for a list of all texts used in the social sciences, Day responded that compliance would be difficult and expensive. "More important, what does the committee intend to infer from such a list? Suppose in some courses Karl Marx's *Das Kapital* is on the list of reading, or sections of the Communist Manifesto. . . . These young people ought to have some acquaintance with these documents. It does not follow because they are cited or used that communism is being taught."[34]

Day sensed that "a witch hunt is developing in this country" and knew that Cornell's board of trustees was not immune from the anticommunist hysteria.[35] When trustee Franklin Olin argued that "our college campuses were riddled with communism," or "calls a New Dealer a communist," or "looked for a red under every bed, even at Cornell," he "just does not know what he is talking about," Day told Frank Gannett. Nonetheless, "in view of Mr. Olin's great wealth" and the prospect that "he might reasonably give us money," Day held his tongue in conversations with Olin himself.[36]

In contrast, Day tried to convince Nicholas Noyes about the values of academic freedom. After reassuring Noyes that he, too, "abhorre[d] communism" and thought communist faculty should be fired, Day illustrated the central role of free discussion in "our American way of life" with the story of a student who had recently "confounded a radical speaker and brought an end to a meeting with a simple question to which he wanted a 'yes' or 'no' answer. If there were a communist government in the United States, would that government permit a meeting such as this?" To Noyes's claim that Cornell was promoting "un-American thinking," Day replied that "most thinking of youth is fuzzy— is not well defined around the edges." The amount of un-American thinking among college students, however, "is negligible." On the "communist issue," the university had used "traditional Cornell methods, methods of thought and persuasion and ultimately conviction . . . methods which invariably bring the most effective and lasting results."[37]

In 1949, two months before his deteriorating heart condition forced him to resign his presidency, Day was interviewed by a Los Angeles radio station affiliated with Mutual Radio News. He defended ejecting communists from teaching positions, "where their fettered minds have no legitimate place." But, he warned, this must "not give rise to a sort of hysteria, in which independent and essentially forward-looking thinkers are scrapped along with real members of the fifth column." Day concluded with a plea that Americans develop an explicit definition "of the essential ingredients of the American way of life." Echoing Carl Becker, Day challenged his radio audience to do what their "founding fathers did not do . . . to spell out the responsibilities, individual and collective, which go along with the rights they established . . . responsibilities without which our rights today cannot be permanently retained."[38]

CORNELL'S TWO ACTING presidents between June 1949 and July 1951, Cornelis de Kiewiet and Theodore P. Wright, were quickly ensnared in controversies over academic freedom issues that rocked the campus. In an October 1950 editorial, the *Cornell Sun* found evidence that "hysteria is mounting" and cautioned Americans to thread "a delicate line between foolish blindness and over-zealous witch-hunting." The *Sun* contrasted Cornell's "healthy attitude" in allowing

Herbert J. Phillips, a University of Washington professor of philosophy who had been fired for membership in the Communist Party, to speak at Willard Straight Hall, with the cancellation of his lecture at the University of Michigan. In another editorial, the *Sun* tried to demonstrate its evenhandedness by condemning the sponsors of the talk, the Labor Youth League, for seeking "a closed, restricted, totalitarian society."[39]

The trustees were divided over the student invitation in December 1950 to Eslanda Robeson, the wife of singer (and political radical) Paul Robeson, to speak at Cornell.[40] When Victor Emmanuel '19, the ardent anticommunist, who had given the university a priceless Wordsworth collection, wondered why she was not banned from campus, as Eugene Dennis had been a year earlier, Arthur Dean '19, JD '23, explained that Mrs. Robeson's son was a Cornell graduate and that, moreover, banning her opened the university to charges of "drawing the color line." Mary Donlon '20 was blunter, writing de Kiewiet, "I certainly do not favor a trustee blacklist of possible campus speakers."[41]

Trustees and alumni sponsored initiatives to encourage anticommunism and Americanism on campus. Myron Taylor, LLB '94, a former U.S. Steel executive and also the personal representative of the president of the United States to Pope Pius XII, made a gift in memory of his wife, Anabel Taylor, in January 1950, to create an interfaith religious center on campus. Since "we are all believers in God and human liberty . . . we must stand together to resist evil," he proclaimed. Taylor hoped his gift would be matched by others so that America could fight "with all our resources" the growth of atheism, sponsored by communism. His new interfaith building (which was completed in October 1952) would help "to clarify the religious issues at stake in the present [Cold War] crisis."[42]

That same year Mrs. John L. Senior of Lenox, Massachusetts, who de Kiewiet described as someone "who had a sense of anxiety about the state of American affairs both socially and politically," established an endowment of $300,000 for a chair in memory of her husband, class of 1901, a leader in the cement industry before his death in 1946. Anchored in neither a college nor department, the chair was intended to be the first professorship in "American values" in the United States. Convinced that the Arts College creation of an American Studies major in 1950, "particularly aimed at good citizenship," was too apolitical, Mrs. Senior urged that the Senior professor "be concerned with the way in which the American faith in the supreme worth of the individual expresses itself in our literature, in our philosophy and in our art, as well as in our system of private enterprise."[43]

While Cornell administrators thought about an appropriate person to fill the handsomely endowed chair, trustee concerns about leftist professors at Cornell came to a head with accusations against Professor Philip Morrison. Morrison first appeared on the trustee radar screen in 1948 and 1949, when he attacked investigations of the loyalty of scientists, opposed a United States monopoly of nuclear secrets, and demanded that America pledge not to be the first to use the H-bomb. While Hans Bethe often appeared alongside Morrison at these Cornell forums, making the same arguments, the Nobel laureate was not interested in Morrison's broader political agenda, including the latter's criticism of the Smith Act, the New York City communist trial, his frequent trips to peace conferences, his attack on the anticommunist McCarran Act, or his speech before two thousand people at a New York City "World Peace" rally, when he followed Paul Robeson's singing of "Peace Will Conquer War."[44]

In April 1949, *Life* magazine described Morrison as one of America's fifty most important "dupes and fellow travelers." A year later, he was singled out as "a member or supporter of various communist activities" in the anticommunist newsletter *Counterattack*, published by a group of ex-FBI agents, and Cornell was urged to fire him. The next month Senator Joseph McCarthy accused him of "belonging to subversive organizations." And in April 1951 a report by the House Un-American Activities Committee cited Morrison as associated with "the current communist peace offensive . . . traveling up and down the country on his Red Mission praising the Soviet Union."[45]

Inaugurating a Cornell Cold War melodrama, Nicholas Noyes wondered "why do we have such men at Cornell?" When board chair Arthur Dean asked if there was solid evidence that Morrison was a communist, trustee Victor Emmanuel indicated that although the FBI could not make available the content of its files "to persons not connected with the government," J. Edgar Hoover was willing to meet with Acting President de Kiewiet to talk about Morrison. De Kiewiet declined.[46] A historian firmly convinced of the virtues of self-reliance and a free-market economy, de Kiewiet had promised trustees that he would "terminate" any teacher "proven to be an active communist." But he reminded them, as well, about the values of vigorous debate at Cornell, citing St. Augustine's observation "that heretics are given to us that we may not remain in ignorance." Campus leftists could "shoot off their mouths," he wrote, because it usually led students to realize "the unacceptable nature" of such views, "strengthening them in their own judgments."[47]

It would be Theodore Wright, the scholarly engineer and acting president after de Kiewiet left for Rochester, who dealt with Morrison, since, as Cornell's presidential papers reveal, some twenty-five letters and calls from trustees arrived at his office in the immediate aftermath of the HUAC report. Making matters worse was Morrison's glib dismissal of Senator Joseph McCarthy in the *Cornell Sun* as someone who "every rational American has long since recognized, speaking under immunity from suit, is willing to degrade the Senatorial dignity by unfounded character blackening."[48]

Wright summoned Morrison to a meeting at which he told him "that his extra-curricular activities were hurting the University." Wright made three requests of Morrison, which he repeated in a follow-up letter. He asked that the Physics professor not accept sponsorship, formal or informal, of student groups not focused on scientific investigation. He asked that Morrison disassociate his own political opinions from those of Cornell University whenever he spoke in public. Finally, he urged Morrison to stop "appearing on platforms in a sympathetic role with avowed and proven communists," citing as an example the meetings of the American Peace Crusade.[49]

Meanwhile, Wright asked Robert Wilson, the Physics Department chair, to evaluate Morrison's importance as a scientist. Wilson replied that Morrison was one of the "best teachers on campus" and ranked him "with Professor Bethe for first honors in our department." His political work, Wilson added, was done "in a small fraction of his spare time, and I have always considered it absolutely none of my business."[50]

On April 18, Morrison thanked Wright for "the reasoned and understanding nature" of their discussion. He agreed not to sponsor student groups and to disassociate himself from Cornell when speaking off campus in nonscientific settings. He would not promise, however, to end his association with the American Peace Crusade. Although he was not a communist and did not endorse the policies of the Soviet Union, he told Wright, "walking through the rubble of Hiroshima" had left him with "the deep conviction that in the true interests of America, my country, it is urgent that some voices speak for peace." It was irrational of trustees to brand his activities harmful to Cornell, especially

The Physics professor Philip Morrison's promotion was delayed because of allegations that he was a communist sympathizer. (Division of Rare and Manuscript Collections of the Cornell University Library)

since he had "always tried to appear in public with the dignity and sincerity which befits a Cornell faculty member."[51]

When Wright reviewed this letter with his "academic cabinet," the minutes note that "there followed an extensive discussion of the desirability and possibility of dismissing Professor Morrison." Wright opposed any such action. Cornell faculty would see it as a violation of academic freedom, he pointed out, and the American Association of University Professors would become involved. But what settled the issue for Wright was his belief that Morrison was not a communist, but "an almost rabid pacifist," a "peace-at-any-price man" with a guilty conscience over his own role in the development of the atom bomb, which had been to help construct the bomb for the first test explosion at Alamogordo, New Mexico, and then join the team on the B-29 base on the Pacific island of Tinian where the atomic bombs dropped on Japan were assembled.[52] These assurances were passed on through Arthur Dean to Nicholas Noyes, Victor Emmanuel, and Frank Gannett. The Morrison crisis appeared to be over.

IT WAS NOT. A year and a half later, in December 1952, a witness testifying before the United States Senate Internal Security Subcommittee claimed that "Dr. Philip Morrison has one of the most incriminating pro-communist records in the entire academic world." He cited the professor's speeches and writings "defending the American Peace Crusade" and worried about the danger Morrison posed "due to his participation on the Los Alamos project." The witness, J. B. Matthews, a Hearst consultant and staff researcher for several congressional communist-hunting committees, chastised Cornell, as well. Despite the university's "full knowledge of Professor Morrison's post-communist activities," it did nothing, using "something known as academic freedom . . . to permit the employment of men who are subversive in their activities with respect to American institutions."[53]

Summoned to deal with the second Morrison crisis was the new Cornell president, Deane Malott, dubbed Cornell's "businessman president" by the *Cornell Sun*. In letters to Gannett and Emmanuel, Malott proclaimed that he was "a Republican," indeed, "extremely conservative." "On the whole," he suspected, the faculty were like him, "very conservative, fervently hoping for a Republican administration."[54] In his controversial inaugural address Malott had warned "against allowing the system of government to sink slowly from the free republic of decentralized government to the welfare state, to the handout state, to the police state." Speaking to the annual dinner of the Ithaca Chamber of Commerce in March 1952, Malott attacked the "so-called great liberals of today" as radicals, "not tinkering with our institutions but out to destroy them." They were "addicts" who sought to have the federal government absorb more and more of the national income.[55] Two weeks later, Malott rejected a petition signed by over 650 students requesting that Cornell ban off-campus housing listings that did not include an "I do not discriminate" clause. He called the petitioners "leftists."[56]

The Cornell Agriculture School's *Country Almanac* was pleased and praised the new president as "a real man and a real American" for defending "old fashioned American free enterprise and free people" from the "concerted program by pinks, and reds, and internationalists" who would turn Cornell into "a radical hot-bed." Not that Cornell students were all that left-leaning in 1952. A mock primary that spring had 1,038 votes for Republican candidates and 312 for Democrats. A year later, when the tiny "Students for Peace" group set up a table at the Straight to encourage Cornellians to send postcards to President Eisenhower urging clemency for the Rosenbergs, other students chanted, "Fry, fry, the Rosenbergs." The table was gone after half a day.[57]

Nonetheless, like his predecessors, Day, de Kiewiet, and Wright, Malott walked the tightrope, balancing pressures from outside the university and the values central to academic inquiry on campus. While personally inclined to conservatism, he wrote a friend, "on the other hand, I have a grave responsibility of preserving Cornell as a free institution, and I am trying very hard to do that."[58] An important step in the evolution of Malott's understanding of this "grave responsibility" was his handling of the reopened Morrison case.

Malott appointed a five-person faculty committee in January 1953 "to consider the problems arising from the unfavorable publicity received by Professor Morrison."[59] In addition to two long sessions with Morrison, committee members took the extraordinary step of visiting Morrison's accuser, J. B. Matthews, in the Hearst building in New York City. Perhaps by design, Matthews was unavailable, but his senior associate, John A. Clements, met with them. According to the two faculty who took notes, Clements boasted that in the six-room suite occupied by his organization was a file with "one million, two hundred thousand cards, documenting communist and communist-front activities." "In most profane language," he accused universities and colleges of having been "arrogant, shameless, and high handed in harboring communists and fellow-travelers." The Cornell faculty should be "ashamed," he fumed, since Morrison "is one of the most active college professors in the country in communist-front affairs." Asked for evidence of Morrison's activities, Clements showed committee members "a pile of about 50 three-by-five cards; each with a date ranging from 1943 to 1952." Clements declined to provide any further information, and the faculty had the impression that the evidence was largely "circumstantial, a record of where he has spoken, to what groups and when."[60]

By contrast, Morrison "impressed the committee as being straight forward, helpful and sincere." Asked "if he were a Marxist," he replied that he supported public ownership of some property, but opposed violent and revolutionary change since "he thought that over the long sweep of years that the natural drift of our society would be in the direction he favors." Asked "if he were a communist," he answered "I certainly am not—but neither am I wholly opposed to them." Although he had joined the American Peace Crusade, Morrison added that he would support the United States if it went to war with the Soviet Union.[61]

The committee unanimously reported to Malott that Morrison's guilty feelings about his work on the atomic bomb had left "a blind or weakened spot in his capacity to think about social and political concepts while having no effect upon the scientific work at which he is indisputably brilliant." Nonetheless, he was "not subversive," and "his scientific work and his more ingenious extra-curricular activities have not blended." Since there was no evidence that either publicly or in private Morrison had ever advocated the overthrow of the government by force or violence, "he should not be charged with any activities which would make him guilty of such misfeasance or malfeasance as makes him unfit to participate in the relationship of teacher to student."[62]

Malott circulated the faculty committee's report to the board of trustees in April 1953.[63] The board was still reeling from an article two weeks earlier in the *American Mercury* magazine in which the ubiquitous Matthews had named Morrison and seven other Cornell faculty, including the literary critic M. H. Abrams, as "communist sympathizers or dupes."[64] Meanwhile, Morrison's case became national news in May, when Morrison, while on leave at MIT, was called to testify before a special session, held in Boston, of the Senate Internal Security Subcommittee. According to the Associated Press, Morrison "answered all questions fully and unhesitatingly," recounting his involvement with the Communist Party in the 1930s and his break with the party in 1939, three years before he joined the Manhattan Project, which developed the atomic bomb. He told the committee that he assumed "his superiors knew of his past connections." The day after his testimony, Morrison was "released as a witness" with no recriminatory comments from the committee.[65]

A university spokesman told the *Cornell Sun* that there seemed to be no grounds for "charges that Prof. Morrison was guilty of misfeasance or nonfeasance."[66] And Professor Robert Wilson, director of Cornell's Laboratory of Nuclear Physics, noted that his colleague's testimony "in no way reflects upon Morrison's ability as a professor of Physics . . . he is an inspiring teacher and an excellent scientist." Although Malott stood by his own faculty committee's report on Morrison, he indicated to trustees that his very visible appearances for the American Peace Crusade continued "to be embarrassing to the University" and that there was "need for some corrective action unless these activities are discontinued."[67]

The president met with the professor when Morrison returned from MIT, with Malott suggesting that "by reason of your past actions, your present activities must be especially discreet." But, interesting enough, when Morrison suggested by return letter that Malott draw up a list of organizations that Morrison "should avoid," the president refused. It was inappropriate, he wrote, for "an administrative officer to keep taboo lists, or to regulate the personal activity of any professor in Cornell University, or to make agreements of permissible conduct." Malott hoped, however, that Morrison would see the advisability "of withdrawing all association from organizations lying outside of your professional field." But "the decision is entirely yours," Malott concluded.[68]

Privately, Malott was reassuring trustees that for his part he had read William F. Buckley Jr.'s *God and Man at Yale* and that no one was subverting the minds of young Cornellians, for "Professor Morrison I do not believe is a communist." Nor had the physicist ever "used his classroom or laboratory in any way to espouse his social causes." In fact, in recent months Morrison had been "extremely quiet," not participating much in "dubious social organizations since I had somewhat of a showdown with him."[69]

Publicly, Malott, the self-proclaimed conservative, defended dissent and free thought. In a published report to the alumni he lamented this "time of widespread hysteria and intolerance of thought, speech and action," reminding them of earlier periods when we "burned witches in Salem" and banned or burned books. Even more emphatically, in a widely read article in the *New York Herald Tribune*, Malott called upon "thinking citizens to stand behind the principles of freedom of thought and expression." The right of dissent, the right to "express some doubt about the existing order of things in democratic America," the right to work for "the utopia of a world organization and international unity" ought not to be confused with "treachery or evil intentions."[70]

But there was to be yet another act in this drama, one in which the trustees and the president had the right and responsibility to play a central role. Morrison had been an associate professor since 1948, and in 1954 his Physics colleagues voted to promote him to full professor. Fearing a divisive debate among the trustees, Malott refused at first to recommend Morrison's promotion to the board. When Malott did pass along the recommendation the next year, a significant number of trustees demanded that a special committee be appointed to investigate Morrison's activities, despite Malott's insistence that "if you turn it down, I am in real trouble—to such an extent that you may have to get a new President."[71]

The unprecedented secret committee of five trustees met in October 1956 and for two lengthy days questioned Morrison, who was accompanied by his Physics colleague and supporter Dale Corson, who had shared an office with Morrison at Berkeley in 1938. Years later Corson noted that he was most worried about Mary Donlon, who "was strongly anti-communist and she saw Morrison as a dangerous leftist." Meanwhile, the full professors in the Physics Department wrote the president and the trustees that it was "a disgrace" to hold up the promotion any further. They threatened to send no more promotions forward until favorable action was taken on Morrison. In January 1957, two and a half years after his colleagues had voted to make him a full professor, the promotion was approved, albeit grudgingly, by the board: "That while the Board of Trustees of Cornell University regrets and deplores certain of the activities of Professor Philip Morrison, nevertheless, on the basis of the evidence so far available to it nothing has been found which would warrant his being brought up on charges before the University faculty."[72]

Other Cold War issues buffeted Malott, as well, testing and helping to forge his commitment to academic freedom. He stood by Knight Biggerstaff when Senator McCarthy questioned the security clearance of the History professor and chair of Cornell's Far Eastern Studies Department. A witness before McCarthy's committee linked Biggerstaff's wartime service in Asia to the "fall of China" to the Communists in 1949, since Biggerstaff had known Mao Tse-tung and Chou En-lai. Malott stood by George Kahin when he was denied a passport because of his criticism of the Philippine government. And he remained on the sidelines in March 1954 when the Cornell University Young Republican Club invited McCarthy to speak on campus, though with the stipulation that the senator "make no nasty aspersions with regard to Cornell or its faculty." Professor C. C. Arnold, the club's faculty adviser, resigned in protest over the invitation. Ten days later McCarthy begged off, claiming he was overburdened with committee work.[73] But Malott could not escape the trustee and alumni explosion that followed the appointment of Dexter Perkins, a professor from the University of Rochester, as the first holder of the John L. Senior Chair.

The trustee Frank Gannett, president of the Gannett Newspapers, was Perkins's principal critic. Gannett reminded Malott that because "president Day leaned a little too much to the left to suit me," he had opposed several candidates for endowed chairs and had been reassured by the president that the Senior professorship "ought to do something to emphasize the American way of life."[74] When Perkins, a relatively apolitical, distinguished historian of American foreign policy, was appointed to the Senior chair, Gannett was furious. Perkins was "too liberal," a "one worlder," who "supported Adlai Stevenson."[75] Mrs. Senior was also upset. After meeting with Perkins at her estate in Massachusetts, she reported that, to her "horror," he wanted to teach a course simply about American foreign policy, not a course on how "communism and socialism are infiltrating every phase of our national life, seeking to destroy our freedom, our government, and our competitive free enterprise system." She suggested that Perkins serve one year and then be replaced by Clarence Randall, an industrialist and author of *A Creed for Free Enterprise*. Mrs. Senior and Gannett contacted several trustees, including Walter Todd '09, Maxwell Upson '99, Nicholas Noyes, John Collyer, and Walter Teagle, urging them to pressure Malott to replace Perkins.[76]

Malott stood firm, supporting the faculty's choice for the chair. Perkins "rates among the foremost historians of America," he wrote Todd, adding that "for your confidential information, Dr. Perkins told me he had given money to the Eisenhower campaign. He can't be all bad!" More important, Malott mobilized his center. He asked trustees Neal Dow Becker '06 and Arthur Dean for help in countering "the kick-up from the ultra reactionaries." If he listened to them and appointed someone "so far to the right to conform to what some of these people think appropriate, he would be laughed off campus by the students as completely ineffective." Perkins was "a liberal conservative and no crackpot." He trusted that Becker and Dean would "not become unduly excited by some of the sentiments which they may hear."[77]

After the appointment was made, Malott declared victory. In his 1954 report to the alumni he announced that the Senior Professor had already had "a significant influence in establishing an understanding of the American way of life," with "several hundred students attending his lectures."[78]

Perkins remained the John L. Senior Chair until his retirement in 1958. He was replaced by Clinton Rossiter '39, the author of *Seedtime of the Republic* and *The American Presidency* and the recipient in 1956 of a grant of $300,000 from the Fund for the Republic to study "the extent of communist penetration into American society, institutions and ideals." No rest, alas, for Malott. Trustee John Olin '13 expressed reservations about the Fund for the Republic and its liberal president, the University of Chicago's Robert Hutchins. Having done his due diligence, Malott pointed out that Arthur Dean was a member of the fund's executive committee and that Rossiter was "no communist or fellow-traveler . . . he happened to be a registered Republican."[79]

Malott was mastering the art of championing academic freedom while sounding like a vigilant anticommunist. He could reassure one alumnus that "confidentially . . . there is an FBI agent in Ithaca with whom we work very closely," while telling another in 1953 that "no one wants our young people taught by Communist influence. But we must keep a free standard of inquiry in the universities of America." A year later, he reminded trustees that "Cornell has always had non-conformity. It is a part of our free tradition." But this was "not to say, of course, that the University is soft, or that the faculty or administration has the slightest intention of fostering Communism or subversion."[80] Malott was about to be tested on this proposition, yet again.

———

MARCUS SINGER, a professor of zoology and nationally recognized expert on neurology and anatomy, whose research had been funded by the American Cancer Society, had come to Cornell in 1951 from Harvard. At Cornell his courses on evolutionary biology were student favorites. Singer had grown up in a working-class neighborhood in Pittsburgh and been a truck driver for four years after high school, before getting his BA at the University of Pittsburgh and his PhD from Harvard. As a graduate student, Singer had been a member of a Marxist study group, though he was never a Communist Party member. By 1945 he had left behind all political interests. In May 1953, Singer was, nonetheless, called to testify before the House Un-American Activities Committee.

Speaking eloquently about his disillusion with Marxism and his realization that his "basic loyalties always were and always will be with my country," Singer refused to supply the names of other members of the study group. When pressed to answer, Singer cited his Fifth Amendment rights against self-incrimination. Harold Velder, chair of the committee, informed Singer that he would ask the Justice Department to rule on whether his selective refusal to answer committee questions should result in an indictment for contempt of Congress.[81] So began Professor Singer's four-year-long legal nightmare.

On April 30, 1954, Singer was indeed cited for contempt by the Un-American Activities Committee, and on May 12 by the whole House of Representatives. The next day, Malott told the *Cornell Sun* that he would take no action on Singer until and unless he was indicted by a federal grand jury. The *Sun* ran editorials strongly "sympathizing with the moral basis of Dr. Singer's testimony and

Found in contempt by the House Un-American Activities Committee for refusing to answer questions, the Zoology professor Marcus Singer was put on leave of absence by President Malott. (Division of Rare and Manuscript Collections of the Cornell University Library)

recognizing his unique contributions to the Cornell community and to the world of science." The editors pleaded with the president "to be courageous and not give in to wealthy alumni who want him fired." The Student Council voted 16–1 in support of Singer and launched a drive to raise money for his defense. The faculty of the College of Arts and Sciences voted unanimously "to express its faith in Professor Singer's loyalty and moral integrity," and it, too, created a committee to help raise funds for the embattled professor.[82]

Malott had already made up his mind. When urged by the dean of Arts and Sciences, Paul M. O'Leary, PhD '29, to simply "relieve Singer of his teaching duties" with a paid leave of absence, "rather than being suspended with pay" in the case of indictment, Malott "answered by phone in general agreement."[83] So on November 23, 1954, the day a federal grand jury indicted Singer for contempt of Congress, the university placed him "on salaried leave and relieved him of his teaching responsibilities pending disposition of the indictment."[84]

The *Sun* insisted that the university take no action unless and until Singer was found guilty. Meanwhile, the professor pleaded innocent in First Federal District Court in Washington and was released on posting $1,000 bond. The government claimed that the Fifth Amendment did not protect individuals from answering questions that did not involve self-incrimination. Trial was set on the twenty-two-count indictment before Judge Burnita S. Matthews and scheduled for February 21, 1955. But nothing moved quickly in the Singer case, and the trial was postponed, first indefinitely, and then until October 24, when Singer's lawyers requested a delay because "cases similar to Dr. Singer's are pending in the courts."[85]

The case was finally heard by Judge Matthews, without a jury, three months later. The prosecution argued that by testifying about himself, Singer had given up his Fifth Amendment rights. The defense argued that since HUAC already knew the identity of those Singer was asked to name, the committee had exceeded "valid legislative purpose" and sought "exposure for exposure's sake." On March 19, 1956, Judge Matthews found Singer guilty of only one of the twenty-two counts with which he was charged, refusing to name those with whom he attended meetings at Harvard in the early 1940s. Singer was sentenced to three months in jail, which was suspended, and was fined $100. Five months later Singer filed an appeal. With his case not settled, Singer's salaried leave from his teaching at Cornell also continued.[86]

Despite the guilty verdict, the trustees exerted little pressure on Malott. They raised no objections to his paid leave of absence. Unlike Morrison, Singer was a student favorite, publicly repentant about his graduate student Marxism, and essentially an apolitical Cornell professor. Alumni letters to the president tended to express support for Singer. "All of our sentiments," Malott wrote to O'Leary, "are I think, entirely with the man."[87] Perhaps the only people on campus not fans of Singer were some colleagues in his own Zoology Department, which had a reputation for anti-Semitism, and whose chairman, H. B. Adelmann '20, MA '22, PhD '24, was reputed to have once told the Zoology librarian to check the bags of Singer and another zoologist, Howard Schneiderman, for stolen books, because "I'm not going to let this library be decimated by some Jews from the slums of Brooklyn."[88]

The chairman of the board of trustees, Arthur Dean, remained concerned that if Singer's sentence involved no jail time and a small fine, and he was restored to teaching, some might conclude that Cornell was "pinning a medal on him." Malott replied that "all of us here" think nothing emerged from the trial indicating Singer was "a serious moral risk as a teacher and he is not at all interested in social problems at the present time." The president shared Dean's view that Singer had been "both legally and morally wrong," but admired how he had handled himself through a long period of uncertainty as well as the "mistaken integrity" that led him to tell all about himself but not "squeal on his fellows." If Singer were jailed, Malott indicated, he would take him off the payroll during the time he was incarcerated. If he were given a suspended sentence or fined, he would reinstate him.[89]

Another year dragged by before Singer's appeal was heard by a three-judge panel of the U.S. Circuit Court of Appeals. Voting 2–1, the court upheld his conviction, with the minority dissenting vote cast by the Chief Judge Henry Edgerton '10, who had been on the faculty of the Cornell Law School from 1927 to 1938. With speculation that Singer might appeal again to the full Circuit Court, Singer remained "relieved" of his teaching duties, despite angry editorials from the *Cornell Sun*, which acknowledged, nonetheless, that president Malott deserved much praise for his handling of the case. "It seems terrifying," the *Sun* indicated, with uncharacteristic understatement, "that there are some college presidents who would fire a professor immediately if they know he had admitted to be in any kind of Marxist study group, but it is true."[90]

The students were not in Ithaca on June 28, 1957, when the full U.S. Court of Appeals sent Singer's case back to Federal District Court, ordering that its decision be reversed. Singer's conviction was overturned on the basis of the Supreme Court's June 17 ruling in the case of a labor leader in the Midwest, John Watkins, whose invocation of the Fifth Amendment was allowed because the committee did not adequately explain the pertinency of its questions. When the students returned in September they were greeted by a bold headline in the *Cornell Sun*, "The End at Last. . . . The Singer Case Is Finished."[91] Singer left Cornell in 1961 for a position at Case Western Reserve.

––––––––––

AFTER THE UNITED states Senate censured Senator McCarthy in 1954, the anti-communist pandemic on American campuses began to wind down, albeit in fits and starts. The *Cornell Daily Sun*'s editor in 1955 and future sportswriter, Richard J. Schaap '55, wrote that year, "There is a pervasive fear here . . . any remark even in jest might rebound upon a student after graduation."[92] The drama of the Cold War at Cornell, indeed, had several more curtain calls. And here, too, not surprisingly, the complex, crosscutting, and contentious presidential balancing act was on display.

Malott and Cornell were commended by the American Association of University Professors (AAUP) in a 1956 report on academic freedom (summarized in great detail in the *New York Times*) for acting correctly in supporting the rights of professors under investigation or accusation by government officials and agencies. Insisting that removal of a faculty member could be justified only by proof "of unfitness to teach because of incompetence, lack of scholarly objectivity or integrity," and not by "the invocation of the Fifth Amendment," the AAUP report also cited five schools for doing it incorrectly. One of them was Rutgers University, which in 1952 had dismissed the classical scholar and historian Moses I. Finley for his refusal to testify before the Senate Internal Security Subcommittee.[93] How ironic that Cornell's president would soon become a central player in Finley's case, taking a position contrary to the principles set forth by the organization that had just praised him.

Between 1956 and 1958, the Cornell History Department tried on several occasions to recruit Finley. But Malott defiantly said no, indicating that he personally "viewed recourse to the Fifth Amendment as both morally and legally indefensible." When the department persisted, Malott sent his executive assistant to interview administrators at Rutgers, only to reaffirm his decision. The History Department then asked the University Faculty Committee on Academic Freedom and Tenure to intervene. The committee met with Malott, but he still refused to budge, indicating that his decision was grounded "upon an overall evaluation of Dr. Finley's character and personal qualifications," which was derived from "confidential information" acquired at Rutgers. The faculty committee, chaired by Milton Konvitz, PhD '33, threw in the towel. Disappointing as it was to them, they concluded that on appointments, in contrast to dismissals, the president and the board of trustees had final authority.[94] Blocking Finley (who became a lecturer in classics at Cambridge University in 1957, a British citizen in 1962, and was knighted in 1979) because he had invoked the Fifth Amendment was one of the few times in the Cold War period when Cornell's president could write the script himself.

With this important exception, the Cold War continued to thaw at Cornell, with, for example, Malott presiding, at times reluctantly, over a six-year process in which the nearly century-old requirement that men students in Cornell's land grant colleges had to be members of ROTC was abandoned. The unraveling began in 1954 with two Cornell students refusing to take the new loyalty oath, added that June as a rider to the Defense Appropriations Bill, mandating that ROTC members swear that they were not members of any group on the attorney general's list of communist-controlled or communist-front organizations. "Of course," Malott wrote, in his balanced way, to Robert Stevens, the secretary of the army, "the whole matter is a tempest in a tea-kettle to my way of thinking, and I personally wouldn't care how many oaths I took." But others in the academic world, he informed "Bob," "think otherwise," and the loyalty oath was being used, he feared, by those intent on abandoning required ROTC programs in America's land grant colleges.[95] Pressure from college presidents like Malott, indeed, led the Defense Department to abandon this new "loyalty" oath in April 1955, but the damage had been done.

That month, a referendum conducted by the Student Council had 2,790 Cornell undergraduates voting in favor of voluntary ROTC and 1,080 against. The next month the faculty, which had ultimate authority in the matter, surprisingly supported compulsory ROTC at a university faculty meeting, where no vote was recorded. But the die was cast. Anti-ROTC had become a national movement. Four years later, 1,752 Cornell students voted for voluntary ROTC and 597 for mandatory ROTC, and this time the university faculty agreed, again with no exact tally reported. So it was that Malott and Arthur Dean wrote Thomas Gates Jr., secretary of defense, on June 16, 1960, that though "many of us felt some considerable regret in the circumstances leading to the decision," the trustees had "approved a strong recommendation from the faculty and administration of the University to operate Cornell's ROTC programs on a basis providing for voluntary enlistment."[96]

By the early 1960s, "the times were a-changing" at Cornell, as they were in the America of the youthful president John F. Kennedy. In August 1961 a letter from trustee J. D. Tuller '09, angry with the appointment of the leftist economist Paul Sweezy as a visiting professor, was answered bluntly by Professor Alfred Kahn, chair of Economics: "He did an outstanding job of teaching for us. I have discussed his performance with a very large number of students, have you? We will continue to be guided solely by academic competence in our staffing." "Your letter to Tuller was superb!!" Malott told Kahn.[97]

In December 1961 Gus Hall, head of the Communist Party of the United States, who had recently been indicted for failing to register the party as an arm of the Soviet Union, spoke to an overflow audience at Bailey Hall. In an interview with the *Cornell Daily Sun*, President Malott noted that he had received "surprisingly few objections from alumni" about Hall's appearance on campus. Perhaps the scheduling three days later of a talk by William F. Buckley Jr. helped in that respect.[98]

And in 1961 Cornell faculty sponsored a rally against nuclear testing, which warmly endorsed the efforts being made by President Kennedy's chief test-ban negotiator, Cornell's own Arthur Dean. But nothing better symbolizes the end of an era at Cornell and throughout America than President Malott's invitation in November 1962, through the Presidium of the USSR Academy of Sciences, to academician I. I. Mints to please visit Cornell in 1963 to give a lecture course on "the development of Soviet society since 1917."[99]

In the years between Day's handling of the Russian Language and Culture Program and Malott's 1962 invitation to the Soviet scholar, there were undoubtedly some socialists and communists among the Cornell faculty—professors who deemed American capitalism destructive and dangerous. But to have such ideas or beliefs did not on its own constitute sedition or mark one as subversive. The faculty understood that in a university there were no restraints on thought itself. They knew, as John Stuart Mill had written, that "there ought to exist the fullest liberty of professing and discussing, as a matter of ethical conviction, any doctrine, however immoral it may be considered," and that "all silencing of discussion is an assumption of infallibility."[100]

The faculty's insistence on these principles weighed heavily on how Cornell's presidents acted during the Cold War, and by and large the presidents acquitted themselves well as they navigated competing pressures from students, alumni, trustees, professors, politicians, and the press. While President Malott insisted that no communist should serve on the faculty, he strongly defended his faculty against unsubstantiated charges. Academic freedom at Cornell weathered the chill of the anticommunist crusade better than it did at many other leading American universities. Many years later, long after Philip Morrison had left Cornell in 1965 for a prestigious professorship at MIT, he wrote then President Emeritus Malott: "I have never made clear to you how much I admire and how often I comment on your fairness and integrity in the bad years of the McCarthy era. . . . Your adherence to the fundamentals of human rights and honesty in dispute . . . was an example of the right conduct for men of responsibility, in a time when too many of them sought the quick expedient."[101]

PART II
1963-1977

4 | The Bureaucratic University and Its Discontents

Like Ezra Cornell, President James Perkins was a Quaker. With a sense of social commitment and an urge to do good, he seemed to be ideally suited to be Cornell's leader during the 1960s. Perkins got off to an auspicious start. With a booming economy in the United States in the first half of the '60s, the New York State Legislature, federal government agencies, and philanthropic foundations made higher education a high priority and allocated substantial sums of money to elite research universities, including Cornell. Faculty hiring in traditional areas and in new fields of specialization accelerated, and interdisciplinary programs, centers, and institutes proliferated. New buildings were constructed, and the size of the administrative and support staff increased dramatically. And the time seemed right for a civil rights revolution at Cornell.

Unfortunately, the "golden age of higher education" at Cornell (and elsewhere) did not last very long. As "stagflation" took hold in the 1970s, Cornell had to run hard just to stay in place. Saddest of all, though he seemed the perfect leader for a time when political unrest swept through university campuses in rebellious 1960s America, Perkins's presidency ended with Cornell providing an iconic visual image of the era, a Pulitzer Prize–winning photograph seen around the world of rifle-toting, bandolier-draped black students striding defiantly out of Willard Straight Hall.

Perkins grew up in suburban Philadelphia; like Malott, he was the son of a banker. He went to Germantown Friends School and then to Swarthmore. After receiving a doctorate in political science in 1937, he became an assistant professor at Princeton, teaching courses on American government and American foreign policy, and assistant director of its School of Public and International Affairs. During World War II Perkins served with the Office of Price Administration and the Foreign Economic Administration. From 1945 to 1950 he was vice president of Swarthmore. This was followed by over a decade with the Carnegie Corporation and Carnegie Foundation for the Advancement of Teaching, where he served as vice president.

James Perkins, president of Cornell from 1963 to 1969. (Division of Rare and Manuscript Collections of the Cornell University Library)

When he arrived at Cornell in 1963, Perkins, at age fifty-two, personified the professional educator, widely networked in the upper reaches of research, education, and government organizations. He was a trustee of the Rand Corporation and the American Council on Foreign Relations. He was a member of the General Advisory Committee of the U.S. Arms Control and Disarmament Agency. He served on the United States Commission for UNESCO and the Herter Committee on Foreign Affairs Personnel. He sat on committees established by New Jersey governor Richard Hughes and the New York Board of Regents to study education. He was chair of the board of trustees of the United Negro College Fund, and from 1953 to 1959, Perkins, the father of five children, also found the time to serve on the local school board of Princeton, New Jersey.

His stature as an educational leader—he was often paired with his friend and Swarthmore classmate Clark Kerr, president of the University of California— was enhanced at Cornell when President Lyndon Johnson appointed him the chair of a General Advisory Committee on Foreign Assistance Programs, and then cochair in 1967 of the International Conference on the World Crisis in Education. It was no secret on campus that these prestigious off-campus commitments often kept Cornell's president away from Ithaca. Perkins spent "25 percent of his time off campus with non-Cornell organizations and institutions," he told the *Cornell Sun*.[1] Dubbed by *Newsweek* "the jet set university president," Perkins flew to his commissions and boards on the university's private plane, the *Far Above*, or on Mohawk Airlines, returning sometimes to student signs reading "Welcome home Jimmy. This is Ithaca. Remember us."[2]

In his account of the Kennedy administration, *A Thousand Days*, the historian Arthur Schlesinger Jr. describes the president and his advisers getting advice on federal appointments after the 1960 election, with Kennedy asking "All I hear is Jim Perkins . . . who in hell is Perkins?" Perkins, Schlesinger added, "was a name that automatically bobbed up whatever the post."[3] Robert Kennedy urged him in 1966 to run for governor of New York against Nelson Rockefeller. Contributing to his standing, as the *New York Times* put it, as one of the "leading spokesmen" for American universities, was his 1966 book, *The University in Transition*, where he balanced concerns about increasingly mobile professors "attracted to the professional and practical life beyond the campus," who were less committed to students and the campus community, against fears that universities might become too inward looking and isolated.[4] Perkins also urged less costly institutional competition in the sciences and more cross-university cooperation. Most important, he emphatically urged greater university involvement with society and institutions more instrumentally relevant to the real world.

University education had traditionally sought to shape virtuous and intellectual character in its students, to pursue knowledge and truth for its own sake, and to maintain standards of excellence. Now, Perkins insisted, universities had to become moral actors directing themselves to the realities of war, poverty, and racism. He made this clear in his inaugural address in the fall of 1963. "The university has a direct stake in the shape and substance of the society in which it will do its work. If free universities require free societies, universities cannot, in my opinion, shirk their obvious responsibilities."[5] Perkins's sense of the university's role echoed themes from Cornell's past, which, as the Eddy Street gate put it, challenged everyone who entered to "gain wisdom" and depart "to serve mankind."

The 1960s was not an easy time to be a university president. Gone were the piety, conformity, and lack of dissent of the 1950s as the civil rights, feminist, and student movements swept through America, with their ideals of emancipation from racial, gender, and generational hierarchies. The principal agents of change in this revolt against traditional authorities were young people, mainly college students, for whom the enlarged and bureaucratized university became the symbol of the misguided authority of elders, and of all the age-old patterns of accepted authority, especially forms of discrimination, sexual and racial.

Perkins had to deal with a politicized campus: students and faculty destroyed draft cards and demanded an end to the war in Vietnam; they demanded changes in the status of women, the creation of a women's studies program, affirmative action in hiring, the creation of a black studies department, participatory power

105

in university decision making, and even the authority to create their own courses.

Perkins transformed Cornell from a virtually all-white institution to what its founders had envisioned, an inclusive college for "any person," including people of color. He introduced his concerns about racial inclusion at the news conference held on his arrival in Ithaca as president-elect on January 5, 1963. In response to a question about "the recent upsurge of student political activity on campuses," Perkins said "I am glad to hear that this is happening. . . . I am enormously in favor of a very burning interest in social questions." He spoke of his eldest daughter, "who has been very active in a student group trying to encourage Negro students onto the campus at Swarthmore. . . . I think the whole business of racial discrimination is one that has pre-occupied student bodies throughout the country and I think that this has been a very good thing for society." Perkins then offered an aside about the upsurge of activism: "Not that this doesn't make life more complicated, sometimes for both faculty and administration."[6]

When Perkins arrived at Cornell, there were ten black undergraduates on campus. By the fall of 1968 there would be nearly 250. Perkins had followed his daughter Barbara's example:

> We decided to encourage them to apply, offered both guidance and scholarship help, put less emphasis on test scores than on teacher recommendation, and gambled on the idea that the Negro could do the work of equal quality if given the chance. After three years we know we are right. With guidance and some catch up courses, these students have proved their capacity for collegiate level study, and the program itself has become something of a pace-setter in the educational world.[7]

Indeed, it was. The *New York Times* in October 1968 reported that in terms of racial integration, "no university has come so far so fast as Cornell."[8]

Perkins's presidency was not only high political drama. He presided over the university's centennial observance in 1964 and 1965. The academic year opened with a major address by Adlai Stevenson, then United States ambassador to the United Nations. "Cornell Week at Lincoln Center" in March 1965 had Perkins moderating a symposium, "The University and the Arts," with panelists August Hecksher, the Architecture dean Burnham Kelly, and the film director Elia Kazan, and concluded with a concert by the New York Philharmonic Orchestra, which featured a new composition by Cornell music professor Robert Palmer. At the Charter Day convocation, April 27, 1965, after a talk by the English professor and university historian Morris Bishop '13, MA '14, PhD '26, Perkins received the university's charter from Governor Nelson Rockefeller, one hundred years to the day after it had been originally granted. That night Eugene Ormandy conducted the Philadelphia Orchestra and the

Cornell University Glee Club and Chorus in a concert at Bailey Hall. Meanwhile, as the *Daily Sun* reported, "about 80 protestors paraded around Barton and in front of the Statler, carrying signs saying 'Cornell Holds Parties While People Are Killed.' Thirty onlookers heckled the picketers. One sign was torn up. . . . Some hecklers threw eggs."[9]

Tall, urbane, and stylish, fluent in French, Spanish, and German, Perkins was as self-confident with students, faculty, and trustees as he was in the world of corporate foundations and government commissions. He was "a man with incredible energy and remarkable buoyancy, who never seemed to tire," Provost Corson recalled, whose off-campus connections served Cornell well: "His wide acquaintance has given him a perspective on problems and on life which few of us will ever achieve. . . . His easy access to the group of outside foundations, agencies, and organizations, which is frequently called 'The Establishment' brought funds to Cornell for a variety of enterprises which could never have been attempted without him."[10]

People close to Perkins described him as masterly in bringing people to consensus, a virtuoso "in managing meetings," with an uncanny ability "to direct and summarize proceedings concisely without killing further discussions." Perkins once described his leadership style as "not conducted from a soapbox. Influence must be felt rather than seen, covert rather than overt." To create a climate for reform, he enlisted members of the university community and "acted as a combination snow-plow and mid-wife, by clearing a path and helping to deliver someone else's baby."[11]

Beyond opening the university's doors to black students, Perkins had an ambitious plan to enhance undergraduate education, to beef up the humanities and social sciences "to match the new focus on the sciences," to "knit together much more tightly the endowed colleges with the statutory colleges," and to make Cornell "a center for creative arts—theater, music, the visual and fine arts."[12] One part of his centennial vision, to be sure, would find no one to clear a path for him: "Taking a long range look ahead, I would think that probably we'll find baseball on the edge of campus rather than on Hoy Field. Football won't be played in Schoellkopf in the year 2000 . . . not because we don't love intercollegiate athletics, but because we want to keep this a walking campus."[13]

In June 1968, Perkins reflected on the tumultuous challenges he had confronted at Cornell. He spoke of the black students he had brought to campus. "Will they insist on being separate?" he wondered. "Once they find their identity, will they give up the notion of living independently? Or is this a permanent feature of our life? We all think that we haven't a trace of prejudice in our bones. We've got it, but don't recognize it because we've never thought about it very much."[14]

Seven months later, on February 28, 1969, while speaking to eight hundred students in Alice Statler Hall about Cornell's investments in South Africa,

Perkins was grabbed on the coat collar by an African American student, spun around, and shoved away from the microphone. Six weeks after that, Willard Straight Hall was occupied, and on May 31, 1969, Perkins resigned. He returned to Princeton, where he founded and chaired the International Council for Educational Development, an organization to identify and analyze problems facing education around the world. In 1995, Thomas W. Jones '69, MRP '72, one of the student leaders in the Straight takeover, then a corporate executive in the Travelers Group, established the annual James Perkins Prize at Cornell for interracial understanding and harmony. Jones stated that Perkins's motivation in significantly increasing the enrollment of African American students was his "conviction that Cornell could serve the nation by nurturing the underutilized reservoir of human talent among minorities, and in the faith that the great American universities should and could lead the way in helping America to surmount the racial agony which was playing out in the civil rights struggles of the 1950s and 1960s. He made a courageous and wise decision and deserves recognition for it."[15]

Perkins died of complications from a fall while vacationing in the Adirondacks in August 1998 at the age of eighty-six.

Appointed Cornell's eighth president in 1969, Dale Corson was the second scientist to head the university (Livingston Farrand was a medical doctor), and only the second president to have come from within the faculty. (Jacob Gould Schurman was the other.) Corson was born in Pittsburg, Kansas, in 1914, the son of a truck driver who later went into the lumber business. His bachelor's degree was from the College of Emporia, his master's from the University of Kansas, and his PhD in physics from the University of California. A distinguished particle physicist, Corson coauthored the book *Introduction to Electromagnetic Fields and Waves*. He helped design and construct the sixty-inch cyclotron at the University of California Radiation Laboratory, as well as Cornell's synchrotron. After wartime service at MIT's Institute of Technology Radiation Laboratory, as technical adviser at U.S. Air Force headquarters in Washington, and as organizer of Sandia Laboratory, the major nuclear weapons engineering facility at Los Alamos, New Mexico, he accepted a job offer from Cornell in 1946 and never left.

Promoted to full professor in 1952, Corson was named chairman of the Department of Physics in 1956. In 1959 his fellow Kansan, Deane Malott, tapped him to be dean of the College of Engineering, and four years later Perkins named him provost. Like Perkins, Corson had extensive professional connections off campus, with the Department of Defense Studies and Advisory Panels, NASA, the Department of Commerce Technical Advisory Boards, and Ford Foundation consultancies. As provost, however, he remained on campus most of the time, acquiring the reputation with the faculty as the indefatigable, accessible, level-headed campus leader. With characteristic bluntness, Corson

Dale Corson, president of Cornell from 1969 to 1977. (Division of Rare and Manuscript Collections of the Cornell University Library)

warned Perkins, whom he referred to as a "semi-resident president," about these faculty perceptions: "The faculty tends to think of me as 'running things,' a situation which distresses me. It is not good for me, it is not good for you, and it is not good for the University."[16]

Whereas Malott had at times intruded himself too much into what faculty saw as their responsibilities and prerogatives, Perkins was perceived as generally uninterested in them. At the end of his presidency, in a memo to the trustee committee searching for his successor, Corson wrote:

> The lack of rapport with the faculty is what did Jim Perkins in in the end. He certainly had enough credentials to command respect from the faculty if he had worked at it, but he did not work at it. Faculty matters bored him. He once told me that it depressed him to eat lunch in the Rathskellar at the Statler. Had he been willing to spend time with the faculty to learn what they were doing they would have come to his aid in the end when he needed it most. Unfortunately, they felt no loyalty to him. . . . The one thing which made it possible for me to survive and to command the help of the faculty was my long association with them.[17]

Corson did "command the help of the faculty" but only after the baptism of fire that was his formal presidential inauguration on June 8, 1970. Having appointed him in the midst of a crisis, the trustees decided to combine the 1970 graduation at Barton Hall with a brief ceremony in which Chairman of the Board Robert Purcell '32, LLB '35, would hand Corson the four-foot gold-and-silver university mace, the formal symbol of authority. Part guerrilla theater and part comic opera ensued. At the "request" of some seniors, the university allowed the event to begin with an "address" by university Catholic chaplain David Connor, who spoke of the "ugly truths of war, and racial and economic injustice." He closed by extending an unauthorized invitation to Gloria Joseph, an associate professor at the Africana Studies and Research Center, to speak. After praising the black seniors for not subscribing to the American dream of individual ambition, Joseph led them in a silent exit from Barton. Meanwhile, throughout the ceremony, a Vietnamese woman in cap and gown carried a placard in front of the stage reading "Vietnamization of the war is not peace!" and printed "anti-programs" were distributed by "concerned seniors" with pictures of the ruins of the Africana Center at 320 Wait Avenue, recently destroyed by arson during spring vacation, and with essays and poetry by Father Daniel Berrigan, written before he left Cornell several years earlier to go "underground as a fugitive from injustice."[18]

Just as Purcell began the formal investiture ceremony, some two dozen graduate students walked toward the stage shouting "Free Black Panthers Bobby Seale and Huey Newton." As they unfurled banners, David Burak '67, the SDS leader still on campus as a graduate student in rural sociology, leaped onstage and grabbed the microphone, shouting "just let me have three minutes." Professor Morris Bishop, the seventy-seven-year-old mace bearer, wielded it to push Burak aside. As Burak was hauled away by the Safety Division, Purcell finally introduced Corson, "the eighth president of the United States." Corson began his remarks by quipping that he had not brought Andrew Jackson's inaugural speech with him. Not bad, even if the eighth president of the United States was Martin Van Buren. Three years later Corson noted that Bishop "had used the mace as it was originally intended to be used, i.e. in defense of the Presidential office."[19]

Corson's presidency saw four building seizures or sit-ins, the most serious the occupation of Carpenter Hall in April 1972. He resisted taking moral positions in the university's name, especially on issues related to corporate investments and ROTC, though he did condemn the Vietnam War, "as a citizen of the community, as a citizen and educator, rather than as President," before a crowd of twenty-five hundred students in the Arts quad. And he reaffirmed Cornell's commitment to "the improvement of education for black students and for accepting an increasing number of them into both the graduate and undergraduate divisions."[20]

Under his low-key leadership the campus climate improved substantially. Corson introduced half-day faculty presentations to board of trustee sessions, with the likes of Robert Kaske of Medieval Studies and David Brion Davis of

History talking about their research. Alumni giving to the university rebounded following a pledge by trustee Nicholas Noyes '06 to give $1 million if alumni gifts reached or exceeded $3 million. It worked, lifting annual giving from $2.5 million to $4 million, never to fall back.

Despite this largesse and Corson's reputation as a prudent manager of money, Cornell's financial health in the inflationary 1970s remained a concern. During his presidency budgets were cut and tuition increased annually, by 1977 doubling to $4,410. In part to reduce heating costs, classes began for the first time before Labor Day, and final exams ended before Christmas. Less revolutionary, but historic and permanent as well, was the 1975 decision to hold commencement in an outdoor ceremony, at Schoellkopf, for the first time in three decades.

As Perkins was articulate and stylish, Corson was laconic and plain. When Malott asked him to be the Engineering dean, Corson hesitated, writing back that he was "a poor speaker," with "insufficient social training and interest." Years later he would suggest that his ordinariness helped him succeed as president: "Coming from a working class environment, I spoke the language of the university staff. I could go into a university shop and run the machine. I'd go to their picnics."[21] While president he remained in his own house, insisting that Perkins's residence at 511 Cayuga Heights Road was too expensive to keep up.

In the summer of 1969, his first as president, he met with the faculty of every college. Unlike Perkins, whose closest advisers were his inner circle of vice presidents, Corson had a "kitchen cabinet" of professors and administrators that included M. H. Abrams, Lisle Carter, Alice Cook, Michael Kammen, David Knapp, Harry Levin, Frank Long, Ian Macneill, Robert Morrison, B. F. Stanton, Ed Cranch, and Bob Plane. When he announced in 1976 that he was stepping down because the presidency had taken "a substantial toll from me and my wife Nellie," and that there was "a need for young blood in the President's office," he noted that he had been provost and president for fourteen years, and "all but the first one or two of these years have been years of crisis of one type or another."[22] His leadership may have lacked flare, but Corson helped restore calm and civility to a troubled campus. He retired in Ithaca, where he lived for over three decades, dying just before his ninety-eighth birthday in 2012.

NINE DAYS AFTER Perkins's announcement that he was asking the trustees to seek his successor, Dale Corson assessed "Perkins the man and Perkins the president." Corson singled out as "the greatest, most dramatic and in my opinion the most important of the Perkins academic innovations the Division of Biological Sciences."[23] Before he took office, Perkins had asked friends and colleagues in the world of educational foundations what discipline at Cornell most needed bolstering. The common response was basic biology. In office, he appointed a committee of distinguished biologists from around the country, headed by Robert Morrison of the Rockefeller Foundation, to chart the way forward.

The Morrison Committee found that "after many years of eminence," biology at Cornell had declined "to a level of mere competence—respectable but undistinguished." This decline had occurred precisely at the time that the biological sciences were making "breakthroughs into fundamental discoveries of enormous impact." The principal reason Cornell lagged behind was fragmentation, with biologists working in "relatively small, isolated, and uncoordinated groups, with a consequent loss of coherence and of mutual stimulation," in eighteen departments in four colleges.[24] Most of basic biology was taught in Agriculture, at some remove from the fields of mathematics, physics, and chemistry in the College of Arts and Sciences.

After receiving the committee's recommendation to establish a separate college of biology, Perkins appointed an implementation committee of Cornell biologists, under the chairmanship of Provost Corson, which settled on "a solution more in keeping with Cornell's structure and with its complex obligations to several constituencies":[25] the creation of an inter-college Division of Biology with responsibility for teaching and research in basic biological sciences, offering programs for undergraduate and graduate students from any Cornell school or college, though admitting no students of its own. The faculty would consist of biologists in the College of Arts and Sciences and the College of Agriculture, who would retain full membership in their respective units.

This major administration innovation did not sail through the faculties of Agriculture or Arts. Charles E. Palm, PhD '35, dean of the College of Agriculture, reported that his faculty was "both confused and concerned, but trying to develop a positive attitude." The Arts College dean, Stuart Brown Jr. '37, PhD '42, passed along claims from the Department of Zoology that the division was "administratively unsound and bound to fail," with faculty responsible to "three masters": department head, dean, and director.[26] Concerns were eased when Morrison was recruited from the Rockefeller Foundation to serve as first division director, and two associate directors were named, one from Agriculture and one from Arts, reporting to their respective deans as well as to Morrison. Furthermore, it was agreed that it would be possible to augment the salaries of some Agriculture faculty, with sums larger than the rigidly structured gradations usually allocated to contract college professors, "in order to attract very outstanding people to positions in biochemistry and botany."[27] And Corson won the support of three influential Cornell biologists, Tom Eisner, William Keeton, PhD '58, and Adrian Srb. Criticism finally evaporated with the announcement of a $4.4 million gift from the Ford Foundation and $2.2 million from the National Institutes of Health, to be used to hire fifteen new faculty for the division. Had this initiative surfaced in the financially constrained 1970s, it may well not have been implemented.

The Division of Biological Sciences was followed in 1965 by the creation of an inter-college Department of Computer Science, bridging Arts and Sciences and Engineering, and funded by a $1 million gift from the Sloan Foundation. Government grants came to Cornell as well for a wide array of initiatives: $2 million to chemists helped build the massive addition to Baker Laboratory in 1967; $2.7 million from the National Science Foundation in 1972 to further support the Materials Science Center; and in 1974 a $500,000 gift from the NSF to establish a Program of Computer Graphics with Professor Donald Greenberg '58, PhD '68, as director. No surprise that Cornell's lobbyist in Washington, Edward Little, heard from Professor Frank Long, the vice president for research in Ithaca, that "Cornell is feeling slightly overwhelmed by the plethora of opportunities which the new federal acts are giving us."[28]

Research flourished in this period, with expenditures in 1966 at $57,273,352, third highest among American universities. Even in the worrisome fiscal year 1975–76, Cornell research expenditures reached a record $71 million, and despite President Corson's constant fears of federal cutbacks, $44 million of that sum came from agencies of the U.S. government. Nor was science the only beneficiary of government and foundation grants. In 1967 alone, the Ford Foundation gave the Center for International Studies $6 million and the Graduate School $4 million over seven years to help students in the humanities and social sciences complete PhDs in four years. By the early 1970s, $500,000 per year came from the federal government, via the National Defense Education Act, for language instruction and area studies centers.

Although external gifts were essential, they sometimes generated political problems for the university, as when NBC television news disclosed in 1967 that ILR had received about $214,000 from the CIA for a labor training program funneled through the Marshall Foundation of Houston, Texas, between 1961 and 1964. Maintaining that "Cornell has never knowingly received any financial assistance from the CIA," Perkins acknowledged that "I cannot say that we have not unsuspectingly received funds from a foundation that had in turn received funds from the CIA."[29] He ordered an investigation, which revealed, the *Sun* reported, that "eight CIA-attached groups contributed funds to Cornell," including two grants of $1,000 each in 1965 and 1966 for a Cornell United Religious Work project in Central America.[30]

Secret research at the university-owned Cornell Aeronautical Laboratory (CAL) in Buffalo, which had fifteen hundred employees and annual contracts worth $32 million, created an even larger controversy. The university disclosed in the fall of 1966 that the Defense Department had sponsored research at CAL involving chemical warfare, photographic reconnaissance, and target recognition. Although forty-four faculty, including three deans, nine department chairs, and many science faculty, demanded the university disaffiliate itself from CAL, many trustees and some faculty, especially in Engineering, opposed its sale. A motion before the university faculty to end Cornell's connection was defeated 164–133, with the faculty then unanimously approving a resolution formalizing past policy since 1946 of banning classified activities from the Ithaca campus.

That fall, in September 1967, a more intense firestorm broke out after the disclosure to the *Sun* that CAL had received $1.5 million from the Defense Department to help design counterinsurgency programs in Thailand. Clinton Rossiter wrote to Perkins that he had often lectured on American institutions in Thailand, but "I'm afraid I'd think twice—and then negatively—before I'd go back there as a scholar identified with Cornell University." Government professor George Kahin weighed in to alert Perkins to the devastating impact such disclosures had on the university's Southeast Asia Program, recently "cited by a major news journal as the outstanding center for Southeast Asian studies in this country. . . . The suspicion that all Cornell research is subordinated to official policy objectives will flourish."[31] Two days later Perkins, who had known nothing about the Thailand project, resigned as chairman of CAL's board, as did Provost Corson, the board's vice chair. A month later, the university faculty reversed itself and voted 240–176 that "there is no acceptable alternative to severance."[32]

At a board of trustees meeting, Perkins responded to claims that CAL "was an extremely valuable asset" and that Cornell "had not only a right but a duty to be involved in research in national defense," by insisting that "classified research is not compatible with the very nature of a university in which the free exchange of information is a keystone."[33] The trustees approved a sale of CAL to EDP Technology Inc. for $25 million. The actual transfer did not take place until 1972, when a State Supreme Court justice's finding that the lab was a public trust that could not be sold to a private profit-making company was overturned.

A paradigmatic example of how important off-campus funding could be in the shaping of university policy is illustrated by the six-year PhD program, the initiative that Perkins deemed second in importance to the revitalization of Biology. Negotiated between the Ford Foundation and College of Arts and Sciences officials in the summer vacation of 1964, the plan, which Perkins touted as a "high-speed Ph.D.," aspired to admit some forty brilliant seniors from the best high schools and confer a BA in three years, a master's in year four, and the doctorate in year six, a total of just one year less than Perkins himself had taken, having received his PhD from Princeton three years after his BA.[34] The idea was presented as a virtual fait accompli for an Arts College vote on October 22, 1964, a week after it was heralded in two *New York Times* stories as a radical departure from how universities traditionally do things. The

Ford Foundation committed $2.3 million to support the first ten years of the "experiment."

With some grumblings from scientists that the explosion of knowledge made acceleration undesirable or impossible, the Arts College faculty approved the program, and Stephen Parrish, an English professor, was appointed its director. Forty-eight "absolutely top-drawer kids," thirty-five boys and thirteen girls, eight from private schools and forty from public high schools, matriculated in the fall of 1966. About 40 percent of them, soon nicknamed "Fuds," said they wanted to concentrate in science or mathematics. The *Sun* quickly criticized the program as "establishing an elite on campus."[35] Exempted from Arts College distribution requirements, the Fuds were placed in small interdisciplinary "seminars" each semester. Receiving generous financial aid, even a free trip to Europe, they lived together, along with several faculty, in the Cornell Heights Residential Club, a former motel off Triphammer Road that was much less fancy than its name. During the program's second semester, in April 1967, a tragic early-morning fire at the "Res Club," the origin of which was never fully ascertained, killed eight of these talented students and an English Department faculty member, putting a pall over its exuberant, experimental beginnings. That night at a previously scheduled Bailey Hall concert Pete Seeger began with "To everything, turn, turn, turn," and then named and paid tribute to each of the nine individuals who had died.

Two years later, in December 1969, Alain Seznec, the Romance Studies professor who had replaced Parrish as director of the program, announced that the Ford Foundation had cut off all funding. Current students would receive support until they completed their six years, and no new class would be admitted. It was unclear why Ford ended the experiment, or whether Perkins's exit from Cornell that summer concerned the foundation. As Seznec put it, "the Ford Foundation gets very interested in a project, then like a child drops it. It's no longer their bag."[36] A possible explanation of Ford's decision may be found in an earlier letter from then provost Corson to Stephen Parrish: "The fact so relatively few of them are continuing for graduate study is disheartening. . . . Will the time and effort and other resources spent on the program benefit society in proportionate amounts?"[37] The six-year PhD program withered away, leaving a legacy in the College of Arts and Sciences, however, with the introduction of the "College Scholar" program, in which students, freed from college distribution and major requirements, are encouraged to do interdisciplinary work.

Corson presided over another innovation in undergraduate admissions, one that would remain a permanent feature of Cornell life. In 1973 he joined the rest of the presidents of the Ivy League and MIT in an agreement on "early admissions." High school students were allowed to apply in the fall of their senior year to one college. If admitted they had to accept the offer and matriculate as freshmen. A small, but significant, number of high schoolers were thus spared several months of anxiety.

The faculty who taught these and other students at Cornell were well rewarded for their work. Endowed college salaries at Cornell ranked sixth in the nation in 1967, with full professors averaging $18,000, associates, $12,700, and assistant professors, $9,900. And they won prizes. History professor David Brion Davis became the first Cornell professor to win a Pulitzer Prize with his 1966 book, *The Problem of Slavery in Western Culture*. He was followed in 1973 by another historian, Michael Kammen, with his *People of Paradox*. Hans Bethe won the Nobel Prize in Physics in 1967—"overwhelmed at the phone call at 6:20 this morning when I thought I received a wrong connection call." And in 1973 the poet A. R. "Archie" Ammons, of the English Department, won the first of two National Book Awards in Poetry for his *Collected Poems: 1951–1971*.

Still, there was concern at Cornell about the faculty as teachers. The vice provost for research and advanced study, Franklin Long, cited the iron law by which "it is almost inevitable that as an individual professor's commitment toward research increases, the extent of his direct concern for undergraduate instruction will decrease. The vital question is, then, are we supplying sufficient additional coverage and concern for our undergraduate teaching to maintain its quality? The answer at present almost surely is, yes, but we cannot assume it will always remain so."[38]

The blue-ribbon committee appointed in 1965 by professor of plant breeding and genetics and dean of the faculty Royse P. Murphy to study undergraduate teaching, and headed by Professors Alfred E. Kahn of the Economics Department and Raymond Bowers of Physics, did not entirely agree. The Kahn-Bowers panel concluded: "This committee is strongly convinced that more attention must be given to improving undergraduate education at Cornell. Such instruction—though generally conscientious, often very good and occasionally brilliant—commands neither the attention nor the status it deserves."[39]

There were the usual suspects: substantial incentives and rewards were mostly directed toward research and graduate training; a lack of attention to teaching in recommendations to tenure; a declining faculty role in advising; an increased reliance on teaching assistants. And Kahn-Bowers offered the usual recommendations: advising and teaching prizes; required teaching appraisals in promotion criteria; senior faculty teaching introductory courses; anonymous student evaluations of courses. All these changes, however, could not transform the quality of undergraduate education without faculty values changing: "There is only one ultimate determinant of the quality of undergraduate instruction and only one ultimate source of its improvement—the individual teacher himself. If the quality of our teaching is not as high as it can and should be—and that is our finding—then the fundamental solution is that each one of us devote a considerably greater effort to making it better."[40]

Advising and teaching awards were introduced in many of Cornell's colleges, along with course evaluations, and departments did look at teaching in tenure decisions, but, along with other research universities, Cornell continued to struggle with the value it placed on teaching. Eight years after Kahn-Bowers, Professor Morris Bishop recalled that in the 1920s professors saw research as important, "but it was not very much practiced, not nearly so much as today." "Today," he added, with tongue in cheek, "the work of research . . . is really so demanding; a professor is lucky if he can get one class in with the rest of it."[41]

LESS ROBUST BUILDERS of the physical plant than Day and Malott, Perkins and Corson built nonetheless. The new home of the School of Business and Public Administration, named Malott Hall, was opened in 1964. Situated between the Baker chemistry labs and Rockefeller Hall, a physical sciences building, seeking to integrate research in chemistry, physics, and astronomy, opened in October 1965, named for W. Van Alan Clark '09, whose $3 million gift made it possible. Campus science capacity was further expanded in 1967 with the dedication of the new space science building, home of Professors Thomas Gold and Carl Sagan, near the A. D. White House and Bailey Hall, built with a facilities grant from NASA, and then with the completion in 1968 of the world's most powerful electron synchrotron, an $11.3 million project, the single largest ever funded by the National Science Foundation. Designed by Professor Robert R. Wilson, director of the Laboratory of Nuclear Studies, the half-mile-long synchrotron, located forty feet below the surface of upper Alumni Field, gave electrons 10 billion volts of energy, accelerating them to nearly the speed of light. In 1969, New York State's $6 million Agronomy Building, several years in construction, was also finished. Subsequently named for Professor Richard Bradfield, an internationally acclaimed specialist in soils and crops, Bradfield Hall, which lodged earth and atmospheric scientists, plant breeders, geneticists, the Northeast Regional Climate Center, and the Water Resources Institute, was the tallest building on campus. To accommodate climate-controlled laboratories, ten of its eleven floors were windowless.

Some new buildings did not serve big science. Noyes Center, Cornell's second student union building, the gift of Jansen Noyes Jr. '39 in 1964, was opened on West Campus in October 1967, with lounges, a cafeteria, and study carrels, to serve the University Hall communities, which after 1971 became coeducational dorms, each with one floor of women and three floors of men. Even though many of Cornell's students lived off campus, once all such restrictions were lifted on women, the university built new dorms between 1968 and 1970. On the old Country Club property north of Mary Donlon Hall, two ten-story "high rise" and five three-story "low rise" dorms opened their doors. The thirteen-acre project on North Campus included a third university union—soon named to honor the chairman of the board of trustees, Robert Purcell—to help feed and serve the 1,080 new students and others already living on North Campus.

Not everyone was happy with the new patterns of residential life. Students still mocked the U-Hall "stables" on West Campus, with their cinderblock walls, structures that, one administrator acknowledged, were "near the cattle pen end of the spectrum."[42] "Cadillac" Bill Smith, the New York state senator who represented Ithaca, was appalled for a different reason. In 1972 he urged the New York Board of Regents to block the university's coeducation residential halls as violations of an 1871 statute prohibiting "immoral pursuits" in dormitories for students in land grant colleges. Smith "did not want a bunch of political radicals dictating who lives in what dorms to our young people of this state."[43]

In 1970 the university constructed a new bookstore across from Willard Straight Hall, built almost totally underground, to meet student and faculty demands that no open grassy space be destroyed. In 1972 the former parking lot between Day and Ives Halls was filled with a social sciences building, Uris Hall, paid for by a diverse set of sources, which provides an interesting snapshot

Designed by I. M. Pei, the Herbert F. Johnson Museum of Art opened in 1973. (Division of Rare and Manuscript Collections of the Cornell University Library)

of university finances in this era: a $2 million gift from Harold Uris '25, an NSF grant of $600,000, a Ford Foundation grant of $240,000, a federal Office of Education grant for $500,000, and New York State Dormitory Authority financing of $5 million. A surprised campus discovered that the building "looks unfinished" and that "rusting was part of the weathering steel process."[44]

Also somewhat controversial was the I. M. Pei–designed Herbert F. Johnson Museum of Art, which opened in 1973 on land that was once the site of Morse Hall. In an early plan (abandoned because of cost and environmental concerns) part of the museum was intended to extend underground beneath University Avenue, through to the Fall Creek gorge, upon which it was designed to look out through windows cut in the stone wall. The building was named to honor a $4 million gift from Herbert Johnson '22, chairman of Johnson Wax Company. Its concrete boxlike slab shape was said to look like "a giant's toy which tumbled out of the Arts Quad." But Kenneth Evett, chair of the Department of Art and art critic for the *New Republic*, opined that "the image of Cornell as a philistine place is changing, and the Johnson Museum is doing much to effect this."[45] In the ensuing decades, most Cornellians have tended to agree with him.

———

THREE COLLEGES CHANGED their names in this period. The College of Home Economics announced in 1964 "plans for a study of the future purposes, organization, and program of the College."[46] The faculty were not pleased that, as the *Alumni News* described it, the college was sometimes derisively known as the "Cook and Sew School," especially since by the middle 1960s it offered virtually no traditional courses in home economics and had made great strides in orienting the curriculum to broader perspectives, focusing on the interdependence of the individual, family, community, and society in the process of human development.[47]

There was also a broader concern over the makeup of the Home Economics student body. A commission appointed by President Perkins to study the college, chaired by Professor Sara Blackwell, Home Economics Education, noted in late 1966 that the "applicants to Home Economics are not so strong scholastically as are the other major groups of women at Cornell."[48] When the commission recommended that the school's name be changed to the "College of Human Development and Environment," Dean Helen Canoyer agreed, albeit reluctantly, that a new name might be an "image builder."[49] Her successor, David Knapp, offered two possibilities: College of Human Development and Resources, or College of Human Development and Environment. In November 1968, the faculty of the College of Home Economics voted unanimously to have the trustees recommend to New York State that "College of Human Ecology" be its name.

The college had researched the change of name carefully. A survey indicated that 90 percent of that year's freshmen understood the term "human ecology," and a spot check of high school students and guidance counselors revealed familiarity with the term. Favorable reactions had come as well from alumni and from deans of similar schools around the country. Along with its new name, the college reorganized itself into five departments: Community Service Education; Consumer Economics and Public Policy; Design and Environmental Analysis; Human Development and Family Studies; and Human Nutrition and Food. In the Corson years the college, with funds from New York State and the U.S. Department of Health, Education, and Welfare, established a Family Life Development Center, among whose purposes was to "disseminate information in order to prevent and treat child abuse."[50] The newly named college became truly coeducational. In 1970, of 225 seniors graduating, only 2 were men. One year later, 150 men applied, and twenty-five were admitted. "The change in name," Dean Knapp declared, "means that men aren't afraid of coming to a home economics school anymore."[51]

Responding in part to a decline in the number of farmers in New York State, the College of Agriculture changed its name as well. A presidential commission's recommendation that the name be the "State University College of Agricultural and Environmental Sciences at Cornell University" was rejected by the college, perhaps because the word "environmental" was being overused.[52] In 1970 the board of trustees asked the New York State Legislature to change the name to New York State College of Agriculture and Life Sciences. Charles Palm, the dean, explained that "recently, concern has been widespread about the interactions of agriculture, biological mechanisms, and the environment. . . . The fast moving pace of scientific achievements, coupled with the expanded demands made on modern agriculture, have broadened our mission."[53]

Undergraduates in the college in these years tended to concentrate in the biological sciences and the social sciences, such as applied economics and business, environmental studies, and rural sociology. Fewer were interested in the actual operation of farms, orchards, and vineyards, or the needs of small farmers, or rural non-farm people in New York State. Students in the college sometimes began their education at one of New York's rural two-year community colleges and if they performed well transferred into Agriculture and Life Sciences as juniors. By graduation the students gravitated into one of two camps, "either eager recruits for agribusiness or proponents of a more people-oriented agriculture."[54]

Whichever camp the students identified with in the renamed college, it was getting more difficult to get into it in the 1970s. In 1969 there were 1,441 applications for a freshman class of 558, and in 1976 there were 3,096 applicants for a first-year class of 580. Many of them were pre-meds, majoring in biological science. Fairly constant, for the moment, was the 85 percent of undergraduates accepted from New York State.

Fully recovered from its wartime slump, with total enrollments rising from eighty students in 1945 to a steady-state five hundred students in the late 1960s, the College of Architecture changed its name in 1967 to the College of Architecture, Art, and Planning. There were no study commissions, no alternative names rejected, nor with its name change did the college seek to signify a more scientifically based research and teaching focus. The change simply granted the departments of Fine Arts and City and Regional Planning equal status with Architecture, while announcing a broader, more protean understanding of the built environment.

The College of Arts and Sciences did not change its name, befitting an enterprise oriented to both the past and to the future, and it created two new departments in this era: the historically focused Semitic Studies and the zealously forward-looking Computer Science. Many features of the college remained the same. Throughout the 1960s and 1970s Arts and Sciences was responsible for 55–60 percent of all university teaching, although it had about 33 percent of the faculty. Much of this teaching was in science or humanities courses required by other colleges, which in the case of the contract colleges led to constant wrangling about "accessory instruction cost," per-credit money transfers from New York State to the Arts College. The other endowed colleges had more of a free ride, with Engineering, for example, absorbing 22 percent of the total Arts and Sciences credit-hours taught.

Concern about the future of the humanities existed in this era, as well. With greater student attention to career preparation, the *Daily Sun* wondered: "Are Liberal Arts Graduates Good for Anything?"[55] A trustees committee was worried enough about "the state and future of humanities at Cornell" to commit several million dollars as part of the centennial campaign fund-raising for the creation of the long-planned Society of Fellows, with perhaps twenty fellowships and its own Humanities Center. In 1966 Cornell's Society for the Humanities opened with a theme of "The Morality of Scholarship" and the participation of the Irish diplomat and writer Conor Cruise O'Brien and the British literary critic F. R. Leavis.

The Society was part of a full-fledged initiative to boost the humanities. President Perkins found funding for A. D. White Visiting Professors, primarily distinguished humanists in the program's early years, who came to Cornell to lecture for several weeks each year during their three- or five-year terms. The College of Arts and Sciences introduced in 1966 a freshman humanities requirement, emphasizing writing in thirty-two seminars offered by several departments as a substitute for the conventional freshman English course. And in late 1969, Dean Stuart Brown Jr., Provost Robert Plane, and President Dale Corson agreed that, given their larger teaching loads, professors in the humanities should have a sabbatical semester leave after six straight semesters of teaching.

There was also growing sentiment that the social science faculty, as Vice President for Academic Affairs Robert Sproul put it, were "in the main competent, with some distinguished, but very few real peaks."[56] Sproul proposed an "Institute for the Social Sciences" and greater use of computer and survey data. When David Knapp, dean of Human Ecology, became provost in 1973, and economist Alfred Kahn was Arts College dean, several social science departments moved into the new steel-and-glass building, Uris Hall, soon to be called "Old Rusty." Knapp was determined to bolster the quality and national standing of the Economics, Sociology, and Psychology Departments, creating in 1975 a "coordination committee" with power to approve or reject all new appointments and new courses in the social sciences.

There was also interest in rebuilding the Government Department, which had lost a group of eminent faculty in the wake of the uproar that accompanied the takeover of Willard Straight Hall by black students in April 1969. The department had always been torn between a social sciences or humanities identity, resisting, for example, the urge after the war to rename itself "political science," as had so many of its peers. In 1970 it voted with its feet. Residing in Sibley Hall along with History since the razing of Boardman Hall in 1959, Government was asked to join social science departments in the soon to be finished Uris Hall or relocate to McGraw, where History was moving. Government consulted its soul and chose McGraw.

Important changes were also occurring in the College of Engineering. Under the leadership of Andrew Schultz Jr. '36, PhD '42, a mechanical engineer, the college in 1965 replaced Solomon Cady Hollister's five-year bachelor's program with a heavier preprofessional four-year curriculum. By the 1970s, Cornell Engineering, which in its infancy had pioneered in civil, electrical, mechanical, and industrial engineering education, was pioneering in biochemical engineering, environmental engineering, materials science, operations research, and computer science.

The College of Industrial and Labor Relations had been on campus long enough to be unsettled about its future. A 1968 study commissioned by Stuart Brown, then university vice president for academic affairs, found a "general malaise" in the college and concerns about its overall mission: "Industrial relations no longer is a social problem of the size and glamour that it was in the late thirties and early forties. The signs are obvious that students aren't interested in the field: the undergraduates come to ILR at best because they have a vague feeling that we are the closest to being socially relevant. At worst, they come as a cheap entry to Cornell."[57]

All the colleges were forced to respond to issues related to gender after 1965 when the university lifted its requirement that all women students reside in university dormitories or sororities, a policy that for decades had generated quotas linking the number of women each college could admit to the total number of university rooms assigned to women. For years the College of Veterinary Medicine, for example, was allocated "bed space" for one or two female admits. A new system began to emerge. A fixed number of women, increasing to around three hundred in 1969, were permitted to live off-campus. By 1970 each college determined how many men and women to accept.

Old habits never die easily. In Arts and Sciences, where so many science majors were males, the number of women did not equal the number of men until the middle of the 1990s. Engineering in the late '60s enrolled a class of 595 men and only 5 women. In 1972 an alumnus of the Vet School threatened to file an official complaint of "sexual bias" with a National Board of Veterinary Medicine committee because so few women had been accepted to the school. Even the Business School was challenged for the small number of women it enrolled: eight, four, and seven in the last three entering classes of the 1960s. Dean H. Justin Davidson explained that "the plain facts of the matter are that women management graduates are not accepted now by business. We had had and will probably continue to have substantial difficulty in placing female students."[58]

An INCREASINGLY DIFFERENT place, physically and programmatically, Cornell became still larger, more complex, and more bureaucratic in the '60s and '70s. Perkins, an inside player in the "organization man" culture of higher education, established three new high-level administrative positions in his first year on campus: a vice president for academic affairs; a vice president for public affairs (public relations and fund-raising); and a vice provost for planning. He made Lisle Carter, an African American faculty member in Business and Public Administration, a special vice president for social and environmental studies in 1968, alongside his professorial appointment to the Business and Public Administration College. The proliferation of vice presidents continued after Perkins left. In January 1970, Samuel Lawrence, a former official of the U.S. Bureau of the Budget, with a PhD in political science, became the first vice president for administration, responsible for the university's business and financial affairs, formerly part of the provost's responsibilities. A new senior vice president was established in 1975 to further free the president and the provost "to devote more time to academic affairs." Corson, who had long sought the creation of the new position to help cope with the university's financial challenges, urged that it be filled by "someone who has ability in business matters."[59] William Herbster, a senior vice president of New York's First National City Bank, filled the position. In that same year the university created a new vice president for New York State land grant affairs and appointed to it Constance Cook '41, JD '43, former Cornell trustee, and fresh from the New York

State Legislature, where she had helped craft legislation legalizing abortion in New York State. Cook became Cornell's first woman vice president.

There was also unprecedented growth in university staff in the Perkins-Corson years. In 1965, the support staff, excluding Extension, numbered 3,900; in 1975 it was 5,700, a growth of 45 percent. Faculty hiring slowed in the 1970s, so that even with the creation in 1974 of the new rank of "senior lecturer," to create a career path for those engaged in teaching but not in scholarly research, faculty grew in those years only 12 percent, from 1,500 to 1,688. New academic centers, divisions, and programs, with no direct connection to departments and no responsibilities for undergraduate teaching, were fruitful and multiplied. By 1975 there were nearly twenty such entities reporting to the provost, each with a faculty director, an administrative associate director, support staff, and physical space needs. No surprise then that the university budget went from $15.6 million in 1960–61 to $47.8 million in 1970–71.

Emblematic of these new "units" on campus was the Center for International Studies, which after 1972 occupied the entire first floor of Uris Hall, with its distinguished area studies programs, crossing departments and colleges, and its directors and staff who used foundation and government grants to fund research and graduate training. The interdisciplinary reach of the Material Science Center extended to sixty faculty from five departments in two colleges at Cornell. The program on Science, Technology, and Society (STS), created in 1969, to stimulate "research on the interaction of science and technology with contemporary society," had affiliated faculty from twenty-three departments and six colleges.[60] In its first five years, STS's full-time administrative support staff grew from one to six, and the three offices it occupied at its inception increased to fifteen in Clark, Baker, and Rockefeller.

Enrollment rose as well in this period—partially to bring in more tuition money during the lean years—from fourteen thousand in 1969 to sixteen thousand in 1974. But the traditional university, with its faculty in departments, teaching and advising these students, in a college, with a dean and an almost nonexistent college administration, was fast disappearing, with a dramatic growth in college administrations and a proliferation of associate deans and advising deans, each with support staff. Since changing professional priorities now took faculty off-campus so frequently, their advising and mentoring role was often shared or even replaced by professional advising staff in the colleges.

The expansion of student services in general contributed to the growth of staff and bureaucratization. Three student unions, new dorms, and dining halls required new campus life directors and assistants. In 1971, a new unit of Gannett was created to disseminate information and counsel students about sexual issues, birth control, and abortion. In May 1963, just before his retirement, the traditionalist Malott had, in fact, issued a general warning against what he saw as the emergent student service university, worrying about "the growth of

124

auxiliary services, such as student health and advising. Though there is need for such services there is some danger of overpampering students."[61]

Perkins's commitment to diversify Cornell's student body produced new programmatic committees around COSEP, the Committee on Special Education Programs, with new staff needed for advising and a Learning Skills Program. Federal directives from the Department of Health, Education, and Welfare in the early 1970s, requiring that Cornell, as a recipient of federal contracts, develop an affirmative action strategy, produced a multilayered affirmative action bureaucracy on campus. By 1974, there was a vice provost for minority affairs, a director of minority educational affairs, and a director of minority employee affairs. Simultaneously, the Financial Aid Office bureaucracy grew as each increase in tuition and fees produced between two hundred and five hundred new financial aid applicants.

As Cornell grew and became more bureaucratically complex, it felt the need, like any rational organization, to keep a record of what was happening. In a 1965 memo, addressed to "Deans, Directors, and Administrative officers," Perkins's vice president for planning, Thomas Mackesey, announced the creation of an Office of Institutional Studies, "to produce, to maintain, and make available information about all aspects of the University's operation."[62] Some years later the office's staff occupied nearly all of the fourth floor of Day Hall, generating data about every conceivable aspect of Cornell. In addition, to improve communication among the university's increasingly numerous component parts, the *Cornell Newsletter* was created in 1965 as an official publication (after September 1969, the *Cornell Chronicle*), published every other week by the Office of Public Information.

One of the newsletter's early issues provided Provost Dale Corson an opportunity, the first of many, to inform the Cornell community that the institution "had undergone in various ways an expansion so rapid that expenses at present have outstripped available sources of support."[63] In the ten years from 1955 to 1965, Corson noted, the cost of running Cornell had tripled, while tuition and fees had doubled. As a result, while state college budgets were required by law to be balanced, the endowed colleges would operate at a deficit in 1965 and remain between $2 million and $3 million in the red each succeeding year.

After four years of deficits and a projected shortfall for 1971 of $4.5 to $5 million, Corson reported that Robert Purcell, the chairman of the board of trustees, "gave a deadline of two years to balance the budget."[64] Corson persuaded the board to give him three years and ordered Provost Robert Plane to ask the deans to reduce their budgets by 4 percent in 1971–72, 3 percent the next year, and another 3 percent in 1973–74. Cornell continued to increase tuition rates about 7 percent a year. Friendly foundations helped out, with Mellon giving Cornell $1.25 million in 1972 "for purposes of prevention of the erosion of quality in universities during times of serious budget problems."[65]

Meanwhile, looking further to the future, Corson appointed a fifteen-member committee (four deans, six professors, three students, and two staff) to recommend actions to strengthen Cornell's long-range financial outlook. Chaired by Engineering dean Edmund T. Cranch '45, PhD '51, the committee issued a 190-page report in October 1972, reprinted in its entirety in the *Cornell Chronicle*, that succeeded in enraging just about everyone on campus. Its tone was captured by repeated references to Cornell's "unplanned ubiquitous growth" spurred on by grants of public funds to create new programs and grow the faculty by 75 percent. The proposed solution was more centralized management of the university, and a commitment of the president, provost, deans, and department chairs to "systematic academic planning," even at the smallest units. Cranch, as the report was inevitably labeled, advocated balancing the budget through an annual 6 percent rise in tuition, an increase in the student body from 15,500 to 17,500 over the next five years, with no growth in faculty, housing, or dining facilities. Financial aid would be capped at a fixed percentage of tuition income each year. There would be no further growth in nonacademic staff, and the university would launch new academic programs and construction "only if they could pay for themselves."[66]

Particularly jarring to faculty was Cranch's suggested use of "such motivation, evaluation, and management techniques as establishing a continuing post-tenure evaluation system, an annual review of each faculty member's achievements." Although the tenure system would be maintained, administrators should have recourse to "possible termination under carefully controlled procedures." Merit pay raises would replace across-the-board salary increases, and faculty would need to "redirect their own activities" to goals established by the central administration, while colleges and departments would specify responsibilities and rewards for individual faculty members.[67] Faculty critics like Peter Stein, of Physics, and L. Pearce Williams '48, PhD '52, chairman of History, blasted the report as a top-down bureaucratic assault on faculty independence.

Having invited campus-wide comment on the Cranch report, Corson issued his own response in April 1973, "Cornell in the Seventies," written with the help of W. Donald Cooke, vice president for research and dean of the Graduate School. The president demurred from fixed long-range planning objectives, since "the factors bearing on our operations are changing much too rapidly." He refused to increase the student body as Cranch had recommended, leaving it to stabilize at around sixteen thousand. And Corson further endeared himself to the faculty by finessing recommendations around goal-setting and post-tenure evaluation with a single sentence: "There simply has been insufficient time to study, and to discuss with those most vitally concerned, such problems as the faculty tenure system."[68]

In early 1974, Corson and the board of trustees announced the first balanced endowed budget in eight years. But good times were fleeting, as rampant inflation and a dramatic decline in the stock market hit Cornell in 1974 and 1975. Cornell's endowment dropped from $318 million to $271 million. The state of New York cut back $3.3 million in payments to Cornell in 1974, resulting in a loss of ninety jobs. Corson returned to gloom and doom. "Since 1956 I have not seen a financial situation so uncertain and so potentially serious as the one we face right now," he noted, even though he understood that "the whole campus is tired of hearing about troubles."[69]

The "troubles" were projected three-year cuts totaling 15 percent (about $10 million) in the endowed budgets. Tuition, which had grown between 5 percent and 7 percent a year in the past decade, to $3,000 in 1973, was increased an additional 10 percent in 1974 and again in 1975. More "troubles" came from members of the "Student Coalition to Fight the Tuition Hikes," about forty of whom occupied Corson's office for thirty-one hours in November 1974. At a hastily arranged meeting with the trustees the next day, according to the *Daily Sun*, "Coalition members alienated students who would normally be sympathetic by their unbelievable rudeness" and their "unrealistic suggestions."[70] The sit-in students were given written reprimands and suspended $25 fines.

In January 1975, Corson asked Professor Ian R. Macneil of the Law School to direct a series of task forces to recommend ways to make the 15 percent cuts. Speaking volumes about the complex place Cornell had become, Macneil apportioned eighty-three faculty members, twenty-four students, and twenty non-faculty staff into twenty-six committees. Their combined reports eight months later amounted to more than a thousand typewritten pages. More to the point, virtually none of their wide-ranging recommendations—like moving academic advising back into the hands of professors, or improving the quality of instruction by assigning fewer teaching assistants and more professors to underclass courses, or disbanding some of the research centers formed during the previous few decades and placing the remaining ones in existing colleges to compete for funds with established departments and disciplines—were ever adopted. Prodded by trustee board chair Stephen Weiss '57, the cuts were made, but by university administrators, working with deans, and not by adherence to task-force suggestions.

Meanwhile, the vice chairman of the board of trustees, Jansen Noyes Jr., announced in the fall of 1975 that he and trustee Austin Kiplinger '39 would head a five-year fund-raising campaign "to help balance the budget."[71] Budgetary equilibrium by 1978 depended in part on a 7–8 percent annual increase in unrestricted gifts. The gift campaign sought to raise $230 million: $170 million from individual alumni, $40 million from foundations, and $20 million from corporations. Only a small portion of the money would go for bricks and mortar, Noyes announced, the rest for professorships, fellowships, and scholarships, along with program support for schools, colleges, the library, the museum, and the endowment. One year later, the campaign had raised $46 million from over thirty thousand alumni.

Cornell's fund-raising strategy had been refined significantly since the centennial campaign. The Development Office added to its focus on the class year of donors a regional approach. Permanent offices had been established in New York, Chicago, Cleveland, Philadelphia, Washington, Miami, Boston, and the West Coast, with capital gift committees in each of them. "Major" gift giving was encouraged with the creation of a new designation, "Presidential Councilor," a title to be held for life by alumni "who had made a clearly outstanding contribution to the University during the active years of their service to Cornell."[72]

There were some problems with persuading alumni to donate money in these years, even before newspaper and television coverage of the exit of armed occupying students from the Straight. Cold War divisions had not died. Newton Farr '09, president of his class, wrote of classmates' reluctance to give and encouraged Corson to have "more representatives of free enterprise visit the campus and talk with professors and students." He believed the ILR School was too "antagonistic to business and prejudiced in favor of labor," and he disliked "women students in men's study rooms, sloppy dress, unkempt hair, frowzy beards, and bare feet in public."[73]

In 1967 Joseph Coors '39 indicated that he and his father, Adolph Coors Sr. '07, would increase their annual gifts only when Cornell dealt with "the trend toward socialistic thinking" on campus and stopped admitting "long haired hippie types" and "rabid far leftists."[74] The university had learned, however, how to deal with gifts bearing strings attached, including creative (re)interpretation of them. When the will of trustee Maxwell Upson '99 stipulated that his endowed professorship in Economics or Government be held "by a man of conservative economic principles and belief in the American system of free enterprise and sound money," the board of trustees noted that the provision "poses no problem for Cornell University in administering the professorship."[75]

Complicating Corson's financial challenges was his experience, first as provost and then as president, of constant negotiations with New York State over money. SUNY officials faulted Cornell in 1965 for refusing to admit enough graduates of two-year state colleges. In 1973 they complained that the university's tendency to arrogate to itself the role of public spokesman for private higher education in New York State had detrimental effects on Cornell-SUNY relationships. For its part, some Cornell administrators hoped that the institution would "throttle the State University and wished it had done so in its infancy, rather than when it got to be a strong adult."[76]

Ambiguity over whether Cornell was an agent of the state or an independent contractor persisted. The university insisted that SUNY had fiscal responsibilities for the statutory colleges, but not administrative and programmatic control. The positions the state took varied, in terms of who was in charge of SUNY. In the late 1960s, for example, Vice Chancellor Harold Syrett informed Corson that "the State University must have complete budgetary and program control."[77] Even as Syrett and subsequent chancellors, such as Ernest Boyer, retreated from such an imperial SUNY role, some Cornell trustees contemplated "cutting the ties between the statutory colleges and SUNY." But "the Ad Hoc Trustee Committee to Study Cornell–State Relations" in 1971 rejected such a radical approach, noting that state appropriations of $34 million that year provided some two-thirds of the total operating income of the four state colleges and that the state financed capital construction for these units. And so, the ad hoc committee recommended that Cornell develop a political and public-relations strategy for presenting to the state a "united front" case for the four statutory colleges.[78]

The committee also recommended the appointment of an administrator, reporting directly to the president, with responsibility for relations with New York State. Corson refused, citing the opposition of college deans to "adding another layer of administration between the President-Provost and the Deans."[79] Four years later he relented, creating the position of vice president for New York State land grant affairs. His decision to create the new position and his appointment of Constance Cook were forged in the context of New York's $3 million cut in funding for Cornell, part of a reduction of SUNY's statewide budget from $685.3 million to $635.5 million, and the changed political climate in Albany, with Governor Rockefeller off to Washington as President Ford's vice president, succeeded by less reliable friends of Cornell, Republican Malcolm Wilson and subsequently Democrat Hugh Carey. Cornell officials were convinced, with some justification, that Cornell had borne a disproportionate share of the SUNY reduction. Corson put the case succinctly and candidly in a confidential memo sent to trustees Purcell, Noyes, Stewart, and Kiplinger:

> There is no recognition of the value of the research done in our statutory colleges. There is a tendency to treat everyone alike, to budget us on the same formula as applied to SUNY Plattsburgh, for example. There are so many full-time equivalent students and, therefore, we qualify for so many full-time faculty positions. . . . Those doing the budget cutting have no understanding or appreciation of the value to the people of the state of the research done in the Agriculture College or the Veterinary College, for example. They have never heard of oat rust or nematodes or Newcastle Disease in poultry flocks. They have no concept of the role of the County Extension Agent or of any other of the roles our four colleges play as part of our Land Grant mission. Research and Extension are viewed as expensive frills. I see little hope for changing this attitude during the next decade if we remain in our present relationship to SUNY and the State.[80]

The university proposed, in fact, to change its nearly thirty-year arrangement with SUNY. In testimony before Governor Carey's commission on post-secondary education, Corson argued that since their research and public service responsibilities made the Cornell statutory units fundamentally different from the large instruction-oriented programs of the state-operated institutions within SUNY, "dissociation of the Cornell administered, State-supported units, from the State University," with budgeting coming directly from the governor and the legislature, should be considered.[81]

It did not come to that. Instead, Corson made sure that a politically savvy vice president made Cornell's case in Albany, supported by a permanent public relations trumpeting of important Cornell land grant contributions to New York State, to its upstate apple growers and its Long Island duck farmers. Set in place, also, were annual pleas by Cornell officials for special treatment from SUNY chancellors, legislative budget makers, and New York State's governors.

Relations with New York State were not helped by persistent tension over the status of Ujamaa Residential College. Opened on North Campus in the fall of 1972, this residential study program focused on the African ideals of family, community, cooperation, and hard work, symbolized by the Swahili word *ujamaa*. The distinguished psychologist Kenneth B. Clark, the only black member of the State Board of Regents, who told the press that he had been discouraged thirty years earlier from applying to Cornell's graduate school "for racial reasons," convinced Ewald Nyquist, New York State commissioner of education, that Cornell "subtly scared students in the direction of segregated residence facilities."[82] Nyquist threatened to order the university to dismantle Ujamaa for violating state laws by discriminating by race in the selection of its residents. And so began a protracted legal memorandum battle between Cornell and the State Board of Regents or the State Education Department. Corson argued that while Ujamaa was 85 percent black, Ecology House was 85 percent Caucasian and Risley, 81 percent. "The point is that all of these units have a theme around which the activities of the dorm revolve (third world development, environment, and arts). Different ethnic groups will show different affinities toward these themes. The percentages reflect affinities and not racial segregation."[83]

Although Corson repeatedly cited the nondiscriminatory clause in the application to live in Ujamaa, and its encouragement for students "representative of the broad diversity in the student population" to apply, and even though he reminded Nyquist and the Regents that federal investigators from the Department of Health, Education, and Welfare in 1973 had determined that Ujamaa was not a segregated residence, they persisted in threatening to close it down.[84] Like the perpetual tension over state finances, friction with the State of New York over Ujamaa ebbed and flowed in the 1970s, along with the political ambitions of state officials and the eagerness or hesitancy of Cornell to claim special treatment from the state.

No less than Cornell's expectations in Albany, the City of Ithaca expected generosity and special treatment from Cornell. All might look rosy on NBC's *Today* show, with host Hugh Downs, in a twenty-minute visit to Ithaca and Cornell in 1964, complete with choral voices singing the alma mater and scenic views of the campus under a soft covering of snow. Concerned with the realities of living in a college town, NBC interviewed Mayor Hunna Johns, who acknowledged that without Cornell Ithaca would be "practically nothing." But the announcer added that "the community is truly overwhelmed by the great university that dominates it."[85]

Four months after the program aired, Johns asked Cornell for a direct contribution of $25,000 for the cost of fire protection. The Cornell legal counsel, Neal Stamp, wrote the mayor that "it does not appear there is any way in which the University can justify such a contribution."[86] Eighteen months of negotiations followed, with Provost Corson finally taking the issue to the board of trustees' executive committee. Claiming campus alarms accounted for 30 percent of its fire responses, the city won its victory in 1967 with Cornell's commitment to an annual "contribution" of $25,000. Two years later, at the urging of Mayor Jack Kiely, Cornell made a $50,000 contribution in lieu of taxes, to include police as well as fire service.

Not that Cornell was not being generous in other ways to "the bustling town." In 1964 it gave $75,000 to provide half of the first three-year costs of the new Industrial Research Park located at Tompkins County Airport. That same year the university invested $500,000 in the city's recently established urban renewal program. In 1965 Cornell pledged $300,000 to the campaign to create an "Ithaca Festival," which was an ambitious plan conceived by Leverett Saltonstall Jr., Cornell agronomy professor and son of the U.S. senator from Massachusetts, the local lawyer Walter J. Wiggins, LLB '51, and David Grossvogel, professor of comparative literature, to build a $2.7 million theater, where each summer dramatic productions, rivaling the Shakespeare festival in Stratford, Ontario, would be staged. It did not happen. In a less sublime gesture, Cornell in the late 1960s started giving an annual contribution of $60,000 to the city for sewer service and about $38,000 per year in lieu of taxes to the Ithaca City School District to defray the costs of school-age children living in the university's married student housing units.

When Collegetown merchants grumbled about Cornell's new calendar, which kept students out of Ithaca for most of January, Vice President for Public Affairs Steven Muller, PhD '58, initiated a series of luncheons between Cornell University and City of Ithaca officials and local merchants. In 1971 the university created a Community Relations Council and appointed Randy Shaw the first full-time coordinator of community relations.

The university's efforts in 1974 to build additional student housing on North Campus, north of Jessup Drive in Cayuga Heights, between Country

Club Road and Triphammer Road, near the "A" parking lot, locked it in conflict once again with professor of history Frederick Marcham, who was now the mayor of Cayuga Heights. With his Village Board, Marcham opposed the construction of a $4.5 million, twelve-acre housing development for five hundred Cornell students in two "serpentine" apartment buildings, designed by the architect Richard Meier '56. Public meetings at the Cayuga Heights School gymnasium, packed with angry residents, some of whom were Cornell faculty, led to a Cornell offer to reduce the student numbers and lower the buildings' height from thirty-four to thirty feet. The start of construction was continually delayed until President Corson announced that Cornell was canceling the project because of its escalating costs. Although Marcham, who had been the university's boxing coach, won this round, seven years later the university built student housing on that Country Club site, its reduced scale finally winning Cayuga Heights approval.

Other town-gown flashpoints were spin-offs of the general campus unrest in the 1960s and 1970s. Some 120 antiwar students in December 1966 rallied in front of the local draft board at 310 North Aurora Street, leading to verbal clashes with passersby. There was some concern downtown in the summer of 1969 when a work-study scholarship program had fifteen black undergraduates studying "the status of black people in Tompkins County." Mayor Kiely welcomed the project, noting that "there may be things we are doing wrong in not encouraging black people," but some Ithacans worried because the project coordinator was Paul DuBois, a graduate student leader of the Cornell Afro-American Society, the central player in the events at the Straight.[87]

By far the most compelling chapter in town-gown relations in this period was the campaign led by the Cornell chapter of SDS in 1968 and 1969 for low-income housing in Ithaca, reflecting the national SDS's strategy to mobilize the poor in northern cities to take control of federal "Great Society" antipoverty initiatives. The Cornell SDS demanded in the fall of 1968 that the university fund the construction of over one thousand units of low- and moderate-income housing in Ithaca, by the following spring, with the planning, building, and administering to be controlled by a local group representative of the low- and moderate-income community. SDS was joined in these demands by MOVE, an antipoverty, antiracism organization, led by English professor Reeve Parker and by TOMPCO, a nonprofit housing corporation created downtown by clergy and community activists and led by James Dunston, who had worked as a technician in Cornell's Center for Radio Physics and Space Research. The three groups negotiated with Cornell officials in what was dubbed the Joint Housing Committee (JHC). In turn, the JHC met several times with a trustee subcommittee on housing headed by architect Philip A. Will Jr. '28 and Patricia Carry Stewart '50, an investment banker from New York.

President Perkins assured SDS that Cornell would "fulfill its proper share of civic responsibility."[88] He and the subcommittee convinced the trustees that Cornell indeed bore great responsibility for the high cost of housing in Ithaca, since its dorms served only 56 percent of its students. The trustees made a commitment to establish a $2 million mortgage fund and to sell fifty acres of Cornell land at $1,000 an acre for community-controlled low-income housing to be administered by TOMPCO. An unusual collaboration of student radicals, middle-class liberal professors, clergy, working-class Ithacans, Cornell officials, and trustees had successfully negotiated an unprecedented and consensual involvement of Cornell in the community, even as it produced a plan somewhat different from SDS's original demands.

There was, of course, always the threat of SDS direct action hovering over the deliberations. The night before the trustees' New York meeting, a group of 450 demonstrators chanting "Housing now" and "Housing or else" marched in a torchlight procession from Willard Straight Hall to Mary Donlon Hall, having at the last minute decided not to proceed to Perkins's home in Cayuga Heights. At its meeting on April 14, with 320 of its members jammed into Goldwin Smith D, there were smiles as SDS claimed victory. The SDS leader Bruce Dancis told the group "I know you've heard a lot of rumors about seizing buildings. Let me tell you those rumors are true. The only way we won was through our threat and our ability to carry it out." When asked for a comment, Provost Corson replied, "Trustees don't react very well to threats."[89]

This dramatic chapter in town-gown relations had a sad ending. In September, Cornell did sell TOMPCO fifty acres, on the north side of Ellis Hollow Road, just to the west of the old Civilian Conservation Corps camp of the 1930s on Game Farm Road. TOMPCO planned to build 115 houses on the site. But in November the political climate in Ithaca changed. The liberal Democrat Mayor Kiely, a champion of low-income housing, who had defeated Hunna Johns in 1967, was defeated in turn by Republican Johns, the owner of a real estate firm, who believed that low-income housing was "worse than cancer for middle-class neighborhoods." So in March 1970, with TOMPCO charging "racial and economic discrimination," the Ithaca Board of Public Works refused to extend city water and sewer lines to the Ellis Hollow Road homes. The project was dead.[90]

The occupation of the Straight in 1969, it could be argued, was an unintended consequence of a different set of town-gown tensions. Since, as will be evident in the next chapter, the central issue informing the takeover was the operation of the campus judicial system, the causal linkage lies in the tragicomic "Trojan Horse" episode, which led to the creation of that system. On Tuesday, January 17, 1967, a day when Cornell's top administrators were at a board of trustees meeting in New York City, Cornell's Safety Division chief, James Herson, ordered the seizure of all copies of the most recently published issue of the *Trojan Horse*, a student literary magazine, because it contained what he considered to be obscene excerpts from an erotic diary. On his own authority Herson also decreed a ban on further sales of the *Horse*—an action that was endorsed by Acting President Don Cooke. The editor of the *Sun*, the president of student government, and other campus activists then persuaded the *Horse* editors to challenge the confiscation and defy the ban.

A "free speech" rally was held at the steps of the Straight on Friday, with hundreds of students chanting "Sell it, sell it," as bundles of the forbidden *Horse* changed hands. Enter the "town" in the person of Tompkins County District Attorney Richard B. Thaler '53, LLB '56, who arrived on campus with two assistant DAs and two plainclothes detectives from the Ithaca police force. Using the rally organizer's bull horn, Thaler told the crowd that the *Horse* was an "obscene, lewd, lascivious, filthy" publication, and if students continued to sell it he would have to arrest them.[91] While scores of students pleaded to be arrested, the city police accommodated five and put them in Thaler's car. When protesters surrounded the car and flattened its tires, Thaler agreed to release the quintet temporarily while he sought an injunction preventing the sale of the magazine. He went downtown and quickly obtained a temporary State Supreme Court writ, which the students agreed to obey, and the rally dissolved.

District Attorney Richard B. Thaler condemns *The Trojan Horse* on January 20, 1967. (Division of Rare and Manuscript Collections of the Cornell University Library)

Early Saturday morning, arrest warrants were served on the five students. The city police, without cooperation from the campus Safety Division, entered their living quarters, on campus and off, and with no advance notice knocked on bedroom doors and served warrants. The students were released on bail, and the Ithaca attorney Walter Wiggins was employed by the New York State branch of the American Civil Liberties Union to defend them. That evening Thaler summoned the university proctor, Lowell George, assistant university counsel Ralph Jones, and Chief Herson to a meeting at Ithaca's Sheraton Hotel, owned by his family. "Fulminating against the President, he insisted that a condition for his refraining from further action would be a commitment by the University to discipline the students."[92]

The final exams that began on Monday kept students diverted from the case, while President Perkins and Arthur Dean '19, JD '23, chairman of the board of trustees, let it be known that they had called the district attorney on Friday, appealing to him to let the university deal with the matter itself. On Friday, January 27, State Supreme Court Justice Harold Sampson sided with the students, declaring "it does, indeed, appear that no matter how worthless, no matter how vile or filthy it may be, if it successfully meets the test against pruriency, a publication is entitled to the protection of the First Amendment and may not be proscribed."[93] Chief Herson resigned, noting that "he felt no longer able to be effective in the position."[94] He soon became Ithaca's chief of police, and Thaler lost his bid for reelection in 1968.

Shocked that for the first time in a hundred years city and county officers had come on campus to arrest students and worried that confrontations like those at the University of California at Berkeley might be down the road, the Faculty Council created a commission to delineate university policy and appropriate jurisdiction with respect to student conduct. Control over student conduct codes had historically been the function of the faculty, except for the short period of Malott's efforts to bring it inside the president's office, but in the 1960s the faculty had delegated it more and more to student government. At the same time, nonacademic administrative staff, like Campus Police and the university proctor—agents technically of the president—presided over the day-to-day enforcement of campus rules and regulations. The acceleration of campus protest and disruption, as well as the unpredictable actions of off-campus officials, like District Attorney Thaler, made clarity about who was in charge on campus imperative. Created in May 1967 and named after its chairman, Government professor Allan Sindler, the Sindler Commission of thirteen faculty, administrators, and students, one of whom was SDS leader David Burak, was charged to work this out. It met twenty-five times before issuing a forty-one-page report in September.

The Sindler Commission recommended that all violations of university codes, and "all but very serious breaches of [local, state, and federal] law be handled internally within the Cornell jurisdiction." Commission members assumed that the university "would exhibit greater understanding and flexibility of action, and be more receptive to and protective of dissent than would civil society." In governing conduct, the paramount concern, they concluded, must be that the university "make its sanctioning power over students serve its educational goals for students, rather than promoting general police functions well represented in general law." In other words, "civil disobedience that did not adversely affect the educational community would be outside Cornell's jurisdiction, e.g. draft card burning." While university regulations should not restrict political or artistic expression, these forms of expression must not interfere with "the right to hear" or subvert "the protection of the community's common rules and their enforcement by requiring student defendants to cooperate with the adjudicatory system."[95]

In accepting these recommendations, the faculty in May 1968 also agreed to the commission's practical reforms, such as shifting enforcement of codes drawn up by student representatives from the proctor to a code administrative officer in the dean of students' office and the creation of a "Student-Faculty Board of Student Conduct," five students and four faculty, which would decide cases brought to it by the code administrator. Any decision there to expel a student would be reviewed by the "Student-Faculty Appellate Board" of five faculty and four students. In an important departure from the commission's recommendations, which would prove momentous a year later, the faculty approved its "right to intervene to overrule actions of the Adjudicatory Board on its own motion."[96]

There was, in fact, a major confrontation between Cornell students and Ithaca police in this period, but it occurred off campus. An antiwar demonstration on Thursday night, May 11, 1972, spilled into Collegetown, where rock-throwing students smashed windows of the branch of the First National Bank and Trust Company. During the incident Herson, Ithaca's police chief, was hit with rocks, and one of his officers was soaked with gasoline, which a demonstrator tried to ignite. On May 13, another confrontation occurred, between about one thousand students and some sixty city police, at an unauthorized Saturday night block party in Collegetown. Twenty-nine people were arrested for disorderly conduct, and ten were injured, including four policemen, in a four-hour melee involving tear gas. A month later Mayor Ed Conley, Herson, and about thirty-six "unknown" policemen were sued by the American Civil Liberties Union on behalf of four Cornell students "for punishing students summarily and without due process of law and without regard to the guilt or innocence of the persons involved."[97] The lawsuit seeking damages from the city was dismissed by the U.S. District Court in Syracuse nineteen months later, long after relative peace had returned to town–gown relations.

Nᴇᴀʀʟʏ ᴇᴠᴇʀʏᴛʜɪɴɢ ᴡᴀs politicized at Cornell in the 1960s and 1970s. The Division of Biological Sciences was denounced by faculty from Government and History, led by Professor Allan Bloom, expressing contempt for those who had tampered with "the traditional structure of the University." Bloom was "profoundly disturbed" that biologists assumed they could understand and control how genes and the environment produce people, and therefore that (more than humanists) they should "play that part not only as means to [finding] a better life but as one of the methods of determining what the good life is." On the contrary, Bloom argued, biologists needed the wisdom of humanists to understand human nature and the good life, concluding "the biological sciences belong in the Arts College and not in splendid isolation."[98] Bloom also opposed the six-year PhD program because it intended to take very bright high school students who had made "a firm career choice" and "rush them through to the start of those careers," instead of letting them follow the "leisurely life of the mind."[99]

The intellectual leader of Cornell's conservative faculty, Bloom was one of the most popular teachers at Cornell in the 1960s; students often burst into applause at the end of his lectures on the wisdom found in the "Great Books." In his early thirties, the charismatic Bloom, a follower of the political theorist Leo Strauss at the University of Chicago, gathered disciples of his own at Cornell, especially among students at Telluride House, where he had lived as a faculty guest for a year and a half. Created in 1911 with a gift from the Colorado Power Company entrepreneur Lucien Lucius Nunn, Telluride provided free room and board to carefully selected students—all of them men, until 1961—who ran the House cooperatively. The intellectual epicenter of Cornell in the 1960s, Telluride was divided into two camps—on the one hand the conservative followers of Bloom and his colleagues Walter Berns in Government and Donald Kagan and L. Pearce Williams in History, and on the other the more radical disciples of the literary theorist Paul de Man, who taught at Cornell until 1966 and spread the theories of Jacques Derrida, the French deconstructionist.

In his 1987 best-selling polemic, *The Closing of the American Mind*, Bloom took Cornell as the model for what he saw as the decline of higher education. This landmark in the "culture wars" of the last third of the twentieth century criticized the intense politicization of campus life in the '60s. Faculty and administrators, Bloom claimed, ceased to see the purpose of a liberal education as finding truth and the nature of a good life. Their relativistic, value-free convictions led them away from the traditional obligation of philosophical professors to perceive objective good and objective evil and to transmit these truths to students. Instead, he lamented, students were left to construct their own curriculum as they sought to realize their own unique selves. Deferring to students as if public opinion finds truth, Bloom wrote, the faculty "no longer provide guidance as to what is important and no longer set standards based on a view of human perfection." The seemingly apolitical consensus on the merit of student course evaluations, introduced in the '60s, epitomized the betrayal of Bloom's vision of the university: "To assert that students, as a matter of principle, have a right to judge the value of a professor or what he teaches is to convert the university into a market in which the sellers must please the buyers and the standard of value is determined by demand."[100]

Among the much larger group of left-leaning faculty on campus, committed less to rational discovery of the good life and more to how the university could combat inequality, racism, and war, there was no counterpart to Bloom, no intellectually dominant personality serving as champion of a just and truly democratic university. Probably the closest claimant was the Economics professor Douglas Dowd, a central player in antiwar activities and racial politics in the 1960s. America in 1967, he told students in Anabel Taylor Hall, was "the very worst society that history has ever known," because it denied people "social justice, which means a world in which men can live decently and freely, in some sort of equality."[101]

The appointing and promoting of faculty were often politicized. The Government Department, dominated by Bloom and Berns, in an unannounced meeting just before Christmas in 1967, hired another Straussian political theorist from the University of Chicago, Werner Dannhauser. The action so enraged absent department member Mario Einaudi that he resolved never to participate in departmental affairs, and, indeed, he spent the rest of his career self-exiled in the Center for International Studies. After the suicide of Clinton Rossiter in July 1970, Arch Dotson, the chair of the Government Department, urged Corson to appoint Daniel Patrick Moynihan, professor of education and urban studies at Harvard and a former counselor to President Nixon, as John L. Senior Professor. Moynihan turned down the offer, but then changed his mind, by which time Corson had received strong expressions of disapproval from Walter LaFeber in History and Urie Bronfenbrenner '38 in Human Ecology, who warned of an angry response by African American students over Moynihan's proposed policy of "benign neglect" to racial issues, crafted when he worked at the Nixon White House, and over his claims about "the pathology" of black families. Corson declined to renew the offer to Moynihan, who was later elected to the United States Senate. For this reason, Corson indicated, "for many years I had strained relations with the Senator." Theodore Lowi, a distinguished liberal political scientist from the University of Chicago, who had taught at Cornell earlier in the 1960s, was given the Senior chair a year later, despite Mrs. Senior's letter reminding Corson that she hoped that Clinton Rossiter's replacement "will present the conservative point of view to the students."[102]

The dismissal of three College of Architecture faculty in 1973 laid bare a different political dimension. Demanding "the school be run more democratically," four hundred students crammed into a Franklin Hall lecture room urging Dean Kermit Parsons, MRP '53, to reverse the denials of tenure or reappointment to Alan Chimacoff '63, Alfred Koetter, MAR '75, and Roger Sherwood '57. The political alignments were surprising, since the students stood here for tradition, insisting that the three were let go because they were architectural "formalists," interested only in design within the built environment. This, the protesters claimed, flew in the face of the school's 1970 decision to reduce the demands of architectural design and introduce students "to the changing economic and social questions of our time," as with the new City and Regional Planning course, "Urban Ghetto Development."[103] The Architecture professors voted 15–10 not to reconsider their denials. The students then took their lost cause to the white Sibley dome, where throughout the '60s and '70s slogans were painted, visible to all in the Arts quad below.

As elsewhere, Cornell students demanded a greater role in shaping their course work. "Student power" advocates complained that the "individual student has very little power over the day to day conditions of his academic life, a situation which serves to alienate him even further from the educational process."[104] Cornell responded in 1969, adding three students to the six professors on the Educational Policy Committee in the Arts College and three students to one-year terms on the Ag School's Faculty Committee on Education Policy. University administrators drew the line on a student-run course. Asking for a $25,000 grant from the university to fund it, SDS proposed "Social Analysis 377X," in which students would "have a significant voice in determining what they will read, who they will hear speak, and the very structure of the presentation (i.e. panel, debate, lecture)." The three-credit course, intended to study conflict and social change in China, Cuba, and the United States, would be ungraded, held in the evening, and open to the public. Even with its detailed syllabus, an aide to Perkins wrote, the course was "of questionable academic merit."[105] SDS eventually mounted the course as part of its own "underground college," housed in Willard Straight Hall.

The trustees also said no to "student power" demands in 1969 that the newly formed University Senate establish a student-dominated committee with veto power over the selection of a new president. In the presidential search of 1976–77, the trustees again refused to allow a student committee to have a veto over its choice. The board did, however, appoint the student trustee Lauryn Guttenplan '77 to the search committee.

The Arts College pursued a strategy of partial concession to student demands in authorizing Philosophy 200, "Social and Philosophic Inquiry," which was "led" rather than "taught" by John Condry, a social psychologist, Douglas Dowd, the economist, and David Lyons, a philosopher. Although the subject was the nature of freedom and authority, Lyons acknowledged "we are playing it by ear." Readings and lecture topics were determined by "the spontaneous interaction" between the instructors and the ninety students in the course, an activity that apparently took up more than half of each class session. The course's greatest strength, according to Dowd, was in "separating education from coercion." Bloom's response to such experiments was that "none of the moves toward student participation . . . have done anything but . . . cause a deterioration of academic standards, an increase of demagogic teaching, and a loss of the sense of a university's purpose."[106]

Academic departments took political positions, as in 1972 when Psychology and Romance Studies voted an end to ROTC. Professors decided to give only A grades in response to draft boards' reliance on grades, and in small courses to replace grades with detailed prose evaluations. The *Sun* editors tried to imagine Selective Service director Hershey "pouring over the recommendations and comments of a student's teachers in order to determine the person's eligibility."[107] Some professors told their students they could buy books for their courses only at the "Resistance Bookstore," while the dean of the faculty worried that proceeds of Resistance were used for political purposes. And some faculty pushed the academic envelope to new boundaries of experimentation. "The Family in Poverty" course, taught in 1967 by Professor Harold Feldman of the College of Home Economics, had no prelim exams, papers, or final exam; one of its unique feature was an exchange, where Cornell students lived downtown with low-income families, while a child of a host family lived in a dorm.

Sage Chapel and Cornell United Religious Work (CURW) were central players in the politicization of campus life. In 1968 a diverse set of critics complained about the character of Sage Chapel's Sunday services: the conservative professor of linguistics Robert Hall Jr.; music professors Tom Sokol, director of the chapel choir, and John Hsu; and the dean of Arts and Sciences, philosophy professor Stuart M. Brown Jr. Sokol and Hsu were offended by the music used in the service and insisted that choosing the selections had been and should still be the responsibility of the Music Department. All four critics were particularly bothered by one Sunday service, when the chapel was decorated with posters "taking a militant line in the cause of American black people" and instead of music by the choir, tape recordings of rock and roll music were played, which Brown found "deeply offensive to people who, like myself, cannot stand the damn stuff."[108]

Mark Barlow, EdD '62, vice president for student affairs, told Perkins that same year that CURW was less interested in "the worship life of students and general pastoral counseling" and "much more involved in social reform . . . in projects such as Brazil or East Harlem." He criticized CURW's director, W. Jack Lewis, and his two associate directors, John Lee Smith and Father Dan Berrigan, for "their self-righteous role as self-anointed prophets."[109] At Barlow's suggestion, Perkins formed a committee, with Milton Konvitz, PhD '33, as chair, to reconsider the role of CURW.

The Konvitz Committee recommended in October 1969 that the decades-long official ties between CURW and the university be ended and that Cornell withdraw the financial support that paid the salaries of the three directors and their staff, to be replaced, committee members hoped, by gifts from "the denominations, their friends among the alumni and elsewhere, and the students." Konvitz characterized the recommendations as the liberation of religion at Cornell, its "complete freedom without hindrance from any official in the University power structure," in keeping with the university's secular roots. CURW survived the break, of course, and in 1971 announced that formal Sunday worship at Sage Chapel would be switched to nonliturgical "convocations" on the role of religion in society, and the chapel choir would perform aesthetic and nonliturgical music. "Since Sage is just loaded with symbol after symbol of Christian theology," Jack Lewis noted, "those who insisted on the present service are guilty of a presumptuous Protestantism which is analogous to unconscious white racism."[110]

ADVOCATES FOR WOMEN'S studies and black studies introduced into university life the identity politics at the center of the feminist and civil rights revolutions roiling American life in this period. Their critics, such as Allan Bloom, saw both initiatives as politically motivated and simply "designed to show that the University is with it, and has something in addition to its traditional specialties."[111] The issue of black studies and racial politics would shake Cornell to its roots and is the focus of the next chapter; here we look at the less traumatic, if equally significant, story of women's studies and gender politics.

The demand for women's studies emerged out of an altered landscape for women at Cornell. Without demonstrating or making nonnegotiable demands, women undergraduates got significant concessions in dorm rules from a university committed to an end of *in loco parentis* practices and concerned about claims that it discriminated, especially after President Lyndon Johnson signed the 1964 Civil Rights Act. By 1969, the quota allowing only about three hundred senior and junior women to live off-campus was dropped, though freshmen and sophomore women were still required to live in dormitories or sororities. Dress regulations had been left to the discretion of each dining area since 1964, and curfews for women students were eliminated by the Faculty Committee on Student Affairs for seniors in 1963, juniors in 1965, sophomores in 1967, and freshmen in 1970.

A chapter of the National Organization for Women (NOW) was founded at Cornell in 1969, a unit of the Women's Liberation Front was established in 1970, and protests and sit-ins were held to gain sex-related medical care. The university responded by inviting Planned Parenthood to set up an office at Sage

Infirmary, with Cornell subsidizing 60 percent of its budget, and by creating the role of sex counselor. In its first year, 1970, 475 Cornell women visited the Planned Parenthood office; in 1975–76 the number was 1,876. Birth-control pills were prescribed, and after New York State legalized abortion in 1970, about ten women with unwanted pregnancies were referred each month to one of four clinics in New York City by University Health Services. The Women's Liberation group also persuaded UHS to sell condoms and contraceptive foam at a "Contraception Information Center" on West Campus and persuaded the university to light badly lit areas on campus. The administration declined to provide an all-night campus bus for women students or a free self-defense course for them. To avoid charges of discrimination, which had held up a $4,500 grant from the Student Finance Commission, the Cornell marching band in 1970 ended its seventy-six-year-long tradition of having all male members and accepted thirteen women. Two years later, the eighty-member Glee Club deleted the word "male" from its constitution, though the club accepted only those with tenor or bass voices.

Women's Studies at Cornell was very much the creation of one woman. In the fall of 1968, Sheila Tobias, a Radcliffe Phi Beta Kappa graduate, recently arrived in Ithaca to take the new position of assistant to the vice president for student affairs, conceived the idea of an "intersession program on women." Tobias assembled an ad hoc committee of faculty, graduate students, undergraduates, spouses of faculty, and women who worked at Cornell to plan the conference. Rather than confine the sessions to concerns about educational and professional opportunities for women, the group decided that "the underlying psychological and sociological questions of women's perceptions of themselves and their role in this society should be explored."[112] Equally ambitious was their invitation list: Betty Friedan, founder of the National Organization for Women, who had spoken to a capacity crowd in Anabel Taylor Hall in 1964, a year after her book *The Feminine Mystique* was published; Ti-Grace Atkinson, militant feminist writer and president of the New York City chapter of NOW; a young instructor from Barnard, Kate Millett, whose readings from her soon-to-be-published *Sexual Politics*, with its provocative discussion of patriarchal culture and suggestion that "the private was public," had galvanized a large Cornell audience that fall; and New York State assemblywoman Constance Cook.

Friedan and Millett attended the conference held in late January 1969, representing, respectively, the liberal and radical camps of feminism, the former seeking women's legal and professional equality with men, the latter convinced that only fundamental cultural changes could liberate women. Cook came and Atkinson declined because men were welcome at the proceedings. Over three days, fifty panelists discussed topics ranging from "How do men look at women and how do women look at themselves?" to "Abortion and contraception" and "The black woman in America." The audience, 60 percent female, totaled over a thousand people. Karen DeCrow, future president of NOW, noted that only 3 percent of doctors and 7 percent of lawyers in America were women. Cornell professors Andrew Hacker, Alice Cook, John Condry, and Harold Feldman, local psychiatrist Howard Feinstein '51, MD '55, PhD '77, and Sarah Lawrence president Esther Raushenbush weighed in, as did a vocal audience of NOW activists from all over the East Coast and Mary Pinotti, a founder of the guerrilla theater group WITCH, "Women's International Terrorist Conspiracy from Hell." One afternoon session began with a rumbling Shakespearean chant from circling witches, "boil and bubble . . . toil and trouble," that ended with a "hex" on the panel of social scientists.[113] The booing came mainly from male SDS students.

Out of Tobias's conference came the Committee for Female Studies, which met weekly after January 1969 and organized a faculty seminar on Female Personality that fall. From the seminar came the experimental course "Evolution of Female Personality: History and Prospects," offered in the Department of Human Development and Family Studies during the spring 1970 semester. Presided over by Professors Joy Osofsky and Harold Feldman, the course included frequent lectures from Tobias, who had been appointed a lecturer for that semester. This first full-credit, interdisciplinary course in female studies taught at a major American university drew 203 students from both endowed and state colleges, among them thirty-four men. An all-day Future of Female Studies conference held at the end of the course in May brought together eighty Cornell faculty and twenty faculty from other universities who taught or conducted research on women's issues. Tobias summed up the concerns of feminist scholars: "Insofar as the curriculum mentioned women at all (and in most cases women's lives and accomplishments were omitted), it trivialized both their problems and their contributions to literature, history, the arts, and the behavioral sciences. On a college campus, we began to realize, feminist politics clearly had a teaching function as well."[114]

Tobias left Cornell that summer to become associate provost of Wesleyan University. She went on to a distinguished scholarly career, writing important books about women in the military and women with math and science anxiety. But her pioneering efforts bore fruit at Cornell. That October, the university announced the creation of a Female Studies program, under the auspices of the university's Center for Research in Education, with a budget of $19,000. Courses for credit were offered in five university units: the "Female Personality" in Human Ecology; "Women and Education" in the Ag School; "Women in Society" in the Division of Biological Sciences; "Women in Literature" in English; and "Women as a Social Force" in Rural Sociology.

Two years later, with a new name, Women's Studies sponsored ten courses and became an Arts College program with Jennie Farley '54, MS '59, PhD '70, an ILR faculty member, as director. "Our ultimate goal is to phase ourselves out," Farley told the *Sun.* "This will happen when women's history, women's art, etc. are taught in the regular courses."[115] The program had its critics. L. Pearce Williams insisted that Women's Studies "is too ideological in content and stresses a raise in consciousness rather than a raise in intellectual inquiry."[116] Opponents brought anti-feminists to campus to question the foundational ideology itself. Before a standing-room-only crowd in 1974, the conservative writer and activist Midge Decter attacked the entire women's movement for depicting women as "fatigued, oppressed, and less than fully human" people, while being "violently anti-male."[117] Women's Studies weathered its critics. By 1975, 635 students enrolled in twenty-nine of its courses, and with several other name changes, it became a permanent part of Cornell life.

When the program was created in 1972 there were 1,453 tenured and tenure-track professors at Cornell; ninety-six were women, and more than half of them were in the College of Human Ecology. Half of the men on the faculty were full professors, while only one-fifth of the women had reached that rank. The College of Arts and Sciences had two women full professors: Eleanor J. Gibson, the first woman in Cornell's history to have an endowed chair, as the Susan Linn Sage Professor of Psychology, and Eleanor Jorden, professor of linguistics. At the Law School, 15 percent of whose students were female, no woman was appointed to the faculty until 1973. Among the two hundred or so "para-faculty at Cornell," lecturers and instructors not on tenure-track appointments and not expected to do research or publish, over a hundred were women.

Of the nearly seven thousand regular, full-time university employees on the Ithaca campus, 45 percent were women, and with the exception of seventy-two librarians, few had professional jobs. In 1972 there were no women in Cornell's central administration, no woman vice president, no woman dean. Of the 146 people with the title "director," as heads of research projects, centers, and administrative units such as admissions and financial aid, six were women, and they tended to head units such as Women's Physical Education and the North Campus Union Craft Shop. In 1972, with a university student body one-third of which was women, there was no woman counselor in Cornell's Career Center.

In response to an executive order from Washington requiring any contractor receiving more than $10,000 in federal money and having more than fifty employees to produce a plan for hiring more women and minority group members, President Corson in 1971 had created an Affirmative Action Office and a Council on Affirmative Action. A "Woman's Action Council," a self-designated group of academic and nonacademic Cornell employees, urged the institution to strive for a 40 percent female faculty, to subsidize day-care centers, provide paid maternity leaves, and freeze the promotion of male employees. The board of trustees took a less militant approach, designed by Constance Cook, Patricia Carry Stewart, and Charlotte Conable '51, future author of a history of women at Cornell. The board created a committee, with Cook as chair, "to study the status of women students, faculty members and employees at Cornell University and to make appropriate recommendations concerning that status."[118]

After a two-year study, the Cook Committee made seventeen recommendations "that will accord equality to women in every aspect of University life, that will promote their intellectual participation at Cornell and that will recognize the especially difficult position of black women."[119] President Corson was charged with increasing the number of women on the faculty, in administrative positions, and on the board of trustees and with eliminating imbalances in employment opportunities between men and women at all levels. Additional funding was recommended for the Women's Studies Program, equal per capita subsidies for men's and women's physical education and athletic programs, and increased career counseling programs for women employees and students.

Positive steps were soon taken. In September the first woman counselor was appointed at Cornell's Career Center, and the following year, 1975, Corson appointed June Fessenden-Raden, from the Division of Biological Sciences, vice provost for undergraduate education, the first woman to hold a major office in the central administration. In 1976, he appointed Constance Cook vice president for New York State land grant affairs, the first woman vice president in the university's history. Judge Mary Donlon Alger, LLB '20, the first woman trustee, endowed a chair that she asked be given only to women. It would go to Mary Beth Norton, the first woman professor in the History Department. Provost David Knapp and Vice President for Research Don Cooke issued regular reports on affirmative action to the trustees. Although their commitment to gender equality never wavered, they engaged in a numbers game, questioning Professor Farley's count of female faculty and deflecting charges of sex discrimination by pointing to the "pipeline" problem, the alleged absence of women demonstrably trained and qualified for academic careers at Cornell. They were also the point people in dismissing the demands of the activist Cornell Women's Caucus that half-time positions be created at the assistant, associate, and full professor ranks to permit greater flexibility in combining family and career, and that financial coverage for abortion be part of the compulsory student health plan.

In an unintended way, the university would leave a permanent stamp on future discussions of the status of women in America and the world. The concept and phrase "sexual harassment" was invented at Cornell by three women working for the Human Affairs Program (HAP), the community outreach program created in 1970 and headed by Professor Ben Nichols '46, MEN '49, of Engineering. Lin Farley, Karen Sauvigne, and Susan Meyer, radical feminist activists and community organizers, ran the seminar for HAP "Women and Work." In 1975, they were asked for help by a former university employee,

Carmita Wood, age forty-four, born and raised in the apple orchard region of Cayuga Lake, and sole supporter of two children. Wood had worked for eight years in Cornell's Department of Nuclear Physics, she told them, and been bothered by a faculty member, who jiggled his crotch when he stood near her desk, deliberately brushed against her breasts when reaching for papers, and cornered her in an elevator at the department Christmas party, planting unwanted kisses on her mouth. To avoid him, she quit her job. When another position at Cornell failed to materialize, she applied for unemployment insurance. Asked by the claim investigator why she left her job after eight years, she answered "for personal reasons," and was turned down. She asked the instructors of "Women and Work" to help her appeal that decision. The HAP seminar leaders, they reported later, "realized that to a person, every one of us—the women on the staff, Carmita, the students—had had an experience like this at some point, you know? And none of us had ever told anyone before. It was one of those *click, aha!* moments. A profound revelation."[120]

They agreed to help with Wood's appeal, but Farley, Sauvigne, and Meyer also decided to hold a public "speak out" protest "to break the silence about this." Brainstorming about what they would call the "this" on their posters, the three rejected "sexual intimidation," "sexual coercion," and "sexual exploitation on the job." Someone came up with "harassment." "*Sexual harassment!* Instantly we agreed. That's what it was."[121] Calling themselves "Working Women United," the three women leafleted Cornell, Ithaca College, and Ithaca's two large factories, Ithaca Gun and Morse Chain. Following mailings to women lawyers in town and secretaries at banks and with stories about Carmita Wood's appeal sent to the *Ithaca Journal* and local radio stations, the "speak out" took place on a rainy spring day, May 4, 1975, downtown at the Greater Ithaca Activities Center, a gathering place for Ithaca's small African American community. This first-ever public rally about "sexual harassment" became national news. In a story that appeared in the *New York Times*, the reporter Enid Nemy described the Ithaca event and Carmita Wood; she wrote of the waitresses who spoke about harassment at work, of stories told by secretaries and assistant professors.

Wood lost her appeal, but Cornell found her a job in a different department. The university ended the HAP program in 1976, and Farley, Sauvigne, and Meyer moved on. But with the help of Eleanor Holmes Norton, New York City's commissioner of human rights, Catharine MacKinnon, author of *Sexual Harassment of Working Women*, and some landmark litigation in the late 1970s, the "this," "sexual harassment," conceptualized at Cornell, became the shorthand for a sexually hostile work environment.

This period also witnessed the first intimations of other fronts in the academic wars over identity. In 1971 a manifesto of the Native American Association (NAA) at Cornell demanded an increase in the number of American

Indian students on campus in the next year from four to twenty-five, as well as a living unit and center for Indian activities. Citing the fact that the university offered only one course on North American Indians, in Anthropology, the association demanded the creation of an Indian Studies Program. Explaining that the History Department planned no new courses in the area, Chairman L. Pearce Williams commented, "If there is a ground swell of opinion to have them, it's a very small swell." The NAA also complained in 1972 that COSEP "had acted in a negligent and discriminatory manner with respect to recruiting Native Americans."[122]

No Indian Studies Program ensued, nor did the numbers of Indian students climb dramatically. The university did sponsor a conference in 1972 on how to provide education for the American Indian population of New York State. Chiefs from each tribe of the Iroquois Confederation attended, as well as American Indian educators, Cornell administrators, and the handful of Indian students on campus. Two years later Cornell agreed to participate in a federally funded program run by St. Lawrence University to provide a network of counseling and tutorial services for Native American students attending colleges in New York State and New Jersey.

Ethnic-group solidarity developed with the creation of the "New Coalition," an alliance of La Asociación del Caribe, the Chicano students' organization, the Asian American Coalition, and the Native American Association. In 1973 the coalition proposed that two positions, filled by Latinos, be added to COSEP's learning skills center, and that an affirmative action officer be hired and "charged with identifying Puerto Rican (and other Latinos), Chicanos and Native Americans to fill positions within the University." Also proposed was a new admissions officer to "actively recruit students in heavily concentrated areas of Latin and Native American groups," as well "as in Asian American communities." Finally, the New Coalition advocated an "Ethnic Studies Program and Center," independent of any department or college, run by "qualified ethnic individuals."[123]

The proposals were turned over to the College of Arts and Sciences dean, Alfred Kahn. Uncertain whether more ethnic students could be recruited to Cornell without an existing ethnic studies program, Kahn urged his colleagues in Day Hall to acknowledge, and New Coalition leaders to recognize, "that the offering of any such promise of setting up programs for other minority students comparable in dimensions to the Africana Center Program is simply unrealistic."[124]

The idea of an umbrella studies program would not die, even as its first proposer, the New Coalition, faded in the mid-1970s, nor did inter-ethnic criticism of COSEP. In 1977 the Asian American Coalition "admonished administrators" for the "total exclusion" of Asian Americans from COSEP. That same year a report by La Asociación Latina claimed that "COSEP has generally played a lukewarm or negative role in the progress of Hispanic education at Cornell," while calling for an ethnic studies program.[125]

———————

NINE CORNELL WOMEN invaded Teagle Hall's steam room in November 1971 demanding that hours be set aside for women to use the male-only facility. The "steam-in" occurred at nine in the morning, when, after a scout determined that there were no men in the vicinity, the women dashed in, stripped off their clothing, and draped themselves with towels. A year and a half later, after the director of physical education refused to allow nude swimming by women in Helen Newman Hall, the norm for men's swimming at Teagle, periodic "nude swim-ins" occurred in the Helen Newman pool. The "Nudist's Manifesto" read, "We have learned to be modest not for ourselves, but in order to restrain men, who put us in this position in the first place. . . . The opportunity to swim nude during all-women swimming hours can help this process of demystifying women to themselves and encouraging women's positive feelings about their bodies."[126] The story of Cornell athletics in this period is as much about its politicization, like everything else on campus, as it is about the emergence of hockey at the heart of Cornell culture.

Women students were angry that in 1971–72 women's intercollegiate athletics received $19,400, less than 4 percent of the total university budgetary allocation for athletics, when the three hundred women intercollegiate athletes constituted 16 percent of the total at Cornell. They were even angrier when after being denied lockers at Teagle and not being allowed to play basketball and volleyball at Barton, they were told "to go to Helen Newman where you belong."[127] Two undergraduates, Laurie Zelon '74, a member of the University Senate, and Jane Danowitz '75, a student trustee, filed a formal complaint with the university in October 1973, seeking an end to sex discrimination in athletic facilities and the development of coeducational PE classes in all but contact sports. Three weeks later, the university partially gave in. A locker room for women was built at a cost of $85,000 under the Barton Hall stands, with 105 storage baskets in racks, 24 half-size lockers, and a shower room with white and turquoise tile. Danowitz told the *Sun*, "I love it. It's gorgeous, I'm so glad they did it in blue instead of pink. But my complaint against the University still stands."[128] She withdrew the complaint four months later when Jon T. Anderson, director of physical education and athletics, announced that a basketball and volleyball court would be set aside for women from 7 to 10 p.m. on weekdays at Barton and that coeducational gym classes would increase in the fall of 1974.

The discrepancies between women's and men's athletic facilities and funding did not go away. Not only did men's sports in the 1970s get subsidized to the tune of half a million dollars to women's $20,000, but female physical education instructors were required to devote some of their time to coaching the women's intercollegiate teams. Some of these issues would explode several years later as part of a suit against the university brought by the "Cornell Eleven."

Race was a nagging issue in Cornell athletics as well. In the wake of the Straight takeover, the CBS-TV newsman Charles Kuralt interviewed Theo Jacobs '70, the African American social psychology major and captain of the varsity football team. Raised in the Bedford-Stuyvesant section of Brooklyn, Jacobs spoke of the pressures of being one of 250 blacks in a student body of 14,000: "I don't think I knew color till I came to this campus and I met what people would call black militants. Well, I consider myself a black militant, but I think the difference is I'm not a hostile black militant in that I don't hate white people because they are white."[129]

The most racially tense sport in the 1970s was basketball. In December 1971, the black players, claiming that Coach Jerry Lace would play no more than three blacks at a time because of alumni pressure, threatened a boycott. Two late nights of secret negotiations, which at various points involved the black players, Athletic Director Robert Kane '34, Jon Anderson, Provost Plane, President Corson, the university ombudsman, Coach Lace, and Gregg Morris '68, MPA '73, the All-Ivy African American captain of the 1968 team, were unsuccessful. All six black players boycotted two games.

When the season ended, black players publicly charged Lace with using a quota system, while white players complained he was incompetent and had forced them to cut their long hair. For good measure, the white players criticized their black teammates for not discussing the boycott with them and for calling their abilities into question. Lace was transferred to an administrative post in the Department of Physical Education and Athletics two months later. He was replaced by Tony Coma, who had compiled a 70–15 win-loss record as basketball coach of Pennsylvania's predominantly black Cheyney State College.

Coma was a disaster. His first-year record, 4–22, was Cornell basketball's worst in sixty-six years, matched only by his second, 3–21. Several blacks were among the four starters who left the team after tense exchanges with the coach. In 1974 Coma resigned when players complained of his drinking and just as the university disclosed that he had violated recruiting rules by paying application fees for prospective students. Ben Bluitt, former head coach of St. Mary of Redford High School in Detroit and the first black head coach in Cornell sports history, replaced him. His teams never did that well, but in 1976 the fifty-five-member Black Athletes Association of Cornell University, under his leadership, formed a ten-team basketball league for preteens and teenagers at the downtown Greater Ithaca Activities Center.

In these years football had its ups and down, uncomplicated, to be sure, by racial issues. Though blessed in his five years as coach with two superstars, Gary Wood '64 and Pete Gogolak '64, both of whom would go on to careers in the National Football League, Coach Tom Harp won only nineteen games while losing twenty-three. Nor did he ever quite adjust to what he saw as Cornell's indifference to big-time football, compared with his years at West Point, or to the university's admissions policies. He wrote to Perkins in 1964: "Is it possible that Cornell will become an 'egghead' university? It would be far better for the University to have an all-around candidate, both scholastically and physically, than to have the so-called intellectuals who move about the campus with beards and dirty clothes and who apparently do not feel any particular loyalty to Cornell while there or in after life."[130]

Harp's successor, Jack Musick, brought back football glory with a shared Ivy League title with Dartmouth in 1971, helped immensely by the great running back Ed Marinaro '72, who became the first college football player in history to rush for over four thousand yards in three seasons. Musick's overall record of 45–33–3 was marred by a final year of 3–5-1. After he was let go in 1974, football reached its nadir with Coach George Seifert, the former defensive coordinator at Stanford, whose two-year record at Cornell was 3–15. Fired in 1976 before the last two games against Columbia and Penn, Seifert went on to football fame, returning to Stanford for an incredibly successful run, and then as head coach of the NFL's San Francisco Forty-Niners, winning the Super Bowl in 1990. He was replaced at Cornell in 1977 by Bob Blackman, the former head coach at Dartmouth, who claimed as soon as he arrived that "other Ivy schools place more emphasis on athletics in admissions decisions," and expressed hope that Cornell would admit "average students who are blue chip athletes."[131]

Hockey is another story. From 1900 to 1947 the Cornell Hockey Club, then Team, played on frozen Beebe Lake, or at opponents' out-of-town rinks. When Beebe wasn't frozen, there was no practice and no game. Frustrated after the war by futile attempts to flood and freeze lower alumni field, the university dropped intercollegiate hockey competition from 1947 until 1957, when Lynah Rink was constructed. For the next five years, Paul Patten, an assistant football coach, who had been a hockey coach at St. Lawrence, rebuilt a competitive Cornell sextet. With the Canadian goalie Laing Kennedy '63 patrolling the nets, Cornell beat Harvard 2–1 at Lynah in 1962, the Crimson's first Ivy defeat in two seasons. It was the turning point for Cornell hockey, allowing the Big Red to finish second in the Ivies that year. And then Ned Harkness arrived.

A native of Ottawa, Canada, Harkness was hired as hockey coach in 1963 after thirteen years as hockey and lacrosse coach at RPI. By 1966, Harkness's uncanny ability to recruit superb Canadian players, including the legendary goalie Ken Dryden '69, led to Cornell's first Ivy League hockey championship. That same year Harkness took over as lacrosse head coach and turned the team's previous year's 4–7 record to 12–0 and another Ivy title. His achievements were Promethean. In the next four years, Harkness hockey teams won two NCAA

Ken Dryden '69, Cornell's greatest goalie, was also an all-star in the National Hockey League. (Cornell Athletics)

national championships. On the way, the 1967–68 teams won twenty-three consecutive victories, and in 1970 Cornell became the first major college hockey team in the post–World War II period to go through an entire regular season of twenty-four games undefeated and then to win its next five for the NCAA title. And from 1966 to 1968 Harkness's lacrosse team was 35–1. In 1969, Richie Moran, a coach at Elmont High School on Long Island, took over lacrosse from Harkness and made it the second front of Cornell's championship sports with a record of 55–11 in his first five years and a 16–0 record and a national title in '75–76.

Harkness became the head coach of the Detroit Red Wings in 1970, telling the *Sun*, "Cornell has been good to me. There is no finer place in the world."[132] He forever transformed the grim winters of Ithaca, filling Lynah with over thirty-eight hundred festive, screaming students and excited townspeople for every hockey game. There was no better proof of hockey's place in Cornell life than the angry letter from three math professors, Carl Herz '50, Jack Kiefer, and Paul Olum, to Robert Kane in 1968:

151

We are fed up with futile waits on line to buy tickets to Cornell hockey games. . . . Two of us arrived for the reserved seat sale two hours before the box office was open only to find that all tickets had been sold two hours before. . . . It strikes us as absurd that faculty members should be asked to stand on line for several hours in order to get hockey tickets. . . . Under the present policy there is no discrimination between the Cornell faculty and the general, non-student public. This strikes us as completely unreasonable.[133]

The architect of postwar athletics at Cornell, Kane retired in 1976 to devote full time to the United States Olympic Committee, where he was executive vice president, soon to be president. A native Ithacan, Kane had emerged as a star sprinter on Cornell's track team, establishing in 1934 a university record for the 200-meter dash. A handsome, well-dressed, and articulate man, he became an assistant to athletic director James Lynah '05 in 1939, and when Lynah left for wartime service with the National Defense Commission, Kane became acting athletic director. It was in that position that he made the crucial call in the legendary "fifth down" 1940 football game with Dartmouth. Reviewing films of the game, he realized that Cornell's winning touchdown in the 7–3 game was scored on an illegal fifth down. Kane offered the victory to Dartmouth, which accepted it. In 1943 he formally became Lynah's successor, and over the next thirty-three years presided over the renaissance of Cornell sports with $9 million spent on new facilities alone, the post–World War II glory years of football, and the emergence of hockey in the 1960s.

Kane's last years at Cornell were difficult, however, convinced as he was that student radicals in the University Senate, which had some jurisdiction over intramural and intercollegiate sports, were intent on a "siege of athletics." In the 1970s, Senate committees opposed the mandatory two-year physical education requirement and complained about large athletic budget deficits. Kane would later write that he had little time to conduct the business of the department "under the constant surveillance and the witness-stand appearances that went on week after week, month after month."[134]

Kane sensed that the persistent criticism created a widespread perception that Cornell "was an exceedingly poor place to coach, about the poorest in the league, and it had all been brought on by our own hari-kari tendencies." He was most upset that, in this trying period, "we weren't defended by anybody."[135] Not only did Corson not rally to his support, but he, too, demanded an end to athletics' annual budget deficits, running as high as $90,000 some years.

During the financially tense 1970s, Kane eliminated support for four sports entirely: rifle, skiing, sailing, and squash. His coaches fought back, through their elected spokesman, rowing coach Todd Jesdale '61, MA '69, ridiculing Senate attacks that "come not from need but from the whimsy of a political body subject to the irregular influence of a few fretful students."[136] Meanwhile,

Kane tried to play off the alumni and trustees against the Senate and Corson. Kane, who had established an alumni-based endowment fund for athletics that surpassed a million dollars, approved the 1975 visit of Richie Moran and Jesdale's crew replacement, Doug Neil, to trustee chair Robert Purcell in his New York City office. Corson later commented that "the two coaches going to talk to Mr. Purcell came about as close to being a totally inappropriate action as it was possible to come without causing a lot of trouble."[137]

The trustees were in a difficult bind, deeply grateful for Corson's campus leadership, while appreciative of Kane's role on the local and national sporting scene. An ad hoc trustee subcommittee on athletics set up in 1974, chaired by trustee Samuel Pierce '47, JD '49, the African American attorney, former Cornell football player, and future Reagan secretary of housing and urban development, praised Cornell's athletic program as "one of the best in the country" and as "serving as a focal point for bringing the diverse elements of the Cornell community together." However, the committee recommended that the accumulated deficit of $346,228 be written off, that Athletics no longer be seen as an enterprise unit, required to pay for itself, but be funded by annual appropriation, and that it bring down its costs, as the president had insisted.[138]

The final showdown occurred in the 1976 search for Kane's replacement as athletics director. The alumni, on their own, appointed a search committee with trustee Bob Engel '53 as chairman, while Corson appointed the official search committee with English professor and Cornell super sports fan M. H. Abrams as chairman. Corson's committee recommended Richard Schultz, from the University of Iowa, and as Corson remembers, the alumni committee supported a former Baltimore Colts football great who "would have been chewed to pieces here." Peace prevailed when the alums invited the president to the Cornell Club in New York City and pledged "to support athletics at Cornell no matter whom I chose."[139] Corson chose Schultz, and then, with the death of the Senate in 1977, the "siege of athletics" came to an end.

———————

IN 1976, TO COMMEMORATE the two hundredth birthday of the United States, Cornell broke with tradition. For the first time in its history, a faculty member delivered the commencement address. On a beautiful day in May, shortly after the trustees accepted Dale Corson's request to begin a search for his replacement, Walter LaFeber, the Marie Underhill Noll Professor of American History, told thirty-two hundred graduates, their parents, faculty, administrators, and guests that the founders of Cornell shared with the founders of the nation a "common commitment, indeed a common passion," to change individual lives and improve society. This goal, he noted, had forced the university to assume the role of "midwife when revolutionary ideas enter an un-revolutionary society." Tensions remained, but LaFeber insisted that Cornell had no choice but to serve as a battleground. To disavow such a role was to abandon responsibility and to risk "losing our own future."[140]

Cornell did not—and could not—turn its back on its responsibility to defend rational discourse and the power of ideas, to extend rights to new social classes, even at a time in which some of the demands placed upon it were unreasonable, the political costs were great, violence was threatened, alumni and friends were alienated, and the institution's financial resources were limited. The Glee Club at commencement may well have been premature when it celebrated in song the light "when the sun riseth, even a morning without clouds." But such a day, indeed, many such days, lay ahead.

5 | Race at Cornell

When Fred Parris '62, a black Cornell undergraduate, appeared on stage singing with the Glee Club at the 1959 Christmas concert in Indianapolis, one audience member and his wife walked out of the room. The audience member was Harry V. Wade '26, CEO of the Standard Life Insurance Company and a six-year member of the Cornell University Trustee Council. President of the city's Cornell Club, Wade had sent word to Professor Thomas Sokol, the director of the Glee Club, earlier that afternoon "that it might be better if Parris went to a movie." If he didn't, Wade noted, after the concert "a local debutante might end up dancing with a Negro Glee Club member at a Cornell sponsored event."[1] Sokol polled the officers of the Glee Club, and they decided that unless all their members sang, none would perform. Six years later, Wade was still angry over the incident, writing to Nicholas Noyes '06, fellow Cornellian and fellow first citizen of Indianapolis (with a carbon copy to President Perkins): "We'll be damned if we want to go to a lot of fuss and trouble to entertain the Glee Club and have them show up with a Sambo in the front row. . . . As far as I am concerned they can have the front row consist of nothing but chimpanzees but I sure don't want them out here in Indianapolis as we are not running that kind of a zoo." Recognizing, no doubt, that these were the attitudes of many in America, even in 1965, Perkins wrote atop his copy of Wade's letter, "Who's this awful man!"[2]

Like the national struggle itself, the civil rights era at Cornell began with an integrationist vision, to be overtaken later in the decade by separatist black power ideals. Martin Luther King Jr. told a Bailey Hall audience of over twenty-six hundred people in April 1961 that "it is human dignity which we are struggling for in the South; and we still have a long, long way to go."[3] He urged white Cornell students to join the "freedom riders" that summer at sit-ins at segregated facilities in Mississippi. The previous year the Executive Board of Student Government had first approved and then, reversing itself, declined to support picketing in front of Ithaca's Woolworth store, for fear that the demonstration would be linked in the public mind to the Malott riots of 1958.

A month after King's visit, a substantial number of Cornell students, joined by students from Ithaca College and Ithaca High School, picketed the Greyhound Bus terminal, demanding that the company desegregate its facilities in the South. That summer Cornellians would, in fact, make up the single largest collegiate group of freedom riders, according to the historian Raymond Arsenault. More than a dozen Cornell students were jailed in Jackson, Mississippi, for sitting in the segregated facilities of the city's railroad terminal. To be sure, not all Cornellians shared those ideals. The *Daily Sun* gave its entire editorial page, two days running, to an essay, "Civil Rights: Too Far and Too Fast," from a recent graduate, Stephen Schleck '59: "I am inclined to believe that we are going too far and too fast, and that continued agitation at this point, without regard for established institutions . . . will not lead to harmonious race relations. . . . The American negro is on the whole a member of an environmentally inferior sub-culture, and cultures (although not individuals) change very slowly."[4]

Michael Schwerner, a member of the class of 1961, who heard King in Bailey Hall, was murdered in a widely publicized case near Philadelphia, Mississippi, with fellow civil rights workers Andrew Goodman, whose parents were both Cornell graduates, and James Chaney in the summer of 1964 as they tried to register black voters. That same year, after what the *Sun* described as "the most highly charged campus debate in years,"[5] students approved, 2,514 for and 1,984 against, a grant of $1,000 of Student Government funds to a Cornell group advised by Professor Douglas Dowd of Economics, aiding black voter registration and poll watching in Fayette County, Tennessee.

Cornell's new president was changing the racial face of Cornell and the Ivy League. In the January 1963 press conference introducing him to the campus community, Perkins telegraphed his intentions by singling out efforts at Swarthmore, where his daughter was a senior, to bring more black students to campus. His commitment to racial equality was a part of his family's heritage. He told Keith Johnson '56 in an interview in 1994 that his mother had once taken him to their maid's home in Philadelphia, and "we were appalled at the circumstances under which she lived. It was absolutely another world. . . . I was sensitized to the fact that the blacks had been given a raw deal." So it was that Perkins devoted many years as a trustee of the United Negro College Fund. When he came to Cornell as president, he discovered that the university stood aloof from the civil rights revolution, which was forever changing that world of his childhood: "The universities like the Ivy League and like Cornell really lived in a world that did not see the inevitable implication of this basic drift towards concern for the equality of opportunity . . . they were living in a dream world. . . . They had to accommodate minority students; they had to set up special programs."[6]

Perkins, with his Quaker convictions, was not alone in thinking that Cornell should involve itself in the civil rights struggle. Several weeks into his presidency, he received a letter from Dale Rogers Marshall '59, the daughter of William Rogers, JD '37, Cornell trustee, Eisenhower attorney general (and future Nixon secretary of state). She had just read Morris Bishop's history of Cornell, published the previous year, and had been moved by Andrew Dickson White's 1862 hope that Cornell would be open to all regardless of sex or color. A future college president (of Wheaton) and Cornell trustee herself, she urged Perkins to "make sure that Cornell takes the leadership in seeking out qualified minority group students."[7]

That is exactly what Perkins did. His initiative was announced that December with the appointment of a Committee on Disadvantaged Students, chaired by Vice President for Student Affairs John Summerskill, the "hero" of 1958. Unlike Perkins's biology reforms and the six-year PhD, this project was implemented unilaterally by the president without faculty approval. The committee—its faculty members were Ben Nichols '41, MEN '49, of Engineering; Al Silverman, Physics; Walter Slatoff, English; Robert Smock, Pomology; and Gordon Varg, Education—was charged to "recommend and initiate programs through which Cornell could make a larger contribution to the education of qualified students who have been disadvantaged by their cultural, economic, and educational environments."[8] When Summerskill left Cornell in 1966 to become president of San Francisco State University, he was replaced as chair for a short while by Dean Robert Beck '42, MED '52, PhD '52, of the Hotel School, and then by Douglas Dowd. The committee's name changed as well that year, to the Committee on Special Educational Projects (COSEP). Providing continuity to the committee throughout Perkins's presidency was its administrative director, Gloria Joseph, PhD '67, a black graduate student in educational psychology and civil rights activist, also serving as assistant dean of students.

From an average of three or four black students entering a year—all middle class and some from abroad—in a class of twenty-four hundred, COSEP raised the numbers to twenty in 1964, thirty-five in 1965, forty-nine in 1966, sixty-seven in 1967, and ninety-four in 1968, most of them from northern ghettos or the South. Student recruitment was facilitated by two referral organizations, the National Scholarship Services for Negro Students and the Cooperative Program for Educational Opportunity, as well as through visits to predominantly black high schools by the newly hired admissions officer, Lincoln Lewis '64, MBA '66. In selecting the students, COSEP paid less attention to SAT scores, roughly 100 points below the overall Cornell medians, than to letters of recommendation from secondary school counselors and teachers and to students' own application essays. A mark of COSEP's success was the formation in the fall of 1966 of a new organization by and for black students. The Afro-American Society (AAS) sought "to discuss and disseminate to the Cornell community information about the cultural heritage of the Negro and his problems in society today."[9]

Most of the COSEP students were admitted to the endowed colleges, with by far the largest number entering the College of Arts and Sciences. Providing financial aid to support these students was made easier by a Rockefeller Foundation grant of $250,000 in April 1967, which supplemented the money that came from the president's special funds. By the end of the decade Cornell was dramatically ahead of the rest of the Ivy League in spending on minority students, providing 52 percent of its freshman financial aid to COSEP minority students. Brown University provided 29 percent of its freshman aid to students of color, Dartmouth 30 percent, Harvard 15 percent, Penn 22 percent, Princeton 33 percent, and Yale 21 percent.

The university's new concern with race took other forms as well. The president urged the Graduate School "to consider methods by which the number of Afro-American graduate students at Cornell can be increased." He wrote the personnel director about the possibility of having 4 percent of Cornell's work force be black because "the black population in greater Ithaca was approximately 4 percent of the total population."[10] A University Committee on Human Rights with power to investigate discrimination on campus was created in 1964, to which Frank Long, vice president for research, reported that "Cornell has one negro now on the teaching staff. He is a lecturer who is simultaneously a graduate student and Arts and Sciences has hired a Negro assistant professor for fall 1965."[11] For several summers an "Upward Bound" program with federal funding brought forty high school students from East Harlem to campus for an intensive six-week academic program, and CURW brought fifty second- and third-graders from Harlem to participate in recreational and educational camp activities with the children of their Ithaca host families.

The presence of several hundred black students on campus created problems for the fraternity and sorority system, which had recently been criticized for discrimination against Jewish students. A prohibition against any discrimination in membership selection that emerged in the early 1960s was finally passed by the trustees in the summer of 1967. The university's vigorous implementation of the new procedures was criticized by some. A New Jersey alumnus complained to Perkins about fraternities being "badgered" by the university. "If you do not object to living with other races that is your privilege, but if you are told that you MUST this will create dislikes rather than eliminate them, in the future." A president of one of the houses anonymously told the *Sun*: "My idea of a fraternity would go down the drain if we let a Negro in. Could you bring your parents over to meet him?"[12] Discriminatory practices persisted in some chapters. Phi Delta Theta was put on social probation in 1966 for charging blacks admission to a party while allowing whites in free. The *Sun* described a black freshman being informed by the rush chairman and president of "Fraternity

X" that they were taking no blacks that year. "They negotiated a deal with the student in which the fraternity agreed to rush Negroes even though they would not be taking any."

Black students were themselves divided on how to relate to the fraternities. When the Interfraternity Council (IFC) president, Samuel "Sandy" R. Berger '67 (future Clinton national security adviser), tried to dispel claims about discrimination against blacks by launching a recruitment campaign in 1967, Tom Jones '69, MRP '72, a member of the predominantly Jewish fraternity Zeta Beta Tau, called on black freshmen, at a meeting of the AAS, to spurn rushing, citing "the refusal of fraternities and sororities to accept Negroes as they are." One black student was quoted by the *Sun* as claiming that "he would like to rush but saying so would result in castigation from the rest of the Negroes present." The next day, an ad hoc group of thirty-five black freshmen and upperclassmen, not connected to the AAS, "putting aside their skepticism," voted not to abstain from rushing "in the interests of racial harmony, though they were prepared to take more radical measures if they detected discrimination."[13]

The split between integrationists and separatists within the black student community was reflected in the clashing voices of the black activists who spoke on campus. While King appeared only once, the moderate head of the Congress for Racial Equality (CORE), James L. Farmer, was a frequent visitor to campus. Many more black nationalists spoke at Cornell. The playwright Leroi Jones labeled blacks who tried to deny their color and culture "traitors and hypocrites." Black Panther chairman Bobby Seale unexpectedly spoke more about community action programs and free public services than guns. Malcolm X appeared in a contentious and tense debate with Farmer, titled "Separation versus Integration." Farmer reminded his audience that blacks "are Americans. . . . This is our country as much as it is white America." Denouncing Farmer as an "Uncle Tom," Malcolm X called for total black separation from white America, even for moving into uninhabited areas in the West.[14]

Stokely Carmichael, the head of the Student Non-Violent Coordinating Committee (SNCC) and along with Charles Hamilton of Columbia University, the popularizer of the notion of "black power," was brought to Ithaca in 1967 to headline a "soul of blackness" week at Cornell. Billed as "the first of its kind on any campus in the country," the joint AAS/IFC project sought to expose the university to "the new direction in civil rights movements . . . the awareness of blackness as a positive entity." Carmichael told a packed Bailey Hall that the alliance between blacks and fraternities "used our name, we used their money," but that it was "neither realistic nor desirable to assimilate Negroes into the white middle class. We must not abolish the black community, but must attain its liberation while maintaining its culture."[15]

CARMICHAEL'S BLACK POWER ideals were championed by the leadership of the AAS, repudiating the integrationist vision of the first set of COSEP students. Earl M. Armstrong '69, one of the AAS founders, speculated, "I think they want to get us into this 'mainstream' thing. They figure that after four years up here in this isolated world, you'll go back and fall into your $20,000-a-year job and never think twice." Edward Whitfield agreed. Black students rejected liberals who "would rather have us as Ralph Bunches going through college than Malcolm Xes in the streets."[16] Originally open to black and white students, the AAS quickly excluded white students, except by special permission. An incident in January 1968 further encouraged separatist attitudes.

Alicia Scott, a black freshman, was removed from her room in Balch Hall during exam period and taken to Sage Hospital after alleged violations of dormitory rules. She was accused of fighting with white students who wanted her to turn down the volume of her music. After examination by a psychologist and psychiatrist, she was deemed "emotionally unstable" and put on a medical leave of absence. The AAS staged what a university spokesman described as a "mild sit-in" at the office of Mark Barlow Jr., EDD '62, vice president for student affairs, demanding that Scott be seen by a black therapist. The university arranged for another examination during intersession at Cornell's New York Hospital, where a white psychiatrist found Scott "to be sane" and not in need of medical leave.[17] Stuart M. Brown Jr. '37, PhD '42, dean of Arts and Sciences, revoked the required leave and put aside the appeal for an interview with a black doctor as no longer necessary.

Two weeks later the AAS and the activist Irene Jennie Smalls '71 requested that the office of the dean of students set up a cooperative residence for black women undergraduates like Elmwood House, a university-owned building at 409 Elmwood Avenue in Collegetown, reserved for black men in 1966. "Sisters," as an undergraduate put it, "just couldn't live in the dormitory context," with the constant obligation to share "one's white corridor-mates' values." Stories were told of black women being accused of smoking marijuana in their rooms, when the "sweet pungent odors" that emerged from behind closed doors turned out to be the smell of burned pressing oil used in hair straightening.[18] Decrying what it saw as the intolerably hostile atmosphere, the AAS declared:

> The present dormitory system, being white in orientation and administration, places the burden of adjustment to communal standards and value, i.e. white middle class, on the black coed and in so doing implies that the cultural background of these black coeds is inferior and not worthy of consideration. One aspect of the new consciousness of blacks today as represented by "Black Power" is a heightened sense of pride in self and race. Any implication of inferiority on blackness, as the dorm system does indeed make, is a direct affront to black people.[19]

The university purchased a three-story house at 208 Dearborn Place on North Campus, near Triphammer Road; twelve black women undergraduates moved in during April 1968. They named their co-op Wari House, *wari* meaning "home" in Swahili. After contemplating a charge of residential racial segregation, the New York State Civil Liberties Union turned away from the issue, and the university defended its action with the words of Ruth Darling, the assistant dean of students: "There has been a great deal of discrimination against blacks in the past, and you have to do more than just say blacks should have an equal chance. You have to move to positive discrimination."[20]

That same semester, Michael McPhelin, a visiting professor in the Economics Department, from Atando University in the Philippines, taught the second part of his year-long course, "Economic Development," Economics 103. A Catholic priest as well as an economist, McPhelin had 338 students in the class, including 8 black students. Three of them, Bert Cooper, Marshall John Garner, and Robert D. Rone, were leaders of the more militant wing of the AAS. Garner was considered by his peers as "the intellectual as well as the spiritual leader of our movement."[21] A student of electrical engineering, from an all-black inner-city school in Dayton, Ohio, Garner became convinced that McPhelin was a racist, who emphasized economic development as found only in European civilization and the product of the rational values and behavior patterns of temperate versus tropical cultures. Particularly upsetting was McPhelin's lecture on March 19, in which he described inner-city poor people as "unambitious, their poverty self-perpetuating, their children's games, sickly and perverted, stressing cunning and survival, as in the jungle. . . . There are no pleasures except those satisfying their baser tastes."[22]

Garner raised a question in the lecture, challenging McPhelin, which the professor ignored. At the end of the class he apologized to Garner for ignoring his question. When Garner insisted a private apology was not enough, McPhelin apologized to the entire class on March 21, the last lecture before the spring recess. Meanwhile, Cooper, Garner, and Rone complained to Vice President Barlow, whose office sent them to Dean Brown, who made an appointment after the break on April 2 for the students to meet with Tom Davis, the chairman of Economics. After hearing their demands that McPhelin be dismissed for incompetence and reprimanded publicly as a racist, Davis told the students that "nothing will be done." They stormed out of his office. Two days later, when McPhelin refused to read a statement, prepared by the trio, acknowledging his racism, insisting that he, McPhelin, "runs the show," Garner read it to the class. McPhelin invited the students to sing "The Star-Spangled Banner" to drown out Garner and dismissed the class amid general disorder.[23]

The three complainants then went to Willard Straight Hall and within minutes emerged with some sixty members of the AAS, who marched with them to the Economics Department's two offices in Goldwin Smith Hall. The protesters closed the offices around 10:30 a.m., letting the secretaries leave, while insisting that Davis remain until their demands for McPhelin's dismissal were met. Some scuffling occurred when occupying students who had left to get food were met on returning by plainclothes members of the university police. No effort was made after that by the police to enter the department offices. The crisis was defused in late afternoon with the arrival of Provost Corson, who negotiated an agreement by which the Economics Department would pay the expenses for an outside lecturer, "of the [African American] Society's choosing," to speak to the class.[24] Corson also pledged to create a special commission that would hold hearings and issue a report by the end of April.

That night Martin Luther King Jr. was assassinated. A large group of black students took over the student radio station, WVBR, to announce on air that "no longer can black people dream, no longer can black people have faith in this white racist society."[25] Fires were set in Collegetown, at Triangle Book Store, and Lyon Tower. The chapel of Anabel Taylor Hall was destroyed by flames. A memorial service for King, sponsored by Cornell United Religious Work, was held the next day in Bailey Hall, with over two thousand in attendance, some seated in areas marked "for blacks only." Classes were canceled four days later, April 9, in observance of King's funeral. At a packed Barton Hall teach-in that night, Perkins and seven professors spoke for three hours and forty minutes about "white racism."

Professor Robin Williams of Sociology, an expert on race relations, chaired the nine-person special commission of faculty, administrators, and three students looking into the McPhelin affair, even as the Cornell Chapter of the American Association of University Professors condemned it as violating McPhelin's right to be judged "by his peers and only by peers."[26] The commission's report, published on April 26, exonerated the visiting professor from accusations of overt racism and rejected demands for his dismissal. "It is our conclusion that Professor McPhelin was not aware of the full cognitive and evaluative interpretation to which his remarks were subject when heard by black American students in 1968 and, more specifically, that he saw no grounds for anticipating the depth and intensity of the response actually encountered."[27] Whether this reflected a general cultural as well as local Cornell "institutional" racism was debated in the report, a position articulated strongly by Gloria Joseph. There was division on the commission as well as to whether the demands of Garner and his allies threatened McPhelin's academic freedom.

Sidestepping that issue, the commission did condemn the students' occupation of the Economics Department, even though Davis had changed his story, no longer feeling that he had been held "hostage." The commissioners recommended, however, that university administrators not punish the students for their actions. A week later Cooper, Garner, and Rone formally appealed to Dean Stuart Brown to dismiss McPhelin "on grounds of incompetence."

Brown declined to take any action against McPhelin, a position supported by Perkins. The three petitioners were disappointed, but neither they, nor members of the AAS, seemed angry. Provost Corson and Dean of the Faculty Robert Miller, PhD '48, had accepted the commission's recommendation that no action be taken against the students, and the university had virtually said they were right in their accusations of "institutional racism." After insisting on the sanctity of faculty academic freedom, the dean of Arts and Sciences wrote:

> It does not follow that the students have no grievance, whether or not one wants to identify the grievance as "racism." On the evidence available to me, I am not prepared to say that he is guilty of "racism," using "racism" with all of its pejorative force. But neither am I prepared to say that he is innocent of it. In some sense of "racist," McPhelin and I and most whites are racists in some degree. We are all in some degree ignorant of and insensitive to the plight of black people everywhere all around the world. And our ignorance and indifference are so combined as to amount in practice to unconscious and well-meaning arrogance and patronage. Black students at Cornell confront this kind of racism both in and out of class, both in their teachers and their fellow students in a massive way. Cooper, Garner and Rone have all affirmed that this is what they as blacks confront.[28]

Perkins wrote that month to the architect Phil Will '28, in Chicago, one of the more liberal trustees, that "it looks as if we will not only get through the year unscathed but we have opened up a constructive set of discussions with our Negro students."[29]

Sympathetic faculty and members of the AAS had begun conceptualizing what they called an "Afro-American Students Study Program" that semester. The McPhelin affair, it seemed to them and others in the university, underscored the need for it. The program would expand the university's 1967 offerings on black subjects beyond Sindler and Hacker's course "The Negro in American Politics and Society" and the visiting black writer Julian Mayfield's seminar at the Society for the Humanities, "Negro Writers of the Twentieth Century." Most important, implicit in these discussions between white faculty and eager students was the assumption of student ownership of the program's content and structure.

The program was conceived at a meeting on March 9, 1968, at 320 Wait Avenue, the old Music building, near the end of Triphammer Road, which was then the home of Cornell's Center for Research in Education. Selected faculty and students had been invited by Ben Nichols, the chairman of the Executive Committee, whose invitation embraced the 1960s ideal of the social justice university. The students of AAS had raised questions that many faculty share, he wrote: "Is it possible to incorporate into the regular academic structure of undergraduate education studies that are directly relevant to current problems of American society? Further is it possible to structure these studies so that they involve not only close analysis of a specific economic, political and social issue but, in addition, aim at producing concrete proposals for action"?[30] The founding group of some ten students and ten faculty, including Dan McCall, Chandler Morse, Douglas Dowd, Walter Slatoff, and Julian Mayfield, plus two administrators, Assistant Dean of Students Gloria Joseph and Assistant to the Vice President of Student Affairs (and Female Studies activist) Sheila Tobias, came up with ten possible courses, whose topics ranged from "Black History in America" to "Urban Ghetto Sociology and Control" and "The Third Stream Era in Black Music." At these late March and early April meetings much discussion was focused on claims from black students who took Mayfield's seminar "that white students are a disruptive influence in a class devoted to aspects of the black experience. They therefore want the courses they are proposing to be for black students only." A consensus emerged that "courses designed for and open exclusively to black students is worthy of experimental trial," although given Cornell's faculty they would be offered by white professors.[31]

The two courses quickly readied for fall 1968, Dowd's "The Economic Development of the Ghetto" and McCall's "Black Literature," needed approval from the Educational Policy Committee (EPC) of the Arts College. Nichols and Tom Jones met with the committee in late April to provide details on the new initiative. Jones, the son of two black professionals, an industrial physicist and a schoolteacher, and who had been elected president of his Cornell freshman class, was becoming more militantly separatist. Afro-American Studies would become his passion. With only History professor Donald Kagan dissenting, the EPC approved the program's courses "so long as the criteria of admission would not exclude white students on grounds of their color."[32] A week later Dowd and McCall met with the committee. Both acknowledged that while black students would be given preference for admission, they did not intend to have an all-black class. Both declined, however, to sign an agreement that they would admit at least one white student.

In mid-May, Dean Brown sent a memo to all members of the Arts College faculty entitled "To still the rumors and allay the fear." The college, he wrote, would insist that the department chair and teacher of the course provide assurances that these courses were not "for black students only."[33] In the fall Dowd interviewed seventy applicants for his course, thirty-five of whom were black. He accepted fifteen black students and four white students. Some black students, including Tom Jones, refused to take the course under these conditions; "The Economic Development of the Ghetto" ended up with twelve black students and one white student. Dowd announced that if blacks believed the white student would disrupt the class, he would try to have him removed. The black students took the matter to the Afro-American Society, which narrowly voted to let the white student stay. Professor McCall had twelve black students in his class and five white students.

That summer, Paul DuBois, a black graduate student in Government, and occasional consultant to Perkins on campus black affairs, conceived what he labeled "an Afro-American Studies Program." "It would," he wrote, "carry forward the spirit of last semester's faculty-student discussions on courses dealing with the Afro-American experience."[34] With some black student friends in Ithaca for the summer and some liberal faculty, he assembled a "Cornell Ad Hoc Committee for African-American Studies." The university found money to fund trips by DuBois and Professor Chandler Morse to Boston- and Chicago-area universities to research Afro-American studies programs.

On August 1, DuBois submitted a detailed proposal to Perkins, Corson, and the deans of each Cornell college on behalf of the ad hoc committee. It called for a scholarly "action oriented" program, organized much like the Asian Studies Program. Students who took courses in the Afro-American experience and culture could receive a degree in Afro-American Studies from the college or graduate field in which they were enrolled. Where the program would fit into the university's structure was left up in the air, nor was there any mention of restricting student eligibility to take these classes. "Special funding" for the program and the appointment of a program director, even if interim, was urgent. "The time for Committee discussions is past; the time for action is now."[35]

The university accepted DuBois's proposal on September 5. Perkins provided $15,000 for the program and appointed the economist Chandler Morse as acting director. In October, Robert Purcell '32, LLB '35, chairman of the board of trustees, gave $1 million to the Afro-American Studies Program, to be used over the next five years. A legal officer for railroads and then president and CEO of an investment company, whose most important client was the Rockefeller family, Purcell would play a crucial role in the events of 1968 and 1969. Like Corson, Purcell always advised against calling local or state police onto campus. All they would do, he told Corson, was "beat people down."[36]

Tom Jones and other students in the AAS, which had played no role in planning the program, were unhappy with its embrace by the university. As bothersome as the white acting director was, even more upsetting was the parallel made to Asian Studies and the assumption that the program would be woven into, and thus buried within, traditional university structures. Nevertheless, the AAS leadership decided to join the program's "Advisory Committee," chaired by Morse, which had six faculty, two deans, and eight black students. This committee moved too deliberately for a group of militants who took over its November meeting, declaring "we can no longer deal with the antagonists . . . there can be no program . . . but rather an Institute run by black students." According to the "concerned black students," a "program" was insufficient; they wanted nothing less than an autonomous "new college to be run for and by black students."[37]

The coup took place December 6. Six of the black students on Morse's committee entered 320 Wait Avenue, where the program had been given several offices, and gave the two white employees and one white professor in the building three minutes to leave. A note was then posted on the door that the building was restricted to members of the "Afro-American Institute." Joined by some forty other students from AAS, the militants allowed no white members of the Advisory Committee into the building except Professor Morse, whom Garner allowed to enter to give an accounting of the funds spent by the committee. A *Sun* reporter was knocked down by a black student outside the building.

The occupying students demanded that Perkins and Corson meet with them at 320 Wait on December 9. Because Perkins was in bed with the flu, Corson came, along with Chandler Morse. Throughout the meeting, the Sociology graduate student, six-foot-six Harry Edwards, MA '66, PhD '73, organizer of the boycott by black athletes at the 1968 Olympic Games, stood by the door so they couldn't leave. The students demanded that Perkins sign within two days a charter creating a new college, run by black students, which would admit students, hire and fire faculty, and begin operating on February 1, 1969. Additional demands called for immediately designating dining at the Straight's Elmhirst Room for the exclusive use of black students and hiring a black psychiatrist. In a statement published in the *Daily Sun* defending "the College of Afro-American Studies," the AAS proclaimed "the right of black people to define the kind of institution most appropriate for them. . . . The issue of who defines is no longer negotiable."[38]

When Perkins and the administration missed the December 11 deadline, mayhem broke out. Several black students, carrying toy guns, upended wastebaskets in Day Hall, then proceeded to Goldwin Smith, where they knocked over candy machines. They proceeded to the Elmhirst Room, which was closing, and demanded to be served. The next day, after Perkins rejected the core demand for a black college—noting that "he could not legally authorize the creation of a College of Afro-American Studies even if he wanted to, and he does not want to"—while agreeing to find a black psychiatrist and a place other than the Elmhirst Room for blacks-only eating, further mayhem ensued.[39] A cart of soft drinks, milk, and rolls provided for the demonstrators outside the president's office was knocked over by students, who then went to Gannett, feigning moans and asking to see a black psychiatrist. From there they walked to the Ivy Room, playing bongos paid for by the university the previous spring and flown up from New York City, dancing on tables, waving toy guns, and upsetting some lunches while chanting "black power" with clenched fists. Then on to Olin, Uris, and the ILR library, where some three thousand books were heaped near the circulation desks, to claims that "they have no relevance to me as a black student."[40] A basketball game was disrupted, a candy machine was overturned in Goldwin Smith, and several students stole pillows from a dormitory lounge. Perkins told the *Sun* that while many on campus "are becoming annoyed, to put it mildly, and wondering how far this is going to go," he had "no desire to constrain these so-called 'exhibitions' as long as they remain peaceful . . . though there is a point they may be detrimental to the morale, sense of stability, and functioning of the University." Charges were brought against seven students, who had knocked over the candy machine and taken the pillows. Meanwhile, some professors at a teach-in angrily criticized Perkins for responding weakly to what they saw as outrageous behavior.[41]

The winter break cooled down the crisis, and the spring semester opened with somewhat less tension. The AAS elected the seemingly more moderate six-year PhD student Edward Whitfield its president, the Garner faction losing some support in the wake of the December excesses. In late December Perkins had appointed his vice provost, College of Agriculture professor Keith Kennedy, chair of a new student-faculty-administration group of fifteen, eight of whom were AAS members. The president wanted the "group" to forge a black studies program with some degree of autonomy and find a director as soon as possible. Enter James Turner, who had been discovered by Jones and Garner at a conference, "Toward the Black University," held at Howard University in mid-November. Still a graduate student in anthropology, the twenty-eight-year-old Turner had led the takeover of a building at Northwestern University, as part of an effort to create a black studies department.

According to Dale Corson, the dean of Northwestern's Graduate School gave Turner a very positive recommendation both as a graduate student and as a responsible leader of protests. Trustee Phil Will told Corson he had seen Turner grilled by TV reporters after the confrontation at Northwestern. Will and his wife "were most impressed by Turner's performance, which was mature, articulate, perceptive and completely principled. . . . On the basis of that performance at least, I would like to see him at Cornell."[42]

Turner visited Cornell in January, which led to an offer of the directorship on January 25. Turner, Tom Jones for the AAS, and Kennedy then conducted intensive negotiations throughout the term, with Turner returning to Ithaca in March. Cornell did not budge on the autonomous black college and proposed an Afro-American Studies Department in the College of Arts and Sciences, which both Turner and Jones rejected. Agreement was finally reached on the model of a center, and announced by Perkins on April 5, two full weeks before the Straight takeover. Turner would become director of the Afro-American Studies Center and "special administrative assistant to the president" as well as an associate professor of Afro-American studies. The university committed $215,000 for the program's first year, 1969–70. Housed at 320 Wait Avenue, the center would report directly to the president, who had the authority to create such units without faculty approval. In a victory for Turner, the center's faculty, recruited and recommended by the director, did not have to be appointed members of an academic department, as was the case with other centers. In a victory for Jones and the AAS, faculty appointments would be reviewed by only three qualified outside scholars in Afro-American Studies until the center had sufficient faculty of its own, and then chosen by a committee, composed of equal numbers of administrators and students selected by the AAS, from a panel of at least fifteen scholars' names submitted by the AAS. Despite the agreement on the center, by semester's end Turner had still not formally accepted its directorship.

This delay, at first a negotiating strategy, then necessitated by the attention-absorbing Straight crisis and its aftermath, was also a by-product of the Hatchett affair. On April 29, Turner had recommended the appointment of the center's first two faculty, J. Congress Mbata and John F. Hatchett. Mbata, a South African educator, antiapartheid activist, and professor of African Studies at Northwestern, was noncontroversial. Hatchett had been a schoolteacher in New York City, a director of NYU's African-American Center, and a graduate student at Columbia. Inquiries by Kennedy revealed serious concerns about him. He had published an article on the opposition to school decentralization with angry denunciations of "the Jews who dominate and control the educational bureaucracy of the New York Public School system . . . a group of people whose entire history should have told them no, this is spiritually and morally wrong." In addition, he had labeled Richard Nixon, Hubert Humphrey, and American Federation of Teachers president Albert Shanker "racist bastards."[43] Turner defended Hatchett, as did the AAS, and also the New York Civil Liberties Union, on the grounds of free speech rights and academic freedom.

When Kennedy discovered that Hatchett's performance on his Columbia comprehensive exams had been unsatisfactory and that he had been dropped from the PhD program, he recommended that Perkins reject the appointment. Four days later, the story appeared in the *New York Times*, and Tom Jones made a speech at Willard Straight, carried on the radio, linking Hatchett's rejection to the still potent power of two Jewish faculty members in the Government Department, Walter Berns and Allan Sindler. On June 1 Turner accepted the Cornell offer, telling the *Daily Sun* that his program had the potential to be "one of the most far-reaching, imaginative, and creative in the country."[44] Robert Purcell wrote to Perkins:

> Tuesday night I saw a television program in which Jim Turner was one of the more active participants. I can see that he will change things at Ithaca in the fall and while he was clearly an activist, I must say that I was impressed by the intelligence which he showed and his approach to the problem. It was also made clear at one point that he thought the struggle of the blacks was their problem and not that of the SDS. Let's keep our fingers crossed that the Turner appointment works out all right. I was both frightened and encouraged by what I saw on television.[45]

THE NEGOTIATIONS IN early 1969 over the nature of the African–American Studies Program took place against a backdrop of general racial tension on campus, ushered in and symbolized by the public humiliation of President Perkins on February 28. Cornell's SDS and the AAS had for some time been demanding that Cornell divest its holdings in companies doing business with South Africa and that Perkins resign as a director of one of them, the Chase Manhattan Bank. Perkins denounced apartheid as "wicked and heinous" but refused to divest, because "the University does not try to tell those people how to run their business as long as they don't tell us how to run our business." Nor would he leave the Chase board, noting that "there isn't a university president in this country who wouldn't swap two or three hundred thousand dollars for that seat. The Chase board has a rich load of foundation and corporation executives."[46] He did agree, however, to speak at a symposium on South Africa, sponsored by the Center for International Studies, featuring an address by New York congressman Allard Lowenstein, on February 28.

Just before the president spoke, an African American student, Eric Evans, commandeered the microphone and told the eight hundred people in Statler Auditorium "that the evening's program would not go on if the audience does not

President Perkins is shoved from the microphone by Gary Patton, at the Statler Auditorium, on February 28, 1969. (Division of Rare and Manuscript Collections of the Cornell University Library)

like Perkins' answers."[47] When the president was allowed to speak, two other African Americans, Gary Patton, an undergraduate, and former student Larry Dickson, mounted the stage, unseen by the president, each carrying a length of wooden two-by-four. Patton approached Perkins from the rear, grabbed him by the coat collar, spun him around, and shoved him away from the microphone. Brandishing his two-by-four, Dickson kept Proctor Lowell George and Safety Division personnel from rescuing the president, who was heard to whisper "You'd better let go of me." Patton released him, and in the ensuing chaos Perkins was able to leave the platform and be escorted home by campus police.

The audience was angered by the actions of Patton and Dickson. SDS saw the incident as a lost opportunity to force the president to defend his South African investment views. An AAS spokesman announced that it had not sanctioned the action and that "we shall as a group move immediately to see that our brother is properly disciplined," though its chairman, Edward Whitfield, added "it is poor reasoning and poor moral arithmetic to equate the suffering, destruction, and oppression of millions of our black brothers with a moment's discomfiture on the part of a university president." After Perkins left, Reverend Gladstone Ntlabati, a visiting South African liberation leader, went to the podium and declared that Perkins should have been allowed to finish. "What happened tonight is against all the principles of what we black people in South Africa believe in."[48] He received a standing ovation.

Perkins, a university administrator noted at the time, "was never the same after he was pulled from the podium at Statler. He had always considered the blacks his friends; evidently, he was deeply shocked and aggrieved by what happened."[49] Ten days later at the Business School's Malott Hall, three Chase Manhattan recruiters were overwhelmed by a largely white group of two hundred SDS students. Barricaded in an office with the dean of students, the dean of the Business School, and Vice President Barlow, the recruiters were not released until university officials agreed to cancel the event.

At a faculty meeting on March 12, which with six hundred present was the largest in the history of the university to that point, Corson berated his colleagues for not speaking out more forcefully about the disruptions at the Statler and Malott. He warned that "the period ahead of us is more critical than any we have ever faced." All the more reason, he claimed, for the faculty to defend "the standards of academic freedom and of scholarly behavior which are commonly held and these must be expressed clearly, publicly and frequently."[50] But the administrators in Day Hall were deeply ambivalent, with Vice President Barlow writing to Perkins,

> In spite of the obvious need to eliminate unacceptable ways of protest, we must understand that the malaise and restlessness among students is real. This malaise can be found in varying degrees among students in numbers far greater than the

few who might participate in a disruptive event. There never has been a protest at Cornell, or probably at any other institution, in which the students were "all wrong." Frequently, their issue is more right than wrong; it is only their style that is often more wrong than right.[51]

The weekend after the faculty meeting, three white students were mugged on the Arts quad. Two were not seriously hurt. A third, Joel H. Klotz '71, MEN '76, was unconscious and in intensive care for more than seventy-two hours. All three described the muggers as blacks of student age. Exactly one month later, on April 17, Chairman Purcell wrote to Perkins about his fears of an occupation of Day Hall. He hoped confidential files were under "lock-box security," and he made clear that given what had happened at other universities, "I do not believe we should contemplate police action to remove the students. . . . I would try to do nothing but keep the rest of the University running until they become either tired, bored, or hungry enough to leave."[52]

The central issue contributing to the racial tension on campus was the semester-long drama of the university's effort to discipline the black students charged with the toy gun disorders of December 12 and 13, specifically for overturning a candy machine in Goldwin Smith and taking cushions from Mary Donlon Hall. Presiding over these judicial proceedings was a new joint faculty-student board, with jurisdiction in cases of student misconduct, created in May 1968 by the faculty on the basis of the Sindler Report's remodeling of the university's legal system. This new Student-Faculty Board on Student Conduct (SFBSC) had four undergraduates, four faculty, and a student chair who voted only to break ties. When it sat on appeals, the board had the same composition, except for a faculty chair who also voted only to break ties. On January 31, 1969, this board, which at the time was all white, formally charged five black students (there had originally been seven, but two had left the university), telling them to appear at the next meeting of the SFBSC on February 13. If the students failed to come, the board noted, it might "proceed to a judgment."[53]

Four days later the five students entered the office of the dean of students and threw their "notices to appear" in the wastebasket. When they did not show up at the board's February 13 meeting, the board rescheduled the hearing for February 27, notifying the students that another failure to appear would have "serious consequences."[54] They failed to appear. A new date, March 13, was set for the hearing, and the board indicated that nonappearance then would lead to automatic suspension. The board vote was 5–2 on the threat of suspension, with the minority claiming that "an attempt to force black students into complying with the conduct board, whose legitimacy has always been tenuous, will only exacerbate if not ensure the destruction of our community."[55]

The whole campus weighed in on the dispute in March. At the large faculty meeting on March 12, a motion supporting free speech on campus and the integrity of the university's judicial system provoked Dowd to suggest re-thinking "the Draconian jurisprudence" of Sindler's structure. Black students "came out of a difficult past . . . so now was hardly the time to demand mech-anistic implementation of the existing disciplinary machinery." The motion passed 306–229, with Sindler apparently "shocked that what he considered a self-evident statement had generated so much controversy." Gloria Joseph also noted that the political activities of the students might "be in opposition to the established rules, regulations, and procedures that exist on the books," but to date "the black students have not, in concert, participated in any radical or violent behavior. Group protests and demonstrations by blacks on this campus have been mild."[56]

The five students did not show up on March 13. Instead, 150 members of the AAS appeared, some of whose members now referred to themselves as the Black Liberation Front. They claimed that the board's charges were a reprisal for political actions by agents of the larger body, the Afro-American Society. The university was "punishing a few for the collective political actions of the many," whose intent was to expose "the legacy of institutionalized racism" at Cornell. "Inevitably there will come situations when the necessities of black people come into conflict with established forms and procedures," the state-ment proclaimed; the all-white board was not competent to handle "cases in-volving political actions by black people."[57] After meeting with the protesters and listening to their claim that the December 12 and 13 actions were minor demonstrations to show black student anger with Perkins's foot-dragging over a black studies program, the SFBSC voted to delay any decision until its parent organization, the Faculty Committee on Student Affairs (FCSA), dealt with the larger jurisdictional and political questions raised by the statement.

A group of black faculty published a statement in the *Sun* the next day. The group included Lisle Carter, former assistant secretary of Health, Education, and Welfare under Kennedy and Johnson, and now a professor of business and public administration and a newly minted vice president for Social and Environmental Studies. The group declared that the pending suspension threatened the creation of the black studies program, which would mean so much to the "mutually ben-eficial relationship (between the races at Cornell) that seems to be emerging." The students had been engaging in "political activity made necessary and inev-itable by the residue of institutionalized racism." They were being offered up as a "ritual sacrifice designed to appease reactionary elements of the community." Acknowledging "the necessity of the University to maintain and preserve an internal judiciary structure," the faculty worried about proceeding "with disci-plinary proceedings in a rigid and mechanical manner."[58]

There were, to be sure, blacks on campus who had a very different take on racial developments at Cornell. Thomas Sowell, a black economist, opposed a black studies program. He rejected a black economics course as well, insisting that black students needed to learn the foundations of economics before they studied Afro-American variations. In June of 1969, Sowell left Cornell; he would emerge in the following decades as one of America's most prominent black conservative intellectuals. Another black conservative who left Cornell that year was Alan Keyes, an undergraduate student in Government, who studied with Allan Bloom. Keyes, who sang with the mostly white Glee Club and dated a white woman, had been threatened with physical violence by AAS members. He transferred to Harvard, where he received his BA and ultimately a doctorate. An assistant secretary of state under President Reagan, he sought the presidential nomination of the Republican Party several times and ran against Barack Obama for a U.S. Senate seat from Illinois.

The intensely anticipated recommendations of the FCSA, drafted mainly by Sindler, were published in the *Sun* on March 26. The committee, which was composed of ten faculty and two students—Art Spitzer '71 and Stephen Wallenstein '69—asked in a forty-five-page report "that students pull back from creating a campus environment of organization endorsed coercion and force which can only lead to a diminution of everyone's freedom." Its most important finding was that "all members of the University community must as individuals bear full responsibility for their actions, whether undertaken on their own initiative or on that of a group to which they belong."[59] Individual responsibility held even if the person's actions were politically motivated. The next day, the SFBSC met and called the six students to appear on April 17.

As the hearing day approached, tension on campus mounted, fueled in part by the university's decision not to bring charges against the white students who had manhandled the Chase Manhattan recruiters at Malott Hall on March 10—a decision perhaps based on fear of provoking SDS, which was rumored to be planning a building takeover if the trustees did not sign on to its Ithaca low-income housing initiative. The existence of a double standard was evident to Walter Slatoff, professor of English and chairman of the Faculty-Student Committee on Human Rights. In an essay in the *Sun*, Slatoff defined "institutional racism" as "this community making a principle of the sanctity of its judicial system only in a case involving black students and black political action."[60] On April 16, the AAS published a statement in the *Sun* blasting the FCSA's failure to acknowledge that the five black students were engaged in permissible political action: "Indeed, it is difficult to imagine a more arrogant, smug, complacent, condescending and totally inflexible document than the one coming out of that Committee. It dismisses all issues raised and proceeds to declare as if by divine fiat, the propriety and legitimacy of the current adjudicative system."[61]

Some sympathizers with the AAS supported its claim that higher law principles justified political action that broke campus rules and regulations. They frequently cited Martin Luther King Jr.'s 1963 *Letter from a Birmingham Jail*, in which he linked his refusal to accept the City of Birmingham's segregation laws to the Christian notion of a higher "natural law" justifying civil disobedience. Other AAS allies noted, however, that even if the comparison of the campus code of conduct to Birmingham's Jim Crow codes could be made, King willingly went to jail for his disobedience. So, too, students should realize, as one letter to the *Sun* put it, that "no civil disobedience is committed without expecting some form of judgment by the whole society. If punishment is to be inflicted, meet it openly, accept it, it will demonstrate sincerity of action and strengthen the movement."[62]

It was not to be. When the five students refused to show up at the SFBSC hearing, the board decided the cases. There were four options: no penalty; a reprimand, involving letters to the parents and deans detailing the seriousness of the misdeeds, which did not become a permanent part of the student's record; suspension from the university for as long as the board determined; and expulsion, which would be a permanent removal. After nearly seven hours of deliberation, the SFBSC announced at 2 a.m. on Friday the eighteenth, more than four months after the actual disruptions had occurred, that the actions of those two days had gone beyond legitimate free speech and political action. The board handed down "reprimands" to three students for overturning the candy machine and acquitted two others in taking cushions from Mary Donlon. In the next hour, eleven false alarms rang out across campus, and at 2:53 a.m. a brick was thrown through the window of the head resident at Wari House. When she looked out the window, she saw a six-foot-high wooden cross, wrapped in cloth, burning on the porch of the black woman's co-op.

THE NEXT MORNING, Saturday, April 19, an unusually chilly day with light snow, fifty to a hundred black men and women students occupied Willard Straight Hall. Angry at what they saw as a run-around in the many months of negotiations between Turner in Chicago and Corson and Perkins in Ithaca over the putative director's salary and the level of funding for Afro-American Studies; furious at the reprimand of the three students by a judicial system that blacks had no role in erecting and that had no blacks on its boards, and for offenses that the AAS construed to be political expression; and now convinced that the university was not thoroughly and seriously enough investigating the cross burning, the students evicted the Straight's forty employees at 5:30 a.m. Having planned since January in the abstract "a building takeover," the AAS concluded the time had come to act; the black students woke and escorted out of the building thirty guests occupying the bedrooms on the Straight's fifth floor, most of them visitors for Cornell's annual Parents Weekend. Parents told of hearing shouts of "The black man has risen," and "We've waited 300 years, and you've got to get out now."[63] By 6:15 all entrances to the building were secured by wire, chains, and rope.

The Campus Police arrived at 6:00 a.m., just as the students, having taken over the campus radio station, WVBR (the Voice of the Big Red), located in the Straight, announced through AAS president Edward Whitfield that they had seized the building because of the university's "racist attitudes" and because it "lacked a program relevant to the black students." At 7 a.m. some fifty SDS members, led by David Burak '67, MFA '80, arrived and formed a picket line outside the building. When several black students arrived, asking to enter the building, the director of the Safety Division, Eugene Dymek, decided to let them, but not the whites, go inside. It remained the police policy throughout the occupation.

Having learned about the takeover on WVBR, a group of some twenty-five white students from Delta Upsilon (DU), the fraternity just down the slope from the Straight, tried to liberate the building by entering through a partially broken ground-level window on the south side of the Straight. The dozen or so who made it in were met by black male students, and after some fighting the whites retreated out the same window. The confrontation resulted in injuries to three whites and one black student and a dramatic escalation of the occupiers' fears of white reprisals. Years later Keith Kennedy noted that "the DU attack was like pouring gasoline on a fire. I could string those DU people up by the ears."[64] Meanwhile, Kennedy, who had been trying unsuccessfully since 7:30 to speak by telephone with Whitfield inside the building, arrived with the university counsel, Neal Stamp '40, JD '42. At 9:15 Dymek, using a bullhorn, demanded the evacuation of the building. A student, Eric Evans, who had transferred to Cornell from West Point, shouted through an open window to the by-now large crowd in front of the Straight, "If any more whites come in . . . you're gonna die here," with "a reign of terror like you've never seen."[65]

The administration had assembled at 8 a.m. in the A. D. White Art Museum in response to rumors of an SDS sympathy takeover of Day Hall. Corson and the dean of the faculty, Robert Miller, were in New York City, so Perkins met with Vice Presidents Mark Barlow Jr. and Steven Muller, PhD '58, Safety Division officials, the faculty trustees, Keith Kennedy, and Stamp. Remembering bitter faculty divisions on the Harvard and Columbia campuses over the police actions of 1968 and concerned with the possible use of police force, they called a Faculty Council meeting for 11 a.m. There were no representatives of student government for the administration to bring in, since there was no student government.

What had begun in 1966 as a humorous Delta Kappa Epsilon campaign "to abolish student government," led by James Patrick Maher '66 and Donald Alford Weadon Jr. '67, gathered support the following year from both SDS students and conservative student leaders like Paul Rahe, columnist for the *Sun* and future professor of political thought. Fed up with what they saw as the ineffectiveness of the Executive Board of Student Government, they all wanted, instead, increased representation on key faculty and faculty-student committees. By the spring of 1968 the students, led by Stephen Hadley '69, future national security adviser to George W. Bush, and Mark Belnick '68, had voted to abolish student government. And so on that Saturday morning a year later, Vice President Barlow had to choose eight students to attend the 11 a.m. Faculty Council meeting. With sentiment running strongly against the use of a court injunction, the augmented council temporarily suspended its meeting at noon, awaiting the AAS demands, which Whitfield had promised to give Kennedy at that hour.

The AAS presented three demands to be met before it would leave the building: the reprimands of the three students had to be nullified; the university had to reopen discussions about housing for the poor in the city of Ithaca with blacks at the table; the university had to conduct a thorough investigation of the cross-burning. In telephone conversations later that afternoon, the students learned from SDS that Ithaca blacks had, in fact, played a large role in the trustees' favorable action about Ithaca housing and replaced the second demand with another, that the university launch a full-scale investigation of the attack by the fraternity students. Meeting at 4 p.m., the Faculty Council reached no clear consensus on what to do; considering itself "a purely advisory group it looked to the administration's executive staff to provide a solution."[66]

On Saturday rumors spread about retaliations against blacks: Wari House was to be burned down, a bomb was going to go off in the Straight; and most ominously, a group of fraternity men, shouting "We're tired of them getting everything they want and doing everything they damn please," was gathering at Noyes Center, armed, drinking, and preparing to drive to the Straight to "get back their building."[67] That night, Whitfield called the president's residence, where Perkins was meeting with Kennedy, Corson, and Dean Miller, both back in Ithaca, and several other members of his executive staff, to say that he heard that eight cars were approaching the Straight with guns. After checking with the Safety Division, Mark Barlow tried to get back to Whitfield to tell him that there was no invasion, but could not reach him.

By then, 10:00 or 10:30 p.m., black students were unloading guns— seventeen rifles and shotguns—at the back door of the Straight. Fearful of being victims of racist violence and moved by the arguments of black power activists like Malcolm X, who urged blacks not to turn the other cheek but to answer violence with violence, the AAS had a stockpile of weapons at 320 Wait Avenue, none of which were brought into the Straight until after the DU "invasion" and the rumors of Saturday afternoon. University administrators knew that the AAS had guns, having been told, according to Corson, by "gun dealers from all over the area." But the university didn't have "anything to worry about," a state policeman had told him, because "it was being done all over the north."[68] Kennedy called Whitfield at 10:30 p.m. about the guns and was told that the occupiers did not trust the campus police to protect them from attacks by armed white students. Assuring Whitfield that no such threat existed, Kennedy urged him to persuade the students to leave or at least to bring the guns out, which he would take away in his own car. Both requests were turned down. As he left Perkins's home, Corson commented, "It's a new ball game."[69]

During the day, the Interfraternity Council, alarmed at the perception of fraternities spread by the rumors, met in emergency session and voted 43–2 to oppose the use of the injunction or intervention by civil authorities, which, the IFC argued, might lead to uncontrollable violence. The fraternity leadership that night cosponsored a Bailey Hall teach-in with SDS, where David Burak promised that SDS would stay outside the Straight "until the University cedes to the black demands."[70] When IFC spokesmen defended the AAS as victims of a breakdown in the university's judicial system, to tumultuous cheering, only Art Spitzer, a student member of the Faculty Committee on Student Activities, defended the judicial process that had led to the reprimands. Perkins arrived at the end of the teach-in, after his crisis team had left his residence, and heard the very clear, if partisan, consensus against "the use of force" that would, everyone assumed, follow an injunction.

After a tense night, with more rumors about bombs, false alarms, and a sniper in Uris Library bell tower (who turned out to be a custodian replacing a burned-out lightbulb), and a real fire at Chi Psi fraternity, Sunday morning saw Perkins's crisis team determined to negotiate a settlement. Even as Ithaca's Mayor Jack Kiely, District Attorney Matt McHugh, and Sheriff Robert Howard contemplated assembling a force of several hundred armed officers in the downtown Woolworth's parking lot, ready if necessary, and even as Stamp did the paperwork on an injunction, if needed, a breakthrough suggestion was made by Dean of the Faculty Miller. If the blacks left the Straight immediately, Miller offered to convene a university faculty meeting on Monday and recommend nullification of the action against the three students involved in the December disturbance. He confirmed his seriousness by telling Whitfield over the phone that if the faculty turned him down he would resign as dean of the faculty.

Miller's proposal was refined throughout the morning, as word spread through campus about the guns at the Straight. Perkins, Corson, and Miller met with members of the Faculty Council, who were very much against the plan, except for Chandler Morse and Ben Nichols. Perkins had phone conversations with board of trustees chairman Purcell and vice chairman Jansen Noyes Jr. '39. What emerged was a sense that the black students would also have to agree to play a part in crafting a new judicial system, acceptable to the whole campus. The president's executive staff chose Keith Kennedy and Steven

Muller, a Cornell PhD and professor of government until his appointment as vice president for public affairs in 1966, to negotiate with the students.

Shortly before noon Kennedy and Muller brought a four-point proposal to Whitfield in the Straight. Dean Miller would ask the faculty to nullify the reprimands Monday; the AAS would participate in the formation of a new judicial system; the university would not prosecute anyone under its judicial system for the Straight seizure, nor, on the other hand, would it interfere with any civil prosecution that might arise. After a discussion of forty-five minutes, Kennedy, Muller, Whitfield, black law student Barry Loncke, JD '70, and former AAS president Robert Jackson '70, PhD '81, arrived at an agreement. The final agreement added three points and redrafted the original fourth point. The university agreed to assume responsibility for all damages to the Straight; provide twenty-four-hour protection for Wari House and 320 Wait Avenue; and investigate the cross-burning and the DU attack and make public its findings. The original final point was given a more positive twist: the university would do its best to secure legal aid for students who might face civil action for the occupation.

When Muller and Kennedy returned to the Straight shortly after 3 p.m., they discussed the theater of exiting the Straight with Whitfield and Zachary Carter '72, the AAS vice chairman. The black students wanted an empty stage, so the 150 SDS pickets were encouraged to leave. Muller and Kennedy wanted the guns left behind, but Whitfield and Carter argued they needed them for protection. Eager to have the students leave quickly, the Cornell negotiators agreed to allow the blacks to depart with their guns unloaded and with breeches open. At 4:10 p.m., thirty-three hours after it began, the occupation of the Straight ended. One hundred and ten students marched out the building, about fifteen carrying rifles, and others clubs and spears made from billiard cues. Fists held high in a black power salute, they were led by Eric Evans and Ed Whitfield, with bandoliers across Evans's chest and a large shotgun in his right hand. The Associated Press photographer Steven Stark, one of the legions of journalists who had flocked to Ithaca over the weekend, exclaimed "Oh, my God, look at those goddamned guns," as he took the picture that would win him a Pulitzer Prize.[71] Tom Jones described the moment:

> We marched out in military formation. We had the sisters in the middle. The brothers with guns were on the outside. We were strategically placed. Different calibers of guns were at different points in the procession, because at all times we were ready. The same maxim applied: "If we die, you are going to die." . . . That moment was a moment in history—armed black people marching out of the student union at Cornell University in military formation! That was a moment that galvanized black people across this nation! . . . We'd taken pains to make sure that the cartridges weren't in the breeches. Uh-huh. I'll admit they were within a flick of being in the breech.[72]

Black students exit the Straight, thirty-three hours after the occupation began. (Division of Rare and Manuscript Collections of the Cornell University Library)

Muller, Kennedy, and the students, who remained silent even as they were cheered, made their way to 320 Wait Avenue, where the agreement was signed on the sidewalk with a line of armed AAS members looming above, on the hillside in front of the building. In a press conference that followed, Muller said the decision to sign the agreement stemmed from the sense "of a growing and imminent threat to life, both black and whites." The students were armed, scared, and "hysterical, and we were afraid scared people would shed blood." The occupiers were, in turn, afraid, Muller added, "that at any moment a mob of police would come running up the hill. They were ready to die."[73] That night and Monday morning the administration was pummeled by criticism from the Faculty Council, the Faculty Committee on Student Affairs, and many prominent professors.

Monday morning, "the whole community seemed to be in a state of great anger," Perkins told the faculty at its much-awaited late-afternoon meeting, and "it had to be made to realize that there was some muscle in the center of the University."[74] This need to show strength, he went on, explained his law-and-order radio statement that morning, banning firearms from campus and prohibiting building occupations. It was the reason he also declared a state

179

Straight takeover agreement is signed at 320 Wait Avenue. (Division of Rare and Manuscript Collections of the Cornell University Library)

of emergency while announcing that suspension would automatically follow any violation of these orders. At the Barton Hall convocation he had convened that morning for 3 p.m., before the faculty meeting, Perkins spoke to a crowd of twelve thousand students, faculty, and employees, for twenty minutes; he never mentioned events on campus over the previous three days, but offered, instead, inspirational challenges to Cornellians "to act as rational and humane men in a time of trial and anguish for our country, for higher education and for Cornell University." Many in the audience were stunned. "I wanted to yell, 'say something already,'" one student told the *Sun*. Many faculty were annoyed at what they perceived as a massive failure of leadership. A *Sun* columnist congratulated Perkins for demonstrating "the difficult art of speaking for 20 minutes without saying anything," while denouncing "the void and vacuum occupying Day Hall." For his part, Perkins reportedly told a professor "that blacks had threatened on the telephone to take over the microphone if he addressed himself to the actual situation."[75]

At the 4:30 faculty meeting at Bailey Hall, with eleven hundred faculty present, a new record attendance, Dean Miller's motion to nullify the reprimands of the three students, grounded in the Sindler reforms giving the faculty the right to overrule actions of the adjudicatory boards, was followed by a

180

substitute motion offered by English professor Cushing Strout on behalf of a group of eminent faculty—M.H. Abrams, Hans Bethe, Max Black, and Herb Carlin, of Electrical Engineering; Henry Guerlac '32, MS '33, and Walter LaFeber, History; Francis Mineka, English; Paul Olum, Mathematics; Adrian Srb and Harry Stinson, Biology—labeling themselves "the center who must be heard." At the heart of their motion, which condemned the takeover of the Straight, the carrying of weapons on campus, and the "despicable attack on the Wari cooperative by the burning of a cross," was the claim that "to reverse [the reprimands of the three students] under coercion and the threat of violence would endanger the future of the University, and we refuse to do it."[76]

Abandoning the dean of the faculty, and at least the spirit of the Straight agreement, Perkins, speaking "as a private member of the assembly," embraced the Strout motion, while offering his own rewording, which Strout quickly agreed to: "The presence of arms and the seizure of Willard Straight Hall make it impossible for the faculty to agree at this meeting to dismiss the penalties imposed on the three students." Perkins proposed that the Faculty Council meet with representatives of the AAS on Tuesday and that the faculty, as a whole, reconvene under "non-pressurized circumstances" on Friday, to revisit "the Afro-American complaints."[77] At the end of its four-hour meeting, the Strout-Perkins motion passed overwhelmingly, 726–281. Dean Miller resigned.

As soon as the faculty left, twenty-five hundred students moved into Bailey Hall for a meeting hastily called by SDS, and voted overwhelmingly to condemn the faculty action. Tom Jones told the group, "Maybe they think we're going to back down, but we're not. The faculty tonight voted to have a showdown. The faculty voted tonight that we are going down. They can do us in, but they go too." In response, the crowd agreed to support the AAS "until the black demands are met."[78] For the first time, the white SDS, preoccupied principally with off-campus issues, and the black AAS, whose separatism denied the value of white allies, made common cause.

On Tuesday, the black students refused to meet with the Faculty Council, and Perkins announced that classes for the rest of the week would be replaced by "discussions of the current issues facing the University." College and department faculties met during the day. The faculty of Arts and Sciences voted to ask Perkins to use his emergency powers "to nullify all judicial decisions of this spring term."[79] The College of Home Economics, the School of Business and Public Administration, and the College of Agriculture and Life Science recommended that the reprimands be nullified, as did the departments of Computer Science and City and Regional Planning. The History and Government Departments were notable exceptions, voting, in fact, to refuse to teach if the faculty voted to nullify the penalties.

That afternoon, the AAS was invited by WHCU, the university-owned radio station, to send a spokesperson to be interviewed that evening. Tom Jones came, and read what seemed like a prepared ultimatum.

> The administration in the person of President Perkins has shown its true colors in terms of his suppressive tactics in declaring martial law. . . . The only violence that occurred over the weekend was when black students were attacked. Why didn't the faculty reprimand that? . . . James Perkins is a racist. Keith Kennedy is a racist. Dale Corson is a racist. Mark Barlow is a racist. And as racists they will be dealt with. Allan Sindler is a racist. Rossiter is a racist. Walter Berns is a racist. And as racists they will be dealt with. . . . Before this is over James Perkins, Allan Sindler and Clinton Rossiter are going to die in the gutter like dogs.

Jones demanded that the faculty meet that night and reverse its Monday vote. "After nine o'clock it's going to be too late. . . . Cornell University has three hours to live."[80] Perkins removed his family from their home, and Sindler and others were given police protection. At 7:30 the Faculty Council voted to call a meeting for Wednesday at noon, and it recommended nullification.

SDS convened another meeting that night, which had to be moved from Goldwin Smith to Bailey and finally to Barton Hall when more than seven thousand people showed up. Jones announced from a podium that had a large poster of Malcolm X on its front that "the pigs are going to die, too, when people like J. P. [Perkins] are going to be dealt with."[81] At midnight, he reported that the AAS had voted unanimously to postpone its threat until after the faculty reconsidered its position at its meeting now called for the next day. David Lyons, the Philosophy professor, read a statement from twenty-eight "concerned faculty" pledging to go on strike and "occupy some University building to show our concern" if the reprimands were not dismissed.[82] Late at night, SDS leader Bruce Dancis urged a takeover of Day Hall to put more pressure on the faculty, which spread excitement through Barton and prompted some students to head to the armory's many doors. Eldon "Bud" Kenworthy, one of the few Government professors sympathetic to the students, defused the effort by grabbing the microphone, and pleading: "If you're really serious about getting the change rather than simply playing out some psychodrama confrontation for confrontation's sake, then wait till tomorrow. Wait! Now is not the time to move. . . . A rational revolutionary would not move now. The faculty meeting is tomorrow at noon; if they don't vote to nullify, then I'll be with you. But let's not move now."[83] Kenworthy's plea was endorsed by Burak, the next speaker, who was worried about the armed deputies downtown, itching to take the offensive against another building takeover, a concern he had passed on to Perkins and the administration that afternoon.

Everyone on campus waited. Once again a huge turnout of eleven hundred faculty appeared at Bailey Hall, having made their way through hundreds of protesters demanding punishment of the black students. This time it took less than two hours for a decision. Perkins spoke first. He applauded the night-long Barton Hall assembly, still going on, and the teach-ins and discussions all over campus, and hoped that "those actions which have most deeply divided this community can be set aside." He urged the faculty to "clear the slate," to create a new judicial system "by which we can all abide," and he reaffirmed the Sunday agreement with the AAS. He ended by calling "upon each and every one of you to join me in the effort to move this University from the edge of disaster toward a new and more harmonious community."[84] The faculty answered with a standing ovation.

Eleven faculty spoke to the motion to nullify the reprimands, made by the acting dean of the faculty, E. F. Roberts, a Law professor; eight spoke in favor, three against. Vance Christian '61, MS '65, an African American assistant professor of hotel administration, spoke at length about the experience of black students at Cornell. As for the seizure of the Straight, he said that he, too, would have sought arms following "the break-in by the white students," and he berated Perkins for referring to the Wari House cross-burning as "a little incident . . . a prank." To a black man, he declared, "it's a hell of an issue." Christian pleaded with the faculty to pass the motion. James John, a professor of medieval history, opposed nullification, noting that if the existence of threats on Monday had been reason not to do so, then "we have a stronger reason for not doing so today." Max Black and Hans Bethe announced they were changing their votes. Black wanted "to say to the world we wish to forget what happened in the immediate past." Bethe wondered "whether the University would continue to exist" and urged nullification to win back "the moderates" from SDS. Amended to commit the university to immediately develop a new judicial system "that all our students will consider fair," the motion carried on a strong voice vote.[85] Reporters present estimated it at three-to-one or four-to-one.

Fear was a factor for some. Blacks had guns, fraternities had guns, and hundreds of armed "deputy sheriffs" waited downtown. William Keeton, PhD '58, professor of biology, told the Barton crowd that morning that "I will vote for nullification from fear for the University. I will lose some self-respect for doing so; I want you to know I terribly resent this." At the faculty meeting Keeton revealed that after speaking at Barton he met with the nine hundred students in his popular introductory biology course, a large majority of whom told him that reversing his position was a matter of justice. His vote, he declared, was "a vote of confidence in his students." Clinton Rossiter, the John L. Senior Professor, who had been the author of the amendments about the new judicial system and one of the three faculty singled out "to be dealt with," assured his colleagues, on the other hand, that "he had changed his mind under reason and not under the gun."[86]

Tuesday's meeting at Barton continued through the night. Insisting they had "occupied" and "seized" the building, the crowd booed when told that

Perkins had declared it "open." By midday Wednesday the Barton crowd had grown to nearly ten thousand, and when word of the faculty vote arrived around 2 p.m., the assembly roared its approval. Tom Jones credited what he called "the Barton Hall Community" for the reversal. "The decision was made right here. The faculty was told by this committee in this room to nullify that act." He added, "the old order has ended."[87] When Perkins arrived a few minutes later, he had to wait his turn to speak, sitting awkwardly on the floor drinking a can of soda—yet another photo in newspapers across America. Eric Evans told the crowd, "You know what just happened up here? JP shook my hand, put a grandfatherly arm around my shoulder and then said, 'sit down, I want to talk.'"[88] Evans finished his talk in a leisurely fashion.

When called to the podium, Perkins repeated his hope "that we may be able to expunge to the fullest extent possible the seizure of Willard Straight Hall from the records of this University and the incidents connected therewith." His tone was ebullient and celebratory. When he finished he was wildly cheered by the huge assembly. Perkins declared that "the Barton Hall Community is one of the most constructive positive forces which has been set in motion in the history of Cornell." When Evans asked the president pointedly on

President Perkins addresses the "Barton Hall Community." (Division of Rare and Manuscript Collections of the Cornell University Library)

mic about the state of emergency and "martial law," Perkins replied that "there is nothing I have said or will say which will not be modified by changing circumstances."[89] Burak, Evans, and Perkins smiled and embraced one another, and the president raised his arms with fists clenched to salute the cheering thousands.

Acting Dean Roberts followed Perkins, reading the nullification resolution and the call for a new "judicial system that all our students consider fair." The love-fest continued with Max Black, the Sage Professor of Philosophy, telling the thousands "we hear you, we care, we are trying to understand you and want together with you to do something . . . we want to be your friends."[90] To complete the ritual of goodwill, the Barton Hall Community gave a standing ovation of several minutes in support of the faculty's request that Robert Miller take back the resignation he submitted to fulfill his promise to the AAS. Miller withdrew his resignation the next day. That same afternoon, Allan Sindler, Government Department chair, resigned from the university.

On Wednesday night Barton Hall was empty, but many people felt the need to talk to each other. What was now called the Barton Hall "general assembly" or simply "the body" was reconvened for small groups of students and faculty to discuss what everyone referred to as "the issues." For the next four days this self-constituted community, its proceedings broadcast live by WVBR, talked about transforming the university: ending racism and giving students a greater role in governance. Guns were seldom mentioned. Thursday afternoon, at a teach-in on racism, the audience of five thousand heard about the injustices of racial life at Cornell, the meaning of black power and separatism, and of opening university admissions to "a wider spectrum of society."[91] The most popular speakers were the black students, cheered whenever they spoke, especially when they announced that the Afro-American Society had officially changed its name to the Black Liberation Front (BLF).

On Friday afternoon a different tone was struck at a teach-in led by members of the History and Government Departments. George Kahin, lionized by radical students for enduring McCarthyite smears in the 1950s and for his opposition to the Vietnam War, quieted "the body" with a magisterial speech about academic freedom and "the New McCarthyism." Defending the commitment of his colleagues Berns, Sindler, and Rossiter to fight racism, Kahin cautioned the crowd that "calling a man a racist does not make him so, any more than McCarthy calling him a communist made him a communist." He then launched a vigorous defense of the faculty's Monday vote. "Behind men armed with guns . . . was the sordid spectacle of a colleague [Perkins] physically pulled from a platform because he expressed views which some of his listeners didn't happen to like." Assisted by inept explanations from the university's administration, Kahin suggested, students had misread the vote. The faculty was not "voting against objectives of the black students, but voting against physical coercion on this campus." Like Professor Keeton, he had "resented deeply having to act [on Wednesday] under the threat of violence." Unlike Sindler, and Berns, who by Friday had also announced his resignation, Kahin pledged to remain at Cornell

and do everything I can to maintain the principle that to me is essential to human progress—the freedom to think, speak, write and advocate whatever a man honestly feels without the threat of physical force, whether under the cloak of political acts, political symbolism or whatever. But I use the word university advisedly—for unless that now terribly endangered principle of academic freedom remains operative here we won't have a university.[92]

The Barton "body" debated a restructured university on Saturday, again with five thousand in the hall, and on Sunday, a sunny summerlike day, with fifteen hundred. The thirty-seven proposals that emerged from the four days of discussion on racism, grades, classes, student power, and academic freedom were assigned to a steering committee that a week later proposed the creation of a representative student-faculty-administration assembly to "investigate and make recommendations for a redistribution of power, to include all relevant constituencies in its governance." While voting 361–59 on May 2 to establish a University Constituent Assembly, the faculty changed the wording to empower it "to make, after appropriate study, recommendations concerning changes in the processes and structures by which the University governs itself."[93] Six weeks after the Straight occupation, on May 30, the Constituent Assembly met for the first time, after elections produced its membership of 117 faculty, 135 students, 27 administration appointees, and 27 nonprofessorial academics and staff. That fall it transformed itself into the University Senate, which fundamentally restructured authority at Cornell in the 1970s, granting faculty, students, and employees legislative authority over the academic calendar, the campus codes of conduct, the university judicial system, and "campus life" (athletics, housing, and dining).

Perkins and the administration kept a low profile throughout the four days of convocations. The *Cornell Alumni News* wondered "Who's in charge?"[94] To be sure, Perkins had asked local authorities on Thursday to send home the several hundred armed sheriff deputies from neighboring counties brought to Ithaca in case of violence. On Sunday night he lifted the "state of emergency," announcing, to the surprise of some, that there were "no unauthorized guns on the Cornell campus."[95] Thirty-two firearms, including two pistols, had been turned in to the Safety Division, and on Sunday the BLF granted the university permission to search 320 Wait Avenue.

On Monday the campus returned to normal, with students and professors in class and people buying tickets in the Straight for a Janis Joplin concert. In an interview in Monday evening's *Ithaca Journal* Perkins was judicious. "It is difficult for anyone who is white to appreciate fully what it is to grow up black in the United States," he noted. Blacks at Cornell had been subjected "to threats, insults, and intimidation," but also bore responsibility for racial tension at Cornell. "A small tightly organized unit of black students" issuing "demands and threats" undermined "the easy communication that makes a community truly humane."[96] Meanwhile, Perkins had to deal with faculty, who were angry that he had "given in to guns."

Walter Berns, former chairman of the Government Department, and Allan Sindler, its current chairman, resigned from Cornell with a blistering letter to the *Daily Sun*. Their indictment began with the administration's failure to speak out for academic freedom when Professor McPhelin was "attacked for his views" the previous spring and ended with its failure "the entire week of April 21–25 this year to resist the forces arrayed against the University." They were horrified by "the shameful, humiliating performance at the surrender ceremony at Barton Hall," blasting Perkins for characterizing the event "not as a surrender but a victory that has astonished newsmen from the national media who have been on campus." What will the Perkins administration do, they asked, when "monitors from the BLF and the SDS complain of the reading Government professors assign?" The president will make promises to preserve academic freedom, but "as he himself said, 'there is nothing I had said or will say which will not be modified by changing circumstances.'"[97] Writing alone, in a response to an April 27 *Sunday New York Times* Tom Wicker interview with Muller, Sindler declared that Cornell should have enlisted "the careful use of the authority and police power of the civil jurisdiction," envisioned by the codes for major infringements on campus of local law, instead of "capitulation."[98]

Walter LaFeber resigned as chairman of the History Department. He indicated that he did "not have any confidence in the administration, with the exception of the Provost," and that he "probably will not be at Cornell after this year."[99] Thirteen of his History colleagues appealed directly to the board of trustees, describing their loss of confidence in an administration that did not comprehend "what a university must be if it is to function."[100] Allan Bloom of Government told the *Sun* that he would happily be on sabbatical the next year "and spared the further acts of this desperate comedy which has left academic freedom at Cornell in a shambles and degraded the faculty."[101] The literary critic Harold Bloom '51, a visiting professor at Cornell in 1968–1969, announced that "when I return to Yale, I shall organize a boycott of Cornell by concerned humanists as long as Perkins is president."[102] Ten faculty, "Cornell Professors for Academic Integrity," the hard-liners, wrote to the trustees and Governor Rockefeller about "the collapse of administrative authority in the University's leadership" and of the need for Perkins to step down. Fifteen members of the Law School faculty threatened to leave if the president didn't do more to see that "freedom of inquiry or freedom of expression was no longer seriously impaired."[103]

Even the forty-one faculty luminaries who on the Sunday night before classes resumed announced their intention to remain at Cornell warned they might leave if the "essential conditions of free teaching and scholarly work are not maintained." The six spokesmen for the "group of 41," M.H. Abrams, Douglas Ashford of Government, Hans Bethe, Max Black, Clinton Rossiter, and Cushing Strout, spoke of "widespread demoralization of the faculty" and worried about future "intimidation" of teachers and students. When asked if they were linked to "faculty factions rumored to be seeking Perkins' resignation," Bethe stated "it would be wrong to ask him to resign. That would add another calamity to the calamities we already have." He then praised Perkins as an innovator who had made Cornell "more than any other university" responsive to young black Americans.[104] Interestingly, several weeks later an informal letter from Psychology professor Ulrich Neisser to all faculty asking for a yes or no vote on a resolution of confidence in Perkins received 261 yes votes and 157 nos.

There was a firestorm off campus as well. President Nixon condemned the occupation and the guns, calling on college administrators "to have the back bone to stand up against this kind of situation."[105] Attorney General John Mitchell urged that campus violence be made a federal crime. Within days, Governor Rockefeller signed legislation banning guns from college campuses in New York State. The press chimed in with relentless descriptions of what was immediately labeled "Cornell's Capitulation" and what the columnists Rowland Evans and Robert Novak described on April 28 as "anarchy at Cornell." Homer Bigart devoted pieces in the *New York Times* to faculty opposition to Perkins. The syndicated humorist Art Buchwald had a column, "The Understanding Professor," on May 1, in which a professor bloodied up by militant students who had taken over his office agrees with a reporter that the behavior was terrible. "Yes, from my point of view it is, but I think we have to look at it from their point of view. Why did they throw me down the stairs? Where have we, as faculty, failed them?" It was a field day for editorial cartoonists, as well, one of whom showed Nixon pointing out to college administrators on a diagram that "the head bone should be connected to the back bone."[106]

Alumni weighed in with telegrams and letters, 130 supportive and 1,163 critical, in the four weeks after April 19. Joseph Coors '39 wrote to Purcell that "we see no future for Cornell University with this man as President, and will withhold financial support unless drastic action is taken by the Board."[107] W. Van Alan Clark '09, the benefactor of Clark Hall, wrote "Jim" Perkins that "we are wasting our money and facilities bringing up men and women who will always be terrorists . . . they must be put in their place."[108] In the same period, forty-nine non-Cornellians wrote letters supportive of Perkins, while 1,616 were not supportive. Much of what came in was ugly and vicious racism, including, for example, claims that "cannibalistic people do not become civilized in the short span of 300 years" and that "these bushmen should be sent back to the Congo."[109]

The day that classes resumed, Perkins told the *Sun* that even though he realized he had "put his utility to the community in question when he urged nullification," and that telegrams and letters were "running 5–1 against him, he had no intention of resigning."[110] That very day, three critics of Perkins—Kahin, LaFeber, and Fred Marcham (Sindler "felt too emotional to attend")—pleaded their case in New York City with a half-dozen trustees, convened by Arthur Dean '19, JD '23, the former chairman of the board.[111] Three days later, on May 1, at a special board meeting in New York, the trustees seemed to express support for Perkins, applauding when he walked into the room. On May 14 Perkins delivered a spirited defense of his handling of the Straight crisis and its immediate aftermath at the annual Tower Club dinner in New York City, which he thought received an "unbelievably sympathetic" response. On May 16, he repeated that he had no intention of resigning. "I feel less negative pressure today than I did two or three weeks ago."[112]

On May 31, Perkins asked the trustees to begin the search for his successor, for "it seemed to me quite clear that one way—a strange way—to contribute to healing the community was to resign."[113] Some years later, Dale Corson reported that "the Trustees never would have asked Perkins for his resignation," and that Perkins had actually intended to serve during the year in which Cornell searched for his successor. But the trustees "were having none of that," and once he said publicly he was going to resign, "they wanted it immediately."[114] In an ironic footnote to this presidency, Perkins, for most of June, was unavailable to comment about the suddenness of his resignation, since, as he himself observed in late July, "previously scheduled commitments in Europe" kept him away from the university.[115]

Harry Edwards wrote Perkins to "applaud your impending resignation" and to criticize the president's references at the Tower Club dinner to "the Black Problem" and to "thoughtless childish pranks such as burning crosses."[116] There were supportive letters to Perkins, as well. Economics professor Alfred Kahn wrote, "You have been an excellent President precisely because of your devotion to the use of reason, discussion, persuasion and to liberal reform." If those policies fail, "it will be the failure of liberalism in a period of revolution."[117] Keith Kennedy and Dale Corson praised Perkins for the COSEP program, while Government professor Andrew Hacker blamed his colleagues for a resignation he regretted: "The failure was the faculty's, not yours. Had you not been the object of constant attack from so many professors, neither the Trustees nor the alumni nor Homer Bigart would have been able to press their advantage."[118]

The "time of troubles," as the spring of 1969 would be remembered, left a festering sore on the Cornell community, a generation of suspicion and mistrust. For those who used historical analogies to "communes" and "constituent assemblies," it ushered in an era of revolutionary change, characterized by civil rights ideals and principles of participatory democracy. For others, the historical analogies were to Nazi storm troopers or to McCarthyism. Not until 1992 would the board of trustees formally approve Perkins's designation as president emeritus.

On a more mundane level, the occupation of the Straight resulted in some $25,000 in damages to the building; it ended the practice of housing in the building for Parents Weekend, which was itself canceled for the next year. Cornell Safety Division personnel started wearing sidearms, and in mid–May charges of "criminal trespass" were brought by District Attorney Matthew McHugh in City Court against eighteen students, a group that included Carter, Jackson, Evans, Jones, and Whitfield. Thirteen months later, in June 1970, City Judge James J. Clynes Jr., JD '48, dismissed the charges against fifteen of them. There were, he ruled, clearly violations of law during the two days of occupation, but the only charge, unlawful entry, could not be sustained for these fifteen, given the easy entrance into and exit from the building in the early Saturday hours. Jones, Evans, and Whitfield pleaded guilty in September to reduced charges of fourth-degree criminal trespass and were unconditionally discharged by the judge.

During the summer two bodies investigated the spring's events. The newly empowered Cornell Constituent Assembly sponsored eleven research groups, for which administrators, faculty, students, and employees wrote detailed studies of topics such as "Problems of Racism," "Minority Groups on Campus," "Black Studies," "the University Code and Adjudicatory System," "Governance," "Academic Freedom," "Financial Resources," even "Crisis and Change in the Governance of Other Universities: Implications for Cornell." Filling a three-inch-wide bound volume of double-sided, single-spaced typed pages, the "Summer Research Projects" received much less attention than another study, the much slimmer sixty-one-page report from the eight-person trustees committee, headed by William Robertson '34, a life insurance executive from Boston.

As the *Sun* reported, the Robertson report resoundingly "hit the University handling of the takeover." Woefully unprepared for a building takeover, Cornell lacked leadership once it happened, issuing no public statement from an administrator until over fifty hours after the Straight had been occupied. There can be no such thing, the report concluded, "as a non-violent building occupation—the very act is a threat of the use of force." With respect to the judiciary system, it insisted that "if freedom and the basic purposes of the University are to mean anything, the University must not in the future negotiate under duress. There must be no amnesty for infractions of the code." The report also asked fundamental questions about administrators' concessions to the occupiers: "No one will ever know if this was the right way to settle this disruption. This was a matter of judgment. These men made the decision to place the protection of life above the reputation of the University. They knew that the price to themselves and to Cornell was great—but was it greater than the price of human life?"[119]

On two contentious issues Robertson's report defended the university. There had been no Cornell police complicity allowing the DU invasion as claimed by the black students. The campus police were handicapped by a shortage of manpower, which left them unable to patrol that side of the Straight. Similarly, the numerous false alarms early Friday pulled Safety Division officers away from Wari House for twenty-two minutes, not insensitivity to the fears of the women residents or lack of interest in finding the culprit. Robertson's committee also investigated the various rumors circulating on campus about who burned the cross and could not come up with a definitive answer. Over twenty years later, Corson claimed that he was "99.9999 percent certain it was set by a black student," but offered no corroborating evidence. So, too, David Burak in 1989 suggested that "the cross burning was an inside job, done to galvanize middle-of-the-road elements in the AAS into action of a militant sort." And, he, too, gave no evidence for his claim.[120]

OVER THE SUMMER of 1969, the university's long-serving controller, Arthur Peterson, to whom the Safety Division, as well as Buildings and Properties, reported, provided the administration with a detailed and confidential set of procedures "On Campus Disorders." A chain of command was spelled out, secure fire-safe vaults built for Day Hall, and communication networks formalized with local political, police, and judicial offices. In September two new positions were created to enhance the maintenance of order on campus. A judicial administrator, Professor Joseph B. Bugliari, JD '59, who had a joint appointment in the College of Agriculture and the School of Business and Public Administration, would investigate alleged violations of university regulations for public order and present charges to a university hearing board. A university ombudsman, Professor Alice Cook of ILR, would assist members of the Cornell community seeking help in handling complaints or grievances against the university or anyone exercising authority in it. And, finally, September saw the first *Cornell Chronicle*, the new weekly of record for the university. That same month, the newly named Black Liberation Front held its first rally between Olin and Uris libraries, where three hundred people heard Ed Whitfield announce that "we must continue to fight until we are free or none of us are left."[121] A week later Acting President Corson reaffirmed Cornell's commitment to the COSEP program, "the improvement of education for black students and for accepting an increasing number of them."[122]

The post-Straight-takeover era in Cornell black-white relations had begun, and with it national black figures again visited the campus, usually accompanied by controversy. Stokely Carmichael's 1971 return bothered Day Hall because it involved a higher admission price for white students ($1.25) than for blacks (75 cents), and, once inside Bailey Hall, white students could only sit in the dress circle, with their coats removed, apparently as a security precaution. No administrative action ensued. A year later, Robert Purcell wrote Corson about sharing a plane ride with his principal client, Laurance Rockefeller, who compared a *Cornell Sun* report of a talk by Black Panther Bobby Seale with an ad in his alma mater's *Daily Princetonian* of a talk sponsored by the conservative group "USA Undergraduates for a Stable America." The contrast, Purcell told Corson, "was almost more than I could bear." He wanted to know how Corson could allow "someone who wishes to overthrow our system to find the welcome mat out at Cornell." Corson bluntly replied:

> I am not prepared to be the censor to decide who is safe for our students to hear and who is not. Furthermore, I believe there should be no such censor. I have long appreciated the Cornell policy which permitted a Gus Hall to speak on campus (and who did more to turn students away from communism than anything that could have been done at that time) and a James Hoffa (who impressed me with the substance of his message).

Corson also reminded Purcell about Princeton "throwing in the towel and abolishing ROTC" while Cornell retained it.[123]

Nothing signified the beginning of the post-Straight era better than the arrival on campus in the fall of 1969 of James Turner, who made his vision of an autonomous, separatist Afro-American Program clear in his first "report" to President Corson. The ten black studies courses with their 160 black students that fall constituted a response of sorts to blacks being "compelled" to learn about the sociopolitical and cultural world of whites; now "the black experience is central to our curricular design and teaching plan." Turner pledged to involve students in all aspects of the program: policy, curriculum, and faculty recruitment. When choosing faculty, academic training and standing would be considered, but "the greatest reliance" would be placed on the candidate's "relevance to the black community and his commitment to work toward the solution of its problems." After enunciating this political test for the center's faculty, Turner wrote candidly about who its students would be. "We have neither the time nor resources to operate a race-relations project wherein well-meaning but inexperienced and dysfunctional white students would occupy positions that might better be filled by blacks. Of course, relevant and equally well-qualified (background, experience, commitment) whites are welcome, but such qualified candidates will undoubtedly be rare."[124]

Turner's vision shaped the operations of the program he directed. It survived criticism from the general faculty concerned about access to Africana Studies Center courses by non-blacks. In fact, Africana's courses remained racially exclusive until 1973, when Mbata allowed three white students to take his history course. And it survived the critique by a committee headed by Lisle Carter, which called for the hiring of more black faculty with joint appointments in other units at Cornell and envisioned the Africana Studies Center more "as an academic program and not as a community service program." It suggested "that all students have access to its courses" and that those courses be more academically focused, noting that earlier Turner had advocated using the center "to equip serious students to work in and for the black community rather than to meet the needs and interests of those students who only wanted some orientation to understanding the black experience."[125]

Efforts were made outside of Turner's new program to recruit more black faculty. In March 1970 the new provost, Robert Plane, wrote the college deans endorsing the federal Department of Health, Education, and Welfare's encouragement of affirmative action. Andrew Schultz '36, PhD 41, the Engineering dean, replied that without raiding black institutions, the supply of "marginally competent black faculty members is . . . practically non-existent." Fred Kahn, dean of Arts and Sciences, asserted "unequivocally that our policies with respect to the hiring of faculty in no sense can be said to discriminate against blacks. The bias, to any extent it exists, is unmistakably in the opposite direction."[126] On the other hand, critics of affirmative action, like L. Pearce Williams '48, PhD '52, LaFeber's successor as chairman of the History Department, deemed it "destructive of the purposes of Cornell." To suggest that universities not hire "the most qualified, but should hire on the basis of race," he wrote the *Daily Sun*, "may well destroy the ability of the University to function properly."[127] Meanwhile, Saunders Redding, hailed by English Department chair Ephim Fogel as "perhaps the most important black man of letters in the country," was appointed the Ernest I. White Professor of American Studies and Humane Letters in 1970, becoming the first black person to hold an endowed chair in Cornell's history.[128]

Turner's arrival ushered in a new era of racial politics at Cornell, with a visible champion of African American students in the administrative structure willing to involve himself and his center in every race-related issue on campus. During his first winter in Ithaca, Turner supported the BLF's proposal that black students themselves handle admissions and that three hundred additional black undergraduates be admitted provisionally each year, at the end of which those with GPAs of 2.0 or over would be kept on as matriculants for degrees. A similar request, with different numbers—120 each year and a 3.0 GPA—was presented by the black graduate students. The proposal further required, Corson wrote in a "memorandum for the record," that "failure to totally fulfill any aspect of these agreements will be tantamount to a vote of no confidence in me as President and as such I will feel obligated to terminate my presidency." Pointing as well to the proposal's projected annual cost of $1 million and of the implications of the administration's relinquishing its authority to make admissions decisions, Corson told the BLF students at a meeting in his office of "the impossibility of my signing any such memorandum." Following this statement, "the BLF members said that there was no use for any further discussion and left the meeting."[129]

Having informed the Black Graduate Student Association that their proposal "was neither practical nor feasible," Corson and Don Cooke, dean of the Graduate School, did meet with graduate field representatives to encourage the admission of black students "whose qualifications are as close to the lower limits of their normal standards as possible."[130] Pleased with the increased black enrollment in the Graduate School from twenty-three in 1969 to seventy in 1970, Corson also announced agreement with the association's goal, a black graduate school population of 15 percent. To which Philip Jones, MFA '72, the head of the Black Graduate Student Association, responded, "Big deal! As we see it, Corson hasn't done one thing to increase the number of black graduate students."[131]

Turner's influence, especially on black undergraduates, was evident in "the Lucas affair." In November 1969 a petition signed by 125 black students demanded the resignation within two weeks of Pearl Lucas, MA '74, a black assistant dean in Arts and Sciences. Their principal grievance was that she "demonstrated an inability to maintain political neutrality" in executing her responsibilities[132] by distributing to incoming COSEP students copies of an article that took a negative view of black college students concentrating on Afro-American studies. Dean Kahn sent Provost Plane the college's draft response to the petition, asking for Day Hall's reaction to it. Black students, Kahn intended to say, had no authority with respect to Lucas's position in the college. "She is an Assistant Dean period. She is not Assistant Dean for blacks; and she is not our black Assistant Dean." If black students had been automatically assigned to her as advisees, on the assumption she could be especially helpful to them, "that practice will end, as of now." He had chastised Lucas for distributing the article without also providing other literature expressing more favorable views on black studies. He also intended to tell the petitioners that they had the right to an alternative adviser. Barring specific instances of misconduct, Kahn suggested, Lucas "should be encouraged to stay."[133] Kahn's proposed response was raised at Corson's executive staff meeting five days later, where "it was agreed that Lucas, who represents the integrationist viewpoint, was needed on campus as a balance for the black students who are not militant segregationists."[134]

Heavy artillery was then brought up by the anti-Lucas forces, in the form of a letter to the *Sun* from four white professors closely associated with

COSEP—Douglas Dowd, Chandler Morse, Ben Nichols, and Walter Slatoff. Lucas, they contended, was the de facto adviser to Arts College black students, "who should have been given a voice in her selection." Having adopted "a role of active opposition to the goals of most of the black students at Cornell," she was not qualified to advise them.[135] Short of resignation, her responsibilities should be changed, the four professors suggested. L. Pearce Williams and Frederick Marcham of History then defended Lucas, "a victim of insinuations and half-truths," in a letter to the *Sun*. She was, they insisted, a professionally trained counselor, a founder of a "freedom school" in Virginia, and a teacher in an acclaimed special program in PS 141 in Harlem.[136]

The two-week deadline came and went. Kahn agreed to set up a three-person committee, one chosen by the students, one by Lucas, and one by himself, to advise him, if formal complaints listing her misconduct and derelictions of duty were lodged. They were never submitted. But pressure for her dismissal from the BLF, COSEP, and from James Turner persisted. Black students refused to meet with her and chose no alternative advisers. Kahn backed down. Citing Lucas's one-week, unauthorized, "self-proclaimed vacation in Florida," his associate dean, Robert Scott, dismissed her in early April.[137] Lucas, who claimed she had notified Scott six to eight weeks before her departure, enrolled as a graduate student that fall, studying English history with Professor Marcham.

Dean Kahn may have given in to the BLF on Lucas in hopes of calming the racial tension that had once again enveloped the campus. On April Fool's Day morning during spring recess, a fire broke out at 320 Wait Avenue, the home of the new Africana Studies Center and the building that had become, as one black student put it, "the only place we could be at home." The blaze destroyed the building, along with its library, its periodical collection, its records, its art, and personal belongings including dissertations and research papers. No one was known to have been in the building when the fire broke out about 1 a.m.[138] Reminding a press conference that it came two months after a fire at the Southside Community Center and five weeks after a lit kerosene-filled flare was thrown on the porch of Wari House, Turner declared he was "sure whites did it, because no black would set fire to a building which had his friends' possessions no matter what his grievances against the University."[139] President Corson pledged "the fire will not impede Cornell's commitment to the Africana Center" and offered protection for the nearly finished new dorm, High Rise 6, on North Campus, where the center was temporarily relocated.[140] He also announced a fund drive for a new center, which received $12,000 by the end of the first week.

When students returned to campus on Monday, April 6, the BLF issued a statement that said, in part, "These attacks must be ended. We, the black community, declare that they will. The time has passed to entrust our safety to our

The remains of the Africana Studies Center, 320 Wait Avenue, destroyed by fire on April 1, 1970. (Division of Rare and Manuscript Collections of the Cornell University Library)

jailors and murderers."[141] Turner was given half the *Sun*'s editorial page for a "Statement: Africana Fire." He contrasted the extensive press coverage of the Straight takeover with the negligible notice given to "the recent efforts in Ithaca of whites to commit murder in cold blood." He pledged that "the hostility, the hatred, and atmosphere of threat of violence" that black people live with in the Cornell community "would not go unanswered."[142]

That afternoon some 175 black students led by Tom Jones, now a graduate student, along with his wife, Stephanie Bell Jones, and Stanford Reaves '72, Irving McPhail '70, and six Africana faculty, including Turner and Gloria Joseph, filled Corson's office, anteroom, and the nearby halls to deliver a "set of demands": that blacks recruited by blacks guard Wari House, the temporary Africana Center, and Turner's home; all the money collected in the Africana fund be turned over to Turner; the center be given several vans for its transportation needs; a new Africana Center be provided by the fall; and that the university fund the rebuilding of the Southside Community Center. If Corson didn't accept "their demands, he would have to accept responsibility for anything that might be done." As they left, the BLF head, Reaves, told the crowd, "The administration doesn't think it has to be accountable to black people. We're going to have to change that. Like we said, somebody is going to have to pay. Now we're going to be moving from here as a group. Let's go."[143]

One hundred of the group went to the newly opened Campus Store next to Day Hall, leaving behind $1,000 worth of damage and taking a reported $3,000 of merchandise. Late that afternoon Corson told the campus, "I can well understand sentiments of rage and anger, but I will not condone acts of vandalism."[144] He promised quick action on what he labeled the "five concerns" expressed that morning in his office. On Wednesday Corson again addressed students who had gathered outside the Campus Store, fast becoming a new focus for student activists. He announced that the Ithaca Fire Department had concluded that the fire was indeed arson, that a $10,000 reward was being offered to find the perpetrator, and that the FBI had been called in. Black guards, as requested, had been hired from a detective agency to safeguard the various locations, and the directors of the Southside Center had assured him "they needed help in other ways than Cornell money."[145]

At 10:30 that night, a large group of black students congregated near the store and burned a pile of material, apparently looted from it. As they moved toward North Campus, they smashed windows in Olin Library and in other Arts quad buildings, overturned cars, broke windows in and vandalized the first floor of Mary Donlon Hall. Corson declared a curfew until 5 a.m. Thursday, and from 11 p.m. to 5 a.m. for subsequent nights. He secured a New York State court-ordered "restraining order," preventing anyone on campus from assembling, exhorting, or committing acts that would provoke violence or disrupt the normal activities of the university. In addition, "show-cause orders" were issued to three black students, Jones, McPhail, and Reaves, three radical white students, Richard Mandell III, David Orden '71, and David Rosoff '70, and a white postdoctoral student at the Society for Humanities, Robert Starobin '61, requiring that they explain to the court why they should not be permanently enjoined from engaging in disruptive activity. Similar orders went to the Black Liberation Front, SDS, and two other militant student organizations. Violating the various orders against violence carried the penalty of contempt of court.

That afternoon a dozen white activists tried to block an entrance to Day Hall, while they "burned the injunction." Escorted away by Cornell officials aided by Tompkins County sheriff Robert Howard, they headed to the Arts quad, where they were joined in the course of the warm sunny afternoon by nearly one thousand students. In defiance of Corson's curfew, about half of them staged a peaceful sit-in on the Arts quad, remaining after 11 p.m. The *Ithaca Journal* speculated that "the Safety Division had been advised to 'cool it' unless there was violence."[146]

As bomb threats and false alarms swept the campus on Thursday and Friday, a group of "faculty volunteers," which swelled from eleven to two hundred, began patrolling the campus, convinced that "the presence of responsible individuals committed to non-violent resolution of conflicts would exert a beneficial moderating influence upon the situation."[147] The intervention helped, even if it did not totally calm the campus. Two Molotov cocktails were hurled into Olin Library over the weekend, and a fire was set in the office of the Constituent Assembly in the Straight. Two firebombs were thrown into the basements of McGraw and Morrill, but failed to ignite. A white student was attacked by six blacks outside Balch. Nor could the patrolling faculty preempt the eleven SDS demonstrators who sat in at Ward Laboratory, the nuclear reactor building, to show "full support from the white community for the black demands"; three of them were arrested and charged with third-degree criminal trespass.[148] The faculty volunteers did succeed, however, in bringing about a two-hour meeting of some forty trustees, in Ithaca for their spring session, with student activists. According to the *Alumni News*, the "initial antagonism" at the meeting "dissipated as the noontime exchange wore on."[149]

Howard K. Smith singled out the past week's tensions at Cornell on his Monday, April 13, ABC-TV news program, in a segment about campus disruptions. "Cornell, once a great and progressive university, is torn up. Tensions and increasing threats have marked the year. That is the price of yielding to the first threat, a year earlier [at the Straight]." Cornell, Smith went on, while "the worst case, is not the only one."[150] Vice President Muller sent a telegram to ABC and the FCC terming Smith's comments "distorted" and a "malicious exaggeration," adding that "no ABC-TV correspondents have been here."[151] He demanded equal time to reply but did not get it.

Relative calm returned to the campus from a combination of court injunctions, patrolling faculty, the appointment of a trustee committee headed by a black trustee, Meredith Gourdine '52, to work with Turner, and final exams. Some 335 university employees signed a petition asking Corson to take action against vandalism and to protect them from threats and lawlessness in their buildings. Even a controversial "Open Letter to Cornell" from eighteen black faculty, including Lisle Carter, Vance Christian, Gloria Joseph, J. Congress Mbata, and James Turner, did not stir things up. It compared the lack of national media interest in the destruction of the Africana Center with the nationwide coverage of the Wednesday night black actions and deemed "unbelievable" rumors that "black people themselves set the fire." "Encouraged by the response to recent events by the Trustees," the black faculty urged the Cornell community to contribute to the Africana Fund. What upset some white faculty was the letter's apparent defense of the black students' behavior: "The actions of [the] black students, in the face of personal danger and anxiety, are expressions of the determination to demonstrate that they are not going to be intimidated by the burning of buildings, the bomb threats, harassing phone calls, or other racist acts."[152]

Gourdine's committee sponsored a university audit of state and federal programs that might support COSEP or the Africana Center and discussed with the board the appropriateness of locating Africana "off campus" at 310

Triphammer Road. On June 15, the university purchased the former site of Alpha Epsilon Pi, a Jewish fraternity, for the new center, with AEP moving to Thurston Avenue. There had been discussion in Day Hall and among trustees about relocating the center in Rockefeller Hall, but, as Corson remembered it, Africana faculty "didn't want that, to come on campus. Their identity was shored up by being outside of campus." It was, he later reflected, "a mistake, they should have been integrated onto the campus."[153] In September the Africana Center moved to 310 Triphammer, where it has been ever since. To this day the person or persons who set fire to 320 Wait Avenue remain unknown.

Meanwhile, questions about COSEP persisted. Thomas Sowell, then a professor of economics at UCLA, in a December 1970 article for the *New York Times Magazine*, attacked "vague humanitarian, socio-political doctrinaires and practical administrators," who, at Cornell, were "concerned with appeasing the most vocal blacks." He accused COSEP "of skipping over competent blacks to admit authentic ghetto types," using, to make his case, the transcript of a middle-class black "passed over" by COSEP, given to him by Pearl Lucas. By then a well-known black conservative, Sowell wrote that one Cornell professor had admitted, "I give them all As and Bs, and to hell with em."[154] Carson Carr Jr., who supervised COSEP admissions, and Douglas Dowd denied the charges in the *Sun*, replying, enigmatically, that "students were not overlooked because they were middle class. . . . To believe that black students are given grades at Cornell is to believe a lie. In this sea of whiteness, academic priority is to all of those who aggressively seek it."[155]

COSEP was accused, as well, in 1971, of maintaining an "academic double standard," with its handbook requiring its students to maintain a 2.0 GPA, while most colleges stipulated that students could continue with 1.7. The handbook directly linked financial aid to academic performance and promised "severe disciplinary action" if students used narcotics. A faculty critic of the program, Alvin Bernstein '61, PhD '69, of History, claimed that, rather than encouraging success, COSEP director Delridge Hunter had "a punitive emphasis," preferring these stricter regulations because he was convinced that "COSEP students were prone to play games and neglect their studies."[156]

A faculty ad hoc committee, appointed to review the COSEP handbook, reported in late 1971 that statements in it did indeed put COSEP in an "unauthorized educational policy-making role." It had no authority to set academic standards, be they "higher or lower than those established by the separate schools and colleges." The committee noted that the basic relationship of COSEP to the university faculty and to the colleges "remains confused and misunderstood." And it reminded everyone that the Robertson Committee had recommended in the summer of 1969 "that all academic advising be removed from the COSEP office and go back to the advising offices of the individual Colleges."[157]

Reenter trustee Robertson. Appointed in January 1974 as the chair of the Cornell Trustee Ad Hoc Committee on the Status of Minorities, an eleven-member panel of trustees, faculty, and non-trustee members of minority groups, Robertson took aim at COSEP once again. Twenty months and seventy-three pages later, his committee recommended increased efforts by Cornell to hire members of minority groups for both the faculty and staff and, to that end, the creation of three new administrative positions, a vice provost for minority affairs, a director of minority educational affairs, and a director of minority employee affairs. More controversial was its recommendation that the residential population of university dormitories with over twenty people not exceed 50 percent from any one minority group, a potentially fatal blow to Wari House and Ujamaa.

Even more controversial, Robertson's committee recommended the dismantling of COSEP. As part of "preparing students for life in a pluralistic society," the committee urged that minority student admissions, financial aid, academic counseling, and remedial tutoring be shifted from COSEP to college offices. This, Robertson told a news conference, "would do away with the separatism that COSEP implies." Trustee James L. Gibbs Jr. '52, the first tenured black professor at Stanford and the founder of its Afro-American Studies Program (and son of the Ithaca-born local civil rights activist James L. Gibbs), told the same press conference that the committee was fully aware that minority students opposed these changes. But "we've taken specific steps to make sure it really works," Gibbs observed. "There will be at least as many advisors in the colleges as are now available in COSEP."[158]

Black students had held several demonstrations the previous spring when the administration had floated similar proposals. Protesters with signs stating "Leave COSEP Alone" charged that college faculty and staff were "not committed to helping minority students and in some cases are overtly racist" and that transferring admissions would weaken the recruitment of new black students.[159] In the wake of the spring protests, Provost David Knapp decided to "postpone" any major changes pending further study.

This retreat prompted some trustees to remind Robertson that the "suggestions in the report were merely recommendations." Provost Knapp announced neutrally that "administrative action would hereafter take into account the priorities and objectives of the report."[160] No matter how many new black faculty and employees the trustees recommended hiring, black students held rallies and protests, rejecting the proposed dismantling of COSEP as well as the end of Ujamaa and Wari House, decisions about which they claimed never even to have been consulted. But for agreeing to aggressive hiring of more minorities, Corson let the Robinson report sit on the table.

In January 1976, yet another report, this one from the "COSEP Advisory Committee," suggested that COSEP and university departments "share responsibility for Cornell's minority program," a modest, but meaningful reform the administration accepted.[161] A tacit truce was in the works. The university let COSEP, as well as predominantly black housing, survive, both to remain pillars of black identity and black solidarity, for a minimal, but symbolically powerful, concession on separateness.

Two months later, however, Corson had another race crisis on his hands, his last as president, in the form of opposition to these efforts to integrate the formerly separate minority programs within the existing structures of the university. On March 10, Herbert Parker, a black assistant director of financial aid, filed a discrimination complaint against Cornell with the New York State Human Rights Commission. The only black in the office since arriving there in 1972, and thus generally considered the university's minority financial aid officer, Parker claimed the university had given promotions to less qualified colleagues and that he had been given additional job assignments without an increase in pay. The university wanted him fired, he added, because he held "unpopular opinions," championing black students while the university sought to cut back on financial aid commitments to them.[162] At a pro-Parker sit-in that delayed the Columbia-Cornell basketball game at Barton Hall for ten minutes, one black student declared, "We realize that Cornell has dedicated itself to the extermination of the black population on this campus."[163]

Two weeks later the university fired Parker for insubordination resulting from a verbal altercation with Robert Walling, the director of financial aid. Parker saw his dismissal as more proof of punishment for his views about (alleged) university cutbacks on minority student aid, a theme that was kept at the center of the developing crisis by Turner, as well. The university declined to elaborate on the firing, deeming it a confidential personnel matter.

About fifty black students, faculty, and administrators met the next day with Provost Knapp, Vice President Barlow, and Walling at the COSEP office. Turner demanded Parker's immediate reinstatement. At the end of what the university described as "a cordial meeting, without angry voices," the Cornell officials stood by the dismissal. After an administrator refused to comment on the details behind the firing, Turner advised, "whether or not you can talk about it, it is going to be talked about. You will not go on consistently treating people the way you do." Another black administrator added, "This is the worst thing that has happened in the history of COSEP. The COSEP office should have been consulted."[164]

Over the next several days, more frightening incidents occurred: a fire set with gasoline in a Balch Hall lounge, a fire in a classroom in Baker Hall, three bomb scares, and the slashing of almost fifty tires on North Campus. An anonymous letter claimed responsibility for the "bomb threats, slit tires, etc.," and added, "We will not be eliminated. The fight has begun. Black power is back."[165] A group of blacks, identifying themselves as the "Coalition of Concerned Black

Administrators, Faculty and Students," separated themselves from such actions, while still insisting on Parker's reinstatement. No one else, they claimed, "has the expertise and training to formulate the complex financial aid packaging process administered through COSEP."[166] Meanwhile, students left campus for spring recess.

When the students returned, so did Stokely Carmichael, this time as the principal speaker on April 18 in Bailey Hall at the end of Black Awareness Week. He was introduced by Herbert Parker. Carmichael told the crowd that "blacks were justified in doing anything that was necessary to achieve justice."[167] The next day, the anniversary of the Straight takeover, Carmichael spoke to a shouting, clapping crowd of three hundred at a rally at the Straight. He railed against capitalism, a topic not uppermost on the minds of his listeners, many of whom began to chant "Herb Parker / Just like him / Dare to struggle / Dare to win."[168] A portion of the crowd, but not Carmichael, marched to Day Hall, and finding the doors locked, entered through a window, marched through the building chanting, and eventually gathered outside. Following instructions from leaders of the demonstration, they dispersed.

The following day, April 20, one hundred black protesters began a sit-in at the university Admissions and Financial Aid office in 410 Thurston Avenue. They left, on their own, after several hours and moved in midafternoon to Day Hall, where some 150 students ejected Corson and other top university administrators, while demanding Parker's reinstatement and unconditional amnesty for anyone involved in the protests. Later in the evening, a crowd of fifty white fraternity students heckled the black students. The occupation ended at 2:30 a.m., with no agreement, after the university obtained a court order ordering the students to leave. Little damage occurred in the ten-hour occupation of Day Hall, but at the Admissions Office doors and locks were broken and vending machines destroyed.

Negotiations took place through the last weeks of the semester, with black students and their white supporters forming picket lines around Day Hall for about thirty to forty-five minutes each day. The university agreed to appoint a black assistant admissions director from the College of Arts and Sciences as an interim replacement for Parker. Administrators refused to have the permanent replacement jointly appointed by the dean of admissions and Financial Aid and the director of COSEP. The selection committee would include minority members, but report only to the dean. There would be no unconditional amnesty and no reinstatement of Parker.

Corson rebutted the rumors about decreases in black student aid, telling the faculty on April 28 that "allocations for minority financial aid have increased—not decreased" and that minority students continued to receive more favorable treatment than others with respect to loans. "These are facts which no amount of rhetoric can put aside," he said. He asserted as well that the "much more deep-seated issue" was the autonomy of minority programs at Cornell and the belief of some that they "can succeed only if they are under minority control." But, an ally now at least of the spirit of the Robertson reforms, he insisted "that all minority educational functions—both academic and non-academic—should be integrated with all University educational functions."[169]

In the middle of the summer the New York State Human Rights Commission dismissed Parker's charges of racial discrimination. Corson had weathered the racial storm and made his point about a pluralist Cornell. Six months later, at his request, the trustees named a new president in a period of relative racial calm on campus. But racial calm was a fragile commodity at Cornell. Episodes of racial tension were now a given at America's newly integrated college campuses; when they occurred at Cornell, they were always accompanied and often magnified by memories of 1969 and 1970, passed on to each new generation of black undergraduates.

6 | The Wars at Home

The semester before she graduated, Janet Reno '60 worried that Cornell students had already been co-opted into the 1950s "silent generation." In a letter to the *Cornell Daily Sun*, Reno, a chemistry major and president of the Women's Self-Government Association—and future attorney general in the Clinton administration—criticized her classmates' "lack of interest" in and "disdain" for politics. While they had recently mobilized in great numbers against university restrictions on their social lives, she contended that they shared the era's pervasive complacency about the larger "off-campus issues of our time" and, like their parents, left public affairs in the hands of professional politicians and bureaucrats. There would be greater campus activism, she wrote, if Cornell faculty offered more courses on pressing political problems.[1]

By the time Reno graduated from Harvard Law School, one of sixteen women in her class of five hundred, and James Perkins was beginning his Cornell presidency, a seismic shift was occurring at Cornell and elsewhere as 1950s campus apathy gave way to the student radicalism of the sixties. This radicalism, which really didn't begin until 1964 and 1965, wasn't produced by professors offering new courses but by the emergence of a new student Left, forged in places such as Berkeley, Ann Arbor, and Ithaca by the Free Speech Movement, the Students for a Democratic Society (SDS), and, most significant, resistance to the war in Vietnam.

The Old Left, rooted in Marxist theory, had seen the Soviet Union and the proletariat, the working class, as the principal agent of revolutionary change. The New Left, shaped to a great extent by postwar intellectuals like Herbert Marcuse and C. Wright Mills, turned its back on the Soviet Union, which it saw as a repressive single-party regime, and on the American working class, which it felt had been co-opted into consumerism, patriotism, and complacent defense of the status quo. The New Left concluded that in America, as in France, Germany, and Japan, it was young people, mainly students, who were thinking and acting in radically transformative ways. Unlike Cornell's Cold War leftists such as Robert Fogel '48, the leadership of its New Left, seldom socialist ideologues, assumed that the principal problem in America, which needed American-style solutions, was that people had lost democratic, participatory control over their lives, that impersonal American institutions left people powerless.

In America's universities—its "knowledge factories," the name Perkins's West Coast friend, the University of California chancellor Clark Kerr, gave to them—students and even faculty, the New Left claimed, had no share in decision making, which increasingly resided in a managerial class of vice presidents and vice provosts. On the national stage, the new student Left saw an electorate powerless to influence the decisions on war and peace increasingly being made, they were convinced, by political, military, and industrial elites. And finally, many in the overwhelmingly white and middle class new student Left were convinced that the materialism of the conventional 1950s lifestyles of their parents, a successful career, a house in the suburbs, all the values of affluent postwar American society, were empty and soulless.

When the class that came to Cornell with Perkins in 1963 was about to graduate in 1967, the tone of annual celebratory rhetoric bespoke the arrival of the radical sixties. The chairman of the Faculty Committee on Student Affairs alerted the board of trustees that "today's students are seriously and sincerely challenging the present order of things as they exist both within the university and on the outside."[2] Meanwhile, Perkins assured the Tower Club at New York's Hotel Pierre that while Cornell was "a restless community," it was just as "vivid, powerful and interesting a place as it was when you were there." He then added, "This does not mean that public issues are going to be discussed sensibly or in a way you find satisfactory."[3]

STUDENT ACTIVISM AT Cornell began in early 1965, in the wake of the fall 1964 sit-ins at Berkeley's Sproul Hall. The first meeting on March 8 of Students for Education (SFE), convened by Nathaniel Pierce '66, had no formal structure or agenda and was simply an open sharing of grievances by the several hundred students who attended. Their concerns were Cornell-specific: large lectures, lack of contact with faculty, the grading system, the horrors of the campus bookstore in Barnes Hall, and Perkins's recurring absences from campus. Offended by Pierce's proposal at the meeting that the university institute "President's Days," when Perkins would be required to be on campus, Perkins declined to meet with anyone from SFE. He left Ithaca for Lincoln Center's celebration of the university's centennial, telling Corson, as his provost remembered it, "This is your problem. I'm going to New York."[4]

Corson responded by inviting to his office the six students whose names he had seen in the *Sun*'s account of the SFE meeting. Changes came quickly.

A coffee shop run by CURW in Anabel Taylor Hall, where faculty could meet students, was promised, as was a study of ways to increase faculty numbers to reduce the size of classes. The precise numerical grading system of 50 to 100, suspected of encouraging competition, was replaced by a new F to A+ scale, making Cornell transcripts similar to those of other colleges. A limited option of "Satisfactory" and "Unsatisfactory" grades was established, as well. At the bookstore, trinkets for sale were replaced by an entire floor stocked with books, including books not even required in courses. Students were appointed to the store's board, and plans were hatched for the Campus Store that would be built five years later. Corson's success with the various student committees of the aggressively leaderless SFE was emblematic, he felt, of how "he was able to communicate on the same wave length with the students better than Jim could. He tended to be formal, and I tended to be more personal about it."[5] The SFE disbanded that spring as campus activism turned to off-campus concerns, for which, however well-intentioned and personable Cornell administrators were, they could not find remedies.

Having campaigned in 1964 against U.S. Senator Barry Goldwater with a pledge not to send United States soldiers to the Far East, President Johnson sent combat units to Vietnam in January 1965 to replace the "advisers" who had been there through the Kennedy administration. On February 7, he launched the first massive bombing of North Vietnam. Four days later, a student-faculty Ad Hoc Committee to End the War in Vietnam was created, and that week on a bitter-cold afternoon about sixty demonstrators, mainly students, marched downtown to the naval recruiting office on West State Street, where a picket line was formed. Half a dozen policemen kept watch as bystanders replied to "Yankee come home" placards with heckling, and, as the *Sun* reported, one elderly woman commented "Hell, in my day, we'd shoot them."[6] A week later, U.S. Senator Wayne Morse visited the campus and before a capacity crowd in Statler Auditorium denounced Johnson's Vietnam policy. In March the eminent French philosopher Jean-Paul Sartre, who was to visit Cornell to give a series of lectures, refused to come, as a protest against the escalating U.S. role in Vietnam. The Vietnam War had come to Cornell.

Three buses full of more than one hundred Cornellians ready to leave Willard Straight Hall on April 18 to join the twenty thousand people at the first National Mobilization protesting the raids in North Vietnam were delayed by counterprotesters who sat down in front of the vehicles. The counterprotesters dispersed only when university proctor Lowell T. George assured them that the marchers had no signs indicating they represented the university student body. George was reported to have also told them, "I'm on your side."[7] A week later, the Ad Hoc Committee organized a twenty-eight-hour antiwar vigil attended initially by 350 students and faculty on the Arts quad, some one hundred sticking it out through the chilly night. A thirty-student counterprotest, the

March to End the Vigil, hovered with signs saying "Gas the Cong."[8] Soon the Committee for Critical Support of the U.S. in Vietnam was established by two Telluride House students: Nathan Tarcov '68 (years later Allan Bloom's successor as a professor of political philosophy at the University of Chicago) and Paul Wolfowitz '65 (years later architect of George W. Bush's Iraq War), with mathematics professor Jacob Wolfowitz, his father, as faculty adviser.

Campus protest escalated with a walkout during the Charter Day convocation on April 27, officially marking Cornell's centennial. As New York State governor Nelson A. Rockefeller began to speak, some seventy-five well-dressed protesters rose from their seats, unfolded antiwar banners, and marched slowly and quietly out of Barton Hall, where they remained, chanting slogans, until the convocation was over. The governor's talk was delayed for six minutes. He responded to the walkout by commending Johnson's Vietnam policy, noting, "It's a wonderful thing that we have a President willing to fight for the freedom of the world."[9] Outside Barton, students booed and threw eggs at the protesters. In early May, the ad hoc committee, now also protesting the April 28 invasion of the Dominican Republic by U.S. marines, drew a crowd of four hundred to a rally on the steps of the Straight; nearby the small and newly formed Tarcov-Wolfowitz group held a silent demonstration in opposition to the larger one.

From Friday evening, May 7, until the early hours of Saturday morning, a "teach-in" attended by two thousand people was sponsored by the Faculty Committee on Vietnam in Bailey Hall, with George Kahin and Douglas Dowd leading the denunciations of the war. Introduced several weeks earlier at the University of Michigan, professorial "teach-ins" soon spread to more than a hundred college campuses, coordinated from Ithaca by a National Teach-In Committee with Pat Griffith, wife of graduate student and chemistry lecturer Joe Griffith, PhD '67, serving as national coordinator. A tireless participant in teach-ins around the country, Kahin, the Southeast Asia specialist, "converted" many undergraduates to opponents of the war with his argument that "the United States cannot exert political leverage where it is counter to the tide of nationalism and the support of the people."[10]

On May 11, the Ad Hoc Committee to End the War in Vietnam staged the first disruptive confrontation of a campus speaker. The Rockefeller walkout had been quiet and respectful, but Ambassador-at-Large W. Averell Harriman's defense of the government's actions in Vietnam and the Dominican Republic before an audience of fifteen hundred in Bailey Hall was greeted with booing, hissing, repeated interruptions, and shrieks of "liar." Frail and visibly shaken, the elderly Harriman finally lashed back: "Why are these bleeding hearts for Communists? How many Communists are there among you? Will those who are Communists please stand up." The career liberal was answered by students: "McCarthyist slander"; "That won't work here"; "We know we're not Communists."[11] After he left, one hundred students "sat in" on the Bailey stage into the next morning, with eleven female students violating the curfew that still existed for first- and second-year women. Campus police made no effort to get the students to leave. The next day the *Cornell Daily Sun*, while critical of Harriman's "incredibly poor and meaningless" defense of President Johnson's foreign policy, denounced the "rampant irrationality" of the disruptive students. "To scream insults at Harriman is unforgiveable."[12] Almost one thousand students signed a letter of apology to the ambassador.

As the attacks on the Vietcong escalated, so did opposition to the war. A televised two-day national "teach-in" held in Washington on May 15 and 16, at which Kahin spoke, along with supporters of the war not usually heard at campus teach-ins, was followed the next day by another, even more confrontational protest by Cornell's Ad Hoc Committee to End the War in Vietnam. After passing out a mimeographed sheet linking ROTC to the "military intervention which prevents self-determination in Vietnam," eighty-four students with linked arms sat down quietly on the floor of Barton Hall, disrupting the annual presidential review of the graduating seniors in Cornell's Reserve Officer Training Corps. Some twenty-five hundred friends of the graduating officers, sitting in Barton's bleachers and, according to the *Sun*, "aching for a fight," threw eggs on the protesters, jeered, and demanded their removal. Proctor George warned the students over the public address system that "no matter what the cause . . . disruption of a regularly scheduled university educational class or event will not be tolerated."[13] He gave the demonstrators sixty seconds to leave. As the students in the stands counted down the seconds, the demonstrators refused to move, but quietly and dutifully gave their student cards to Safety Division officers, summoned by the proctor.

Perkins then arrived to begin the ritualistic presidential officers review, which eased the tension somewhat as the demonstrators, ROTC members, and the seated friends—some rumored to be carrying stones and brass knuckles—all stood for the "Star-Spangled Banner." Even though they sat back on the floor, the protesters' concession to tradition seemed to calm the pro-ROTC audience. Perkins's amplified comments deftly maintained the standoff. "The University is very much on trial here," he said, urging respect for both the demonstrators' "right to protest" and "the audience and their capacity for restraint and compassion." A shortened review was held. Instead of the corps passing before Perkins, he walked down their stationary line, which stood at attention, with the demonstrators still quietly sitting on the floor. They rose slowly for the alma mater, and as the audience shouted "Throw them out," Perkins told the campus police to form a circle around the protesters, protecting them as they left Barton Hall.[14]

The next day a petition signed by 750 students asking for "prompt and firm action" against the protesters was sent to Perkins. On May 20, the Undergraduate Judiciary Board recommended the relatively mild rebuke of "reprimands"

The Ad Hoc Committee to End the War disrupts ROTC graduation ceremonies, 1965. (Division of Rare and Manuscript Collections of the Cornell University Library)

for the students from the options in order of severity: warning, reprimand, disciplinary probation, suspension, and expulsion. The UJB warned that a second offense might lead to separation from the university. The protesters maintained in a statement to the board that they had "a duty and a legal right" to stage the ROTC demonstration, which had been "orderly and responsible and violated no university regulations." Four days later, the Faculty Committee on Student Conduct, exercising its authority to rehear cases, increased the penalty by one degree, placing the students on "disciplinary probation," since they acted "in such a fashion as to constitute disorderly and irresponsible conduct." Even a sincere moral belief, the FCSC held, "does not give one the right to determine the legitimacy or to obstruct the freedom of others."[15] The probationary sentence was for the remainder of the semester, a matter of only several days until commencement.

Perkins was pleased that the university's difficult centennial spring semester had ended with relative calm. The faculty, at his urging, had also responded to the Harriman affair with a resolution recording its concern "at the jeopardy in which the right to hear and be heard was placed" and insisting on "the preservation of all conditions essential to freedom of expression" at Cornell.[16] Walter

Berns, chairman of the Government Department, wrote Perkins "that you deserve only the highest praise for the way you have handled the problem of free speech," thwarting "the group on this campus that may be trying to produce a Berkeley-like situation here at Cornell."[17] At commencement, Perkins's pleasure at what he saw as the university's principled response to protest and confrontation was evident. "I think," the president told the assembled celebrants, "we came to a more sophisticated view of the reciprocal rights to speak and to be heard," and "that it is not within the spirit of the university to use physical pressure, whether violently or peacefully, as a substitute for reason."[18] In a late May personal note to Vice President Mark Barlow Jr., EdD '62, he shared his belief "that we may be through the worst of it, although I may be wrong. Those who are leading the Ad Hoc Committee on Vietnam are determined to make a public circus of their concern, but by this time the campus seems to be pretty well united in its view that this sort of thing is out of order. Perhaps we had to have the events themselves in order to demonstrate the point."[19]

————————

PERKINS WAS WRONG. In the next three years Cornell would become one of the central sites of student antiwar activism on America's campuses because of the moral and strategic leadership provided by Cornell United Religious Work (CURW) and the Cornell chapter of SDS.

The priest and poet Dan Berrigan arrived on campus in 1966 to be the assistant director of CURW and a chaplain to the Cornell Catholic community. He led marches, vigils, and campus fasts against the war in 1967, while refusing to pay his taxes. In January 1968, during the Tet offensive, he went to North Vietnam with Boston University professor Howard Zinn, to receive three American POW airmen. That May, along with eight other Catholic activists, Berrigan was arrested for destroying nearly four hundred files of the Catonsville, Maryland, draft board, claiming "we did it to serve our soul and manhood."[20] In a pretrial "rally" at Bailey Hall, he spoke briefly and read poetry to over two thousand students, who were told by the event's organizers that the dean of students had "granted University excuses for students going to Baltimore for the trial of the Catonsville 9."[21] Some 275 Cornellians attended the trial, where Berrigan was convicted. Sentenced to three years in prison, he instead went into hiding, eluding the FBI for three years, even as he occasionally showed up and quickly disappeared from Cornell events, as he did on April 20, 1970, speaking to the five thousand people gathered at Barton Hall, at the celebration of "the spirit of non-violence" organized by the local activist Jack Goldman, coincidentally scheduled on the first anniversary of the Willard Straight Hall takeover. Berrigan was apprehended later that year, sent to prison, and released in 1972.

Berrigan was not alone; others at CURW also bore witness against the war at the organization's new "Commons" coffeehouse in Anabel Taylor Hall, equipped with the only espresso machine in Tompkins County. Thirty-year-old David Connor, another Catholic chaplain, and a former Cornell football player, mailed his draft card to his Geneseo, New York, local board in 1967 and was notified immediately that he was reclassified "Delinquent 1A" and ordered to report for induction. Accompanied by some ninety Cornell students and a few faculty, Connor refused to be inducted into the army at the Buffalo induction center. Paul Gibbons, thirty-four, a Protestant chaplain at Cornell since 1963 and married father of three small children, mailed his draft card to his White Plains, New York, board and was also peremptorily called up for induction. He refused to serve "not out of bitterness, but out of concern and love for my country."[22] In the spring of 1970, CURW went "on strike," closing Anabel Taylor, it told the *Sun*, "to put at least one department of the university on record as officially opposed to the war. . . . Enough is enough."[23]

SDS, founded in 1962 by Tom Hayden at the University of Michigan, burst on the scene at Cornell in the academic year 1965–66, quickly replacing the Ad Hoc Committee to End the War as the epicenter of antiwar activism. By 1969, the Cornell chapter, with Douglas Dowd as its faculty adviser and with 250 members, was the third-largest in the country, behind Harvard and Columbia. It had recruiters and organizers in most dorms and even in the Ithaca public school system, much to the ire of parents at DeWitt Middle School. The Cornell chapter had lengthy, consensus-seeking meetings where anyone could speak, though members recall that male students did most of the talking, and a leadership that rotated among the omnipresent David Burak '67, MFA '80, and his roommate, Chip Marshall '68, both of whom were former members of Sigma Nu fraternity, and the charismatic Bruce Dancis. While the leadership of Cornell's SDS was predominantly male, as in most chapters, there was a significant number of women students active in the antiwar movement on campus, within and outside SDS. Mary Jo Ghory '69, for example, doused three marine recruiters at Barton Hall with cans of paint in 1969.

Cornell administrators had their channels to the overwhelmingly white SDS student radicals, which they lacked with the AAS. Burak, for example, who occasionally wrote for the *Ithaca Journal*, was hired by Perkins at one point to provide him a paper on the "various positions and points of view of the New Left." And Provost Corson, years later, claimed that a member of the faculty "kept me informed about what was going on, even leaving meetings of SDS to telephone me to tell me what they were planning."[24]

Such was the prominence and clout of Cornell SDS that Burak got approval from the office of the dean of students in early 1969 to allow the chapter to host the SDS National Convention that June. Following the takeover of the Straight, permission was withdrawn by Corson on June 3, because "tension on the campus makes it impossible for him to allow us to meet here."[25] Not that there was much common cause between black and white student militancy at Cornell in

1969 or in the late '60s in general, even if it was their voter registration work in Tennessee's Fayette County in the summers of 1964 and 1965 that helped radicalize Dowd and the Griffiths. There was some mutual support: black students helped with the SDS "housing for Ithaca's poor" initiative, and SDS opposed apartheid and supported the Straight takeover, leading the Barton Hall Community that followed it. Perkins gave his interpretation in a June 1968 talk to university presidents at the Carnegie Corporation: "The black students at Cornell think they've brought the internal problems of the university to the surface, and therefore that they are the real radicals. They feel the SDS is concerned with problems outside the university, blacks with problems inside it."[26]

The dramatic new role for SDS at Cornell was ushered in by the arrival of the freshman Bruce Dancis from the Bronx, who soon made common cause with Professor Robert Greenblatt, the Math Department's antiwar foil to the hawkish Professor Wolfowitz. Greenblatt organized a massive antiwar teach-in at the beginning of Dancis's second semester on campus, at which he, Kahin, and Walter LaFeber spoke. In April, Greenblatt led a march of four hundred students from the Arts quad to DeWitt Park in downtown Ithaca, getting himself arrested following a fracas with the police. Four weeks later, in response to new national exams held on campus, required for college students seeking draft exemption, Dancis, with six other students, led by Tom Bell, SDS president, and with Greenblatt's support, "sat-in" President Perkins's office for eleven hours "to assert that Cornell University in administering the exam is deeply involved in the war, as an agent of the federal government," collaborating with the military and the Selective Service system.[27] A two-hour meeting with Perkins, in which the group was joined by the one hundred other students and faculty, including Greenblatt, who had been assembled outside the president's office all along, ended with Perkins agreeing to the group's demand that the university reconsider Cornell's policy on administering the Selective Service exam, after the already scheduled May and June tests.

Trespassing charges against the six students were dismissed by the Undergraduate Judiciary Board, citing First Amendment rights and "their efforts to be orderly and responsible." Perkins appointed a committee "to explore the Draft and the university's relationship to it."[28] The campus was ambivalent. Some colleges, like Arts, defied the government's classification of the lower 50 percent of the class as subject to the draft by eliminating class rankings. At the same time, the faculty voted two-to-one in favor of some system of student deferment. In a huge referendum, students voted narrowly in favor, 3,300 to 3,242, of Cornell continuing to calculate and record class standings, but two-to-one—4,423 to 2,138—against using university facilities to administer the Selective Service qualification test, on which a score of 90 percent or better allowed a student to maintain his deferment.

There was no end of complications in the university's "relationship" to the draft. In 1966 Cornell reversed its policy, announcing that the registrar would no longer supply local draft boards with an academic transcript unless requested to do so by the student. In a memo to Perkins, Corson refined the policy to allow a student "to sign a statement saying he does not want such information released under any circumstances." At most, the registrar was allowed to certify that a student was "pursuing satisfactorily a course of full-time study at Cornell for the current academic year," which was enough to persuade most draft boards to grant exemption from the draft.[29] On the other hand, the university continued to allow the Selective Service exam to be held on campus. Meanwhile, the Educational Policy Committee of Arts and Sciences refused in 1967 to approve yet another antiwar math professor's plan to give his students in Math 122 only A's. Undeterred, Professor Len Silver told the *Sun* "I'm confident the students in my Math sections will be earning their A's."[30]

(A's proliferated in the late '60s with the beginning of the "grade inflation" that persists at Cornell and elsewhere to this day. Absent any provable causal connections, be they draft concerns or the spread of student "course evaluations," it is indisputable that in the turbulent decade from 1966 to 1976 the number of all undergraduate A grades at Cornell climbed by 64 percent, from 17 percent of all grades to 29 percent, and the number of C's dropped by 35 percent, from 32 percent to 20 percent. Hotel, Human Ecology, and Arts experienced the most pronounced increase, and ILR the least. Arts College dean Alfred Kahn noted that "the inexorable and sharp increase represented by these averages is absurd.")[31]

Dancis was the son of a World War II conscientious objector and a passionate opponent of the war. As co-chairman of Cornell SDS in the fall of 1966, he organized one of the country's first "We Won't Go" groups. On December 14, standing on the steps of Olin Hall before a crowd of two hundred, which included TV news crews and FBI agents, Dancis became the first college student and first SDS member in the U.S. to destroy his draft card, ripping it into four pieces and mailing it to Local Board 26 in the Bronx. A recently enacted federal law had made it a crime to mutilate a draft card, with a penalty of not more than $10,000 and/or imprisonment for no more than five years. Having become a national symbol of the "Resistance Movement," Dancis left Cornell to become the principal planner of a mass draft card burning in New York City on April 15, 1967, at the Spring Mobilization to End the War in Vietnam. "Powerful resistance," Dancis urged with a statement written by fellow Cornellian Burton Weiss, "is now demanded: radical, illegal, unpleasant, sustained." He wanted five hundred people to participate in the New York "burn in."[32]

Still living in Ithaca that spring term, Dancis, other SDS students, and Professor Greenblatt (soon to leave Cornell to be the national coordinator of the Mobilization to End the War), talked up the "burn in" at fraternity houses and

Bruce Dancis rips his draft card into four pieces. (Courtesy *Cornell Daily Sun*)

dorms. They set up tables in the Straight lobby in March, soliciting student pledges to burn cards in New York three weeks later. The Straight's board of managers refused to allow solicitation for an illegal act. Art Kaminsky '68, the chairman of the student committee that supervised all other student groups, while sympathetic to the war protesters' actions, grudgingly went along with the decision. Dancis and SDS persisted, continuing to occupy the lobby every day at noon for a week. Scuffles broke out between SDS students and Proctor George, who resuscitated and politicized the assumed dead doctrine of *in loco parentis*, because he was convinced that Cornell had an obligation to stop students from engaging in illegal activities. Burak argued, in turn, that the SDS students "recognized higher laws" than Cornell's or America's. Dancis agreed. "We're saying that we will no longer go along blindly, or go along without doing anything, while our government is committing what we consider to be mass murder in Vietnam. We are willing to risk five years in jail and a fine of $10,000 to stop this murder. We are saying that the university rules and Proctor George are irrelevant to this killing."[33] The formal charges against nineteen students for violating university rules were dismissed by the UJB, which termed their actions "responsible dissent."[34]

More than twelve hundred Cornellians went by bus and car to New York on Friday, April 14, their departure delayed for an hour when some seventy-five students blocked their vehicles. Led by the Hotel student Seth Bramson '69 from Miami, Florida, the Society to Oppose Protesters (STOP) sought "to show that there are those on the campus who are repulsed by the complete disregard and contempt for duly constituted authority."[35] They dispersed only when the ever-busy Lowell George intervened. Once at the mobilization, the Cornell contingent announced itself to the nearly quarter of a million people in Central Park with a huge white banner "We Won't Go—Cornell." After taking pictures of Martin Luther King Jr., Harry Belafonte, Dr. Benjamin Spock, and Stokely Carmichael, reporters and FBI agents moved to the Dancis group's scheduled "burn in." He did not get his 500 people. About 170 people, 20 of them Cornellians, put their draft cards into the flaming coffee can he held while supporters cried "Resist! Resist!"[36]

Dancis, who had been indicted ten days earlier for his December Olin Hall draft card destruction, discovered years later from his own FBI file, that J. Edgar

The Society to Oppose Protestors (STOP) blocks vehicles taking demonstrators to the Spring Mobilization to End the War in Vietnam in New York City in April 1967. (Division of Rare and Manuscript Collections of the Cornell University Library)

Hoover, hoping to discourage others by going after draft resistance leaders, had sent a memo to the U.S. attorney for upstate New York, stating, "It's very important that you indict Dancis before April 15."[37] Dancis was sentenced in November 1968 to a maximum of six years in jail. He was released on bail, pending a possible appeal, largely as the result of a petition to the court signed by five thousand Cornell students and President Perkins, who also sent a private letter to the U.S. Court of Appeals favoring release on bail, which the court made public, causing a fuss the *New York Times* made much of. When he returned to campus, a standing-room-only crowd of about five hundred jammed into the Straight's Memorial Room to welcome him. Dancis eventually served nineteen months in a Kentucky federal prison.

General Lewis Hershey, director of Selective Service, issued an edict in late 1967, calling for the immediate induction of draft obstructers. Perkins, who wrote to Hershey denouncing the policy, was put on the spot in early 1968 when a noontime SDS rally at Willard Straight attended by some 350 students protested the December letter sent to a Mount Vernon, New York, draft board by Cornell's assistant registrar C. Edward Maynard, urging that board to take away the student deferment of Michael Singer '68. It did, after learning that Singer had burned his draft card. Perkins settled what quickly was dubbed the "Singer Case" repudiating Maynard's intervention as "totally unauthorized in terms of university policy."[38] He asked the draft board to disregard Maynard's letter and insisted that Maynard send a personal apology to Singer. Two months later, the registrar's office was relieved of all but perfunctory Selective Service functions, and the office of the dean of students became the central administrative resource for Selective Service issues and information on campus.

Efforts were made on campus in 1967 to have a civil and rational debate about the war. A four-day national student conference on Vietnam was held on campus, chaired by the student government activist Mark Belnick '68. The more than 150 delegates from forty colleges and universities heard antiwar arguments from national figures including Marcus Raskin and David Dellinger, and locals George Kahin and Pat Griffith. Supporting the war were Professor Wesley Fischel of Michigan State University and Professor I. Milton Sacks of Brandeis. In the same spirit of open discussion, President Johnson's secretary of state, Dean Rusk, whose son Richard '69 was then a Cornell undergraduate and antiwar activist, was invited to speak on campus. After agreeing to come, he canceled, citing a scheduling conflict, though letters to the *Sun* suggested a fear "of a hostile reception which might be waiting."[39] In March, however, Rusk spoke to a generally supportive crowd of twenty-two hundred in Bailey Hall. When he was introduced by President Perkins, fifteen people silently walked out, and another fifty donned white death masks and sat quietly with their backs to him. When Rusk declined to answer a post-talk question about antipersonnel weapons, he was hissed and booed.

Everyone on campus was considering or reconsidering his or her views on the war. In a letter to President Johnson, reprinted in the *Daily Sun*, 293 Cornell faculty, the vice president for student affairs, the dean of students, and the dean of the faculty made what they deemed "a reasoned and compelling argument for the immediate halt to the bombing of North Vietnam."[40] After lengthy deliberations, the Executive Board of Student Government voted 7–1 for the immediate cessation of bombing and withdrawal of U.S. support for the Nguyen Cao Ky regime in South Vietnam, and, in a massive referendum sponsored by the executive board, an end to bombing was favored 3,497 to 2,994. Students made nuanced distinctions in their expressions of antiwar sentiment. An executive board proposal in October to pay the expenses of buses going from campus to the Pentagon protest with student government funds was defeated in a referendum by a three-to-one margin, 1,229 yes and 3,511 no. About half the no votes, including write-ins, were along the lines of "if they want to take a trip, deport them."[41]

Despite their rebuff on using student funds for the buses, Cornell's antiwar protesters were galvanized by the October 21, 1967, March on the Pentagon. The charismatic priest David Connor led some fifty students in a four-day fast for peace before they left for Washington, joined there by Father Dan Berrigan. The Cornell contingent, smaller by hundreds than those who had gone the shorter distance to the Spring Mobilization, joined the October "assault on the Pentagon" that Norman Mailer forever engraved on the American psyche in the best seller *The Armies of the Night*. Seventeen Cornellians, including Father Berrigan, were among the 430 people arrested at the protest. Two years later, the journalist and feminist writer Susan Brownmiller, who had been a student at Cornell in the 1950s, also wrote about the event in *Esquire* magazine. Janet Reno would have been pleased:

> Norman Mailer's account of "notables" there be damned. Was he aware that the first brigade to charge the barricades of that awesome military citadel carried a Cornell banner? Cornell, let me repeat. My school. To a member of the class of 1956—a solemn representative of the Silent Generation—a Cornell banner leading the charge of the Pentagon has more historic importance than the comings and goings of Norman's friends. Well, I exaggerate my case. But NOBODY carried any banners at Cornell in my day, except to and from a football rally.[42]

Less than a month after their confrontation with armed military police at the Pentagon, three hundred Cornell antiwar protesters led by Father Connor and Bruce Dancis, still free on bail, trudged through the snow from a rally at the Straight, accompanied by fifty counterprotesters, to obstruct two crew-cut Marine recruiters in the lobby of Barton Hall. Surrounding them and blocking access to their recruitment table for two hours, protesters asked, "Why are you killing innocent women and children in Vietnam?" One recruiter, a decorated thirteen-month veteran of Vietnam, replied "I have never heard of any such orders being given, or any such actions being taken." Counterprotesters shouted

"Communists" at the protesters, who shouted back "Nazis." When asked by the students to cancel a planned second day of recruiting because the marines "failed to engage in open and free debate," Perkins refused. Cornell had to be an open campus, he insisted, welcome to all visitors, including military and corporate recruiters.[43] Charges were lodged against 132 students who refused to obey the proctor's orders to clear an aisle to the recruiters' table.

Typical campus ambivalence, uncertainty, and indecisiveness about the war followed. The Undergraduate Judiciary Board voted 4–3 to take "no action" against the 132 demonstrators, holding that "no action" was not acquittal, the protesters were "basically peaceful" and "the actions did not warrant punishment."[44] The UJB worried as well about General Hershey's edict and its threat to free speech and dissent on campus. The next day the Faculty Council, which had earlier sided with Perkins, voting that "the campus should remain open to all recruitment for legal employment," banned military recruiters on campus if Hershey's call for immediate induction of those obstructing the draft were not promptly rescinded.[45] Nine days later, the Faculty Committee on Student Conduct (FCSC) overturned the UJB's decision to take no action against the 132 students, "reprimanded" 129, and placed three others on "disciplinary probation," on the grounds that "obstruction and interference with a regularly scheduled university event constituted serious misconduct." One member of the FCSC, Sociology professor Robert McGinnis, resigned, charging that the committee had "disregarded the propriety of dissent."[46] Three members of the UJB, one of whom was Tom Jones '69, MRP '72, quit as well.

Two months later eight hundred students marched in an orderly double picket line around Malott Hall where four recruiters from Dow Chemical Company, the makers of napalm, were interviewing students from the Graduate School of Business and Public Administration. People were allowed to walk freely across the picket lines, in and out of the building, encountering signs that read "Burn draft cards, not children" and "Dow shalt not kill."[47]

To be sure, not all Cornell students were at odds with the United States government in these years. In striking contrast to campus antiwar protest, the Cornell Glee Club in late 1965 accepted an invitation from the U.S. State Department's Office of Cultural Presentations to be goodwill ambassadors in Asia. Forty-one members spent the entire spring 1966 semester singing over seventy concerts in ten Asian countries, often appearing on radio and television, as well. A Taiwanese general who saw a performance on TV flew the Glee Club on a C-110 cargo plane to the island of Quemoy, where a hastily arranged concert for his troops was held in a large underground hall carved out of rock. All this ten miles from Red China. The singers, who were not officially enrolled in classes during the semester and therefore subject to the draft, received special deferments from the U.S. government.

THE VIETCONG'S JANUARY Tet offensive throughout South Vietnam, defying the optimistic predictions of President Johnson in Washington and General William Westmoreland in Saigon, ushered in the dramatic set of events that punctuated 1968. In March, Johnson announced he would not seek reelection. In April, an assassin killed Martin Luther King Jr. As black ghettos exploded, SDS students, barricaded in Columbia University buildings, were pummeled by university and New York City police. In June, the morning after defeating Eugene McCarthy and Vice President Hubert Humphrey in the California Democratic presidential primary, Robert Kennedy was murdered in the kitchen of a Los Angeles hotel. And in August, Chicago's mayor Richard Daley used massive force to quell the antiwar "days of rage" intended to disrupt the Democratic National Convention.

Father Connor and 130 students drove to New Hampshire to work a weekend for antiwar candidate Eugene McCarthy in that state's early presidential primary. Forty-four administrators and professors, including Hans Bethe, Mark Barlow, and Steven Muller, PhD '58, signed a statement endorsing McCarthy. Two visitors were deeply, though differently, struck by the antiwar passion on campus. In Ithaca for a weekend with his undergraduate daughter in April 1968, a "dismayed and disturbed" parent wrote to Perkins that at a Saturday evening concert of the singers Simon and Garfunkel, he was held "captive to their un-American distasteful utterances. . . . It hurt me to hear applause from America's youth for two such seditious individuals."[48] In contrast, the Republican senator from New York Charles Goodell attributed his conversion from staunch supporter of the war to one of the Senate's leading doves to his soul-searching after a tense meeting with militant antiwar students on a visit to Cornell. Meanwhile, President Perkins wrote to a trustee that the Columbia University disaster bolstered his belief "that Cornell's investment of time and energy in dealing reasonably with students has paid off and it is disastrous not to do so." At Cornell, he told the *Ithaca Journal* in June, "The things that have led to militancy elsewhere have been better handled. Students have the feelings that somebody's likely to listen to their complaints."[49]

When Richard Nixon defeated Hubert Humphrey that November, Professor Douglas Dowd was a candidate for vice president of the United States. A believer in nonviolent civil disobedience, who had supported the more nonviolent faction in Cornell's SDS in the many meetings he sat through as faculty adviser and who had urged moderation at the Democratic Convention's chaotic street protests, Dowd was on the Peace and Freedom Party ticket with its presidential candidate, Black Panther leader Eldridge Cleaver. His party managed to round up enough signatures to be on the ballot in California and New York. Dowd's nineteen-year-old son, Jeffrey, a college student on Long Island, was arrested with nine Cornell undergraduates by Cornell police the following

May Day in an SDS disruption of an ROTC practice drill in a gun cage at Barton Hall. Cornell chose to bring the charges against the "Barton Hall Ten" to the City Court in Ithaca. SDS was bringing the war at home to the entities it considered the most visible sign on campus of the "American war machine" and of Cornell's "complicity with the military": the air force, army, and navy ROTC units in Barton Hall. After the May 1 protest, the Cornell SDS chapter demanded in a letter to Perkins that charges be dropped against the Barton Hall Ten and that the university "abolish the ROTC program."[50]

Still in his law-and-order mood just weeks after the Straight takeover and recently urged by the trustees to make "firm and appropriate responses to campus disturbances," Perkins defended the civil charges brought against the ten, claiming that "to have allowed these acts to go unnoticed would put in jeopardy all of the efforts to assure the rest of the community that the administration and faculty meant what it said, that breaking the rules would require punishment."[51] Surprisingly, one of the leading critics of Perkins's actions was Allan Sindler, the Government Department chairman, who had already announced his resignation from Cornell at the end of term. While he decried SDS's Barton Hall action, Sindler felt that the decision to prosecute off-campus was a "gross violation" of the existing system; because the action did not "constitute a very serious breach of the law" it should have been "handled exclusively within the campus adjudicative system."[52]

The case was heard by Judge James J. Clynes Jr., JD '48, without a jury, in late September. The trial, the first face-off between radical students and established "authority" since the Straight episode, attracted a good deal of attention. Law professor Harrop Freeman '29, LLB '30, JD '46, a familiar defender of student activists, argued that the SDS protesters were exercising their constitutional rights of free speech. And for six days a parade of witnesses, which included Cornell trustees, Day Hall officials, and university faculty, answered questions about whether or not they considered the SDS actions at Barton a "serious breach of the law," which according to the code alone merited downtown prosecution. In his testimony, trustee William R. Robertson '34, chairman of the committee that reviewed that spring's campus unrest, said that in light of the Straight takeover, he "didn't consider the Barton Hall incident a serious breach of the law."[53]

Judge Clynes never had to settle the sticky jurisdictional issue. In early December, three of the Barton Hall Ten—Chip Marshall and Joe Kelly '68, and Jeffrey Dowd—preferring to be lawbreakers, pleaded guilty to a charge of third-degree criminal trespass. They were each fined $50 and released with orders that they could not participate in any unlawful activities in Tompkins County for one year. A week later, Clynes dismissed the charges against the others "because of insufficient evidence to prove the defendants' presence with criminal intent in the fenced off ROTC area."[54]

Based on voluntary enlistment since 1960, and in 1969 totaling around 350 men, ROTC did not sit that easily with the Cornell faculty. A Presidential Commission on Military Training, appointed by Perkins in September 1968 and headed by his vice provost Keith Kennedy, MS '41, PhD '47, recommended retaining ROTC, but urged fundamental changes such as dropping university credit for courses in military skills and having academic departments instead of military officers teach courses with political or policy content. In 1969, by a 60 percent majority, the faculty rejected a commission recommendation championed by Professor Paul Olum of Mathematics that would make military training an extracurricular and noncredit activity, conducted off campus, preferably in summer programs. In a closer vote several months later, the faculty defeated by a nine-vote margin the motion by Law professor David Ratner to eliminate ROTC altogether, while retaining the university's responsibility under the Morrill Land Grant Act to provide instruction in "military tactics" through a program "limited to providing academic instruction, within the framework of the university's regular departments."[55]

In his first semester as president, the fall of 1969, Corson, who had spent three years in the Pentagon during World War II, visited the assistant director of ROTC programs at the Department of Defense. He urged free discussion of controversial issues in ROTC classrooms, and no penalties for students who left the program as upperclassmen. In a memorandum for the record, he wrote, "I came away with the impression that we will be encouraged to suggest modifications in the existing ROTC program, and that we will at least be heard with interest." On his return to campus, Corson recommended that Cornell continue ROTC "because a civilian influence on the nation's corps of military advisors is healthy."[56] It would be best if the policymaking part of the military were trained in major universities, not military academies, he advised. Reassured by Corson, the faculty voted 385–99 to retain ROTC, with some modifications that put it under closer civilian scrutiny of the faculty.

That evening sixty-five SDS protesters crossed rope barriers and chanted during the naval ROTC drill in Barton. This time internal university charges were brought against eight of the protesters, including David Burak and Professor Dowd, by the judicial administrator, Professor Joseph Bugliari, JD '59, before the University Hearing Board, both offices recently created in post-Straight-takeover campus judicial reforms. They were found guilty of disrupting a university event and were "reprimanded."

Despite President Nixon's plan for a gradual "Vietnamization" of the war, protest continued. In August 1969, forty-five Cornell SDS students picketed the U.S. Marine recruiting office on State Street, shouting "two, four, six, eight, organize to smash the state."[57] Marching with Cornell students was Mark Rudd, SDS national secretary and leader of the Columbia antiwar movement in 1968. Three months later, in an unprecedented expression of public dissent, more than two million opponents of Nixon's policies stopped work on the morning of October 14. At Cornell, the "Moratorium" found most classes canceled, or, as in one organic chemistry lecture, 32 of the enrolled 273 students in attendance. Senator Goodell spoke to seventy-five hundred people in Barton Hall, where President Corson and a number of his vice presidents sat on hard wooden benches. Early in the afternoon, Corson spoke to about three thousand people on the Arts quad, denouncing the war "as a citizen of this community, as a citizen and educator, rather than as President."[58]

Then came Cambodia and Kent State. Nixon announced the U.S. bombing and invasion of Cambodia on the evening of April 30, 1970. That next morning he told reporters, "You will now see these bums, you know blowing up the campuses . . . burning up the books."[59] Four days later, Ohio National Guardsmen shot and killed four students at an antiwar demonstration at Kent State University, with Nixon insisting that the protesters bore the responsibility for their own deaths. These momentous events occurred after a month in which racial and political rage had already engulfed Cornell's campus: the Africana Studies Center at 320 Wait had been destroyed by fire; on April 19, the first

Antiwar rally, 1969. (Division of Rare and Manuscript Collections of the Cornell University Library)

anniversary of the Straight takeover, the fugitive Daniel Berrigan had shown up at a massive "Freedom Seder" in Barton Hall; Dowd, returned from a visit of academics and clergy to North Vietnam, had told students about the Vietcong's humane treatment of POWs and of his gift of a copy of Berrigan's newest book of poetry to Prime Minister Pham Van Dong; the Cornell police and dean of students' office had acknowledged they were compiling a photographic file of students at both racial and antiwar demonstrations.

After Kent State, student "strikes" spread to hundreds of colleges. Eight thousand students in Barton Hall voted about four-to-one on Monday night, May 9, to boycott classes. A handful of black students proposed, and then declined to bring to a vote, that the university publicly support Black Panthers awaiting trial in New Haven. That same day, a group of 125 nonacademic employees voted to join the national "strike" against the war, even if their pay was docked for the time away from work. And CURW closed its Anabel Taylor doors for twenty-four hours. College deans insisted that classes and laboratories continue to meet, while acknowledging that individual faculty members had discretion over their classes. Recovering from a back injury, President Corson issued a statement from his New York hospital bed that "the university must officially go on." He shared the students' despair over the broadening of the war and the shootings at Kent State but pointed out that while "some will find it impossible to go on . . . closing the university is not an effective means for expressing these concerns."[60]

Claiming the invasion of Cambodia was unconstitutional, sixty-eight Cornell faculty called for President Nixon's impeachment. The faculty in the College of Arts and Science voted 110–44 to urge individual faculty members to suspend classes. Across the university some faculty canceled term-paper assignments, postponed or canceled exams, and declared that final course grades would be based on work done to that point in the term, since there was only a week of classes left. At a meeting with 750 present, the university faculty, expressing "horror and anger" at the shootings at Kent State, announced officially that students participating in antiwar activities could either take an "incomplete" or receive a letter grade or a Satisfactory/Unsatisfactory for work completed through May 4.[61] All other students would complete all class work as previously scheduled.

An estimated one-half of the student body observed the strike. Some 450 of them put on shirts and ties or dresses to talk to residents of Ithaca and Tompkins County about the expansion of the Vietnam War into Cambodia. They carried antiwar petitions with about forty-five hundred signatures to the area's congressman, Howard Robinson (R–Owego), and the state's two Republican senators, Jacob Javits and Charles Goodell. Other students used sawhorses, cinderblocks, old tires, fallen branches, and inoperable automobiles to erect street barricades and roadblocks on and near campus, hoping to bring university operations to a standstill. A small group of students answering a flyer call to

Cornell Vietnam Mobilization
Committee, 1970. (Division of Rare
and Manuscript Collections of the
Cornell University Library)

meet on the grassy roof of the Campus Store for a "riot," dispersed after two hours, having hurled stones and bottles at the store, breaking three panes of glass worth $1,500. The week ended with seven chartered buses and forty rented cars taking between five and six hundred Cornellians to Washington to join a thousand more Cornellians already there, as part of the huge national antiwar weekend effort to lobby representatives and senators.

Still smoldering, campus tensions hijacked the combined commencement and formal inauguration of President Corson in Barton Hall a month later. Father Connor indicted the war and racial injustice, black students walked out, a Vietnamese woman in graduation robes held a placard throughout the ceremony reading "Vietnamization of the war is not peace," and David Burak tussled with Professor Morris Bishop '13, PhD '26, the mace bearer. Corson, who ordered Burak banned from campus and had him arrested for trespass several months later, was nonetheless pleased to tell the thousands of alumni who returned to campus a week later for reunion that "the Cornell campus behaved in an extremely mature fashion after the Cambodian announcement and the Kent State tragedy compared with other institutions in the nation."[62]

A "citizenship recess" was observed that fall from October 24 to November 4 to allow students to participate in activities related to the midterm national elections. The unprecedented revision of the academic calendar, which had been approved by the new University Senate at its second meeting in late spring after Kent State, was opposed, unsuccessfully, by an editorial in the *Cornell Daily Sun* and by a small number of History and Government faculty. L. Pearce Williams '48, PhD '52, Mack Walker, Alvin Bernstein '61, PhD '69, Arch Dotson, and Werner Dannhauser informed the *Sun* that "during the so-called citizenship recess we will do what we continue as our privilege and duty to do: we will teach."[63]

In the next semester, as the war continued, the second spring Vietnam War "Moratorium," on May 5, 1971, saw several Cornellians arrested in Washington protests. In Ithaca, a thousand students gathered in front of the Campus Store to hear Democratic senator Vance Hartke from Indiana and President Corson denounce the war. By the end of the day, 128 letters and 222 telegrams had been sent to Washington legislators, and sixteen hundred people had signed petitions urging support of the bipartisan Hatfield-McGovern amendment cutting off all funding of the war by the end of the year. According to the *Sun*, however, "the vast majority of the students attended classes as usual."[64]

The dramatic and unexpected re-escalation of the war a year later on April 15, 1972, with massive B-52 bombings of Hanoi and Haiphong for the first time since 1968 and thousands of civilian casualties, set in motion a sequence of events that led to the most disruptive event of the by-then seven years of Cornell antiwar protest—the occupation of Carpenter Hall. Just two days before the resumption of bombing, a teach-in organized by the Concerned Asian Scholars drew eight hundred people to Bailey Hall to hear representatives of the Vietnamese and Cambodian liberation movements. An antiwar parade of 350 people around campus on April 18 took a vote and narrowly decided against seizing a university building. The University Senate then condemned the bombing and called on Cornell to join other universities on Friday, April 21, for a nationwide student strike demanding immediate cessation of U.S. involvement in the war. The university remained open, with a few classes called off, but in the largest demonstration since May 1970, sixteen hundred Cornell students marched downtown to Washington Park, where, joined by two hundred Ithaca College students and townspeople, they heard antiwar speeches.

That same month students demanded that Cornell sell its holdings in Gulf Oil if the company did not stop assisting the repression of anticolonial movements in Portuguese Africa. Some three hundred students, nearly all black, organized as STOP—the acronym this time for "Students to Oppose Persecution"—went to Day Hall on April 24 with an anti-Gulf petition that had seventeen hundred signatures, including Provost Bob Plane's. That day, however, the Trustee Investment Committee reaffirmed the view of Chairman

225

Robert Purcell '33, LLB '35, that "we can't use the investment portfolio as a primary instrument to affect social change." STOP pledged "to keep pressure on our enemies" but also not to take over any campus buildings.[65] Two days later, Wednesday, April 26, an "anti-war, anti-imperialist" noontime rally of some two hundred mainly white students and a handful of faculty, angry with the trustees' vote, set out to occupy Barton Hall. They proceeded first into the Engineering administration and library building, Carpenter Hall, telling the occupants to leave. After chaining the doors closed, seventy-five protesters remained in the building. No blacks took part in the Carpenter Hall occupation.

Two dozen campus policemen smashed their way into the building the first day, battering down a huge plate glass window, whereupon the occupiers retreated to the library. After some scuffling and harsh words, an uneasy truce ensued, with the police settling in to occupy and keep open the rest of the building, while preventing any of the several thousand students who surrounded Carpenter that night from entering it. Windows were opened, nonetheless, and the ranks of protesters in the library grew to between 200 and 250, some bringing bags of food with them. The first action of the protesters, denouncing "Cornell's complicity in the War machine," while chanting "U.S. out of Indochina—Cornell out of Gulf," was to rename Carpenter "Giap-Cabral Hall."[66] Vo Nguyen Giap was the principal military strategist of Vietnam's twenty-five-year anti-imperialist struggle against the Japanese and the French; Amílcar Cabral was a leader of the freedom movement in Portugal's African colonies.

President Corson was at a meeting of university presidents at Northwestern that day, so it was Provost Plane who arrived about midnight Wednesday to meet with the protesters. He informed them they were violating the rules for maintaining public order, which the state legislature had mandated for New York colleges after the Straight takeover. In turn, they presented him with four "negotiable demands": that Cornell end all war-related and Defense Department research on campus; that it get rid of the Buffalo-based Cornell Aeronautical Laboratory, a decision already made but not yet finalized; that it "force Gulf Oil out of Portuguese African colonies"; that it phase out ROTC from campus. Plane remained in the library for a while to "talk and listen" but not "to negotiate over their demands."[67] He told reporters that there were no plans to remove the students if they decided to stay overnight. The university would, instead, temporarily suspend anyone who could be identified from photos that had been taken by the police during the takeover of the building.

Cutting short his trip, Corson returned the next day and met with the students for thirty minutes at 2:30 Friday morning. He would later write, "I was politely received . . . and there was none of the ugly, threatening mood which had characterized some of the earlier campus troubles." They were "flailing about . . . seeking to do something in opposition to the war, no matter how

Carpenter Hall takeover, April 26, 1972. (Division of Rare and Manuscript Collections of the Cornell University Library)

ineffective and useless it might be." Corson decided not to remove the protesters by force. He did not want "the spectacle of police carrying out limp students through the inevitable hostile crowd, four policemen to each student. I had had enough of unhappy newspaper photographs in the Willard Straight episode in 1969." The president concurred with trustee chair Robert Purcell's advice: "Just let them sit; they'll get tired of it after a while." Meanwhile, the *Ithaca Journal* speculated that Corson's decision stemmed "from his personal commitment to non-violence and his sympathy for the protestors' general goals."[68]

Corson did obtain a temporary restraining order from the New York State Supreme Court, which deemed anyone who continued to remain in the building in contempt of court, even as the occupiers used a rigged-up window service to provide library books requested by Engineering students. Although they voted unanimously to stay and face suspension or possible arrest, the weekend erosion of campus support turned the tide. Forty to fifty Engineering faculty tried unsuccessfully to "open" the library and talk to the protesters on Saturday, while a group of students marched on Day Hall demanding that the library resume normal operations. A spring weekend featuring the gala Hotel Ezra Cornell and Risley College's Medieval Fair attracted thousands, compared with the dwindling crowd of several hundred outside Carpenter Hall, where the protesters ate a steady diet of peanut butter and jelly sandwiches. There were varsity baseball and tennis matches against Brown, and lots of students were "just basking in the warm spring sun."[69] Equally devastating to the protest was the cutting of the cord to its sound amplifier by an angry Law School professor, William Tucker Dean, who at the time was also the Justice of the Peace in Cayuga Heights.

On Monday, the beginning of finals week, a series of contempt summonses were served, and the occupiers marched out of Carpenter, declaring "victory." They could credibly do so because that day, in New York City, the Trustee Investment Committee, headed by Jansen Noyes Jr. '39, decided for the first time ever to oppose management in a proxy vote—not involving Gulf Oil, to be sure, but General Motors' involvement in South Africa. A Day Hall staffer, Tom Tobin, director of university relations, noted "the general consensus was that Dale Corson must have really laid it on the line to the Investment Committee."[70] Later in May, the University Hearing Board convicted twenty-six of the Carpenter Hall students of violating Cornell University rules for the maintenance of public order. They were each given one year of probation and a fine of $250. Downtown, seventeen occupiers of Carpenter Hall were found guilty of civil contempt of court for violating the restraining order issued by State Supreme Court justice Frederick B. Bryant. Eight of them paid fines, and nine, including Professor Chandler Morse, served two-week jail sentences.

Morse's Economics Department colleague, Douglas Dowd, played no role in the Giap-Cabral events; he had left Cornell for San José State University in 1971. He told the *Sun* he had been in Ithaca since 1953 and had had enough. "People at Cornell know they've got it made and spend their time simply enjoying themselves," Dowd said. "I'm tired of teaching rich kids to feel guilty enough to try to solve the problems of the poor."[71] Bruce Dancis did not return to complete his degree requirements after serving his jail sentence, and Father Berrigan went to Fordham after his time in prison. Barred from campus, Burak also turned to college teaching in California, as the National SDS itself disintegrated in the early 1970s from factional bickering. Fifteen months after the occupation of Carpenter Hall, United States military involvement in Vietnam ended, in August 1973, and with it the draft.

RICHARD ALPERT AND Timothy Leary, peripatetic missionaries for the hallucinogenic LSD cult, both visited Cornell in the middle 1960s. The university insisted, at the conclusion of Alpert's moderately well attended 1965 talk, that a doctor from the medical school be allowed to read a statement about the dangers of drugs, an intervention that elicited several angry letters to the *Sun*. A panel discussion with two medical experts describing the need to restrict the use of LSD drew three hundred people to Bailey Hall in the fall of 1966, including Burton I. Weiss, who leapt onstage to claim the university was "one sided by not including advocates of the free use of hallucinogenic drugs."[72] A leading antiwar activist as well, Weiss was placed on "disciplinary probation" for two semesters.

A week later, Timothy Leary, brought to campus by Watermargin, told an overflow crowd of three thousand at Bailey that "modern society is an insane asylum." His new religion, the "Legion of Spiritual Discovery" (LSD), preached "the divinity of the individual, where everybody is a god, within himself." Leary urged the students not to "beat up" their repressive and conformist parents, but "when you're spiritually ready, go home and turn them on," preferably in "a private family shrine," dedicated to his new faith, LSD.[73]

A central feature of the 1960s collegiate assault on conformity and authority, the drug culture sat uneasily with political activism on campus. The "do your own thing" and "turn on, tune in, drop out" of Leary's religion and the general hippy quest for marijuana-based harmony, love, and understanding in a "new age of Aquarius" preached retreat and withdrawal to rural communes in Vermont and Colorado or urban flower culture sanctuaries in San Francisco, not collective action against political elites. Suspect as well to the disciples of enlightenment through drugs, heavily influenced by Eastern mystical spiritual traditions, was the rule of reason, science, and technology in the postwar university.

Estimates of drug use on campus in these years varied widely. In 1966 the university reported eight cases of "hallucinogenic drug use" to a U.S. Senate hearing conducted by New York's Robert Kennedy. The following year, the dean of students, Stanley Davis '47, PhD '51, claimed there were "around 90 users of LSD at Cornell last year," and that while some 15 percent of students had tried marijuana once, the "frequent users were less than 100." What had changed, Davis noted, was that "many students no longer consider marijuana use a crime or even especially dangerous."[74] By 1971, the consensus was that a majority of students were pot smokers—"more students who turn on than there are who don't." As one university official put it, "Don't get the idea that it's just the hippie type Collegetown group that's involved. In perhaps more cases, it's the typical square-looking fraternity and sorority type that's moved into this new culture."[75] The clientele were anything but square, however; in April 1967 about five hundred Cornellians gathered on a Saturday "to assert their love of love" at Cornell's first ever counterculture "be-in." Activities included "ring around the rosy" and "follow the piper." The *Daily Sun* reporter overheard some parents asking "Where have we gone wrong?"[76]

Cornell administrators were uncertain and ambivalent in their attitudes and policies toward drugs. On one hand, some felt the need to defend the academy's commitment to reason and rational inquiry against the apostles of unreason and irrationality, while a lingering sense of *in loco parentis* caused others to worry about student health and tacit "approval" of an illegal activity. On the other hand, there was a sense that the university had no place taking a moral stand on individual drug use, especially of marijuana, when it did not harm others. Moreover, use was almost impossible to detect and prevent, though trafficking in it was another matter. Complicating the university perspective was the widespread, legal, and traditionally approved consumption of alcohol by students over eighteen. Indeed, the Faculty Committee on Student Affairs had unanimously repealed the prohibition on alcoholic beverages in freshman dormitories in November 1967.

President Perkins announced in early 1965 that marijuana users on campus would be reported to the Tompkins County district attorney's office. He was concerned about easy access to pot in the Cornell community "and its use by even a few students." Cornell intended to do all it could, he added, "to remove the opportunity for life-long harm that grows out of the availability of narcotics."[77] A month later the district attorney, Richard Thaler '53, LLB '56, subpoenaed seven Cornell students to appear before the grand jury and then handed down two indictments, one against a student who had just left the university and the other against a senior in the Arts College. They were charged with selling marijuana, a felony, but were allowed to plead guilty to misdemeanor charges. On campus, the Judiciary Board and the FCSC placed the senior on disciplinary probation with mandatory counseling.

Rumors swept through campus in late 1966, denied by Mark Barlow and Thaler, that a crackdown on marijuana was imminent. A Cornell source told the *Sun* that "there has been an extraordinary increase in the amount of pot on campus since last year."[78] Several months into the next term, Thaler did indeed stage a dramatic predawn arrest by city and state police of eleven people in Collegetown and around Ithaca, on charges of possession or sale of LSD, marijuana, and other drugs. The group, which included several Cornell undergraduates and graduate students, as well as a "42 year old house man" at a fraternity and a "cashier in the Straight cafeteria," was rounded up as part of simultaneous drug busts in New York City and Montreal.[79]

In May, about a pound of marijuana was seized on campus, with two students taken before Thaler and promised immunity from prosecution if they cooperated. The *Sun* editorialized that the university's effort to control marijuana use on campus and its list of "suspected users" was an "abominable witch hunt."[80] In response, the administration clarified its position. Provost Corson defended efforts "to suppress the traffic of marijuana and other illegal drugs on its campus" and pledged to continue "cooperating with civil law enforcement officials on this matter." President Perkins added that "the university will make every effort to suppress traffic in drugs on the university campus." Barlow announced that Cornell would take no action against users of marijuana "unless it is determined that the use can be disruptive to the educational environment," but "trafficking will be referred to civil authorities."[81]

Two years later, the FCSC removed marijuana use, but not trafficking, as a sanctionable offense from the Campus Code of Conduct. Corson, now president, clarified the university's position in a press release announcing that drug abuse would henceforth be dealt with solely "on a counseling and medical care basis," unless such use "leads to a destructive disorderly or disruptive situation," in which case action would be initiated against the individuals involved. Even as he committed the university "not to employ undercover agents," Corson announced that any evidence of "the sale, exchange, or transfer of drugs would be communicated to public law enforcement officials."[82]

This retreat from a punitive *in loco parentis* role had an unexpected victim—the venerable Cornell institution of the university proctor, who had played a substantive part in the drug and Vietnam wars that roiled the campus in the mid- to late 1960s. Patterned on the disciplinary officer in Oxford and Cambridge colleges, the proctor at Cornell was responsible for maintaining order on campus, the institutional personification of *in loco parentis* authority. The exact nature of his power, especially vis-à-vis the Safety Division, the campus police, was always vague, lost in earlier Cornell traditions. Typically the proctor was informed of an alleged student misconduct, requested an "interview" with the student, and then decided whether or not to cite the student with charges. He was present during the deliberations of the Undergraduate Judiciary Board.

Misgivings about the proctor's role were bound to intensify in the contentious politicization of campus life in the sixties. There were due-process issues, students generally unaware that their "conversations" with the proctor formed the basis of disciplinary action, and the blurring of prosecutorial with adjudicative roles in the proctor's consultant function with the UJB. More important, between 1965 and 1967 the seeming omnipresence of the proctor at campus demonstrations, rallies, and actions, in the name of maintaining order, partly filled the vacuum left by the administration's reluctance to call for a local or university police presence, which itself might become an issue in the protest. The proctor's role in those years was also shaped by Lowell George's disdainful personal views of the drug culture and antiwar activism—views that were much less permissive than those of Cornell administrators and faculty.

Concerns abounded that the proctor, by tradition also a deputy sheriff of Tompkins County, was too close to District Attorney Thaler. George and Thaler were allies in the *Trojan Horse* episode in January 1967 and in the drug bust two months later. George repeatedly cited students for "trespass," for "disrupting normal operating procedures" and "refusing to leave when requested by a university official," as he did with Day Hall protesters in May 1966, only to see the UJB "take no action." His was a lonely administration voice on campus, at odds with the uneasy, often conflicted, and at times inconsistent tolerance of the rest of Day Hall.

Campus-wide criticism was leveled at Proctor George in late 1966 and early 1967 when an assistant proctor pushed and shoved Bruce Dancis down the steps of the Straight. Dancis was one of a group of students wearing large buttons inscribed "I am not yet convinced that the Proctor is a horse's ass" and a smaller button that read "I am convinced." In what the *Sun* labeled "the Button Brawl," President Perkins reprimanded Assistant Proctor Richard Travis for "his unwise display of temper, which seriously reflects upon the stature of the Proctor's office," while "branding the buttons as provocative" and endorsing the Faculty Council characterization of them "as discourteous, juvenile and cowardly."[83] In March, when Dancis and SDS tried to sign up draft card destroyers in the Straight lobby, a tense two-hour confrontation occurred between Lowell George and button-wearing SDS students.

The next day, George received a petition signed by nearly five hundred students apologizing to him "for the inexcusably rude treatment of the student body."[84] Nevertheless, the contradictions and anomalies inherent in the office, and George's actions, were doing it in. The final blow was the wielding of emergency power by George, which for some time had been lodged in the never-before-used rules of the Faculty Committee on Student Conduct, to temporarily suspend students on the spot. George had applied it to nine students the previous day in order to bring the fracas in the Straight to an end. A campus campaign to eliminate the office of proctor, led by SDS, was launched. A flyer insisting that "the Proctor can't be our man and Thaler's" demanded "the Proctor must go." A group of faculty asked for a student referendum "to do away with the University Proctor." Noting that "some campus elements are pressing to eliminate the Office of the Proctor," Provost Corson suggested at the May 1967 presidential staff meeting that the administration postpone a decision until the Sindler Commission made its report in the fall.[85]

The commission recommended, among many things, "stripping the University Proctor of all but investigatory powers." In January, Provost Corson circulated an internal memorandum for the record, promulgating "A Policy on Student Disturbances," which included the commitment not to arrest students on the spot but to do so later, if appropriate. It concluded with a resolve that the "transference of the role in judicial procedures from Lowell George to the Dean of Students Office will be gradual with George phased out by July 1."[86] The proctor's duties would eventually be shared between the dean of students office and, after 1969, the judicial administrator. Lowell George was appointed to the much more circumscribed position of head of the university's Safety Division, after James Herson left in the wake of the *Trojan Horse* affair to become

Ithaca's chief of police. There would never be another university proctor. *In loco parentis* was truly dead and buried.

An *ITHACA JOURNAL* headline in 1974 announced "This year, Campus was still." The cease-fire agreement signed in Paris, the end of the draft, and the last U.S. troops leaving Vietnam had "eliminated many reasons for protest." Fraternities, the numbers of which had dropped from fifty-three to forty-five in the sixties, were experiencing a revival, "getting better and stronger." An academic adviser to Delta Kappa Epsilon noted that because of activism on campus in the late '60s "it wasn't considered cool to be in a fraternity. The attraction then was torn faded blue jeans, unkempt hair, and a hovel in Collegetown." It was, he and others claimed, "a new era for fraternities . . . moving away from the nostalgic rah, rah, rah days to a more diverse brotherhood, community action programs, and emphasis on academic achievement." In the 1975 commencement issue of the *Sun*, senior editor David Green '75 acknowledged, as well, "the end of the age of student protest," when opposition to the war and Washington "was an acceptable emotional and social substitute for the comforts of rah rah college tradition." Since the "movement took its famous nosedive," Green was not going "to sneer and hoot" at collegiate life; he was going "to wear a cap and gown to graduation."[87]

Nothing indicates how far the campus had moved from the era of unrest than the administration's pleasure that students, like the *Sun*'s editor, would come to commencement fully clothed. A fad of streaking, running through campus stripped to nothing but sneakers, had led to fears of naked students disrupting graduation. Ever prepared, Arthur Brodeur, university public affairs officer, had sent a memo to Corson suggesting "in case there are streakers at Commencement you should say 'apparently those people are the late-arriving doctoral candidates in dermatology.' "[88] None appeared. Another sign of a campus back to normal was the return of the war against dogs. After a large canine, growling menacingly, bit four students during a chemistry exam being administered to about 450 undergraduates by Professor Walter Galenson in 1973, much to the consternation of *Sun* columnists satirizing "Arts Profs who bitch at dogs," the university started enforcing a 1971 requirement that all dogs on campus had to be leashed. Lowell George's Safety Division announced "it would pick up any stray animal," and Arts College dean Alfred Kahn sent a detailed memo "giving faculty the right to expel dogs from their classes."[89]

A sadder concluding bookend to the era was the demise of the beloved "stump" in front of Willard Straight. The campus woke on the morning of November 6, 1975, to discover that during the night the five-foot-high stump, the remains of a tree that in 1967 had succumbed to Dutch elm disease and had since been both a public kiosk with painted political messages and the site for protest rallies, had been sawed off again. A classified ad in the *Sun* suggested a ransom payment would result in the return of the missing three feet. Money was collected and offered to anyone who came forward. Painted on the shortened stump was "outrage" in large red letters, along with "foul bloody murder!" and "the assassin shall be tarred and feathered and run out of town." The "power saw vandals" were never apprehended.[90]

Campus protest was not totally dead. There were new off-campus issues. A 1972 Morrison Hall meeting of the dean and department chairs in the College of Agriculture and Life Sciences was disrupted by students and staff angry that the college had not replied to their demands that they more vocally support New York State farmworkers, including seasonal and migrant laborers. After three separate and courteous requests from Dean Charles E. Palm, PhD '35, that the protesters wait until the meeting was finished were rejected, Palm and the department heads left the room. For the next several years Ag and ILR students on the University Senate clashed often with administrators and staff over directives that the university buy, when available, only lettuce from California and the Southwest that had Cesar Chavez's United Farm Workers union labels. In 1975 several hundred demonstrators protested the Soviet Union's treatment of Jews, prior to a performance by the Moscow State Symphony at Bailey Hall. Marching in two circles in front of the hall with candles and placards reading "KGB goons go home," they did not block the entrance to the hall.

There were even final reprises for Vietnam issues and protest. In response to the Arts College faculty refusal to give college credit to an ROTC course called "The Anatomy of Warfare," because ROTC officers were allegedly "not free to speak critically about United States military policy," L. Pearce Williams decided in the fall of 1973 to grant independent reading course credit in History for it, following a review of the students' exams and papers. "I think it is a legitimate course," he told the *Sun*; the only reason credit was not permitted was political, "anti-military prejudice." But, he went on, "in this matter no one is my superior. That is known as academic freedom." Dean Kahn reluctantly conceded "I don't approve, but I have no control over what professors choose to view as acceptable work in their reading courses." In early 1974 the Arts and Sciences faculty voted once again, by a more than two-to-one margin, against credit for the course, but Williams continued to offer his independent studies, denouncing the vote as a political decision of "the mindless left." It seems, he observed, "that the radical scum that tried to ruin the university years ago is now radical scum faculty."[91]

Vietnam's most dramatic campus curtain call, however, occurred on December 9, 1975, with the appearance at Bailey Hall of Nguyen Cao Ky, "Marshal Ky," the former prime minister and vice president of South Vietnam. Living in California and on a speaking tour of colleges, Ky was brought to campus by Jay S. Walker '77, future founder of the popular website Priceline, then an undergraduate in ILR and head of both the Interfraternity Council and the Oliphant Speaker's Committee of Sigma Phi fraternity. Having come up with the $1,500 speaker's fee, fraternity brothers were given reserved floor seats in Bailey Hall, while protesters, summoned for days by posters announcing an antiwar "reunion," filled the mezzanines and balcony.

In the thirty minutes before the announced time of the speech, protesters, led by a young woman dressed as Hitler and a man with an oversize papier-mâché head of Richard Nixon, chanted "Hitler rose, Hitler fell, fascist Ky go to hell." Banners claiming "the blood of millions is on his hands" hung from balcony railings.[92] As pandemonium reigned, Walker, the evening's moderator, worried that Ky could not make it through his prepared speech and sought out Michael Parenti, a visiting professor in the Government Department, who had taken a lead role in orchestrating the demonstration. Parenti convinced Walker that if he, Parenti, announced that the event had been changed to a question-and-answer session, Ky's critics would hold back. Walker reluctantly agreed to the format change. To Walker's surprise, however, Parenti went to the stage and first labeled Ky "a mass murderer, assassin and fascist who jailed, tortured and killed tens of thousands of people," and then announced that the meeting had been changed to an "open forum between the people and the dictator, a people's court."[93] Walker then remained on the stage with Marshal Ky.

Mainly hostile questions followed, from hastily arranged microphones in the aisles, accompanied by booing, catcalls, and chanting. Had Ky not fled Vietnam with millions in gold and heroin? Had Ky not made statements to the press about admiring Hitler? Twenty-five minutes into the chaotic proceedings, Richard Miller, an assistant professor of philosophy, asked Ky how he could sleep at night and then declared, "In people's courts if someone was a murderer you shoot him. We can't do that tonight, but I don't think we should be having an academic discussion with this creep."[94] Chaos ensued with eggs and wadded paper hurled at the stage, accompanied by persistent chanting and rhythmic clapping. After about five minutes, Ky left the stage. Protesters took over, shouting "We have set a precedent. We have sent him away. The place is now ours." Ky returned to Sigma Phi fraternity house, where he was spending the night. Before a private late-evening reception for members of the fraternity, he spoke to reporters. Yes, he told them, "it had been the worst situation on his 13 campus speaking tour."[95]

A firestorm of anger against the Ky events spread through the campus, despite Mark Barlow Jr.'s claim that "the clapping was not increasing, had not become infectious, and that Ky might have continued had someone responsible on the platform made a strong effort to control the audience."[96] The next day, President Corson directed the university's judicial administrator, Barbara Kauber, to investigate possible violations of the Campus Code's regulations for the maintenance of public order. At a special meeting of the faculty attended by four hundred people, convened two days later by Dean of the Faculty Byron Saunders, Corson declared that he was "indignant that such an event could occur at Cornell. I can only feel outrage." He defended free speech, denouncing what he saw as a trend at universities to treat people "with disrespect and contempt, to shout obscenities, and to vilify in countless ways." Violations of free speech, Corson suggested, should be met with penalties for students ranging from reprimands to dismissal; for faculty, penalties might even include "termination of tenure."[97]

The meeting concluded with a motion from S. Cushing Strout, professor of English and chairman of the Faculty Committee on Freedom of Teaching and Learning. Informed by reports "that members of the faculty played prominent roles in creating a climate hostile to the preservation of free speech," Strout's motion, which carried by a vote of 248–82, called for an investigation by his committee "of the event and the responsibility of particular individuals."[98] Four months later, in March 1976, as the incident received national publicity in a column by William F. Buckley Jr., accusing Ky's Cornell detractors of the very Nazism he had been accused of, Strout's committee issued its report. It condemned the hecklers for violating Ky's right to speak and singled out Parenti for changing the format, which brought on the disruption. The report deferred recommending sanctions, lest this prejudice the judicial administrator's ongoing investigation.

That March also saw a visit to campus by William Colby, director of the CIA during the last years of the Vietnam War. He, too, was brought by the Interfraternity Council and the Oliphant Committee of Sigma Phi fraternity, joined this time by the Cornell Forum and the University Unions. Groups that had joined in the anti-Ky protest announced they did not intend to disrupt Colby's talk, but would mount a picket line outside Bailey and boo him for three minutes when he was introduced. A panel with four other panelists was arranged, including two law professors, and a professor served as moderator. When Colby, who received $2,000 for his appearance, spoke to a packed Bailey on "Secrecy in a Democracy," he was interrupted many times by heckling and applause. He paused until the noise diminished, remaining composed and seemingly unfazed by it all.

The judicial administrator concluded her investigation of the Ky events in September. She filed formal disciplinary charges against Professor Miller for violating Article I, Section 2, of the Campus Code of Conduct, which prohibited interfering or attempting to interfere with the lawful exercise of freedom of speech. One month later, during a five-hour public hearing, Miller's attorney, Elizabeth Bixler, convinced the University Hearing Board that his speech "was not especially inflammatory given the context," that no questioners were denied access to the microphones, and that a tape recording showed that at the crucial moment Jay Walker told Ky he could leave the stage temporarily or end the forum.[99] The board dismissed the charge against Miller, holding that Ky had left the Bailey Hall stage "voluntarily." The campus war over Vietnam was finally over.

BY 1976 IT was apparent that there was flagging interest in the University Senate, born in the heady idealism of the "Barton Hall Community" in the week after the Straight takeover. Unfilled seats, low voter participation in elections, declining attendance at meetings, and frequent quorum failures prompted Corson to recommend its abolition in 1977 as one of his last acts as president. The death of the Senate, the embodiment of New Left egalitarian ideals of nonhierarchical, "communal" control of the university by students, faculty, and administrators, with its power to choose student trustees and to superintend important areas of campus life such as housing, dining, and athletics, symbolized the return to academic business as usual. Some years later, Corson, who had presided over the entire era, either as provost or president, captured that historic moment:

> It was a poor form of government. But given the circumstances, the distrust of authority, the demand for participation in decision making that existed at that time, it might have been the only sensible way to proceed. It was participatory democracy; it was awkward, and it didn't work well. As soon as things quieted down, interest in it faded, after three or four years. By 1975 it was obvious that it could not survive. Finally . . . I went to the Board of Trustees with the recommendation that it be dissolved—back to normal university operations.[100]

PART III
1977–1995

7 | The Rhodes Years

It did not take long to select a successor for Dale Corson. The board of trustees search committee, chaired by Austin Kiplinger '39, identified only one finalist—Frank H. T. Rhodes—and moved quickly to invite him to campus for discussions with faculty, staff, and members of the community. At that point, in 1977, Rhodes expressed surprise that Cornell had sought him out and claimed not to be familiar with a single faculty member outside of the Geology Department. He had been to Ithaca only once, to deliver a guest lecture in 1960 in the middle of winter, when his plane had been delayed and his bags lost.

Ten minutes into Rhodes's first meeting with the search committee, trustee Stephen H. Weiss '57 recalled, the candidate, who seemed to know everything about Cornell, had won them over. Confessing that he could "listen endlessly" to Rhodes's "flow of elegant English and his penetrating consideration of Cornell's problems," trustee Les Severinghaus '21 gushed that although it was out of order to declare "love at first sight," he had come close.[1] On February 2, 1977, the committee unanimously and enthusiastically recommended that Rhodes be named Cornell's ninth president, a position he would keep for eighteen years. Although Dean of the Faculty Byron Saunders groused that more than one candidate should have been brought to campus before a decision was made, the faculty search committee, chaired by William Austin, professor of music, endorsed him as well in an overwhelmingly affirmative straw vote.[2] Detecting "a sense of beginning anew—and an optimism unparalleled on campus in recent years," the editors of the *Cornell Daily Sun* agreed that the "imperturbably suave" Rhodes was a terrific choice.[3]

When he stepped down in 1995, in an era when college presidents came and went quickly, Rhodes was hailed as one of the greatest and most beloved leaders in the history of Cornell and one of the most outstanding academic administrators in the United States. Rhodes once joked that taking credit for achievements in a great university "is a bit like giving the jockey the beautiful

241

Frank H. T. Rhodes, president of Cornell
University from 1977 to 1995. (Division
of Rare and Manuscript Collections of
the Cornell University Library)

cup when the horse wins the race."[4] Nonetheless, he had a hand in massive increases in funding for research; major initiatives in astronomy, nanofabrication, supercomputing, and biotechnology; dramatic growth in applications to the undergraduate colleges; construction projects ranging from a Theory Center to a Center for the Performing Arts; and an expansion of Cornell's global reputation and its contacts with Asia. Most important, perhaps, he played an indispensable role in rekindling pride in Cornell among faculty, students, and especially alumni, making it possible for the university to reach its $1.25 billion campaign "super goal" at the end of his presidency.

Cornell was far less turbulent during the Rhodes years than it had been in the 1960s and early '70s. It is not surprising, though, given the multiple constituencies and multiplicity of views in Cornell's multiversity, that the Rhodes administration had its share of conflicts and critics. Strikes by service and maintenance workers divided the campus in 1980, 1981, and 1987, with some Cornellians refusing to cross picket lines. More than one thousand people were arrested in 1985 amid protests over Cornell's divestment policy in South Africa. Black students and faculty ardently denounced proposals to institute random housing assignments for first-year students as an attack on Ujamaa Residential College. And a few days before Thanksgiving 1993, Latinos occupied Day Hall, vowing to stay there until the administration agreed to establish a Latino living unit.

"We have a long way to go," Rhodes acknowledged in 1995. Nonetheless, although his knees were weak and he no longer played squash three times a week, he had never doubted, even when times were tough, that being president of Cornell "was a terrific job."[5]

Born in Warwickshire, England, in 1926, Rhodes received a bachelor of science degree with first class honors (1948), a PhD (1950), and a doctor of science degree (1963) from the University of Birmingham. He taught at the University of Durham and the University of Wales, Swansea, where he also served as dean of the faculty of science. In the United States, Rhodes was a National Science Foundation Senior Visiting Research Fellow at Ohio State and a Fulbright Scholar, director of the geological field station, professor of geology, department chair, and dean of the faculty of sciences at the University of Illinois. He served the University of Michigan as professor, dean of the College of Literature, Science, and the Arts, and vice president for academic affairs, the position he held when he was named president of Cornell.

A prolific scholar, Rhodes published numerous journal articles and six books, including *The Evolution of Life* (1962), which had been recommended reading for geology students at Cornell, and *The Paleobiology of Condononts* (1972), which described a group of extinct organisms useful in determining the age of some types of rocks.

In many ways, Rhodes's inauguration on November 10, 1977, foreshadowed the tone and turmoil that characterized his presidency. He began his address by predicting that hard times and hard decisions lay ahead. He expressed hope as well, pointing to Cornell's partnerships with New York State, loyal alumni, supporters, friends, and foundations, and the company of men and women who love learning "and defend it well." Promising to be a spokesman and servant for the university on and beyond the campus, Rhodes indicated that he would not be in thrall to the status quo or to any particular constituency, nor would he stand on the sidewalk, watching "collisions between propelled vehicles, each on its own side of the road, each sounding its horn and each stationary." He affirmed a commitment to four principles necessary to secure Cornell's future. In the "uncertain years that lie ahead," he indicated, Cornell must embrace "the power and priority of reason"; support affirmative action and robust financial aid policies because learning flourishes not in isolation, but in a "give and take, question and debate," tolerant, trusting, and respectful community of diversity; recognize that the university has a responsibility to research as well as teaching, as part of the range of questioning and creating "which is the glory and burden of our common humanity"; and serve a much wider community than the campus itself.

The new president declared that he shared the ire and indignation of Cornell professor Morris Bishop '13, PhD '26, at a "foreign author" who claimed that only a handful of American universities—"Harvard, Yale, Princeton, and perhaps Cornell"—were truly distinguished. Haunted by these words, he promised to use them "not as an uninformed and pompous judgment of our past, but as a hope and challenge for our future." Someday, he predicted, an observer seeking "the essentially American college "will specify Cornell University. And perhaps Harvard, Yale, and Princeton."[6]

About 250 members of the inaugural audience had less lofty views of Cornell. Sitting in Barton, where security was tight (a Safety Division officer refused to admit a young man with a walking stick until he proved he limped without it), protesters from the Financial Aid Project, the Minority Student Coalition, and the Cornell Liberation Army held placards during the proceedings before silently marching out with raised fists during Rhodes's remarks. Departing from his prepared address, the president regretted that the dissenters had "another engagement," which prevented them from listening to comments relevant to their concerns. Later that day, he declared that the demonstrators were "disciplined, well-behaved and expressed a legitimate concern which I share." The young men and women, added Fine Arts professor Jason Seley '40, chair of the inauguration planning committee, were "just another example of diversity at Cornell."[7]

Along with college and university presidents across the country, Rhodes struggled throughout his tenure to keep budgets balanced, maintain financial support from the state and federal governments, and contain rapidly rising tuition and fees. He worked, as well, to recruit and retain the best and brightest faculty and students, repair and enhance the physical plant, understand and adapt to racial and ethnic identity politics, and decide whether the university should take a stand on urgent social and moral issues.

As he spent more time off-campus, visiting alumni, foundations, and government officials, Rhodes relied on his provosts to help manage these challenges. The chief academic officers of the institution, with considerable authority over budgets, Cornell's provosts worked with the deans of the colleges to set priorities for the university. Appointed provost in 1978, following the resignation of David Knapp, W. Keith Kennedy, MS '41, PhD '47, who, along with Steven Muller, had negotiated the settlement in the Straight takeover, was the quintessential institutional insider. He had joined the Cornell faculty in 1949 as a professor of agronomy, became associate dean of the College of Agriculture in 1965, and was appointed dean and director of the New York State Agricultural Experiment Station in Geneva seven years later. Knowledgeable, blunt, and tough, Kennedy managed to balance the university's budget, which had been in the red for years. A plaque on the wall of his Day Hall office read: "If you don't want to join the parade, at least stay out of the way."[8]

Following Kennedy's retirement in 1984, Robert Barker, who had served Cornell as professor of biochemistry, director of the Division of Biological Sciences, and vice president for research, became provost. Appointed senior provost and chief operating officer five years later, Barker focused on strategic planning and the long-range capital needs of the university. On his recommendation, Cornell made it a practice to reinvest a portion of the interest earned by the endowment each year.

He was replaced as provost by Malden Nesheim, PhD '59, another Cornell "lifer." A Cornell PhD in nutrition and animal science, Nesheim joined the faculty of the College of Agriculture in 1959. He served for years as director of the Division of Nutrition Sciences, building a nationally recognized program in research, teaching, and public service. Appointed vice provost for planning and budget in 1987, and provost two years later, Nesheim kept Cornell on a strong financial footing, met regularly with the deans of the colleges, provided resources to recruit women and underrepresented minorities to the faculty, and played a key role during the occupation of Day Hall by Latino students and their supporters.

Rhodes's administrative colleagues allowed him to do what he did best: serve as ambassador to students, parents, alumni, and friends of the university. Slim, handsome, and unfailingly gracious, Rhodes had a superhuman capacity to remember names and faces, and to persuade high-powered members of the board of trustees—many more of whom by now had made their mark on Wall Street rather than in manufacturing—that they should "keep their noses in and their fingers out." He was a masterful public speaker, who talked without notes in a captivating British accent and made frequent use of two shoeboxes of index cards, cross-referenced by author and subject, with quotations from sources ranging from race car drivers to movie stars to politicians. "There's nothing worse," Senior Vice President William Herbster observed, "than preceding or following Frank Rhodes."[9] When he ended each commencement address with a Gaelic blessing ("And until we meet again, may God hold you in the palm of his hand"), thousands of listeners, young and old, felt connected to him—and to Cornell.

In 1995, at the time of his retirement, Frank Rhodes was a Cornell icon. At a send-off celebration for him on campus, more than seventy groups, colleges, and departments marched in a parade, accompanied by the president in a wagon pulled by a pair of Belgian horses. The theme was Rhodes's claim that Cornell was "the best place in the world to be." Marchers included building care employees with floor waxing machines, vacuum cleaners, and brooms, ROTC cadets, Sitara dancers, engineers who had built a hybrid electric car, and food scientists with a wedge-shaped sign that read "Farewell to the Big Cheese."

At the time, almost half the university's 122,895 living undergraduate alumni had attended Cornell when he was president. Acknowledging that some faculty believed Rhodes had been insufficiently attentive to academic issues, Robert Johnson, director of Cornell United Religious Work, thought that no one could deny that "this guy has been incredible, and has given Cornell a voice and a place in the world landscape of education that we didn't have before. There aren't many people like Frank Rhodes. There just aren't."[10] Normally no friend of administrators, Theodore Lowi, the John L. Senior Professor of American Institutions, wanted Rhodes to "stay on till he keels over."[11]

In retirement, Rhodes remained more in demand than any other potential speaker at Cornell reunions, traveled the world in behalf of the university, served on prestigious national and international science and higher education boards, and advised colleges and universities on several continents. And he wrote two major books. Published in 2001, *The Creation of the Future* made a compelling case that research universities are essential national resources and laid out the challenges they face. *Earth: A Tenant's Manual* (2012) examined the natural systems that govern our planet, assessed the consequences of human activity on it, and offered suggestions for their remedy and repair, and for sustainable growth.

A YEAR BEFORE he relinquished the reins to Rhodes, Dale Corson dissected Cornell's financial challenges in a confidential and characteristically candid memorandum to the executive committee of the board of trustees. Tough decisions had been made, the president reported. Less successful programs, including the Human Affairs Program, the Center for Urban Development Research, and the Center for Innovation on Education, had been eliminated or scaled back. Faced with "grim realities," the college deans were complying with the reductions assigned to them by Day Hall.

With the national economy ravaged by "stagflation," Corson believed that by "cutting at every obvious point," spreading reductions in the size of the faculty over four years, maximizing gift income, and "channeling support selectively to critically important areas," Cornell might be able to "avoid the shattering effect of excising major portions of the academic program." Given decreases in appropriations from New York State, Corson concluded, even this modest goal would be virtually impossible to achieve in the statutory colleges.[12]

Less prone to pessimism than his predecessor in public and private communications, Frank Rhodes acknowledged in a message to the campus community in fall 1978 that "the current budget squeeze" was likely "to be with us for a least a generation." While painful decisions had to be made, however, he insisted there was no reason to despair: "Cornell has faced adversity in the past and has emerged with renewed strength. In the period ahead we shall do the same."[13]

Keenly aware of the burden on students and their families, Rhodes reluctantly supported double-digit increases in tuition—the one source of income controlled by Cornell—as long as inflation persisted. Along with aggressive efforts to increase gifts, tuition revenue made it possible to support academic initiatives, improve faculty salaries, and make investments in the physical plant. When critics pointed out that between 1977 and 1995, endowed tuition at Cornell rose from $4,400 to $20,000 a year, more than twice the rate of inflation, Rhodes replied that the story was much the same at every Ivy League institution.

The policy did not go unchallenged. In March 1981, following a rally at the Straight attended by over seven hundred people, more than a dozen students took over the president's office in Day Hall to protest tuition hikes. When Joy Wagner, Rhodes's assistant, tried to call for help, a young woman "swooped over to her desk" and slammed down the phone. Incidents of "scuffling, shoving, and pushing," Wagner reported, alternated with two students typing term papers they said were overdue. Three hours after the occupation began, fifteen Safety Division officers in riot gear arrested the protesters.[14] Charged with violating the Campus Code of Conduct, they were convicted by a University Hearing Board and sentenced to fifty-dollar fines and seventeen hours of community service.

The "hard line" on tuition stemmed in part from a realization that cost reductions beyond those already made by Dale Corson would be difficult to achieve. Between 1975 and 1979, for example, endowed units in Ithaca had reduced general fund budgets by more than 10 percent. And as Joseph Ballantyne, vice president for research and advanced studies, indicated in a memorandum to his Day Hall colleagues, Cornell was compelled to spend more to maintain its status as a great research university. Conservation, preservation, automation (Olin Library announced plans to abandon its card catalog in 1988), and the "knowledge explosion," Ballantyne pointed out, pushed library costs higher. Computerizing the campus—and servicing machines and users—was expensive. Laboratory equipment consistent with modern technology was also costly and, because of the pace of innovation, had "a shorter useful life." Federal regulations for accountability and compliance in areas such as the care of animals used in instruction and research, the use of human subjects in research, and affirmative action required additional support staff. And the cost of research, which was rarely fully funded by external grants, took a big bite out of discretionary spending.[15]

Financial aid put additional pressure on the annual budget. Until 1976, the size of the financial aid package offered by Cornell to successful applicants from economically disadvantaged families varied by individual, and some high school students were admitted with no offer of aid (referred to by admissions professionals as "admit/deny"). By taking advantage of substantial increases in federal funding for scholarships, work study, and low-interest loans, Cornell began in 1977 to meet the financial needs of all accepted students. By 1980, however, federal support had begun to level off. The Reagan administration restricted eligibility and reduced the overall expenditures for financial aid. In testimony to the U.S. House of Representatives, Reagan's budget director

247

David Stockman declared, "I do not accept the notion that the federal govern-ment has an obligation to fund generous grants to anybody who wants to go to college. It seems to me that if people want to go to college bad enough [sic], then there is opportunity and responsibility on their part to finance their way as best they can."[16] In constant dollars, federal aid awarded to postsecondary students decreased from $13.73 billion in 1980–81 to $11.63 billion in 1985–86. The distribution of government aid among grants, loans, and work study shifted dra-matically as well. In 1975–76, grants constituted 80.3 percent of total aid; ten years later they accounted for 46.7 percent, while loans increased to 50 percent.

A relatively small number of institutions reaffirmed their commitment to "need-blind" admissions and need-based aid, allocating internal resources to make it possible for young men and women of all economic, ethnic, and geo-graphic backgrounds to attend the colleges of their choice. At Cornell, the de-cision to do so was by no means unanimous. Committed to a balanced budget and to addressing "inadequate faculty salaries, inadequate faculty support funds, and unmaintained teaching facilities," trustee Jansen Noyes Jr. '39, a member of the board's executive committee, advised President Rhodes in 1978 that the board was tired of "nickel and diming the colleges in order to give more free education and cheaper education than our peers." Noyes and his col-leagues no longer felt "a social obligation to maintain this position."[17] As a first step, Noyes recommended accepting fewer scholarship students.

However, after debating the alternatives—admit/deny, aid-conscious ad-mission (a limitation on the number of students offered financial assistance), and "gapping" (aid packages providing less than the student's demonstrated need)— the administration proposed, and the board approved, continuing the policy of working with families to meet full need. The founder's democratic vision and the institution's land grant mission, they indicated, conferred a special obligation on Cornell to provide opportunities to "students who can best benefit from its education programs regardless of socio-economic background."[18]

The decision came with a hefty price tag. Despite increases in the "self-help" expectations for students, Provost Barker announced in a letter to the *Daily Sun*, Cornell's annual undergraduate financial aid bill increased from $10.3 million in 1981–82 to $16.7 million in 1985–86. At the same time, Barker indicated, Cornell had to find resources to "improve facilities and programs to assure our continued position of leadership in teaching and research."[19]

Throughout Rhodes's tenure as president, tuition and financial aid at Cor-nell were locked in an inflationary spiral: an increase in one dictated an in-crease in the other. In 1991–92, about $26.5 million of the financial aid bill for undergraduates was paid by Cornell. On top of that, $4.8 million came from the federal government, $6.2 million from New York State (whose economic woes made reductions in higher education allocations likely), and $4.4 million from outside sources, such as National Merit Scholarships. During the 1980s, the cost of financial aid rose twice as fast as tuition.

As the U.S. economy improved in the mid-'80s, Cornell's protracted budgetary crisis eased. It did not go away. Cornell "is a financially strong university," Provost Barker declared in 1989, but the institution needed to find a way to solve its "2% problem." Because tuition and fees accounted for 65 percent of income but had to pay for almost all the necessary (or, some would say, desired) increases in annual expenditures, a 5 percent rise in the overall budget required a 7 percent jump in tuition and fees. If the endowment grew by 50 percent or a tenth of the university's restricted and designated gifts could be diverted to current use, the problem would go away. In the meantime, Barker concluded, Cornell had to "make adjustments to assure that we live within our means."[20]

To that end, Senior Vice President James E. Morley Jr. tried to apply "Total Quality Management" to Cornell. Developed by several management consultants in the 1980s, TQM sought to provide continuous improvement of products, processes, and services and enhance customer satisfaction by involving all employees in modeling, measuring, and, if appropriate, modifying the institution's culture and structures.

In 1992, Morley tasked twenty-two "Problem Solving Teams" and many "Service Delivery Teams" to generate "cost avoidances," while improving programs and services. Five hundred faculty and staff were trained in the use of "Total Quality" tools and techniques, and an additional six hundred participated in Quality Improvement Awareness programs. Although he acknowledged that TQM had gotten off to a "rocky start," Morley claimed in the fall of 1993 that the initiative was succeeding. Over $156,000 had been saved over three years in postage, with over five hundred thousand packages removed "from the Cornell mailstream." By providing students with ID cards before registration and modifying bills, the "Bursar Team" had improved customer satisfaction and staff efficiency. Thousands of labor hours and dollars had been saved by installing standard vendor bar codes in the Campus Store.[21]

TQM was viewed with skepticism by staff and ridiculed by faculty as an initiative far better suited to corporations than universities. Straining to be diplomatic, Alan Merten, dean of the Johnson Graduate School of Management, and Don Randel, dean of the College of Arts and Sciences, complained to Provost Nesheim that TQM was "short range and narrowly focused," providing little or no help in identifying significant problems or enabling faculty and staff to work together. Savings could well be achieved, they implied, without such a drain on time and resources. By 1995, TQM had been abandoned.[22]

The administration also expected a downsizing of the faculty to help generate cost savings. In 1989, Rhodes proposed—and the Faculty Council of Representatives (FCR) endorsed—a plan to cut faculty and staff positions by 4 percent over two years, largely through attrition, so that faculty salaries, which had not kept pace with salaries in comparable institutions, could be increased by 10 percent a year, financial aid policies could be maintained, and tuition increases held to slightly above the rate of inflation.

A year later, responding in part to concerns that because the student-faculty ratio at Cornell was already too high and that students would be the victims of reductions in the size of the faculty, the FCR changed its mind. Shrugging off the claims of Richard Schuler, professor of economics and chair of the Financial Policies Committee of the FCR, that the original proposal was "a modest trade-off," given a "choice between a number of stone walls,"[23] the FCR voted 36–19 to hold tuition increases to inflation plus worker productivity and preserve need-blind admissions and need-based aid, but rejected any reductions in the workforce. "What disturbs me," Schuler fumed, "is that the FCR gave the committee a mandate to suggest ways to help the University plan into the future with a balanced budget and then votes for a program that won't balance the budget."[24] No wonder, then, that atop the financial statement for 1990–91 prepared for President Rhodes, a denizen of Day Hall wrote, "Due to the current financial crisis the light at the end of the tunnel will be turned off until further notice."[25]

————

DESPITE ITS FINANCIAL CHALLENGES, Cornell burnished its reputation as a research university during the Rhodes years. Total research expenditures at the university rose from $88.2 million in 1977–78 to $301.3 million in 1993–94. "Research is the foundation of our national progress," Rhodes told the U.S. House of Representatives Committee on Science and Technology in 1984. "Our economic strength, our industrial productivity, our cultural vitality, our people's health, our international leadership, our national security—all these and more depend on it." Support for universities engaged in "creative research and vigorous development," he emphasized, "is not one claim amongst countless competing claims, however admirable or worthy their goals may be. It is the prerequisite for all other goals, the best hope for their achievement, the foundation for their eventual implementation, the basis of our national being."[26]

Although they did not necessarily disagree with these sentiments, critics pointed out that research appetites and expectations also involved Faustian bargains, with implications for university priorities, the rising costs of higher education, the influence of state and federal agencies and corporate sponsors, and undergraduate teaching. In the late twentieth century, however, even they did not know how—or whether—to turn the clock back.

"Big science" continued to dominate the research university. In 1987–88, for example, the physical sciences received $46.8 million for research from external sources, the life sciences $43.4 million, engineering $36.8 million, and the humanities $719, 668. In a memorandum written a few years earlier to his colleagues in Day Hall, W. Donald Cooke, professor of chemistry and vice president for research, endorsed the idea that "Cornell is a science-oriented institution," which should make significant investments in equipment, labs and buildings. At "the risk of sounding like a traitor to the cause," however, he noted that scientists got what they wanted (including reduced teaching loads) so often because they were numerous, well organized, and willing to take an approach that "can be classified as bullying," while a constituency advancing the interests of humanists and social scientists "hardly exists." Fearing that he "might lose some friends of thirty years," Cooke asked that his memo not be shared with anyone outside the executive staff.[27]

Federal agencies, especially the National Science Foundation, the Office of Naval Research, and (increasingly) the National Institutes of Health, were, by far, the biggest sponsors of research, providing about 62 percent of the $259.5 million total in 1987–88 (with the Medical College in New York City included in the calculations). New York State and local governments were a distant second, foundations and nonprofits third, and the university chipped in $19.7 million of its own resources, almost 8 percent of the total. Corporate support remained relatively small, in part because the university was reluctant to shift from basic to applied research, relinquish patent rights, keep the results of research secret, and take on projects that might not be in the best interest of the society at large.

Most grants, of course, went to individual "principal investigators" based in departments. Increasingly, however, they were awarded to multidisciplinary institutes or centers, composed of faculty members with shared research interests and capable of making multiyear commitments to set up and run complicated projects with expensive equipment (such as supercomputers and synchrotrons). In 1979–80, these units received about $2.1 million in university general purpose (GP) funds and obtained nearly ten times that amount from external sources. Not surprisingly, they were dominated by the sciences and engineering, with the Newman Laboratory of Nuclear Studies, the National Astronomy and Ionosphere Center, the Materials Science Center, the Center for Radiophysics and Space Research, and the Laboratory of Atomic and Solid State Physics bringing in millions of dollars. The Society for the Humanities, in contrast, spent $66,000 of GP money—and garnered $86,000 in outside support. While acknowledging "compelling reasons" for establishing centers and institutes "on a selective basis," Provost Kennedy warned, as had so many of his predecessors since the 1950s, that "the quality of teaching" might be reduced by organizational structures devoted primarily or exclusively to research.[28]

Since the 1940s, grants from federal agencies were especially important to universities because they paid the indirect (overhead) as well as the direct costs related to the proposed research. Expenses such as the maintenance and operation of the physical plant, for example, were eligible for indirect cost recovery, as were the use of space and equipment, department and general administrative expenses, library operations, student services (for graduate research assistants), and computing services. University administrators argued that the indirect cost rate set by the agencies did not cover the full cost of research, which they believed should include, among other things, the replacement of faculty members whose project work relieved them of undergraduate teaching obligations. They pointed out as well that university overhead rates were substantially below those used by the government for industry contractors (who were allowed, for example, to recover money spent on internal research and development) and by the government itself. If the defense industry had been limited to the rates mandated for universities, Senior Provost Barker indicated, "we would still be defended by flying fortresses and would never have been to the moon."[29] Nonetheless, indirect cost recovery constituted a significant component of the budgets of research universities. In 1990, for example, Cornell recovered about $47 million in indirect costs for federally sponsored research.

These indirect costs were difficult to calculate, however. They varied from agency to agency, institution to institution (they were different in Cornell's endowed and statutory units), and from year to year. Professors did not like them because they increased the size of grant applications and, in their view, made them less competitive. Responding to tight federal budgets, agencies began to reduce the rates and require universities to provide matching funds to cover some of the direct costs of the projects.

In the early 1990s, the previously arcane issue of indirect cost recovery became a public scandal. Government auditors claimed that Stanford University had overcharged for indirect costs by as much as $200 million to $400 million, billing for such activities as the wedding ceremony of its president. The two parties settled, with Stanford agreeing to pay the (far less sensational) sum of $1.5 million. But the damage had been done. Universities throughout the country scrubbed their own accounts, ahead of a possible audit. Cornell removed $319,000 for travel, entertainment, and upkeep on President Rhodes's home from its calculations of indirect costs.

More important, despite intensive lobbying by Cornell and other research universities, government indirect cost recovery rates went down. Between 1991 and 1997, the rate at Cornell's endowed units fell from 75 percent to 55 percent. The university made up the shortfall, which was estimated at about $10 million, by moderating salary increases, hiring fewer new faculty, and pushing tuition a bit higher.

Meanwhile, the grants themselves had become more politicized. Under pressure from members of the House of Representatives and the Senate to fund projects for their constituents, federal agencies began to spread awards throughout the

United States. This "pork barrel" policy, Vice President Ballantyne pointed out, "subverted the basic elements of scientific merit and peer review." If the trend continued, he predicted, the quality of the scientific enterprise at Cornell and other first-rate research universities would suffer.[30]

In December 1985, Cornell got a chance to practice what it preached. Shortly before ending its session, Congress approved $55.6 million in Department of Defense grants for ten research universities, including the University of Nevada at Las Vegas, Oklahoma State University, and Wichita State University. Inserted into a massive spending bill, none of the grants had gone through the usual peer-review process. One of the beneficiaries was Cornell, which received $10 million from the Defense Advanced Research Projects Agency (DARPA) to purchase a supercomputer for the Theory Center. However, following discussions with Professor Ken Wilson, the director of the Theory Center and winner of the Nobel Prize in Physics in 1982, and other stakeholders, President Rhodes notified Congress that Cornell would not accept funds that were not the product of merit review by the relevant agency. "If the gateway to federal support is political influence," he wrote, in a letter distributed to all Cornell faculty, "science, industry and the nation will soon be the poorer." And Cornell would be less likely to get awards in the future.[31]

In an appearance on the *MacNeil/Lehrer NewsHour*, Rhodes gave a little ground, acknowledging that "part of merit will be the geographical situation." But he held firm to the fundamental proposition that if the government "spread funding between each congressional district, that's going to really lose the international race." He used his platform as well to decry "the very serious crisis" of general government reductions in appropriations for new facilities and equipment in the sciences and engineering.[32]

The issue did not go away. Indeed, with hundreds of millions of dollars at stake, drawing the line between "political pork" and awards based solely on merit became more and more difficult. In 1993, Secretary of Energy Hazel O'Leary selected the Linear Accelerator Center at Stanford University (SLAC) as the site for the construction of a "B factory" in high-energy physics (to better understand the relationship between matter and antimatter). Cornell cried foul. SLAC, Rhodes pointed out, specialized in linear accelerators and colliders. The "B factory," however, was a storage ring, "and the most successful storage ring operating in the B meson energy range is the Cornell-Electron-Positron Storage Ring." Cornell's proposal to upgrade its facility, moreover, would cost $116 million, as opposed to the $225 million promised to Stanford. Senator Diane Feinstein and "our friends in California," Rhodes suggested, "are determined to do whatever they can to obviate the need for a thorough examination" of an upgrade as a viable alternative to the construction of a new facility. Attempting to thread the needle, Rhodes appealed for redress to Governor Cuomo, U.S. Senators Moynihan and D'Amato, and the entire

New York congressional delegation. In addition to Cornell staff, he noted, more than three hundred jobs were at stake. Cornell did not seek a "special earmark," he insisted, but rather "a full and fair review" based on scientific and technical merit and the costs to society.[33] The decision, however, was not overturned.

In 1994, the Strategic Planning Task Force titled the "Generation and Application of Knowledge" summarized the challenges Cornell faced in retaining and enhancing its position of leadership in research: a decline in support, especially for basic research; rapidly escalating costs for "big science"; and competition from other institutions. To succeed in this "tougher environment," the task force recommended a "bottom-up approach," in which faculty would identify strategic enabling areas in the sciences and engineering and make them university priorities. The seventy separately organized multidisciplinary centers, institutes, programs, and laboratories, the task force suggested, gave Cornell a "significant edge," which should be maintained through carefully selected new initiatives. Noting that the Cornell land grant model, which combined research, application, and outreach, had spread agricultural innovation throughout the world, the task force indicated as well that "whole new areas of the University" should adapt it "to a wide range of contemporary problems." The task force devoted a section of its report to exhort faculty to "provide unique opportunities to undergraduate students to understand and participate in the process of original scholarship and research." But the primary goal was clear: sustaining Cornell as "a research university of the first rank in the world" by maintaining programs "at the forefront of science and other disciplines that represent Cornell's greatest strengths."[34]

WORLD-CLASS RESEARCH UNIVERSITIES require world-class facilities—and during his eighteen-year tenure, Frank Rhodes presided over the construction of more buildings than any other president of Cornell. Scattered across the campus, the buildings, more often than not, were designed for scientists. But an addition to Olin Library, a Center for Performing Arts, a new hotel, and a multicultural living center dedicated to Native Americans were built as well. To get some of the projects off the ground, however, Cornell administrators had to overcome the objections of environmentalists and historic preservationists.

Plans to demolish three buildings on the Ag quad—Stone, Roberts, and East Roberts—met ferocious opposition. Arguing that the buildings were obsolete and hazardous, with wasteful and woefully inadequate heating, plumbing, and electrical facilities, and that the cost of renovation exceeded the cost of new construction, Provost Kennedy and David Call '54, MS '58, PhD '60, dean of Agriculture and Life Sciences, secured funding from New York State to replace them with two new buildings. Academic I, at the end of the quad, would contain classrooms, administrative offices, and space for Cooperative Extension, the Departments of Communication Arts and Education, and the Landscape Architecture Program. Located across Tower Road, on Lower Alumni Field, Academic II would house the Department of Entomology, biology laboratories, and Media Services.

When the plans became public, members of Historic Ithaca and the Ithaca Landmarks Commission sought to have Roberts, East Roberts, and Stone included in the National Register of Historic Places. In January 1980, Orin Lehman, commissioner of parks, recreation, and historic preservation, turned them down, declaring that the substantial price tag of rehabilitation could not be justified. The preservationists soldiered on, however, until 1986, when a judgment from the New York State Court of Appeals ended their efforts to save Stone Hall. Featuring a six-hundred-seat auditorium (subsequently named for Dean Call), a four-hundred-seat dining facility (called Trillium), and a three-story-high passageway providing access to and from the Bailey-Malott Plaza and the Ag quad, Academic I would bear the name of Keith Kennedy. Academic II honored Cornell professor Isaac Roberts, "the father of agricultural science in the United States."

During the 1980s, the university drew on $20 million of New York State funds (two-thirds of the total cost) to put a Biotechnology Building on Campus Road. Designed to help university researchers transfer new technologies for the manufacture of products to the agriculture, food, and pharmaceuticals industries, the building attracted donations from Union Carbide, Corning Glass, General Foods, Eastman Kodak, and other corporate sponsors. A five-story structure, with interior space of 171,000 square feet, Biotech, as it was called, was the largest single building devoted to research on the campus. The academic home of three dozen faculty, fifty postdocs, and about one hundred graduate students, it provided laboratories and facilities for protein and nucleic synthesis and sequencing, fluorescence and electron microscopic imaging, and X-ray and NMR spectroscopy.

A few steps away on Tower Road was another new facility, completed in 1982, that was designed for researchers in Neurobiology and Behavior, and Ecology and Systematics. It contained 128 laboratories; woodworking and machine shops; accommodations for crickets, lizards, snakes, and opossums; aquariums with fresh- and saltwater environments; and symmetrical free-flight rooms for the simulated study of the migratory habits of birds. Rooftop greenhouses and growth chambers provided a range of conditions for plant studies. A four-story atrium linked the east and west buildings with walkways, while providing some solar heating. The beneficiary of a substantial grant from the Seeley G. Mudd Fund, the building complex was named for the late Dr. Mudd, a physician, expert on radiation and X-ray therapy, dean of the University of Southern

California School of Medicine, and trustee of the Carnegie Institution in Washington, D.C. And for Dale Corson. At the dedication of Corson-Mudd, which featured a colloquium on evolution, ecology, and biology, Corson was in typically understated form. "I have never had a building named in my honor before," the former president quipped, "and I don't exactly know how to act."[35]

Nestled between Hollister Hall and Cascadilla Creek, Snee Hall (named for William Snee '24, MA '26, who developed a process for using hydrofluoric acid to increase production in gas and oil wells), opened in 1984. A 44,000-square-foot, $10.9 million structure, designed specifically for Geology, Frank Rhodes's department, Snee contained state-of-the-art laboratories, a "clean room" for analysis of trace elements and isotopes, and a video system for instruction in microscopy. The L-shaped atrium displayed rock and mineral specimens and featured dinosaur tracks.

Far more controversial than Snee was a proposed building on the other side of the Engineering quad, designed to accommodate programs of the Center for Theory and Simulation in Science and Engineering and four allied units: Computer Science, Mechanical and Aerospace Engineering, Materials Science and Engineering, and Operations Research and Industrial Engineering. Established at Cornell in 1985 with a $21.9 million grant from the National Science Foundation, the Theory Center was one of five such facilities in the United States. Its principal aim, according to Ken Wilson, was to provide nationwide access (through a web of high-speed data links) to "supercomputers" capable of performing billions of mathematical operations per second, and making it possible to study complex phenomena and systems under conditions impossible to achieve in laboratories. By the end of the century, Wilson predicted, one million scientists would use supercomputers. Computer simulation could well enable them to "map the structure of genes, model the global economy, and track the evolution of quasars."[36]

With a commitment of $10 million in loans and grants from the New York State Development Corporation, the university prepared to authorize construction of the $29 million facility next to Cascadilla Gorge in 1987. A not inconsequential number of Cornell faculty, Ithaca residents, and local officials opposed the plan. The eight-story, 252,000-square-foot building, they claimed, constituted a threat to the ecology of the gorge. Marvin Adleman, a professor of landscape architecture, did not mince words. Violating a 1972 board of trustees edict that visual access to the gorges remain "open and undiminished," the proposal, he fumed, was "a gross mistake of a magnitude which will dwarf all campus planning and design errors of the past and, for at least the next century, will be a blatant reminder of the university's insensitivity to the visual and physical consequences of piecemeal planning with expedience as its excuse." The City of Ithaca Planning Board agreed. Extremely concerned that the siting of the building would "destroy forever the beauty of the gorge," the planning board voted unanimously to oppose it. "It's so easy once the first bite has been taken to keep taking smaller nibbles," the environmental activist Betsy Darlington predicted. Before long, the gorge, "a living laboratory," would be lost.[37]

Following an environmental impact study and extensive negotiations with Mayor Gutenberger and planning board chair Susan Blumenthal, MRP '78, the university agreed to move the building from twenty to thirty feet away from the gorge tree line and decrease its height. Despite $1 million in additional costs and lengthy delays, John Burness, vice president for university relations, declared, "the controversy has yielded a much better design." Giving his blessing to "a very handsome building," the mayor proclaimed that he was "very pleased that the University not only listened to the concerns of the community, but clearly took them to heart."[38] The Engineering and Theory Center opened its doors in 1990. Its greatest attraction, according to some staff members, was an "outdoor skybox" on the fifth-floor terrace, which on a clear, sunny day provided a picture-perfect view of baseball games played on nearby Hoy Field.[39] In 1995, the board of trustees renamed the building Frank H. T. Rhodes Hall.

Many humanists, still doing research the old-fashioned way, in libraries, and upset that tens of thousands of "lesser-used" library materials had been transferred to an annex in the Cornell apple orchards, lobbied for more space on central campus for monographs and "special collections." They got their wish. Designed by the architectural firm Shepley, Bulfinch, Richardson and Abbott, and named for Carl Kroch '35, a bibliophile, who transformed Kroch and Brentano's, his family's Chicago-based business, into the largest privately owned bookstore chain in the United States, an addition to Olin Library responded imaginatively to their needs while honoring the university's commitment to open spaces and unimpeded views on the Arts quad. "The Kroch," as it came to be called, was located completely underground. The project required construction crews to blast through eighty thousand feet of dirt and rock. Comprising three levels, the lowest of them fifty feet below the surface, and with four skylights in the courtyard between Stimson and Goldwin Smith the only evidence of its existence to passersby on the quad, the Kroch used mirrors to reflect and diffuse natural light throughout the three-story atrium at its center. Within its 97,000 square feet were thirty miles of shelving, providing space for 1.3 million volumes and twenty thousand cubic feet of manuscript collections. Opened in 1992, it housed the university's Rare and Manuscript Collections and extraordinarily rich holdings related to Southeast Asia, East Asia, and South Asia.

Carl Kroch contributed as well to the Performing Arts Center (later named the Schwartz Center for the Performing Arts in honor of Richard Schwartz '60 and his wife, Sheila), which posed a difficult fund-raising challenge. Noting that Drummond Studio, the Willard Straight Theater, the Alice Statler Auditorium,

"The Kroch," the underground addition to Olin Library, opened in 1992. (Division of Rare and Manuscript Collections of the Cornell University Library)

and Bailey Hall were woefully inadequate theatrical spaces, the Council for the Creative and Performing Arts pressed for a new facility as early as 1968. Ten years later Marvin Carlson, PhD '61, resigned as chair of Theater Arts when Harry Levin, dean of Arts and Sciences, dropped plans for such a facility because the cost was prohibitive. In 1979, however, with support from a new dean, Alain Seznec, an amateur thespian who had appeared in many Straight plays, President Rhodes made the center, designed exclusively for theater and dance, a priority of his administration. He promised, as well, to renovate other performing arts facilities, especially for music, as soon as he could generate funds to do so.

A sufficient number of major gift donors, however, did not come forward, and as time passed, the cost rose to almost $26 million. Rhodes and Seznec forged ahead, making appeals to alumni and philanthropic foundations and selling named seats in the proscenium theater, one by one. In 1989 the building opened for business in upper Collegetown. Designed by the English architect James Stirling, the complex was based on a classical Italian village, with a central commons containing a theatrical church and an adjoining octagonal baptistery. The main building of the Performing Arts Center had a marble façade, originally intended to be brick and limestone (and, rumor had it, vetoed by the president). Inside, spread over six levels, were the main theater, which seated 456 people, two smaller theaters, three dance studios, labs for courses in scenic, costume, lighting, and property design, editing rooms, twelve faculty offices, two seminar rooms, and a library. After the ribbon-cutting ceremony on April 10, President Rhodes sang an impromptu version of "I Am Thinking Tonight of My Old College Town" and "The Evening Song," with Herbert Gussman '33 accompanying him on the baby grand piano he had donated, along with the center's grand lobby.[40]

Cornell's building boom (critics called it an "edifice complex"), including the new Statler Hall, which had its grand opening in 1989, did not mean that every worthy proposal got a green light. In 1989, for example, a consulting firm pointed out that the university provided housing for only 41 percent of its undergraduates and recommended adding 1,570 beds at a cost of $68 million. The administration, which had constructed town houses on North Campus in 1983 for undergraduates and renovated the U-Halls on West Campus, deferred action. The only new building for undergraduates completed during these years was Akwe:kon (pronounced ah-Gway-go), a multicultural residential center for thirty-five students, half of whom were Native Americans, located at the corner of Triphammer and Jessup Roads. At its opening in 1991, Rhodes celebrated Akwe:kon as "a call, not simply to sharing and understanding, but to living together on this small fragile planet we call home."[41]

As BUILDINGS WENT UP, a more positive attitude began to take hold in Cornell's colleges. Finances remained fragile, to be sure. Nonetheless, budgets were balanced, the endowment was growing, undergraduate applications from increasingly well-qualified high school students rose every year, and some resources were being directed to new academic initiatives. Realists called it a recovery; optimists a renewal.

The College of Arts and Sciences began the Rhodes years on the brink of bankruptcy. Citing "fundamental differences" with the central administration about how to address the college's deficit, Dean Levin resigned effective June 30, 1978.[42] Alain Seznec, his successor, made a compelling case that Arts and Sciences was underfunded, opposed any increases in teaching loads, and made a substantial increase in the college's base budget a condition for accepting the position. President Rhodes, who sometimes saw reducing faculty as necessary to save money, this time said, "You do not increase faculty productivity by asking the quartet to be a trio and to play faster," and agreed.[43] In exchange for reductions in personnel, a reorganization of the dean's office, and a "commitment to a systematic process of long-range planning," Rhodes added more than $2 million to the A&S budget, to cover general expenses and "academic development."[44]

These resources helped Arts and Sciences recruit and retain outstanding faculty, who in turn helped the college maintain its preeminence in the sciences and humanities. In 1981, a year before Ken Wilson made his trip to Stockholm, Roald Hoffmann won a Nobel Prize in Chemistry for finding ways of determining where electrons are in molecules. In 1996, a year after Rhodes retired, two more Cornell Physics professors, Robert Richardson and David Lee, became Nobel laureates as well. Shared with Douglas Osheroff, MS '71, PhD '73, their Nobel recognized their discovery of the property of superfluidity in helium-3 atoms.

In a long career at Cornell, the iconoclastic Thomas Gold used his base in astronomy to branch out into biophysics, geology, and aerospace engineering. Gold helped Cornell establish the world's largest radio telescope at Arecibo Observatory in Puerto Rico, predicted that the moon was covered with a fine layer of dust, risked funding for his own proposals by criticizing NASA's Space Shuttle program, and speculated that oil and coal were produced through

The astronomer Carl Sagan, one of the world's most admired scientists. (From *Time* magazine, October 20, 1980 © 1980 Time Inc. Used under license.)

tectonic forces, not through fossil decomposition. And then, of course, there was Carl Sagan, director of Cornell's Laboratory for Planetary Studies. With *The Dragons of Eden*, which won a Pulitzer Prize for General Non-Fiction (1978); *Cosmos: A Personal Voyage*, an award-winning television series (1980); *Contact*, a best-selling science fiction novel (1985); and frequent appearances on *The Tonight Show Starring Johnny Carson*, where he became associated with the phrase "billions and billions," Sagan became the most recognizable scientist in the world.

The English Department remained one of the best in the country, although it had to suffer through a scandal that attracted the attention of the national media. In 1977, in a British publication, M. S. Allen of Princeton and W. F. Bolton of Rutgers University identified numerous grammatical errors, misspellings, and awkward constructions in English professor Robert Farrell's critical edition of two Old English works. When the Washington Post News Service learned that Farrell also served as the director of Cornell's Freshmen Writing Program, it spread the by-now irresistible story, including exchanges between Farrell and his most persistent and acerbic on-campus adversary, History professor L. Pearce Williams '48, PhD '52. The controversy became fodder for traditionalist critics of higher education, who lamented the lack of instruction in "the basics" of reading and writing. "Among the values that ought to be conserved (I say this as a practicing conservative)," wrote the syndicated columnist James J. Kilpatrick, "is the purity of the English language." With luck, Kilpatrick concluded, "high above Cayuga's waters, the students of Cornell may yet learn the English language, how she should be writ!" Bemoaning the phrase "war on illiteracy," Roger Rosenblatt, in a *Washington Post* column, referred to Cornell's writing program "as a model of how not to tackle a problem." And a publication at Glassboro Teachers College rejoiced that Robert Farrell "has been exposed and humiliated."[45]

Farrell was replaced as director, the press moved on, and so did the English Department. Following the retirement of M. H. Abrams in 1982, Jonathan Culler, an interpreter of structuralism, post-structuralism, and deconstruction, became the department's leading literary theorist. A. R. Ammons won two National Book Awards for Poetry (in 1973 and 1993) and a MacArthur ("genius") Fellowship in 1981, the year the award was established. Hired away from Yale, Henry Louis Gates Jr., another MacArthur Award winner and an indefatigable academic entrepreneur, promised to make Cornell the strongest center for African American Studies in the United States.

Celebrated on campus for teaching as well as scholarship, the History Department had a constellation of stars, including Walter LaFeber; Brian Tierney, an authority on medieval church history and papal infallibility; David Wyatt, PhD '66, the most respected historian of Thailand in the English-speaking world; and L. Pearce Williams, historian of science, extraordinarily popular teacher of "Introduction to Western Civilization," campus conservative, and self-proclaimed "big mouth."

Deans of Arts and Sciences—and provosts—continued to struggle to strengthen the social sciences during the Rhodes years. Sociology and Rural Sociology (in Agriculture and Life Sciences) had conversations about joint searches and appointments, shared instructional responsibilities, and a merger of the two departments. Noting that the Economics Department was not a high priority of Arts and Sciences and that the research quality of economists across the institution "varied widely," a university-wide committee pleaded for funds to "attract truly first-rate" faculty. It recommended as well that searches be conducted with representation from distinguished economists, even if they had appointments in other colleges, and that tenure standards be raised.[46] In 1995, a consensus had not been reached.

Although the college spent virtually all of its money on departments, Arts and Sciences did launch several multidisciplinary programs during the Rhodes years. The History and Philosophy of Science and Technology—a program designed by L. Pearce Williams and Astronomy professor Martin Harwit— sought to provide students with insights into the actual conduct of science. Initially a "concentration," it merged with Science, Technology, and Society (STS) in 1991 to become a full-fledged department. The Program in Ethics and Public Life sought to train students to learn about, evaluate, and apply ethical principles in their personal and professional lives, according to its founders, Government professor Isaac Kramnick; Walter Lynn, a professor of environmental engineering and director of STS; and David Lyons, who had appointments in Philosophy and Law. And in 1991, by a unanimous vote of the A&S faculty, Religious Studies, which had been a concentration for fifteen years, became a major. Because Ezra Cornell and Andrew White had decreed that the university not be tied to any religious denomination, noted Barry Adams, a professor of English, vice provost for undergraduate education, and the initiative's prime mover, Cornell had been "resistant not only to sectarian influence but to religion at large." Broadly conceived and eclectic, Religious Studies, Adams insisted, was consistent with the vision of the founders.[47]

In the College of Agriculture and Life Sciences, priorities were established and implemented by David Call, a professor of agricultural economics, who served as dean for all but one of the Rhodes years. When he stepped down in 1995, Call had hired half of the current crop of CALS faculty, increased women faculty from six to fifty-five, helped raise $120 million for the college, presided over computerization, expanded the alumni network, and weathered budget cuts and building demolitions. Call was respected by professors, virtually all of whom he knew by name, as well as by politicians in Albany. David Brown, a professor in Rural Sociology, praised Call as "an exciting dean even when resources were scarce."[48]

Call worked with his colleagues to reimagine a curriculum in a state in which less than 2 percent of the population were farmers. Responding to developments in food processing, distribution, and retailing, which engaged one of five workers in New York, and to a modern agricultural system that relied on skills in the biological sciences, environmental management, and international trade and development, they identified three areas of emphasis for undergraduate and graduate courses: science and technology, management, and communication and education. Building on strength in animal and plant sciences, entomology and ecology, neurobiology and behavior (the academic home of Thomas Eisner, a pioneer in the study of the chemical defenses of insects), the college poured resources into biotechnology and supported international agriculture as an integral component of its teaching, research, and extension missions.

The College of Engineering responded to the post–Cold War shift from defense-related engineering projects funded by the federal government to those related to the design, manufacture, and marketing of consumer products, by collaborating with CALS on biotechnology and by forging university-industry partnerships, including a Design Research Institute (with Xerox) and an Electronic Packaging Alliance (with IBM, Digital Equipment, Carborundum, and AMP). Most important, it committed resources to the Department of Electrical and Computer Engineering, Applied Engineering Physics, Materials Science, Operations Research, and Systems Engineering.

Because many Engineering graduates abandoned the field they majored in within a decade, often gravitating to managerial or administrative positions, the college reduced the number of required courses and encouraged study in business, computer science, the humanities, and the social sciences. To foster teamwork and provide hands-on experiences, Engineering opened labs to first-year students and allocated funds for designing and building an SAE formula race car and a hybrid electric automobile, a concrete canoe, and a pedestrian bridge. To increase retention, the college reduced the size of first-year calculus and computer science courses and established a tutorial program in which faculty advisers met their advisees once a week to discuss topics related to engineering. And Engineering redoubled its efforts to recruit minority students and women and keep them in the field. The college needed to show that engineering "is an area where you interact with people, a field that is important to many national problems," Dean (and professor of computer science) John Hopcroft declared in 1994. As long as they are excellent, "it doesn't matter if it's a man, woman, minority . . . that's the driving force of the college."[49]

Cornell's smaller colleges extended their reach as well, "matching possibilities," as the *Cornell Chronicle* put it, "with existing realities."[50] No longer able—or willing—to rely exclusively on appropriations from New York State, Human Ecology and ILR (along with Agriculture and Life Sciences) turned to alumni to endow professorships and fund innovation in research and academic programs. Francille Firebaugh, PhD '62, dean of Human Ecology for more than a decade, awarded the college's first two privately endowed chairs to Phyllis Moen, the director of the Life Course Institute, and Stephen Ceci, a professor of human development, with expertise on the reliability of the testimony of children in court. In 1994, seven new faculty members, a lecturer, and three senior extension associates were hired—and external funding for projects in nutrition and health, human development, economic and social well-being, and environmental design and technology exceeded $24 million, the highest level ever.

The college highlighted the work of three institutes, which, Firebaugh suggested, were "uniquely poised to find creative solutions to contemporary human problems."[51] Created in 1988, The Family Life Development Center conducted research and offered workshops on family stress, child abuse, and parent education. The Cornell Food and Nutrition Policy Program investigated nutrition in developing countries and provided training on food policies based on the results of its studies. The Life Course Institute supported multidisciplinary work on aging and family development and crafted concrete proposals to help people function amid uncertainty. In 1994, the Life Course Center was named for Urie Bronfenbrenner '38, a professor emeritus of human development and family studies, who had gained national recognition for his comparison of childhood in the United States and the Soviet Union, his ecology systems theory, and his role as a cofounder of the Head Start Program.

Despite efforts to refute "old and mistaken stereotypes," Human Ecology continued to struggle to close its gender gap. Two-thirds of the undergraduates enrolled in the college in 1993 were women. They constituted the vast majority of majors in Human Development and Family Studies, Human Service Studies, and Textiles and Apparel. There was a trend toward gender balance, however, with men attracted by Biology and Science (often as a pre-med option), Consumer Economics and Housing, and Policy Analysis. "We've tried to tell our story right," Brenda Bricker, the college's director of admissions, indicated, "but we aren't going to change the story for men."[52]

As for ILR, its "story" was changing with the times. In 1986 unions enlisted only 18 percent of nonagricultural workers in the United States and only one in ten of the college's graduates employed by them. ILR responded by overhauling its curriculum, offering majors in human resources and organizational behavior, directing students to take courses in statistics, computer science, and finance, and recruiting professors with pro-management as well as pro-labor perspectives. The college launched two new research centers, the Institute for Collective Bargaining and the Institute for Labor Market Policies. ILR got support from fifty-four corporations for its Center for Advanced Human Resource Studies. And the college moved into international workplace studies, requiring students to take courses in comparative labor, encouraging them to study foreign languages, offering extension and public service programs in foreign countries, and adding two faculty who specialized in the North American Free Trade Agreement.

To fund these initiatives, ILR used tuition, gifts, and off-campus programs for union members, managers, and employment assistance professionals that generated surpluses for the school. Out of a budget of $22.5 million in 1992, for example, $9.7 million came from Albany, $6.3 million from tuition and fees, $3.7 million from "service courses," and the remainder from contributions from alumni and friends, endowment income, and other sources.

Of all the colleges, the Hotel School was best suited to thrive during the Rhodes years. Except for student financial aid, the school did not depend all that much on Albany or Washington. But it could count on the support of a large, loyal contingent of alumni, who dominated the hospitality industry in the United States and around the world. "Hotelies are sociable by nature," Dean David Dittman noted. "Not only are they joiners, but they are often instigators and organizers of charitable activities."[53] Alumni helped make the Cornell Hotel School "brand" so well recognized and well respected that the president of Cornell College in Mount Vernon, Iowa, received VIP treatment in hotels whenever he traveled abroad because managers confused his liberal arts institution with "the real deal."

To strengthen its position in the marketplace, the Hotel School offered industry supervisors, middle managers, and senior executives a comprehensive executive education program. In 1992, Hotel redesigned its Professional Masters program, adding courses to train students to put theories into practice. The school revised its undergraduate curriculum as well, adding a foreign language requirement and reorganizing management courses into organizational behavior, human resources, and strategic planning. Through a Rooms Division course, first-year students rotated through the various services of the new Statler Hotel. And it beefed up Career Services, upgrading the Management Intern Program and adding an industry-student mentor program.

In contrast to Hotel, the College of Architecture, Art, and Planning was perennially impoverished. Labor intensive, with a high faculty-to-student ratio and relatively few "major gift" alumni donors, the college, Provost Kennedy indicated in 1984, generated net unrecovered costs to the university of about $3,000 per student. Because the Architecture program was recognized as one of the best in the nation, Kennedy resisted proposals to abolish AAP by moving Architecture to Engineering, Art to Arts and Sciences, and City and Regional Planning (CRP) to several units, including A&S and Human Ecology. Hoping to focus the attention of the faculty of the college on its "a serious financial problem," the provost did propose merging CRP with Human Ecology and a permanent $1 million reduction in the base budget, which could be recovered through a differential tuition. The "shock wave," however, was "more than the faculty could handle." Kennedy modified his goal to a $500,000 cut and/or increased income and left the problem to his successor.[54]

AAP's financial woes persisted. Making Architecture a graduate program and transferring Art and CRP to Arts and Sciences remained on the table in Day Hall. Making matters worse, in 1993 the visiting team of the National Architecture Accrediting Board deemed Cornell's facilities "the worst" they had ever seen. "I'd rather have the world's best school in horrible buildings than a horrible school in the world's best buildings," Dean William McMinn declared.[55] McMinn realized, however, that neither he nor President Rhodes could raise the $20–30 million needed to renovate Rand, Sibley, and Tjaden Halls.

Understanding that "the trick is to increase income without increasing costs," the college searched for outside support for its programs. It wasn't easy to find. To be sure, Professor Donald Greenberg '55, PhD '68, a pioneer in computer graphics, persuaded an advertising agency in New York City to donate work stations with computers, laser scanners and printers, and give students summer internships. In a partnership with Olive Press, the college invited ten artists to campus for weeklong visits to make limited-edition prints (with the help of student apprentices) to be sold by the press. Most telling, McMinn offered his college as the host location for an interdisciplinary graduate program in real estate but cautioned that in addition to tuition, funds for it would have to come primarily from alumni.

Like Cornell's undergraduate colleges, each of the professional schools operated under its own unique set of circumstances and constraints during the Rhodes years. Perennially at or near the top of the national rankings, the College of Veterinary Medicine was a large and complex operation. In addition to training the next generation of veterinarians and conducting cutting-edge biomedical research, the Vet School ran a hospital, a Diagnostic Laboratory, an Equine Drug Testing Program, a Poultry Diagnostic Laboratory, a Duck Research Laboratory, a Mastitis Control Program, a Bovine Research Center, a Quality Milk Promotion Project, a Feline Health Center, an Institute for Animal Health, and ambulatory clinics for animals throughout the Northeast.

Because tuition generated a relatively small percentage of its annual budget, and few veterinarians were wealthy enough to make major gifts, the college was tethered to appropriations from Albany. The financial woes of the state forced the Vet School to cut back in the '80s, but as it prepared to celebrate its centennial in 1993–94, the school got the go-ahead for Phase 1 of an expansion that had been in the works for quite some time. The largest single construction project ever undertaken at a New York State–supported institution of higher education, with a price tag of $82 million, Phase 1 provided 183,000 square feet for laboratories, classrooms, a library, a new small-animal clinic in the hospital, and a renovation of the large-animal clinic. Phase 2, an overhaul of

Schurman Hall, the laboratory-office-classroom building at the end of Tower Road, awaited a hike in the state's cap on bonding.

As its facilities caught up with the growth of its programs, the Vet School also altered its admissions practices, curriculum, and pedagogy. By the 1990s, more than three-quarters of the entering DVM class were women, up from 55 percent in 1982 and 15 percent in 1972. And in 1993, the college implemented a "learning in context" approach to veterinary education, featuring problem-based case studies and a curriculum organized around interdisciplinary courses rather than the traditional disciplines. Today's veterinarians, noted Dean Robert Phemister, DVM '60, needed to communicate more effectively, become more sensitive to the cost of animal care, and "understand the role of medicine in the larger context of society."[56]

The Law School, thanks in part to the generosity of its alumni, was financially self-sufficient and relatively easy to manage, Dean Russell Osgood noted in 1992: with thirty-five faculty, six hundred students, one building, one discipline, and no departments, "we're able to focus on the one business at hand."[57] That business, of course, was evolving. Starting in 1990, the Law School introduced students to feminist legal theory, with courses such as "Gender Discrimination" and "Feminist Jurisprudence." It added a program in Law and Economics and one on Ethics, expanded the Legal Aid Clinic, and responded to the revolution in technology with a Legal Information Institute, under the direction of Professor Peter Martin '61, that developed and disseminated information on the Internet. Convinced that international law, an essential component of multinational economic activity, was a growth area in the profession, the Law School expanded its International Legal Studies Program with a Summer Institute, offered in collaboration with the University of Paris I (Sorbonne-Pantheon).

The Graduate School of Business and Public Administration also made international studies a priority. But it took a while to get there. Still suffering the aftershocks of stagflation and recession and convinced that the school's comparative advantage was in the functional areas of business (accounting, finance, marketing, operations management, and organizational behavior), faculty and administrators made the difficult decision to eliminate the Public Administration and Health Administration programs in 1983. A year later, Samuel Curtis Johnson Jr. '50, who had transformed his family's Racine, Wisconsin, wax business into a multibillion dollar global giant, made the largest gift ever made to a business school. His $20 million donation was used to increase the size of the full-time faculty in the Samuel Curtis Johnson School of Management (named for Sam's great-grandfather, the founder of Johnson Wax) from thirty-one to forty-five.

In the '80s, with attention riveted on Japan, the Johnson School gave MBA students opportunities (through course work and summer internships) to learn that country's language, customs, and business practices. In the '90s, with one-third of the entering class coming from about three dozen foreign countries, the Johnson School offered team-taught courses, including "The World Geopolitical Environment of Business," with appearances by the historian Walter LaFeber and the economist Alfred Kahn—and sent almost 10 percent of its second-year students for a semester abroad. "Keep your differences," Dean Alan Merten urged his students, "but learn from each other."[58]

To ADDRESS THE needs of the statutory colleges, Rhodes and his provosts set out to stabilize and sustain support from New York State. Convinced that as New York's only land grant university, with tripartite responsibilities of research, teaching, and extension, Cornell was fundamentally different from other public institutions, they believed that Cornell's needs were not "incorporated properly into funding formulas and the budget process." To ensure that Cornell had greater freedom to set policies bearing on its unique functions and the resources required to maintain the preeminence of its statutory colleges, they revisited the ideas proposed during the Corson administration for fundamental changes in relationships with SUNY, the State Education Department, the New York State Legislature, and the Governor's Budget Office.[59]

A document prepared for internal consumption in 1977 by Constance Cook '41, JD '43, vice president for land grant affairs, conceded that Cornell's critics were right: the university did indeed want money but did not want to be told how to spend it. And so, she added, the university's task was to convince decision makers in Albany that "such a system is the best way to guarantee the state the maximum return on its investment." Noting that Cornell had only begun to build a broad base of political support (it was, at present, strongest among Republicans in the Senate and weakest among Democrats in the Assembly) and that there was a deep-seated and pervasive view in the state capitol that the statutory colleges were "too expensive," Cook was not optimistic about the chances of achieving substantial change in the near future.[60]

Four years later, amid intensifying concerns that SUNY's enrollment-driven model shortchanged Cornell's research and extension activities and its need for salaries that were competitive with its peers, Keith Kennedy, by then provost emeritus, raised the possibility of "a complete separation of the statutory colleges from SUNY." But secession, Kennedy reminded his colleagues, imperiled the financing of current and future physical facilities. If the statutory colleges were divorced from the State University Construction Fund, the legislature would have to pass a bill designating a portion of its funds to them every time a building was built or renovated. Moreover, even if the State Dormitory Authority issued bonds for capital construction at Cornell, the Budget Office would have to set aside money each year for debt service, and the legislature would have to approve. The best option for Cornell, Kennedy concluded, would be a grant of authority to forward requests to the Budget Office, with an opportunity for SUNY to comment on but not alter them.[61]

In the ensuing years, disputes between Cornell and SUNY intensified and became more public. A SUNY-appointed commission asked for greater autonomy for SUNY, but no change in Cornell's relationship with SUNY. When SUNY failed to incorporate a request for additional funding for the College of Veterinary Medicine into its annual budget application, Cornell went directly to the governor and legislature and got their approval. And when John Dyson '65, chairman of the New York State Power Authority and a governor-appointed member of the Cornell Board of Trustees, told a joint meeting of all legislative committees on higher education that SUNY's "unwillingness to make hard choices for excellence" was responsible for the Vet School's fall from first place in the national rankings and near decertification, SUNY chancellor Clifford Wharton Jr. characterized his comments as "a series of lies, half-truths and unfair innuendoes."[62]

In his testimony before the Senate and Assembly Higher Education Committee in March 1985, President Rhodes criticized SUNY for failing to achieve "a position of leadership in research and graduate education." The continued success of Cornell's statutory colleges, "which are among the most distinguished in the nation," he insisted, depended on "giving them the same freedom of program development SUNY seeks for itself, through the right of direct access to the governor and the legislature." Under the present arrangement, Cornell's budget proposals were "submerged" in a massive SUNY effort "to deal with 59 other and very dissimilar institutions, including 20 state-operated units and 30 community colleges." Commending Chancellor Wharton for his willingness to listen, Rhodes noted that the two men had not reached an agreement and called on the legislature to give Cornell the right to make its own case.[63]

Combined with an improving New York State economy, Cornell's full-court press had an impact. Cornell won the right to present its budget to the legislature, without modifications to it by SUNY. In 1988, the university and the state agreed to tie annual increases in accessory instruction (the costs associated with the enrollment of statutory students in courses offered by endowed colleges) to the Higher Education Price Index (which tended to be higher than the Consumer Price Index). A cap on expenditures for accessory instruction remained in place, which meant that the state did not pay the whole bill.

Critically important, as well, was an agreement between Cornell and Governor Mario Cuomo in 1988 to restore an $800,000 appropriation for the Cornell Theory Center that had been removed by the legislature because of a projected revenue shortfall. The agreement to support technology and a supercomputer, assurance of continued funding at that level, and a commitment of

$10 million for a new building came at the right time. A National Science Foundation committee had just arrived in Ithaca to review a proposal for six years of funding, at a total cost to the federal government of $111 million, to create a national Center for Theory and Simulation in Science at Engineering at Cornell. The NSF would not take a proposal to the National Science Board, an official told Cornell administrators, without a commitment from New York State to the project.

As things changed, however, they also remained the same. Between July 1988 and December 1989, Provost Nesheim indicated, Cornell's four state-supported units absorbed five separate reductions, totaling more than $2.8 million. In 1990–91, an additional $5.6 million disappeared, including a $2.6 million December "surprise." Over twenty years, Nesheim calculated, New York State–funded positions declined by almost 20 percent. The university could no longer merely tighten its belt in response to what appeared to be a chronic fiscal crisis.

In 1995, three months before Rhodes stepped down, he reported to the board of trustees that the "Albany situation" was not encouraging. If enacted into law, Governor George Pataki's budget would necessitate layoffs of such magnitude that the university had placed a freeze on external staff hiring in the endowed colleges to create space for statutory staff. Well over $1 million in cuts in the state Tuition Assistance Program (TAP), Bundy Financial Aid, and Educational Opportunity Programs would have to be replaced by Cornell, necessitating sizable increases in tuition.[64] Although not all the cuts were made, Rhodes, in his exit interview with the *Cornell Daily Sun*, claimed that "times are tough"—"they're tough in Albany, they're tough in Washington, and they're tough in the City of Ithaca. And I don't think they're going to change in the next year or two. . . . On the other hand, they've been tough for eighteen years."[65]

WHATEVER THE STATE of the state, relations between Cornell and its four municipalities— the City of Ithaca, the Town of Ithaca, Cayuga Heights, and Tompkins County— involved a delicate balancing act on all sides. By far the largest employer in the county, attracting thousands of visitors to the area each year and generating hundreds of thousands of dollars in sales taxes, the university, Cornell associate counsel Thomas Santoro declared, had "a fairly imposing presence in the community." Without Cornell, Town Supervisor Noel Desch agreed, "Ithaca would be like any other town."[66]

Still, with so much offered to the community, Cornell also engendered costs to it. Although Cornell students, staff, and faculty used public transportation, schools, fire and police protection, and other services, the university, a nonprofit institution, paid no property taxes. At times, it encroached on residential neighborhoods, competed with local businesses, and removed buildings and land from the tax roll. During the Rhodes years, the administration and local officials struggled, with mixed success, to build trust and agree on an appropriate "voluntary" contribution to defray expenses incurred by local governments.

A major initiative for a "new Collegetown" illustrated the challenges facing town and gown in working together even on an initiative designed to benefit both. Commissioned by Ithaca and Cornell, American City Consultants characterized Collegetown in 1981 as "a rundown hodgepodge of stores, housing, and other student-related uses," lacking focus and direction. Recommending new construction for the East Hill commercial and housing district, the consultants indicated that the blocks closest to campus could contain a Performing Arts Center (though the building had been authorized by the trustees, its site had not yet been chosen); a renovated Sheldon Court, repurposed as a dormitory; a parking garage for 350 cars, to be built by the city; and housing, retail stores, and office buildings, to be financed by private developers.[67]

The consultants predicted that the cost to taxpayers would be offset by increases in sales and property taxes, parking fees, and special "benefit" assessments. They suggested that Ithaca apply for an Urban Development Action Grant from the federal government. Although H. Matthys Van Cort, the city's planning director, warned about "a lot of ifs," he claimed that Collegetown was "a sexy site" for developers: "you're downtown for a university of 20,000 people."[68] Forty-seven Collegetown merchants endorsed the plan. Any short-term inconveniences, declared Stephen Fontana '79, owner of a shoe store on Eddy Street, would be outweighed by long-term benefits. Only one retailer, whom Fontana declined to identify, demurred. She preferred keeping Collegetown small.

Opponents of the plan made themselves heard as well. Complaining that more and more students and staff parked their cars, legally and illegally, at metered and unmetered spots in Collegetown, as Cornell increased fees for permits, some residents worried that a Performing Arts Center and the construction of high-rise apartment buildings would exacerbate the problem, even with a parking garage. The Progressive Citizens Alliance lobbied against city financing. "It would be wise for the government to keep in mind that this is Ithaca, New York, and not Cornell, New York," Edward Abbott, the spokesman for the organization, suggested.[69]

"You've gotta believe, you've got to keep pushing ahead," said John Gutenberger, the owner of the IGA supermarket on College Avenue.[70] In 1983, a few months before Gutenberger was elected mayor, the Common Council of Ithaca authorized Mack Travis, a local developer, to undertake a feasibility study for a hotel and parking garage in Collegetown. In 1984, citing high construction costs and interest rates, Travis backed out.

Cornell's commitment to put the Performing Arts Center in Collegetown (the only one of seventeen proposed sites within Ithaca's city limits), however, kept the project alive. When the university donated land that allowed access to and from a proposed garage site on Dryden Road, the city agreed to build the garage. Cornell also rehabilitated Stone Arch Bridge connecting campus to C-Town. And the first-floor retail space in Sheldon Court was included in the tax-benefit district to help pay for street lighting and landscape improvements.

Battle lines formed as well in Cornell Heights, an area between Fall Creek gorge, North Campus, and Cayuga Heights. Kept awake by firecrackers, raucous parties, obscenities, and the newly faddish primal screams emanating from fraternities, sororities, and houses owned by Cornell, residents demanded stronger enforcement of noise ordinances and better property maintenance by the university. "We feel threatened, even scared for the future," Bryant Robey, a member of the Common Council and spokesman for the Cornell Heights Civic Association, told the *Ithaca Journal* in 1980.[71] The university's decision to convert more single-family houses into multiple dwellings, move its publications office to Fall Creek Drive, and make a home on Wait Avenue the headquarters of the Modern Indonesia Project, Robey indicated, violated the spirit and letter of city zoning, which designated Cornell Heights for residential use. Further encroachment by the university, he added, would make it difficult for residents "to sell their homes to other families."[72]

To mollify Cornell Heights home owners, many of whom worked for Cornell, the university appointed James Kidney, director of buildings and grounds, as "special liaison" to the neighborhood and announced plans to rehabilitate and upgrade its properties. Administrators insisted, however, that educational institutions were exempt from zoning laws. The dispute went to the Board of Zoning Appeals, the Common Council, the New York State Supreme Court, and, ultimately, to the court's Appellate Division, which ruled that Ithaca could not restrict the university from occupying property in a residential area but ordered Cornell to return to the zoning board for a special permit.

A definitive resolution did not come until 1989, when the city supported an effort by Cornell Heights residents to have their neighborhood designated a historic district. A representative for the city and a member of the Cornell Heights Civic Association squared off against university counsel Walter Relihan in the Albany office of Orin Lehman. Following their presentations, Lehman ordered that Cornell Heights be added to the New York State Register of Historic Places. The university would have to look elsewhere to expand.

Neither courts nor commissioners, however, could resolve the most persistent problem in town-gown relations: the demand that Cornell make larger payments to the community in lieu of taxes. During his campaign for mayor, John Gutenberger told Cornell administrators that voters complained about a "deliberate change in 'the corporate philosophy' of the University toward the city." They cited fees for Ithacans borrowing books from the library, attempts to get fraternities and sororities off the tax rolls, and an unwillingness to contribute "a fair share" for Collegetown parking. Calls to Gutenberger's campaign headquarters ran about five-to-one in favor of his view that Cornell should "pay more."[73]

Pressure came from Tompkins County officials as well. In 1984, the County Division of Assessment placed three Cornell buildings on the tentative taxable roll: Gannett Clinic, which set aside space for physicians to treat private patients; Lynah Rink, which was used by non-Cornell groups; and Sage House on East State Street, which assigned a room for an engineering magazine for blacks. Three years later, arguing that "Entrepot," a branch of the Campus Store, was selling goods to the community, the county put the operation on the property tax assessment list, but backed off after Cornell got a restraining order from the New York State Supreme Court.

"If Cornell wishes to play hardball with the county of Tompkins," Representative Donald Lifton '67, PhD '88, declared, "we should return in kind." After subtracting items he felt were not relevant, Lifton estimated that Cornell paid about $175,000 in property taxes, not including water, sewer, and fire assessments, and $268,000 in lieu of taxes for school districts, fire departments, and Ithaca Transit. Lifton asked his colleagues to join him in demanding an increase to $1.2 million each year for the next ten years. If the university agreed, the county tax rate could drop by 13 percent.[74] University officials disputed Lifton's calculations, pointed out that the Campus Store produced $1.2 million in sales tax, $514,000 of which remained in the county, and promised to study Cornell's financial contributions to Tompkins County.

Town–gown relations became even more acrimonious when Ben Nichols '46, MEN '49, was elected mayor of Ithaca in 1989. A retired professor of electrical and computer engineering, Nichols had worked on radio waves in the ionosphere but switched to science education for primary school students because he feared that his research might assist the United States military. A socialist and a champion of equal opportunity and justice for African Americans, Nichols had been a combative critic of Cornell policies in the '60s and '70s. As mayor, he made increasing the university's voluntary contributions for city services one of his highest priorities. Citing studies indicating that some Cornell workers lived below the poverty level, he pressed as well for some municipal involvement in assessing the wages and benefits of Cornell employees.

In 1992, Cornell responded to the recommendations of the Mayor's Commission on Cornell-City Relations. The university, administrators noted, provided $3.5 million to Ithaca and its municipal neighbors in direct cash transfers, subsidies, and voluntary payments: "Taken together, these revenues easily outweigh the cost of services provided to the University." And, in a shot across Nichols's bow, the university reasserted its position that, while it was paying attention to "the special problems of working class families," collective bargaining "and its own human resources programs are the appropriate vehicles concerning employee compensation and related matters."[75] President Rhodes, in a letter to the mayor, expressed sympathy for the fiscal pressures prompting the city to seek additional sources of revenue, but emphasized that Cornell's need to keep tuition rates as low as possible, "and the budgetary stringencies that will result" meant that the institution's capacity to provide relief for Ithaca "is quite limited."[76]

By 1995, Rhodes had delegated negotiating responsibilities to Henrik Dullea '61, vice president for university relations and former director of state operations and policy management for Governor Cuomo. In a letter to Nichols on January 10, Dullea bristled at the mayor's claim that when it came to payment for services, "Cornell was no different than the Woolworth's Department Store across the street from your office." He labeled Nichols's bid for a voluntary contribution of $2.4 million above "the $145,000 we presently contribute" an "ultimatum." And he blasted the city's "concerns" about zoning, building construction, laboratory renovation, and parking as "just a smokescreen—your leverage to extract direct cash payments from the University for City services, payments the City is not entitled to under law." Dullea concluded his letter with the hope that "improved relations would develop during the rest of the New Year."[77] Although he knew it was desirable to "remove yet another issue from the list that will greet Hunter Rawlings," Cornell's president-elect, Dullea noted five months later, he was uncertain about "the way forward."[78]

DURING THE 1980s many service, maintenance, and clerical employees felt that they had borne the brunt of the budget cuts. Having made do with pay increases far short of inflation for years, they listened to union organizers who promised that by banding together they could improve wages and working conditions. And so it was that Cornell would experience the most intense decade of labor strife in its history.

Thirty-six workers in the heating, filtration, and chilled water plants, organized by Local 71–71A of the International Union of Operating Engineers in September 1979, went on strike in March 1980. Ron Bess, business agent for the union, claimed that the university had dragged its feet during contract negotiations: "They don't like unions. It's possible they're trying to make an example of us in light of other union organizing efforts."[79]

Cornell was forced to shut down the water filtration plant and pump two million gallons of water from the Bolton Point facility in Lansing and deployed supervisors and secretaries to continue operations at the plant on Oak Hill Road that heated more than four hundred buildings on campus. Meanwhile, some faculty and students joined strikers on the picket lines amid rumors, later proven to be false, that scabs had been hired—and Cornell appeared before the National Labor Relations Board to contest a petition to unionize thirty-three grounds workers in the United Food and Commercial Workers International. After twelve days, the strike was settled. Both sides claimed to be pleased with the outcome, and President Rhodes insisted that strikes never yield "any winners." Union organizing efforts in other sectors of the Cornell workforce accelerated.[80]

In October 1980, after a nine-month gestation period, organizers petitioned the National Labor Relations Board to hold an election to determine whether the United Automobile Workers would represent about one thousand janitorial, maintenance, grounds, and dining workers at Cornell. According to Catherine Valentino, a pre-print secretary at Newman Laboratory, the union had collected authorization cards from well over one-third of the potential bargaining unit, the minimum required by the NLRB. "This is the first stage of an overall plan," she announced. A second petition, on behalf of clerical and technical workers, would follow shortly.[81]

Two months earlier, in a long letter to Provost Kennedy and Vice President William Herbster, Charles Rehmus, dean of the School of Industrial and Labor Relations, warned that the university's public positions "are or are perceived as anti-union." Rehmus commended President Rhodes for issuing proclamations of neutrality and instructing staff to provide employees "the fullest information concerning University practices and policies," including fringe benefits, compensation levels, and grievance procedures. He objected, however, to articles in *CONTACT*, a university publication, that implied that the main function of a union at Cornell would be to collect dues "and use it to finance strikes in the automobile industry," emphasized that unionization had a harmful impact on the relationships between workers and supervisors, and concluded that once a union is voted in it is virtually impossible to eliminate it. Encouraging supervisors who lacked training in labor-management relations to discuss the pros and cons of unionization, moreover, "almost inevitably means that many unfair labor practices will be committed."

Cornell's decision to appeal an NLRB award of bargaining rights to two butchers, Rehmus suggested, also poisoned the well. He understood objections to carving the institution up into small units. But taking the matter to the federal courts while refusing to bargain was not only expensive but certain to be labeled "typical anti-union legalism." If, despite Cornell's "communication efforts," the UAW gained representation rights, Rehmus declared, the costs "in ill will" might well be substantial: "Strikes are more common when the organizing campaign has been hard fought."[82]

Rehmus's warning went largely unheeded. The campaign was rancorous, with charges of unfair practices made and denied by both sides. A petition supporting unionization was signed by two hundred faculty and printed as a paid advertisement in the *Ithaca Journal*. And in a round of talks a week before the vote, President Rhodes reminded workers that "voting either for or against the union will not automatically create more money. . . . The fact is, of course, that our income is limited."[83]

On February 24, 1981, the UAW and the university provided transportation to polls set up in Barton Hall. That evening, four NLRB officials tallied the bright pink ballots, announcing each vote to four counters—two for Cornell, two for the union. They were scrutinized, the *Ithaca Journal* reported, by "a stern-faced crowd" of about one hundred workers, many of them wearing UAW T-shirts, caps, and buttons, who packed a small room at the west end of Barton. When the final tally was announced—483 yes, 375 no—they cheered; some of them hummed "Solidarity Forever," the classic union song. Later, union officials attributed the relatively slim margin of victory to "scare tactics" by Cornell, a claim the university strenuously denied.[84]

Contract negotiations began almost immediately—and went nowhere. Rejecting the UAW demand for a 57 percent wage increase spread over three years, Cornell charged that the union was bargaining in bad faith and asked federal labor officials to appoint a mediator. The union followed suit. According to Pam Mackesey '89, a gardener at Cornell Plantations and the chair of the seven-person bargaining committee, "their attitude at the bargaining table has been arrogant and uncompromising."[85] At a meeting held in August at the VFW Hall on State Street, workers authorized their representatives to call a strike.

Unable to resolve differences with the university on about thirty of forty outstanding issues, including alleged threats of disciplinary action against members of the bargaining committee for spending time away from their jobs preparing for negotiations, union leaders scheduled a three-day walkout for the last weekend in September, when two thousand visitors arrived on campus for the sixth annual Parents Weekend, and a general strike if a contract was not signed by midnight, October 3.

Not surprisingly, the two sides differed about the impact of the September job action. The union estimated that 80 percent of its members, about 760 people, did not report to work. Mackesey also claimed that United Parcel workers, and some members of the Buildings Trade Council, the New York State Electric & Gas Company, and New York Telephone refused to cross picket lines. Noting that many employees do not usually work on weekends, the university set the job action number at five hundred. Except for "Elements of Cross-Country Gourmet," a twenty-five-dollar-per-person Saturday night dinner, for which one hundred people had signed up, Ronald Loomis, director of unions and activities, reported, no Parents Weekend events were canceled.

Responding to a request from Governor Hugh Carey to extend negotiations for three weeks, about seven hundred UAW members, meeting at the Strand Theater, set the strike deadline for October 5. Vice President Herbster called the threat "the worst kind of brinksmanship."[86] Tom Fricano, UAW director for western New York, pointed out that while the cost of living had increased more than 157 percent between 1969 and 1981, a Cornell worker earned $3.39 an hour in 1969 and $5.91 twelve years later, a 76.4 percent increase.[87] "Cornell may hold all the cards," Dick Tompkins, a custodian at Willard Straight Hall acknowledged. "But we're not ready to cut the deck. We're not going to shuffle along anymore. But you don't cut the deck until the cards are stacked." Another worker, who chose to be anonymous, indicated that he did not like the union but would not cross the picket line: "I never can feel you get back what you lose in a strike. But we don't have a choice. We just get dragged into it."[88]

On Monday, October 5, a steady downpour soaked pickets stationed at three dozen locations across the campus. The UAW offered them hot meals and day care services for their children. No classes were canceled, but six dining halls were closed. In other units, supervisors and administrative personnel filled in. "I think the strike's kind of silly," a student told an *Ithaca Journal* reporter. "They're probably not making that much, but they're making more than if they weren't working."[89] On October 6, three students were arrested and charged with harassment and DWI after they sprayed a picket with a fire extinguisher. Other students expressed sympathy with the strikers.

On October 11, one hundred strikers formed a semicircle around Barton Hall, as two thousand employees and their relatives sat down for an Employee Day chicken barbecue. As the Big Red Band marched in and cheerleaders with scarlet pom-poms in their hands moved in front of them, the strikers chanted "We want dignity." Later, when the sounds of "Give My Regards to Davy" drifted outside Barton, the pickets countered with "Solidarity Forever."[90] As the strike wore on, university officials indicated that 60 percent of the bargaining unit was not at work, but maintained that "things seem to be running smoothly."[91] "We know they are hurting," Catherine Valentino countered.[92]

Meanwhile, negotiations intensified. On October 15, a tentative agreement was reached. A 413–29 vote at a meeting at Statler Hall brought the twelve-day strike to an end. Although the contract provided for wage increases, retroactive payments, and a new grievance procedure, the UAW and the university differed on whether it provided better salaries and benefits than those earned by nonunion workers. Nonetheless, both sides expressed relief. Thanking individuals who worked during the strike and welcoming back the strikers, President Rhodes concluded that "Although the University has come through these weeks with remarkably little inconvenience and disruption, any strike is bound to be divisive. But the strike is now over and we must pick up the threads."

Service workers went out on strike three times during the 1980s. (Division of Rare and Manuscript Collections of the Cornell University Library)

Rhodes hoped that the agreement would bring "an opportunity for new understanding and a new conciliation."[93]

Instead, during most of the 1980s, conflict intensified. In December 1982, by a vote of 50–17, security officers voted to be represented by the independent Cornell University Employees Union. Three months later twelve building guards, averaging eighteen years of service, and thirty-two other employees were terminated. A union spokesman charged that "Cornell has cynically seized upon New York State mandated layoffs to get in a little union-busting on the side."[94] The National Labor Relations Board agreed, finding that the actions constituted an unfair labor practice. The university agreed to offer new jobs to all but two or three of the men, who had decided to retire.

Cornell and UAW Local 2300, led by Al Davidoff '80, a Buffalo native who worked as a janitor while completing his degree at the School of Industrial and Labor Relations, went up to or over the brink in virtually every contract negotiation. In 1983, as the union tried to organize 650 technicians and conclude an agreement for its service and maintenance workers, Jansen Noyes Jr., chairman of the board of trustees, announced that the board had decided to abandon its position of neutrality on unionization. Denying that any change in policy had occurred, Vice President Herbster acknowledged that the administration would inform employees of its concerns about the UAW. Indeed, the *Ithaca Journal* reported, a communication to technicians in May declared: "There should be no misunderstanding. We do not believe that further unionization of Cornell employees is either necessary or desirable."[95]

The technicians decided against union representation. So did service and maintenance workers at the New York State Agricultural Experiment Station in Geneva. But Local 2300 and Al Davidoff would not go away. In July 1983, a settlement came five hours ahead of a strike deadline. Two years later, a three-day strike disrupted freshmen orientation. And in 1987, negotiations broke down again. The university offered a 5 percent wage increase, the same package given to nonunion employees. The union demanded nothing less than 13 percent. "We are paying what we think we can afford; they feel they don't make enough. We are both probably right. But they aren't going to tear the fabric of the University apart," President Rhodes declared in response to pickets at a breakfast of cider and doughnuts at the Memorial Room of Willard Straight Hall during Parents Weekend.[96]

Workers walked out in October. The union, Davidoff indicated, was counting on support from students and faculty, several of whom appeared at Day Hall with placards reading "How much does Rhodes make?"[97] The strike lasted three days. The settlement, which Davidoff called "a slight advance for workers," raised salaries by about 5 percent and eliminated the very lowest wage level. Vice President Morley called it "a fair arrangement for both parties."[98]

The times were changing. Following a recession in 1981–82, the economy was recovering and increasingly robust. And after Ronald Reagan's firing of air traffic controllers, unions had less and less power, nationally and locally. In 1988, Local 2300 and Cornell agreed on a four-year contract. "There wasn't a lot of the game playing that there was in the past," declared Pete Tufford '69, a former varsity hockey player now serving as Cornell's chief labor negotiator. Characterizing the negotiations as "healthy and constructive," Davidoff concluded that the process "bodes well for the future."[99] At the ratification meeting, held in James Law Auditorium at the College of Veterinary Medicine, Plantations worker James Huested, the union's sergeant-at-arms and a former member of the bargaining team, was perhaps more realistic. Shaking his head from side to side, Huested told his colleagues: "I guess I'd call it fair. It would be nice to have a little more money, but I think this is all the University is going to pay."[100]

CONFRONTED BY CLAIMS on Cornell's coffers from just about everywhere, President Rhodes looked to philanthropy to supplement tuition revenues. In addition to maximizing investment income, he recognized that the university had to increase the endowment—which was valued at $270 million in 1978, far smaller per student than those of Cornell's peers—and "current use" gifts. For "development" goals to be reached and, he hoped, exceeded, moreover, he had to engage and erase alumni hostility related to the takeover of Willard Straight Hall in 1969.

Rhodes worked closely with Richard Ramin '51, the vice president for public affairs, hundreds of professionals in Alumni Affairs and Development and thousands of alumni volunteers and became an incredibly successful fundraiser. Alumni adored spending time with him, even when they knew the visit would end with a solicitation. Over breakfast at the Cornell Club in New York City, for example, the president discussed the university's capital campaign with trustee Stephen Fillo '59, an investment banker. "We'd like a few minutes to discuss your own gift, Steve, and anything we can do to help your thinking," Rhodes said. By the time the two men had finished their meal, Fillo had pledged $1 million—and felt honored that he had been asked.[101]

Raising money took an enormous amount of time and energy. Early on, Rhodes and Ramin agreed that the president would spend about two hundred hours a year raising funds. In 1982, he exceeded that number by early November. "There is no hope that I can keep up the present pace," he told Ramin, "and still devote adequate time to other aspects of the University's affairs." If Cornell was to meet its goals, however, he concluded that he had to devote a week or two—or more—each month to public affairs activities.[102]

Rhodes breathed new life into the university's five-year campaign, begun in October 1975, with a "super-goal" of $230 million. By the end of 1980, Cornell hit $250 million. About $88 million came from alumni, $22 million from non-alumni, $26 million from corporations, $38 million from foundations, and $74 million from bequests. Donors designated $95.7 million for the endowment (including endowed professorships and financial aid), $36.1 million for construction and renovation of facilities, and $52 million for unrestricted support of the operating budget. The remainder of the gifts went to a variety of specified needs, including equipment, program support, guest lectures, and concerts.

Throughout the 1980s, Cornell, in essence, engaged in a "continuous campaign." Substantial assistance came from one alumnus with whom Rhodes established an important and enduring relationship and whose gifts would transform campus life. Born in 1931 in Elizabeth, New Jersey, Charles Francis Feeney '56 served overseas during the Korean War before entering Cornell's Hotel School in 1952. He supplemented his GI Bill stipend by selling sandwiches at fraternity houses. After graduation, he went to Europe, and in time, with his classmate and partner, Robert Miller '55, he began selling tax-free merchandise to overseas tourists. By the 1970s, as Duty Free Shoppers Ltd.

became extraordinarily successful, Feeney decided to begin giving back. His first major gift went to Cornell. For its twenty-fifth reunion in 1981, the class of 1956 set a goal of $250,000 for the entire class. Feeney contributed $700,000.

To prevent publicity and the requests for money that accompanied it, Feeney decided to give anonymously. He set up the Atlantic Philanthropies, a charitable foundation, in Bermuda to avoid disclosure regulations in the United States and made an irrevocable gift to it in 1984. No other philanthropist had ever relinquished so high a percentage of his assets while he was still alive. Cornell remained his principal beneficiary. With "more than a simple diploma," he explained to students during a campus visit, Cornell "prepared me. When you come out of Cornell you have good baggage."[103]

Influenced by Rhodes's recommendations, Feeney directed his gifts to the university's highest priorities and to areas of personal interest to him. To "prime the pump" in the class of 1956, "the anonymous donor" matched any individual gift of $5,000. In 1983, his $2 million commitment made it possible for Dean Jack Clark, PhD '69, to replace the Statler Hotel with a new, 150-room, $50 million facility. That same year, he donated $2 million to the Performing Arts Center. An athlete who liked to play pick-up basketball with his Cornell buddies, Feeney pledged $4 million to athletics in 1984. Between 1986 and 1988, he gave more than $15 million for a Cornell Club in New York City. In 1989, he pledged $25 million to the Cornell University Library. And in 1990, he promised $7.5 million to the Cornell Institute for Food and Agricultural Development.

Feeney made numerous "smaller" gifts as well: $250,000 for Chemistry Television Production; $10 million to the Commitment to Diversity Project; $700,000 to Computer Graphics; $300,000 to Faculty Fellows in Residence; $150,000 to the Global Climate Change Initiative; $1 million to the Johnson Graduate School of Management Campaign; $500,000 to the Law School Campaign; $725,000 to the Reason, Social Values and Policy Program; $100,000 to Southeast Asia Fellowships; $500,000 for Mobile Satellite Uplinks. As a mark of his affection and respect for Frank Rhodes, Feeney directed $5 million to the President's Discretionary Fund in 1986.

Feeney's most innovative contribution to Cornell in the 1980s was over $13 million to establish Cornell Tradition Fellowships. Using a "hand up rather than hand out" approach that appealed to Feeney, as it had to Ezra Cornell, the Cornell Tradition Fellowships drew on alumni networks to identify summer jobs to enable undergraduates to explore careers, get valuable work experience, and reduce the loan portions of their aid packages. Selection criteria included achievement (at least a 2.3 grade-point average), initiative, leadership, scholarship, and a demonstrated commitment (through a minimum of 360 hours of academic year work-study) to take personal responsibility for meeting the costs of an education. In 1983–84, the Tradition's first full year of operation, the student employment office provided jobs for 415 undergraduates. The Tradition reimbursed 40 percent of the wages for employment with private companies and 70 percent to public and nonprofit agencies. Frank Rhodes called the Tradition "a unique response to the increasing costs of financing higher education."

By the late 1980s, as Cornell closed in on its goal of becoming the university with the largest amount of annual private contributions, Rhodes and the board of trustees decided to authorize another university-wide fund-raising campaign. When it was completed, Rhodes told a joint meeting of the board and the University Council in October 1990, the five-year, $1.2 billion drive, which depended on a 50 percent increase in annual gifts and commitments, would make "things possible for those who have the affairs of the next century on their horizon." Dedicated to "reinforce what we are already doing," Rhodes indicated, the campaign targeted five major university priorities: $450 million to support teaching and learning programs; $250 million to endow professorships and other positions; $175 million for undergraduate and graduate financial aid; $75 million for the library; and $300 million for the renovation and construction of buildings, laboratories, and other facilities. "I believe it is a turning point in Cornell history," he concluded.[104]

Before the formal announcement, during the "silent phase" of the campaign, when Cornell's best friends were solicited, Feeney committed $25 million a year for the duration of the fund-raising drive. Rhodes agreed to postpone his retirement until it was certain that the campaign goal would be reached. Describing his role as "super-active," he was on the road 128 days during the penultimate year of his presidency. Despite the recession of the early '90s, Cornell was six months ahead of schedule when Rhodes left office in 1995. Ninety-seven percent of the $1.25 billion had been secured, in gifts and commitments. "Enough bricks to last well into the new century," the *Cornell Alumni Magazine* declared. Enough bricks "for new generations of dreamers."[105]

IN 1990, CORNELL celebrated its 125th anniversary. Spread throughout the year—and held in New York City, Washington, D.C., Chicago, Boston, Tokyo, and Hong Kong as well as Ithaca—symposia focused on undergraduate teaching, international affairs, family and workplace issues, science and technology, the arts, professional ethics, and values. On Reunion Weekend in June, Walter LaFeber and Alfred Kahn discussed "Problems and Prospects in the New Post–Cold War Era" before a packed crowd in Bailey Hall.

The 125th celebrations lasted until October 1991, when thousands of alumni gathered in the San Francisco Bay area for a four-day grand finale. A luncheon at the Commonwealth Club featured President Rhodes; Donald Kennedy, the president of Stanford University; and Chang-Lin Tien, the chancellor of the University of California at Berkeley. In a spirited defense of research universities, Rhodes decried the notion advanced by former secretary of education William Bennett that they should develop "no frills, plain vanilla programs." America's undergraduates, Rhodes declared, "are the seed core of the future leadership of our nation. Deny them opportunity, and we impoverish the nation."[106]

At the banquet that evening, Big Red Bears danced, and diners devoured a chocolate clock-tower. As he toasted the joint anniversaries of two great universities (Cornell's 125th and Stanford's 100th), Donald Kennedy said that Leland Stanford chose just the right model when he patterned Stanford after Cornell and selected the Cornellian David Starr Jordan '72 as its first president. On the next day came what the *San Francisco Examiner* called "a matchup nobody wants"—a football game between Stanford and Cornell. Taking note of the 43.5-point spread, sportswriter Mark Purdy joked, "Toyota may be patterned after Chrysler, but at least Toyota doesn't throw a party and bash in Chrysler's brains to celebrate it."[107]

For Cornell's athletic programs, the Rhodes years had been a time of triumphs and tribulations. Men's varsity teams had given Big Red fans many memorable moments. Although the hockey team could not sustain the record achieved by Ken Dryden '69 and his teammates, it came out of nowhere to win the ECAC title in 1980—the first time an eighth-seeded team had made it to the finals, let alone become champions—won Ivy League titles in 1983 and 1984, and another ECAC championship in 1986. Still led by legendary coach Richie Moran, the lacrosse team made it to the NCAA Division 1 championship game in 1987 and 1988. And in 1988, the previously lackluster basketball squad lost to Penn and Princeton on the last weekend of the season, but backed into the Ivy League title when Yale beat Dartmouth.

For the football team, it had been the best of times and the worst. In 1983 Maxie Baughan, who had been an All-American at Georgia Tech and an All-Pro linebacker for the Philadelphia Eagles and Los Angeles Rams in the National Football League, was hired and proceeded to build a formidable team. In 1986, with an end-of-season 31–21 loss to Penn, its only Ivy League defeat of the year, and before twenty-two thousand fans at Schoellkopf Field, the largest crowd in fifteen years, Cornell fell just short of the Ivy League championship. Two years later, the Red topped previously unbeaten Penn, 19–16, to share a spot at the top. But the glory would be short lived.

In 1989, following accusations of an affair with the wife of one of his assistant coaches, Baughan resigned—and the football program imploded. As it tried to rebuild Cornell football, the Department of Athletics and Physical Education also struggled to eliminate annual deficits, then over $400,000, that had persisted since Corson had been president. At the very time Cornellians were gathering in the Bay area, the department was putting the final touches on a plan titled Vision 2000. Released to the public in early 1992, Vision 2000 reduced the administrative budget by $260,000, eliminated the men's and women's gymnastics and fencing teams, and required men's lightweight football and squash and the men's and women's equestrian polo teams to rely entirely on their own fund-raising efforts. The decision, Athletic Director Laing Kennedy '63 indicated, was "a last option." Cornell, he hastened to add, would still maintain one of the largest and most diverse athletic programs in the nation, with thirty-one varsity intercollegiate sports teams, extensive offerings in intramural sports, and 150 PE courses, which enrolled ten thousand students each year in everything from Adirondack skiing to yoga.[108]

The weekend at Stanford did not produce a Hollywood ending for Cornell athletics. To be sure, the heavyweight, lightweight, and women's crew teams bested their Stanford opponents. But in the first—and many hoped, the last— football contest between Stanford and Cornell, thirty thousand spectators in the stands watched (or didn't) as the Cardinal drubbed the Bear, 56–6. The game wasn't so bad, the *Cornell Chronicle* opined. The Big Red showed a lot of class on the gridiron. And "no one on the Cornell team was injured." Most important, enthusiasm was undiminished. The bay "glistened under warm and sunny skies, and even the great San Andreas Fault remained tranquil, on this, the second anniversary of the Loma Prieta earthquake." According to the *Chronicle* writer, some people were beginning to ask "Is God a Cornellian?"[109]

8 | Academic Identity Politics

"For at least four years," Harry Levin, dean of Arts and Sciences, reminded Provost David Knapp in 1977, Cornell had responded to students' requests for various ethnic studies programs "by putting them off." Led on, "cynically," by the administration, the students had worked hard and in good faith. Levin was "amazed at their patience." Acknowledging that "ethnicity is in vogue," Levin urged frankness and shared with Knapp his "firm decision" to oppose ethnic studies programs. Although the proposals had "been dressed in the guise of providing appropriate courses that have intellectual merit," Levin believed the students' primary motivation was to bolster "morale and self-esteem."

Courses emphasizing ethnic origins, he added, were extraordinarily difficult to design and teach. A course in Jewish American literature, a candidate for an endowed chair in the English Department had told him, would have to explore Yiddish literature, examine American literature taught by Jewish writers, compare the two, in part by supplying relevant social contexts, and then establish a theoretical foundation for understanding modern novels. The professor (and Levin) doubted "the exercise would add much to our understanding of contemporary fiction."

The prospects for a first-rate curriculum in Hispanic American, American Indian, and Asian American studies were even dimmer. Although a few professors in the college had expertise in these areas, Levin did not think they were sufficient in number to staff full-fledged programs. Equally important, he objected to allocating additional faculty lines to ethnic studies: "We have many, many priorities which take precedence." For these reasons, Levin opted out of discussions for an initiative "which is not likely to come into being."[1]

As Levin recognized, ethnic studies had come a long way in a short time. As late as 1965, the University of California, Berkeley, sociologist Nathan Glazer asserted that "for the moment, ethnic self-assertiveness is in eclipse and even in bad odor."[2] In that year, however, President Lyndon Johnson signed an executive order that required all government employers to take "affirmative action" to hire individuals without regard to their race, religion, or national origin. The Immigration and Nationality Act of 1965 substantially increased the number of immigrants outside of Europe who were eligible to enter the United States. In the late '60s and early '70s, moreover, the black power movement, with its emphasis on cultural pride, nationalism, and self-segregation, became a model for members of other groups.

As Harry Levin wrote his memorandum, ethnic studies had become a component of what came to be called "multiculturalism" or "identity politics." Declaring that they were "unmeltable" or unwilling to assimilate into a white, male "American" melting pot, partisans of identity politics viewed themselves as victims of oppression. They demanded opportunities to learn about and celebrate their history and heritage, and safe, secure, and separate spaces for members of their group. In time, their numbers included African Americans, Asian Americans, Latino Americans, Native Americans, women, and gays, as well as some "white ethnics" (including Jewish, Irish, and Italian Americans).

Identity politics took hold with greater force and ferocity in colleges and universities than in other institutions in the United States. Many professors in the humanities and social sciences were eager to reconceptualize society, history, and culture from the perspectives of previously "silenced" men and women. Legitimate and valuable in its own right, this testimony could also be used to expose what they viewed as the flaws at the core of American society. For students, many of whom were teenagers in the process of forming a stable sense of self, the appeal of identity politics, with its self-confirming dynamic and its demand for recognition and respect, was self-evident. "Having been told they were nobodies," the Columbia University sociologist Todd Gitlin has noted, "they were now in a position to insist that they were somebodies."[3] Administrators, who recoiled at the prospect of unrest, protest, violence, and bad publicity and endorsed affirmative action as a worthy principle and policy, found identity politics hard to resist—except when it hardened into separatism.

Identity politics became a fact of life at Cornell during the Rhodes years. Ethnic studies programs proliferated and "black" residence halls and affirmative action were hotly debated. Hispanic students took over Day Hall, Orthodox Jews got a kosher dining hall, and gays demanded their own living and learning center. Amid concern that groups were turning into fortified enclaves, there was an effort as well, implemented in fits and starts, to configure the campus as a more cohesive "community."

———

MANY STUDENTS BARELY noticed, were indifferent about, or hostile to identity politics. They preferred to live up (or down) to Cornell "musts," myths, and modes of operation, and, on occasion, to introduce new ones. There was a lot to do on campus. In an *Alumni News* story about her graduating class, Diana Katcher Bletter '78 claimed that in one week she had heard a lecture on Polish poetry, attended a class in Japanese Noh dancing, listened to a reading by Allen Ginsberg, jumped on a trampoline, taken a wine-tasting test, camped out near Cayuga Lake, and joined a political protest at the Straight.[4] Mark Schwartz '84 told the *Sun* that "you are not a true Cornellian" unless you climb to the top of the clock tower, tromp through the apple orchards, swim in the gorge, and take "a seemingly irrelevant course."[5] Surprisingly, perhaps, his list did not include throwing fish on the ice or tying a chicken to the net during a Cornell-Harvard hockey game.

Whether or not their courses seemed relevant, Cornell students studied a lot. They crowded into Uris Library, sneaked into the stacks at Olin, which at the time was not open to undergraduates, or set up shop in the Green Dragon in Sibley or in a classroom on the first floor of Goldwin Smith, which was always unlocked. In 1994, the Student Assembly asked the administration to maintain twenty-four-hour study spaces. Of course, students also wanted to see or be seen. An old game had a new name, an aspiring poet announced in the *Alumni Magazine* in 1981:

> If you want to know the places where the facetime is great,
> Then try the Ivy Room, the Fishbowl, or the steps of the Straight,
> History 340 or Psych 101,
> At Statler High or Uris Libe you're bound to get some,
> The window seat at Ruloffs or the Uni-Del,
> Hit the Nines or the Connection
> 'Cause you never can tell,
> Where there's facetime (at Cornell).[6]

Nonetheless, Cornell had a reputation as a pressure cooker, where cutthroat competition was the norm. Pre-meds, engineers, and architects felt stress most acutely, but students in all colleges were certain, rightly or wrongly, that they had more rigorous workloads than their friends at other schools. Noting that papers, prelims, and pop quizzes in all his courses came in the same week, Christopher Morris '96, a communications major, admitted, "If I were paranoid, I would feel there was a conspiracy against me by all the faculty. At times, it seems as if my schedule was written by Stephen King."[7]

A low attrition rate—96 percent of first-year students returned for their sophomore year—didn't alleviate anxiety. Neither did grade inflation. In 1979, 29.3 percent of all grades at Cornell were A's, 44.1 percent were B's, and 20 percent were C's. In 1992, 38.3 percent were A's, 43.2 percent were B's, 14.4 percent were C's, and undergraduates chose the pass-fail option twice as often as they had a decade earlier. Since grade inflation was rampant throughout the rest of the Ivy League as well, and students still felt they needed a leg up in the stiff competition for spots in professional schools and good jobs, an (unidentified) ILR professor lamented to the *Alumni News*, the young men and women in his class often viewed a grade on a paper as his "opening bid."[8]

Some students cheated, as they had in the past. A 1987 survey of three hundred Cornell undergraduates documented the extent of academic dishonesty and the varied forms it took. Ten percent of the students said they changed an answer on a returned exam and then asked for a re-grade; 11 percent indicated that they used a "cheat sheet" during an exam; 25 percent admitted that they allowed a classmate to look at their answers; 32 percent said they made up an excuse to get an extension; 33 percent plagiarized; 37 percent shared the content of an exam with a friend before he or she sat for it; 72 percent worked on a lab report, problem set, or term paper with another student without the permission of the instructor.

Many of the students found ways to rationalize their behavior. Some 70 percent said they had been psychologically intimidated by a course or a professor; 59 percent believed they were at a disadvantage because their classmates had access to assignments, notes, term papers, and tests stored in fraternity files; and, interestingly, only 27 percent granted that they had violated the Academic Code of Conduct. "I'm sure I did," one student wrote on his survey, "since I answered yes to so many of these questions, but I don't feel like I have." Perhaps most devastating of all was the judgment of another student: "I think that people will lie on this survey. They won't even admit this stuff to themselves."[9]

Empathy, Assistance, and Referral Service (EARS), a peer-counseling organization, promised to help students cope with stress with no questions asked about violations of academic integrity. Also on call were professionals at Gannett Health Services. In 1980, North Campus and West Campus residents let off steam by using a technique developed by the California psychologist Arthur Janov to help people "empty their heads of pools of pain." On weeknights, at 11 p.m., they opened their windows and delivered opinions about Chem 207 or on other weighty topics to the dorm next door in a "primal scream." By day, they wore T-shirts that read "Primates" on the front and "Primal Scream Club" on the back.[10] Yoram Szekeley, a librarian at Uris, denounced the screamers as "infantile and inconsiderate" and warned them not to be "surprised if some irate neighbor throws a rock at you. I certainly would if you were close enough for your howling to bother me." When students in the dorms were asked to change the scream time to 10 p.m., Eric Birenbaum '84 agreed to comply, but declared "We're not going away unless they cart us away."[11]

While primal screaming was a fad, drinking was a staple of the "work hard, play hard" Cornell culture. Students drank to forget stress, lower inhibitions, and, quite often, because their friends were drinking and they could not come up with anything better to do. They drank in their dorms, in Collegetown bars, and at "keg parties" sponsored by the Greeks (about 35–40 percent of male and female undergraduates joined sororities and fraternities during the Rhodes years). And they drank at tailgating parties outside Schoellkopf Field, ice hockey games at Lynah Rink, Dragon Day, Fun in the Sun Day, and, of course, at Springfest (soon to be known as Slope Day).

Things changed on December 1, 1985, when New York State raised the minimum age for the purchase of alcohol to twenty-one. The law made students unhappy and bar owners unhappier. Duffy's on College Avenue closed in February 1986. Johnny's Big Red Grill on Dryden Road, where Peter Yarrow '59 sang, Harry Chapin got his first gig, Richard Fariña was a regular, and, rumor had it, Vladimir Nabokov once lived upstairs, followed two months later (its neon sign, which the City of Ithaca had given landmark status, stayed up). The Chapter House, the once legendary tavern on Stewart Avenue, began inviting students to drown their sorrows with fruit juice "mocktails." Some bars were more diligent than others about verifying the age of patrons, but businessmen took notice when Tompkins County district attorney Benjamin Bucko cracked down on fake IDs, threatening students who were caught with them with a year's probation and a $5,000 fine and bar owners who accepted them with escalating penalties, including loss of licenses to sell alcohol.

Some traditions disappeared. Cornell's annual Mardi Gras, held at Robert Purcell Union, was only half full in 1986 and never recovered. The Phi Psi 500, a race through Collegetown with about fifteen hundred beer-fueled contestants, who donated the proceeds to the Ithaca Rape Crisis Center, Suicide Prevention, and other social service organizations, was canceled. Phi Kappa Psi members considered purchasing a $10 million, twelve-hour insurance policy, but decided that the $5,000 price tag was too high. They concluded as well that students would not spend ten dollars for a T-shirt and five cups of Coke, even if the money were going to charity.

With the university no longer willing to register events attended by people under twenty-one at which alcohol was served, drinking went underground. David Drinkwater, the aptly named dean of students, saw "a big increase in events such as student-faculty teas at the Pub and other establishments on campus."[12] Underage imbibers, however, found ways to get high above Cayuga's waters. Residence hall directors noted a marked increase in alcohol consumption and property damage. During Slope Day in 1992, the only public event where drinking was still "tolerated," seven students with alcohol poisoning were carted off in ambulances, and an additional twenty-two required on-the-spot emergency medical assistance. Citing surveys indicating that 85 percent of Cornell undergraduates drank, with perhaps 20 percent fitting the definition of "heavy drinker," a task force headed by professor of law John Siliciano '75 warned in 1993 that "abuse of alcohol is a widespread, entrenched and enduring social problem."[13]

Drunk or sober, the vast majority of students seemed pleased with their experiences at Cornell, according to journalists covering the campus. Although Fun in the Sun was dry, and Jell-O wrestling, keg rides, and appliance destruction had been banned as unsafe and likely to do damage to the Arts quad, attendance topped five thousand in 1986. "It's not what's here," Bill Watson '86 told the *Ithaca Journal*, "but how you feel. Fun in the Sun is a state of mind."[14] A chimes recital prompted another undergraduate to leave a note tacked to the doors on the ground level of Uris Tower: "I was feeling blue. The concert today really picked me up."[15] "Life sucks, and then you get hockey tickets," Michael DiTonto '87 declared to another reporter.[16] Acknowledging for the *Alumni News* that she was "romanticizing, diving heart first into sentimentality," Diana Bletter brushed aside "Cornell's bureaucracy, its lack of compassion, computerized registration forms, racial tensions, pre-professional grinding, and competition" to confess: "I loved it here, I did."[17]

B LETTER WAS RIGHT about the existence of racial tension on campus. As Day Hall saw it, Cornell was making substantial progress. By the early 1980s blacks made up about 7–9 percent of the undergraduate population in the statutory colleges and a bit less than 5 percent in the endowed units. As part of the university's commitment to increase these numbers, student volunteers, minority counselors, and faculty were asked to be aggressive in urging minority students to accept offers of admissions. And hundreds of thousands of dollars had been added to the COSEP budget. Growth in the number of black faculty was occurring more slowly, in part, administrators explained, because relatively few African Americans were getting doctorates in mathematics, engineering, and the sciences.

In 1978, moreover, Cornell found a way to resolve a formal complaint that Ujamaa violated New York State laws against segregation and discrimination in access to educational facilities, without fundamentally changing its composition and character. In a consent decree approved by the Board of Regents, the university agreed to establish a procedure to investigate concerns about access to "any Special Project Unit based on race, color or national origin" and to stop distributing handbooks that could be construed as solicitations of members of a single ethnic minority and substitute brochures emphasizing the availability, attractiveness, and nondiscriminatory nature of all Special Project Units.[18]

Where Day Hall saw progress, black student activists, faculty members in the Africana Studies and Research Center (AS&RC), and their allies saw insincerity, insensitivity, and institutional racism. They pointed to numerous bias incidents—a brick painted black and thrown through a window of Ujamaa during a conference on black studies; the theft and burning of a black nationalist flag; and the harassment of a black student on North Campus by ten white males. And they rejected the explanations of administrators as an excuse to do nothing, insisting that Cornell, like the rest of the country, was not as free of bigoted acts as they would like it to be.

In 1978, Rhodes's first year as president, trustee Robert Purcell '32, LLB '35, infuriated blacks on campus. He suggested that Cornell should consider integrating "the black community into the white man's world" by dismantling the Africana Center and redirecting his $1 million endowment for Black Studies to financial aid for minority students. He retreated within days, apologizing for a use of words that was "offensive to some people."[19] Chanting "Cornell, Purcell, think racism is swell" and "Africana yes, racism, no, death to apartheid, blow by blow," two hundred students blockaded the Johnson Museum that April, trapping Rhodes and the Executive Committee of the trustees inside for ninety minutes. They dispersed only when Rhodes agreed to hold an open session to discuss the university's investments in South Africa and the future of Africana Studies. James Turner, the director of the Africana Studies and Research Center, accused the president of "a clear insensitivity to what's happening."[20]

Backed by a petition signed by seventy faculty members, the Student Alliance against Racism demanded that the board of trustees respond constructively to five demands. They wanted Africana to remain intact, autonomous

President Rhodes and Professor Turner at the Johnson Museum during a board of trustees meeting, 1978. (Division of Rare and Manuscript Collections of the Cornell University Library)

291

and not subject to reviews required of all centers, and moved closer to campus; the establishment of a Third World Student Union, with its own information office and bookstore and control over minority programming; an end to the planned "centralization" of COSEP and the replacement of its director, Darwin Williams, whom they saw as too accommodationist; the creation of an advisory council, with substantial student representation, to coordinate ethnic studies courses; and the cessation of investments in banks and corporations that did business in South Africa. To preserve its integrity, the faculty petitioners wrote, Cornell "must stop backing away from strong commitments to social justice."[21]

The administration and the board decided against any major revisions to Cornell's minority programs. The trustees resolved only to study "the social, fiduciary and financial impacts" of divestment. Agreeing to look for a home for Africana closer to central campus, Day Hall announced that COSEP would continue in its current form, a Third World Student Union would not be built, an end to reviews of Africana violated faculty legislation, and ethnic studies programs were the purview of departments and colleges.

These issues were contested throughout the 1980s. In 1983, administrators also felt compelled to respond to a two-year decline in applications and acceptances from black and Hispanic students. In a guest column in the *Daily Sun*, Provost Kennedy refuted allegations that Cornell had reduced support staff and financial aid packages. In eight years, he indicated, the university had doubled the number of minority program staff from twenty-one to forty-two. And Cornell offered one of the most generous financial aid packages in the country for minority students with family incomes of $30,000 or less. From 1979–80 to 1982–83, he pointed out, expenditures for financial aid for COSEP students increased from $1.6 million to $3.1 million. "Substantial progress" had been made, Kennedy concluded, and the university was determined to "maintain a strong and effective minority education program."[22]

In 1984, after a year-long study, a board of trustees Committee on Minority Education issued its report. Chaired by Ithaca native and Stanford professor of anthropology James L. Gibbs Jr. '52, the fourteen-member committee praised Cornell's commitment to diversity as "strong and genuine" and affirmed that "truly significant changes" had been made. The "major issue," the report suggested, was a "discrepancy between perception and reality" on campus, with a feeling among many students that "little is being done" and that the university's efforts were "half-hearted or on the verge of being withdrawn."[23]

The committee urged efforts by all students and faculty to achieve mutual understanding and cooperation. Busy with their own interests and careers, the report indicated, white students "appear to be indifferent to the intensely felt concerns of minority students." At the same time, "many minority students reflect an insecurity and distrust of non-minority students and faculty." Preparing students for life in a pluralistic society and "striking a balance between preserving ethnic identity on the one hand, and integration with non-minorities on the other is difficult," committee members acknowledged. There were honest and entrenched differences "about where that balance should be struck or indeed whether a balance should be struck at all."[24]

The Gibbs committee endorsed intensified recruitment efforts, with special attention to those most in need of the special services available at Cornell as well as those most highly qualified, and greater use of financial aid as a tool to achieve a more diverse undergraduate student body. To help alleviate "the anxiety and anger" of some minority students, it suggested greater attention be given to "the needs and feelings of the various groups that made up a pluralistic community." Important as well was a "more visible" ethnic studies curriculum, with greater use of minority-based course material and a greater representation of minorities in faculty and staff positions. Finally, the committee recommended that the Africana Studies and Research Center, which reported to the provost, become part of the College of Arts of Sciences, moved to the center of the campus, and that the term of the director be limited to a fixed number of years.[25]

The report created a firestorm on campus. Black students denounced the assertion that perception—and not reality—was the principal problem with minority education at Cornell. They joined Africana faculty, who characterized the report as "a threat to the integrity of all academic components at Cornell."[26] As the rhetoric heated up, Provost Kennedy promised to make no changes to Africana without discussing them first with its faculty. AS&RC was not moved to Arts and Sciences. In 1986, however, Professor Turner, who had served as director since the founding of AS&RC, stepped down "to pursue scholarly interests." He was replaced by Professor Robert Harris Jr. The change in leadership, AS&RC professor William Cross indicated, was unrelated to the report of the Gibbs committee.[27]

Many Africana faculty viewed parts of the diversity initiative proposed by Henry Louis ("Skip") Gates Jr., the black professor of English who came to Cornell in 1985, as another threat to the autonomy of their center. To be sure, they supported the framework presented in "The Crisis of Minority Faculty at Cornell," a report Gates coauthored with professor of comparative literature Walter Cohen. Gates and Cohen demanded that Cornell stop counting foreign people of color and part-time and temporary faculty in its statistics. They recommended that the university expand the number of professorial lines dedicated to minority scholars by at least one a year for thirty years, encourage all departments to design affirmative action plans, and establish visiting professorships for blacks, Latinos, and Asian Americans to facilitate recruitment.

Far less palatable to Africana faculty was Gates's strong support for joint appointments, which he laid out in a confidential memorandum to Provost

Barker. Every new hire in Africana, Gates indicated, should also have an appointment in an appropriate department in the humanities or the social sciences. Each search committee should include two or three members of the relevant department, and its choice should be voted on by both departments. Following the appointment, teaching assignments, salaries, and promotions would be considered jointly as well. And the professors would have offices in each of their academic homes. "It is difficult to imagine a more ideal system," Gates wrote, to guarantee that faculty in Africana satisfy "the highest academic standards" in the university.

Gates pressed the provost to add four lines right away in "strong departments" such as English, History, and Philosophy. Departments "should be made to compete" for authorization to search for subsequent joint-tenure-track positions to ensure the appointment of extraordinarily qualified candidates. Given the increasingly large pool of well-trained black graduate students, he claimed, finding first-rate faculty "should provide no problem for a university of Cornell's standing."

Although he believed that "no reasonable faculty would refuse an opportunity to expand," Gates realized that, "given the remarkably political character" of the Africana Studies and Research Center, his plan "cannot be imposed by the Administration." Therefore, he advised the provost to appoint an external review committee, composed of the directors of the very best black studies programs in the country, to "address these questions."[28]

Gates practiced what he preached. He brought Kwame Anthony Appiah, a philosopher and cultural theorist to Cornell. A rising star (he became the W. E. B. Du Bois Professor at Cornell in 1988), Gates had the clout—and the strategic sense—to ask for a lot and get what he wanted. In 1989, however, he left Cornell, along with Appiah, for Duke University. Two years later, Harvard made Gates professor of English and director of its Institute for African and African American Research. He used this platform to become one of the nation's most prominent public intellectuals.

With Gates's departure, the momentum for joint appointments diminished while attention shifted unexpectedly back to Ujamaa. Amid ongoing complaints from alumni and a renewed threat of legal action against "the segregated residences on Cornell's campus," Larry Palmer, professor of law and vice president for academic affairs and student programs, convened the "Task Force on Freshman Housing Assignment" in December 1991. Dominated by members of the board of trustees and the Cornell University Council, the task force issued its preliminary report the following March. Although "multiculturalism can and should be a constructive force on campus and an integral part of Cornell students' educational experience," it concluded, undergraduates often "get insufficient direct exposure or training regarding the concerns, ideals and social traits of people from cultural, racial, ethnic, and national backgrounds different from their own." To help first-year students "honor and explore their own identities, affinities, and talents and, at the same time, look beyond surface differences and experience the similarities among one another as Cornellians and as human beings," a "strong majority" of task force members recommended that housing assignments be made for students randomly by professionals in the Department of Residence Life, based on guidelines that conformed with the university's educational values. Ideally, it was suggested, each residence hall would approximate the demographic makeup of the class.[29]

Based in part on concerns about "balkanization and cultural separation" on campus, the task force report was a shot across the bow of Ujamaa, which had a high percentage of first-year students of color who chose to live there. On March 5, about 350 protesters gathered outside Willard Straight Hall, protesting the random housing plan. Ujamaa Residential College was the reason she came to Cornell, Josina Reaves '95 told the crowd: "I want to be with people who understand me." Other speakers characterized the report as another attack on Cornell's black power base.[30]

After an hour of speeches, many of the protesters filed into the Memorial Room, where task force members were holding an open forum. At 5 p.m. several dozen of the protesters encircled the room and blocked the doors. Calling the proposal "a done deal," Professor Turner castigated task force members for "engaging us in a charade." About an hour later, Vice President Palmer arrived, and, after a tense stand-off and his assurance that no changes would occur until the fall of 1994 at the earliest, task force members were permitted to leave. "It was uncomfortable, unpleasant," trustee Mary Falvey Fuller '63, the chair of the task force, indicated. "I don't think it was constructive."[31]

Sometime later, the Africana faculty issued a statement opposing random housing. Rejecting the implication that the preferences and behavior of minority students was the source of the problem, they declared that the proposal "shifts the burden away from the dominant majority community" and diminishes the right of people of color "to choose associations, to maintain institutions of their own design and accentuate cultural identity positively." Africana faculty directed their sharpest attack at Larry Palmer, a black man. Cornell "has seen fit to put in charge of its diversity efforts a person who has repeatedly and publicly stated his preference for an assimilationist perspective," they wrote; he "must bear responsibility for the tension that has occurred." Concluding with a claim that formal and informal associations of racial and ethnic groups are "a positive, not a negative," they suggested that the university authorize a two-year study by a commission composed of faculty, undergraduate and graduate students, and staff and cochaired by a male and a female, "since so many gender issues transcend the entire diversity discourse."[32]

In April, a few weeks after vandals slashed holes in the Tennis Bubble on Kite Hill and spray-painted "NRH" (No Random Housing) on the facility, a

Student Response Task Force, appointed by Palmer, weighed in. Random housing, its members insisted, could well isolate minority students, rob them of support networks, and have an adverse impact on recruitment and retention. Instead, they advocated greater outreach by the "program houses," including Ujamaa, alternate residential locations for the COSEP Summer Program (to avoid unduly influencing first-year housing preferences), and more courses with multicultural content.[33]

Palmer put the random housing plan on hold. He asked Dean of Students (and professor of policy analysis and management) John Ford to develop a plan to redefine the freshman experience and look at housing within that context. Determined to have representation from all constituencies, Ford enlisted forty-one people to join his task force, assuring them and everyone else on campus that random housing would not be considered. Students interviewed in the *Sun* chimed in against the initial Palmer plan. "People's mindsets must be changed, not their housing," proclaimed Lynell James '93. J. J. Noonan Jr. '93 agreed that students should be able to "choose to live where they feel they belong."[34]

Ford's task force issued its report in April 1993. It proposed the appointment of a dean for first-year students and a university-wide requirement that all students take at least one course on multiculturalism. Ford acknowledged, however, that as soon as random housing was dropped, interest in his task force "diminished."[35]

Two years later, President Rhodes responded to an inquiry about possible segregation from Donald Nolan, New York State's deputy commissioner of higher and professional education, with a detailed description of the operation of Cornell's ten residential program houses (Akwe:kon, Ecology House, the International Living Center, Just About Music, Language House, Latino Living Center, the Multicultural Living Learning Unit, Risley Residential College, the Transfer Center, and Ujamaa Residential College). He emphasized that any student could apply for a spot in any of these houses. Applicants had the option of identifying their racial or ethnic background but were not required to do so. A committee of student residents and staff made the selections. The program houses, Rhodes concluded, helped link the academic and residential experiences of students in concrete ways: "It is our firm view that these facilities do not violate Section 19.4 of the Rules of the Board of Regents or any other applicable state or federal statute or regulation."[36]

AFRICANA FACULTY did not elaborate on their observation that "so many gender issues transcend the entire diversity discourse." It is clear, however, that the issue of women's rights, which, as we saw in Chapter 4, was much discussed at Cornell in the late 1960s and early '70s, was an important component of academic identity politics during the Rhodes years. Feminist students often made common cause with professors in demanding that the university comply with Title IX, end sexual harassment, incorporate affirmative action principles in recruiting and retaining faculty and staff, and eliminate gender-based salary inequities.

Consciousness-raising at Cornell took a variety of forms. In 1979, about one hundred (male and female) protesters pestered David Chan, a photographer for *Playboy* magazine, as he interviewed applicants for the "Women of the Ivy League" issue. Carrying posters warning that "Baring your ass takes away my dignity as a woman," they reminded passersby that *Playboy* portrayed women as sexual objects, whose primary function was pleasing men. Some of their classmates did not share their outrage. The protest drew 250 spectators—many of whom refused to accept leaflets handed to them—twenty hecklers, and two dozen fraternity members wearing only athletic supporters. One woman scrawled on a poster, "Restricting my choice takes away my freedom as a person." About 225 women signed up to meet with Chan.[37]

Less sensational but more critical were complaints that Cornell was not in full compliance with Title IX. Signed into law in 1972 as part of a reauthorization of the Higher Education Act, Title IX provided that no one, on the basis

Pro-choice rally, c. 1985. (Division of Rare and Manuscript Collections of the Cornell University Library)

of sex, should be subjected to discrimination in any education program receiving assistance from the United States government. Although it made no explicit mention of sports, Title IX had its most profound impact on high school and collegiate athletics.

The law gave colleges and universities several years to comply, and Cornell scrambled to do so. By 1979, the Department of Physical Education and Athletics had spent $77,000 on travel and equipment for women's sports, upgraded athletic facilities for them, and expanded the women's coaching staff. A full-time trainer for women was hired, along with a part-time staff writer, assigned to promote women's sports. The department also made a "fair assignment" of practice time and the scheduling of facilities, and "appropriate adjustments" to the salaries of coaches. Work still to be done, at an estimated cost of $425,000–$465,000, included construction of a boathouse for women's crew, locker rooms for women in Teagle Hall and Lynah Rink, the addition of two tennis courts at Helen Newman, and a modification of showers and dressing rooms in the Grumman squash courts.[38]

During the next fifteen years, the department added two full-time assistant coaches to the women's basketball team and started a junior varsity program. It expanded the previously part-time assistant coach jobs in women's crew and lacrosse and the head coach in ice hockey into full-time positions. Women's soccer was elevated from a club team to varsity status, given a full-time coach, and provided a dedicated practice and playing field. Women's softball also became a varsity sport. And the recruiting budget for all women's intercollegiate teams was increased.[39]

When the department did not provide retroactive remuneration for women's coaches, six of them filed discrimination complaints with the New York State Division of Human Rights. All but one settled for three months' back pay with interest. In 1979, thirty-four-year-old Gretchen Dowsing, who had raised gymnastics from a club sport to a national power, went to court, asking for $45,696—the difference between what she was paid and what a man with equivalent qualifications would have received during the five years she worked at Cornell. Claiming that she had never thought of "anything but coaching at Cornell" for the rest of her life, Dowsing claimed that she had resigned because of the "attitude of contempt" toward women's athletics and would never coach again: "I'm not a vindictive person. I just want what I deserve."[40]

Sex discrimination, according to the Cornell Women's Caucus, was not confined to athletics. Focusing on the College of Arts and Sciences "because of time pressures and lack of information," and factoring in the number of PhDs granted annually to women in each discipline throughout the United States, the caucus claimed in 1979 that if Cornell had hired and promoted on the basis of availability since 1965, the college should have had forty-nine associate and full female professors, instead of seventeen. To refute arguments that the female

applicant pool was not excellent, the caucus noted as well that the best universities were granting about the same proportion of PhDs to women as less prestigious institutions. Emphasizing a shortfall due to "past and present
discrimination" against at least sixty female assistant, associate, and full professors in Arts and Sciences, the caucus report concluded that, in an era of reduced
hiring, the strategy of hiring a few female faculty members in proportion to
their current availability "is not a workable solution."[41]

By the university's own calculations, gender-based salary inequities existed
across all ranks in all the colleges. Responding to a routine Labor Department
investigation in 1977 (undertaken for all institutions receiving more than
$1 million in grants from the federal government), which required Cornell to
furnish statistics on the hiring and promotion of women and minorities, Vice
President Don Cooke informed Provost Knapp in a confidential communication that the university was "on the horns of a dilemma." The salaries of women
faculty, adjusted for years of service, were lower than those of males by about
5 percent. The differential was somewhat smaller in the Social Sciences, and,
Cooke noted, there "are no female professors in the Physical Sciences." The
statistics "do not prove in any way that there has been discrimination," he
added, "but when the information is released there will certainly be questions
raised . . . and perhaps a law suit."[42]

Cooke suggested that Knapp consider withholding information about salaries for 1976–77 and trying to "patch up some of the holes and redo the whole
thing based on 77–78." With an allocation of about $75,000, he estimated, "the
entire female gap" could be closed. If "we do move this way," Cooke cautioned, "each dean with a potential problem should be contacted individually,"
and awards should be made on merit to avoid suits by male professors alleging
that salaries were awarded on the basis of sex without a court order to do so.[43]

There is no evidence that Knapp implemented Cooke's recommendations.
In any event, a group of women, including five assistant professors who were
denied tenure or reappointment, soon to be known as the "Cornell Eleven" (to
include the coaches) filed a sex discrimination suit against Cornell in 1980.
During the lengthy court fight that ensued, Gretchen Dowsing settled with the
university (on terms not made public by either side), but the faculty members
sought to broaden the scope of their legal action by asking the federal court to
grant them class-action status so that all women on the Cornell faculty since
1974 and those who would have been employed "but for the discrimination of
the defendant" would be represented.[44]

Students, faculty, alumni, and interested Ithacans mobilized in support of
the Cornell Eleven. A petition signed by 232 individuals called on President
Rhodes to avoid litigation that would damage the university's reputation and
divert funds "from essential academic activities." The executive board of the
Women's Studies Program criticized Cornell's contention that the university

"has not engaged in widespread sex discrimination."[45] Supportive rallies were held on campus, and funds were solicited. "We've been raising money right along, at a fairly regular, if low rate," Alice Cook, ILR professor emerita and cochair of the "Friends of the Cornell Eleven," announced.[46] Feelings ran deep on both sides. Rejecting a "speedy settlement," Rhodes called for support of decisions "based on the best academic judgment of the faculty."[47] An advertisement submitted by the Friends of the Cornell Eleven was rejected by Charles Williams '44, general manager of the *Alumni Magazine*, because its assertion that the institution used "alumni dollars" to pay the costs of insurance and outside counsel was "at considerable variance" with information supplied by the university.[48]

In 1983, U.S. District Judge Howard Munson rejected the claims of the Cornell Eleven. In a summary judgment, he deemed it an "understatement to say that Cornell has come forward with legitimate, non-discriminatory reasons for plaintiffs' failure to receive tenure."[49] The U.S. Court of Appeals subsequently agreed, deeming the statistical evidence provided by the women circumstantial and therefore not directly germane. In September 1984, the parties agreed to a settlement, in which Cornell promised to pay $100,000 to be divided among the plaintiffs (the psychologist Donna Zahorik; the sociologist Judith Long; Jacqueline Livingston of Art and Architecture; Antonia Glass of Russian Literature; and Charlotte Ferris, Human Service Studies), $25,000 toward legal fees, "$65,000 to their attorneys, and to establish a $60,000 professional development fund to be used by women faculty members at Cornell."

The case, university officials declared, "immeasurably strengthened the historic right of the colleges and universities of the nation, through their own faculties, to define the qualifications of those who shall teach."[50] In a letter to the *Cornell Daily Sun*, the plaintiff Jacqueline Livingston indicated that the experience left her feeling "violated, battered and maligned." To fight discrimination, she wrote, she and her colleagues had put their careers at risk only to see their allegations dismissed as technicalities. She was buoyed, however, by the knowledge that because the case received more publicity than any other sex discrimination suit in academia, "no woman will ever find herself in as helpless a situation" as she had been.[51]

Women's rights issues, of course, affected students as well as faculty. Unlike employment discrimination, which did not yet touch many students directly, sexual harassment constituted a clear and present danger to females on campus. In a survey of 786 upperclass and graduate female students conducted by the Cornell Institute for Social and Economic Research in 1986, 61 percent of respondents indicated that they had been subject to some form of unwanted sexual attention from a person in a position of authority over them, ranging from verbal comments to explicit propositions, coercion, kissing, touching, and assault. Of that group, 46 percent said the incident involved a professor or lecturer, 22 percent a graduate student, 20 percent a staff member, 4 percent an academic adviser, and 2 percent a department chair. Of all respondents, 78 percent reported unwanted sexual attention from fellow students. Concerned that less than 1 percent of the respondents who experienced sexual harassment filed a complaint, President Rhodes declared that no form of harassment "will be tolerated" and assured victims that "their concerns will be treated with confidentiality" and they would not suffer retaliation for having reported the incident.[52]

A year later, the College of Arts and Sciences began implementing a plan to overcome the reluctance of women to come forward. The new procedures gave students the option of talking, informally and confidentially, to one of eight specially trained sexual harassment counselors selected from the faculty and staff, whose names and office hours were announced each semester. With the student's permission, the counselor might bring the complaint to a dean or associate dean. At any time, the student might also file a formal charge with the Office of Equal Opportunity in Day Hall.

Although they had already been used several times, the Arts and Sciences procedures and the university's system for dealing with allegations of sexual harassment were put to the test in the fall of 1994, with accusations against Professor James Maas, MA '63, PhD '66, Cornell's most popular teacher, whose Psychology 101 course filled Bailey Hall every fall. In response to complaints current and former students made to an Arts and Sciences counselor, the college's Professional Ethics Committee determined that although Maas had neither sought nor had an intimate sexual relationship with any of his accusers, he had "repeatedly behaved unprofessionally and inappropriately" with three students and "committed harassment of a more manifestly sexual and egregious sort" with a fourth. Dean Don Randel imposed sanctions related to Maas's teaching, advising, and student employment responsibilities.[53]

Details of the case were leaked to the *Cornell Daily Sun* and eventually made their way to the *New York Times*. Acting on Maas's behalf, the Center for Individual Rights, a Washington, D.C.–based advocacy group committed to fighting "political correctness," filed a $1.5 million suit against Cornell. Maas's lawyers asserted that their client "was subjected to an adjudicatory process that was administered by fanatical faculty members and devoid of even the most basic elements of procedural fairness," including vagueness in the definition of sexual harassment and denials of the defendant's right to face his accusers and to adequate representation by an attorney.[54]

In a series of decisions, the last of which was issued by the Appellate Division of the Supreme Court in 1999, the New York State judiciary affirmed that Cornell properly adopted its sexual harassment guidelines, properly applied its procedures, and had no legal obligation to prevent breaches of confidentiality by the participants in the Maas case. Cornell provided the accused "far more 'process' than the law requires," university counsel James Mingle declared. "We hope that Professor Maas will now put the matter behind him."[55]

In the aftermath of these trials and tribulations—over Title IX compliance, employment discrimination, and sexual harassment—lessons were learned. Belying Jacqueline Livingston's prediction that Cornell would never change, the university hired many female faculty in all fields, including the sciences and engineering. The institution addressed gender-based salary inequities and worked hard to eradicate sexual harassment.

Women at Cornell learned that organization promotes influence and power. They established academic and nonacademic affinity groups throughout the campus. Created in 1990, the President's Council of Cornell Women provided a symbolic and substantive example of an "old girls' network." Composed of alumni who achieved a high level of accomplishment in their professional endeavors despite invisible "glass ceilings," the PCCW provided role models and mentors for female students and faculty members, helped seniors find jobs and climb into positions of leadership in corporations, and pushed for the recruitment of women into high-level administrative roles in colleges and universities. In 1991, the PCCW set out to raise $100,000 to support administration initiatives to combat sexism, date rape, and sexual harassment. "When women get out into the work world, they are not part of a fraternity," Marlene Jupiter '78 told the *Sun*. "We want them to go as far as we did, but we want it to be easier for them."[56]

CORNELL IS LOCATED in the heart of Iroquois country, and for decades the university provided assistance in farming and home economics to American Indian families through Cooperative Extension. But it did not address the needs and ambitions of American Indian students or contemplate creating an American Indian Studies Program until the 1970s. In 1972, teachers, administrators, and Native American students formed an American Indian Affairs Committee. Despite limited resources, the committee, working with the North American Indians at Cornell (NAIC), a student organization, sponsored an annual Indian Solidarity Day, an American Indian Week, two conferences on Native American Law, and student-faculty dinners. Largely through the efforts of Barbara Adams, assistant director of COSEP and a Tonawanda Seneca, the number of Indian students on campus grew from three in 1975 to thirty in 1981. And the development of American Indian Studies into a lively and important field in History, Anthropology, Sociology, Economics, and Law led to the formation of an ad hoc faculty committee to identify the necessary steps to establish a formal program at Cornell.

In 1981, the Committee argued that the university's commitment to providing educational opportunities to students from "all backgrounds" would "be greatly advanced by the availability of an American Indian Studies Program." Awareness of "the unique cultural heritage of American Indians" and their "perception of the relationship of people to their environment" would benefit non-Indian students as well. Given the interest and expertise of faculty already on campus, committee members claimed that putting a program in place "should be neither difficult nor expensive." They recommended that a director be hired, with responsibility for coordinating the efforts of program faculty and the staff member from COSEP who was responsible for recruiting, counseling, and providing support services to Indian students. Once in place, the director would chair a search for a faculty member qualified to teach "The Indian in Contemporary Society" and a "Survey of Native American Studies."[57]

With funds supplied by Dean David Call '54, MS '58, PhD '60, who also provided a home for American Indian Studies in the College of Agriculture and Life Sciences, the program became self-sustaining in the 1980s. By the end of the decade, about twelve hundred non-Indian students were taking courses offered by it. As the curriculum took shape, faculty and staff developed additional support structures to reduce the high attrition rate of Native American students. Working with faculty and COSEP staff, the Cayuga chief Frank Bonamie acted as an advocate for the undergraduates. He intervened, for example, to get permission for a young woman to miss some classes so that she could return home for an important religious holiday. In time, according to Dean Call, Cornell "had one of the best retention rates for Indian students in the country."[58]

Dressed in feather headdresses, ribbon shirts, deerskin leggings—and dashikis, kimonos, kilts, and yarmulkes—for the dedication in 1991 of Akwe:kon (a Mohawk word meaning "all of us"), the American Indian residential program house on North Campus, the residents paid tribute to its significance for Native Americans and for multiculturalism at Cornell. Onondaga chief Irving Powless noted that like the first encounter between the Iroquois and Dutch settlers in the 1600s, groups at Cornell promised "to recognize each other's differences, but respect each other's differences." Powless presented President Rhodes with a Mohawk sweetgrass basket to symbolize the young men and women his community had sent to Ithaca: "We leave our children in your hands and the community of Cornell." Rhodes gave Powless a Steuben glass eagle because the bird "holds a special place in American Indian lore and is the American national emblem." At an open house following a luncheon for four hundred guests, Evelyn Arce '93, MAT '98, described what living in Akwe:kon meant to her: "People who know their culture know themselves. This American Indian dorm, for some reason, has a spirit to it."[59]

Opening of Akwe:kon, the American Indian residential program house, 1993. (Division of Rare and Manuscript Collections of the Cornell University Library)

Mᴀɴʏ Jᴇᴡɪsʜ Aᴍᴇʀɪᴄᴀɴ students knew little or nothing at all about manifestations of anti-Semitism at Cornell and throughout the Ivy League in the first half of the twentieth century. With barriers against their admission long since removed, Jews were overrepresented in elite colleges and universities (based on their percentage of the population of the United States)—and not regarded as a minority group in need of special attention in recruitment and retention. Nonetheless, at Cornell, as at many other colleges and universities, some Jewish students pushed for the establishment of an ethnic studies program and for facilities and services appropriate to those among them who observed religious rites and regulations.

Throughout the Rhodes years, a group of faculty, led by ILR professor Milton Konvitz, PhD '33, lobbied for a more vibrant program in Jewish studies. Several deans of the College of Arts and Sciences, directors of the Development Office, and President Rhodes, Konvitz recalled, could testify that he "became a thorn in their flesh" when he pressed for a "mini-campaign" to generate re-sources for more courses and more professors in Jewish Studies.[60] Pushed by Harold Tanner '52, an influential trustee, and "impressed with the self-evident interest of many undergraduates in courses related to Judaica," the college agreed to initiate a fund-raising drive in 1987, following a review of the offer-ings at fifteen peer institutions.[61] Significantly, A&S placed Jewish Studies in the department of Near Eastern Studies and initially authorized searches for two positions, instead of the four that had been requested by Konvitz and his colleagues, while adding an Arabic language lecturer and a non-tenure-track appointment in Turkish History to Islamic Studies, also housed within NES. In time, the campaign for Jewish Studies reached and exceeded its goals, providing resources for endowed chairs, lecture series, and library acquisitions. Although Jewish Studies did not offer a major or a minor, several courses, especially one on the Holocaust, proved to be very popular with students.

Outside the classroom, Cornell seemed somewhat less accommodating to Jewish students, especially Orthodox Jews. To be sure, the university acknowl-edged Jewish holidays as "excused absences" and provided space for services on Rosh Hashanah, Yom Kippur, and Passover. Unlike at other Ivies and SUNY Buffalo, Binghamton, and Albany, however, kosher food was in short supply. Students had to order a box lunch or supper a day in advance or eat salad and milk in a dining hall. After hearing administrators assure undergraduates that "We are here to serve you," Lawrence Pomerantz '90 felt compelled to reply in the *Sun*, "For now, my service is provided at Tops" (the local supermarket that stocked kosher food).[62]

Into the breach stepped Norman Turkish '56, MBA '60, the president of Cornell's Young Israel Alumni Association. An Ithaca resident, Turkish per-suaded university officials in the summer of 1987 to support his plan to reno-vate Young Israel House and build a Center for Jewish Living adjacent to it, on West Avenue, below the Law School. The centerpiece of the $600,000 facility was a kosher dining unit with about 230 seats. Cornell provided a ground lease for the property. Responsibility for funding the project, however, rested with National Council of Young Israel.

The Kosher Dining Hall opened in 1989, at a cost of almost $2.5 million. More than fifty students, most of them Young Israel residents, ate there every day. One hundred or more attended Shabbat dinners, two hundred appeared for Rosh Hashanah, and over four hundred for Passover. Having contributed about $1 million of his own money, Turkish made the Center for Jewish Living his home away from home. He chose everything from guest speakers to the silverware and chastised students who did not dress appropriately or clean up after themselves.

Turkish was a flawed visionary. The *Cornell Daily Sun* revealed that in 1978 he had been convicted of five counts of criminal activity, stemming from trades he made on the now defunct crude oil market of the New York Cotton Exchange. Turkish paid a fine, lost his brokerage rights, and spent about three months in prison. A major difference between Lewisburg Penitentiary and Cornell University, he told the *Sun*, was that the former but not the latter served kosher food.

The Center for Jewish Living had other problems as well. Dining revenues did not cover operating expenses. A $300,000 loan from Marine Midland Bank became due in September 1989. Giordano Contracting and Norton Electric filed suit for $288,000 and $76,000 in unpaid bills for labor and parts. The complainants went after Cornell as well as Young Israel—and the university, in turn, filed a counterclaim against Young Israel's National Council, citing a guarantee in the ground lease indemnifying Cornell.

At the end of October, the Kosher Dining Hall shut its doors. Turkish and Young Israel demanded that Cornell Dining assume its contractual obligations to operate the unit. William Gurowitz '53, vice president for campus affairs, refused. The clause in the ground lease outlining the responsibilities of Cornell Dining, he pointed out, had not been signed because Turkish and university officials could not agree on its terms. Not structured to run small units, Cornell Dining would provide advice and reimburse the Kosher Dining Hall for co-op meals. Gurowitz suggested that Turkish and Young Israel "get a staff equivalent to a fraternity or sorority."[63]

Some Jewish students demanded that the impasse be resolved. In a letter to the *Sun*, David Fuller '90, the president of Young Israel, and Lisa Ross '92, the president of Hillel, noted that "diversity cannot exist" when people's dietary needs are not met.[64] Petitions were circulated at Willard Straight Hall. And on October 26, the eve of Trustee Council Weekend, protesters marched from the Kosher Dining Hall to Day Hall, where they met with Senior Provost Barker.

In December, Rabbi Laurence Edwards, director of the Hillel Foundation at Cornell, intervened to resolve the stalemate. There was "more than enough blame to go around in this mess," he noted, including his own "blind hope" that the Jewish community could get a kosher dining facility "at little or no cost." Norman Turkish had poured his time, energy, and money into the project. He had not hidden what he was doing from anyone, though "he did use some obfuscatory tactics to bring it about." Having "run amok with the grandiosity of his vision," Edwards claimed, Turkish "built a magnificent building and brought it to the brink of disaster." Cornell, however, "was at least as culpable." The university failed to apply its own standard practices to the project: it did not exercise appropriate oversight, set no limits on expenditures in the ground lease, and did not require that a substantial fraction of the money be raised before construction began.

Edwards asked Norman Turkish to step aside. He asked Cornell to "swallow its pride," allocate $1.5 million over ten years to pay off the capital debt "with some cushion for maintenance," and direct Residence Life and Cornell Dining to manage Young Israel and run the Kosher Dining Hall. "As we have often acknowledged to each other," Edwards told Gurowitz, it is the students who were hurt by the financial and legal fiasco. "And now that their expectations have been raised, we cannot expect them to be patient forever."[65]

After Edwards set up a Kosher Dining Advisory Board to oversee the operation of the facility and manage a bank account for the Kosher Dining Hall, the university agreed to run the Center for Jewish Living. Eventually renamed 104 West, so as to welcome Muslims and vegetarians who might be attracted by the cuisine, the dining unit became a popular destination for observant Jews (including Norman Turkish) on Friday nights and religious holidays.

DURING THE LAST quarter of the twentieth century, Asian Americans were often characterized—and stereotyped—as a "model minority." Much like Jewish Americans, they were highly successful compared with other ethnic and racial groups, as measured by household income, professional achievement, and family stability—and were overrepresented in colleges and universities. They were generally regarded by the public at large as ambitious, smart, and studious, yet also diffident and deferential, to their elders and those in authority.

At Cornell, as at virtually all elite universities, administrators, faculty, and Asian Americans themselves differed on the group's status as "minority." In 1982, for example, Asians constituted 1.5 percent of the population of the United States and 6.4 percent and 2.2 percent of the undergraduate population of the endowed and statutory colleges. As these percentages increased (to 10 percent of all undergraduates in 1985 and over 20 percent of first-year students in the College of Arts and Sciences and the College of Engineering in 1991), the university decided to stop treating Asian Americans as a homogeneous group and concentrate its recruitment efforts—and the provision of academic and support services through COSEP—on individuals from economically disadvantaged families and/or underrepresented nationalities (including Thai, Vietnamese, and Cambodian).

Asian American students and faculty were generally supportive of these changes. Some perceived their minority status, and especially inclusion in COSEP, as a stigma. Others, however, suggested that the university used the "myth of the model minority" to justify policies that diverted resources to other racial groups. Lee C. Lee, professor of human development and family studies and adviser to the Asian American Coalition, described COSEP as "abominable" in dealing with Asian American students, expressing shock and outrage that the office did not employ a single Asian American counselor. Asian Americans, Lee pointed out, still faced discrimination; many of them had problems adjusting to life at Cornell. Even those Asian American students who excelled in their classes, added Helen Huang '88, the program coordinator for AAC, needed role models and support networks.[66]

Noting that many of their fellow students did not know very much about Asian history, heritage, and traditions, AAC members were encouraged that a 1984 board of trustees' Subcommittee Report on Minority Education recommended the addition of courses of special interest to Asian Americans—and that, in response, the Asian Studies Department put "Asian-American Literature and Film," a course that had previously been taught on an ad hoc basis, into its permanent curriculum.

In 1986, Cornell convened a conference of Asian American faculty to design and launch a Program in Asian American Studies. With start-up funds from the provost and the President's Fund for Educational Initiatives, it came to life in 1987, the first comprehensive program of its kind in the Ivy League (and on, or more precisely near, the East Coast). Lee Lee was the director. The first course, "Asian-Americans from Exclusion to 'Model Minority,'" a survey of the experiences of Chinese, Japanese, Koreans, Filipinos, East Indians, and Vietnamese since the mid-nineteenth century, was taught by the sociologist Sharon Lee (no relation to Lee Lee), who also served as associate director. Lee and Lee enlisted fifteen program affiliates, from History, Sociology, Rural Sociology, Art, Human Development and Family Studies, and Asian Studies to cross-list courses with Asian American Studies and serve as advisers (and, where appropriate, as role models). The program offered $4,000 grants to faculty members who introduced Asian American materials into their "mainstream" courses or who conducted research on Asian American topics. In 1989, the program opened an Asian American Studies Resource Center, with library materials, videos, a conference room, and study lounges. Designed to encourage Asian American undergraduates and faculty members, many of whom were in mathematics, the sciences, and engineering, to get to know one another, the Resource Center also welcomed non–Asian American students and members of the Ithaca community. Viewing the program as part of the whole university, not a separate entity, Lee Lee emphasized that "Ethnic Studies should be for all students."[67]

LIKE "ASIAN AMERICAN," the terms "Hispanic American" and "Latino" could encompass many nationalities, cultures, and societies. Until the mid-1960s, when President Perkins included Puerto Ricans among the minority students he sought to bring to Cornell through COSEP, relatively few Hispanic Americans matriculated as undergraduates. In the 1970s and '80s, the university made a commitment to recruit and retain members of all "underrepresented" ethnic and racial groups. In an initiative called "Taking Cornell Home," the Admissions Office enlisted members of Black Students United, North American

Indians at Cornell, La Asociación Latina, the Asian Student Coalition, and the Mexican American Student Association to visit homes and conduct phone-a-thons to reach out to high school students who expressed an interest in attending Cornell. During a weekend in the spring, the university also brought to the campus two hundred minority students who had been offered admission. Most important, Cornell continued its policy of meeting the financial needs of these students. These efforts bore fruit. Black enrollment increased by an admittedly modest 11.4 percent between 1976 and 1986, but the undergraduate population of Asian/Pacific Islanders shot up by 240 percent and of Hispanics by 136 percent.

Soon after they arrived on campus, Puerto Rican students lobbied for a Puerto Rican Studies Program. They were not successful, but in 1987, the same year the Asian American Studies Program was established, Cornell created a Hispanic American Studies Program (HASP). Hiring professors to teach in it proved to be a daunting challenge, in part, it was said, because Hispanic Americans didn't feel all that comfortable in Ithaca, New York. In April 1991, concerns about the future of financial aid, and an unsuccessful search for a director of the program, led Hispanic American students, joined by black students, to block entrances to Day Hall. Assured that the university would make up the shortfall from reductions in financial aid appropriations by New York State, the students lifted their siege after four and a half hours. That same week about two hundred students met in the Memorial Room of Willard Straight Hall for an open forum, "Building a Multicultural University," organized by Vice President Larry Palmer. Speakers criticized professors and administrators for not offering more non-Western courses, for excluding the works of non-whites from syllabi, and, most vociferously, for failing to hire minority faculty.

When students learned that the leading candidate for HASP director had withdrawn from the search and that the committee had suspended efforts to hire a professor from outside of Cornell, three hundred of them marched through campus, chanting "Keep the pressure on!"—a reference to financial aid as well as faculty recruitment. Although the protesters, most of whom were Hispanic Americans and African Americans, stopped traffic, Cornell public safety officers made no arrests. Maintaining that he remained strongly committed to HASP, Palmer declared that he did not want "to be an impediment. I want to do what's good for the institution" and resigned as chair of the search committee.[68] He was replaced by Nutritional Sciences professor Cutberto Garza. After several more organizational stumbles, José Piedra, a professor of Romance studies at Cornell, became the director of the Hispanic American Studies Program.

Piedra didn't have it easy. Citing "a rejected list, broken protocol and feeble promises" in a joint search for a specialist in U.S.-Latino literature conducted by HASP and the English Department—a search that ended when faculty on the committee rejected Hispanic American candidates because they were

Rally in support of Hispanic American students, 1991. (Division of Rare and Manuscript Collections of the Cornell University Library)

"under-theorized"—Hispanic students vandalized English Department offices, leaving graffiti on the walls, in the spring of 1993. Sharing their frustration, Piedra wrote an angry letter to the *Cornell Daily Sun* in April 1993. Despite the "valiant efforts" of Provost Nesheim ("and too few others"), he indicated, "500 years of Spanish-American history are rapidly going down the drain at this University." Piedra was tired of hearing prejudices against Hispanics framed as questions: "What do you call yourselves? Where are the candidates? Would you give us a list? Haven't we already done enough? Why don't you get us the money to appoint one of you?" He could barely contain himself when an on-campus recruiter expressed delight that Anglo students were learning about Hispanic issues "because they will be managing Hispanics."

Rebellions "are ugly for all," Piedra declared, "but unnecessary only for those who have already had them." He regretted violence, whether it was the Boston Tea Party or a "momentary takeover" of the English Department. After the joint search failed, he, too, might have joined students in spray-painting the walls of that department's Goldwin Smith offices "after years of letter writing, knocking at doors and other more acceptable forms of demanding what is ours." But "graffiti or not the facts remain the same": only fifteen tenured or tenure-track faculty and three administrators at Cornell were Hispanic, "most of us having arrived in the past couple of years."

310

Piedra warned that Hispanics "refuse to be treated as charity cases, marginals or outsiders." The time had come for members of the Cornell community to think long and hard about why Hispanics complain. "Or would you prefer to continue targeting us for academic ethnic cleansing?"[69] In the fall, someone set fire to a bulletin board in a mailroom in the Class of '28 dormitory on West Campus. Two hundred students were evacuated; no one was injured. Claiming that Cornell was not acting in good faith to hire Hispanic professors, a member of the militant organization Tupac Amaru III (named after Tupac Amaru, the last indigenous monarch of the Inca state of Peru and Tupac Amaru II, a leader of an uprising against the Spanish in Peru in 1780), which had vandalized the English Department office, claimed responsibility for the fire. President Rhodes condemned "this intimidation with all the energy at my command." Dean Randel vowed that academic decisions would "not be guided by acts of violence."[70]

Latino students led the way in condemning Tupac Amaru, but tried to use the incident to ratchet up the pressure on the Cornell administration to add more Latinos (by this time "Latino" had supplanted "Hispanic" as the preferred term of many faculty and students). Criticizing "irresponsible and destructive acts" that alienate the very people in a position to help, the U.S. Latino Graduate Student Coalition asked the militants to think about "how your anonymous, and therefore cowardly, actions" affected other Latino students. The Student Coalition leaders acknowledged, however, that "activism has its place and we will not deny that the graffiti incident last spring helped to jump-start, but only to jump start, the temporarily stalled" joint search with English.[71]

Eduardo Peñalver '94, president of La Asociación Latina, responded in a somewhat different way. Peñalver indicted *Cornell Daily Sun* editors for automatically accepting a claim of responsibility for the fire by an anonymous caller. Inclined to believe it had been a "set-up," Peñalver claimed that a predisposition to conclude that a Latino was an arsonist was evidence of a pervasive "racist credulity" on the campus. He, too, did not condone setting fire to the dormitory, in part because he did not believe that "students are our adversaries in the struggle" for greater Latino representation at Cornell: "Were I to set fire to a building (which I would not do), it certainly would not be a residence hall." Peñalver did, however, approve of the graffiti in the English Department because "it had the desired effect"—the appointment of a professor in U.S. Latino Studies.[72]

Late in the fall semester of 1993, Peñalver became the leader of a takeover of Day Hall. In November, *The Castle Is Burning*, a series of eight-foot-tall wooden panels, painted in black tar, sponsored by the Johnson Museum and installed on the Arts quad by the artist Daniel Martinez to commemorate the student occupation of the Sorbonne in Paris in 1968, was repeatedly vandalized. On November 19, 150 students joined hands around the project, preventing passersby from crossing their human chain. About seventy-five of the protesters then moved to Day Hall, where they insisted that the Cornell police, who had taken the position that Martinez wanted students to interact with his work, punish anyone found defacing it. President Rhodes and Provost Nesheim, they discovered, were in Philadelphia to celebrate the one hundredth Cornell-Penn football game. In a rambling ninety-minute exchange with Larry Palmer outside the president's office, the students demanded an "immediate condemnation" of the racial epithets spray painted on *The Castle Is Burning*, police protection for the installation, a timetable for hiring Latino professors, more funds for recruitment of and financial aid for Latino students, the establishment of a Latino Living Center, and a written guarantee that Rhodes would appear at an open meeting at the Memorial Room at the Straight. Following a phone conversation with Rhodes, Palmer proposed a private meeting with student leaders on December 3, the last day of classes. The protesters refused, and at 6 p.m. Palmer ended negotiations. "The building is closed," he declared, as he walked out the door, and "you're in violation of the Campus Code."

The students began organizing a sit-in. They used pay phones to ask friends to bring food, books, and blankets to Day Hall and hoist them up to a third-floor bathroom. Police blocked entrances to prevent anyone else from entering the building but did not attempt to remove the students and allowed the supplies to be delivered. Late at night, the occupiers were studying, listening to music, and chatting from open windows with supporters gathered outside in a candlelight vigil. The protest took a more ominous turn early Saturday morning, when about sixty students burst through the doors and rushed inside. Two officers sustained injuries during the melee. The police decided not to resist in the event of another forced entry. "There is no way we can fight them off without using sticks," an officer said.[73]

On Saturday night, Rhodes, who had returned in haste from Philadelphia, entered Day Hall, accompanied by Provost Nesheim and Henrik Dullea '61, vice president for university relations. Concerned that the president might "create fear and awe" among people who "were not used to dealing with him on a regular basis," Peñalver ordered the protesters not to listen. As Rhodes repeated his offer to meet with Latino student leaders, they walked away, covering their ears and chanting hymns. Rhodes left the building. He issued a public statement on Sunday, acknowledging that the university had "a long way to go," affirming a commitment to address concerns expressed "by the Latino/Hispanic community and other groups within the campus," but insisting that "continued occupation of Day Hall does not further that objective."[74]

During the weekend, periods of calm alternated with tense moments inside Day Hall. The students, whose ranks included Latinos, a sizable number of African Americans, and smaller contingents of Asian Americans and whites, slept on bedding that had been passed up through the windows; mopped, swept, and vacuumed the floors; danced to music blaring from radios; signed a sympathy note to the injured officers; did their homework; played cards; and held hands to express unity of purpose. As rumors circulated that the Cornell police were preparing to evict them, the mood changed. At 2 a.m. on Monday, they were formally warned that those who did not leave the building would face disciplinary action, including suspension.

Campus reaction to the occupation was mixed. After heated debate, the Student Assembly endorsed both the demands of the Latino community and the relevant provisions of the Campus Code of Conduct they were violating, asked for leniency for the protesters, and expressed concern about "the paralysis of the daily activities of students and staff." One student praised the students as "inspirational," another denounced them as "craven, vile terrorists," and a third said she didn't know enough about what had happened to take a position.[75]

Following lengthy negotiations and a threat by eight HASP professors to resign en masse if the protesters were punished, the occupation ended on Monday evening. The students marched out of Day Hall, some of them with tears in their eyes. They were greeted by about 250 students, who had organized a rally on their behalf. The university lifted the threat of suspensions, pledged not to act on any alleged violations of the Campus Code, and agreed to keep in place for one week the poems, quotations, and letters placed on the third-floor walls of Day Hall and the artwork on the Arts quad. The president, provost, Dean Randel, and Dean Ford agreed as well to meet with eight Latino leaders, ten student observers, four faculty members, and one Hispanic alumnus on November 30, with the proceedings to be videotaped and made available to any interested parties. The protesters, the *Daily Sun* reported, had split on whether to stay or leave. Some opposed accepting an offer that had been made on Friday, but Peñalver's view—that remaining in the building any longer "was counter-productive"—prevailed.[76]

Within a week, student leaders and university officials agreed in principle on next steps. Influenced by Nesheim and Randel, both of whom had close personal and professional ties to the Latino community, President Rhodes affirmed a prior commitment to add six new faculty members to HASP over the next three or four years and welcomed participation by a student from a Latino organization in each of these searches. Although details remained to be fleshed out, he consented as well to establishing a living center to house students, promote Latino culture, and host Latino faculty.

In a series of communications—an editorial in the *Cornell Daily Sun*, letters to alumni, and a presentation to the board of trustees—Rhodes explained (and defended) these decisions. No complaint, however legitimate, he wrote in the *Sun*, "can justify the unlawful occupation or blockade of campus buildings." At the same time, "we must accept controversy and conflicting viewpoints, not as differences to be suppressed, but as opportunities for better understanding." Rhodes hoped that Cornell could provide "a new model in this endeavor,

313

respecting diversity, while at the same time renouncing the divisions that too often continue to characterize our larger society."[77]

To alumni, many of whom expressed outrage at the granting of amnesty to the students who occupied Day Hall, the president indicated that he understood "the disposition to insist on punishment." The behavior "was wrong and of course I denounced it as wrong." Nonetheless, Rhodes claimed that the seventy-five Latino students "were not the menacing, violent protestors of a generation ago." Courteous and respectful of property, "they seemed sincerely to believe that certain concerns of Latino-Americans were not known to the administrators." After the building had been cleared and discussions began, Rhodes decided "this was a time when leniency would serve everyone's interest."[78]

In a report to the board of trustees on January 21, 1994, Rhodes reiterated his "grave reservations" about the desirability of creating entities on campus "that would tend to separate rather than integrate." The recently agreed upon Latino Living Center differed substantially from the proposals he had previously rejected, he insisted. Most significant, it would be an academic unit, under the direction of the Hispanic American Studies Program. As such, it would be reviewed by the Faculty Council of Representatives. And Rhodes assured board members that the proposal "specifically guarantees the inclusion of a substantial number of non-Latinos."[79]

Two months later, following a referendum in which 57 percent of undergraduates opposed the idea, the Student Assembly declined to endorse a Latino Living Center. By a narrow margin, however, the trustees authorized the administration to go ahead. Located at first on West Campus and later moved to Anna Comstock Hall, across the street from Risley, the center became home to about fifty students.

For Eduardo Peñalver, 1993–94 was a good year. Praised by Rhodes as a "serious and active young man," he had seen his agenda adopted by the administration. A week after he ended the occupation of Day Hall, Peñalver, a College Scholar from Puyallup, Washington, who was analyzing U.S.-Bolivia relations in his honors thesis, learned that he had been named a Rhodes Scholar. History professor Tim Borstelman, Peñalver's faculty adviser, praised him as "extraordinarily thoughtful and engaged," a religious person, devoted to his family, "who is unusually serious about the truth, wants to do right and thinks about what he ought to do with the gifts he has been given."[80]

Before he left for Oxford University to study philosophy and theology in the summer of 1994, Peñalver sent a handwritten "note of appreciation" to Provost Nesheim. "Looking back on the year's events," Peñalver confessed that he was "often upset with myself and embarrassed for many mistakes, overstatements and perhaps an overly-confrontational style." He had taken positions with which he did not fully agree, he claimed, "in order to maintain community cohesiveness and because, as a representative, I could not simply represent my own views and desires." In retrospect, Peñalver was "not at all comfortable with the role

I played—I'm not much of a politician. I just hope and pray that the change in which I participated is change for the better. I think it was, but I am never certain."[81] After he completed his degree at Oxford, Peñalver went to Yale Law School. After graduation, he clerked for Supreme Court Justice John Paul Stevens. An expert in property law, Peñalver joined the faculty of the Cornell Law School in 2006. He left Cornell for the University of Chicago Law School in 2013. Peñalver returned to Cornell as dean of the Law School in 2014. His appointment, he told former provost Nesheim, might prove to be penance for the grief he gave administrators when he was an undergraduate.

MANY GAY STUDENTS at Cornell watched the developments involving the Latino Living Center with interest and indignation. They believed that they were not getting the recognition and respect accorded to other minority groups. Homosexuals began to "come out" in appreciable numbers at the university in the 1960s. In 1968, with the assistance of Daniel Berrigan, the outspoken Jesuit priest, six students founded the Student Homophile League (later renamed Gay People at Cornell), the first organization of its kind in the state outside of New York City. The group lobbied to prohibit discrimination on grounds of sexual preference on campus and in 1981 helped persuade the Ithaca Common Council to include sexual orientation in the equal opportunity section of its affirmative action plan. Around this time, a Cornell Gay and Lesbian Alumni Organization and a local chapter of Dignity, a Catholic gay group, were formed.

In the 1970s and '80s, many students and faculty kept their homosexuality a secret from their parents and friends. Coming out at Cornell, after all, had consequences. Athletic teams, fraternities, and ROTC did not tolerate openly gay students, and gays encountered hostility and harassment in many forms. In 1978, Roger Cramton, dean of the Law School, expressed concern about the university's "enlarged" affirmative action policy (that now included gender and sexual orientation) in a letter to President Rhodes. "Despite the propaganda of the Gay Liberation Front," he maintained, homosexuality was "abnormal and to be discouraged." Although it "is desirable to be tolerant and merciful toward those who have problems, whether they take the form of behavior quirks, alcoholism, or homosexuality, each of these problems, and not only the first two, are relevant in making institutional decisions."[82] Five years later, "in accordance with the University's commitment to racial, ethnic and gender diversity," the Faculty Council of Representatives voted to take affirmative action considerations into account in the evaluation of faculty for tenure and promotion. Following the vote (35 yeas and 22 nays), Chemistry professor James Burlitch gathered fifty-two signatures for a motion to rescind. Brought before the whole university faculty on May 18, 1983, Burlitch's motion failed, but the 81–170 vote indicated that a substantial number of professors opposed the "enlarged" affirmative action policy.[83]

It was not surprising, then, as one undergraduate put it, that gays sometimes "made a big deal out of being gay because other people make a big deal out of it."[84] Gays also attended the free movies sponsored by GayPac, renamed the Straight "Willard Gay Hall," showed up in force at the annual May Gay Festival at Buttermilk Falls, and in 1986 inaugurated Lesbian, Gay, and Bi-Sexual Awareness Month.

Galvanized in part by the AIDS epidemic and a desire to counteract the influence of antigay groups such as the Moral Majority and Anita Bryant's Save the Children Crusade, gay activists pressed Cornell to go beyond toleration to create a more affirming environment for homosexuals and lesbians. The Cornell Gay Alumni Organization and David Goodstein '54, a pioneer in the use of computers in financial analysis, prominent horseman, collector of priceless paintings, publisher of the Los Angeles–based gay newspaper the *Advocate*, and founder of personal growth seminars for gay men and women, helped lead the way. In 1982, several gay alumni offered to establish a library endowment fund for a collection in gay literature. Indicating that the subject area was not broad enough, Louis Martin, the university librarian, declined it, but reversed himself after the Gay Alumni Association asked President Rhodes to intervene. Goodstein, who had contributed money for a minority student scholarship fund in the 1960s, proposed a financial aid endowment for gay students. Citing the difficulties of inquiring about and verifying the sexual orientation of applicants to Cornell, Larry Palmer turned him down. "If they don't want it," Goodstein declared, "I suspect there will be other universities that will."[85]

In 1983, Goodstein gave his alma mater another chance. He offered the university the massive collection of books, archival material, films and videotapes on human sexuality in general, with special attention on homosexuality, then housed in his Mariposa Education and Research Foundation. University officials hesitated. "Instantly obvious," one of them wrote in 1985, in an unsigned position paper circulated within Day Hall, "is the fact that this collection deals with an issue that is sensitive, socially, morally and politically." Since some of the material was "obscene and pornographic," access would have to be limited to serious scholars, with "no browsing allowed." Possible "adverse impacts" of acceptance included "recruitment of students and faculty, relationships with current students, faculty and alumni, and on fund-raising." It was also possible that Cornell "might be inappropriately labeled as a 'gay center.'" The position paper suggested that the university schedule focus group sessions with alumni, "to get an early reading of their reactions."[86]

Between 1983 and 1985, the Mariposa collection was reviewed by two senior Cornell faculty members, the Library Board, and a group of non-Cornell experts in the field. All of them concluded that the collection was of great importance to scholars studying human sexuality. The external group noted that it would be invaluable as well to historians interested in social movements, civil rights, law and public health; sociologists investigating the treatment of "deviance and marginal groups"; political scientists examining community conflict and community organizing; psychologists examining belief and attitude change; therapists dealing with sexual preference; and art historians, folklorists, and specialists in popular culture.

Recognizing that David Goodstein "was angry and hurt by our treatment" and concerned that continued fussing "will make matters worse," Provost Barker advised President Rhodes in the fall of 1984 that Cornell should "face the matter squarely, deal with the gift pretty much as we would with any other," and accept the collection contingent on the creation of an endowment with sufficient funds to maintain it.[87] With the approval of the board of trustees, the library established a Human Sexuality Collection, with the Mariposa materials as its centerpiece, in 1988, three years after the death of David Goodstein.

In 1990 and 1991, graduate students who were using the Mariposa collection lobbied for institutional recognition of the research they had been pursuing independently. They proposed and the faculty agreed to establish a graduate minor in Lesbian, Bisexual, and Gay Studies to complement work in their major fields of study. Twelve professors from ten different disciplines in the College of Arts and Sciences joined the new field. Twenty graduate students enrolled in the course "Issues in Lesbian, Bisexual, and Gay Studies." Forty undergraduates signed up for "Lesbian Writing and Theory," offered jointly by Women's Studies and Government. And more than one hundred people attended a three-day conference, sponsored by the field, called "Perverting the Academy or Camping Out at the (A.D.) White House."

Detractors continued to snipe at the Mariposa collection. In 1994, the *Chronicle of Higher Education* published an item in its "Give & Take" column: "Cornell University wants advice on buying dirty movies—in the name of scholarship, of course." And Olin Library received a postcard that said, among other things, "You disgust me. You are sick." Such responses, however, were rare.[88] "The University has changed because the world has changed," said Nelly Furman, professor of Romance studies. "A healthy society is a society that doesn't hide itself or parts of itself."[89]

Gay students, faculty, and their supporters also began to demand changes in several of the university's nonacademic policies and priorities. On October 2, 1991, the Law School faculty voted to comply with a new American Association of Law Schools guideline barring employers who discriminated on the basis of sexual orientation from interviewing on campus or using an institution's placement facilities. The next day, "Queer Nation, Ithaca" and the "Cornell Lesbian, Gay and Bisexual Coalition" urged President Rhodes to stop "evading the issue by using legal technicalities"—provided by Walter Relihan '52, JD '59, "the very conservative University Counsel"—and to exclude representatives of the U.S. military from campus because it "continues to resist junking its outdated and irrational policy" toward individuals "it discovers or believes to be homosexual."[90]

Local, state, and federal laws appeared to be in conflict. Because Section 2-A of the New York State Education Law obliged colleges and universities to make facilities available to military recruiters if it opened them to any other recruiters, President Rhodes informed Russell Osgood, dean of the Law School, representatives of the armed forces could not be banned from the campus. At the same time, however, resolutions adopted by the Cornell Faculty Council of Representatives, the Cornell Student Assembly, the Tompkins County Board of Representatives, and other provisions of state and federal law prohibited discrimination based on sexual orientation. In March 1992, moreover, the Cornell Board of Trustees required any employer using its facilities to interview students to comply with all applicable laws "prohibiting unlawful discrimination in hiring." Provost Nesheim wrote Secretary of Defense Dick Cheney to affirm Cornell's two proud traditions, providing support for the armed services and opposing discrimination, and to ask for "full and fair consideration of this matter."[91] The secretary provided no solution, and for a more than a decade military recruiters decided to preempt protests by gay activists by renting space off campus.

Determined to attain the recognition, empowerment, and safety granted to other minority groups, Cornell gays proposed a living/learning unit, modeled along the lines of Ujamaa and Akwe:kon, for gay, lesbian, and bisexual students. Joseph Barrios '93, the GLB representative to the Student Assembly, drafted a resolution in December 1992 calling for a "safe haven" on campus where gays who felt "disenfranchised, unprotected from bodily harm, and disconnected from their cultural heritage" could "connect with their peers and their heritage." Although the resolution indicated a willingness to consider an alternative site, it identified sixty rooms in one wing of a floor in Clara Dickson Hall for students who wanted to increase their understanding of and respect for gay, lesbian, and bisexual people. Dickson was chosen because its single rooms eliminated the objection to same-sex homosexual couples living together, which heterosexual couples were not permitted to do, and because singles provide an added incentive for sophomores, juniors, and seniors to participate.[92]

The Student Assembly passed the resolution. In a letter of transmittal to President Rhodes, Pankaj Talwar '93, president of the Assembly, noted that the university had "done little to provide a clear affirmation of support" for gay students. Rhodes responded in early January that he would not make a decision until the issue had been more fully assessed by the entire Cornell community. The Assembly convened a public forum, commissioned a telephone poll of three hundred students (in which 38 percent indicated support for the unit, 33 percent disapproved, and 29 percent had no opinion) and then passed a second resolution that was virtually identical to the first. This resolution was delivered to Rhodes less than a week after Student Assembly elections, which included a referendum asking students if they were willing to live in a gay/lesbian/bisexual residence hall. A total of 3,631 said no, but 768 said yes—more than enough, supporters of the resolution noted, to fill the sixty slots in Clara Dickson.[93]

Rhodes made his decision in April 1993. Conceding that the university had "done little to provide a clear affirmation to members of the Gay/Lesbian/Bisexual community that they are today and will continue to be in the future valued Cornellians, whether they be students, faculty or staff," he promised to appoint a "Working Group" of senior administrators "to develop appropriate recommendations to accomplish this objective." That said, he rejected the resolution because he had "the deepest reservation about the increasing tendency within the campus to define ourselves in terms of groups or factions. I would express this same view if presented with requests for similar living units from other racial, religious, ethnic or special interest groups." Rhodes did not doubt that Cornell should try to find "the proper balance" between "fostering self-identity on the one hand and facilitating group interaction on the other." He believed, however, that the proposed living unit failed to strike that balance. He was also convinced that it did not contribute to keeping the university as "a place of inquiry rather than one of institutionally-supported political and social advocacy." Emphasizing that his decision did not give "tacit support" to intolerant attitudes and behavior, Rhodes concluded that gays "are our children, our students, our colleagues, our friends, and our neighbors. In a free and just society, it is our responsibility to find the most appropriate ways we can to live together in harmony and mutual support."[94]

In response, gays held a noon rally in front of Willard Straight Hall, which drew four hundred people, about half of whom then marched on Day Hall. Observers noted that the protesters were remarkably restrained. Indeed, Barrios had declined an invitation to appear on television on *The Maury Povich Show*, fearing that it would turn into a "media circus." Nonetheless, he refused to accept a distinction between the gay/lesbian/bisexual living center and existing residence halls with ties to academic programs, citing courses in Human Ecology on sexuality to which the proposed unit could be linked. Barrios deemed Rhodes's reasoning "the most discriminatory double standard I've ever heard." He also told the crowd outside the Straight that "a new day has dawned for minorities at this university."[95]

The outrage of gays intensified when the administration agreed to establish the Latino Living Center. Distinctions between the Latino center and the gay unit were "hypocritical" and "circular," *Cornell Sun* editors claimed. While there was no formal undergraduate program in gay studies (a concentration was approved by the College of Arts and Sciences in 1995), Women's Studies, Psychology, and Human Service Studies offered relevant courses that could be linked to the residence hall. If gay leaders could garner support from the faculty,

Gay pride rally, 1993. (Division of Rare and Manuscript Collections of the Cornell University Library)

the *Sun* editorial writers believed, they should be permitted to form a living center. A letter to the *Sun* (published the same day) from professors in Women's Studies and the graduate field in Lesbian, Gay, and Bisexual Studies offered that support.[96]

Meanwhile, Dean Randel shared his thoughts with President Rhodes about how a gay center differed from a Latino living-learning center. "There is only one ground of principle" on which to reject the former, "however much learning may go on there," he suggested, "in a University that does not view homosexuality as wrong in and of itself." That ground "has to do with the sexual behavior of undergraduates." Even in an age of coeducational housing, Randel noted, colleges and universities do not assign rooms or dorms "according to sexual preference." They would not allow the creation of a living unit of heterosexuals "whose unifying principle was their common interest in heterosexuality, however important and beautiful heterosexuality might be in human affairs and however worthy of serious study."

Resistance to a GLB living unit ("at least mine and probably that of most trustees"), Randel wrote, without addressing the role of single rooms in Barrios's plan, derived from "a belief that it would somehow approve or encourage or facilitate sexual activity" and was not motivated by discrimination. Because eighteen-year-olds "of whatever preference do not understand the long term consequences of, or assume personal responsibility for, sexual activity," the university should offer a "degree of protection or shelter to them," even as it recognizes that "it will not prevent this activity." Opportunities "to live as and with whom they please" off campus provide a further justification for a policy maintaining slight distance between students with a sexual preference for one another. Talking about sex in this context, Randel realized, "may be even harder than talking about what has occupied us until now." But if sex was not the issue, there might well be no valid way to distinguish in principle between a GLB unit and those that already existed or might be proposed in the future. "And we are not likely to be rid of them all," he concluded, with a display of mordant wit, "especially in the context of our tolerance for fraternities and sororities, unless we are willing to say that students may not live together based on intellectual interests but only on anti-intellectual ones."[97]

Gay students submitted a proposal designed to meet the criteria laid down by President Rhodes in his endorsement of a Latino Living Center. Once again Rhodes said no. In 1995, Rhodes's "Working Group" recommended the establishment of a Gay-Lesbian Resource Center. Still skittish about the word "Center," Day Hall expressed a preference for "Office."[98]

PRESIDENT RHODES BELIEVED that identity politics "brought to the fore the issue of community." Throughout his presidency he searched for ways "to make the whole more than the sum of its parts."[99] He formed a Commission on Common Learning in 1983. The initiative grew out of his belief that at Cornell and at colleges and universities throughout the United States the undergraduate curriculum had become increasingly specialized and that students "with varying backgrounds and viewpoints" needed general education courses to help them better understand common "questions of values, social priorities and global concern."[100] Chaired by Urie Bronfenbrenner '38, professor of human development and family studies, and Larry Palmer, with professor of economics Peter McClelland as faculty coordinator, the thirteen-member commission used a $90,000 grant from the Mellon Foundation to develop a pilot program that focused on "the shared use of symbols, shared memberships in groups and institutions, shared activities of consumption and production, shared relationships with nature, a shared sense of time, and shared values and beliefs."[101]

Offered to junior and seniors, with enrollments limited to twenty students, multidisciplinary Common Learning courses were taught by a lead professor, with five additional faculty members participating as well. They were organized around subjects of significance to contemporary society and required a substantial amount of writing by the undergraduates. Initial offerings included ILR 451, "Science, Technology, and the American Economy," taught by Professor Vernon Briggs Jr.; HD&FS 485, "Human Development in Post-Industrialized Societies," taught by Bronfenbrenner; ALS 300: "Perspectives on the World Food Situation," taught by Professor Ed Oyer; and History 448: "The Conflict between Science and Religion," taught by Professor Will Provine.

Although students and faculty participants found "the undertaking to be an exciting and rewarding intellectual adventure," the Common Learning Program did not continue much beyond the two-year pilot funded by Mellon.[102] The courses were labor intensive and expensive. The program reached a relatively small number of students, and, as critics pointed out, it did not really constitute common learning at Cornell.

The university kept on trying. Appointed dean of students in 1992, John Ford, an African American, made building a sense of community a high priority. Convinced that the first-year experience was critically important, Ford advocated sending accepted students some "material to think about" before fall orientation, "to focus their attention on issues that stimulate the life of the mind, such as ideas about multicultural awareness and the role and responsibility of faculty." He combined this idea (the genesis of the "Freshmen Book Project" that was put in place by Provost Carolyn "Biddy" Martin a decade later) with an aspiration to improve faculty advising and an admittedly vague notion that programs needed to be developed to "help students feel comfortable in reaching out to others whose backgrounds are different from their own." It is "only the beginning," Ford acknowledged.[103]

As he prepared to leave office, Frank Rhodes agreed: "It is something Cornell must continue to work on. But at least there is now recognition that community is an important goal."[104]

9 | Political Engagement, Divestment, and Cornell's Two-China Policy

When the United States invaded Grenada in 1983, protest rallies once again enlivened the Cornell campus. And that fall three hundred people gathered outside Willard Straight Hall to demand that the board of trustees stop investing university funds in companies doing business with South Africa's apartheid regime. Despite these events, however, political activists felt that during the Rhodes years rallies had grown rarer, quieter, and less likely to attract widespread support on campus than they had been in the 1960s and early '70s.

In the new era protestors were often greeted with hostility and derision. In 1977, after a question-and-answer session with Walter Wriston, chairman of the board of Citicorp, was terminated early after two hecklers, dressed in Ku Klux Klan hoods, presented him with a citation for services allegedly rendered to white supremacy in South Africa, Justin Davidson, dean of the Business School, demanded that the judicial administrator appoint a special investigator to look into the case. In a letter of apology to Wriston, Davidson declared, "Within the Cornell community, and most other university communities, a small number of true-believers and Yahoos unfortunately exist. They suffer from a peculiar arrest in moral development which leaves them full of truth, righteousness and total disrespect for the opinions of others. They deserve your contempt. They have mine."[1] Six years later, David Brown '83, a History major and self-styled libertarian, told the *Ithaca Journal* that left-wing campus activists "just take what is served up on the current ideological platter." Cornell students, Brown declared, were no longer buying what the radicals were selling: "You hear people say, 'Ah, those idiots, they're out in front of the Straight again.'"[2]

Nonetheless, political activism over issues in the world beyond Cornell did not vanish during the Rhodes years. Students and faculty protested against the nuclear arms race. Conservatives became more visible on campus with a newspaper, the *Cornell Review*, advancing their point of view and skewering what they perceived as the "political correctness" exhibited by the university, including affirmative action and a ban on displaying American flags outside dormitory windows. And a movement for divestment from South Africa gathered strength on the campus, culminating in the construction of a "shantytown" and mass arrests in 1985 and 1986.

Cornell administrators were ambivalent about the political engagement of faculty and students. They supported free speech, wanted Cornellians to be well-informed about political issues, and for the institution to be a "player" on the national and international scene. To these ends, they intensified lobbying activities in Washington, D.C., and Albany, established a Cornell in Washington program for undergraduates, made study abroad more available and affordable, and reached out to Japan and China. At the same time, they were determined to keep mass demonstrations from getting out of hand, and, for example, amended the Campus Code of Conduct in 1985 to specifically include

Front page, *Cornell Review* (founded in 1984), March 1986, vol. 3, no. 3. (Courtesy *Cornell Review*)

as a violation the act of unlawfully remaining in a building and to make suspension of students possible if they interfered with the normal operations of the university.

President Rhodes, moreover, was acutely aware of the dangers of endorsing controversial political positions—in his own name and on behalf of the university. Since his appointment as president, he indicated in a confidential memorandum to his assistant, Joy Wagner, he had had requests to speak on "everything from nuclear freeze and nuclear power . . . to abortion, campaigns for financial aid, federal support for research, suppression of academic freedom in the Soviet Union, Republican candidates for Senate and Democratic candidates for the House." He had to "pick and choose," he realized, and in doing so to "shelter the argument, that's the essential point, and not commit the university in a way that would, on the one hand, destruct [sic] the freedom of its own members, or on the other hand, jeopardize the extraordinary freedom which society encourages it to exercise."[3]

In choosing "constructive engagement" over divestment in South Africa, Rhodes was opposed by a substantial majority of faculty (and perhaps a majority of students as well). In insisting on Cornell's right to invite Lee Teng-hui, PhD '68, the president of Taiwan, to travel to Ithaca to receive an award, he garnered more support but ran afoul of advocates of a United States government policy that withheld diplomatic recognition of the island in deference to China, which branded Taiwan a breakaway republic. On a campus as large and as diverse as Cornell, Rhodes declared, shortly before he retired, "You can't pretend you're one small happy family."[4]

THEODORE LOWI, the John L. Senior Professor of American Institutions, was the founding father of the Cornell in Washington program. Responding to an invitation to all faculty (during the university's celebration in 1976 of the bicentennial of the United States) to make proposals for Cornell's next century, Lowi told President Corson and Provost Knapp that the nation's capital had become "the center of the universe." It would be "foolish to argue," he added, that the quality of education and research at Cornell would not be improved by direct access to the policymakers, archives, and culture in the city. Lowi proposed that interested undergraduates spend a semester in Washington, taking courses from Cornell professors who might be "detached from service in Ithaca" to teach there or travel back and forth each week to offer a seminar. Courses could engage government, culture, planning, or economics with the workings of the city. In addition to their course work, students would get practical public policy experience by interning at a federal agency, on Capitol Hill, at the White House, or with a "think tank," and write an honors thesis. As an ancillary benefit, the program, Lowi suggested, would allow Cornell to better coordinate "government grant and contract competition," relationships with alumni living in the D.C. area, and efforts to place graduates in positions in the private and public sectors.[5]

Corson and Knapp expressed interest but left office before taking formal action. President Rhodes and Provost Keith Kennedy, MS '41, PhD '47, approved the project in the fall of 1979. Cornell in Washington (CIW) opened its doors the following spring on the second floor of a building at 1606 Twentieth Street NW. Six undergraduates enrolled in two team-taught courses, "Foreign Policy and the American Political Process" and "Science, Government, and Society." Internship sponsors included Congressman Robert Walker, a Republican from Lancaster, Pennsylvania, and Congressman Edward Beard, a Rhode Island Democrat. The CIW pioneers found their own housing, and, Carol Dreyer '81 boasted, "we figured out the damned computerized Metro transit system."[6]

In 1985, Cornell in Washington acquired a permanent home. On Saturday, April 20, President Rhodes formally opened the Cornell Center at 2148 O Street NW. Ivy from the Plantations was transplanted on the walls of the four-story building, which contained classrooms, offices, and beds for fifty-five to sixty students (establishing the maximum enrollment for the program). Participating faculty that year included Lowi, James Turner, History professors Walter LaFeber and Joel Silbey, the economist Robert Frank, the sociologist Rose K. Goldsen, professor of resource economics David Allee '53, MS '54, PhD '61, and professor of architecture Barclay Jones. Among the rapidly expanding list of internship sponsors were the State Department, the Commerce Department, Common Cause, and the Federal Elections Commission. Popular with undergraduates, especially those majoring in Government, Cornell in Washington restricted enrollment to juniors or seniors with a grade-point average of at least 3.0. Putting a premium on small seminars, with substantive interactions between faculty and students, the program was at once rigorous and "a dazzling way to learn." Government professor Arch Dotson, the director of CIW, announced: "We take no prisoners. There are no incompletes for academic reasons at Cornell in Washington. . . . But to succeed in the program, what you really need is brains and an interest in public policy—we do the rest."[7]

Over time, the curriculum in Cornell in Washington grew: two tracks, one in public policy and another in American studies, were offered; students were required to take a seminar in research methods and assigned tutors to assist them with their honors theses. Although CIW relied increasingly on adjunct faculty, based in Washington, and enrollments became less robust, the program remained an important option for Cornell undergraduates interested in politics and public policy. Some of them returned to Washington for careers in government service.

Whether or not they agreed that Washington, D.C., was the center of the universe, many students, faculty, and administrators believed that Cornell should extend its educational reach well beyond the borders of the United States. Great universities, according to President Rhodes, should be "campus rooted but internationally oriented . . . and cosmopolitan in character." Their curricula, the makeup of their graduate and undergraduate student bodies, and the research and teaching activities of their faculty should be "conspicuously international." To respond to an increasingly global economy and the political imperatives associated with it, Rhodes supported new research partnerships, teaching exchanges, scholarly consortia, institutional memoranda of understanding, directed community service, internships, and study abroad. He even entertained the possibility that Ithaca would become "the American campus of an international university."[8]

The emphasis on global outreach was, of course, not new; for decades Cornell faculty and graduate students had helped developing countries adopt better methods of growing and harvesting rice, coconuts, coffee, and citrus, combat diseases and pests threatening crops, and improve different breeds of animals. International involvement intensified, however, during the Rhodes years. In 1985, for example, the theme for Trustee Council Weekend was "Cornell in the World"; lecture and symposia topics included "Power and Influence in Today's World," "Revolutionary Nostalgia and Cultural Administration in Japan," and "Do Third World Workers Share in Economic Growth?"

Throughout the academic year, three dozen American students promised not to use their native tongue when they entered their dormitory, Anna Comstock Hall, to speak only French and Spanish and hone their language skills by sharing meals five nights a week, screening foreign films, and reading foreign periodicals. German language students were affiliated with the Language House as well, sharing space in Anna Comstock for meetings and parties. A Language House section in Chinese would soon be established, as well.

With a grant of $2.4 million from the United States Agency for International Development, the Division of Nutritional Sciences helped train officials in developing countries to monitor diets and factors affecting malnutrition. And Cornell's International Agriculture Program, which had been established in 1963, was conducting activities in nearly two dozen countries, including the Philippines, Bangladesh, Panama, and the People's Republic of China; more than one hundred informal contacts also had been forged between faculty in the College of Agriculture and Life Sciences (which had 343 graduate students from foreign countries, nearly three-quarters of them from developing nations) and their counterparts in universities around the world.[9]

In 1990, CALS received $7.5 million from anonymous donors (later revealed to be Atlantic Philanthropies), the largest grant in its history, to establish the Cornell International Institute for Food, Agriculture and Development to combat poverty, hunger, and malnutrition in Africa, Latin America, and Asia. Noting that three-quarters of the world's people lived in less developed countries, Daniel Sisler, PhD '62, professor of agricultural economics and an authority on the impact of technology on food production, suggested that the "threat to the balance between population, resources, and the environment and the need for careful management to counter that threat have never been greater." Commenting on the initiative, Barber Conable '43, LLB '48, a former congressman from New York State and at the time president of the World Bank, declared that "anyone who travels knows that Cornell is a global institution. . . . The new institute adds a new dimension to the University's presence abroad."[10]

Study Abroad added yet another dimension. Before 1985, students interested in enrolling in a university outside the United States for a semester or a year of academic work had to identify an appropriate institution on their own, complete an application, register in absentia once they were accepted, find housing, and seek to transfer the credits back to Cornell when they returned to Ithaca. Often they could not apply financial aid grants to pay their tuition. It is not surprising that very few Cornell undergraduates—fewer than two hundred out of twelve thousand—studied abroad each year.

At the request of President Rhodes and Provost Kennedy, the Center for International Studies designed a Study Abroad program suitable for Cornell. The center tapped Professor Dotson, who left Cornell in Washington and became the first director of Cornell Abroad, to negotiate agreements with institutions able to offer courses equivalent in quality to those available in Ithaca to reserve a specific number of spaces for Cornell students. Dotson also established centers in Spain and Germany, directed by Cornell faculty members in collaboration with the University of Seville and the University of Hamburg. A Study Abroad office advised students about their options, ranked applications, and sent them off. The university extended financial aid to those who needed it.

In 1985–86, its first full year of operation, more than three hundred Cornell undergraduates studied at dozens of institutions in Europe, the Middle East, and Asia. A substantial majority of them were from the College of Arts and Sciences, though the College of Agriculture and Life Sciences and Human Ecology sent a fair share of students, as well. The most popular destination, by far, was Great Britain. Others studied in Seville with Urbain "Ben" DeWinter, director of admissions in the College of Arts and Sciences, who taught courses on the philosopher Miguel de Unamuno and Spanish novels written between 1914 and 1936. Ten students accompanied H. Peter Kahn, professor emeritus of the history of art, to Hamburg. A few individuals ventured to Denmark, Geneva, Switzerland, Israel, Egypt, Nepal, Japan, and China. "No person can be considered educated in the full sense of the word without some knowledge of other cultures and nations," Dotson declared. The change in policy, he added, "makes foreign education an integral part of a Cornell education."[11]

———————

INTEREST IN NATIONAL and international affairs prompted small numbers of dedicated and determined students and faculty to political activism and public protests. They addressed a wide variety of subjects in several different forums. On a Sunday afternoon in April 1979, following an accident at a nuclear power plant near Harrisburg, Pennsylvania, about 450 Cornellians and Ithaca residents assembled downtown for a two-hour rally featuring songs, skits, and speeches. Organizers circulated petitions to state and federal legislators demanding a moratorium on the construction of nuclear power plants and more stringent regulations on the disposal of nuclear waste.

In December of that year, supporters and opponents of the recently deposed shah of Iran clashed in front of Willard Straight Hall. When some students raised the red, white, and green Iranian flag, others pulled it down and burned it, as hecklers shouted "Free U.S. Hostages" and sang the national anthem and "America the Beautiful." After a barrage of water balloons hit the speakers' platform and Safety Division officers moved in to separate the combatants, Vice President William Gurowitz '53 appealed to the crowd to support freedom of speech and forswear violence. Gurowitz could barely be heard. Although five hundred people milled about, the *Ithaca Journal* reported, only a few dozen on each side seemed to be seriously involved in the demonstration. When a speaker asked, "If we go to war, would you fight in Iran?" some students shouted back, "Yes," and laughed. During the flag burning, the paper noted, a young man turned to his friend and said, "Let's go eat man. Who wants to burn a flag when you're hungry?"[12]

Students and faculty organized "Survival Week" in April 1982, to analyze and dramatize the impact of nuclear war. A noontime theater production on the Arts quad on Monday included the response of fifteen students to a mock air-raid siren. On Tuesday, protesters marched through the campus, wearing black clothes and white skull-like makeup, announcing to sunbathers that a bomb had just landed, leveling everything within a two-mile radius. The week ended with a lecture, "Civilian Based Non-Violent Defense," in Anabel Taylor Auditorium, a workshop, "Educating about the Arms Race," at the Greater Ithaca Activities Center on Albany Street, and two Bailey Hall convocations, featuring U.S. Senator Daniel Patrick Moynihan, Economics professor Alfred Kahn, and Physics professor Hans Bethe.[13]

In 1984, more than one hundred students and staff marched around Barnes Hall to protest the presence of CIA recruiters on the Cornell campus. When twenty of them blocked an entrance to the building, the British dean of students David Drinkwater told them, "I am going to invite everyone in a nice, sweet English way to vacate the passageway." They refused to move, were arrested by public safety officers, and charged with violating the Campus Code of Conduct. At a rally that afternoon, Government professor Eldon Kenworthy told a crowd of about 150 people that through its covert support of insurgents seeking to topple the government of Nicaragua, the CIA "has brought death and destruction" to Central America.[14] The next year, CIA recruiters returned, and so did about forty protesters, this time carrying a black cardboard coffin garnished with flowers. Sixteen students, in whiteface and wearing black makeup, sitting in a circle holding hands in front of the door of the Career Center in Barnes, were arrested and detained.

Students and faculty also mobilized in opposition to the Reagan administration's plan for mandatory drug testing of employees of the federal government in 1986. At a rally at the Straight, at which nonalcoholic beverages were served, a group facetiously calling itself "Patriotic Individuals Supporting Screening for Evil Drugs" (PISSED), collected urine samples from 139 individuals in a pile of three-ounce plastic cups, none of which was labeled by name, which were then packed and shipped to the White House. Graduate student Ron Boznack and his German shepherd–Doberman pup were the first to enter the portable toilets. "It was a trick getting Cheyenne to cooperate," Boznack said, "but both of us have spoken our minds on this issue and feel good about it, so to speak." Deeply concerned about a "growing threat to personal liberty," Jan Grygier, PhD '83, a research associate in civil and environmental engineering, declared that the tests were "a direct and blatant violation" of Fourth Amendment protections against search and seizure, and that the $300 million allocated to the program would be far better spent on drug education and rehabilitation.[15]

The atmosphere was not nearly as light when Rabbi Meir Kahane, the American expatriate, right-wing member of the Israeli parliament, and supporter of expelling Arabs from the Gaza Strip, the West Bank, and Israel, appeared on campus in November 1986. Kahane told an audience of about two hundred people that peace with "Arabs who want us dead" was impossible. When he spotted a Palestinian flag in the lecture hall, he proclaimed "it's wonderful to see that flag in Ithaca because it will never fly in Israel." "There will be no more Auschwitzes," he added. "There will be no more Holocausts. Never! Never! Never!" Kahane was interrupted so often by hecklers from an organization called "Jews against Zionism" that Dean Drinkwater threatened to prosecute anyone who continued to yell and scream. He ended the question–and–answer session when Kahane refused to recognize a Palestinian man who wanted responses to a written list of concerns.[16]

In 1988, political activists found a different outlet to support the United Farm Workers' call for a boycott on California grapes. Following a speech at Cornell by UFW president Cesar Chavez, they lobbied the Student Assembly, which had legislative authority over Cornell Dining, to prohibit grapes from being served in any dining halls on campus, at the Entrepot Store, or by Cornell Catering. Although the Ithaca Common Council had also endorsed the boycott, the Student Assembly vote, activists boasted, was "the first time we've actually gotten grapes removed from someplace."[17]

Clearly, public protests at Cornell were most often initiated by the political Left. Perennially anti–Establishment, and feeling disenfranchised by the Reagan revolution, radicals (and some liberals) believed that demonstrations were the best way to bring attention to their causes. By the 1980s, however, conservatives were increasingly willing to enter the public square to challenge them. Citing the establishment in 1977 of a Center for the Study of American Political Economy, which sponsored courses in "the American private enterprise system," and a concerted effort by the Business School to bring corporate executives to Ithaca to discuss problems and opportunities, the *Cornell Alumni News* asked in 1982, "Are the Winds of Conservatism Being Felt on This Campus?"[18] Two years later, editor-in-chief James Keller '84 announced the debut of the *Cornell Review*, "an opinion journal dedicated to traditional values and conservative principles of government." Modeled on the *Dartmouth Review*, the first avowedly conservative newspaper at an elite university campus, the *Cornell Review* spoke out, bluntly, about what it regarded as the misguided and malignant policies being pursued in Day Hall, Albany, and Washington, D.C. And the Cornell Republicans became a larger and more visible campus organization, registering students in election years, inviting prominent conservatives to Ithaca, and weighing in on the issues of the day.[19]

In 1991, conservatives mobilized against a manifestation of what they labeled "political correctness." That February, as an expression of solidarity with American soldiers fighting against Iraq in the Persian Gulf, Diane Schieu '94 hung a yellow ribbon outside her window in Lyon Hall, and Nathaniel Brackett '94 displayed a United States flag outside his window at McFaddin. Informed that they had violated a provision in their dorm contracts (inserted in 1988 to prevent the showing of a Confederate flag), Schieu and Brackett, both of whom had cousins stationed in the Gulf, protested. Twelve students in Mary Donlon Hall supported them by hanging flags from the fifth floor of that dorm, and students in Risley hung a banner that read, "Hasn't the Department of Residence Life implied that you can break the rules if you have the right ideology? Would a 'No Blood for Oil' banner have elicited the same spineless response? Have a nice day." The last line referred to the "smiley button" always pinned to the sport jacket of Vice President Bill Gurowitz.[20]

University officials backed down. "A flag is symbolic speech and is potentially offensive," Vice President Palmer maintained. "I prefer discourse, but perhaps there should be more space for symbolic speech if that is the consensus of the University community." Citing the "strong and negative reaction inside and outside" Cornell, Palmer declared that "rational discussion is not possible—the issue is too emotional." Since "banning American flags is not something any of us feels comfortable doing," he suspended the rule and promised not to pursue disciplinary action against Schieu and Brackett.[21]

ONE POLITICAL ISSUE dominated the first decade of the Rhodes years: a movement to help end apartheid by persuading the board of trustees to divest from companies doing business in South Africa. Divestment was first advocated in United Nations General Assembly Resolution 1761, which established a Special Committee against Apartheid and called on all nations to impose economic sanctions on South Africa. A divestment campaign in the United States began to gain critical mass in the 1970s with the founding of the Interfaith Center on Corporate Responsibility, revulsion at the torture and murder of the South African anti-apartheid activist Steve Biko while he was in police custody in 1977, and the publication that same year of the so-called Sullivan principles. An African American minister based in Philadelphia, and a member of the board of General Motors, Leon Sullivan called on corporations to require as a condition of doing business there that all employees in South Africa be treated equally and work in an integrated setting. Criticized by some as lacking mechanisms of enforcement, the Sullivan principles were designed to enlist international corporations in pressuring South Africa to end apartheid.

The divestment initiative spread to several university campuses in the late 1970s. Following teach-ins and demonstrations, Hampshire College, Michigan State University, and Columbia stopped investing in companies that traded with or maintained operations in South Africa. At Cornell, as we have seen, divestment was linked with demands related to financial aid for African American students and the Africana Studies and Research Center in the 1970s. The movement took center stage as Frank Rhodes took office, when protesters lambasted the trustees for "shirking humanitarian aims to avoid insulting corporations in which Cornell has a stake" and called for an institution "dedicated to freedom to speak out against tyranny."[22]

In April 1978, several hundred protesters marched from Ujamaa to Day Hall, then across the Arts quad to the Johnson Museum of Art, where they presented a divestment petition with two thousand signatures to administrators and trustees meeting there and demanded to address the board's Executive Committee. Knowing that a confrontation was likely, Edward Sills '77, JD '80, quipped in the *Cornell Sun*, the trustees "should have convened at Oxley Polo Arena, where escape on horseback is easy."[23]

Of course, the confrontation was not a laughing matter. The board allowed four students to address the committee for fifteen minutes, thanked them, and asked them to leave. When the meeting ended, board members found that the demonstrators were blocking the exits to the museum. After a tense, ninety-minute standoff, Rhodes and several trustees agreed to attend an open forum on divestment to be held before the end of the month. Commiserating with the new president that he had had "to face this kind of trouble so soon," Dale Corson reminded Rhodes that "threats are the chief weapon of your adversaries," who were testing him: on one hand, "Once you alter a position or give ground under pressure, every issue will be pressed relentlessly." On the other hand, "every position rationally and firmly held makes the next assault more responsible and more restrained." Expressing confidence "that the Trustees will back you completely if you have a rational position (or even if you don't—to a point)," Corson advised Rhodes to avoid large public meetings wherever possible and to make sure he retained "credibility with the faculty."[24]

On April 26, seven trustees and administrators and eight members of the Student Alliance against Racism appeared onstage at Bailey Hall to discuss divestment, corporate responsibility, and the Africana Center. Rhodes's claims that U.S. corporations trained black South Africans and raised the standard of living in the country were received with derision by most of the twelve hundred people in the audience. The session ended with no agreement—and a pledge by the trustees to appoint a committee to investigate divestment. The issue was complicated, as the editors of the *Cornell Daily Sun* acknowledged. The argument that corporations improved conditions for black South Africans had "been proven dead wrong, most recently in a U.S. Senate report," they declared. Insisting that "Cornell must pull out of South Africa, now," the *Sun* editors also noted the "strong arguments against divestment," including the distinct possibility of a drop in the endowment and a decline in corporate gifts. Convincing trustees that morality required divestment "even at the expense of some income loss," they concluded, "will take some time."[25]

A similar debate raged inside Day Hall. Cornell's divestment would have little or no impact on American corporations, Provost Kennedy suggested to President Rhodes, and a loss of funds available to the university "during a period of retrenchment cannot be ignored." Still, divestment would send "a very positive symbol" to the campus. "I have reached an impasse in my own argument," Kennedy confessed, "and hence am waiting to hear the conclusion of the Investment Committee."[26]

In a report issued in December 1978, the committee unanimously opposed divestment. The trustees declared that foreign policy was the responsibility of the government of the United States, while contending that corporations could comply with the Sullivan principles on their own and constitute a force for progressive social change in South Africa. They estimated the cost of divestment at $1 million immediately and another million in each subsequent year and predicted that purchasers of the shares Cornell sold would almost certainly be less socially responsible than the university. They did recommend, however, that Cornell not invest in firms that did most of their business in South Africa or hold shares in banks that made new loans or expanded existing loans to the apartheid government. They proposed, as well, that the university assist black schools in South Africa and fund fellowships to bring black South African students to Cornell. The report, the *Cornell Sun* editors opined, was an advance on the board's previous position that the weight of the institution should not be put "behind a particular social concern." But the struggle, they predicted, "is not over."[27]

Divestment activity at campuses throughout the United States, including Cornell, receded but then swelled in the mid-1980s, when a violent crackdown against the "People's Campaign" of the African National Congress inside South Africa was covered extensively by the American mass media. This time, many divestment initiatives succeeded. By the end of the decade, twenty-six states, twenty-two counties, and more than ninety cities had taken some action against companies doing business with South Africa, including selective purchasing policies and restrictions on pension fund investments. And more than three hundred colleges and universities had partially or fully divested.

On April 18, 1985, at Cornell, which had not divested, protesters sat in at the lobby of Day Hall and two adjoining hallways near the financial aid and bursar's offices for six hours. A few hundred yards away, outside Willard Straight Hall, representatives of American Express were distributing free bottles of Coca-Cola to anyone who signed up for a credit card, three individuals were protesting President Reagan's "Star Wars" Strategic Defense Initiative, and Chun-Hsaing Chu '88, one of 250 students participating in a "faculty auction" to raise funds for the classes of 1985 and 1986, was bidding $95 to have lunch on a powerboat with Vice President William Herbster. The divestment activists, who by this time were predominantly white, renamed Day Hall "Biko Hall" and demanded that Cornell sell $112 million of its $700 million endowment, which they believed was supporting apartheid, directly or indirectly. They paid particular attention to Johnson Wax Company, dousing an effigy of trustee Samuel Johnson '50, the chairman of the company, with Future, a floor wax, and placing it in the branches of a tree. When the protesters refused to leave the building at 5 p.m., closing time, public safety officers detained 144 of them, the largest mass arrest to date in the history of Cornell. Buses carried many of the young men and women to Barton Hall, where they were formally charged with violating the Campus Code of Conduct; others locked hands with their comrades, walked to Barton, and turned themselves in. "What we have started here is not going to stop," Michael Rinder '86, a member of the Cornell Congress for a Free South Africa, proclaimed. "No one is going to tell me that this was insignificant."[28]

The protesters returned to Day Hall on Friday, April 19, 1985. This time 190 of them were arrested. On Monday, 211 were taken in custody; on Tuesday,

130. Fourteen Cornell faculty members joined the sit-in on Tuesday, marking the first time professors as well as students were arrested. An announcement that three-time offenders would be suspended and charges of third-degree trespass referred to Ithaca City Court, against a few individuals, had some deterrent effect, but in any event the protesters changed tactics that week. A small number announced hunger strikes, while many others constructed a "shantytown" on the west side of Day Hall. Within a week, fifteen shanties and two tents, built out of cardboard, plastic, and pieces of wood, had gone up. About two dozen demonstrators slept in the shanties, which had been supplied with camping stoves and stocked with food. One of them, the "Inhumanities Library," contained antiapartheid and divestment brochures and pamphlets. "This is our home until Cornell divests," said Gregory Holbein, an Agricultural Economics major from Auburn, New York.[29]

The protesters called on students and faculty to boycott classes in a "No Business as Usual Day" on April 29, which had been scheduled as well at dozens of colleges and universities. On the Cornell campus, it featured a "No Campus Tour as Usual" at 1 p.m., a "No Dancing as Usual" party at the Big Red Barn at 7:30 p.m., and workshops at the shanties on the university's financial ties to

Divestment sit-in, Day Hall, April 1985. (Division of Rare and Manuscript Collections of the Cornell University Library)

South Africa, racism, the history of Native Americans, sex education for women, and the oppression of young people.[30]

As the tension mounted and police responded to bomb threats in Day Hall and Hollister, President Rhodes laid out the university's position on South Africa, the protests, "and the prospects for the coming weeks" in a letter published in the *Sun*. He emphasized that his administration and the board of trustees viewed apartheid as "morally repugnant and cruel and repressive in its effects." After summarizing board actions, including the sale of stock in three companies that did not comply with the Sullivan principles, he announced that a Proxy Review Committee, consisting of four trustees, one of them a student trustee and another a faculty trustee, was reviewing investment policies in a study involving fourteen other universities and would hold a public hearing on campus on May 2. Rhodes claimed that the demonstrators had made their point and "have been heard." But, he added, "the events of the last few days have moved beyond reasoned discussion. Dissent is one thing. Disruption is another." It "will not result in divestment, let alone contribute to an eradication of that oppressive system." The president concluded by pleading for recognition that "simple solutions rarely exist" in a complex world and urging that everyone at Cornell needed to express views without disguising differences but with "good will, mutual respect and restraint."[31]

On May 1, 1985, the faculty debated a resolution, introduced by Michael Latham, professor of nutritional science, urging the trustees to divest in "as expeditious a manner as possible." "Repression, injustice and cruelty are as entrenched in South Africa today as they were in Nazi Germany in the 1930s," Latham declared. To claims that the withdrawal of corporations would hurt black workers, Latham replied that "in the long run the whole black population would benefit." The abolition of slavery led to some job losses, he added, as would ending the operations of the Mafia in New York City, but that was no reason to oppose such actions. With but three or four exceptions, speaker after speaker agreed with Latham. As the meeting wound down and the question was called, Rhodes asked to speak. A motion to end debate, which required a two-thirds vote, failed (165 yeas and 140 nays), and he took the floor, "as a faculty member who also has administrative responsibility." To audible expressions of disapproval, Rhodes denounced apartheid but opposed the nonbinding resolution. Casting doubt on the impact of divestment and reminding his colleagues of the fiduciary responsibilities of the board of trustees, Rhodes asked whether Cornell should divest "simply as a symbolic gesture." He wondered whether divestment included a rejection of student fellowships, joint research projects, and equipment purchases from corporations, and suggested that it would open the door to divisive debates about other political issues "waiting in the wings for action to be taken." Emphasizing that the trustees "are open to change," Rhodes asked the Cornell faculty to wait for the report of the Proxy

Committee.[32] The question was called, and by a vote of 323–72, Latham's resolution was adopted. In response to a petition subsequently circulated by opponents of divestment, a mail referendum on the issue was scheduled to be sent to the entire faculty in the fall.

Meanwhile, administrators struggled to decide how to deal with the protesters in light of the mixed signals sent by judicial bodies on campus and downtown. On May 6, the Campus Hearing Board in a 3–2 vote dismissed charges against fifty-one students who had refused to leave Day Hall on the first day of the sit-ins on the grounds that they did not know they were violating the Campus Code of Conduct and had acted in good faith. After dismissing 288 similar cases for individuals arrested on the first two days, Roseanne Mayer '75, the judicial administrator, reserved the right to prosecute those who entered the building on subsequent dates and/or repeatedly disobeyed lawful orders. The board also upheld the authority of the president to suspend students for "good cause" but lifted the temporary suspensions because the circumstances surrounding them "had changed."[33]

On May 10, Acting City Judge M. John Sherman deplored that Cornell was "either incapable or unwilling to impose even the minimal administrative sanctions set under its own disciplinary rules" and threw out charges of trespass against 241 students, faculty, staff, and non-Cornellians. Given "the lack of any demonstrated threat to the health and safety of the community, the essentially petty nature of the charges . . . and the possible expense involved in the trial of these cases," Sherman concluded that "there are sufficient compelling circumstances to clearly demonstrate that prosecution or conviction of these defendants would constitute an injustice." Walter Relihan '52, JD '59, Cornell's chief counsel, replied that the university had the right to "avail itself" of the laws of trespass "in the same manner as any other citizen" and expressed a concern that Cornell might become a "free zone" for trespassers.[34]

Even more vexing was the question of what to do about the shantytown. Having been granted a permit by the university through May 30, the residents settled in, welcoming the folksinger Pete Seeger, who visited them before giving a concert at Bailey Hall. To dismantle the shantytown on May 30, administrators recognized, would almost certainly disrupt Senior Week and Cornell's commencement. To allow the buildings to remain during commencement, however, would prolong the controversy and increase "public and Trustee discontent." If the structures stayed up during Reunion in early June, "the line of least resistance," administrators feared that alumni would be angry and the shantytown might become a permanent fixture on the campus.[35]

On May 10, a fire destroyed one of the seven-foot-high shanties. Ignited by a cigarette placed in a mayonnaise jar used as an ashtray that tipped over, the fire raged for fifteen minutes, destroying bedding and injuring Robert Forness '87, while he was trying to douse the flames. It was put out by students, campus

Shantytown, 1985. (Division of Rare and Manuscript Collections of the Cornell University Library)

security officers, and city firefighters. Asked by Cornell officials to investigate the site, City of Ithaca deputy fire chief P. K. Reeves declared it a fire hazard and ordered the removal of all "combustible waste and refuse."[36] Dean Drinkwater informed the protesters that the permit for the shantytown had been revoked and asked them to pack up their personal possessions and leave.

The next morning, Cornell groundskeepers arrived to dismantle the shantytown. The residents locked arms in front of a backhoe and tethered themselves to the shanties. Cornell police cut the wires and began dragging them from the makeshift structures, but then backed off and left the area to avoid a violent confrontation. Over the weekend, the students removed flammable materials and replaced the cardboard shanties with huts and tents made of wood and tin. They passed out leaflets asking for support to "stop the bulldozers and trucks from destroying a living monument to the black South Africans who don't have the luxury of Fire Protection and Building Codes."[37]

On May 13, 14, 15, and 17, 1985, Vice Presidents Gurowitz and Herbster conferred with six shantytown representatives to discuss a "mutually satisfactory resolution" to the impasse. Citing safety concerns, Gurowitz suggested that the shantytown be replaced by an alternate site, "a table at the Straight." The proposal, he indicated, was greeted with "much laughter."[38] The students insisted on staying there through commencement, Reunion, Fall Freshman Orientation, and October 11, a national day of protest. They agreed to take down the shantytown on October 15 if the (nonresidential) Inhumanities Library remained open, with an office, telephones, a computer with a modem, and a budget supplied by the university. Gurowitz offered to move the Inhumanities Library to the plaza "somewhere between Willard Straight and the Campus Store" if the rest of the shantytown was dismantled by the end of the week.[39] When students refused, he agreed to let the structures stay up until the day after graduation. The students countered with an offer to remove the shantytown by September 15 if the university granted them a speaker at commencement and a summer budget. "It seems we have no reason to meet further," Gurowitz declared. "I regret we could not come to an agreement."[40]

Cornell Faculty and Staff against Apartheid organized a series of events on commencement weekend, which coincided with a meeting of the board of trustees. They picketed every building at which trustees gathered, offered sleep-ins and tours of the shantytown, and sponsored a "Divestment Convocation" at Anabel Taylor Hall on Saturday, June 1, featuring Dennis Brutus, a black South African poet, and Prexy Nesbitt, chair of the Illinois Coalition for Divestment.[41] They distributed literature to family and friends of the graduates as they entered the Campus Store, sold divestment T-shirts, and promised to be out in force, wearing red armbands, during the academic procession and commencement exercises on Sunday. And they began planning for Reunion by "putting together a list of sympathetic alumni."[42]

On Sunday, June 2, a sunny day, President Rhodes was greeted by graduates with chants of "Frank" as he made his way across Schoellkopf Field. As he began his address, about a dozen members of the class of 1985 stood and looked away from the podium. Citing Winston Churchill's advice, "never speak to a group that knows more about a subject than you do," Rhodes added that Churchill, "alas, gave no advice about speaking to those whose backs are turned toward you. I respect your moral commitment, but my remarks are for *all* of you here today. Whatever our differences we shall solve them only by squarely facing one another." Praising the concern, exhibited "passionately and determinedly," by antiapartheid activists, Rhodes indicated that he was "troubled by some of their methods. . . . Turmoil, disruption and abuse will not beget the understanding, respect and agreement needed to reach the worthwhile goals we seek." Borrowing his theme from Rabbi Harold Kushner, the baccalaureate speaker, the president concluded that forgiveness and love "are the weapons

God has given us to live fully, bravely, and meaningfully in this less than perfect world." His address was greeted with thunderous applause and the launching of scores of helium–filled black divestment balloons.[43]

After commencement, the administration and the protesters remained deadlocked. On June 3, in response to the statement of Cornell spokesman David Stewart that the shantytown "will be removed at the convenience of the buildings and grounds department," twelve students, three staff members, and two individuals not affiliated with Cornell were arrested and charged with criminal trespass following a sit-in at Day Hall.[44] Six faculty members, English professors H. Scott McMillin Jr., Kenneth McClane '73, MA '74, MFA '76, and Satya Mohanty; Philip Lewis in Romance Studies; Donald Barr in Human Ecology; and Risa Lieberwitz in ILR, met in the president's office the next day to urge Rhodes and Provost Barker to "give the highest priority to avoidance of confrontation" and consider "simply tolerating the continuation of the Shanty Town protest." Rhodes indicated a willingness to compromise, emphasized that every effort would be made to ensure proper conduct by the police, while stressing the dangers that the continuing existence of the shanties presented to members of the Cornell community, including the protesters.[45]

On June 6, Barker met with student members of the Cornell Coalition for Divestment, Professor McClane, and Philosophy professor David Lyons. The students offered to limit the shantytown to the Inhumanities Library plus five buildings and to remove "wire, tank traps, the blockhouse and tents."[46] After consulting with Rhodes, Barker agreed to "allow a single symbolic structure, such as the Inhumanities Library," to remain on site until October 12, if all the residents cooperated in the dismantling of all other structures. He agreed, as well, to organize a symposium related to divestment, invite trustees to it, and to arrange an antiapartheid concert for the fall.[47] With "great regret," the students expressed dissatisfaction with the negotiations and asked for a two–week "cooling off period."[48] There is no record of a reply by Barker.

Fearing that the university would act before Reunion, the Divestment Coalition went to court, seeking a temporary restraining order protecting the shantytown "prior to final adjudication of administrative complaints." The coalition's lawyer, Peter Costanza, JD '78, argued that dismantling the site infringed on the free speech rights of supporters of divestment under Cornell's Campus Code of Conduct and the First Amendment to the United States Constitution. On June 11, Judge Howard Munson of the U.S. District Court in Albany turned them down.[49]

Reunion came and went. A panel discussion on investments in South Africa in Kaufmann Auditorium in Goldwin Smith Hall, with presentations by antiapartheid activists and university officials, took place without major disruptions. Less than two weeks later, on June 24, at 6:30 a.m., a dozen Cornell maintenance workers, accompanied by two dozen helmeted Safety Division officers, arrived at the shantytown, ordered the eight people sleeping there to remove themselves and their belongings in two minutes, loaded the cinder-blocks, wood, and debris onto trucks, and drove off. The operation took less than an hour. Three shantytown residents, Adria Moskowitz '87, Barbara Ebert, and Richard Ryan, were charged with obstructing governmental administration and resisting arrest. Tents and personal property found in the area, David Stewart announced, could be picked up by their owners at a warehouse on Route 366, near the Apple Orchards. The restoration of the shantytown area "to its natural condition, it is hoped, will permit a return to a meaningful discussion in an atmosphere of mutual respect for divergent views," he added.[50] Protesters met that evening to discuss next steps. "It's going back up," Catherine Ouellette '88 declared. "As far as I'm concerned, it's going back up."[51]

The next afternoon, about one hundred demonstrators appeared on the lawn between Day Hall and Sage Chapel. Some of them took down the orange plastic fence that cordoned off the area, carried in wood and cardboard, and quickly constructed five crude structures. In the scuffle that followed, David Whitehead and Karl Zweerink '86 were arrested. As the safety officers tried to drive away with the pair in custody, forty protesters surrounded the car. Liz Danzig '85 complained that she was struck in the chest with a nightstick and barely escaped being run over. That evening New York State Supreme Court Justice Richard F. Kuhnen issued a temporary restraining order prohibiting protesters from creating a new shantytown, employing force or the threat of force on university property, inciting others to engage in similar activity, or blocking entrances to buildings "in ways that interfered with the normal functioning of the University." He ordered thirty-five named defendants to appear in court to show cause why a permanent injunction should not be issued against them. Tuesday night, the protesters removed the structures.[52]

On June 27, at a hearing before New York State Supreme Court judge Howard Ellison, Cornell attorney Thomas Santoro insisted that the dispute involved the university's right to control its property, not free speech. He characterized attempts to defend the shantytown as tactics to "force physical confrontations." Professor Lyons, one of the thirty-five named defendants, called that claim "at best a misrepresentation."[53] On July 1, Judge Ellison ruled that Cornell had acted lawfully. Affirming that "the rights the First Amendment grants are not absolute and must be balanced with the rights of others and the public welfare," he made permanent the temporary restraining order issued by Judge Kuhnen.[54]

The protesters refused to be deterred. On July 12, 120 of them jammed the hallways of Day Hall. Diarmuid Maguire, MA '86, PhD '90, a graduate student in Government, was arrested for refusing to leave the building at 5 p.m. Less than a week later, following another Day Hall sit-in, held in honor of the birthday of Nelson Mandela, twenty-seven individuals were charged with criminal trespass. When students returned for the fall 1985 semester, antiapartheid activity accelerated. In a document labeled "off the record for journalists" (and acquired by Day Hall when a copy was inadvertently left at a cashier's station), Maguire proposed that protesters "burn every bridge the administration builds to escape from the siege of Day Hall until they agree to cross the one that we have built for them, immediate divestment." He advocated sit-ins at Day Hall, followed by mass arrests on September 23, 30, and October 11, with an escalation of disruption that might include bringing "kazoos and other noise-making equipment" into the building. On October 11, teach-ins, speeches, songs, and films should be accompanied by prayer vigils outside Day Hall. To create an enduring organization, increase efficiency and "maximum democracy in the movement," Maguire urged the election of a movement coordinator, a fundraiser, a publicity coordinator, and a legal coordinator. Assuming that "revolution has not occurred in South Africa and that Cornell has not divested by October 11," he predicted that "we will have to rethink our strategy" in light of the recommendations of the Proxy Review Committee "and the general state of the movement."[55]

Maguire's plan was implemented. In late September and early October, protesters assembled each day in Day Hall. All but two of them, who agreed to be arrested, left the building at 5 p.m. One such volunteer was English professor Alison Lurie. Winner of the Pulitzer Prize for her novel *Foreign Affairs* in 1985, Lurie arrived at the bursar's office at 4:15 p.m. on October 2, placed a Cornell Student Directory on the floor, and sat on it to protect her silk suit. An hour later, she became the fiftieth faculty member to be arrested for divestment-related activities. Charged with trespass, Lurie was fingerprinted, released without bail, and ordered to appear in City Court on October 7. "Thank God I'm getting arrested in Ithaca, New York, instead of Johannesburg, South Africa," she said. In a prepared statement, Lurie condemned Cornell: "A college that continues to invest in South Africa today is like a merchant who has his choice of customers but goes on manufacturing sheets for the Ku Klux Klan, with the excuse that he himself is an equal opportunity employer."[56]

On October 9, to demonstrate continued large-scale support for divestment, protesters rallied inside the Day Hall courtyard. Fifty of them were arrested. On November 21, 450 students and faculty marked the anniversary of sit-ins at the South African embassy in Washington, D.C., with a silent candlelight vigil. They stood outside Day Hall, then walked to the Straight, where they listened to a series of speakers describe the day-to-day experiences of blacks under apartheid.

Cornell administrators appeared to be unmoved. When the faculty, in the mail ballot completed in September, voted 651–516 to recommend divestment, the administration suggested that the results proved that professors were divided on the issue. And when the State University of New York Board of

Trustees decided to stop investing in businesses with ties to South Africa, Walter Relihan indicated that the action "would be of considerable interest" to Cornell's trustees, but that it "has nothing to do with the assets of Cornell."[57] In his "State of the University" talk to the Trustee Council in mid-October, Frank Rhodes asserted that the principles on which Cornell is based were "being strained by those who seek to impose their views on others, not by reasoned review and persuasive discussion, but by repeated confrontation."[58]

The long-awaited report of the Proxy Review Committee of the board of trustees was made public on December 5. Its five members—Patricia Carry Stewart '50, vice president of the Edna McConnell Clark Foundation and chair of the committee; Aubrey E. Robinson Jr. '43, LLB '47, Federal District Court chief judge for the District of Columbia; Paul Tregurtha '57, president of Moore McCormack Resources; professor of economics Erik Thorbecke; and Kenneth W. Williams '85, JD '88, a student trustee—expressed their outrage at apartheid, which was "particularly reprehensible because of its explicit insistence upon domination by one race over another." They stressed, however, that by retaining shares in companies doing business in South Africa on condition that they abide by the Sullivan principles, Cornell was exerting a beneficial influence. The committee called for a strengthened policy of selective divestment in companies that were not working actively and publicly to end systematic violations of human rights and recommended that Cornell consider total divestment in three years if "it appears that private sector efforts . . . have resulted in insufficient progress towards ending apartheid."[59]

On January 31, 1986, the full board convened at the Cornell University Medical College in New York City. When the meeting was disrupted by about forty-five protesters, who shouted the names of trustees they claimed had conflicts of interest, calling them "fascists and scum," Chairman Austin Kiplinger '39 declared a recess; as the trustees moved to a another location, security officers with billy clubs escorted the protesters out of the building.[60] Maintaining that total divestment had "substantial long-term risks and negative financial consequences" for the university and was "tantamount to total abandonment" of any role in improving conditions in South Africa through "responsible corporate citizenship," the board voted 33–7 to adopt the recommendations of the Proxy Committee.[61]

Supporters of divestment reacted with disappointment and defiance. In an open letter published in the *Cornell Chronicle*, Romance Studies professor Philip Lewis dismissed the Proxy Committee's defense of selective divestment as "farcical." He made "one last appeal, formed of passionate conviction and dispassionate judgment," to President Rhodes and the board of trustees, "to face up to the challenge of leadership that the case for divestment has put within your reach."[62]

For a time, however, the protesters were stymied by the Cornell administration. The court injunction banning the construction of shanties remained in force. And in January 1986, the Executive Committee of the board of trustees revised the university's "Regulations for the Maintenance of Public Order" to forbid individuals from "entering or remaining" in Day Hall unless they were transacting business. The new rule was not challenged until May, when thirty people sat down in the bursar's office. The students were charged with failing to comply with the regulations; the nonstudents were charged with trespass. More arrests came after 5 p.m., when ten of fifty protesters refused to leave the main lobby of Day Hall. Nine of the ten had been arrested in the earlier confrontation in the bursar's office.[63]

In October 1986, protesters defied the shantytown injunction. Following an afternoon antiapartheid rally attended by two hundred people on October 8, two shanties went up just north of the statue of Andrew D. White on the Arts quad. Just after dark, about twenty Safety Division officers arrived to take them down. As a crowd of about one hundred onlookers chanted pro-divestment slogans, the protesters locked arms around the structures; some of the protesters were pushed face-down into the ground and had their arms twisted or placed in pressure-point holds before they were handcuffed and carried away. Twenty-three individuals, three Ithacans and twenty students, were arrested. Acknowledging that safety officers handled them "vigorously," David Stewart, the university spokesman, maintained that they had been warned four times and that the treatment was commensurate with the resistance they offered.[64] The next day, protesters hastily constructed shanties on the Arts quad, at the Johnson Museum, and near the Campus Store, and Safety Division officers just as quickly took them down. "After seeing what happened last night," said Weiben Wang '89, "I felt it was something I had to do." At the end of the day, only a cardboard box with the word "shanty" on it, tied to the statue of Ezra Cornell, remained in place.[65] More shanties appeared on October 17, during Trustee Council Weekend; maintenance workers dismantled them the next day.

By this time, substantial numbers of faculty had become more involved. Deeming the actions of the administration "rigid and intolerant," the faculty of the College of Arts and Sciences on October 30 endorsed a resolution drafted by Philip Lewis and Comparative Literature professor Walter Cohen that asked President Rhodes to stop enforcing the injunction against building shanties on campus and to exercise greater restraint in responding to nonviolent protests. The vote was 108–11. Denied a permit to build a shanty, about eighty faculty announced on November 5 that they intended to build a structure, which they would remove after two days, on the slope about twenty yards in front of the entrance to the A. D. White House, as part of a homecoming forum on racial oppression in South Africa and Cornell's complicity in it. "It is possible," the professors indicated, "that the University will regard this forum as an illegal act."[66]

When the administration took no action for two days, faculty members declared that professors and students were being treated differently and that temporary shanties constituted symbolic speech, not covered by the injunction. Government professor Ron King proclaimed that "the shanty has returned to Cornell as a non–disruptive" tactic of the pro-divestment movement.[67]

In late January 1987, the antiapartheid activists and Cornell administrators finally reached an agreement. The administration dropped contempt of court citations (which carried a six-month jail term and a fine) against five demonstrators and allowed the construction of one shanty at a time, within a strict set of safety guidelines, on either the Arts quad, the Ag quad, or the east side of Willard Straight plaza. The shanty had to be no larger than ten feet by ten feet by eight feet and must not stand overnight. The plan was approved by Judge Ellison, who issued a new permanent injunction specifying these requirements.

The struggle over divestment continued, however. Two months later, two thousand crosses, with splotches of red paint, were planted around the campus to commemorate the Sharpeville Massacre, when sixty-seven unarmed blacks were killed by South African police. In April, more than a dozen students were forcibly removed from Day Hall, as they shouted "Before Cornell divests, how many more arrests?"[68] That same month, a shanty that had been constructed behind Day Hall (without a permit) was taken down.

The movement, however, was losing steam. On January 27, 1989, in a 23–11 vote, the board of trustees rejected divestment and reaffirmed its current policy as "a responsible and principled approach."[69] In a letter published in the *Sun*, President Rhodes supported the board's action. Cornell, he insisted, "does have a principled divestment policy"; total divestment would have "no effect on the government of South Africa" and would impose costs "we can ill afford" in a time of "severe financial strain."[70] Alumni trustee Joseph Holland '78, MA '79, had a different view. The decision, he predicted, would "set off the bomb which will explode the soul of Cornell into a thousand pieces of disharmony."[71]

It didn't. To be sure, Kenneth McClane gave voice in the *Sun* to a "nearly uncontrollable rage." Having remained at Cornell for nearly two decades, as an undergraduate, a graduate student, and a professor, he had often spoken of his love for Cornell: "I am ashamed to be here now."[72] Another black man, Philosophy professor Kwame Anthony Appiah, claimed that he had intended to turn down an attractive offer from Duke University until "the Cornell trustees voted not to divest."[73]

In 1990, when Nelson Mandela was released from prison, events began to overtake the divestment movement. In time, student advocates of divestment departed from the campus. Many faculty members and administrators, of course, stayed on. They agreed, no doubt, with President Rhodes that the challenge for "our generation" was to preserve the university "as a place of extraordinary freedom . . . hospitable to every viewpoint, without infringing on the sense of order and responsibility upon which any reasonable discussion depends."[74] They did not agree, however, about how successfully that challenge had been met.

———————

WHILE RHODES WAS debating South Africa divestment, he was reaching out to China. Close connections between Cornell and China had been forged soon after the founding of the university. Cornell offered courses in Chinese languages in the 1870s. Helped by Willard Straight '01, who had served there in the Foreign Service, the university began to assemble for its libraries materials in Chinese studies that became part of one of the world's greatest collections in the field. At the beginning of the twentieth century, scores of Chinese students used their U.S. government–funded Boxer Indemnity Scholarships (which were designed to influence future leaders of the country) to come to Ithaca as undergraduates or graduate students. When they returned to China, they remembered Cornell with affection and respect. The most famous of them, Hu Shih '14, led a movement to replace China's classical language with vernacular literature (*baihua*), a transformation comparable to the break with Latin in Western Europe. Appointed China's ambassador to the United States in 1938, he was asked by Chiang Kai-shek to run for president a decade later but declined, indicating that a person who could not keep his desk in order should not try to manage a government. English professor Martin Sampson once said of him, "It is entirely possible that one thousand years from now Cornell may be known as the place where Hu Shih went to college."[75] Returning often to his alma mater, where he had been president of the Chinese Students Club, won the Hiram Corson Prize in English for an essay on Robert Browning, and was selected to Phi Beta Kappa, Hu once showed History professor Knight Biggerstaff the chair in Goldwin Smith where he was seated when he decided to transfer from the College of Agriculture to Arts and Sciences (and a philosophy major). Hu's son, Tsu-wang, was one of about 3,500 Chinese students to graduate from Cornell during the university's first hundred years.

Connections between Cornell and mainland China had been attenuated by the Communist Revolution and the Cold War. Encouraged by the rupture between the People's Republic and the Soviet Union and President Nixon's historic trip to China in 1972, Rhodes made reestablishing academic and cultural ties with the mainland (while retaining a close relationship with the Republic of China, which was established on Taiwan in 1949) a priority of his administration. In 1979, five official delegations of scientists from the People's Republic traveled to Ithaca. In the same year, staff from Cornell University Libraries visited the mainland to acquire books and manuscripts. In March 1980, six professors from Agriculture and Life Sciences joined Dean David Call '54, MS '58, PhD '60, in a trip to China to examine programs in research and education and make contact with two dozen alumni working in leading agricultural universities. And in July 1980, at the invitation of the Chinese Academy of Sciences, Rhodes led a ten-member delegation of faculty and administrators on a three-week-long tour of six Chinese cities, Beijing, Xi'an (the ancient capital), Chengdu, Emeishan (on the eastern margin of the Tibetan-Himalayan plateau), Wuhan (in south central China), and Shanghai, the point of departure. In a news conference following their return, the president summarized the purposes of the visit: to get a better understanding of higher education in China; investigate developments in science and technology; explore the possibility of exchange relationships with Chinese universities; and meet with alumni, who held senior and responsible positions in virtually every institution of any size.

Devastated by the Cultural Revolution, higher education in China, Rhodes noted, was in "a period of reorientation and recovery," with "a new sense of freedom on the campuses" and an "openness to the West and what it has to offer." Because China had six million high school graduates, 4.7 million of whom applied to college, and space for only three hundred thousand first-year college students, Rhodes reported, officials were under no delusions about the distance they had to travel to expand the number and quality of colleges and universities, increase the number of students studying abroad while new institutions were built, and train a new generation of researchers and teachers. At the end of the trip, Cornell became the first American university to sign a comprehensive exchange agreement, involving faculty and students, with the Chinese Academy of Sciences.[76]

During his courtship of China, Rhodes also sought to strengthen Cornell's ties to Taiwan, the fifth-largest trading partner of the United States and the arch-enemy of the People's Republic. Accompanied by a delegation that included Walter LaFeber, Alfred Kahn, Asian Studies professors Karen Brazell and Mei Tsu-lin, vice president for public affairs Richard Ramin '51, and vice president for research and advanced studies Norman Scott, PhD '62, Rhodes visited Japan, South Korea, Hong Kong, and the Republic of China in 1990. A major topic of conversation during the trip concerned America's policies toward the two Chinas. At a session at the Regent Hotel, overlooking Hong Kong harbor, Professor LaFeber told an audience of 150 alumni that, in contrast to Asian nations, the United States was well behind, "badly divided and almost leaderless" in dealing with the "China problem."[77]

In Taipei, the capital of Taiwan, an island nation with about twenty-one million inhabitants that is about the size of West Virginia, Rhodes presented an outstanding alumni citation, inscribed on parchment in black and red letters, and two large photographs of the Cornell campus to Lee Teng-hui, the president of the Republic of China. The ceremony, Lee indicated, brought back "beautiful memories—the calm and tranquility of Ithaca, the thought-evoking paths on the campus, the classic beauty of the library and the enchantment of beautiful Beebe Lake."[78]

The first Taiwanese native to head the government of the Republic of China, Lee had become president in 1988 and was beginning to institute political reforms that contributed to his reputation as "the father of Taiwan's democracy." Born into a prosperous family of tea farmers in 1923 in northern Taiwan, which was then part of Japan, he served as a second lieutenant in the Japanese army during World War II, earned a bachelor's degree from National Taiwan University in 1948, became a member of the Communist Party (albeit briefly), received a master's in agricultural economics from Iowa State University in 1953, and returned home with an appointment to a Joint Commission on Rural Reconstruction, which had a mandate to modernize the economy and implement land reform. In 1965, "T.H." as he was then called, came to Cornell to complete a PhD in agricultural economics. A superb student, he spent little time outside of the library, except for many rounds of golf at the Robert Trent Jones course near the campus. Lee's dissertation, "Intersectoral Capital Flows in the Economic Development of Taiwan, 1896–1960," later published as a book, was honored as the best doctoral thesis in the field for 1968 by the American Association of Agricultural Economics. Back in Taiwan, Lee joined the cabinet of the Kuomintang government in 1971, became mayor of Taipei in 1978, governor of Taiwan Province in 1981, and vice president of the country in 1984.

When he succeeded to the presidency four years later, following the death of Chiang Ching-kuo, the son of Chiang Kai-shek, one of his first official acts was a renunciation of the use of force to achieve national reunification with the mainland. In an address in May 1990, however, Lee rejected the proposal of Deng Xiao-ping, the "Paramount Leader" of the People's Republic, that the two Chinas become "one country, two systems," with Taiwan retaining some control over domestic policy but relinquishing autonomy in international affairs. Reunification was not possible, Lee insisted, without substantial democratic reforms by the People's Republic and the preservation of Taiwan's right to negotiate with other countries. Emphasizing that he was in no hurry to reunify, Lee observed, sometime later, that "we will talk even if it takes 100 times and 100 years. If we talk 100 times and we fail, that's all right."[79]

Frank Rhodes made two more trips to Taiwan before he retired. In April 1995 he visited Taipei for two days, signing a scholarly exchange agreement with Academia Sinica, Taiwan's premier national research institute, thanking President Lee's friends in person for endowing the Lee Teng-hui Professorship in World Affairs at Cornell, and renewing the invitation he had made to Lee in 1990, to come back to campus, this time to deliver the annual Olin Lecture at Reunion in June.

The invitation ignited an international incident. By the 1990s, Taiwan had suffered a series of diplomatic setbacks. In 1971, the United Nations voted to expel Taiwan, awarding its seat to the government in Beijing. Eight years later, following decades in which it treated the Taiwan government as the legitimate representative of all Chinese, the United States severed formal ties with Taipei and officially recognized the People's Republic. In 1995, only twenty-nine nations maintained diplomatic relations with Taiwan; dozens of countries, including the United States, dealt with the Republic of China through its trade representatives.

In this context, the People's Republic viewed any overture to Taiwan as a hostile act. Frank Rhodes delivered the alumni award to President Lee in Taiwan in 1990 because the State Department would not allow Lee to travel to Ithaca. In 1995, Cornell officials hoped for a compromise, in which Lee would be granted a transit visa, allowing him to pass through the United States and visit the Cornell campus on his way to another destination. Noting Lee's close ties to Cornell, Rhodes asked President Clinton to "transcend the rigid formulas that have governed past decisions" related to Taiwan.[80] Clinton replied on May 2. Indicating that his administration had been "responsive to many of Taiwan's continuing concerns," the president declared that he could not "reconcile the most senior level visits with the unofficial relationship" between Taiwan and the United States.[81]

This time, however, Republicans, who had gained control of Congress in 1994, pressured the White House to reverse course. On May 2, the House passed a nonbinding resolution to that effect by a vote of 360–0. The Senate followed suit, with a 97–1 vote (J. Bennett Johnston, Democrat of Louisiana, was the lone dissenter). Senator Frank Murkowski (R–Alaska), the sponsor of the resolution, deemed it "unmistakable proof that the U.S. Congress believes it is in our nation's best interest to improve relations with Taiwan" by permitting its leader "to at least spend the night on U.S. soil."[82] Tapping the still potent anticommunist sentiment in the country, Murkowski thundered that Americans should not let China "dictate who can visit the United States."[83]

The Chinese Embassy responded immediately with a statement expressing its government's firm opposition to any visit by President Lee "in whatever capacity, under whatever pretext and in whatever form." After praising Lee Teng-hui for consolidating democracy in Taiwan, John Ohta, a spokesman for the U.S. State Department, announced that the administration would not rethink its position. Whether or not Lee's visit was termed "private," Ohta maintained that it "would unavoidably be seen by the People's Republic as removing an essential element of unofficiality in the U.S.-Taiwan relationship."[84]

Congressional action and the likelihood of a binding resolution forced the hand of the Clinton administration. The about-face was announced on May 22 by press secretary Mike McCurry, who noted that during his stay Lee would not meet any officials of the U.S. government. It was especially galling to the Chinese because no invitation, official or unofficial, had ever been extended to their president, Jiang Zemin. National Security Adviser Anthony Lake met Li Daoyu, the Chinese ambassador, to assure him that approval of Lee's visit did not signal a change in U.S.-China relations. Daoyu responded that the decision "gravely harmed" bilateral relations.[85] After a tense meeting with J. Stapleton Roy, the U.S. ambassador to China, Foreign Minister Qian Qichen issued a long statement denouncing the Americans for duplicity and perfidy: "If the U.S. Administration succumbs to pressure of some pro-Taiwanese elements in total disregard of the feelings of the 1.2 billion Chinese people and infringes upon the fundamental rights of China, Sino–U.S. relations can only retrogress instead of making progress."[86]

On Thursday, June 8, 1995, Lee Teng-hui was among the thirty-seven passengers on USAir flight 3706 to land in Ithaca. He received an enthusiastic reception. Taiwanese émigrés, faculty, and students—who in April had organized "Speak Up for Lee Teng-hui" at Willard Straight Hall, reportedly the largest political gathering of Asian students ever held at Cornell, and had collected twenty-six hundred signatures on a petition to President Clinton—turned out in force to greet him. They sang two folk songs, "Yearning for a Spring Breeze" and "Open the Window of Your Mind."[87] At the C&A Restaurant on Dryden Road, owned by the Liu family of Ithaca, a window banner read "The President and His Wife Are Welcome."[88] And in the Severinghaus Reading Room of the Kroch Library, curators displayed twenty-five works in English and Chinese written by or about Lee, and the gift he had made in 1990: a five-hundred-volume set of classical Chinese texts.

Not everyone was pleased to have Lee Teng-hui on American soil. In early June, about seventy-five former and current Cornell students and scholars, from the Ad Hoc Committee of the Chinese Cornellian Association, the Beijing chapter of the Cornell Alumni Association, the Chinese Students and Scholars Association in Washington, D.C., and the Chinese Students and Scholars Association at the University of California, San Diego, wrote to President Rhodes and the board of trustees to indicate that they were "shocked and deeply disturbed" at the invitation. Through visits to the United States, they claimed, President Lee was trying to "advance his agenda of gaining Taiwan the status of a nation-state" and "finally separate Taiwan from China." Receiving money from Lee and then "facilitating" his political goals "disgraces the fine reputation of the University," they added, and "has caused profound anger and outrage among Chinese Cornellians." The letter ended with a plea to the Cornell administration to "stop trampling upon the Chinese people's deepest collective feelings with imperialist cultural arrogance and show basic respect for international practice."[89]

The campus was turned upside down during President Lee's visit, which occurred on Reunion weekend. To accommodate more than four hundred journalists covering the story, Lynah Rink became a media center, complete with fax machines and computers and interpreters to help translate instructions into Mandarin available all day and night. And security was tight. When Lee arrived on campus in a motorcade on June 8, 1995, a New York State helicopter hovered overhead. "It's been a long uphill climb," Lee declared when he stepped out on the Ag quad, "but the view is worthwhile. Finally, I am back here in

Ithaca after a solid 27 years." Before the doors opened to a hot and steamy New-man Arena in Alberding Field House for Lee's Olin Lecture on June 9, security officers and bomb-sniffing dogs searched the building. Outside, about two hundred pro-Taiwan and pro-Beijing protesters took up positions on opposite sides of the street. As alumni walked by on their way to the lecture, the pickets waved flags, held banners, sang, cheered, and jeered a bit.[90]

Journalists, including CNN International, which broadcast Lee's speech live and in its entirety, barely noticed the protests. The weekend belonged to President Lee. In his forty-minute Olin Lecture, entitled "Always in My Heart" and delivered to a fan-waving and enthusiastic audience of five thousand alumni, the seventy-two-year-old leader recalled with fondness "the long, exhausting evenings in the libraries, the soothing and reflective hours at church, the hurried shuttling between classrooms, the evening strolls hand in hand." He suggested that a round of golf during his visit should be called "The U.S. Open for Lee Teng-hui." He boasted that his country, with meager resources, generated $180 billion in trade and had a high per capita income. And he spoke boldly and bluntly about his vision for all the Chinese people. Declaring that communism "is dead or dying," Lee offered "The Taiwan experience" as a new model, held

Lee Teng-hui, PhD '68, president of Taiwan, during his controversial visit to Cornell, 1995. (Division of Rare and Manuscript Collections of the Cornell University Library)

out the possibility of a meeting with Jiang Zemin, and pledged his determination to play "a peaceful and constructive role among the family of nations."[91]

The weekend also belonged to President Rhodes. In his State of the University Address at Bailey Hall on June 10, Rhodes proclaimed, to frequent bursts of applause, that "President Lee has saved Taiwan by his exertions and has styled her free world by his example." For its part, he stated, "Cornell has not been content for the world to come to campus; it has also reached out to the world. Its land-grant mission has been writ large." The university, in his view, was meeting its "obligation to produce global citizens for a world that is shrinking before our eyes and where alliances and interrelationships change on an almost daily basis." Following a review of Cornell's international initiatives, Rhodes predicted that as soon as a newly designed International Network for Graduate Student Exchange was in operation, "a graduate student from National Taiwan University could spend a year at Beijing University, a year at Cornell, and, if he or she could speak Russian, a third year at Moscow State." In a world of continuing division, Rhodes concluded, "where local tribalism, on the one hand, and obsessive nationalism, on the other, threaten to plunge us into wars of unpredictable proportions, global education is our best hope for peace, for prosperity and for humane action."[92]

"In the 1980s," the editors of the *Ithaca Journal* gushed, when the United States "was basking in the glow of Reaganomics and the Soviet Union was very much together," Rhodes had talked about internationalization "as the most important challenge for the next quarter century." As president, he had "promoted Cornell's leadership on every continent." Rhodes's "global vision and dreams will be missed when he leaves office this month," the editorial concluded. "The man is going out on top."[93]

Rhodes took a victory lap in 1996, the year in which Lee Teng-hui was reelected president of Taiwan. Rhodes represented Cornell at the inauguration ceremonies in Taipei in May. "It was quite astonishing," he said. "I would walk down the street and complete strangers would come up to me to thank me for Lee's visit to Cornell." Now a president emeritus and a world away in time and space from the political hurly-burly he had experienced for eighteen years in Ithaca, Rhodes allowed himself to indicate which of the two Chinas was his favorite. "This nation of 22 million," he observed, "really pulled itself up by the bootstraps to become one of the great economic powers of the world." And, reflecting on the election in Taiwan, the "noisy opposition," and "the belligerent behavior of the People's Republic of China" during the contest, Rhodes was all the more impressed that "once the result was announced, the people were very pleased that there was not a single act of violence or challenge to the outcome. It was quite remarkable."[94]

PART IV
1995–2015

10 | Into the Twenty-First Century

In the early 1990s research universities faced a wave of challenges. In 1994, President Rhodes enumerated the "important and rapid changes" in higher education in the United States that directly threatened the health of Cornell and fellow institutions. These changes included a growing public resistance to tuition increases in excess of inflation; uneven and uncertain growth in federal government funding of research; budget cuts by the state; demographic shifts in the college-age population; and public dissatisfaction with the education and training of undergraduates. Because the stakes were so high, Rhodes declared, it was "imperative that we think carefully about our strengths, weaknesses and societal role. To do less will threaten the gains we have made and jeopardize our position for continued leadership in the 21st century." Fortunately, Rhodes added, Cornell could engage in these efforts from a position of strength. Among its strategic advantages were a strong financial foundation; the breadth and quality of its academic programs, public service initiatives, and research; its skill in forging productive cross-disciplinary alliances; the commitment of its alumni; and a demand for excellence "in all it undertakes."[1]

As Cornell responded to political, social, and economic changes, both within the university and in the world beyond, it had to contend as well with the motto of its founder. When Ezra Cornell proclaimed "I would found an institution where any person can find instruction in any study," observed Ronald Ehrenberg, vice president for academic programs, planning and budgeting, and professor of Industrial and Labor Relations and economics, he "sort of put a curse on the university. He's been taken too literally. We don't have the resources to do as many things as we currently do. We need to look at what businesses we can get out of." Colleges and universities, however, including Cornell, were not very good at making such hard choices.[2]

In the two decades between 1995 and the celebration of its sesquicentennial in 2015, Cornell did a considerable amount of soul-searching. Three

presents—Hunter Rawlings, Jeffrey Lehman '77, and David Skorton—
addressed a wide array of opportunities and challenges, some quite familiar
and others unanticipated and new. With varying degrees of success, they collaborated with faculty, staff, students, and alumni to build on Cornell's firm
foundation, ask hard questions about traditional ways of doing things, and reimagine academic structures, the residential life of undergraduates, and what
historian Carl Becker called "the central isolation" of Ithaca, New York.

In December 1994, Stephen Weiss '57, chairman of the board of trustees,
announced the appointment of Hunter Ripley Rawlings III as Cornell's tenth
(and, at six feet, seven inches, its tallest) president. Born in 1944 in Norfolk,
Virginia, where his father and grandfather worked for a wholesale hardware
company, Rawlings was introduced to Homer's *Iliad* by his mother when he
was about ten, the beginning of a love affair with Greek and Latin writers, historians, and philosophers. At Haverford College, he majored in classics and was
a standout student-athlete. With Rawlings playing center, the Haverford basketball team won thirty-nine games and lost twenty-one. Baseball, however,
was his favorite sport. A left-handed pitcher, "Hunt" had earned a tryout with
his favorite team, the Baltimore Orioles. When the scouting report concluded
"Good fastball. No curve. Go back to school," he returned to classics.[3] For
Haverford, he had a 2.17 earned run average in ninety-one games. After receiving his BA with honors, Rawlings completed a PhD at Princeton in 1970,
with a dissertation on Thucydides's *History of the Peloponnesian War*, and then
joined the faculty of the University of Colorado at Boulder. On occasion, however, he still fantasized about a career with the Orioles: "When I watch somebody make a fat pitch and give up a home run . . . I think, with a little regret, 'I
could have tried at least.'" But the life of an academic "is even better than
throwing a good fastball past a cleanup hitter."[4]

While Rawlings was at Colorado, his book, *The Structure of Thucydides' History*, was published by Princeton University Press; and he served as editor of the
Classical Journal. He also began to climb the career ladder in university administration. Rawlings became chair of his department in 1978, was named associate vice chancellor for instruction in 1980, and vice president for academic
affairs and research and dean of the Graduate School in 1984. In 1988, he was
appointed president of the University of Iowa. During his seven-year tenure at
Iowa, Rawlings completed a capital campaign; lobbied legislators, many of
whom were hostile to aid to higher education or partisans of Iowa State University; presided over an increase in externally funded grants and contracts
from $115 million to $188 million; and tried, unsuccessfully, to persuade the
NCAA to prohibit freshman from playing intercollegiate sports. Determined
to feed his intellectual curiosity, he continued to teach and to read (developing
expertise in the life and work of James Madison). "I didn't grow up wanting to
be a college president," Rawlings emphasized. "I grew up wanting to be a

Hunter R. Rawlings III, president of Cornell from 1995 to 2003; interim president, 2005–2006. (Cornell University Photography)

professor. There's a big difference."[5] Administrators and faculty in Iowa City characterized him as straightforward, down to earth, principled, direct, and decisive.

A few months after taking office at Cornell, Rawlings identified the priorities that would characterize his tenure as president. With the budget "still a major challenge," he indicated, clarifying Cornell's role in New York State and SUNY and increasing support from alumni and friends of the university "become all the more important." To augment resources for teaching and research and improve faculty and staff compensation, Rawlings intended to restructure and streamline nonacademic services. He hoped to stimulate multidisciplinary teaching and research and create "greater synergy" among departments and colleges.[6] And he was determined to involve undergraduates "as whole beings in the life of the mind" by bringing together their intellectual and social experiences, which were "often light years apart," and foster "greater interaction, greater intimacy" between professors and students.[7] To begin the process, in October 1995 he announced the establishment of a Cornell Research Scholars Program, a four-year pilot project designed to provide three hundred students with opportunities to do research with members of the faculty.

That same month, Rawlings mended fences with Mayor Ben Nichols '41, MEN '49, and the City of Ithaca. Nichols's efforts the previous year to get a larger voluntary contribution from Cornell had led to a tense confrontation.

357

When the mayor began to deny building permits to the university, Day Hall administrators cried foul, and hundreds of construction workers, angry that they bore the brunt of the delays that ensued, marched on City Hall in May. Rawlings reached out to the city to break the impasse. A memorandum of understanding acknowledged the "significant fiscal and regulatory pressures" faced by both parties and pledged to "understand and accommodate their respective interests in furtherance of the common good of the entire community." They agreed to form a Cornell-city "working group" charged with analyzing issues of common concern and making specific proposals to address them. City officials promised to review university applications for building permits and other municipal authorizations "in a professional, expeditious, and cost-conscious manner." Cornell vowed to "exercise its purchasing power, to the extent practicable, to support the local economy" and to encourage students, faculty, and staff to volunteer their services to Ithaca. Most important, without waiving its tax-exempt status or entering into a contractual agreement for payments in lieu of taxes, Cornell agreed to a schedule of contributions over a thirteen-year period, 1995–2007, that gradually increased annual contributions for fire protection from $225,000 to $600,000 and for other municipal services from $25,000 to $400,000. The city affirmed that during that period it would take no action, "through judicial, legislative or other means" to alter Cornell's financial obligations to Ithaca.[8] A town-gown détente followed the swift ratification of the memorandum by the City of Ithaca Common Council and the Cornell University Board of Trustees. When Alan Cohen '81 replaced Nichols as mayor in 1996, the city and Cornell worked collaboratively (and often cordially) on several initiatives, including a downtown development project that permanently relocated more than two hundred university staff to offices on Seneca Street above a new hotel, the Hilton Garden Inn.

On Thursday, October 12, 1995, with the temperature reaching an unseasonal eighty degrees for the outdoor ceremony, Hunter Rawlings was formally installed as Cornell's tenth president. His inaugural address, "To Compose Cornell: Cultivating the Mind," was a surprisingly specific clarion call to members of the Cornell community to reinvent, reinvigorate, and refocus on the central mission of the university by promoting intellectual activity for the sake of the individual and in service to the state, the nation, and the world. Noting that a half century earlier, President Day had worried about the "divisive and distracting forces of contemporary society," Rawlings observed that Day, could he have lived to see 1995, would have been equally concerned about the presence of those forces "within the university." On American campuses, Rawlings indicated, Left and Right "rage sanctimoniously against each other," and virtually everything had become politicized.[9]

To compose Cornell, Rawlings endorsed "sustained, reasonable discussion, greater composure, less anger and vituperation." He used Cornell's topography as the central metaphor for creating community "in a place of multiple strengths and remarkable diversity." The first bridge atop Cascadilla Gorge, he pointed out, was made of wood. It was replaced by an iron structure, but in 1898, metal gave way to the "sturdy and picturesque stone arch that we still use today." Almost a century later, "in a country of fissures and fault lines," Rawlings declared, Cornell "is called upon to build sturdier bridges, to compose itself anew." He left no doubt where those bridges should be located. If the university of Janet Reno '60, Toni Morrison, MA '55, Ruth Bader Ginsburg '54, and the scientist and Nobel Prize winner Barbara McClintock '23, MA '25, PhD '27, still tolerated "barriers to women's advancement," he said, "then let us have the nerve to reduce them to rubble." If "an invisible rift down the center of Garden Avenue" separates endowed and statutory colleges, "let us plumb its depths." If "a more serious cultural divide" isolates North and West Campus undergraduates along racial lines, "let us explore and measure it honestly." And if a chasm was found to exist between students' intellectual and personal lives, between college and Collegetown, "then let us fling a rope bridge, however narrow and tenuous, across that abyss."[10] Rawlings concluded by reading a verse from Emily Dickinson ("The Brain Is wider Than the Sky") and expressing the hope that "our endeavor will bring us to a deeper understanding of each other."[11]

Rawlings built many of the bridges he imagined in his inaugural address during his tenure as president. As we will see, he conceived and carried out a residential initiative for North Campus that transformed the first-year experience of undergraduates and one for West Campus that brought faculty and students together in "colleges" presided over by house professors. He promoted diversity for Cornell's faculty, staff, and students, appointing ten women and minorities to senior positions in his administration (including Carolyn "Biddy" Martin, an openly gay woman, as Cornell's provost in 2000). He worked as well to take down departmental and collegiate disciplinary silos. Imperfectly realized, to be sure, Rawlings's reforms were designed, he often emphasized, to make Cornell "the best research university for an undergraduate education in the United States."

AT THE END of the twentieth century, academics and administrators engaged in a serious and substantive reassessment of the nature, practice, and organization of research in universities. Departmental boundaries in the sciences, social sciences, and humanities had become more elastic and permeable. Chemists incorporated chemical biology and physics. Psychologists studied neurobiology. Professors of literature delved into history and cultural studies. The history of art expanded to include mass media and other visual studies. Areas of inquiry with significant societal implications—such as the environment, energy, and health care—relied on multidisciplinary work. And with financial support for research from the federal government reaching a plateau in some fields and declining in others, it was clear that universities needed to set broadly based research priorities.

In 1997, President Rawlings appointed the seventeen-member "Task Force on Physical Sciences and Engineering and Their Relationship with Biological Sciences," chaired by John Hopcroft, dean of the College of Engineering, and Norman Scott, PhD '62, vice president for research and advanced studies, to identify "strategic enabling areas" in these fields and design strategies to support them. The task force report, made public in October 1997, acknowledged that concerns about "top down" management of research priorities and a loss of department autonomy were legitimate. Nonetheless, it maintained that Cornell "cannot do everything" and must make "well-informed and wise resource commitments" or risk losing its position as a world-class research university. To this end, the report reiterated Cornell's strong commitment to basic research in all sciences and identified three areas that were likely to influence scientific inquiry for decades: (1) genomics and integrative molecular biology, which were at the cutting edge of a life sciences revolution that integrated information for whole organisms, physiological systems, and behavior; (2) information sciences, which facilitated connections "unconstrained by physical location" and the accumulation, dissemination, and analysis of massive amounts of data; and (3) advanced materials sciences, including nanotechnology, which fundamentally transformed knowledge of the structure and composition of matter. Task force members realized that they "faced a significant challenge" in suggesting a plan for building strength in these areas. "Departments have been and are key," they wrote, but since they were, at times, narrow, inward looking, and tradition-bound, the report recommended engaging "a broader set of individuals" to design organizational structures and common facilities, participate in faculty searches, and ensure collaboration among disciplines.[12]

The task force attempted to build on existing strengths. Convinced that it had chosen the members of the task force wisely and well, the Rawlings administration moved aggressively to implement its recommendations. Cornell was already at the forefront of research in nanotechnology (the science of the small). A "sub-micron" facility had opened on campus in 1978, and nine years later a nanofabrication laboratory, funded by the National Science Foundation, attracted engineers, biologists, chemists, and physicists. In the summer of 1997, as the task force was deliberating, a team of scientists working under the supervision of Professor Harold Craighead, MS '77, PhD '80, carved out of crystalline silicon the world's smallest guitar, an instrument with six strings, each about fifty nanometers (fifty billionths of a meter) wide and ten nanometers long. In 1999, Cornell became the lead institution (in a cooperative effort with Princeton, Clark Atlanta University, Howard University, Oregon Health Sciences

University, and the New York State Department of Health's Wadsworth Center) of the nation's first Nanobiotechnology Center, housed in the Biotech Building. Applying the computer revolution to the life sciences, researchers at the center looked for the E. coli pathogen, tried to create "neuron repair kits" to treat Parkinson's disease and Alzheimer's, and began to experiment with restoring the sight of blind people with computerized artificial retinas. The center also supported the work of thirty-five graduate students and fulfilled its pedagogical responsibilities in a variety of ways, including teaching primary school students about size and scale through games offered at Ithaca's annual summer festival and funding a nanobiotechnology club for high school girls.[13]

With financial support from David Duffield '62, MBA '64, the founder and chairman of PeopleSoft Inc., Rawlings authorized the construction of a 150,000-square-foot, $62 million addition to the Engineering quad, connected to Phillips and Upson Halls by a large atrium, and devoted to nanofabrication. "I have made a zillion dollars," Duffield said, following his $20 million commitment, "and I don't want it all to go to my kids."[14] Duffield Hall, which opened in 2004, was filled with state-of-the-art equipment (with science-fiction names such as "optical lithography steppers" and "ion beam etching systems") and laboratories. Unlike the "clean rooms" of "regular" labs, which had between 100,000 and 1 million particles of 10 microns or less in a cubic foot of air, Duffield's clean rooms had fewer than 100 such particles. "At the sizes we're dealing with," Hopcroft pointed out, "a particle of dirt looks like Mount Everest." Because the technology had a downside—it might lead to diseases as well as cure them—the College of Engineering established a professorship in ethics in 2000. Meanwhile, Cornell nanofabricators, sensing that their field was in its infancy, became more confident that in time they would be able to make almost anything that exists in nature.[15]

Although it too built on strength, the initiative in information sciences took a different form. Founded in 1965, Cornell's Computer Science Department has been ranked among the top five departments of its kind ever since. In 1996, its twenty-six faculty members crafted a "Vision for the Next Decade" and challenged President Rawlings "to 'will into being' the model American research university of the information age." Taking note of skyrocketing undergraduate course enrollments and majors (the department was based in Engineering and Arts and Sciences), the distinguished quality of PhD students, and recent efforts to balance theory with high-impact applications in the curriculum and in research, CS faculty cited the impact of information sciences on speech recognition, visual processing, architecture, digital imaging, computational finance, cognitive psychology, electrical engineering, fluid mechanics, and nanotechnology. The science behind computing was so deep and the technology so pervasive, they claimed, "that they are relevant to every subject in the university." To ensure the preeminence of the department and make it a catalyst for engaging other departments, "indeed for helping to break down departmental barriers," the report advocated increasing the quality, breadth, and influence of education and research in information sciences, enhancing Cornell's computing infrastructure, and adding ten new faculty positions (two a year) over five years to the department.[16]

In the wake of the department's "vision statement" and the Hopcroft-Scott task force report, Provost Don Randel, in collaboration with the Faculty Senate, appointed a committee early in 1999 to make recommendations for advancing computing and information science. In June, the committee issued an initial report proposing the creation of a university-wide academic unit, called the Faculty of Computing and Information (FCI), "with some of the attributes of a college and some of the structure of fields in the Graduate School," to incubate new concentrations, programs, and majors and provide new channels for cross-disciplinary activity to faculty across the institution. Randel responded quickly. To ensure that discussions benefited from "vigorous intellectual leadership," he appointed Professor Robert Constable, chair of Computer Science, to the position of dean of FCI in August. Randel asked Constable to develop pilot administrative procedures for the new entity (including authority for budget and human resource functions, and authority to conduct fund-raising activities and expand partnerships with industries). At the same time, Randel emphasized that "no new department, college, school, center, faculty etc. has been predetermined, much less put in place. Any such new organization will require approvals on campus and by the Board of Trustees." As if to explain his sense of urgency, the provost reminded deans, directors, and department heads that "Cornell can, and it must, seize an opportunity to lead in bringing to bear on the broadest range of disciplines the remarkable advances in computing and information sciences now taking place."[17]

Randel's announcement, acknowledged Charles Van Loan, the new chair of the Computer Science Department, "very definitely created a buzz." Van Loan heard "the words 'fait accompli' a hundred times."[18] "This was done in the summer," a faculty member complained at a forum sponsored by the dean of the faculty in September; "for us that's the middle of the night."[19] Rumors circulated that the provost had made his decision, which was not supported by Dean Hopcroft, the former chair of Computer Science, to prevent a well-regarded faculty member from accepting an offer from another institution. Concerns about substance as well as process also surfaced. Van Loan predicted that "venom would flow . . . because the structure envisioned looks like a set up for CS domination." Deans wondered whether "seed money" and the annual operating budget for the new entity would come from funds previously allocated to them. And whether "their" prospective donors would be redirected to FCI. Faculty in the School of Electrical Engineering unanimously declared that the new entity would "severely hinder" educators and scholars at Cornell.

Hiring, tenure, and promotion decisions would be dominated by Computer Science faculty "with vested interests." And internal and external resources would be diverted to the Faculty of Computing and Information. They asked Rawlings and Randel to meet with them "for a frank and friendly discussion."[20]

Many frank, if not always friendly, discussions ensued. The forum at Call Auditorium sponsored by Dean of the Faculty J. Robert Cooke attracted three hundred faculty members, with strong opinions expressed on both sides. Whether or not it was a fait accompli, with Computer Science "foxes in charge of the hen house," the initiative moved forward. Although one of the Faculty Senate's resolutions deemed it unlikely that FCI would "accomplish the aims announced for it and may obstruct the evolution of more useful mechanisms for smaller, more coherent faculty groups to engage with the information age," the Senate approved a motion to endorse the appointment of a dean to implement "the visions, goals and principles that will grow out of the Task Force and other efforts."[21] Up and running in 2000, FCI (soon to be renamed Faculty of Computing and Information Science) had sixty faculty "affiliates" within a few years, with plans to expand to eighty, spread across almost two dozen departments. An Information Science program, offering a major and a PhD, was in place in three colleges, and undergraduates in every college could complete a minor. The university also revealed plans to build a state-of-the-art building, as part of an "information campus," appropriate for twenty-first-century teaching and cross-disciplinary research. "We're in the middle of a revolution today," Dean Constable proclaimed, "and we haven't even hit the most interesting part yet."[22]

The life sciences were in the middle of a revolution as well. Rawlings's New Life Sciences Initiative, which became the most expensive and ambitious academic undertaking in Cornell's history, began with yet another task force, this one charged with examining the intercollegiate Division of Biological Sciences, and chaired by William R. "Ronnie" Coffman, PhD '71, associate dean for research in the College of Agriculture and Life Sciences, and Biddy Martin, associate dean in the College of Arts and Sciences. In a report made public in March 1998, the task force found that the division, which had been created during the presidency of James Perkins, worked well for the organization of undergraduate teaching, the promotion of outreach initiatives, and, "to some extent," for faculty recruiting and retention. It did not perform well, however, in promoting interaction with biologists who were not in the division; reallocating resources, such as vacant faculty positions; promoting faculty research and scholarship; and "creating excellence in key fields in the biological sciences by providing vision, identifying new directions, and sustaining the flexibility required to move in those directions." Genomics, task force members indicated, had "shifted the ground from underneath the Division structure." The result was serious funding shortages for facilities and technical expertise, uneven quality among faculty in the field, a lack of distinction and poor national rankings in important research areas, and the perception of a vacuum in leadership. The task force recommended maintaining the undergraduate major (which was available to students in Arts and Sciences, Agriculture and Life Sciences, and Human Ecology) and the Advising Center, located in Stimson Hall, supervised by a director of undergraduate biology. It also proposed dismantling the division and replacing the "sections" in it with departments, each of which would report to the dean of a college.[23]

The report was not well received by many faculty members in the division. At a Faculty Senate meeting on November 11, 1998, Howard Howland, PhD '68, professor of neurobiology and behavior, deemed the recommendation to dismantle the division "illogical, parochial, ill-thought out, and in its effect downright destructive." It would "abolish the home of basic biology on this campus, scatter its parts to three colleges, and throw away more than thirty years of basic biology on this campus. With all my heart, I urge the administration to reject it."[24]

On November 17, Rawlings announced his decision. Although he took "particular care" to assure faculty that the undergraduate program would continue to be administered from the complex in Stimson by a director with authority to "maintain the current commitments of faculty, teaching assistants and material support" and work with colleagues to revamp the curriculum and improve advising, Rawlings dismantled the division. Convinced that units of twenty to forty faculty "are optimal" for building strong programs, Rawlings mandated that faculty be assigned to departments in Plant Sciences, Ecology and Evolutionary Biology, Neurobiology and Behavioral Science, Molecular Biology and Genetics, Microbiology, and Physiology. Administrative responsibility for these departments was assigned either to the dean of Arts and Sciences, Agriculture and Life Sciences, or Veterinary Medicine. To assuage "another important reservation expressed by advocates of maintaining the Division," the president required the deans to draw up a "substantial agreement of cooperation," subject to approval by the provost, specifying resource commitments and standards and procedures applicable to hiring and promotion. Finally, in light of the enormous breadth and significance of the field and the "need for attention to direction and cohesion," Rawlings indicated that the vice provost for life sciences (professor of biology Kraig Adler) would represent the administration in the sphere of biology and create a local and an external board of distinguished scientists to review ongoing developments, discuss matters of concern, and "pay particular attention to our attempts to strengthen molecular and cell biology."[25]

The restructuring of Biological Sciences added momentum to what was then called the Cornell Genomics Initiative, to which the Rawlings administration committed $25 million between 1997 and 2002. Twenty distinguished scientists were hired by search committees composed of professors from across the campus, as well as members of the departments that "owned" the positions. The approach, insisted Charles "Chip" Aquadro, professor of molecular biology and genetics, was "not an attempt to usurp the departments' role, but to enhance it."[26] An Institute for Genomic Diversity, directed by professor of plant breeding Stephen Kresovich, was established, and Aquadro started a program in comparative and evolutionary genetics. Cornell's DNA sequencing capability doubled, and genotyping and micro-array facilities became available to all faculty, staff, and students. Faculty designed a new undergraduate concentration in computational biology. The College of Veterinary Medicine opened a twelve-thousand-square-foot pathogen-free mouse facility to genetically transform and breed the most-used animal model in biomedical research. All this activity prompted the New York State Office of Science, Technology and Academic Research to designate Cornell as the site for a genomics technology center and the U.S. Department of Agriculture to select the university as the site for its Center for Agricultural Bioinformatics.

To ensure that Cornell became one of the top five institutions in life science research and education within ten years, the administration officially launched the $500 million New Life Sciences Initiative (NLSI) in 2002. At a celebratory reception at Lincoln Hall on April 30, Rawlings and Provost Martin announced that the ambitious initiative would encompass seven colleges, hundreds of faculty, sixty departments, the New York State Experiment Station in Geneva, the Boyce Thompson Institute on campus, and the USDA's Agricultural Research Service and Plant, Soil and Nutrition Laboratory. NLSI aspired to support the hiring of fifty faculty, broaden educational opportunities for undergraduates, create one hundred graduate fellowships, and make possible the construction of new facilities, including a New Life Sciences Technology building, a physical sciences structure in the Baker Hall / Clark Hall precinct, Duffield Hall, and laboratory renovations across the campus. About $100 million of the $500 million, Rawlings revealed, was already in hand. Acknowledging that Cornell had to "educate" potential donors, Inge Reichenbach, vice president for alumni affairs and development, was optimistic that the remainder of the funds could be raised within five years. Everyone agreed, however, that "a lot of hard work is yet to be done."[27]

The social sciences and humanities enjoyed some benefits from the initiatives in Computing and Information and the Life Sciences. CIS gave funds for faculty positions in digital art, communication, science and technology studies, and other fields. NLSI directed resources to the study of ethical, legal, and social issues emanating from research in the life sciences. Between 1995 and 2003, moreover, social scientists and humanists, who recognized that they did not have the same clout as their brethren in the sciences and engineering, also created academic structures to promote multidisciplinary collaboration in teaching and scholarship.

In January 1999 a Task Force on the Future of the Social Sciences at Cornell submitted its report to the provost. The report identified social adaptation and decision making, life course transitions and social policy, and wealth, poverty, and international development as significant conceptual clusters." The task force recommendations prompted a modest initiative in the social sciences, with a price tag of $1.5 million a year. The administration appropriated funds for two junior faculty positions in the Government and Economics Departments, for the recruitment of senior professors in the social sciences, and to establish an Institute for the Social Sciences, modeled in part on the Society for the Humanities, to bring together about a dozen Cornell-based and visiting scholars working on a common theme. Housed in Noyes Lodge, the institute opened its doors in 2005.

Meanwhile, multidisciplinary institutes and programs brought together social scientists and humanists with common research and teaching interests. The Cognitive Studies Program enlisted faculty in linguistics, philosophy, modern languages, computer science, and human development. Arguing that statistics was an essential tool for behavioral and social scientists as well as for scientists and engineers, professors from ILR, Plant Breeding and Biometry, Mathematics, and Operations Research and Industrial Engineering joined forces to advocate a "virtual department" that would offer an undergraduate concentration in several colleges, a master's in applied statistics, and a PhD.

The greatest activity occurred in applied economics. In 1997, the departments of Consumer Economics and Housing and Human Services in Human Ecology merged to become the Department of Policy Analysis and Management. Two years later, ILR established the Institute in Workplace Studies, directed by Professor Samuel Bacharach, to build bridges between researchers in Ithaca and the practitioner community in New York City. And in 2002, the Department of Applied Economics and Management (which had been Agricultural Economics and then Agricultural Resource and Managerial Economics) received accreditation as an undergraduate business program, the second of its kind in the Ivy League. AEM featured courses in business, food management, agribusiness, farm management and finance, environmental and resource economics, and agricultural economics. "The agricultural portion is not going away," Professor James Hagen emphasized. "It is part of our strength."[28] His colleagues understood, however, that many of the students who were attracted to the major would not pursue careers in agriculture. With forty-two professors, instructors, and lecturers, seven hundred majors, and thousands of students inside and outside the College of Agriculture and Life Sciences clamoring to enroll in its courses, Andrew Novakovic, chair of AEM, recognized that the department needed more resources and staff support. With enrollments declining in other departments in the college, he also realized that his problems were good ones to have.

ILR, the Hotel School, and the Johnson Graduate School of Management modernized their facilities. A renovated Ives Hall opened to mixed reviews in 1998. Some thought the exterior looked cold and forbidding. Inside, however, Ives had two large lecture halls, one seating 330, the other 140, and three amphitheaters, two of them equipped for distance learning. That same year, the Johnson Graduate School of Management moved from Malott Hall to Sage. At a cost of $38 million, the 1874 landmark structure, which had been designed to accommodate Cornell's first female students, had been completely renovated. Sage's exterior remained intact; its spire, which had been missing for fifty years, was discovered and restored to its place on top of the building. Providing Johnson School students and faculty 60 percent more space than Malott, Sage boasted an atrium, one thousand computer ports, classrooms wired for distance learning, a negotiations laboratory, and a trading center supplied with live data from financial markets around the world (which made possible the establishment of a student-managed, faculty-supervised equity hedge fund). And early in 2003, construction began on the Beck Center, a thirty-five-thousand-square-foot facility, attached to the eastern end of Statler Hall, named for Robert Beck '42, MED '52, PhD '54, the former dean of the Hotel School. Featuring a three-story glass-walled atrium and interior balconies, the Beck Center had high-tech classrooms, a computer lab, and, of course, a hospitality suite.

Concerned that the place of the liberal arts at many universities had become "smaller and seemingly peripheral," Rawlings maintained that at Cornell the humanities "stand at the center of the curriculum and reinforce the university's traditional role as independent thinker and critic."[29] To keep them there, he and Provost Martin helped draft a $1.4 million proposal, subsequently approved by the Mellon Foundation, to fund postdoctoral fellowships and multidisciplinary seminars in the humanities and persuaded the Atlantic Philanthropies foundation to provide $6 million to hire junior faculty in English, History, and Government, support research, and develop team-taught seminars in American and comparative studies.

The administration also authorized large-scale capital projects for the humanities and performing arts. In 1998, following an $8 million renovation of its 42,500-square-foot interior, Olive Tjaden Hall (formerly Franklin Hall) reopened as the home of the Department of Art in the College of Architecture, Art, and Planning. The building contained multimedia classrooms, a studio for performance and installation art, a six-story atrium, photography labs and a darkroom, print-making workshops, and a gallery. Next door, White Hall, one of Cornell's original "Stone Row" buildings, had its interior completely redesigned, with an atrium in the center, seminar rooms, and an art gallery, while the Florentine-style exterior remained untouched. "This is not a restoration," explained Gary Wilhelm, the project manager, "but a sympathetic renovation that retains the 19th century character of the building while improving it."[30]

When the project was finished in 2003, at a cost of $12 million, White welcomed the Government and Near Eastern Studies Departments. That same year, Cornell broke ground for a renovation and expansion of the Africana Studies and Research Center on North Triphammer Road. Taking up 5,480 square feet, the new building contained the center's library and a multipurpose room.

Across the Arts quad, Lincoln Hall, the home of the Music Department, received a $19 million renovation and the addition of a nineteen-thousand-square-foot wing attached to its east façade. Completed in 2000, the new Lincoln contained 70 percent more space for its music library, fifteen streamed digital sound stations, an Internet-accessible computer lab with MIDI keyboards and music software, acoustically engineered classrooms and practice rooms, a two-story gamelan room, space for chamber music rehearsals and storage for instruments, and a climate-controlled system that protected temperature- and humidity-sensitive instruments, including Professor Malcolm Bilson's fortepianos. Plans were laid as well early in the twenty-first century to renovate Bailey Hall, Cornell's multipurpose venue and principal concert space. At an estimated cost of $13 million, the Bailey makeover, the first since its foundation was laid in 1913, included the replacement of two thousand wooden seats with fourteen hundred larger and more comfortable ones; handicap-accessible bathrooms, stairs, and aisles; and rewiring and air-conditioning.

The fate of a report by a faculty committee on the humanities, however, underscored the inability of Cornell humanists to arrive at a consensus about priorities and lobby effectively for resources—and the capacity of identity politics to disrupt and derail their deliberations. Mindful of the pressures on the College of Arts and Sciences budget, Dean Philip Lewis asked the twelve (soon to be seventeen) members of the State of the Humanities Committee to build on strengths and compensate for weaknesses in the humanities without incurring substantial additional expenses. Issued in the fall of 1998, their report, according to English professor Timothy Murray, was designed "to catalyze further reflection" without serving "as a prescriptive policy-making instrument."[31] It proposed the establishment of a program in French Studies, dedicated to teaching and research related to the language, literature, and culture of the Francophone world, and the replacement of the Medieval Studies program—which remained "at odds with critical trends and turns in the humanities" and therefore was perceived by graduate students as "arcane, inaccessible, over-specialized and irrelevant"—by Mediterranean Studies. It advocated supplanting History of Art with a Department of Visual Studies that would specialize in theory and culture, cinema and video, the history of art, and digital studies; a required course in the humanities for first-year students in Arts and Sciences; and further investigation of a core curriculum for all A&S undergraduates. Declaring that "the entire spectrum of ethnic and minority discourse at Cornell has been marginalized and isolated," the committee also suggested linking American Indian Studies, Asian American Studies, Latino Studies, and the Africana Studies and Research Center to the Program in American Studies and moving all of them into a single building, on or adjacent to the Arts quad.[32]

Public reactions to the report were overwhelmingly negative. Professors of French, Spanish, and Italian literature declared that a separate French Studies program would destroy the Romance Studies Department. History of Art professor Robert Calkins insisted that abolishing his department would make Cornell "the laughingstock of the Ivy League." Classics professor Danuta Shanzer proclaimed the report's characterization of the Medieval Studies program "slanderous and offensive."[33]

Faculty in ethnic studies programs and the Africana Studies and Research Center were even angrier. Jane Mt. Pleasant '80, MS '82, professor of soil, crop, and atmospheric sciences and director of the American Indian Studies Program, expressed astonishment at the "arrogance of people who would suggest a solution like that" without consulting those who were most affected.[34] At a College of Arts and Sciences faculty forum on October 28, set up by Dean Lewis to discuss the recommendations, Africana Studies and Research Center faculty denounced the report as "a declaration of war," as their students, who packed the Hollis Cornell Auditorium in Goldwin Smith, stamped their feet and chanted.[35]

That night Lewis wrote to James Turner, who was again serving as the director of the Africana Center. "Just so the record is clear," he indicated, "I would definitely prefer a more central location for Africana Studies." Lewis assumed that an attractive space at or near the center of campus might appeal to Turner and his colleagues: "If this supposition is invalid, it will suffice for you to say so." On the question of "Africana's (relative) autonomy and the status of ethnic studies," Lewis added, he was "not prepared to be reduced by either colleagues or students to the stereotype of a bureaucrat advocating some facile 'consolidation' that I have never envisaged." Instead, he stood ready to work together with faculty, "as intellectual allies, without giving in to masters who might wish to deny ethnic difference or to agglomerate curricula for purely administrative reasons." He left the choice, however, to Turner. If "you decide against talking with us" about subjects of "common interest," Lewis promised to "leave aside the section on ethnic studies entirely" and oppose "attempts to bring concrete proposals affecting Africana Studies before the college faculty."[36]

Apparently unaware of these developments, Africana students staged a sit-in at Dean Lewis's office in Goldwin Smith in early November, vowing to return each day until the humanities report was withdrawn. On November 9, Lewis announced that discussion of ethnic studies "is not going to be able to continue in the public forum."[37] With the restoration of collegial harmony "clearly the order of the day," Lewis also put substantive deliberations about French Studies,

Medieval Studies, the History of Art Department, and ways to introduce undergraduates "to vital issues and scholarly practices in the humanities" on hold, pending conversations with the faculty in the college.[38] Professor Shanzer wondered whether "the issues in the report are too hot to handle and are going to get put underground and pulled up and endorsed by fiat." Modern Languages professor Carol Rosen observed, more accurately, that Lewis's cancellation of the faculty forums placed the recommendations "face down in the bottom drawer underneath the winter socks. He has cut the rope and let the Humanities report sink."[39]

THE ACADEMIC INITIATIVES and the building boom—including the transformation of undergraduate residence halls that was soon to come—cost a lot of money. Cornell did not always have the cash it needed on hand. A prosperous national economy and a rising stock market in the 1990s helped. The endowment of the university grew, and alumni were increasingly generous. With interest rates low and economic expectations rising, Day Hall administrators decided to take on a substantial amount of debt. At the same time, they continued to struggle to reduce expenses and raise revenues.

Adding to the financial pressure was a restive and increasingly aggressive faculty. Between 1988 and 1998, while the size of the undergraduate student body remained stable, at about 13,000, the number of faculty declined about 5 percent, from 1,617 to 1,525, with the heaviest losses, about 58 positions, in the College of Agriculture and Life Sciences. Along with administrators, Cornell professors worried that the end of mandatory retirement in colleges and universities, which went into effect in 1994, was clogging the system (in 1997, thirty professors age seventy or more were still working) and reducing the number of assistant professors. Most important, faculty noticed that their salaries were no longer competitive with those at peer institutions in the United States. Cornell paid a market salary for junior faculty, but full professors had fallen far behind. In the endowed colleges they were in twenty-first place; in the statutory units, they ranked thirty-fourth.

Cornell professors relied on the newly organized Faculty Senate to persuade the administration to make salaries its top priority. Adopted by a mail ballot vote of 684–78 in November 1995, the Senate had a governance structure, including representatives chosen by each department, designed to make it more influential than its predecessor. A nine-member University Faculty Council met regularly with the president and provost. And the Senate chose half the members of all university committees (the other half were chosen by Day Hall administrators). Joined by an Arts and Sciences Ad Hoc Committee on Faculty Salaries, the Senate Financial Policies Committee compiled comparative data on salaries and benefits and refuted arguments that the cost of living in Ithaca justified lower salaries. In April 2000, President Rawlings indicated that the board of trustees was receptive to their message. In August, he and Provost Martin announced a five-year salary improvement program. In 2001–2, salaries for professors in the endowed colleges went up, on average, by 7 percent (the peer group average increase was 4.4 percent); statutory college salaries increased 6.5 percent (the peer average was 2.6 percent). At the end of five years, Cornell professors had made up a good deal of the ground they had lost in the preceding decade.

The money had to come from somewhere. It seemed clear, however, that not enough of it would come from New York State and SUNY. In November 1999, Vice President Henrik Dullea '61 revealed that the $130 million allocation from SUNY was about $4.6 million short "of what it would require for us to continue our current operations."[40] Agriculture and Life Sciences felt compelled to reduce its budget by about $1 million and to increase tuition more substantially than originally planned. In the ensuing months, negotiations with SUNY, the New York State Legislature, and Governor George Pataki resulted in some additional appropriations. The more fundamental differences between SUNY and Cornell, however, were not resolved. Much like their predecessors, Rawlings and Provosts Randel and Martin complained that SUNY's enrollment-driven formula, in essence, punished Cornell for trying "to get better, not bigger."[41] As they had so often in the past, they argued that SUNY failed to account for the extensive—and expensive—extension and research activities engaged in by the university in support of its land grant mission. In the absence of a formula that recognized the distinctive quality of Cornell, however, they realized that, at best, Cornell's statutory colleges would continue to run in place. In 2002, they claimed that resources from New York State "have decreased and are expected to decrease further."[42]

Blessed and cursed with the founder's motto, Cornell was loath to eliminate any academic program, regardless of the money to be saved. The political price to be paid for shutting down a research facility became abundantly clear in 2001 when Vice Provost for Research and Nobel laureate Robert C. Richardson recommended decommissioning the five-hundred-kilowatt TRIGA (an acronym for Teaching, Research, Isotope, and General Atomics) Mark II nuclear reactor and phasing out the activities at the Ward Center for Nuclear Sciences, which had an annual operating budget of $500,000. Scheduled to be reviewed for relicensing in 2002–3 by the Nuclear Regulatory Commission, the forty-year-old reactor, Richardson pointed out, had been underused since 1995, when the College of Engineering disbanded its Nuclear Science and Engineering program. Ward also contained nuclear fuel, which posed problems associated with the removal of waste and took up twenty thousand square feet of "valuable space on the campus."[43] Richardson proposed maintaining only the Ward Center's cobalt-60 gamma cell, a dry irradiation facility, used by researchers in Veterinary Medicine and Agriculture and Life Sciences for sterilization, radiation testing, and the cross-linking of polymers.

The Ward reactor did not go quietly. Although the Local Advisory Committee, a standing committee of the Faculty Senate, unanimously supported the move to decommission, and the Senate's Committee on Academic Programs and Policies agreed, the body as a whole voted 36–19 (with 9 abstentions) for a resolution urging the university to maintain the reactor, the gamma cell, and the associated activities of the center. "I listened to both sides," Microbiology professor Eugene Madsen, MS '81, PhD '85, said, "and came away completely convinced by both."[44] "Compassion for colleagues," Dean of the Faculty J. Robert Cooke suggested, may well have influenced the vote.[45] He was referring, no doubt, to Kenan Ünlü, the director of the Ward Center, who deemed closure a betrayal of Ezra Cornell's "mission statement" for the university.[46] And also to Classics professor Peter Kuniholm, who used the reactor to date artifacts, and Suzanne Kay, of Earth and Atmospheric Sciences, who needed it to study the formation, evolution, and destruction of the continental crust. The university offered to ship their samples to other reactors but acknowledged that the time and expense would slow the research.

Cornell students mobilized to save the Ward reactor, creating a website to drum up support for their petition campaign. "The projects being conducted at the lab are for the good of humanity and all students have a stake in its closing," Danielle Houck '03 insisted. In the end, the point of view advanced by a member of the Faculty Senate—"Everything's good, but the question is, is it $500,000 good?"—prevailed,[47] but only because the board of trustees voted unanimously in May to authorize the administration to close down the Ward Center for Nuclear Studies.

In the 1990s, using technology to modernize administrative systems appeared to be the best way to provide budget relief at Cornell. In March 1996, eight months after he became president, Rawlings introduced "Project 2000: Creating a Best Managed University" to the campus community. By reconfiguring the way it conducted its business, he indicated, the university would be able to direct its resources to its core mission—excellence in teaching, research, and service. Conceived by Senior Vice President and Chief Financial Officer Fred Rogers, who was given a $30.9 million incremental budget to manage the initiative, Project 2000 was expected to increase efficiency in human resource and payroll administration, financial and accounting systems, student services, endowment management, and alumni development. Systems applications and service would be provided by PeopleSoft, a coup for the relatively new company founded by Cornell alumnus David Duffield, which was eager to land a prestigious university as a customer. Rogers claimed that the new systems would be fully implemented between 1997 and 1999. By the turn of the century, Cornell "should be the best managed" university in the United States.[48]

As the university changed "from a growth paradigm to a quality paradigm," eliminating "duplicative and unnecessary processes," Rawlings and Rogers subsequently added, at an Employee Assembly open forum at Bailey Hall, Cornell's workforce would shrink. Anticipating that the number of jobs lost would be roughly equal to the annual attrition rate of 8 percent, they did not envision a substantial number of layoffs.[49]

Project 2000 was a fiasco. By the end of 1997, Rogers was trying to refute claims that "the project will cost twice as much as anticipated and save us nothing," asking Rawlings and Randel for more money, and revising the "timetable, scope, and consequences" of the initiative.[50] In May 1998, Helen Mohrmann, a senior officer of Project 2000, laid out the options in a confidential e-mail to Randel. Concluding that "we still do not know how to organize ourselves to manage" the implementation of more than one new system, Mohrmann opposed allocating "$10 million a year to keep pursuing the current strategy." Although she understood that "the Duffield relationship is still important in the long term," she proposed finishing the Human Resources and payroll systems and suspending PeopleSoft work on student services. The justification on campus "for this change of approach," Mohrmann wrote, "could be that 'we've learned a lot and now we ought to take stock and catch our breath.'"[51]

In September, Rogers announced that the student service module had been delayed for one year. Standardizing systems, he said, "was a lot more complicated than we thought. Every detail and nuance has to be dealt with."[52] In August 1999, Randel notified staff, students, and faculty of further delays: "Originally we envisioned a suite of five major integrated systems by the year 2000. In reality it takes more time and money. . . . We had to add people to save the new systems."[53] At the end of 2001, money was in short supply, for reasons, some devastating, no Cornell administrators could have planned for. The World Trade Center and the Pentagon had suffered terrorist attacks that would leave few aspects of life undisrupted. The dot-com stock market bubble had burst, Cornell's endowment had declined by 7.8 percent—the largest drop in twenty years—and New York State faced a serious budget crisis. "We do not yet know the precise financial consequences," Rawlings stated, "but we do know there will be consequences." Deeming it "imperative that we undertake a series of prudent actions now," Rawlings ordered a campus-wide hiring freeze that would last until June 30, 2002.[54] Although Cornell continued to implement new software systems, he never again mentioned Project 2000.

_____

ONE FACILITIES INITIATIVE turned out to be the most ingenious money-saving project during these years. In 1995, about 40 percent of Cornell's buildings were cooled by a central circulating chilled water system, consisting of seven large electricity-driven refrigerator units (or "chillers") and an insulated storage tank. The system was approaching its capacity, and the chillers, which used environmentally dangerous chlorofluorocarbons, were reaching the end of their useful lives. The estimated cost of new chillers (designed to use alternative refrigerants) was $22 million by the year 2000 and an additional $69 million by 2030. After weighing the options and investigating an area in Stockholm, Sweden, that was cooled by ocean water, Cornell engineer W.S. "Lanny" Joyce '81 and three colleagues in Cornell's utilities division recommended a process that became known as lake source cooling. Water from the campus cooling system, chilled through conventional refrigeration to about 55–60 degrees Fahrenheit, would make a two-mile journey through pipes to a facility on the shores of Cayuga Lake, where it ran alongside other pipes containing colder lake water (39–41 degrees) drawn from a depth of 250 feet. Separated by stainless steel exchangers, the two flows of water would not make physical contact, but heat would pass from one set of pipes to the other. The lake water, now warmer at 48–56 degrees, would then be deposited in a shallower part of the lake, while the Cornell water, now colder at 45 degrees, was pumped back up to the buildings on campus to cool laboratories, lecture halls, and offices. At a projected cost of $58 million, lake source cooling, the first project of its kind in the United States, was touted as a more efficient, cheaper, and more environmentally friendly way to air condition the campus. If the system were adopted, proponents said, the use of electricity for air-conditioning at Cornell would drop by 80 percent; the annual savings in the initial years of operation would exceed $1 million. Lake source cooling, Joyce declared, is "a really long-term solution to what is a continuous expense—and a recurring problem right now."[55]

At first, the permitting process went smoothly. Scientists indicated that the impact on Cayuga Lake would be negligible, comparable to about four or five additional hours of sunlight per year. After reviewing Cornell's fifteen-hundred-page environmental impact statement, the New York State Department of Environmental Conservation approved the project in January 1998. Pleased that lake source cooling would provide jobs and assured by Cornell that the university would pay to rebuild the roads and sidewalks torn up to install the pipes, the City of Ithaca provided the necessary permits. The Ithaca City School District, which expected to reduce its utility costs when the project cooled its high school buildings, authorized the university to run lines underneath its property, and the Town of Ithaca provided a permit for the construction of the heat transfer facility, following an "unrelated transaction" in which Cornell donated a parcel of land for a marina.[56]

Laying forty-two-inch pipes from Libe Slope to East Shore Drive, however, was bound to be controversial. "You're talking about invading space, big time," Lanny Joyce noted. As he praised Cornell for openness and flexibility, Ithaca mayor Alan Cohen predicted as well that "given the nature of the community,

The interior of the lake source cooling facility. (Cornell University Photography)

there will be knee-jerk naysayers."[57] In September 1998, Save the Lake, a group of local environmentalists, filed suit to delay or stop the project. In December, a New York State Supreme Court judge dismissed their claim that the city, town, and school district had violated procedures in granting permits. Construction of lake source cooling began in March 1999 and was completed in 2000. Designed to last seventy-five to one hundred years, the system, according to its proponents, taps a renewable resource, reduces Cornell's reliance on fossil fuels, and has done no damage to Cayuga Lake, Ithaca's recreational jewel. Critics, however, have not gone away. Increased levels of phosphorus in the lake, attributable to lake source cooling, they claim, have damaged the ecosystem. In 2013, the New York State Department of Environmental Conservation renewed Cornell's State Pollutant Discharge Elimination System permit for lake source cooling, but mandated that the university fund a $2.1 million collaborative study of the sources and the impact of elevated phosphorous levels in the lake.

IN MARCH 2002, Hunter Rawlings informed the board of trustees that he would step down as president on June 30, 2003. After fifteen years as a university president (seven at the University of Iowa and eight at Cornell), he wanted to return to his first love, teaching classics. During the fifteen months Rawlings had remaining in office, board chair Harold Tanner '52 noted, "he intends to be a strong and vigorous president."[58] And, indeed, these months were filled with contention and combat. Rawlings fought off an attempt by graduate students to unionize, forced the resignation of the dean of the College of Arts and Sciences, and threatened to abolish the College of Architecture, Art, and Planning.

Cornell's graduate students had expressed dissatisfaction with working conditions, wages, and benefits for quite some time. After meetings with Day Hall officials, the self-constituted Graduate Advocacy Organization reported in a newsletter circulated in April 1989, "We are always graciously thanked for our 'input,' assured of their 'concern,' told our information has been 'helpful,' and praised for participating in 'a useful dialogue.' But input can't buy groceries." After pointing out that 57 percent of a teaching assistant stipend was needed to pay the rent on a two-bedroom unit in Hasbrouck (a university-owned apartment complex for graduate students), and another 10 percent went to utilities, the GAO maintained that graduate students would make significant gains only through unionization and collective bargaining agreements with their employers. At a GAO-sponsored rally outside Day Hall on April 21, students brought copies of rent, food, and utility bills, attached them to their pay stubs, and presented them to then provost Robert Barker. Nothing happened.[59]

Six years later, in the spring of 1995, Walter Cohen, professor of comparative literature and dean of the Graduate School, wrote a detailed memorandum to President-elect Rawlings about graduate education. Cohen noted that the GAO "was in an advanced state of decomposition," expressed sympathy with their proposals, indicated that the Graduate and Professional Student Assembly, which was established by the university in 1993, was "too boring and anti-confrontational to get the attention of many graduate students," and called attention to "numerous defects in their education and life" that deserved to be addressed.[60] In 1997, Cornell increased its graduate student stipends and benefits to levels approximating those offered by peer institutions. "We're back in the game," Cohen announced.[61] Some graduate students, however, especially those in the humanities, where the job market was poorest, deemed the new package inadequate.

In November 2000, in a case involving New York University, a three-member panel of the National Labor Relations Board held that graduate students who worked as research and teaching assistants in private universities had the right to form unions, reversing the previous NLRB policy that they were students and not employees. Soon after the decision was announced, graduate students at Columbia and Brown voted to determine whether they wanted to unionize; the results were sealed because the two universities appealed the NLRB ruling. In May 2002, the Cornell Association of Student Employees (CASE), an affiliate of the United Auto Workers union, filed a petition seeking recognition as the legal bargaining agent for graduate student employees at Cornell. CASE/UAW cited low wages, inadequate health and dental benefits, and a lack of influence in working conditions as reasons for the union drive. At What Cost?, an ad hoc antiunion student organization, urged graduate students to vote "no." An election was set for October 23 and 24, 2002.

Rawlings opposed unions for graduate students. In a statement issued to the campus community on September 4, he indicated that, unlike Columbia and Brown, Cornell had sought no legal or procedural delay, negotiated in good faith with CASE/UAW to define the bargaining unit of students who were eligible to vote, and set a date for the election. He made clear, however, his conviction that unionization "will inevitably introduce standardization," complicate the relationship between graduate students and their faculty mentors, and deprive departments of their ability to respond to the needs and goals of individual students. Despite a sidebar agreement with the union that academic issues would not be subject to collective bargaining, Rawlings predicted that "even with the best of good will on both sides," it would not be easy to disentangle academic issues from "employment matters." The real question, he concluded, was whether unionization was "the best solution." He urged all eligible graduate assistants to vote "in an election that has such significance for the entire campus, not only today, but also for many years to come."[62]

Casting ballots at two polling places on the Ithaca campus and one at the Agricultural Experiment Station in Geneva, New York, 2,049 graduate students, 88.4 percent of those on the final bargaining unit list, voted overwhelmingly—1,351 to 580 (118 votes were challenged and voided)—to reject representation by CASE/UAW. Cornell administrators attributed the results to the competitive stipends and benefit packages, including payment, starting in 2001, of the full premium for a health insurance plan, and the relatively low costs of living of graduate students in Ithaca. Relevant as well was the decision of negotiators for the university to insist on the largest possible bargaining unit, to ensure inclusion of graduate assistants in the sciences and engineering, who tended to be far less favorable to unionization than were humanists and social scientists. Many voters were also convinced that the UAW, which had lost many members in the previous two decades, was neither knowledgeable about nor interested in graduate students, apart from the opportunity to charge them dues. "A lot of people like unionization," Amanda Holland-Minkley, MS '99, PhD '04, a founder of At What Cost? noted, "but don't like this union." Some paper ballots, it turned out, contained handwritten messages such as "no, absolutely not, no way."[63]

Although another unionization vote could not be held for at least one year, Day Hall administrators believed that the UAW might well try again. In congratulating graduate students for making informed choices, Rawlings pledged to work with them "to see that their educational experience here at Cornell continues to be of the highest quality." In February 2003, four months after the election, Alison "Sunny" Power, professor of science and technology studies and dean of the Graduate School, announced an increase in graduate student wages from $13,850 to $14,530 per year, the largest boost in a decade. Graduate students "were trying to send the administration a message that there were still issues," Power declared. "We wanted to indicate our responsiveness to their concerns."[64]

Unlike unionization, where the ideological battle lines were clearly drawn, the clash between President Rawlings and Dean Philip Lewis involved differences in temperament and tone more than disputes over policy. Once he made a decision, Rawlings moved on and expected those around him, including deans, to move on as well. As his behavior as an advocate for divestment from South Africa during the Rhodes years demonstrated, Lewis was principled, persistent, and loath to give in or give up.

A specialist in French literature and critical theory and practice, Lewis had served as chair of the Romance Studies Department and associate dean of Arts and Sciences. In 1995, when Rawlings chose Don Randel as his provost, Lewis was named acting dean of the college. He became dean a year later and was reappointed in 2000. Extraordinarily knowledgeable and hardworking, Lewis managed the college's resources well, recruited about one hundred new Arts and Sciences faculty, added career counseling to an integrated Office of Admissions and Advising, and presided over the renaissance of Lincoln Hall and the renovation of White.

During Lewis's first term as dean, his relationship with Day Hall was relatively cordial. In 1996, in a letter to the *Cornell Daily Sun*, he commended Rawlings's controversial North Campus residential initiative as a "principled enactment of social, ethnic and racial integration" for first-year students.[65] In turn, the president and provost applauded Lewis's decision to dissolve the Modern Languages Department and integrate language instruction with literature and cultural studies. Over time, however, Rawlings and Provost Biddy Martin (Lewis's senior associate dean, who became his boss in 2000, when Randel was appointed president of the University of Chicago) became increasingly exasperated with Lewis. In their view, he pressed his views, on matters great and small, settled and unsettled, with excessive frequency and at inordinate length. Lewis raised concerns about the impact on Arts and Sciences of the initiatives in Computing and Information Science and the Life Sciences. He protested against what he deemed intensified pressure on his college to lower its academic standards and admit recruits for varsity athletic teams. He objected to the new Cornell logo, a red box that he and others deemed too much like the trademark of J.C. Penney. And he blasted a new brochure on the humanities, prepared by University Communications and Media Relations without consultation with him or Arts and Sciences faculty, for "painting a picture that accords essentially no attention to the College's role or long term efforts in this sphere."[66]

The concerns of Rawlings and Martin about what they considered Lewis's "negativism" and his "corrosive style" intensified in 2002. Rawlings curtailed his one-on-one meetings with him. In February, Martin warned him that it was "time to shape up." In April, following a characteristically detailed letter from Lewis to the forty alumni members of the Arts and Sciences Advisory Council that included criticism of the university's approach to program review, genomics, and financial and capital issues, Martin told Lewis that Rawlings and Peter Meinig '61, the chair of the board of trustees, expected more restraint, diplomacy, and "positive discourse" from him in the future. That summer, while Lewis was in Paris, he continued to spar with the provost over university initiatives in the social sciences—and she sent him an e-mail asking him to re-sign effective June 30, 2003. "After much reflection" and an assessment of his options, he agreed to do so.[67]

Martin maintained that she and Rawlings did not ask Lewis to resign be-cause of disagreements over policy: "Our decision came after lengthy delibera-tions and a conclusion, made with great reluctance, that the working relationship between Lewis and University administrators had broken down and that the breakdown was irreparable."[68] In private, Lewis blamed Rawlings for choosing "peremptorily" to devastate his career "in a brutally punitive and malicious way."[69] In public, he insisted that "no employee of the University—not even those who serve at the pleasure of the President—should have to resign without an opportunity for an exchange that could produce a mutually acceptable ac-count of the decision."[70]

After returning from their summer break, professors in Arts and Sciences defended their besieged dean. He was a "deep thinker," Charles Van Loan, chair of Computer Science, observed, who had an admirable capacity to "frame academic issues and make people think." Jonathan Culler, senior associate dean of Arts and Sciences, praised Lewis for wanting to "reflect seriously before go-ing down one path or another." Upset by the timing of the decision, the lack of consultation, and "the air of mystery that surrounds it," a large group of faculty asked the board of trustees for an explanation. Replying on behalf of the board, Meinig stated that it was the responsibility of the president and provost to select deans and work with them.[71]

In September 2003, Linda Grace-Kobas, interim vice president for com-munications and media relations, acknowledged that she did not know why Lewis had been forced to resign. "Things happen behind closed doors," she said. "Rumors get out, stories get out, and very often each side will tell its side of the story. In my long experience at the university, there is always a history and there is never a simple answer."[72] Lewis returned to the Romance Studies Department in the fall of 2003. In 2007, Don Randel, then president of the

Andrew W. Mellon Foundation, appointed him Mellon's vice president for liberal arts college programs.

In July 2002, at the very time they were seeking the resignation of Dean Lewis, Rawlings and Martin summoned Porus Olpadwala, MBA '73, MRP '76, PhD '79, dean of Architecture, Art, and Planning, and the three department chairs in his college to a meeting in Day Hall, where they were informed that the administration intended to dissolve the college. They were asked to submit a "realignment" plan. Concerned about the lack of academic integration among the three departments (there were no college-wide course requirements), two recent unsuccessful dean searches, and a recurring $1 million annual deficit, the president maintained that "it is possible that the faculty of Architecture, Art and Planning could create stronger intellectual ties with other departments at Cornell by joining other colleges, and that the University could thereby realize administrative and budgetary savings." This idea, he added, "is not new—it was first proposed some 20 years ago and has been re-examined periodically." Although discussions, "which will be led by the academic leadership of the College," were "in a very preliminary stage and no decisions have been made," Rawlings required Olpadwala to submit a plan in time for approval by the board of trustees at its January 2003 meeting.[73]

The announcement in August of "the alignment review," which Olpadwala and others viewed as a prelude to the college's dissolution, hit the college like a bombshell. The faculty was split. Professors in Art and City and Regional Planning wished to stay together and stay put, while many in Architecture preferred their own school and refused to explore other options (such as affiliation with Engineering) until their first choice was "removed from the table." Current AAP students were anxious, of course. Admissions officers scrambled to design a strategy to persuade high school seniors to apply to a college that might be on the brink of extinction. And alumni were outraged.[74]

Olpadwala convened a core planning council to lobby the central administration. As the news spread, hundreds of AAP graduates, administrators of architecture and design programs around the country, and members of professional and accrediting associations sent e-mails and letters. Many of them emphasized that the undergraduate program in architecture was ranked number one in the United States. Others pointed to interdepartmental college endeavors such as the Historic Preservation Program and Cornell in Rome, a semester-long study abroad program. And undergraduates organized rallies on campus. At varsity football games, they handed out placards to students in the west stands of Schoellkopf Stadium that spelled "Go Cornell" on one side and "Save AAP" on the other. Each time Cornell scored, the students rose, shouted "Go Cornell," and when fans turned to them, displayed the second message.[75]

In the fall, as the architects realized that Rawlings would not allow them autonomy, a poll of all the AAP faculty revealed a clear preference for retaining the college. Franklin "Buzz" Spector, chair of the Art Department and the college's Committee on Realignment, assured members of the Faculty Senate that his colleagues now had a "sense of shared responsibility" around curriculum reform and the allocation of resources.[76]

The cascade of opposition from faculty, students, staff, and alumni apparently had an impact. In December 2002, Rawlings and Martin announced that they had decided not to recommend dissolving the college. They declared that AAP "will come under renewed scrutiny in order to enhance its intellectual unity within current budget constraints"[77] and created both an internal and external committee to develop a strategic plan, organized around the core concept of "design and the built environment." Budgetary authority was shifted from individual departments to the dean. And Day Hall went forward with a search for Olpadwala's successor.[78] Rawlings and Martin subsequently claimed that they never intended to disband AAP but merely to give the college, which was widely regarded as either ungoverned or ungovernable, a wake-up call. Although Olpadwala acknowledged that the problems of academic governance were substantive and serious, he labeled this claim "disingenuous"[79] and insisted that their "precipitous" move was "far too Draconian."[80]

In time, the dissolution genie was put back in the bottle. Finances became more stable, and AAP got a new building on the Arts quad. However, discussions about restructuring the college as a school of design continued.

On April, 28, 2003, the Cornell community saluted the departing President Rawlings. "It's enjoyable," Rawlings said, "to have people come up and say they've appreciated what I've done." At a dinner that evening in the Memorial Room at the Straight, his colleagues in Day Hall gave him a first edition of *The Papers of James Madison* and a nineteenth-century volume about Thucydides.[81] Rawlings's supporters—and his critics—agreed that he had strong opinions, set a bold path, stuck to it, even in the face of criticism, and turned ideas into realities. "Following Frank Rhodes was an almost impossible task and he succeeded in making the transition," Ronald Ehrenberg claimed. "He has a *Field of Dreams* type vision for running universities. He doesn't take resources as being an absolute constraint. He has the vision that if you propose a good idea, the resources will show up." In an "environment of needs," where "you can't be all things to all people," said Vice President Susan Murphy, '73, PhD '94, "one of Hunter's strengths is his willingness to make tough calls, but that sometimes has a downside. I wouldn't call him abrasive, personally, but I wouldn't disagree that there's a top-down leadership approach." His style was, at times, necessary, Murphy added, "because not all choices are win-win."[82]

After a semester-long leave of absence, Rawlings returned to Cornell in the spring of 2004 as a professor of classics and history. He had been accused by some, he joked, "of taking the comparatively simple and undemanding job of university president" so that he could get tenure in two Cornell departments.[83] Professor Rawlings taught a popular undergraduate class on Periclean Athens, which included a reenactment of the trial of Socrates; a graduate-level course, "Advanced Readings in Greek"; and a course for the History Department on classical influences on the American founding. When he wasn't in his office in Goldwin Smith, he could often be found in the Friedman Wrestling Center, the first arena in the nation built solely for the sport. Named for Stephen Friedman '59, a former CEO of Goldman Sachs and economics adviser to President George W. Bush, and Barbara Benioff Friedman '59, vice chair of the Cornell Board of Trustees, the fifteen-thousand-square-foot building, which held its first intercollegiate match in 2003, boasted state-of-the art training and weight rooms and an arena with eleven hundred seats. A knowledgeable and noisy fan, prone to leaping to his feet and pumping his fists, Rawlings did not hesitate to let referees know they had made a bad call.

AT A SPECIAL meeting held in Ithaca on December 14, 2002, the board of trustees appointed Jeffrey S. Lehman as Cornell's eleventh president. The search committee had sought a candidate "with passion to lead, passion to learn, and passion for Cornell," its chairman, Edwin Morgens '63, declared. "Jeffrey Lehman embodied all of those things." A native New Yorker, Lehman had received a BA in mathematics at Cornell, where his extracurricular activities included membership on the table tennis club team, cochairmanship of the concert commission that brought the Grateful Dead to campus, and coauthorship (with Jay Walker '77, the moderator during the "Ky incident" and founder of Priceline.com) of the book *1,000 Ways to Win Monopoly Games*. After completing a law degree and a master's in public policy from the University of Michigan, he served as a clerk for Supreme Court justice John Paul Stevens and practiced tax law in Washington, D.C., for four years before joining the faculty at the University of Michigan Law School in 1987. When he became dean seven years later, the *National Law Journal* deemed him one of forty "Rising Stars in the Law." As dean, Lehman gained national attention when he was named as a defendant in *Grutter v. Bollinger*, a case involving the law school's affirmative action policy in admissions, which was held to be constitutional by the U.S. Supreme Court in 2003. The first alumnus to serve as president of the university, Lehman declared that "Cornell has never been far from my heart. By the time you graduate, Cornell is in every cell of your being."[84]

To underscore his conviction that "great universities must continue to nurture a transnational perspective," Lehman scheduled a "triple inauguration," spanning five days and five thousand miles[85]—on October, 12, 2003, at the Doha, Qatar, campus of Weill Cornell Medical College, the first branch of an

Jeffrey S. Lehman, president of Cornell from 2003 to 2005. (Cornell University Photography)

American medical school ever established overseas; in New York City on October 15 at the Weill Cornell Medical College and the ILR offices on Thirty-Fourth Street; and, of course, in Ithaca. On the morning of October 16, at the Tompkins County Public Library, Lehman declared his intention to increase Cornell's annual contribution to the city and extend the memorandum of understanding to 2023. That afternoon at Barton Hall, after an introduction by U.S. Supreme Court justice Ruth Bader Ginsburg, Lehman invoked a "revolutionary" and a "beloved" Cornell in a beautifully crafted inaugural address. He compared the response of the Catholic Church to Copernicus's 1543 work, *On the Revolution of the Heavenly Spheres*, a copy of which Andrew D. White had contributed to Cornell's library, with the criticism of some Americans to the founding of Cornell, with its revolutionary ideas about coeducation, nonsectarianism, racial diversity, and equal respect for traditional, theoretical, and applied subjects. Citing another "intellectual treasure," the novel *Beloved*, by the Nobel laureate Toni Morrison, Lehman noted that a member of Cornell's first graduating class had written (during the period covered by the novel) "that we in undergraduate enthusiasm cry out" that Cornell is a success "if only for the fact that it has inspired love." In light of its tradition of innovation and its "legacy of devotion in the hearts and minds of those who studied here," Lehman concluded by asking Cornellians to consider "fundamental questions" about what "we think a beloved, revolutionary, truly superb, comprehensive research university should be offering to its students and to humanity."[86]

383

Inaugural revelers returned to Barton Hall after dinner for "Ezra and Andy's Big Red Adventure," a ninety-minute showcase of student ensembles. A few minutes into the festivities, a phone rang. "It's for you," Jacob Lehman '06 told his dad. The caller was NASA astronaut Ed Lu '84, speaking from the International Space Station some 240 miles above the Pacific Ocean while orbiting the earth at about seventeen thousand miles an hour.[87]

In November, Lehman formalized the "call to engagement" he had issued in his inaugural address. He invited Cornellians to send him ideas about how the university should evolve during the years leading up to its sesquicentennial in 2015. To help focus the discussion he posed a series of broad questions: What intellectual dispositions, character traits, and essential knowledge should Cornell nurture in its students? How might new technologies improve pedagogy? What mix of undergraduates, professional students, and graduate students is best for Cornell? How much further, where, and how should Cornell extend itself? What forms of extension and public service are necessary for a twenty-first-century version of Cornell's land grant mission? What institutional partnerships, domestic and international, would allow the university to accomplish things it cannot do alone? Are there special domains of research and emphasis where Cornell is especially well situated to make significant contributions? Finally, how might changes in organization help advance individual and institutional goals? Lehman promised to read all the responses himself, reflect on them, and develop concrete proposals within a year.[88]

In the meantime, the president acted on his goal of enhancing Cornell's national and international image. He removed Henrik Dullea and split the office of vice president for university relations into two units: Government and Community Relations, and Communications and Media Relations, charging the latter with updating the university's website and logo. The president and his university basked in the reflected glory of the near-perfect landing on Mars of the rover vehicle *Spirit* and its twin, *Opportunity*, in January 2004. Appearing on *ABC World News Tonight*, which named him "Person of the Week," Astronomy professor Steven Squyres '78, PhD '81, the principal science investigator for the mission, described how he fell in love with space exploration while he was a graduate student: "I went into the place at Cornell where they kept the pictures that the *Viking* orbiter was sending back from Mars at that time. . . . I came out of that room four hours later knowing exactly what I wanted to do with the rest of my life." After the ABC News segment aired, the *PBS NewsHour with Jim Lehrer* interviewed the Cornell astronomer James F. Bell, who led the panoramic camera team. Sharing the latest images from the "Pancams" and infrared data from the rover's Mini-TES instrument, Bell identified the hot spots and rocky cool spots on the red planet.[89]

That same month, Lehman congratulated Steven Tanksley, professor of plant breeding and chair of the Genomics Initiative Task Force, when he won the

Wolf Foundation Prize in Agriculture, one of the most prestigious scientific awards in the world, for his "innovative development of hybrid rice and discovery of the genetic basis of heterosis in this important food staple."[90] In February, he served as on-campus host to Bill Gates, the founder and CEO of Microsoft. In March, he met with the Chinese ambassador to the United States to discuss his own forthcoming trip to the People's Republic, where he planned to sign agreements with Peking University and Tsinghua University. And in April 2005, he would hail Professor Steven Stucky, MFA '73, DMA '78, who had been awarded the Pulitzer Prize for Music Composition for his *Second Concerto for Orchestra*.

In October 2004, after sifting through over one thousand pages of recommendations, which had been organized for him, chronologically and thematically, in two large loose-leaf notebooks, Lehman issued his "Reflections on the Call to Engagement," which included about twenty pages of summary and commentary, and unveiled his road map for the future in his State of the University Address to the board of trustees and Trustee Council. Characterizing the responses he received as "insightful, witty, and internally contradictory," Lehman maintained that their influence in crystallizing his thinking could not be overestimated.[91] In the next decade, he claimed, Cornell would face two special challenges: ensuring that students, regardless of family income, could attend the university without incurring a substantial burden of debt; and expanding its presence around the globe. As it emerged as a transnational university, still revolutionary and beloved, Lehman thought Cornell should address three great challenges facing humanity: "life in the age of the genome," "wisdom in the age of digital information," and "sustainability in the age of development," each of which would involve research not only in the sciences but also in economics, ethics, political science, and many other fields. "All of these areas are very big. They are very important and they require the marshaling of a lot of human and financial resources," Lehman concluded. And, at the same time, Cornell had to support "our core strength in every discipline on campus. That is a critical challenge."[92]

Less than eight months later, on June 11, 2005, Lehman listed some accomplishments of his administration—including a record year in fund-raising and a 17.4 percent increase in applications to the undergraduate colleges—in a State of the University Address to a Reunion audience of seven hundred Cornellians in a steamy Newman Arena in Bartels Hall. After summarizing the three challenges he had identified in the aftermath of the "Call to Engagement," Lehman stunned the crowd by declaring,

> But as encouraging as these signs are for Cornell's future, there is today an important obstacle to Cornell's ability to realize its full potential. Over the past few months, it has become apparent to me that the Board of Trustees and I have different approaches to how the University can best realize its long term vision. These

differences are profound, and it has become absolutely clear to me that they cannot be resolved. Imagine for a moment an airplane that is supposed to fly from New York to the beautiful island of Bali. It can get there by going east. Or it can get there by flying west. But even if the pilot and co-pilot are each highly skilled, even if they have the highest regard for one another, the plane will not reach the destination if they are unable to agree about which direction to take. Cornell University is meant to fly. Its pilot and co-pilot must agree on the strategic direction to be taken. Since I now understand that it is impossible for such an agreement to emerge as long as I am President, I have notified the Chairman of the Board, Peter Meinig, that I will step down as Cornell's eleventh president at the end of the month.

As the crowd gasped, Lehman emphasized that Cornell "had entered his soul and would never leave." He had served "with all the ability that was mine to offer," he said. "Thank you for giving me the opportunity to do so." Lehman left the stage to a standing ovation and exited the building. Meinig walked slowly to the podium, thanked Lehman for his work, announced that Hunter Rawlings, who was in the audience, had agreed to become Cornell's interim president, indicated that the board would appoint a committee to search for a new president very quickly, and led the singing of the alma mater.[93]

On campus and in cyberspace, speculation swirled over what caused the end of the shortest presidential term in Cornell's history. A non-disparagement clause in the separation agreement between the parties, the *Cornell Alumni Magazine* reported, barred Lehman and the trustees from specifying reasons for the decision. Nonetheless, in an article published in the fall of 2005, the magazine's staff indicated that "a clearer picture had emerged": the executive committee of the board and senior administrators in Day Hall had lost confidence in Lehman's judgment, leadership, and management skills. Some of them were troubled by what they perceived to be Lehman's undue emphasis on the university's transnational role and a travel schedule that prevented him from dealing with more pressing issues in Ithaca. There was disappointment as well about his inability to convert the "Call to Engagement" into a concrete plan of action. Lehman's "three themes," they indicated, had no real connection with the call; two of them repackaged Rawlings's initiatives, and "sustainability" was a vague concept, not clearly related to the priorities identified in Cornell's $3 billion capital campaign.[94]

There was deep concern as well over how Lehman managed the university and its personnel. When they appointed Lehman, the trustees had chosen a young man with great promise but without substantial experience managing a large, complex research university. "Jeff ran the law school very well at Michigan," board chair emeritus Stephen Weiss claimed, "but I don't think anyone would argue that that's a major administrative position." Many trustees came to believe that Lehman relied far too much on a small "kitchen cabinet" that included Barbara Krause, JD '86, and Kathy Okun, Lehman's wife. Lehman named Krause—who had previously served as Cornell's judicial administrator, associate university counsel, and then executive secretary of the Presidential Search Committee—as "senior advisor to the president." In response to criticism that Krause was undiplomatic and ineffective, he reduced her role in April 2005. Okun, a former associate vice president for development at Michigan, became "senior university advisor" at Cornell when Lehman became president. Although her portfolio focused primarily on faculty recruiting and community relations, Okun did not hesitate to weigh in on other matters at senior staff meetings. Inge Reichenbach, the highly regarded vice president for alumni affairs and development, was especially uncomfortable with Okun's interventions and her influence. Lehman, however, was not receptive to suggestions that Okun's role be clarified. In April 2005, Reichenbach resigned to accept a position at Yale. According to the *Alumni Magazine* it was "a defining moment" in the deteriorating relationship between the president and the trustees.[95]

Not surprising, instant assessments of Lehman's resignation and legacy ran the gamut. "There was genuine intellectual engagement with the faculty," Dean of the Faculty Charles Walcott, PhD '59, observed. Rolf Frantz '66, MEN '67, president of the Cornell Alumni Federation, pointed out that many alumni "appreciated being invited to share their thoughts, opinions, and suggestions" in the "Call to Engagement." The president "asked a lot of good questions and you could tell he was really trying to make the effort to learn more," student-elected trustee Douglas Mitarotonda '02, MEN '03, PhD '09, declared. Alex Shapero '06 was impressed when Lehman showed up at a Latin-Israeli dance practice and "put more energy in it than I could have." There were naysayers as well, of course. Former *Cornell Daily Sun* editor Andrew Guess '05 concluded that Lehman was "a lovable dork" who failed to follow through on "the big ideas" in his "grandiose speeches." As he often did, Stephen Weiss made the most balanced assessment: "Jeff worked very hard, he loved the place, and he did a lot of good things. . . . I don't think this is a good/ bad guy situation, but one where the chemistry didn't work for a lot of reasons."[96]

Lehman spent 2005–6 as a senior scholar at the Woodrow Wilson Center in Washington, D.C. He subsequently served as the founding dean of the Peking University School of Transnational Law in Shenzhen, China, and in 2012 was named the vice chancellor and CEO of New York University Shanghai.

——————

As INTERIM PRESIDENT for the 2005–6 academic year, Hunter Rawlings tried to "ensure that the capital campaign gains momentum," academic priorities "move along briskly," the deans "continue with their initiatives," and students are "well-served in their education."[97] Determined to keep the West Campus initiative on schedule, he sustained President Lehman's decision to authorize the construction of a parking lot on a site environmental activists called Redbud Woods. And in what was probably the most notable achievement of his interim presidency, he departed from the practice of presidents at Cornell and other institutions of higher education and addressed a politically controversial topic in his State of the University Address. On October 21, 2005, at the Statler Auditorium, Rawlings dissected "the challenge to science posed by religiously based opposition to evolution." A surrogate for creationism, Rawlings declared, "intelligent design" was, "at its core, a religious belief" and therefore did not deserve a place in the curriculum. He called on humanists, social scientists, and scientists at the university to help the public understand this issue, and to "speak out, frequently and forcefully," in the great tradition of Ezra Cornell, Andrew D. White, and Cornell's land grant mission.[98]

Declaring January 21, 2006, "a terribly, terribly exciting day," Peter Meinig told a press conference at the Beck Center of Statler Hall that David J. Skorton had been appointed the twelfth president of Cornell, professor of biomedical engineering in Ithaca, and professor of pediatrics and internal medicine at Weill Cornell in New York City.[99] Skorton was the second medical doctor to be president of Cornell; Livingston Farrand (1921–37) was the first. The son of a Belarusian immigrant to the United States who sold shoes, Skorton was the first member of his family to complete college, enrolling first at UCLA and then completing his undergraduate and MD degrees at Northwestern. A pediatric cardiologist and researcher in cardiac imaging and computer image processing, he was hired as an instructor at the University of Iowa in 1980, rose through the faculty ranks, and was cofounder and codirector of the Adolescent and Adult Congenital Heart Disease Clinic. In 1992 he was appointed by Hunter Rawlings as Iowa's vice president for research, and later added the duties of vice president for external relations. Skorton was named president of the University of Iowa in 2003. Declining to relinquish his clinical practice, he continued to see patients while he was an administrator. In his "free time," the *Cornell Daily Sun* revealed, he played the flute and jazz saxophone, and cohosted a jazz program on the National Public Radio station in Iowa City. An early adopter of Facebook, he had over forty-three hundred "friends" at Iowa.[100]

David Skorton's inauguration was held outdoors on a stage installed in front of the statue of Ezra Cornell on the Arts quad on September 7, 2006. In his self-deprecatory inaugural address, which used dance as a unifying motif and was punctuated three times by musical selections, Skorton emphasized the importance of the creative arts in a university dominated by the sciences and engineering, downplayed the role of the president, and set priorities designed to ensure continuity with the visions of his predecessors.

Skorton's five priorities struck familiar chords. He promised to build on the North Campus and West Campus initiatives to "achieve our goal of making Cornell the finest research university and provider of undergraduate education

David J. Skorton became Cornell's twelfth president in 2006. (Cornell University Photography)

in the world." He pledged to improve the environment for the staff by promoting professional development, work-life balance, employee diversity, and opportunities for dual-career couples. He hoped to "draw the disparate geography" of Cornell's colleges and campuses "into one community." He vowed to "appropriately support the arts, humanities and social sciences." Drawing "inspiration and resolve" from Cornell's land grant mission, he indicated that he would use the institution's "enormous and varied resources and talents to positively impact the world outside our gates." To that end, he announced the establishment of the Jeffrey Sean Lehman Fund for Scholarly Exchange with China and asked the former president to stand and receive the applause that followed. "We must set our collective vision such that there will never be a boundary to where our imagination may wander, nor artificial limits to what we may accomplish," Skorton concluded. "One alone, a dyad, more, many, a society of dancers are we."[101]

During Skorton's tenure, Cornell experienced the best of times and the worst of times. The university weathered one of the most challenging financial crises in its history—and won a competition, sponsored by Mayor Michael Bloomberg, to establish a tech campus in New York City. In March 2014, Skorton announced that he would leave the presidency on June 30, 2015, following the celebrations of Cornell's Sesquicentennial, to become Secretary of the Smithsonian Institution in Washington, D.C.

THE SKORTON ADMINISTRATION got off to an auspicious start. In August 2006, the president and his wife, Robin Davisson, professor of biomedical sciences, lived in a faculty residence suite in the freshman dorm Mary Donlon for a few days to get to know members of the class of 2010. In September, in his first full address to the Cornell staff, Skorton shared his e-mail address, noted that Cornell had been named one of the top one hundred employers for parents in the United States, and promised to address concerns about compensation and benefits. A year later, the university broke ground, just north of the "A" parking lot on Pleasant Grove Road, on a new child care center, with capacity for 158 children, ages six weeks to five years, of staff, faculty, and students. And Skorton reached out to faculty, in dozens of meetings. "With Skorton," Mohsen Mostafavi, dean of Architecture, Art, and Planning, told reporters, "there isn't a split between the sciences and the humanities. With his interests in music and language, he'll be able to mediate between all the various realms at Cornell." Nonetheless, Mostafavi cautioned that the atmosphere of optimism was to be expected so early in a presidency.[102]

In October 2006, Cornell kicked off a $4 billion capital campaign for the Ithaca campus and Weill Cornell Medical College. Taking the name "Far Above . . . The Campaign for Cornell," the fund-raising drive focused on three priorities: recruiting and retaining the next generation of faculty (to replace at least six hundred professors expected to retire in the next decade); building state-of-the-art facilities; and ensuring that all accepted students, regardless of the financial circumstances of their families, could attend Cornell without incurring an inordinate amount of debt. A year later, in October 2007, Cornell was ahead of schedule. In the 2006–7 fiscal year, the university raised $754.8 million in new gifts and commitments, about $300 million directed to the Ithaca campus and the balance to Weill Cornell. Gifts to the Cornell Annual Fund reached record levels as well, at $18.4 million, a 29 percent increase over the previous year. Acknowledging that fund-raising usually slows down as campaigns progress, Charles Phlegar, vice president for alumni affairs and development, predicted that this one would be different: as "key donors" spent time with Skorton, heard about his ideas, and shared his enthusiasm, "I think it will get easier in this campaign, not harder."[103]

With the expectation that the campaign would reach (or exceed) its goals, the building boom continued. In September 2007, construction began on a new physical sciences building on East Avenue between Rockefeller Hall and Baker Lab. With eighty laboratories, a 120-seat auditorium, buffered, noise-free, vibration-proof rooms in the basement (to develop instruments for atomic-scale fabrication and manipulation and tools to explore the structure of molecules, materials, and cells), an atrium, a café, an exquisite view of Cayuga Lake, and various niches and nooks, the building, proclaimed architects for the

Boston–based firm Koetter, Kim & Associates, would encourage planned collaboration in biophysics, microscopy, and nanobiotechnology and "the serendipity of informal intellectual collisions."[104]

In 2008, Cornell broke ground on a new Animal Health Diagnostic Center. A partnership between the New York State Department of Agriculture and Markets and the College of Veterinary Medicine, the 125,000–square–foot facility was funded by a $56 million grant from New York State and $24 million from Cornell and other sources. To improve the health of animals that produce food and fiber, and of companion animals and wildlife, the facility made possible the rapid diagnosis and control of infectious diseases and zoonotic diseases, like avian flu and West Nile virus, that migrate from animals to humans. AHDC, said Michael Kotlikoff, dean of the Vet School, "will continue to inspire 21st century discovery, strengthen our ability to successfully respond to emergencies and protect the animals and citizens of New York State."[105]

The dedication ceremonies for Weill Hall on October 16, 2008, marked a milestone for the New Life Sciences Initiative. Named for Sanford I. Weill '55, chairman emeritus of Citigroup Inc., and Joan Weill, the 265,000–square–foot building, which cost $162 million, was one of the largest research facilities in New York State. Working closely with faculty planners, architect Richard Meier '56 facilitated multidisciplinary collaboration by arranging overlapping laboratories, not separated by walls, in long, open, sunlit spaces along the length of each floor of the south wing and one floor of the north wing. Equipped with microscopes, centrifuges, freezers, mixers, cold rooms, dark rooms for processing films for experiments using radioactive stains, and the latest videoconferencing technology, Weill provided office space, support rooms, and an atrium as well, for researchers in the departments of Biomedical Engineering, Biological Statistics and Computational Biology, the Division of Nutritional Sciences,

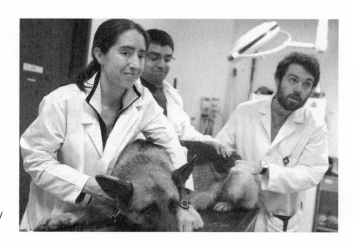

A patient at the Animal Health Diagnostic Center. (Cornell University Photography)

and affiliates of the Center for Venture Development in the Life Sciences. Filling Weill Hall's south wing was the Weill Institute for Cell and Molecular Biology. Under the direction of Professor Scott Emr, ICMB focused on understanding how cells work, through signaling, member trafficking, and the movement of proteins across cellular membranes (the area in which Emr developed his influential "yeast cell model"), and how cells are shaped and internally organized. Weill Hall faculty had already begun interacting with their counterparts at Weill Cornell Medical College with annual symposia, meetings on topics of mutual interest, and jointly conducted studies of the role of small strokes in the onset of Alzheimer's disease and the development of laser-based therapy for epilepsy. Cornell wanted to nurture "innovation and creativity that we didn't think about ten years ago," Stephen Kresovich, vice provost for the life sciences, pointed out. "In the long run, we'll be measured by how that building, as a keystone, impacts life sciences at Cornell."[106]

Although "big science" got the big-ticket buildings, several facilities for the arts, humanities, and social sciences were built. Construction began in 2008 to replace Human Ecology's North Martha Van Rensselaer Hall, which had been closed in 2001 because of structural deficiencies and demolished in 2006. And the Herbert F. Johnson Museum of Art broke ground in May 2008 for a $20 million, sixteen-thousand-square-foot addition to architect I.M. Pei's distinctive structure, with its marvelous views of Cayuga Lake, located on University and Central Avenues. The project was the last major initiative of Frank Robinson, the director of the museum, who had vastly increased community outreach and worked closely with faculty members to integrate exhibits with the courses they offered. Largely sited underground, and adorned by a Japanese garden, the addition contained a 150-seat auditorium, a workshop studio, new galleries, and storage and office space. Renovations to the existing building created additional room on the fifth floor, making possible exhibitions featuring additional works of African, pre-Columbian, Asian, and decorative art.

As buildings went up in the statutory and endowed colleges, Cornell also resolved its relationship with SUNY after decades of contention. In 2009, the governor's executive budget proposal for higher education included a provision prohibiting SUNY from reallocating funds directed to Cornell's statutory units to other colleges within the system. The provision was included in each subsequent budget, and the Cornell proportion of the SUNY budget was not challenged.

Cornell also committed substantial resources during these years to financial aid. In January 2008, Provost Martin announced that within two years the university would eliminate need-based loans for undergraduates from families whose income was below $75,000 and cap them at $3,000 per year for students from families with incomes between $75,000 and $120,000. Skorton praised the initiative, which was expected to affect about forty-five hundred students, as appropriate and necessary for what he called "the original opportunity university" (which made work-study part of its fundamental philosophy, awarded need-based grants as early as 1879, and established its first endowed scholarship fund in 1892). As it strengthened the mission laid out by Ezra Cornell, the program, Skorton wrote, would provide "a superb liberal education across the full range of disciplines to the best and brightest students from all walks of life, regardless of their resources." Making Cornell more economically diverse, it also freed students to choose majors—and careers—that matched their interests and aptitudes rather than those likely to help them repay their loans. Cornell administrators estimated that when fully implemented, the new program would add an additional $14 million per year to the $117 million of the university's resources already being spent on undergraduate financial aid. They promised as well to review "this program on an annual basis to make sure our actions keep pace with changes in family incomes. We will also evaluate the size of the family contribution we require from students from our neediest families."[107]

As Cornell made these commitments, and many others, and took on debt to see them through, the United States was entering its worst economic crisis since the Great Depression of the 1930s. The meltdown was triggered by a complex and interrelated array of policies, including easy access to home loans, the overvaluing of bundled sub-prime mortgages by rating agencies, the use of high-risk alternative investment instruments, the failure of financial institutions to retain sufficient capital to back the commitments they made, and ineffective government regulation. The crisis reached its most critical stage in September 2008, when, following the bankruptcy of Lehman Brothers, $144 billion was withdrawn from money markets in one week (compared with $7 billion in the previous seven days), and the Bush administration proposed a $700 billion bailout of financial institutions. The U.S. stock market plunged, with the Dow Jones Industrial Average dropping from a high of over 14,000 in 2007 to 6,600 in March 2009. In the fourth quarter of 2008 and the first quarter of 2009, the output of goods and services in the United States decreased at an annual rate of 6 percent. Unemployment skyrocketed to over 10 percent in 2009.

The Great Recession had a profound impact on Cornell. "We were overleveraged," Skorton subsequently acknowledged. "We built buildings like crazy." To lock in relatively high interest rates on its bond holdings, moreover, Cornell used derivatives known as forward swaps, a strategy that backfired when the financial bubble burst, with the university forced to pay millions in termination fees to unwind agreements.[108] And a 26 percent, $1.5 billion decline in the endowment in the 2008–9 fiscal year left an $80 million hole in the operating budget for 2009–10. If the university failed to take corrective action, President Skorton revealed early in 2009, the perfect storm—significant reductions in New York State appropriations, federal research funding, philanthropy, endowment income, and short-term investments—would produce an annual deficit on the Ithaca campus of about $215 million (about 10 percent of the operating budget) by 2014.

"As part of an overall management philosophy that will require us to live within our means," Skorton announced, the university would cut annual budgets by 5 percent and suspend the Salary Improvement Program for faculty and staff in 2009–10. He eliminated the position of executive vice president for finance and administration and canceled many faculty searches, while banning the hiring of nonacademic staff from outside the institution so that open positions would be filled by those whose jobs had been eliminated. Skorton mandated a construction pause and took $175 million from reserve accounts throughout the campus ($43 million in the colleges and $132 million in the central administration). He paid down lines of credit, reduced the payout from the endowment yet further to approximate the earning power of the long-term investment pool, and moved significant sums of money into more liquid investments. The board of trustees, the president indicated, had also agreed to sell $500 million of taxable bonds to supply additional working capital and withdraw $35 million a year for five years to help pay for need-based financial aid for undergraduates.[109]

To "identify our aspirations for the future and plan for a leaner and stronger institution," Skorton and Kent Fuchs (the former dean of Engineering, who became provost in January 2009, after Biddy Martin was appointed chancellor of the University of Wisconsin–Madison) called for university-wide planning, led by the vice presidents and deans, with input from the Student Assembly, the Graduate and Professional Student Assembly, the Faculty Senate, and the Employee Assembly, in a process they called "Reimagining Cornell."[110] To help improve administrative functions, Cornell hired Bain & Company, a consulting firm. To make recommendations on academic programs, Fuchs appointed task forces in each college and multidisciplinary committees for broad areas such as the life sciences and social sciences. An all-faculty strategic planning task force, chaired by Edward J. Lawler, former dean of ILR, was asked to identify institutional priorities and find ways to enhance the core mission of teaching, research, and engagement in an era of scarce resources. And Fuchs introduced a new budget model, designed to make the revenues and expenses of academic and administrative units more transparent.

In appearances throughout the campus, Skorton tried to be candid, optimistic, and reassuring. At an employee forum, which drew well over two hundred people, he maintained that "everything is on the table," pledged that protecting jobs was his highest priority and that Cornell would not "take a meat cleaver" to benefits. "I know you're picking up the slack," he said. "We cannot continue to go forward just by telling everyone that you're going to work more and work harder, stay later, skip your lunch hour." At a forum attended by about two hundred faculty members, Skorton indicated that balancing the budget meant that Cornell "can again pursue the initiatives, hiring and projects that we want to—reaching our aspirations without concern that one more aspiration will require the decrease of spending or activity in another area." Although only a dozen individuals showed up at a student forum, Skorton declared "Your engagement is critical. This is not fluff."[111]

In 2009, Cornell offered a one-time-only retirement package to members of the staff age fifty-five or older with at least ten years of service to the university. The incentives included a lump-sum payment, based on the employee's base salary, and an enhanced contribution to the individual's retirement program. By the June 30 deadline, 432 staff members—about a third of those who were eligible, and many more than the administration had anticipated—elected to accept the Staff Retirement Incentive. Mary Opperman, vice president for human resources, pointed out that some of them took the option because they feared they might lose their jobs. SRI actually helped minimize layoffs, Opperman added, although "these might not have been the people or positions we would have chosen." Because about three-quarters of the retiring staff were not replaced, the program saved Cornell about $25 million in annual payroll. A smaller number of employees opted for the phased retirement program, which allowed anyone currently working at least thirty hours a week to cut back to twenty hours for up to three years before retiring. With these retirements and several hundred layoffs, Cornell reduced its workforce by about 7–8 percent by 2010.[112]

The administration was less successful in implementing the cost-cutting recommendations of the consultants at Bain. To be sure, some operations, including the *Cornell Chronicle*, which ended the print version of its publication, went paperless. Resistance throughout the university to the general idea and the means used to implement it, however, largely thwarted efforts to centralize the purchasing of goods and services, ranging from lab equipment, office furniture, and computers to car rentals and hotel bookings, to increase leverage with vendors. The university also did not meet Bain targets in reducing the number of "spans and layers" separating supervisors and those who reported to them.

To bring in more revenue, Skorton, Fuchs, the deans, and the board of trustees agreed to increase tuition substantially more than the rate of inflation for all undergraduates and even more steeply for non–New York State residents enrolled in the statutory colleges. They decided, however, not to expand undergraduate enrollments beyond the unanticipated addition of one hundred freshmen in the fall of 2009. "If you have to invest in new facilities to provide for the students, you're losing money," Fuchs noted. "We also must carefully consider the impact on faculty research and scholarship and on the quality of education."[113]

"The situation is grave," Fuchs told the Faculty Senate in February 2009. "If we do nothing, this institution is at great risk."[114] Therefore, in 2009–10, the size of the faculty, including non-tenure-track teaching staff, which had not increased during the preceding decade, would go down. Although he embraced Ezra Cornell's vision of a university accessible to everyone and broad in its offerings, Fuchs claimed that the economic crisis "has made us face the following question: should we have an institution where our investment is spread thin or where it is deep?" When resources are constrained, "we may have to stop doing things. We should probably end a few programs, close some centers and merge some departments to create more focus and visibility."[115] For about three years, Fuchs predicted, Cornell would tighten its belt and reduce expenditures. "Then we'll come out of this refocused with a set of strategic priorities in which we will invest."[116]

In 2009–10, many academic units faced tough choices. The Cornell University Library (CUL) system, with eighteen units scattered around the campus, completing over one million transactions a year, and with interlibrary loan requests up sharply, retained its top spot for student satisfaction among campus services and facilities. Asked to shave 10 percent from its $44 million budget, university librarian Anne Kenney had to decide whether CUL could remain one of the top ten university libraries in the United States or close some of its branches, because "it can't do both." In the short term, as its collections budget failed to keep pace with its competitors, CUL fell in the national rankings, and Kenney postponed an extensive renovation of Olin Library and presided over staff reductions and library consolidations and closings. Asserting to somewhat skeptical faculty that "maintaining a significant number of physical facilities in an increasingly digital world bleeds our ability to provide critical scholarly resources," Kenney presided over a shift of books and periodicals from the Hotel School and the Johnson School to the ILR Library.[117] At the end of 2009, the Engineering Library and the Physical Sciences Library shut their doors as well. Heavily used collections were stored in adjacent libraries; lesser-used materials were transferred to the annex near the Apple Orchards, where they could be retrieved in twenty-four hours; and subject specialists continued to offer assistance to users, as well as support for electronic resources. Leah Solla, coordinator of the Physical Sciences Library at Clark Hall, promised that she and her colleagues "will flex, reach out in many directions and think well beyond the traditional branch library . . . to support the evolving research environment for the 21st century."[118]

Although she pointed out that the libraries acquired more than one hundred thousand books each year, requiring about two miles of shelves to house them, Kenney assured proponents of browsing in the stacks (and the serendipitous discoveries they associated with it) that Olin, Kroch, and Uris libraries would contain at least the same number of volumes as they currently did throughout her tenure. At the same time, operating on the premise that access to books was far more important than ownership of them, Cornell and Columbia University agreed to coordinate collection development and share the services of expert librarians and cataloguers. Starting in 2011, students and faculty could register for library cards, check out circulating material in either institution, and enjoy expedited delivery. With only a 35 percent duplication rate in the holdings of the libraries at the two universities, access to hitherto unavailable items grew substantially.

CUL also moved aggressively into the digital world. By 2011, digital services and publications accounted for about 60 percent of the library's $16 million collections budget. About five million articles were downloaded from CUL's digital subscriptions, and its "virtual library" saw ten million visits. Among the scholarly information systems managed by the library was arXiv.org (pronounced "archive"), a service founded in the 1990s by Paul Ginsparg, PhD '81, when he was at Los Alamos National Laboratory, a decade before he returned to Cornell as professor of physics and information science. The service facilitated the posting of "pre-prints" of research papers, not subject to peer review, in mathematics, astrophysics, computer science, and biology and statistics as "e-prints," available to anyone anywhere in the world with an Internet connection. Run on three servers in Rhodes Hall and fifteen sites around the world, arXiv.org stored more than 770,000 papers and provided ways to search, mine data, and detect plagiarism. In 2011, over seventy-five thousand papers were submitted to "archive," and more than seventy million articles were downloaded. Kenney remained quite concerned that her acquisitions budget for "traditional" materials was small compared with those of Cornell's peers, but she insisted that "digital access doesn't threaten library services or spaces, it just gives us new avenues to reach users."[119]

While CUL consolidated and closed libraries, the College of Agriculture and Life Sciences consolidated and closed departments in agricultural sciences in part, critics said, to accommodate growth in Agricultural Economics and Management. CALS integrated academic units in Food Science, Plant Pathology and Plant Microbe Biology, Horticulture, and Entomology at the New York State Agricultural Experiment Station in Geneva, with those in Ithaca. In 2011, the college began consolidating five departments—Horticulture, Crop and Soil Sciences, Plant Breeding and Genetics, Microbiology and Plant Biology, and Plant Pathology—each of which was consistently ranked within the top ten in its field, into larger academic units. The reorganized Plant Sciences program, in which faculty shared support staff to maximize efficiency, struck a balance between foundational, translational, and applied sciences, encouraged collaboration, coordinated the teaching of undergraduates and graduate students, and maintained extension outreach and international agricultural development initiatives.

Even more consequential was the announcement of CALS dean (and professor of food science) Kathryn Boor '80 in 2010 that the Department of Education, a part of the college for decades, would be shut down. Noting that the department was small relative to its peers at other institutions, Boor indicated that she had "come to the difficult conclusion that we do not have the resources that would need to be invested in the program to ensure its preeminence as we move into the future." The process was phased in over two years to permit students to complete their degrees. The eleven faculty members in Education were relocated to social science departments as closely aligned with their areas of expertise as possible. Eight administrative staff and six academic staff members received assistance in getting jobs within the college. Extension and outreach programs, including Agricultural Outreach and Education and the Community Learning and Service Partnership, were incorporated into other departments. CALS renewed its commitment to agricultural science education, a popular program, and promised to investigate possible partnerships with SUNY colleges to allow Cornell students to obtain teacher certification in science, technology, engineering, and mathematics.[120]

Like the other colleges at Cornell, Arts and Sciences made cuts here and there, postponing searches and reducing the number of teaching assistants and appropriations for travel and entertainment. But A&S implemented some permanent changes as well. In 2010, despite the strenuous objection of faculty in the department, the college eliminated funding for postdoctoral students and visiting professors who taught introductory mathematics courses, dramatically increasing the size of classes. The college merged the Russian Literature Department with Comparative Literature and ended instruction in Dutch, Modern Greek, Turkish, Quechua, Swedish, and English for Academic Purposes (for foreign students) as well. In 2011, faced with massive reductions in U.S. Department of Education Title VI funding for less frequently taught languages—Burmese, Tagalog, Indonesian, Khmer, Vietnamese, Thai, Bengali, Nepali, Hindi, Farsi, and Sinhala—Provost Fuchs provided temporary support, and the college used a $1.2 million grant from the Andrew Mellon Foundation to expand partnerships with Columbia and Yale to provide videoconferencing courses in some of these languages. "The obvious move for institutions is to try to pool students because it's hard to have a financial model that only supports a handful of students taking them," Arts and Sciences dean (and professor of physics) Peter Lepage indicated. "I don't know if that'll solve the problem, but I suspect it'll be more and more a part of the future."[121]

Having concluded that across-the-board cuts would not promote excellence, Lepage targeted "departments that have unusually large expenditures falling outside their professorial budgets" and told Theater, Film, and Dance to plan for a budget reduction of about $1 million.[122] Declaring that they had no choice, a majority of faculty in the department voted to shift from the current regional theater model, which offered six high-quality productions each year, often with Equity actors (who also taught introductory courses) in leading roles, to a far less expensive student-driven performance model. Theater, Film, and Dance eliminated its cutter/draper, audience services manager, scenic artist, master carpenter, box office manager, master electrician, and stage manager. "We have a running joke in the Theater Department," said Brendan Komala, the master carpenter. "We've been re-imagined."[123] "Everything will now be related to coursework or theory and divorced from practice," Professor (and director) Bruce Levitt declared. Many of his colleagues, he implied, were not unhappy to have it that way. In 2011, the department stopped offering a major in dance and eliminated nontenured instructors. A year later, the department, which was "looking not just to stay abreast of trends in our discipline but to forge them," changed its name to Performing and Media Arts, offered a single major, and emphasized the study of digital arts, mass media, and body-technology convergences.[124]

Along with reductions in staff and restructuring in the colleges, Cornell scaled back on its expenditures for financial aid. In many respects, the 2008 financial aid initiatives were a success. In 2011, 34 percent of undergraduates borrowed money during the academic year, down from 43 percent four years earlier. The average cumulative debt from student loans at graduation decreased as well, from $23,936 for 2007 graduates to $19,180 for 2011 graduates. The cost of the initiative, however, was substantial. Cornell, larger than its Ivy League competitors, had a higher percentage of students receiving assistance (51 percent) and a much smaller per capita endowment. In fiscal year 2011, the university's total grant aid expenditure reached $204 million, a 64 percent increase (about $31 million a year) since 2008. With appropriations from the state and federal governments relatively flat, about 80 percent of need-based financial aid came from university resources, most of it from the annual operating budget.

The growth resulted from a 21 percent rise in the number of grant-assisted students (the Great Recession made more students eligible for aid), a 55 percent increase in average grants, and a 19 percent increase in tuition and fees, along with a 13 percent increase in room and board (which also made more students eligible). Adding to the costs was a policy instituted in 2010, in part to help Cornell recruit varsity athletes, to match the financial aid offers made to any applicant by other Ivy League universities and peer institutions. There was growing sentiment as well to provide some financial aid to highly qualified foreign students. In April 2012, an Undergraduate Financial Aid Task Force, chaired by Vice Provost and Dean of the Graduate School Barbara Knuth, whose portfolio included admissions and financial aid, concluded that the current policies were unsustainable: "leaving this issue unaddressed will significantly hinder the University's ability to address other academic priorities including faculty renewal."[125]

That summer, Cornell reaffirmed its long-standing commitment to remain one of the few institutions in the United States to offer need-blind admissions and need-based aid—and adjusted its financial aid policies. The packages for students with family incomes below $60,000 would not change. Beginning with undergraduates matriculating in the fall of 2013, however, individuals with family incomes between $60,000 and $75,000 would have loan expectations, which were capped at $2,500 a year. Men and women from families whose income ranged from $75,000 to $120,000 would be asked to take on loans no greater than $5,000 a year. Cornell also raised its expectations for work done by aid recipients during the academic year, which had not changed for two decades, from $2,000 to $2,500. Noting that the adjustments were in line with those made by several of Cornell's peers, Provost Fuchs declared that "the entire academic community benefits from our ability to enroll a talented and diverse student body, while ensuring that their choices after graduation are not constrained by debt." The revised policy, which saved about $20 million a year when fully implemented, "sustained that promise into the future" in ways that were "not only durable but enduring," while making it possible for Cornell to meet "other top priorities at the same time."[126] President Skorton agreed. He himself had "borrowed much more money than we're asking students to borrow," he noted, taking twenty-one years to pay off his loans. Skorton wanted to make a promise to future generations "that my successors can keep: that we have a sustainable commitment to need-blind admission and need-based financial aid."[127]

CORNELL RECOVERED FROM the Great Recession, albeit slowly. To be sure, Moody's Investors Service, a major credit-rating agency, warned in 2012 that Cornell faced a "higher amount of debt and thinner operating cash flow" than its Ivy League peers, should expect declines in government funding, and might not be able to continue hiking tuition to generate revenue.[128] Despite these challenges, the university was on track to balance its books well before 2015. "There isn't as much urgency to cut back," claimed Max Pfeffer, professor of development sociology and senior associate dean in the College of Agriculture and Life Sciences. "People are learning to live within the budget we have now."[129] In his State of the University Address in October 2011, Skorton declared that Cornell now had "resources to recruit hundreds of new faculty, stabilize our superb staff workforce, continue our commitment to need-based student financial aid, and think deeply, clearly and creatively about who we are and what we can become."[130]

Skorton did not believe, however, that Cornell had sufficient resources to substantially increase its annual voluntary contribution to the financially strapped City of Ithaca. And so, town-gown tensions, which were never far from the surface, returned. In response to a question at a public meeting on the city's budget on October 1, 2013, Svante Myrick '09, one of the youngest mayors in American history, complained that while "Cornell is thriving and booming and we're struggling," the university, as measured by dollars spent for its host city, per endowment and per resident, "is dead last to all the schools that it compares itself to and competes with." Acknowledging that Ithaca had little leverage in negotiations with President Skorton, Myrick vowed to "work hard" to convince him that "an increased contribution is in Cornell's best interest."[131] In response, the university deplored "us versus them charges and characterizations," insisting that its contributions to the city and the Ithaca City School District compared favorably to those of its peers. It emphasized its enormous positive impact on the local economy and quality of life, while agreeing to work collaboratively with the mayor on "mutually beneficial solutions to difficult problems."[132] For the city and its university, it appeared, the more things changed the more they remained the same.

In 2011, Cornell resumed its campaign to replace its faculty, half of whom were above the age of fifty-five, with a new generation of world-class scholars and teachers. "If you ask almost any professor," asserted Joseph Burns, PhD '66, professor of mechanical engineering and astronomy and dean of the faculty, "they would much rather have better colleagues than better buildings."[133] Just as it was getting started, the $100 million faculty renewal initiative, half of which was to come from donors, had been stopped in its tracks by the Great Recession. The Ithaca campus had about sixteen hundred professors, a number that had not changed since 1982, despite significant increases in undergraduate and graduate enrollments and in staff headcounts during the same period. Given financial constraints, it was not likely to grow in the foreseeable future. Failing even to keep pace with retirements, moreover, Cornell made only forty-two tenure-track appointments in 2009–10, and a mere twenty-seven the next year. In 2011–12, the number jumped to seventy-one, and subsequently remained at that level or higher. With other universities facing the same demographic realities, the market for the most talented professors was extraordinarily competitive.

Cornell was on the way toward achieving its aspiration to be widely recognized as a top-ten research university, Skorton emphasized. According to Academic Analytics, a higher-education research organization, Cornell had forty-seven programs (not counting those at Weill Cornell Medical College) ranked in the top ten of their disciplines in 2012, more than any other university. To stay there, Cornell had to recruit and retain "exceptional faculty who discover, create, innovate, transform individual lives, and change the world for the better." So far, Skorton indicated, the university had been successful "in attracting rising stars as well as senior level colleagues."[134]

As the Great Recession lifted, members of the faculty, old and new, did create multidisciplinary, multi-college academic programs. In 2011, professors of economics in five colleges joined a single department. An outgrowth of one of Provost Fuchs's task forces, the new department, according to Policy Analysis and Management professor Donald Kenkel, was designed to give the field greater visibility and recognition, and counter perceptions among Cornell's peers that a "critical mass didn't seem to be there" and the reality that "the whole was less than the sum of its parts."[135] The integrated department, which existed alongside departments in Arts and Sciences, Agriculture and Life Sciences, Human Ecology, ILR, and the Johnson Graduate School of Management, had the ability to coordinate the hiring of faculty, build on strength in labor economics, focus on emerging areas in computer science and economics and behavioral economics, and provide better education to majors (20 percent of students in A&S majored in economics, and all nine hundred ILR students took labor economics courses) and all undergraduates, five thousand of whom took at least one course in economics each year.

The new Economics Department had its own office and staff, responsible (along with professors) for advising students about course choices and career planning, fostering a sense of community, and creating a website and an alumni network. Concerned that 36 percent of undergraduate majors in the class of 2012 did not have a single economics course with fewer than fifty students in it, the department planned a seminar-like "capstone experience" and small courses for no more than thirty seniors on, for example, "Bank Management and Regulation" and "The Economic Analysis of Politics." Large lecture courses included "Networks, Crowds and Markets: Reasoning about a Highly Connected World," taught by professor of economics David Easley and Jon Kleinberg '93, professor of computer science and winner of the MacArthur "genius" Award, and "Why People Earn What They Earn and What You Can Do Now to Make More," taught by ILR professor Kevin Hallock. "We believe we should have a top 10 Economics Department," Senior Vice Provost Ronald Seeber said. "The better we are perceived, the better students we'll attract, the better faculty we'll attract—it's a spiral upward."[136]

Economics had already gotten a boost in 2010 when John Dyson '65 (the commissioner of commerce who developed the "I Love New York" campaign in the 1970s, deputy mayor of New York City under Rudolph Giuliani, and founder and chairman of Millbrook Capital Management) and his three siblings honored their father by giving $25 million to establish the Charles H. Dyson School of Applied Economics and Management in the College of Agriculture and Life Sciences. With about seven hundred undergraduate majors, ninety graduate students, and fifty faculty members, the Dyson School (formerly the Department of Applied Economics and Management) was ranked near the top of undergraduate business programs in the United States. Noting that he used skills from his accounting classes at Cornell every day, John Dyson declared that "most business schools are too theoretical. They do not have the breadth of framing and grounding in reality that Cornell has had for 100 years."[137]

The university's most ambitious academic initiative in these years involved sustainability. During Reunion weekend in June 2007, Skorton had pointed out that Cornell was one of two universities in the United States (Oregon State University was the other) designated by the federal government as a land-grant, sea-grant, space-grant, and sun-grant institution. Its wide-ranging achievements in sustainability included discovering uses for plant biomass in energy and chemical production and fuel development; sending fifteen professors from a variety of disciplines to provide humanitarian aid and agricultural assistance to Zambia; lake source cooling; and dozens of other policies and practices that put Cornell on schedule to exceed its own Kyoto Protocol commitment to reduce greenhouse gases on campus to 7 percent below 1990 levels in 2012. These practices included the diversion of 117,000 pounds of dining waste to compost every month, cutting the size of the landfill by half, and the construction of Silver, Gold, and Platinum LEED (Leadership in Energy and Environmental Design) certified facilities. Skorton promised one thousand alumni and friends assembled in Bailey Hall that the university would "put the full force of our teaching, research, and outreach" behind sustainability.[138]

Skorton knew that the College of Agriculture and Life Sciences Advisory Council, whose members included David Atkinson '60, a private investor with a deep understanding of climate change, had recommended that Cornell create a sustainability center. In 2007, with seed money provided by Atkinson and his wife, Patricia, the university did just that. Frank DiSalvo, professor of chemistry and chemical biology, became the director. In 2010, after an external panel composed of experts in the field concluded that the work of the Cornell Center for a Sustainable Future was "nothing short of remarkable," the Atkinsons committed $80 million, the largest single gift to the Ithaca campus from an individual or family, to establish the David R. Atkinson Center for a Sustainable Future.[139]

Some 270 faculty members from sixty-five departments across Cornell were affiliated with the Atkinson Center, which funded dozens of multidisciplinary research projects and launched mini-fellowship programs in agrarian transformation and sustainable biodiversity. "We're matchmaking all the time," DiSalvo explained. "Most major universities have an energy center. Many have some kind of environmental center, and then some have development or poverty centers. Cornell is almost unique in putting all the pieces together."[140] Atkinson envisioned the center as "a source of unbiased information; a catalyst bringing different disciplines together; and a partner with entrepreneurs, businesses, NGOs and government to magnify the impact of the knowledge and ingenuity at Cornell."[141] By 2012, the center had leveraged $9 million of its own resources to attract $90 million in external funding. Its research teams produced biofuels using aquatic micro-algae. They investigated pyrolysis, which made biofuels and biochar from corn husks and chicken manure. Atkinson Center researchers also harvested energy from the wind that swirls around buildings, developed tools to forecast mosquito-borne infections, designed methods for comparing the sustainability of different food systems, and enlisted mathematics and engineering as well as social science to understand poverty and its causes.

Cornell professors, it is clear, still wanted better buildings as well as better faculty. In the run-up to the sesquicentennial, they got quite a few of them, a vivid sign of Cornell's economic recovery. A new eighty-nine-thousand-square-foot Human Ecology Building, located behind Martha Van Rensselaer Hall, was dedicated in October 2011. Environmentally friendly, HEB featured on-site gardens, extensive use of natural light, and a ventilation system that regulated carbon dioxide levels. More than 90 percent of the timber used in the building was harvested by the Forest Stewardship Council, 60 percent of the furniture came from existing inventory, and 1,050 tons of waste was recycled as construction material. In addition to classrooms and administrative and faculty offices, the building contained apparel, interior design, and drawing studios, labs for researchers using biomedical materials and implants, 3-D scanners, and the Cornell Costume and Textile Collection, with over nine thousand garments dating back to the eighteenth century. By providing centralized space for the college, HEB promoted "integrated learning." A colleague teaching an environmental psychology course, reported Professor Paul Eshelman, now "has his students acting as behavioral consultants to the design students I'm working with."[142]

In the fall of 2010, construction began on a $105 million New York State–funded project to replace Stocking Hall, which housed the Food Science Department and the iconic Cornell Dairy Bar, with a new four-story building on Tower Road. Fully operational in 2014, the new Stocking contained laboratories for wine production, sensory studies of food, food safety, and food and biomaterial processing, a "crush pad" for viticulture and enology students, modern classrooms, and networked meeting spaces. The Dairy Bar's ice cream freezer, tanks, and pasteurization equipment were replaced with computer-controlled machinery. From a balcony above the Dairy Plant, visitors to Stocking could observe ice cream, milk, pudding, and yogurt as the items made their way from processing to pasteurization to packaging.

A few years earlier, in November 2011, the $140 million Physical Sciences Building between Baker and Clark Halls was finished. With glass walls offering

The new Human Ecology Building, October 2011. (Cornell University Photography)

writing surfaces for creative thinking and an open design that encouraged chance encounters, it, too, fostered collaboration, this time among faculty and students in Physics, Chemistry and Chemical Biology, and Applied and Engineering Physics. According to Provost Fuchs, the building was also essential for faculty recruitment. Each professor, he pointed out, "typically now has twice as many people working in his or her group as in the past. Equipment also now takes up more space. So the departments have had positions to fill but not space to put them in."[143]

Milstein Hall was a long time in coming. In the early 1990s, the Boston firm of Schwartz/Silver produced a plan for Architecture, Art, and Planning that extended the existing floors of Rand Hall northward and added a floor, attached a glass block to the north face of Sibley Dome, and gutted and rebuilt Franklin Hall. Without sufficient funds to pay for the whole project, the university refurbished Franklin, which reopened as Olive Tjaden Hall. In 1999, the real estate developer and financer Howard Milstein '73 facilitated a gift from his mother, Irma Milstein, to help pay for a new building, to be named for his father, Paul. AAP opted for an open competition to pick the architect. Seventeen firms expressed interest, and in 2001, following presentations by the four finalists at Bailey Hall, the jury unanimously chose Steven Holl Architects of New York City. Within months, however, Day Hall administrators, faculty, and alumni expressed grave doubts about the amount of space, openness, circulation, and flexibility in Holl's design and about the budget. A "Cornell Alumni Committee for an Intelligent Solution to a New Architecture School Building" wrote to the dean, the president, trustees, and the *Alumni Magazine*, and

405

placed two full-page advertisements in the *Cornell Daily Sun*. As opposition intensified, an impasse developed with Holl, who seemed wedded to the original design, and the relationship with him was severed in May 2002. In November, Dean Olpadwala chose a new architect, Barkow Leibinger, but in 2004, his successor as dean, Mohsen Mostafavi, terminated the contract and appointed the architectural icon Rem Koolhaas and his associates in the Office for Metropolitan Architecture, based in Rotterdam in the Netherlands.

Dogged by controversy, Milstein experienced delay after delay, despite concerns that the undergraduate architecture program might lose its accreditation if inadequate facilities were not rehabilitated or replaced. To address objections raised by the City of Ithaca Planning Board and other authorizing agencies about the impact on University Avenue of supporting columns for the building, Koolhaas changed to a cantilever design. Raising the remainder of the funds for the $40 million structure took time, especially after the stock market crash. And professors, alumni, and members of the community continued to complain about the "extravagant expense" (at a time in which the university "was pinching pennies and starving other programs") and the "provocative, setting-discordant design" by a flamboyant "starchitect."[144] Ultimately, ground was broken in 2009, and the building, which was connected to Rand and Sibley, officially opened two years later. Milstein's "bump," forming a dome on the first floor and its open workspace for architects, with floor-to-ceiling views of campus, on the second floor, became campus attractions. A 257-seat auditorium with digital audiovisual and wireless technology was used for large lectures and, at Milstein's request, for meetings of the board of trustees. "It's absolutely beautiful, it's absolutely gorgeous," gushed Architecture student Ben Waters '14. "I can't believe it's ours. We got the facilities that reflect the caliber of the program."[145]

Gates Hall, which was completed in 2014, had a lengthy gestation period as well. In January 2006, two years after Bill Gates's visit to campus, the Bill and Melinda Gates Foundation donated $25 million to support the building. The remainder of the $60 million budget for it (Skorton and the board of trustees mandated in 2009 that all the funds for major capital projects had to be in hand before construction could begin) was not raised until late 2010. Rising on the site of the Hoy Field parking lot, on Campus Road across from Barton Hall, the one-hundred-thousand-square-foot building brought Computer Science and Information Science, which had outgrown its rented space on College Avenue, together under one roof. Along with offices and classrooms, the striking modern glass structure contained research and teaching labs, including work stations equipped for cyber-security, human-computer interaction, computational sustainability, robotics, and computer vision. It became home to Haym Hirsch, an expert in artificial intelligence and data mining and the former director of the Division of Information and Intelligent Systems at the National

Science Foundation, who was named dean of Computing and Information Science in 2013. Hirsch was attracted to Cornell, he indicated, because of Gates Hall and an "academic org chart that facilitates wide ranging collaborations."[146]

"As a practical matter, we are bursting at the seams," Dean Stewart Schwab told Law School alumni in 2012. When Myron Taylor Hall opened, the Law School had fourteen professors and 157 students. Eighty years later, the building complex accommodated fifty full-time faculty members and 695 students, along with forty student groups, eleven research centers, institutes, and programs (including the Legal Information Institute, the Death Penalty Project, the Initiative for Law and Development in the Middle East, the Program in East Asian Law and Culture, the Institute for the Study and Practice of Business Law, the Labor Law Clinic, the Center for Women and Justice, the Advocacy for Lesbian, Gay and Bisexual and Transgender Communities Clinic, and the Juvenile Justice Clinic), as well as visiting scholars and exchange students. Among the "loftier reasons" for the first major expansion and renovation of space in a quarter century, Schwab noted, was a responsibility to "emphasize the accessibility of the law and the relation between law and culture in an increasingly diverse world. Our physical space must reflect these ideals. Indeed, our physical space can foster these ideals."[147]

The expansion began with a new wing placed in the hill east of the Law School courtyard. Accessible from the courtyard at ground level as well as from an entrance on College Avenue, the addition, which contained study spaces and three classrooms, welcomed students throughout the university, some of whom were enrolled in a six-year joint JD–PhD in psychology program, offered with the College of Human Ecology, and a new, three-year JD–MBA program, offered in partnership with the Johnson School of Management. Skorton predicted the facility would help the Law School "remain a school of large vision within one of the world's great universities."[148]

In the summer of 2013, Cornell broke ground on the first building constructed exclusively for the humanities since 1905. At a cost of $61 million, Klarman Hall, named for the hedge fund manager Seth Klarman '79 and his wife, Betty Klarman, was attached to Goldwin Smith Hall. It featured the largest auditorium on the Arts quad and an atrium near East Avenue formerly embraced by Goldwin Smith, faculty offices, courtyards, green roofs, and a transparent glass entrance wall. For Gretchen Ritter '83, the large lecture hall testified to the hope that the recent decline in enrollments in humanities courses and in majors would be reversed. Ritter, a professor of political science (and former vice provost for undergraduate education and faculty governance) at the University of Texas at Austin, became the first female dean of Arts and Sciences in 2013. By making Klarman "the first building not already in the pipeline to be built after the economic crisis," an Arts and Sciences professor proclaimed, the university "spoke volumes about its commitment to the centrality of the humanities. . . . As long as people exist, the humanities is going to be vital to any worthy enterprise."[149]

After December 16, 2011, all of the impressive construction on the Ithaca campus had to be seen from a different perspective. After a yearlong competition initiated by Mayor Michael Bloomberg, Cornell won the right to build a two-million-square-foot applied sciences campus on Roosevelt Island in New York City. Scheduled to be completed in 2037, at a total cost of more than $2 billion, Cornell NYC Tech, as we shall see in Chapter 12, was designed to do for New York City what Silicon Valley did for the San Francisco Bay area in California. It was a historic opportunity for Cornell—and a big gamble. For institutions as much as for individuals, timing can change the course of history. Had Bloomberg announced the competition in December 2008, during the depths of the Great Recession, instead of December 2010, Cornell might not have jumped at it.

11 | The New Normal in Student Life

In the late 1990s, a transformation of undergraduate life was under way. Observers of higher education suggested that colleges and universities had begun to adopt an updated and subtler version of *in loco parentis*. They asserted that many baby-boomer parents expected more college involvement in their child's activities outside the classroom, that students were more accustomed to guidance by adults than they had been in the 1960s and '70s, for example, and they were more amenable to residing in living and learning communities presided over, or at least shared with, faculty and staff.

They were only partly right. *In loco parentis* was not really making a comeback. The regime of surveillance and supervision over the personal lives of students—with curfews, dress codes, and parietal rules (including the requirement of "three feet on the floor" and open doors when a male and female were in the same dorm room)—was still in the distant past and in the late 1990s remained as it had been for more than three decades, virtually nonexistent. Handbooks contained no restrictions on deportment. Deans of students did not evoke fear or trembling in any undergraduate. Several institutions repealed their speech codes, leaving students free to speak up or speak out on just about any subject. Workshops concerned with the exploration of personal identity and racial, gender, and sexual differences were offered, but the protocols they promoted were left to the student to carry out. Undergraduates retained considerable autonomy over their own activities and their associations, their beliefs, and their behavior. And they would have it no other way.[1]

As the observers indicated, however, colleges and universities across the country had begun to reconceive and reconstruct the residential environment and thus the student experience. A consensus was emerging that dormitories, along with fraternities and sororities, should not be intellect-free zones. To demonstrate that exchanging ideas could be a fulfilling and enjoyable activity outside the classroom, many institutions provided undergraduates with opportunities for frequent contact with faculty members and graduate and professional students, at meals and on social occasions, and in classes, seminars, and advising and career services offered in the residence halls. Moreover, the transformation of residential culture did not stop there. Motivated in part by a desire to minimize liability and litigation, many colleges and universities took some steps to regulate drinking and drug use, end hazing in fraternities and sororities, and protect and promote the physical and mental health of their students.

Between 1995 and 2015, Cornell tried to find better ideas to replace *in loco parentis*. To broaden the intellectual, cultural, and social experiences of first-year students and promote interaction across racial, ethnic, and college identities, the university mandated that they reside as a class on North Campus and read a book assigned to them during the summer and discuss it during freshman orientation. The West Campus initiative aspired to link the academic and nonacademic lives of sophomores, juniors, and seniors into a cohesive whole by replacing the much maligned U-Halls (which had long corridors and virtually no public spaces) with five new residence halls, each of which had a dining room, library, classrooms, study spaces, a resident house professor, affiliated faculty fellows, and a self-governance structure.

During these years, Cornell administrators also attempted to foster "wellness" (a buzzword of the new century). They introduced healthier dietary choices in dining facilities. And they tightened restrictions on the consumption of alcohol by underage students in places owned or controlled by Cornell. Following a spate of hazing incidents, one of which resulted in the death of an undergraduate, they directed leaders in the Greek system to make fundamental changes in pledging, the probationary period in which new recruits were sometimes compelled to engage in demeaning or dangerous behavior. Cornell also mobilized a series of strategies including augmented mental health services, crisis management, peer counseling, and the installation of protective fences and nets on the gorge-spanning bridges around campus to prevent student suicide.

Under the aegis of *in loco parentis*, Christine Schelhas–Miller, a senior lecturer in human development and a student services specialist, pointed out, undergraduates had not had much room to experiment and learn from their mistakes. In contrast, in the twenty-first century, she said, using traditional Cornell distinctions, they "have more freedom, but it may take them time to learn the responsibility piece. It's our job at the university to teach them that."[2]

LIKE THE GENERATIONS that preceded them, Cornell's "millennial" students were a diverse lot in their tastes and temperaments as well as their backgrounds. The class of 2017 was the most diverse in the history of the university. Some 16 percent were Asian, 12 percent Hispanic, and 7 percent African American. More than 2 percent of first-year students were biracial, multiracial, or non–Hispanic underrepresented minorities. Eleven percent were international students. Many Cornell students embraced school traditions. Others ignored or disdained them. Some were apathetic about politics; others chose to be activists on issues related to group identity and, increasingly, to health and the environment. More than a few did their own thing, occasionally in ways that attracted the attention of the whole campus—and disobeyed regulations and regulators. No matter what their racial and ethnic heritage or their country of origin, students expressed their individuality and asserted their identities as Cornellians.

For almost every men's varsity hockey game, students packed Lynah Rink, ostentatiously and audaciously read newspapers while the lineup of the opposing team was announced, then crumpled them up and threw them on the ice. In 2002–3, they cheered wildly as the Big Red posted a 15–0 home record, won the Ivy League championship and the ECAC regular season and tournament titles, only to fall to New Hampshire in the semifinal of the Frozen Four in Buffalo's HSBC Arena. The team brought home a bucketful of awards. Mike Schafer '86 was named ECAC Coach of the Year, the only person ever to win the award twice in a row. Doug Murray was selected ECAC Defensive Defenseman of the Year, Stephen Baby '03 the Best Defensive Forward, and David LeNeveu the Best Goalie, Co-Player of the Year, and the Most Valuable Player in the tournament.

Students did not always show up in force for other varsity sports. Crowds swelled in 2007, however, when the men's lacrosse team, led by first-team All-Americans Max Seibald '09, Mitch Belisle '07, and Matt McGonagle '07, posted its first undefeated regular season in three decades, won the Ivy League title for the fifth straight year, and dropped a heartbreaker to Duke in the last three seconds of the NCAA semifinal game. In 2007–8, students clocked lots of face time at Newman Arena when Cornell became the first school to have its men's and women's basketball teams win Ivy League championships in the same year.

Some traditions ended during these years. Since 1960, Bob Petrillose had sold food to hungry Cornellians, night and day, from a red-and-white truck parked on Stewart Avenue. He adopted the name "Hot Truck" to differentiate his menu—PMP, or poor man's pizza, and MBC, meatball and cheese, which used French bread from his father's restaurant, Johnny's Big Red Grill—from the cold sandwiches sold by his West Campus competitor, Louie's Lunch. In 2000, Albert Smith '71, owner of the Short Stop Deli in downtown Ithaca, bought the business. In 2009, Cornell hockey fans also bid a fond farewell to Dave Nulle, a former ballroom dance instructor, who drove Lynah Rink's Zamboni for thirty years, decked out in outlandish costumes.

The most emotional good-bye was extended in 2006 to Walter LaFeber, a fabled teacher, scholar, and mentor at the university since 1959. Taught on

Tuesdays, Thursdays, and Saturdays every semester, his "History of American Foreign Policy" course attracted hundreds of students, who applauded at the end of every class. LaFeber delivered his "last lecture," titled "A Half Century of Friends, Foreign Policy and Great Losers," in his signature conversational style, without notes, to an overflow crowd at the Beacon Theater in New York City.[3]

Students refused to say good-bye to Slope Day, the most popular tradition at Cornell, which made David Letterman's list of the best campus parties in the country. The event dates back to 1902, when students marked Spring Day with tugs of war, whistles, toy balloons, and games of marbles. In the decades that followed, there were mock bullfights, parades, clowns, and circus tents as well. Alcohol was very much in evidence, even during Prohibition. Between the 1920s and '40s, the festivities included a dance with live music in Barton Hall, provided on one occasion by Glenn Miller's band. Spring Day seems to have disappeared in the tense and contentious 1960s, only to return at the end of the '70s, when Cornell Dining held a Springfest barbecue on the last day of classes to thank students for putting up with renovations to Willard Straight Hall. In 1986, with the change in the legal drinking age from eighteen to twenty-one, the university stopped serving alcohol on what was by then called Slope Day. Students began to skip the last day of classes and show up on the Slope already stoked and well-stocked with their own supplies. Following the treatment of several dozen students for alcohol-related emergencies in the early '90s, university administrators tried to end Slope Day by refusing to book bands and other performers. Even without a concert, however, as many as three-quarters of the undergraduates kept on coming, some of them wearing "Take Back the Slope" T-shirts.

Although they worried about whether their involvement exposed Cornell to lawsuits, administrators felt compelled to plan and supervise Slope Day. Staff in the Office of the Dean of Students encouraged leaders of student organizations, fraternities, and sororities to urge their members to behave responsibly. Administrators cautioned against drinking to excess or getting "glory scars" from sliding down the Slope into broken glass bottles. They dispensed free bottled water, put portable potties at or near Libe Slope, locked the doors of Olin Library and buildings on the Arts quad, enlisted volunteers to patrol the area (which, in time, was fenced in), kept paramedics on hand, and turned Gannett Health Center into a MASH unit with mattresses on the floors and lots of intravenous bags on hand. They promoted a dry alternative, called "Hope Day," on the Engineering quad. Despite their efforts, however, Slope Day, which by then boasted A-list bands, attracted many students who were intent on drinking themselves into oblivion.

Millennial students invented some traditions of their own—and added to university lore. In the dark hours of October 7–8, 1997, just before fall break,

Slope Day, 2009. (Cornell University Photography)

someone placed what appeared to be a hollowed-out pumpkin on top of the McGraw Tower spire, 173 feet above ground. The *New York Times*, CNN, MTV, and NBC's *Today Show* gave prominent attention to the stunt, which was a whodunit as well as a howdunit. Some speculated that a skilled rock climber got access to a maintenance hatch six feet below the point of the tower, lassoed a rope onto the lightning rod from there, rappelled to the top, and attached the vegetable (or was it an object made of clay, Styrofoam, plastic, or papier-mâché?) to the spire. "It was aliens," declared Andy Pierson '01, MEN '03. Hunter Rawlings quipped that he, standing on tiptoes, had done it himself.[4]

Cornell administrators decided neither to erect scaffolding nor secure a crane to remove it. Instead, the university installed bright orange fences around McGraw Tower, posted warning signs to alert passersby that a sixty-pound unidentified flying object might be on its way down, and waited for it to rot. Oliver Habicht '97, a staff member in Academic Technology Services, stationed a webcam on the seventh floor of Olin Library that provided twenty-four-hour live images of the gourd. In February 1998, Provost Don Randel offered a competition for undergraduates to identify the composition of the orange entity. The victorious individual or team would receive a $250 voucher for the

413

"The Great Pumpkin," 1997.
(Cornell University Photography)

purchase of books, a signed lithograph of Charles Schulz's cartoon "The Great Pumpkin," a Cornell pumpkin T-shirt, and a video exploring the life of the McGraw Pumpkin.

On March 13, the day Randel was scheduled to ride a crane-hoisted gondola to the top of the tower to retrieve the now famous object, the basket that workmen were testing banged into the spire and dislodged the object from its perch. Plummeting twenty feet to a scaffold (which was there because a column in the belfry of the tower was being replaced), the pumpkin remained intact, having frozen solid overnight. A faculty panel, chaired by John Kingsbury, professor emeritus of plant biology, declared that the evidence "leads to a single, harmonious conclusion: It's a pumpkin!" and presented Randel with a certificate of authenticity. William Streett, former dean of Engineering, announced that four seniors in Physics and Astronomy had won the provost's competition. Modeling their technique on planetary exploration, Team 318 had deployed a remote-controlled weather balloon, fitted with a drill bit and a webcam. To confirm that the object was a pumpkin, the quartet used a scanning electron microscope and adapted an analytical method known as polymerase chain reaction. They concluded that the pumpkin had been hollowed out before being placed on the tower. With less water in it and more interior ventilation, it had become a "leathery husk, which could cling to the spire for decades."[5]

For its finale, the famous pumpkin, after being freeze-dried and installed in a glass display case, was paraded into the Memorial Room of Willard Straight Hall in a mock academic processional, complete with the accompaniment of a brass quintet, and at last came to rest in Day Hall. The perpetrator(s) of the greatest prank in Cornell's history never came forward.[6]

On the ground as well as atop the bell tower, the new normal for Cornell students included the extensive, often incessant, use of technology. Millennials spent more time in front of a computer screen than a television. Tethered to cell phones, they texted and tweeted. They "friended" family, friends, and friends of friends. They subscribed to Napster, iTunes, and Ruckus and often downloaded music illegally. Some of them directed questions about love, sex, and whether graduate schools examined Facebook profiles to "Dear Uncle Ezra," an anonymous Cornell staffer, at the world's first online advice column, which had opened its portals in 1986.

At 1:18 p.m. on Monday, September 22, 2003, between fifty and a hundred students assembled on Ho Plaza for Cornell's first "flash mob." A flamboyant example of Internet connectivity, the phenomenon (sudden gatherings of people at predetermined locations and predetermined times) dated to the anti–World Trade Organization protests in Seattle in 1999. On the Ithaca campus, each of the flash mob participants, who learned about "Project Free Love" from instant messages, texts, and weblogs, showed up, "mono style," stretched out their arms to identify themselves to others, synchronized watches without talking, and at the appointed time hugged three people and dispersed within two minutes. Matthew Nagowski '05, the organizer of the event, hoped that the flash mob would become a twenty-first-century Cornell tradition. It didn't.[7]

But the phenomenon did not disappear entirely. At 2:30 p.m. on Friday, February 26, 2010, with roads and many campus facilities closed in the wake of a storm that dumped two feet of snow on Ithaca, more than three hundred students appeared on the Arts quad and began to pelt one another with snowballs. Anticipated to last fifteen minutes, the battle had not let up after an hour, spreading to the patio of Olin Library, where missiles were launched from higher ground. Harrison Gill '12, who created the Facebook event, "watched in amazement" as the RSVPs "began creeping up. I didn't realize how big it had gotten until Friday morning when I overhead people in class talking about going."[8]

———

SOME CORNELL STUDENTS promoted political and social agendas. They were most visible—and effective—with voter registration drives during presidential elections, especially Barack Obama's campaign in 2008; when championing environmental causes with local implications; and in responding to sexual assaults and racial incidents. Even then, however, activists found it difficult to mobilize large numbers of students and focus the attention of the campus on an issue for more than a few days. In accounting for the "apathy" of his generation, Steve Grossman '07, program chair of the Cornell Democrats, spoke for many student leaders. Compared with the Vietnam era, Grossman claimed, the challenges of the twenty-first century were not "as immediate" to his contemporaries, who were, after all, preoccupied with getting good jobs.[9]

Of course, the attacks on the World Trade Center and the Pentagon on September 11, 2001, commanded the attention of everyone on campus. Twenty alumni died as a result of the attacks, eighteen at the World Trade Center towers and two on United Airlines Flight 93, which crashed in Pennsylvania. One of the casualties, Eamon McEneaney '77, an executive at Cantor Fitzgerald, who had led sixty-five colleagues down a smoke-filled stairway following the bombing of the World Trade Center in 1993, was considered one of the greatest players in the history of college lacrosse. At a candlelight vigil on the evening of September 11, President Rawlings asked his audience to reach out to New Yorkers and each other. Three days later, classes were canceled over the noon hour, and more than twelve thousand students, staff, and faculty huddled together in the chilly weather at a memorial convocation on the Arts quad. The Reverend Kenneth Clark, director of Cornell United Religious Work, prayed "that from the ashes of these horrible events there will emerge a phoenix of justice and truth, peace and understanding, respect and acceptance." Declaring that the community was united in condemning terrorism and in sympathy for its victims, President Rawlings promised that the university would "do what we do best: educate our students in open classrooms and campus-wide teach-ins; conduct our research and scholarship in open labs and libraries; publish our work in open journals and airways." And Professor LaFeber reminded listeners of the importance of understanding global affairs and exercising civic responsibility.[10]

The Cornell community came together again in September 2005 to assist victims of Hurricane Katrina. Over seventy organizations mobilized to collect donations and organize blood drives. Faculty and students from the Colleges of Engineering and Architecture, Art, and Planning traveled to New Orleans to help rebuild the city. And Cornell offered students from Tulane University, Dillard University, Xavier University, and the University of New Orleans (all of which had been forced to close their doors while they repaired the damage) a tuition-free semester and free housing. About two hundred students appeared in Ithaca, apparently the largest number to find refuge at a school outside of Louisiana and Texas. Staff members in the School of Continuing Education and Summer Sessions worked through the Labor Day weekend to advise the "extramural" students (all but a handful from Tulane), enroll them in classes, and assure them that credits would transfer back when they returned home in January. Emeritus professors volunteered to teach extra courses and discussion sections. Students in dormitories, fraternities, sororities, and off-campus apartments and houses found room for them. "Our image of the cutthroat Cornell student has vanished over the past few days," said Tulane undergraduate Lindsay Oliver. "They've been offering us notes before we could ask. . . . And the professors have been amazing. You tell them you're from Tulane and everything changes."[11]

In the absence of a disaster of the proportions of 9/11 or Katrina, activists divided along partisan and ideological lines. In March 2003, for example, about two hundred students opposed to the impending war with Iraq marched through more than a dozen buildings on campus before rallying at Day Hall. Coordinated with 230 universities across the country by the National Youth and Student Peace Coalition, their protest was designed to make the point that government spending on education would decrease when bombs started falling on Baghdad. At the end of the month, Cornell Republicans countered with a rally on Ho Plaza to express solidarity with combat troops in Iraq and approval of President Bush's decision to remove Saddam Hussein from power. Estimating that at its peak the crowd numbered more than one hundred people, Ryan Horn '02, MPA '04, chair of the Cornell Republicans, declared that the "vast majority" of students "are patriotic people and they support the troops in the field."[12] As the war in Iraq and the conflict in Afghanistan wore on, year after year, Cornell students rallied, occasionally, but not ever with the passion or in the numbers they had in the Vietnam era.

Labor activists got more traction because their target was Day Hall administrators, who were predisposed to support their arguments, and not the White House. Responding to pressure from Students Against Sweatshops, President Rawlings pledged in 1999 to "work vigorously" to eliminate the use of sweatshop labor in the production of any products licensed by Cornell. He would attempt as well to require licensees (for themselves and on behalf of their contractors, subcontractors, and manufacturers) to recognize and respect the right of employees to freedom of association and collective bargaining, negotiate in good faith with any union they choose, subject no person to unlawful on-the-job discrimination, ensure women equal pay for equal work, and take affirmative actions to protect women workers' reproductive health. And he agreed to meet with student representatives at least twice a semester "to assess the progress of compliance with these principles."[13] With the problem still not resolved to its satisfaction in 2005, the Cornell chapter of United Students Against Sweatshops (CSAS) submitted petitions, sponsored teach-ins, and brought foreign textile workers to campus. The following spring, upon the recommendation of a committee of faculty members, administrators, and students, Day Hall endorsed the principles in the proposed Designated Suppliers Program, which included requiring any factories that produced clothing with a Cornell logo to pay a living wage, allow workers to unionize, and prohibit sweatshop conditions. However, the university acknowledged "the significant challenges presented in implementing and sustaining such an effort."[14] In the ensuing years, the CSAS continued to push Cornell to limit the manufacture of clothing with its logo to designated supplier factories.

Environmental activists also criticized the university, specifically on Cornell's approach to climate change. On April 11, 2001, seven members of the Cornell branch of Kyoto Now!—a national organization demanding compliance with the 1997 Kyoto Protocol on climate change—staged a sit-in at Day Hall. Signed by the Clinton administration, the Kyoto treaty, which was opposed by the George W. Bush administration and never ratified by the United States, committed signatories to reduce greenhouse gas emissions by 7 percent below 1990 levels. The protesters wanted the university to implement the Kyoto Protocol for the Ithaca campus. After four hours, the protesters were removed by Cornell police; they regrouped outside Day Hall, and within five days collected three thousand signatures on their petitions. On April 19, Harold Craft Jr. '60, PhD '70, vice president for administration and chief financial officer of the university, while characterizing his discussions with the protesters as "substantive and creative," emphasized that it would be "very difficult" to reach the Kyoto targets by 2008, but committed Cornell "to do everything within its ability, consistent with the university's obligations for teaching, research, service, and extension," to do so.[15] In the ensuing years, Cornell substantially reduced greenhouse gases by providing alternative transportation options to employees, replacing fossil fuels with renewables, and building energy-efficient buildings. A Climate Action Plan provided a road map to reduce carbon emissions to net zero by 2050.

In 2012 Kyoto Now! upped the ante. As Cornell worked toward carbon neutrality, Anna-Lisa Castle '14, copresident of Kyoto Now! pointed out that the institution was investing endowment funds in fossil fuel companies. Joining organizations on three hundred campuses in the United States and more than twenty student organizations in Ithaca, Cornell Kyoto Now! asked the university to fully withdraw its investments in the fossil fuel industry by 2020 and reinvest 30 percent of the funds in companies involved in renewable energy initiatives. The Cornell Faculty Senate would make a similar recommendation in the fall of 2013. In May 2013, two dozen students staged a "die-in" in front of Day Hall to dramatize the potential consequences of fossil-fuel-induced global warming. Citing concerns about the consequences of divestment on the endowment and Cornell's annual operating budget, the effectiveness of the proposed strategy in achieving "the desired result," and the use of the university's financial clout to advance political and social agendas "that fall outside our primary missions," President Skorton declared that "Cornell had no plans to remove holdings in the fossil industry from the endowment in the foreseeable future."[16] Urging students to continue raising environmental concerns, reminding them that he had placed a moratorium on the controversial practice of "hydro-fracking" for natural gas on Cornell lands, and that the Sierra Club had ranked Cornell fifth among the nation's "Ten Coolest Schools" for its sustainability and conservation initiatives, Skorton added that "this is going to be a long-term conversation between us."[17]

THE POLITICS OF racial, ethnic, and gender identity remained a significant factor at Cornell during the millennial years. In 2009 the university established an Asian & Asian American Center (A3C) in temporary quarters in Willard Straight Hall. Patricia Nguyen, the first assistant dean of students with a portfolio focused on a single race, worked closely with individual students and Asian and Asian American organizations and helped raise money from alumni to fund the center. She made special efforts as well to avoid "self-segregation" by connecting with other minority constituencies on campus, including the African American, Latino, and the gay, bisexual, lesbian, and transgender communities. In 2011, A3C relocated to the Center for Intercultural Dialogue at 626 Thurston Avenue.[18]

In 2013 the university established a Muslim Cultural Center. Located in 208 Willard Straight Hall, the center showcased the diversity of Muslim culture and provided support for any person who identified as a Muslim. Working with the Committee for the Advancement of Muslim Culture, the center reached out to other communities, including Jews, as well. Its very presence, according to Vice President Susan Murphy '73, PhD '94, "makes it very clear that we have a vibrant Muslim student community and a leadership we value."[19]

The university also struggled to satisfy the demands for a "gender neutral" campus environment. Student activists asked for bathrooms that could be used by members of either sex and gender-neutral housing for individuals who did not self-identify as "male" or "female." In the resolution he submitted on the latter subject to the Student Assembly in 2007, Vince Hartman '08 claimed that "by denying students the right to choose their roommates based on their preferences regardless of gender, the university discriminates with the assumption that heterosexuality is universal."[20] By a 9–2 vote the Assembly passed the resolution, which requested that a number of suites on West Campus be set aside as gender neutral. Administrators maintained, however, that they would continue to figure out what worked best for transgendered students by tailoring housing "to individual needs rather than one size fits all." In 2012, by a vote of 23–1, the Student Assembly again endorsed a "Gender-Inclusive Housing Policy," and President Skorton agreed to provide gender-inclusive options in all university residences open to sophomores, juniors, and seniors.[21] In the fall of

2013, for the first time in Cornell's history, students in on-campus housing had a roommate of another gender. Of 3,340 undergraduates who signed up for the residential lottery, twenty-six opted for gender-inclusive housing on West Campus. All of them chose gender-inclusive suites, not gender-inclusive rooms.

Conflicts over the campus climate for African Americans continued to be the most persistent—and contentious—issue of identity politics at Cornell. On April 17, 1997, the *Cornell Review*, the self-proclaimed "conservative voice" on campus, published an unsigned parody of Ebonics, the vernacular English used by some African Americans. The article offered a translation for a description for "Racism in American Society," a course offered by the Africana Studies and Research Center: "Da white man be evil an he tryin to keep da brotherman down."[22] Angry students held a demonstration, demanded that the *Review* be banished, and burned a handful of copies of the offending issue in a trash basket. As students began to take final exams, however, protests subsided. In a statement issued on May 1, President Rawlings deplored "race-baiting, stereotyping and intentionally degrading attacks on the African-American community" but emphasized that "demands for restrictions on free speech and for other repressive actions only escalate intolerance and feed hostility."[23]

The controversy was reignited in October 1997 when the *Cornell Review* published a cartoon showing a Ku Klux Klan rally, a Nazi soldier, and a doctor in an abortion clinic. The caption read: "Which one of these kills more blacks?" Offended students renewed their demand that the administration censor or ban the publication. On October 28, one individual took copies of the newspaper (estimates varied between fifty and two hundred copies) from three locations, placed them in a duffel bag, and burned them. Alleging that the burning constituted theft and the destruction of private property, the editors of the *Review* asked Barbara Krause, JD '86, the judicial administrator, to take action. On December 4, Krause concluded that because the paper was offered to anyone on campus "at no cost," and that there was "not a systematic effort to take large numbers of the *Review* out of circulation," thereby violating the right of free speech, the burning did not constitute a violation of the Campus Code of Conduct. The staff of the *Review* and supporters of the newspaper, who regarded themselves as a beleaguered minority at Cornell, were outraged.[24]

In the fall of 2000, four bias-related incidents, involving physical or verbal assaults (or both) on Asian American students, galvanized the campus. At a rally on Ho Plaza, members of the Cornell Asian Pacific Islander Student Union, La Asociación Latina, and the Black Students United declared that none of the assaults, or for that matter any others like them in the country, should be called "isolated incidents." Forty student organizations proposed a series of actions to "transform the cultural, intellectual and environmental climate at Cornell," including a course required of all undergraduates that addressed diversity, intolerance, and discrimination.[25] The university's response, a white paper titled "To Transform the Climate of the Larger Campus Community," reaffirmed Cornell's commitment to "civility, decency, and respect for others." It identified safety as the primary imperative, promising improvements in the Blue Light Services (which included emergency phones to reach the Cornell Police, a security escort service, and free bus rides in the evening) and the specification of consequences for anyone found guilty of a hate crime. Instead of instituting a required course, administrators began planning small group discussions during orientation to introduce first-year students to the "complexities and pleasures" of living in a diverse community.[26]

When Nathan Poffenbarger, a white student in ILR who had been binge drinking, shouted racial epithets at and then stabbed Charles Holliday, an African American Union College undergraduate who was visiting West Campus, on February 18, 2006, these issues rose to the surface again. At a rally on Ho Plaza on February 26, organized by the Africana Studies and Research Center, students and faculty members called for a mandatory course on diversity and an end to what they called "institutional racism" at Cornell. A forum held the next day turned into a tense confrontation between the 120 students, faculty, staff, and community members who crowded into the Memorial Room at the Straight and Interim President Rawlings and Tompkins County District Attorney Gwen Wilkinson. Rawlings acknowledged that the university had been ineffective in disseminating information about the assault, but pushed back at critics of the university. He stressed that required courses were the purview of the faculty. Noting that the "vast majority of violent incidents on campus are directly related to alcohol use," he wondered why Cornell students were not more concerned about binge drinking. Agreeing that racism was all too prevalent in the United States, he maintained that Cornell was not "institutionally racist."[27]

In subsequent years, bias-related behavior continued to result in skirmishes over "institutional racism." In 2010, however, attention shifted to another perennial issue in racial identity politics at Cornell: the status of the Africana Studies and Research Center. AS&RC was experiencing generational change. Several senior faculty, including James Turner, were preparing to retire. Professors at the center still did not agree about the best way to promote excellence in research and teaching. Some supported the approach recommended by Henry Louis Gates Jr. in the 1980s: searches conducted with other departments and joint appointments; others preferred to go it alone.

Personal and professional cleavages in AS&RC provided the backdrop to an ugly incident in February 2010. Grant Farred, a professor of English and Africana studies, invited two female graduate students to accompany him to a conference at the University of Rochester titled "Theorizing Black Studies." According to one of the students, when the women arrived late to a panel presentation, Farred allegedly made a comment to them that included the term "black bitches."[28]

421

He apologized when they told him his comment was offensive. He subsequently characterized his remark as an ill-conceived attempt at edgy humor. Upon returning to Ithaca, the women told several AS&RC faculty and graduate students what had happened. Farred was removed from his position as director of graduate studies for AS&RC and told not to participate in a fortieth-anniversary celebration of the center. Some students, faculty, and alumni of AS&RC expressed their outrage at Farred's behavior and their sadness that it came at a time when the community was preparing to celebrate "the inspiring institution that was built under the leadership of its founding director, James Turner," while condemning Salah Hassan, professor of the history of art and director of AS&RC, for consulting with only two Africana professors and failing to make a public statement about the hostile climate created by Farred until early April.[29] At a heated forum held at the Africana Center on April 14, Hassan explained that although Farred's comment was clearly "racist, sexist and utterly disgusting," formal investigations of tenured professors took time and occurred behind closed doors. Many in the room, the *Sun* reported, "left unsettled."[30]

In December 2010, Provost Kent Fuchs announced that the Africana Studies and Research Center, which had historically reported to his office, would become part of the College of Arts and Sciences, effective July 1, 2011. Making no mention of the Farred incident, which was not a factor in his decision, Fuchs explained that in the wake of the recent economic crisis he had cut staff in the provost's office, evaluated programs reporting to him, and concluded that some of them, including Africana, needed "better support" than he could provide.[31] The move would allow Africana to add a PhD program and double the size of its faculty, mostly through joint appointments with departments in Arts and Sciences. Fuchs cited the 2005 "Report of the Visiting Committee to the Africana Studies and Research Center" as "critical" to his decision. Characterizing Africana's place in the provost's office as a "peculiar arrangement," the visiting committee had recommended that the university reexamine the decision. Referring to the national rankings of departments and programs, Fuchs stated, "the past of Africana has been good, but what I want is what's excellent, not just good. I'm not going to win the most popular provost award but Cornell will be better."[32] In response to criticism, he said that he had not consulted with students because they would not be affected by the move but noted that he had had conversations with the previous and current directors before making his decision. And he took exception to the argument that his action stripped the center of its autonomy. The provost, he indicated, had always had and often exercised the power to increase or reduce budgets and authorize the hiring of faculty: "So I've been their virtual Dean." Fuchs claimed that he was not alone in believing that "twenty years from now, Africana faculty, students, alumni and staff will look back and say, 'This is the best thing that ever happened to us.' "[33]

Some students and faculty of color didn't see it that way. On December 3, several dozen of them marched to Day Hall, protesting the lack of consultation as well as the decision itself. Banging drums, they chanted "What do we want? Reversal! When do we want it? Now!"[34] "I don't think this university respects its students at all," said Tia Hicks '12, an Africana Studies major. Denouncing the "simple use of raw power in an autocratic undemocratic manner," Professor Turner said he had never seen anything like it "in 41 years of service at Cornell."[35] Professor Robert Harris Jr., who had succeeded Hassan as director of AS&RC, claimed that a majority of the ten-member Africana faculty opposed Fuchs's decree because it undermined the center's tradition of autonomy from administrative interference. Describing himself as "very careful" about using the term "racism," Harris suggested that "we would have to talk about institutional, systemic, societal racism." Denouncing "what they did" as "arrogant and condescending," Professor N'Dri T. Assié-Lumumba found it evidence of "institutional racism." Comparing Fuchs's model of decision making to the U.S. invasion of Iraq, Professor Carole Boyce Davies used the term "structural racism."[36]

Protests continued throughout the spring of 2011. Africana alumni, black studies professors at other colleges and universities, and elected officials and community leaders in the city of Ithaca and Tompkins County sent e-mails and petitions. Students and faculty with close ties to Africana held several rallies and marched on Day Hall. And Robert Harris refused to meet with the provost to discuss the center's budget unless Fuchs rescinded his decision.

In public statements and in a series of meetings, David Skorton supported his provost. "The African American community in general, even outside of Cornell, has a right to talk about this and hear about it," Skorton declared, but he emphatically rejected the claim of institutional racism "by any design, strategy, policy, or tactic." The objective of the administration, he emphasized, "was to improve the resources at the disposal of the same people who are running the Africana Center." Skorton maintained that putting the center under the auspices of the dean of Arts and Sciences "is what every other top-ranked Africana program—every single one, not most of them, not 90 percent, but 100 percent of them—do." And the president reminded those who asserted that the decision "came out of nowhere" that it "has been talked about for at least five years."[37]

On June 2, 2011, Fuchs affirmed his decision. As he had promised, the structure of the center and its faculty's control over the curriculum remained intact. Along with many other departments, programs, and centers at Cornell, however, its personnel were changing. James Turner retired in 2011. Robert Harris stepped down two years later. In 2012, Gerard Aching, MA '90, PhD '92, a professor of Africana studies and Spanish and French literature, was named the director of the center. The dean of Arts and Sciences authorized

AS&RC faculty to conduct searches for several junior faculty, some of whom would have joint appointments. In December 2013, the College of Arts and Sciences announced that a PhD would be offered in Africana Studies—the first such program in New York State and one of only ten in the United States. "None of this would have been possible without the faith, good will, and support of the administration at Cornell, from the offices of the President, Provost, and Dean of the Faculty and the efforts of the graduate school dean and her staff," said Professor Noliwe Rooks, the interim director of graduate studies for the AS&RC.[38]

Hunter Rawlings's decision to require all first-year students to live on North Campus also had its origins in racial identity politics. In 1991, as we have seen, a task force recommended that housing assignments be made for students randomly by staff members in the Department of Residential Life. Following protests by black students and Africana faculty, the plan was put on hold. But concerns about balkanization and cultural separation on campus did not go away. Indeed, Hunter Rawlings shared them. In March 1996, Rawlings declared that Cornell "had a particularly important interest in assuring that students, especially freshmen, are given the widest possible exposure to the full range of intellectual, cultural and social opportunities on campus." To that end, the president proposed a ban—to be phased in over five to seven years—on first-year students living in program houses. He knew, of course, that freshmen made up about half the residents living in the program houses, which included Akwe:kon, Ecology House, the International Living Center, Just about Music, the Language House, Risley Residential College, the Multicultural Living Learning Unit, the Transfer Center, the Latino Living Center, and Ujamaa Residential College.[39]

The response was as vehement as it had been in 1991. At a Student Assembly meeting in early April, Solomon Smart '97 declared that "this is not about creating community. It's about eliminating Ujamaa."[40] In the middle of the month, 250 students rallied outside the Straight and then delivered a statement drafted by the Ujamaa Residential Communities to the president's office. At the end of April, at a "Day of Outrage" rally outside Day Hall, Hubert Neal, an undergraduate, proclaimed "As long as we live in a racist society, this university will be racist, and we will be fighting for Ujamaa. This is a training ground for the real world."[41] The featured speaker, the Reverend Al Sharpton, who had been invited to campus by the Cornell chapter of the NAACP, explained that "the reason I rode to come here today is to tell President Reynolds [sic] . . . that these young students come from homes, communities. When you mess with them, they will all come."[42] And just before classes ended for the semester, about two hundred students blocked traffic and disrupted crosswalks, disabling central campus for four hours. No attempt was made to remove them; no one was charged with disorderly conduct.

Citing student concerns, Rawlings asked the board of trustees to postpone a vote on his proposal. "What we have done is say, 'We hear you,'" he claimed. "You're concerned about the program houses. So are we."[43] Rawlings denied that his recommendation was "a subterfuge for the 'real' plan, which is alleged to have as its goal the eventual elimination of the ethnically-related program houses such as Ujamaa, Akwe:kon and the Latino/a Living Center." He reaffirmed his commitment to recruit, enroll, and retain a diverse student body. Rawlings repeated, however, that he was not convinced by the argument that permitting freshmen to live in "affinity or interest groupings immediately upon their arrival is the best alternative." He promised that a new policy for first-year students would not go into effect until a plan for improving all residential communities, with input from all relevant constituencies, was completed. The comprehensive plan should include expanding the number of rooms on campus, attracting more sophomores, juniors, and seniors to campus housing, engaging more faculty in residential communities, establishing a more supportive environment, especially on West Campus (where 78 percent of students were white), and providing a common experience for freshmen.[44]

In April 1997, the Residential Communities Steering Committee, composed of faculty and staff and chaired by Vice President Murphy, endorsed the principle of assuring that first-year students had "the widest possible exposure to the full range of intellectual, cultural and social opportunities available at Cornell" and made twenty-two specific proposals for addressing residential community issues, but, in essence, endorsed a continuation of the student housing status quo. The report, the *Cornell Sun* editorialized, put Rawlings "in an unenviable lose-lose situation. If he decided to follow through with his initial proposal to phase freshmen out of the theme houses, he will be accused of once again disregarding community opinion. If, however, he accepted the recommendations of the steering committee he will be seen as backing down because of student outcry."[45]

On October 8, Rawlings praised the steering committee report "as an excellent starting point" but brushed aside its proposals as "limited in scope and incremental in approach." The president declared that "integration, particularly racial and ethnic integration," was a goal of Cornell as well as American society generally, and need not entail "the assimilation of minorities into the majority population and the consequent loss of their identity." Although he recognized that "freedom with responsibility is a value long cherished at Cornell," Rawlings claimed that "choice" in residential housing "neither addresses the problem of the self-segregation of new students into West Campus and North Campus made possible by our current housing options, nor does it confront the need for effective programming for all freshmen." To preserve freedom of choice, "to

425

the extent feasible," and also to "move decisively" to provide a "unifying educational experience" for first-year students to "experience the full diversity of the freshman class," he mandated that within three years all freshmen be housed on North Campus—and that new residences be constructed to accommodate them. Program houses on North Campus could house first-year students but had to participate in cross-residential programming; if a program house did not fill all its beds, the Office of Campus Life was authorized to fill the spaces. Harking back to his inaugural address, Rawlings concluded that the time had come "to bridge the chasms."[46]

Students opposed the initiative. In a survey commissioned by the *Sun*, only 22 percent endorsed the notion that all freshmen should be assigned to North Campus. "It doesn't surprise me," Susan Murphy said. "Anytime there's a change, you're apt to get more negative responses."[47] Hunter Rawlings asserted that although the administration would listen to students during implementation, the broad principles in his report were "no longer under discussion."[48]

In 1998 the board of trustees authorized construction of what would become first-choice housing for many freshmen, two new residences accommodating 558 students, on a thirty-three-acre site on North Campus that had been a playing field and situated near Donlon and Dickson Halls and the high rises. One of the new complexes, Court Hall, formed a courtyard with Balch and Clara Dickson. The other, Mews Hall, was named for an English term for an alleyway created by two buildings. Both residence halls were made of brick and "Llenroc," the shale-dense limestone distinctive to the region and offered air conditioning. Nearby would be a new Community Commons building, a glass-and-brick cube that glowed at night, with a thirty-two-hundred-square-foot fitness center, a large multipurpose room, a copy center, a school supplies store, a café, and a dining hall, with 625 seats. To make room for replacement recreational fields, the adjacent Pleasant Grove Apartments, which for decades housed graduate students, would be demolished. The estimated cost for the whole project was $65 million.

On Friday, August 24, 2001, 3,029 first-year students moved into their rooms on North Campus. The main welcoming event was an alcohol-free First Night celebration, featuring games, dancing, food, and "a night of madness under the moon." Acknowledging that he did not have "hard data," Rawlings cited "anecdotal" evidence of a link between the high priority Cornell was assigning to the freshman experience and the restructuring of its student housing, which had been, he suggested, Cornell's competitive Achilles' heel, and the 6.5 percent increase in undergraduate applications, to 21,519 for the fall of 2001. He predicted that the initiative would have "a transforming effect on the freshmen experience for decades to come."[49]

As Rawlings knew, efforts had been made to connect faculty and students on North Campus. With the addition of apartments for them in Court and

Mews, the number of faculty-in-residence rose to thirteen. They often collaborated with the many nonresident faculty fellows. A "Conversations with Faculty" program was launched as well. Nine freshmen writing courses were offered mornings and evenings in Robert Purcell Community Center, Court and Mews, and in the newly created Carol Tatkon Center for New Student Programs, which had taken over the former dining area in Balch Hall. To encourage informal interaction with their students, instructors in these seminars received free meal passes. With only six hundred sophomores, juniors, and seniors now living on North Campus (in program houses), a Residential Fellows program enlisted upperclass students as mentors, who might also provide links with West Campus.

Members of the class of '05 were the first to participate in what would become a new Cornell freshmen orientation tradition, called "the book project." Already adopted by many colleges and universities in the United States, the concept was designed to provide a common intellectual experience for students and professors. During the summer preceding their arrival on campus, first-year students were all required to read the same book—in this case, *Guns, Germs, and Steel: The Fates of Human Societies*, by Jared Diamond, a professor of physiology at the UCLA School of Medicine. Awarded the Pulitzer Prize in 1998, the book sought to explain the development of human societies on different continents. Success or failure, Diamond argued, was due more to geographical and environmental factors, including the availability of food and other natural resources and animals that could be domesticated, than to the innate (that is, genetic) attributes of the people themselves. Provost Biddy Martin, the champion of the book project, chose *Guns, Germs, and Steel* because it made a bold and controversial argument about a big issue and because it drew on many disciplines, "and thus fits Cornell's multi-college campus well."[50]

On Sunday, August 26, 2001, three thousand students came together for a symposium at Barton Hall, where faculty members along with a graduate student led them in an exploration of the book. That evening and throughout the next day, first-year students flexed their intellectual muscles in small discussion groups, most of them led by faculty. Rawlings and Martin were among the discussion leaders. *Guns, Germs, and Steel* was also incorporated into assignments in some fall semester first-year writing seminars. On September 25, the Cornell community gathered to hear the author's own analysis when Jared Diamond appeared at Bailey Hall.

While acknowledging that there may have been some students who were underwhelmed by the book project, Provost Martin said she thought it had achieved success in sending a signal that they were attending "a serious academic institution where they're going to be expected to work hard and participate in intellectual debate, take responsibility for their own education, and not simply listen to other people."[51]

The project's second-year assignment, in 2002, was *Frankenstein* by Mary Shelley, a novel that provoked questions about science, ethics, and the nature of humanity. The university broadened the scope of the book project, encouraging alumni to form discussion groups and drawing the surrounding community into the conversation by distributing over fifteen hundred free books to the Tompkins County Library, local high schools, senior citizens centers, and other civic organizations. In 2003, to honor Rawlings in his last year as president, the university chose *Antigone* by Sophocles, and an adaption of the play was presented at the Schwartz Center for the Performing Arts. In subsequent years, contemporary works of fiction and nonfiction (including *Lincoln at Gettysburg* by Garry Wills, *Do Androids Dream of Electric Sheep?* by Philip K. Dick, *Homer and Langley* by E. L. Doctorow, *The Pickup* by Nadine Gordimer, and *When the Emperor Was Divine*, by Julie Otsuka) were selected. In 2008, the *Cornell Alumni Magazine* looked back at the North Campus initiative. Although the experiment was still evolving, the magazine found substantial evidence of student satisfaction.

In addition to the book project, new students arriving on campus met such traditions as the Dump and Run recycling sale (in which donated clothing and household goods left by departing students the previous semester were sold) and "freshman migration," a trek across the Thurston Avenue bridge to central campus. As measured in surveys of graduating seniors, overall satisfaction with the housing and accessibility of faculty during freshman year was at an all-time high at Cornell. Casey Stevenson '05 acknowledged that a residence hall closer to Engineering would be nice, especially in the snow, "but it's worth being farther away to be all together as a class."[52] Students also singled out the bright and sunny public spaces and the dorm rooms in Court and Mews, and the dining and recreational facilities in Appel Commons, the second student union on North Campus (named for Robert Appel '53 and Helen Appel '55).

Cornell administrators knew that students who had a successful first year at college were much more likely to be well adjusted throughout their time on campus. Gregory Eells, director of Psychological Services at Gannett Health Center, suggested that having first-year students share the same space and many of the same experiences helped them balance their aspirations for independence and their need to act responsibly. At age eighteen, Eells indicated, Cornell freshmen were adults in the eyes of the law but had frontal cortexes that were not as developed as they would be at age twenty-five. Many of them experimented with new distance from the "helicopter parents" who for so long had hovered over them. Consequently, they were likely "to be more impulsive and less able to predict consequences." With professors and trained professionals on hand, the North Campus initiative allowed Cornell "to create more of a safety net."[53]

Wʜᴀᴛ ᴛᴏ ᴅᴏ then with the freshman-free West Campus? President Rawlings promised to make the living and learning environment on West Campus "architecturally and programmatically attractive to upperclass students." Ways to meet their needs and interests, he indicated, might include an adaptation of "the residential college model used effectively at a number of other universities."[54] In September 1998, a committee composed of professors, administrators (in Student and Academic Services and Campus Life), and undergraduates, chaired by Dean of Students John Ford, recommended a framework for housing approximately eighteen hundred post-freshmen on West Campus. Noting that numerous studies on housing since 1966 had preceded their report, committee members pointed to a "heightened concern" in colleges and universities in general, and at Cornell in particular, about the role of residential life in the intellectual, social, and cultural development of undergraduates. They made four core recommendations: (1) establish an environment on West Campus that has "faculty leadership as its primary principle"; (2) develop living-learning houses, whose "personality" would evolve over time, based in part on the interests and needs of the faculty members and students residing in them; (3) redesign or construct four or five houses, each with communal dining, seminar rooms, faculty offices, guest apartments, a library, and social spaces; and (4) recruit distinguished senior Cornell faculty with their families as live-in "house heads" and in other important roles.[55]

In fall 1998, Vice President Murphy appointed professors, administrators, and students to a West Campus Planning Group and asked them to specify the structure and programmatic content of the visionary goals laid out by the Ford Committee. Chaired by professor of government Isaac Kramnick, who became the intellectual leader, principal advocate, and driving force behind the West Campus initiative, the planning group produced a detailed plan in May 2000 that proposed a root and branch transformation of West Campus. The U-Halls would be demolished and replaced by five new houses, presided over by house professors. Some twenty or twenty-five other faculty, administrators, and coaches would be affiliated with each house, having meal privileges to encourage interaction with students. Undergraduate resident advisers, an entrenched tradition at Cornell, would be replaced by resident graduate students. Spaces would be provided in each house for small classes as well as for concerts and other cultural events. The planning group insisted that a dining hall in each house (and a mandatory meal plan for every resident) "was essential to building community." The group presented its proposals "as a landmark opportunity to enhance fundamentally the undergraduate experience at Cornell."[56]

Hunter Rawlings agreed. He authorized the demolition of the U-Halls by 2004 and the construction of five residential colleges, each of them with the capacity to house about 350 students. And he asked Kramnick, who had become the university's first vice provost for undergraduate education, and Edna Dugan, assistant vice president for student and academic services, to cochair a new West Campus Council, to plan and oversee the initiative. The president emphasized that, unlike the houses at Harvard and Yale, in which all undergraduates were required to live, the West Campus houses would provide another choice among Cornell's many residential options. When leaders of the Greek system complained that the initiative covertly intended to undercut fraternities and sororities by reducing the pool of potential pledges, Rawlings replied, "Let the competition begin." Recognizing that raising $200 million for the physical and programmatic transformation of West Campus would be especially difficult because the council had decided that each of the buildings was to carry the name of a legendary (deceased) Cornell professor, Rawlings turned to "the anonymous donor," persuading the Atlantic Philanthropies to contribute $100 million. "This magnificent pledge," Rawlings announced in October 1999, "gives us a solid path, not a narrow and tenuous rope bridge, along which to develop the plans for the transformation of West Campus."[57]

On April 28, 2003, ground was broken for the first West Campus house, to be named for ILR professor Alice Cook, one of the first scholars to study the experiences of working women in the United States. Ross Brann, professor of Judeo-Islamic studies and chair of the Near Eastern Studies Department, agreed to serve as Cook House professor and dean. "Cornell is big, with all of the resources that come with a major research institution," Brann noted, "but it succeeds best when it creates smaller intellectual and social communities." Led by faculty and run by students, Alice Cook, he claimed, would be such a community. In 2023, Edna Dugan predicted, alumni would say " 'I was a member of Alice Cook House,' the way a classmate might say, 'I was a member of the Glee Club or hockey team.' It provides another positive sense of identity, which we all need."[58]

In August 2004, 360 students and staff walked past a "Rock the Vote" van, stationed there to register students for the presidential election, and joined Ross Brann for the grand opening of Alice Cook, whose exterior design was intended to echo the adjacent "Gothic" structures (Boldt Hall, Baker Tower, and Baker Hall North), with their sloped roofs, stone, and chimney-like ventilation shafts. Many of the residents, the *Daily Sun* reported, chose to live at Alice Cook because it was brand new. Others, however, "were drawn by the allure of the community atmosphere."[59]

Construction on West Campus was slowed by a protracted dispute over a parking lot. To provide parking for house students, staff, and faculty, the administration planned to build a 176-space lot, east of University Avenue, on nearly three acres of the former Treman estate, dubbed "Redbud Woods." The lot would replace 195 spots lost under the Alice Cook House footprint. Environmentalists argued that it would deprive the community of green space, destroy

Alice Cook House, the first West Campus residential college, 2004. (Cornell University Photography)

the ecology of the area, eliminate sanctuaries for wildlife, and generate water runoff from pavement that would flood downstream basements. Maintaining that there was already an excess of cars in the neighborhood, they championed alternatives, suggesting that Cornell give bus passes to students, limit or eliminate parking privileges for freshmen, and find other ways to encourage the use of more environmentally responsible transportation. In 2003, the Ithaca Planning Board, which supported virtually all other aspects of the West Campus initiative, voted to deny Cornell approval for a parking area, as did the Ithaca Landmarks Preservation Commission. Fifty-two faculty, headed by Cornell's distinguished professor of entomology Tom Eisner, wrote to President Lehman to object to the parking lot. Arguing that as an educational entity it was exempt from zoning restrictions, Cornell sued the city and the commission, prevailing in the New York State Supreme Court in June 2004 and in the Appellate Division of the State Supreme Court in March 2005.

The Redbud Woods Working Group, a coalition of students, faculty, and community activists, fought on. Vowing to make this "the Waterloo of parking lots," their leader, Danny Pearlstein '05, MRP '07, declared "We have seen the other way of life, and it's totally livable."[60] On April 13, 2005, about a hundred protesters dressed in red, thumping empty buckets, and chanting "Don't pave paradise," appeared in front of Day Hall, where high school students and their parents were beginning their campus tours.[61] Two weeks later, two students used reinforced steel pipes to lock their arms around a tree, as fifty of their fellow protestors held a vigil outside Day Hall. They told passersby that the Student Assembly had passed two resolutions in favor of preserving Redbud Woods, asked them to join hundreds of others in signing a petition, and held up posters inscribed "Lehman, be a tree."[62]

Following a scheduled meeting in President Lehman's office on April 28 that ended at 12:30 p.m., and which both sides characterized as civil and productive, eight students, who would become known as the Redbud Eight, five of them chained together with PVC piping, shut down Day Hall for six hours. They claimed they would not leave until Lehman agreed that no parking lots would be constructed on green spaces, issued a public apology to the community, and granted amnesty to all Redbud Woods activists. Meanwhile, other members of the working group tried to enter Day Hall but were turned away. At 5:45 p.m. police came into the president's office and detached the protesters. Three of them left the building. Pearlstein and coleader Jordan Wells '07 were handcuffed and placed in a police car, but when protesters prevented the vehicle from leaving the scene, they were brought back into the building and then released, along with three others. Five of the students were charged with trespassing and resisting arrest; three of them with trespassing. "You have disgraced the University today," Pearlstein told Vice President Murphy, who had allegedly refused to allow him to take a photograph of his handcuffed wrists.[63]

On May 4, protesters deposited dozens of pounds of soil and plants at the entrance to the Day Hall parking lot, parked three cars in front of the building, and removed the wheels from them. One car contained a wooden coffin with the branch of a tree from Redbud Woods. Its roof and trunk door had been torn off to showcase plantings from "The Jeffrey S. Lehman Urban Garden." That day, dozens of faculty, staff, and graduate students published a letter in the *Cornell Daily Sun* urging "respect for the nonviolent actions of the Redbud Eight" and asking the administration to agree to a six-month moratorium on construction of the parking lot and to consultation with constituencies on and off campus. The *Sun* also noted, however, that "a fair share" of the Cornell community opposed the protests. Some thought the issue at hand was incommensurate with the claims of the working group that transparency, democracy, and sustainability had been betrayed by the administration. Others arrived at Day Hall with posters declaring, "Don't Save It, Pave It!"[64]

Starting on June 6, the start date for construction of the parking lot, protesters occupied Redbud Woods. When several of them scrambled up trees or chained themselves to heavy objects on the ground, the national media began to cover the story. On July 15, the administration ordered the activists to leave the site immediately. A construction fence was put up around the area, and Cornell Police issued more than seventy citations for trespassing. After a weekend of negotiations, Hunter Rawlings, who had become interim president a few weeks earlier, signed an agreement with members of the Redbud Woods Working Group that ended the standoff. On condition that the protesters leave of their own volition and not impede construction or engage in acts of vandalism, Rawlings promised to drop trespassing charges, issue free transportation passes to all new students who did not request parking permits, and work with student and faculty committees and a neighborhood council to draft and implement environmentally sustainable transportation policies. Standing alongside Pearlstein, Rawlings asserted that the outcome was "good for everyone concerned."

The night before the agreement was signed, Asian Studies professor Jane Marie Law, who had earlier been arrested for trespassing, spent several hours in the woods. Because it "was a beautiful space where you could see the lake and the crescent moon," she felt she had been part of "a life and death struggle," she later recalled. As disappointed as Professor Law, Patrick Young '06, a leader of the protest, endorsed the agreement because it was "the only thing we could do to keep our friends from being hurt." Seven individuals, none of them members of the working group, refused to leave the site. One of them chained himself to a pipe near the gate on University Avenue and started a hunger strike. The police removed him at 3 a.m. on July 20. The next day, the remaining protesters left Redbud Woods. By then, Cornell groundskeepers had salvaged black walnut and other hardwood trees for use by local woodworkers and removed and potted more than fifty redbud saplings, which were offered to anyone interested in replanting them.[65]

Protesters gather as loggers start clearing Redbud Woods, July 2005. (Courtesy *Ithaca Journal*)

433

A month later, West Campus had moved forward, opening its second residence as house professor and dean Cindy Hazan, a professor of human development, welcomed students to Carl Becker House. Along with her husband, Richard Canfield, a senior research associate in Nutritional Sciences, Hazan adopted many of the practices introduced by Ross Brann. In 2005–6, Becker hosted Bill Nye '77, "the Science Guy," in its guest suite (an event patterned on the visit of Janet Reno '60 to Alice Cook), as well as an expert on Japanese hip-hop from MIT and a masseuse, who helped students combat stress during study week.

In January 2007 the new Noyes Community and Recreation Center opened on West Campus. The building boasted a convenience store with a diversity of foods including a full line of kosher products, a thirteen-foot climbing wall, air hockey tables, an outdoor basketball and volleyball court, a fitness center, three lounges equipped with "RedRover" wireless, and a multipurpose room. The facility became a valuable resource for all West Campus residents.

January 15, 2007, was move-in day at Hans Bethe House for about 320 students, many of whom had lived in Class of '18 and Class of '26 halls the previous fall. The house bore the name of the man who, according to Hunter Rawlings, "controlled the entire field of physics in his head" and "changed the way much of contemporary science is done."[66] The first house professor and dean of Bethe House was Porus Olpadwala, MBA '73, MRP '76, PhD '79, a professor of city and regional planning (who had been dean of Architecture, Art, and Planning from 1998 to 2004). A specialist in urban and economic development and environmental issues in developing countries, he also brought to Bethe an interest in and intimate knowledge of the culture, society, and politics of India.

Keeton House opened its doors in August 2008. An expert in avian navigation, including pigeon homing, William Keeton had revolutionized the teaching of biology with his standing-room-only introductory lecture course, until his death at age forty-seven in 1980. The first house professor and dean at Keeton was Jefferson Cowie, an ILR professor, whose interests included labor history and American popular culture.

Flora Rose House, the fifth and final West Campus house, was finished in the fall of 2008 and officially open its doors in August 2009. It bore the name of the nutritionist who, along with Martha Van Rensselaer, established a department of home economics that later became the College of Human Ecology. House professor and dean Shirley Samuels, an English professor, who wrote and taught about American literature and photography, praised Flora Rose "as a testament to the possibilities Cornell provided then and still provides today."[67]

As he marked the opening of Rose House, President Skorton celebrated "a new Cornell where the West Campus Housing system is not just a vision or a dream but is a reality."[68] Completed ahead of time and on budget, West Campus was the largest capital expenditure and the most innovative program in residential education on the campus since 1868. Undergraduates were clamoring to secure rooms in one of the houses, and 150 faculty members had agreed to be affiliates. Although no one was prepared to declare that student culture had already been fundamentally transformed, the new normal on West Campus and North Campus, animated by a vision of students sharing the intellectual and social potential of college and residential life, represented singular achievements in the history of Cornell.

SOME TRADITIONS DIE hard. Some do not die at all. Hazing has been a pervasive practice in clubs, teams, fraternities, and sororities in colleges and universities for generations. A 2008 study by the National Collaborative for Hazing Research and Prevention found that more than half the members of these organizations (and 73 percent of Greeks) reported being hazed. The National Study of Student Hazing revealed that same year that the vast majority of hazing incidents were unreported. In its moderate form, according to its defenders, hazing was a rite of passage that promoted knowledge of and dedication to the organization and bonding with its members. Critics pointed out, however, that hazing can be extreme and often endangers physical and mental health, through the forced consumption of alcohol, sleep deprivation, beatings, humiliation, and sexual acts. In the U.S. at least one hazing-related death has occurred on a college campus each year since 1970 (when records began to be kept).

At Cornell in the twenty-first century, most of the attention to hazing was directed at fraternities and sororities—and to "pledging," the "probationary" period between a "bid" (an invitation to join) and full and formal acceptance as a chapter member. Hazing, Vice President Murphy declared, "runs counter to every value we have regarding student life and our core missions." Because a vocal few continued to believe that the practice was positive and necessary, she noted, hazing had been perpetuated. "The reality is that the perceived benefits of hazing are largely unrealized," she said.[69] Hazing was prohibited by the Cornell Campus Code of Conduct, the Fraternity and Sorority Judicial Code, and New York State law. In 2004, Cornell's Interfraternity Council, Panhellenic Association, and the Multicultural Greek Council adopted a "sunshine policy," mandating that all reports of hazing incidents be made accessible to the public. The next year, the university launched a website, hazing.cornell.edu, which provided information about hazing, allowing visitors to report incidents and read about alternative organization-building activities. The website revealed graphic details about hazing. One fraternity, a post alleged, forced pledges to take off their clothes, lie in a pool with six inches of ice water, urine, beer, and kitchen garbage, while other new members took turns dropping raw eggs into their mouths.

In 2010, following the suspension of Kappa Sigma by the fraternity's national organization for hosting a party with alcohol without alerting their regional manager or registering with the Interfraternity Council, Cornell gave Greek leaders two years to completely eliminate alcohol from all recruitment and pledging activities. The directive was "not our idea at all," Interfraternity Council president Allen Miller '11 declared: "We've spent so much time trying to argue with the Administration. . . . We're at a point where we know things aren't negotiable."[70] When the board of trustees approved the policy changes, however, Miller acknowledged that compliance would be a challenge but promised that the Greeks would "focus on getting to know people in a safe and healthier environment."[71] Hazing continued at Cornell, however. In 2010, complaints were filed following 13 percent of all Greek events, more than double the percentage in 2005. The number of disciplinary cases, many of them involving hazing, increased as well.

On Friday, February 25, 2011, George Desdunes, a sophomore in Human Ecology, majoring in biology and society, and a member of Sigma Alpha Epsilon, was found unconscious on a couch in the fraternity house, a three-story Tudor-style building called Hillcrest. Desdunes was transported to Cayuga Medical Center, where he died. In a "reverse" hazing incident, the *New York Times* subsequently revealed, Desdunes and another Cornell sophomore had been kidnapped by freshmen pledges and driven to a townhouse on campus. After downing a shot of vodka each time they failed to answer a trivia question about the fraternity, the two men consumed "pixy stix," a concoction of chocolate powder, strawberry syrup, hot sauce, and a bite of a sandwich. Apparently, Desdunes passed out, and his colleague vomited into a garbage pail. The two young men were placed in the back seat of a car and driven to the library of the fraternity, where they were left on a leather couch, blindfolded, their wrists and ankles bound with zip ties and duct tape. After tilting Desdunes's head so that he would throw up on the floor and not choke, the kidnappers went to the kitchen, got something to eat, and went to bed. Around 7 a.m., after the maintenance worker picked up plastic cups, straightened out the furniture, and scrubbed the toilets—the aftereffects of a beer pong tournament that had ended at 1:30 a.m.—he noticed someone in a brown hoodie on the couch, "with vomit or mucous in his mouth," tried to wake him up, and called 911. When rescue workers arrived on the scene, they did not find a single fraternity member in sight.

In March, Cornell revoked recognition of the SAE chapter (which had been suspended for a semester for hazing violations in 2006) for five years and ordered that Hillcrest, which was owned by the university, be vacated. Three students were charged with misdemeanor hazing in connection with the case; the records of a fourth, a juvenile, were sealed. Through one of their lawyers, Raymond Schlather, JD '76, the pledges alleged that Desdunes had a history of binge drinking, had consumed a significant amount of alcohol before the kidnapping, and went along with the prank, which would have ended had he asked them to stop.[72] In June 2012, Judge Judith Rossiter, JD '86, of Tompkins County Court found that Desdunes had been drinking heavily before the kidnapping and had a reputation for holding his liquor and acquitted three defendants of hazing in the first degree and unlawfully dealing with a child (serving alcohol to a person under twenty-one), both misdemeanors. Because the fourth defendant was a minor, the charges against him were resolved separately and not disclosed. The fraternity did not defend itself and was found guilty of hazing and other related charges.

In a series of public statements on campus and an op-ed published in the *New York Times*, President Skorton declared that the tragedy had convinced him that "it was time—long past time—to remedy practices of the fraternity system that continue to foster hazing, which has persisted at Cornell." Over the past decade, he indicated, almost 60 percent of fraternity and sorority chapters had been deemed responsible for activities defined as hazing by the Cornell Code of Conduct. Skorton directed leaders of the Greek system to develop approaches to member recruitment and initiation that did not involve pledging or encourage hazing and other risky behavior, either directly or indirectly. He urged national fraternities and sororities to end pledging across all campuses and for Cornell students to lead the way.[73]

Skorton suggested that bright young people subjected themselves to hazing because they wanted to forge their own identities and be accepted into a group—and because constraints on organizational activities that perpetuated bad behavior were ineffective. He called attention as well to the role of substance abuse in hazing. High-risk drinking and drug use, he pointed out, were two to three times more prevalent among fraternity and sorority members than among the rest of the student population. "Alcohol makes it easier for members to subject recruits to physical and mental abuse without feeling remorse and to excuse bad behavior on the ground of intoxication," he wrote. "It provides a social lubricant, but it impairs the judgment of those being hazed and lowers their ability to resist." Calling attention to a "pressing need for better ways to bring students together in socially productive, enjoyable and memorable ways," such as Sigma Phi Epsilon's "Balanced Man Program," which emphasized community service, Skorton concluded that pledging "and the humiliation and bullying that go with it—can no longer be the price of entry" to fraternities and sororities.[74]

A twenty-four-person task force was constituted to respond to Skorton's challenge to Cornell's sixty-four fraternities and sororities and their 3,647 members—26 percent of all undergraduates—to remove the power differential between members and pledges, which often led to coercive behavior during the initiation process, and move to a "membership development" model focused on the chapter's core values that extended from recruitment through initiation into active membership. The task force, which included staff, alumni, and faculty, as well as thirteen students, took on the acronym RARE—Recruitment, Acceptance, Retention, and Education—a reference to its goal of redefining pledging to encompass all these objectives. Change would not come swiftly, IFC president Chris Sanders '13 emphasized, and it required preserving the Greek system's structures. "No one solution will be the silver bullet to the end of this very complex societal issue. All culture change takes time, but as it becomes the norm people will grow to accept it," he added. "That being said, we as a community will continue to take it on ourselves to facilitate these changes."[75]

RARE issued its report in fall 2012. Titled "Meeting the Challenge: The Evolution of Cornell's Greek Community," it recommended a comprehensive approach, to be fully implemented in 2014–15, to address "destructive, coercive and dangerous activities" by building on "the exceptional values of Greek life," including leadership, fellowship, scholarship, and philanthropy, "and emphasizing that hazing is not compatible with these values." The task force put forward several proposals for consideration by Greek chapters, their umbrella organizations, and university administrators. RARE wanted to eliminate the terms "pledge" and "pledging" and other derogatory terms meant to separate new and continuing members and shorten the "new member intake process" from eight to four weeks, effective before spring 2014. The report recommended that Cornell offer intensive education and social programs (including a sophomore "Break the Cycle" initiative and antihazing training) and direct all chapters to submit detailed plans for events they planned to hold, for approval by the Office of Fraternity and Sorority Affairs. It suggested that off-campus chapter houses be provided access to Cornell emergency responders (in the past, some houses turned away help from EMS personnel because they feared it would subject them to disciplinary action for hosting unauthorized parties or serving alcohol to underage students) and that the university post online all guilty verdicts and corresponding penalties assessed by the Greek Judicial Board, the Fraternity and Sorority Review Board, and the Interfraternity, Panhellenic, and Multicultural Greek Judicial Councils. Most controversial, the task force recommended a required "live in adviser" for new and "at risk" houses and raised the possibility of mandating one for all fraternities and sororities.[76]

In November 2012, President Skorton applauded the work done by the RARE task force. Singling out the reduction in the period between the acceptance of a bid and formal induction and the substantive redefinition of "pledging," he indicated that the recommendations in the report constituted "important first steps." Nonetheless, since decisions had yet to be made about the most important proposals in the report, including live-in advisers in chapter houses, Skorton insisted that "it is equally clear that we are not yet where we need to be."[77]

Although some students, faculty, and administrators thought the recommendations, if adopted, would not fully "eliminate pledging as we know it," as Skorton had mandated, many officers and rank-and-file members of fraternities and sororities thought they went too far. Heightened enforcement of university rules, including the ban on first-semester freshmen from attending their parties, they claimed, would drive risky behavior from fraternity houses to less safe environments. They were most upset, however, at the prospect of a loss of autonomy in various aspects of Greek life, especially if live-in advisers were looking over their shoulders. Convinced that, in the wake of the death of George Desdunes, change was necessary to preserve the system, Interfraternity Council president Chris Sanders '13 cautioned his fellow students that "self-governance is a privilege that is granted by the Administration and by the Trustees. That privilege comes with a sense of responsibility, and I don't think we've lived up to that responsibility. If behavior like we saw near the end of this semester continues, we run the risk of further distancing ourselves from that privilege."[78]

Sanders was referring to actions taken in 2012 against four houses—Tau Epsilon Phi, Phi Sigma Kappa, Pi Kappa Phi, and Acacia—for incidents involving hazing or underage and excessive drinking, or both. These behaviors, it appeared, remained pervasive at Cornell. An online survey of 615 sophomores, conducted in fall 2012, revealed that 32 percent of the freshmen who joined a fraternity or sorority were hazed. According to Tim Marchell '82, director of mental health initiatives at Gannett Health Services, the challenge was complicated by the finding that many of them did not identify their experience as "hazing" because they did not know that university policy deemed physically or psychologically harmful activities to be hazing, regardless of the person's "consent" to participate. Although 86 percent of the students in the sample agreed that humiliation and intimidation should not be part of joining a group or organization, Marchell added, "they weren't so sure that others believe those types of activities were unacceptable." Greek student leaders took solace in the fact that Cornell was well below the national average for hazing in fraternities and sororities.[79]

Fraternities and sororities did not fare any better in 2013. In January, Cornell withdrew recognition from Tau Epsilon Phi after two pledges were hospitalized following an alcohol-related, sexually humiliating incident, in which their underwear was ripped off their bodies. In February and March, Sigma Nu, Chi Psi, and Delta Phi were suspended, following documented instances of hazing. Phi Kappa Psi was suspended in April. In December, incidents of underage and binge drinking prompted Cornell to revoke recognition of Delta Kappa Epsilon for a minimum of two years. Also in fall 2013, moreover, Athletic Director Andy Noel canceled the exhibition games of the varsity men's lacrosse team after a hazing incident that involved coerced consumption of alcohol by a freshman. "Team bonding is important," Noel noted, "and there are many ways to achieve it that don't involve hazing."[80]

Vice President Murphy and Travis Apgar, associate dean of students for fraternity and sorority affairs, suggested that increased reporting of infractions was evidence of progress. "It feels negative, because you hate to hear bad news," Murphy acknowledged. "But I take it as a sign that people understand what's okay and what's not okay, and they don't have tolerance for [what is] not okay."[81] While Apgar pointed out that "education is not nearly as effective as enforcement when it comes to hazing and alcohol abuse," he also noticed a shift in norms.[82] Although a few chapters "had taken backward steps" and succumbed to pressure from upperclassmen to use "certain activities" to make new members "prove themselves," he said, many others were embracing change.[83]

Greek student leaders agreed, but worried about the future of fraternities and sororities at Cornell. Michael Reynolds '15, president of Zeta Psi, claimed that Greeks had been "greatly mischaracterized" as "mindless animals that do nothing but drink"—and not recognized for their contributions to philanthropy and campus engagement. Although he deemed university administrators well-intentioned, with a legitimate responsibility to protect the well-being of students, Reynolds, resurrecting the old indictment of *in loco parentis*, did not think they should "babysit" undergraduates: "We want to be treated as responsible adults and be put on an equal field as anyone else." If changes were to be made, he concluded, "they should be done slowly. That is the only way to ensure a lasting change that meets halfway between the Greek system and the administration."[84]

As Cornell approached its sesquicentennial, it remained a house divided. Administrators and the student leaders of Cornell's thirty-seven Interfraternity Council fraternities, twelve Panhellenic Council sororities, and fourteen Multicultural Greek Letter Council chapters did not agree about what it meant to "end pledging as we know it" and how to eliminate the stereotypical behaviors, including hazing and underage and excessive drinking, associated with fraternities and sororities. The system will "remain strong," Colin Foley '14, president of the Interfraternity Council, predicted. "Fraternities and sororities will continue to be an integral part of campus life, a home away from home for one third of our student body."[85] And, according to the 2013 "Cornell Perceptions of Undergraduate Life and Student Experiences Survey," an online questionnaire filled out by 45 percent of the student body, 49 percent of undergraduates either disagreed or strongly disagreed that they "enjoy what the Greek system contributes to Cornell University."[86]

SINCE ITS FOUNDING, Cornell has taken on more and more responsibilities for the health and welfare of its students. In 1870, the university set aside rooms for sick students; seven years later, a medical examiner was appointed to evaluate students seeking exemption from military duties on the grounds of ill health. Following the death of Henry Sage in 1897, his mansion on East State Street became the Cornell infirmary. An addition to it was completed in 1912. The infirmary provided beds, board, and some nursing care. Until about 1940, Cornell viewed diagnosis and treatment as the responsibility of the students and their families. In the 1950s, university administrators concluded that the infirmary was poorly located and outdated, and with the financial support of the Gannett Foundation built the Gannett Health Clinic. By the time Gannett expanded to its west side in 1979, bringing it to thirty-nine thousand square feet of interior space, professionals were on staff to deliver preventive, diagnostic, and therapeutic care related to mental as well as physical health. In the 1980s and '90s, Gannett responded aggressively to the AIDS epidemic. In 1986, Cornell became one of the first universities to provide free and anonymous HIV antibody testing to students, faculty, and staff.

In the twenty-first century, University Health Services (UHS) provided a comprehensive approach to student health. Services included clinical care; educational programs on eating disorders, sleep, stress, substance abuse, hazing, and sexual health; after-hours calling services; physical therapy (at Schoellkopf Hall); mobile clinics for flu shots; occupational medicine; disability services; oversight for animal and human subject research; electronic health records; and liaison with local and state health departments. The new normal of university life—international travel, ever increasing expectations for academic performance, medical management that allowed sicker individuals to attend college, and state and federal government mandates—led to new challenges. In the millennial years, UHS played the central role on campus in responding to global infectious disease pandemics and a suicide cluster that claimed six lives.

Between 2002 and 2003, SARS (severe acute respiratory syndrome), which had spread from southern China and Hong Kong to thirty-seven countries, nearly became a pandemic, but did not devastate Ithaca, New York. Neither did the much-publicized "avian flu" a few years later. In the summer of 2009, after outbreaks of the H1N1 "swine flu" in Mexico and the United States, the World Health Organization declared the disease a pandemic, and the Cornell campus braced itself for an invasion of the virus when students returned for the fall semester. Accompanied by fever, sore throat, coughing, chills, and, occasionally, diarrhea and vomiting, the flu was usually mild, with most people recovering within four to seven days with self-care at home. But it could be deadly. In college and university settings, especially those with significant numbers of international students, the U.S. Center for Disease Control and Prevention warned, it could spread very rapidly.

The fall semester of 2009 at Cornell began with a raft of cases. In a two-week period in September, over one hundred students per day were diagnosed with H1N1 symptoms. Implementing a plan that had been crafted in 2008, a "flu incident lead team" monitored developments, with guidance from the CDC and the New York State Department of Health, and managed day-to-day operations. Gannett staff canceled less-urgent appointments, offered vaccinations, and used follow-up telephone calls to monitor the progress of patients. To reduce the pressure on Gannett, a Cornell "flu line" was established, staffed by volunteers from University Communications, Campus Life, and the Office of the Dean of Students, trained to answer questions about the disease. The Interfraternity Council imposed a moratorium on social events to help curb the spread of the H1N1. Professors posted assignments, lecture notes, and course materials online for anyone unable to attend class. If the pandemic turned out to be more severe than anticipated, Provost Fuchs indicated in a letter to faculty, "a general suspension of instruction may be necessary."[87]

On September 11, Warren Schor, a junior majoring in applied economics and management, died from complications related to H1N1. Underlying medical conditions, the *Daily Sun* reported, had put him at greater risk of serious consequences from the disease. By the end of the month, however, the number of new cases had declined dramatically to around twenty or twenty-five per day. At the end of the semester, 1,628 students had been diagnosed as probable H1N1 victims. When students returned in the spring 2010, the threat of this new strain of flu had largely passed. But the next potential pandemic often appeared near or on the horizon—and university officials had to spend time and money preparing for it, just in case.

For entirely different reasons, the spring of 2010 turned out to be deadlier than the fall of 2009. On February 17, rescue workers found the body of Bradley Ginsburg, a freshman in Arts and Sciences, in Fall Creek Gorge, under the Thurston Avenue Bridge. On March 11, a utility crew doing work on the underside of the bridge discovered the remains of William Sinclair, a sophomore in the College of Engineering. And the very next day, police responded to a call from a motorist driving along Stewart Avenue who observed a person, later identified as Matt Zika, a junior in the College of Engineering, jump from the Suspension Bridge. These three fatalities were part of a "suicide cluster" in the 2009–10 academic year, involving six students (three of whom used other means to take their lives). The ensuing national coverage, experts informed university officials, elevated the risk for future "copycat" suicides by vulnerable people living in Ithaca.

In an e-mail sent on Friday, March 12, President Skorton implored students to remember that they were not alone. "If you learn anything at Cornell," he emphasized, "please learn to ask for help. It is a sign of wisdom and strength." Provost Fuchs and Dean of the Faculty William Fry, PhD '70, asked faculty members to reach out to their students. University staff knocked on the doors of every dormitory room and checked on the residents. Gannett opened its doors on Saturday and Sunday. Hand-made notes posted on the bridges encouraged students to "smile" and remember that "your prelim grade isn't as bad as being mauled by a bear." And Cornell Police Department officers, EMS workers, and private security employees were stationed, night and day, on all the bridges.[88]

On Wednesday, March 17, one thousand students, faculty, and staff gathered on the Arts quad in an event called "Lift Your Spirits." They made paper cranes with members of the Origami Club, threw Frisbees, talked with peer counselors from Empathy, Assistance, and Referral Service (EARS) and Gannett staff, and listened to David Skorton exhort them to connect with one another. Two days later, most Cornell undergraduates left for spring break, giving them some needed time off and an opportunity to regroup.

WHILE THE STUDENTS were gone, Cornell varsity athletes gave all Cornellians lots of reasons to lift their spirits. On March 19, the women's hockey team, winner of the ECAC title, made its first appearance in an NCAA Division I Women's Hockey Frozen Four. Led by Laura Fortino, Lauriane Rougeau '13, and Catherine White '12, each of whom was named a Division 1 All-American, the Big Red defeated number-one-ranked Mercyhurst College, 3–2, in overtime. The championship game on March 20 lasted 119 minutes and 26 seconds of playing time, the longest hockey game in Cornell history, with the University of Minnesota–Duluth winning, 3–2.

Following suit, the Cornell men's hockey team competed in the ECAC championships in Albany, New York. On March 19, led by Locke Jillson '12, John Esposito '13, and goalie Ben Scrivens '10, the Big Read defeated Brown University 3–0 and advanced to the finals. The next night, Cornell faced off against Union College and again won 3–0, with Scrivens recording a school-record nineteenth career shutout. A week later, the season ended with a 6–2 loss to New Hampshire in the first round of the NCAA tournament.

Starting on March 18, one day earlier than their peers on the hockey teams, the men's wrestling team, which had won its eighth straight Ivy League title, competed for the NCAA championship in Omaha, Nebraska. After a disappointing first day, only Mack Lewnes '11, Cam Simaz '12, and Kyle Dake '13, a freshman from nearby Lansing, New York, remained in contention for individual championships. Lewnes and Dake made the finals, with the latter winning his championship. Cornell's second-place finish was the best ever for Cornell, and for any Ivy League men's wrestling team. Compiling an overall record of 137 wins and 4 losses, Dake went on to make history, becoming the first wrestler to win NCAA titles at four different weight classes. In the spring of 2013, he became *Sports Illustrated*'s inaugural male College Athlete of the Year.

The 2010 men's varsity basketball team at the NCAA Tournament, Jacksonville, Florida, 2010. (Cornell University Photography)

Capping what may well have been the greatest Cornell sports weekend, the men's varsity basketball team, which had won its third straight Ivy League championship, journeyed to Veterans Memorial Arena in Jacksonville, Florida, for the NCAA "March Madness" championship. On March 19, Cornell defeated Temple University, 78–65, and became the first team in school history to advance to the second round of the tournament. Led by Louis Dale '10, Ryan Wittman '10, and Jeff Foote '10, the team beat the University of Wisconsin, 87–69, the next day, to advance to the "Sweet Sixteen." Cornell's Cinderella season ended the following Thursday night at the Carrier Dome in Syracuse, New York, with a 62–45 loss to number-one-seeded Kentucky. Near the end of the game, the *Cornell Daily Sun* reported, coach Steve Donahue replaced his starters with reserve players, to a chant from fans in the stands that, according to the *Sun*, "could not have been more appropriate: 'Thank you seniors.' "[89]

WHEN UNDERGRADUATES RETURNED to campus, the university celebrated Cornell's historic sports season with a big bash. No one could fail to notice, however, that while they were gone the university had moved forward with one immediate response to recent tragedies. It installed ten-foot-high chain-link safety fences on the bridges it owned, and construction had begun as well on the

444

Thurston Avenue bridge and the two bridges on Stewart Avenue owned by the City of Ithaca, after Mayor Carolyn Peterson issued an emergency declaration allowing Cornell to install them. The chain-link fences were temporary, university officials reported, and would remain in place until the long-term solution was determined. "As an architect," Dean of Students Kent Hubbell '69 indicated, "I look forward to the day when we have much more pleasing, permanent approaches for enhancing safety while preserving the natural and man-made beauty of our campus."[90]

It was not the first time Cornell had considered building bridge barriers, and the intervention was not without controversy. In 1977, following three suicides in the gorges, a suit by a bereaved parent, and lobbying by Nina Miller, the director of the Suicide Prevention and Crisis Service, university officials announced plans to install six-and-a-half-foot metal bars on the Collegetown bridge. "Students' freedom to run their lives as adults will be mocked as they stare through the prison-like bars," the editors of the *Cornell Daily Sun* fumed. In letters to the paper, some undergraduates, graduate students, and faculty bemoaned the destruction of the "pristine view" as a detriment to mental health, recommended redirecting the resources to academic counseling and psychiatric health programs, and pointed to the absence of hard evidence that suicide barriers were effective. Cornell administrators suspended the metal-bars plan.[91]

In 2010, however, Vice President Murphy claimed that experts in the field considered the use of "means restrictions," especially in locations such as Ithaca's gorges, the "best practice." Although "the fences inject our idyllic campus with prison yard imagery," serve as constant reminders of the tragedies, and might scare off potential students, the editors of the *Sun* agreed that the barriers were necessary to break the "suicide contagion." Nonetheless, they added, since "fences have not been conclusively proven to decrease the overall suicide rate," they should be regarded as a temporary solution.[92]

Students had mixed feelings about the bridge barriers. Some of them believed that since "impulsivity" was a factor in suicides, barriers might deter individuals long enough for them to reconsider their decisions. "I love the fences," Deirdre Mulligan '11, who remembered Matt Zika as "a brilliant, funny, warm, caring person," declared. "The sight of a fence could never be as painful as the sight of your best friend's tombstone."[93] Others deemed the fences impractical, pointing to the suicides that were not gorge related. The cluster might be a statistical anomaly, Jordan Kent-Bryant '12 suggested, and was unlikely to recur in 2011 even if the university did nothing, "because of a regression towards the mean."[94] In an op-ed titled "President Skorton, Tear Down These Fences," Steven Zhang '12 observed that Cornell's suicide rate did not exceed the national average (for a college-age population its size) and that the university "had received a disproportionate amount of scrutiny" because of the spectacular way some of its students had chosen to die. Zhang endorsed a strategy that addressed "all of those who are in trouble, not only those who commit suicide by impulse."[95]

To assess its long-term options, Cornell hired three experts—Annette Beautrais, senior research associate at Yale University School of Medicine; Madelyn Gould, professor of psychiatry and public health at Columbia University; and Eric Caine '69, professor of psychiatry at the University of Rochester Medical Center. In their extended report, issued in July 2010, Beautrais, Gould, and Caine acknowledged that Cornell's rate of suicide "has been consistent with national data in higher education, despite its reputation as having had an elevated rate." In light of the suicide cluster, however, they applauded the decision of university administrators to offer crisis support and augment educational and counseling services. Placing temporary barriers on six of the seven bridges over local gorges and closing the seventh, they asserted, "was an essential demonstration of the University's commitment to safety above all else, and entirely in keeping with what has been shown to work in other settings." All of the admittedly small number of studies formally evaluating the impact of installing barriers at suicide "hotspots," they indicated, found barriers "effective in reducing suicides from that site, without displacement to neighboring sites." Acutely aware that "viewing natural scenes, being in natural settings, and walking amongst trees together constitute a restorative environment, which has psychological, cognitive, physical benefits," the consultants recommended that Cornell install permanent barriers on all the bridges (because "in essence, Cornell and Ithaca are handcuffed one to the other") that "are minimally intrusive" and in keeping with the landscape. The report concluded with a warning that Cornell had no alternative. Sooner or later, the consultants predicted, another suicide would occur. "If the barriers are removed . . . there will be speculation regarding why barriers were taken down, when 'experts' now point to 'best evidence' suggesting they should be installed permanently. There will be media-led speculation (and assignment of responsibility) about who estimated the risk and assessed the value of life (lives) lost versus the cost or aesthetics of barriers."[96]

That summer, Cornell hired Nader Tehrani, a professor at the Massachusetts Institute of Technology and a principal at Office dA, a design firm based in Boston. Working with the City of Ithaca–Cornell Long-Term Bridge Means Restriction Committee, Tehrani developed plans to install steel mesh nets beneath the four Cornell-owned bridges (the Suspension Bridge, Beebe Dam Bridge, Stone Arch Bridge, and Trolley Bridge) and three city-owned bridges (the Stewart Avenue bridges and the Thurston Avenue Bridge). The university bore the entire estimated $1 million per bridge project cost, as well as maintenance and repair costs. On November 22, 2011, Ithaca's Planning and Development Board voted unanimously that the nets would have no significant adverse impact on the environment. Formal approval of the site plans by the Ithaca Common Council came in December.

In May 2013, with the nets in place, workers took down the temporary fences. A horizontal net system under each bridge extended about fifteen feet to either side (except for the Suspension Bridge, which had a vertical mesh "sock" installed during the summer). Cameras stationed nearby allowed police to identify anyone lingering on the site, tampering with the nets, or throwing anything into them. Any time a person landed on the net, an alarm would be triggered, a staff person from Environmental Health and Safety would be sent to investigate, and the Fire Department would perform the rescue. The project director John Keefe warned would-be pranksters that the experience would be like "jumping into a cheese grater"—and discovering that you can't get out. Most important, the nets created a stopping point, where an individual might reevaluate, decide he or she needed assistance, and get it.[97]

The suicide cluster, the hazing incidents, and the H1N1 pandemic underscored the role of the university in providing physical and mental health care services to its twenty-one thousand students. The demand for those services was growing. In fiscal year 2013, UHS had an operating budget of $19.3 million and 158 full-time-equivalent workers, including clinical, support, and administrative staff. On the pre-matriculation forms they submitted, about a third of Cornell students reported a significant health concern. Gannett experienced almost one hundred thousand visits each year (85 percent of them by students and about 15 percent by faculty, staff, and other users), a figure projected to grow by 20 percent if the ten-dollar user fee for professional visits put in place in the mid-1990s was replaced by a prepaid health fee. Tens of thousands more had "non-visit clinical encounters," through after-hours calls, secure messaging for the delivery of laboratory results and follow-up instructions, educational outreach, emergency room and hospitalization consultations, and conversations with partners and parents. Three-quarters of students used UHS at least once during each academic year. Mental health services were provided to about 15 percent of the student body.[98]

With increased demand a virtual certainty—including among "at risk" students—a population larger than at peer institutions (most of which had an academic medical center on campus), and a medical staff size far below peer average (mental health staffing was slightly above peer average), Janet Corson-Rikert, director of health services, and Vice President Murphy pressed for additional resources and renovated and expanded facilities. Since the completion of the addition to Gannett in 1979, they pointed out, student enrollment at Cornell had gone up by 30 percent. Gannett lacked an adequate number of examination rooms. Waiting rooms were so small that sick and well students often sat (or stood) in an unhealthy proximity to one another. Holding rooms had been converted into exam rooms, forcing staff to transfer patients who needed observation or IV fluids to emergency rooms. And the doubling, tripling, and even quadrupling of office-space occupants compromised student privacy.

In March 2013, the administration asked the board of trustees to authorize a $55 million project to upgrade Gannett Health Center. Several site alternatives had been considered and rejected, Skorton, Fuchs, and Murphy reported. A new facility on the Ag quad was incompatible with existing academic priorities. The Grumman squash court site was rejected "due to low visibility and pedestrian access." Leasing a facility in Collegetown from a developer generated annual rental costs in perpetuity and was also deemed incompatible with "site selection criteria." And administrators concluded that the cost of putting up a new building on the Gannett site, which was estimated at $120 million, would put an undue burden on internal resources and philanthropy. The plan ultimately approved by the board included renovation of the facility's thirty thousand existing square feet; a fifty-eight-thousand-square-foot addition on the southern and western ends of Gannett; and replacement of the lobby (which, according to the designers, made "inefficient use of that portion of the facility footprint") with an additional eight thousand square feet of useful space. The project would be funded with a combination of Student and Academic Services reserves and those from other administrative and academic units (covering two-thirds of the total expenses) and philanthropy (covering the remaining one-third). Construction was slated to begin in March 2015 and be completed in June 2017.[99]

"As a university president, physician and parent, I know how important good health is to the achievement of both immediate and lifelong goals," Skorton declared. "We can be proud that our campus health center is a national model for integrating the delivery of physical, mental and public health services."[100] The upgrading of Gannett's facilities, he added, "will enable University Health Services to continue its pioneering work in preventive, diagnostic and therapeutic services with the focus on identifying and reaching those at risk."[101]

Along with the North Campus and West Campus initiatives and the response to hazing and suicides, the renovated Gannett was part of a new residential environment at Cornell. *In loco parentis* and a regime of surveillance, supervision, and discipline had not returned. The university, however, committed itself to promoting the exchange of ideas in and beyond the classroom and to protecting the physical and mental health of members of the community.

12 | Going Global

Three days after September 11, 2001, at the memorial convocation for some twelve thousand members of the Cornell and Ithaca community—possibly the largest gathering on the Arts quad in the university's history—Walter LaFeber, one of America's most respected historians of foreign policy, offered a geopolitical perspective. LaFeber noted that the United States was "the world's most powerful nation, militarily strong while others feel defenseless; rich, while others are poor; often culturally dominant, while others fear the loss of their ancient traditions." A serious study of history, he cautioned, reveals that these disparities "will inevitably change." If Americans were "fortunate and wise," they might be able to guide that change. In an age of instant mass communication and disappearing borders, LaFeber claimed, wisdom consisted in no small measure in remembering that the United States cannot be "ignorant of other peoples" and "intolerant of great cultures and races with which we share a shrinking planet and remain free."[1]

From its earliest days, Cornell had been international in its aspiration and, to an extent, in its outreach. Early in the twentieth century, as we have seen, students from China completed undergraduate and graduate degrees on the Ithaca campus. In the 1920s, the Cornell-Nanjing Crop Improvement Project became the first of many programs designed by the university to improve plant breeding and food production across the globe. Over time, the international content of many courses increased, the number of international students and scholars grew, and faculty with international roots and experiences were recruited. And Cornell excelled in international studies (understanding the history, culture, demography, politics, and economics of other nations and people) and international engagement (deploying resources and expertise worldwide to effect positive change).

Between 1995 and 2015 Cornell strove to become, as President Rhodes put it, "the land grant university to the world." Acting opportunistically, in

9/11 Convocation on the Arts quad. (Cornell University Photography)

response to the priorities of individual faculty, departments, donors, government agencies, and (would-be) foreign partners, and at other times with a somewhat clearer and more coherent strategic vision, the university deepened its commitment to infuse international and comparative perspectives into teaching, learning, research, and engagement. On the eve of the sesquicentennial, Cornell's approach to international studies and international engagement, along with many other priorities common to modern research universities, remained a work in progress.

S INCE 1995, THE number of Cornell students receiving academic credit for study abroad remained fairly stable (except for a dip following the economic crisis of 2008–9). In 2000–2001 and in 2012–13, almost five hundred undergraduates spent a semester or a year abroad, studying at universities in the host countries (in Paris, Rome, and Seville under the auspices of a Cornell program). In 2013–14, enrollments rose in study abroad programs and foreign exchange programs. The United Kingdom was the most popular destination, while substantial numbers of students enrolled in programs all around the globe. About 60 percent of these students came from endowed colleges at

Cornell and 40 percent from the contract colleges. Some students received academic credit for short-term study, during the summer, the mid-semester break in January, and leaves of absence. In sum, about 27 percent of undergraduates had some study-abroad experience during their Cornell careers. About forty research universities in the United States (including Dartmouth, Yale, Georgetown, Tufts, and Notre Dame, all of which sent at least 50 percent of their undergraduates abroad) and many small colleges had higher participation rates. The reluctance of Cornell students majoring in the sciences and engineering to spend a semester at an institution whose curriculum might not fit their expectations and needs was a factor in the relatively lower participation rates. And, as President Skorton pointed out, the administrative fee at Cornell (which was used to pay overhead and financial aid costs) was the highest in the country and more than twice as high as that in any of the other Ivies, making study abroad "unaffordable for many, particularly New York State residents in the contract colleges who do not qualify for financial aid." In a white paper issued in January 2012, Skorton proposed that Cornell act to ensure that no less than 50 percent of undergraduates have an international experience by the time they earn their degrees.[2]

The growth of international students on the Ithaca campus during these years, however, was dramatic. In 1994–95, 2,567 young men and women, from 126 countries, were enrolled in degree-granting programs at Cornell, about one thousand more than had matriculated a decade earlier. Some 70 percent of them were graduate and professional students; 30 percent were undergraduates. International students constituted 5.6 percent of total undergraduate enrollment and 31.1 percent of graduate and professional school enrollment. The top five providers of students were Canada, Taiwan, India, Japan, and China.

By 2012–13, the numbers had risen to 4,098 international students, representing 119 countries, enrolled at Cornell, which was among the top twenty-five universities in the United States in the number of foreign student matriculants. The countries sending the largest numbers to Cornell included China, India, and Canada, but, compared with the decade before, South Korea and Singapore now replaced Japan and Taiwan in the top five. International students made up 44.1 percent of the graduate student body, 23.9 percent of professional school enrollments, and 9.6 percent of all undergraduates (12.3 percent in the endowed schools and 5.5 percent in the contract colleges). These percentages, by all accounts, were likely to increase. Like most leading research universities, Cornell did not distinguish between U.S. citizens and foreign nationals in admissions of graduate students or the financial aid packages it offered them. Governments of emerging economies in China, India, Brazil, and Indonesia, moreover, were investing substantial sums in graduate education and undergraduate exchanges, and affluent families in those countries and elsewhere seemed increasingly willing to send their children abroad for an undergraduate degree. Along with many faculty and administrators, President Skorton believed that bringing the best and brightest international undergraduates to Ithaca, regardless of their country of origin or ability to pay, as some of Cornell's peers were doing, would burnish the university's reputation as a world-class institution and "greatly benefit all students as we seek to prepare them to live in a multi-cultural world." In January 2012 he proposed that Cornell find a way—despite the strain on its resources for financial aid for U.S. citizens—to add to the "extremely limited" pool of money dedicated to need-based undergraduate financial aid for international students.[3]

At Cornell, the Mario Einaudi Center for International Studies was the principal forum for interdisciplinary work on global affairs, serving as a key sponsor, catalyst, and coordinator of research, teaching, and outreach on campus and abroad. Established in 1961, the Center for International Studies changed its name thirty years later to honor professor of government Mario Einaudi, its founding director, whose father had been president of Italy after World War II. In 2012–13, over eight hundred faculty were involved in the center's core and affiliate programs. The Einaudi Center also brought visiting scholars, politicians, and activists to campus, and provided travel grants to graduate students and seed money to faculty to incubate new initiatives.

Most of Einaudi's core programs were for "area studies"—the examination of the history, culture, politics, economy, international relations, and languages of a society or societies—which had been, and to some extent remained, a jewel in the crown of international studies at Cornell. In 2012–13, the Southeast Asia Program (SEAP), the South Asia Program, and the East Asia Program retained their prestigious designations as National Resource Centers (NRC), eligible for substantial funding under Title VI of the U.S. Department of Education (SEAP was the oldest continuously supported NRC in the United States). Area studies, however, had given way to theory, comparative political economy, and econometrics as the preferred methodologies among many scholars and was less a priority of federal agencies. Cuts in Department of Education funding (and the retirement of some distinguished area studies Cornell faculty) had resulted in loss of NRC status at the Institute of European Studies and the Latin American Studies Program. And, as we have seen, retrenchment by the federal government had also put at risk the teaching of some foreign languages.

In October 2012, a task force on internationalization, appointed by President Skorton, Provost Kent Fuchs, and Weill Cornell Medical College dean Laurie Glimcher, composed of ten faculty members, and chaired by Alfonso Torres, a professor and associate dean for public policy in the College of Veterinary Medicine, recommended expanding the scope of the Einaudi Center to include additional faculty from engineering and the natural, applied, environmental, and health sciences, and changing "the area study programs from a traditional model driven by the National Resource Centers and the U.S. Department of Education to a multi-disciplinary approach" that incorporated "problem-based development in thematic programs."[4]

Einaudi affiliate programs were already engaged in an impressive array of "problem-based" international initiatives. Many of them were developed and implemented by International Programs of the College of Agriculture and Life Sciences (IP-CALS). Established in 1963, IP-CALS was dubbed "the fourth dimension" of the college by Dean Charles Palm, PhD '35, who sought to give international engagement the status and visibility equivalent to research, teaching, and extension. With the support of the Ford Foundation, international professors and support staff were appointed and resources set aside for graduate fellowships and travel. Between 1974 and 1995, IP-CALS received substantial funds from the federal government, with twenty of sixty major projects funded by USAID. A $15 million grant from the Atlantic Philanthropies made possible the establishment in 1990 of the Cornell International Institute for Food, Agriculture and Development (CIIFAD), which was located within IP-CALS but operated separately to increase participation by faculty members in other colleges.

In the fifteen years covered by the Atlantic Philanthropies grant, CIIFAD promoted sustainable agricultural practices and resource use through collaborative research and education and leadership development programs in Bolivia, the Dominican Republic, Ghana, Kenya, Madagascar, the Philippines, and Zimbabwe. Among CIIFAD's signature achievements were the introduction of a sustainable way to greatly increase rice production for farmers in developing countries, and a relationship with the Amhara Regional Agricultural Institute, Bahir Dar, in Ethiopia, to promote integrated water management, which resulted (through a grant provided by the World Bank's Development Initiative Fund) in the establishment in 2007 of a joint Master of Professional Studies program designed to train Ethiopian nationals in this field.[5]

In the 1990s, professionals in Uganda and at the Pan-American School of Agriculture at Zamorano in Honduras received advanced education and training thanks to IP-CALS. In the new century, IP-CALS infrastructure projects included providing the administrative and financial headquarters for the International Service for the Acquisition of Agri-Biotech Applications, a nonprofit organization that shared information about crop biotechnology with appropriate stakeholders, especially farmers in developing countries, and a Cornell Transnational Learning Program that develops video-learning modules to help institutions in Africa enhance food security. IP-CALS faculty also worked with scientists in Uganda to reverse the decline in the production of the Matoke banana caused by diseases and pests, and led a collaborative effort by seventeen research universities (supported by the United Kingdom Department for International Development and the Bill and Melinda Gates Foundation) to develop strains of wheat that can resist the Ug99 pathogen and other races of stem rust.

IP-CALS partnered with scientists in Uganda and Nigeria and at the Boyce Thompson Institute for Plant Research at Cornell and the U.S. Department of Energy Joint Genomic Institute (in another Gates Foundation–funded initiative) to design a new breeding method based on statistical modeling to "unlock the full potential of cassava," a staple crop in Africa (and elsewhere). And it used genomic selection (in a third project supported by the Gateses) to help "at risk" farmers in Africa, Asia, and Latin America improve maize and wheat crop yields.[6]

Turning its attention to undergraduate education, the Einaudi Center coordinated the university-wide, multidisciplinary International Relations minor at Cornell. Offered to students in all the undergraduate colleges, the minor required one core and one elective course in four subject areas (international economics and development; world politics and foreign policy; transnational processes and policy; and cultural studies), and completion of two foreign languages at "proficiency" level or one at a higher "facility" level. IR minors were encouraged to study abroad, join the Cornell International Affairs Society, and write for or serve on the editorial board of the student-run *Cornell International Affairs Review*. In 2013, thirty-three students completed the IR minor—about 80 percent of them from the College of Arts and Sciences. Fredrik Logevall (Einaudi Center director, professor of history, vice provost for international relations, and winner of the 2013 Pulitzer Prize in History) claimed that the language requirement was "a practical obstacle to participation" for many students in colleges other than Arts and Sciences.[7]

———

To BOOST INTERNATIONAL studies and international engagement, Cornell signed formal agreements with institutions in host countries to offer joint and dual degrees. The advantage for students on both sides of these partnerships included more choice for postsecondary educational opportunities while each school enjoyed an increase in intellectual capital, research capacity, organizational experience, and resources at its own institution. In addition to the professional master's degree at Bahir Dar, Cornell offered a dual degree in law with several universities in Europe and a program in food science with Tamil Nadu Agricultural University in India. In 2004, the Cornell School of Hotel Administration began offering a joint master of hospitality management degree with Nanyang Technological University in Singapore.

Cornell was less inclined than many of its peers to establish "branch campuses" abroad, in which the curriculum was set and the faculty hired by the American university, and budget neutrality or better was the precondition for launching the initiative. According to critics, the educational quality of branch campuses rarely equaled that of the parent school, which was often forced to divert time and resources from its "core mission" to the new initiative. The approach, moreover, did not necessarily augment the capacity of existing universities in the host country to improve pedagogy and conduct research. Nor did the model of the American university always fit or function well in the host culture.

In 2001, Cornell set these concerns aside to create the Weill Cornell Medical College in Qatar, a tiny, oil-rich Persian Gulf nation with a population of about 750,000, about two-thirds of whom were "temporary" foreign workers. The initiative was part of an ambitious plan by the Qatar Foundation for Education, Science and Community Development, a charitable entity established in 1995 by Sheikh Hamad Bin Khalifa Al-Thani, the country's emir and head of state, to establish an "Education City" in Doha, Qatar's capital.

Developed under the leadership of Sheikha Mozah Bint Nasser Al-Misnad, a wife of the emir and the chair of the foundation, Education City, which covers nearly five and a half square miles in Doha, used the branch campus model because it was faster and more efficient than building universities from scratch. Education City opened its doors in 1998 when the Virginia Commonwealth University in Qatar School of the Arts offered a bachelor of fine arts in fashion design, interior design, painting, or printmaking and a master's of fine arts and design studies. In little over a decade, in addition to VCU and Weill Cornell Medical College, Education City housed branch campuses from Texas A&M, Carnegie Mellon University, Georgetown, Northwestern, Hautes études commerciales de Paris, and University College of London. Also on site were a Qatari university, the Qatar Faculty of Islamic Studies, which began enrolling master's degree students in 2007, and Qatar Science and Technology Park, home to about two dozen companies involved in research and development.

A meeting in spring 1999 between Sheikha Mozah and Susan Kelly, a member of the U.S. House of Representatives from New York, who was in the

Qatar premedical students in the biology lab. (Courtesy John Samples, Weill Cornell Medical College in Qatar)

country to observe its first municipal election (which also marked the first time in Qatar that women could vote and run for office) launched the Cornell-Qatar connection. Sheikha Mozah asked Kelly to recommend a university that might be willing to collaborate to build (and run) Qatar's first medical school. Kelly thought of Cornell and approached Antonio Gotto Jr., dean of Weill Cornell Medical College, who had established an Office of International Health Care at his school in 1997. Gotto knew there were many reasons to say no: "It's far away. It could be dangerous. They have very different customs. You might dilute your resources and distract your management. You may not be able to recruit faculty or find students. Some of your alumni and friends may not understand it."[8] Following extensive negotiations, however, the Qatar Foundation agreed to allocate $750 million over eleven years to the project, to pay Weill Cornell a substantial management fee, and make a donation to it. Members of the Cornell Board of Trustees and the Weill Cornell Board of Overseers and leaders of the university, some of them skeptical about the proposal, visited Doha and returned as converts. Responding to concerns that the initiative might entangle Cornell in the political conflicts in the region, Sanford I. Weill '55, chairman of the Weill Cornell Board of Overseers, claimed, "This is about health care, medical education and medical research. We're not in the political business; we're in the science business, the education business."[9] President Rawlings agreed. "Establishing a Qatar branch of the Weill Cornell Medical College is an unprecedented example of the strength of American education, and it reflects the common commitment to educational opportunity that links all nations and peoples," he declared. "This history-making venture is educational diplomacy at its finest."[10]

The proposal was vetted in Ithaca as well because it included the creation of a non-degree-granting premedical program to help prepare high school graduates, especially young men and women from Qatar, for the Medical College Admission Test (MCAT) and for medical school. Administered by the School of Continuing Education and Summer Sessions, which was empowered to grant Cornell credits for extramural study, the two-year program, offered in English, featured courses and labs in biology, chemistry, physics, genetics, anatomy, and physiology, which were designed to be identical in content to those offered in Ithaca. The relevant departments in Ithaca had to approve each course and the appointment of every faculty member.

Faculty and students on the Ithaca campus raised a host of objections to the joint venture. Considered progressive by regional standards, Qatar, they pointed out, was a monarchy that had banned political demonstrations and required all private organizations to register with the government. In 2000, for example, a Kent State student had been arrested and put in jail for maintaining a website that criticized government policies. Although women had the right to dress as they pleased, drive cars, and hold professional positions, gender segregation in public places was the norm, and Qatari law allowed husbands and fathers to prevent females in their families from traveling. Homosexuality was a criminal offense in the country. Although an Israeli trade office had opened in Qatar in 1996, pro-Palestinian and anti-Zionist sentiment was pervasive. For many years, moreover, Israelis were forbidden from entering Qatar. "I think you are going to have a lot of Jews and Israelis saying, 'I'm not going to go there; it isn't safe for me,'" Gershon Lewental '03, president of the Cornell Israeli Student Association, said.[11] Finally, some faculty expressed concerns about whether first-rate faculty could be recruited to teach in the pre-med program, wondered about safety in the event of a war or a coup, and warned that despite the promise of autonomy for Cornell in all academic matters, the Qatar Foundation, which held the purse strings, might exert influence in subtle ways, including funding research projects of interest to the royal family.

Rawlings, Provost Biddy Martin, and Dean Gotto assured them that the foundation was contractually bound to a nondiscrimination policy and had pledged to issue visas to Jewish and/or Israeli students, staff, and faculty. Acknowledging that Education City was Qatar's first foray into coeducation, they emphasized that increasing opportunities for Arab women was a high priority for Sheikha Mozah, that Qataris considered medicine a respectable profession for women, and predicted that the majority of applicants to their school would be female. They noted as well that Cornell ran many programs in countries in Asia, Africa, and Latin America whose governments restricted free speech and religious freedom and violated human rights. Weill Cornell in Qatar "will position us to have a significant impact on medical education and culture there," Dean Gotto claimed. "We would like to think we may even contribute to peace in the Middle East."[12]

Operating in offices and classrooms at the Qatar Academy while a permanent facility was under construction, the Weill Cornell Premedical Program was launched in October 2002. The opening took place amid escalating tensions between the United States and Iraq and the possibility that Qatar might allow President Bush to use a military base there to launch an attack against the regime of Saddam Hussein. Dean Gotto indicated that an evacuation plan was in place in case the situation deteriorated and lives were at risk. At present, he indicated, "it is safe and calm there. Children continue to play outside."[13]

The impasse between the United States and Iraq and the war and occupation that ensued did not interfere with the program. After receiving just over one hundred applications and interviewing fifty-five students, administrators had accepted thirty-one young men and women, twenty-seven of whom enrolled. Daniel Alonso, dean of the Weill Cornell Medical College in Qatar, predicted, accurately, that very soon fifty to sixty new students would matriculate each year. Hailing from several nations, including Jordan, India, Iran, the United States, and Qatar, every member of the pre-med program's first class had a familial connection to the Middle East. Some 70 percent of the premedical students were women. In what would prove to be an ongoing challenge for administrators of the program, 60 percent of the students were Qatari citizens, less than the aspirational goal of 70 percent set by the foundation. Attracted by a generous package of salary and benefits, as well as their idealism and a sense of adventure, seven faculty members, several of them nontenured lecturers and instructors from Cornell–Ithaca, and three teaching assistants, were on hand to provide instruction.

The Weill Cornell Medical College in Qatar opened in fall 2004. Four years later, sixteen students, thirteen of them from the premedical program, got their MDs, the first class to do so from an American program conducted outside the United States. American students were second only to Qataris in the student body. Looking ahead and acknowledging that "these are still early days," Dean Alonso expected a substantial number of graduates of the medical college to work as clinicians, scientists, and educators in the region and for Weill Cornell in Qatar to work with the new Sidra Medical and Research Center in Doha to build a biomedical research capacity that excelled in basic science and clinical investigation.[14]

LIKE WEILL CORNELL in Qatar, the Arecibo Observatory, located in a mountainous area fifty miles west of San Juan, Puerto Rico, provided tangible evidence of the university's geographical scope and global mission. Arecibo was "an icon for astronomy," Professor Joseph Burns, PhD '66, vice provost for physical sciences and engineering, and a specialist in planetary sciences, claimed in 2007. "It speaks to Cornell's expansiveness—to be able to go to a distant place and use special geography there to look out at the universe."[15] A federal government facility, Arecibo was conceived and then administered by Cornell, through a contract with the National Science Foundation, since it became operational in the mid-1960s. The facility housed the most sensitive radio telescope in the world, with a 305-meter-wide-dish, made up of thirty-nine thousand perforated aluminum panels (fixed to the ground in a way that people could walk or drive under it) and instruments suspended above it from three towers. For decades, at the behest of the Search for Extraterrestrial Intelligence (SETI), the dish scanned the skies for signs of alien life. On November 16, 1974, Cornell astronomers Carl Sagan and Frank Drake '51 broadcast an interstellar greeting to anyone who might be able to receive it. In the twenty-first century, the facility had more users than ever before, with some three hundred researchers from 150 universities worldwide selected each year in a highly competitive peer review process. Arecibo was responsible for several important discoveries, including Nobel Prize–winning verification of Einstein's work on the existence of gravitational radiation, the molten core of the planet Mercury, detections of pulsars, and what may be "a dark galaxy," with a large mass but no stars. And the dish was cast as the headquarters of the villain in the James Bond movie *GoldenEye* (1995), with special effects making it possible for it to rise up from under a lake.

In 2006, a senior review committee of the Division of Astronomical Sciences at the National Science Foundation prescribed cutting the annual appropriation for Arecibo from $10.5 million to $8 million in fiscal 2009 and $4 million in 2011. An appropriation of $2 million a year from the Division of Atmospheric Sciences, another branch of the NSF, was left untouched (and subsequently increased, along with funds from NASA, to make up part of the shortfall). No one doubted the scientific merit of the observatory or any other facility targeted for reduced funding, C. Wayne Van Citters, the director of the NSF's Division of Astronomical Sciences, maintained. "It's just a question of scientific priorities and having to withdraw funding from some things to do new things that are extremely exciting too." Van Citters, however, also raised the possibility of decommissioning the observatory as more advanced telescopic instrumentation was constructed at other sites.[16]

Administrators at Arecibo hoped for a budget reprieve but eliminated a quarter of the 150 positions at the facility and limited observations to sky-wide surveys (rather than examination of individual objects), performed during night-time hours. And they tried to identify alternative funding sources, including

The radio telescope at Arecibo. (Cornell University Photography)

support from the National Aeronautics and Space Administration, and the government of Puerto Rico, which relied on the observatory to boost tourism and stimulate interest in science among primary and secondary school students. In 2011, however, the National Science Foundation awarded a five-year contract to Stanford Research Institute International and a consortium of other universities to administer the facility. The result of a competitive bidding process, the decision, Cornell Astronomy professor James Cordes speculated, may have been the result of an NSF mandate (ignored in this case for decades) to rotate management periodically. "It wasn't a scientific decision," added Cordes, who had conducted research at Arecibo since 1972, "it was a management decision," made in a weak fiscal climate "that always puts pressure" on the existing management team. In addition, the NSF may have preferred to have operations headquarters on site, rather than in Ithaca.[17]

By then, Cornell astronomers were hard at work on an exciting "new thing." In 2004 Cornell and California Institute of Technology agreed to become the lead partners in a $150 million project to build the largest, most accurate, and highest astronomical facility in the world. The two universities committed to identifying the sources for full funding of the project, which they expected to include a substantial grant from the NSF. At twenty-five meters (eighty-two feet) in diameter, the Cerro Chajnantor Atacama Telescope (CCAT) would be situated on a mountain 18,400 feet above the Atacama Desert in Chile, where the arid climate and high altitude would make it possible to detect radiation at submillimeter wavelengths (longer than visible light but shorter than radio waves) blocked to ground-based telescopes because it is absorbed by water in the Earth's atmosphere. "CCAT is designed to optimize our ability to study the genesis of structures in the universe," said Riccardo Giovanelli, professor of astronomy and CCAT project director. "It will allow us to explore the process of formation of galaxies, which saw its heyday about a billion years after the Big Bang, some 13.7 billion years ago; to peek into the interior of the dusty molecular clouds within which stars and planets form; and to survey the pristine chunks of material left intact for billions of years on the outskirts of our solar system."[18] Pointing to the involvement of the University of Colorado; Associated Universities Inc., a not-for-profit organization based in Washington, D.C.; the United Kingdom Astronomy Center; and a consortium of German and Canadian researchers, Giovanelli emphasized that "international cooperation is a hallmark of this evolving process." Proponents of CCAT hoped that "first light," a standard benchmark to measure progress toward completion of an observatory, would be attained sometime after 2017.[19]

DURING THE MILLENNIAL years, Cornell established a long-term presence in the world's two most populous countries, India and China. In 2004, IP-CALS, which had been active in India for decades, used a USAID grant to launch two new programs. An undergraduate course, "Agriculture in Developing Countries—India," required students to select one of several themes—agriculture education and extension; agricultural biotechnology; food processing and post-harvest; global marketing and export agriculture; livestock development; and tropical cropping systems—for special emphasis. Members of the class then had the option of taking a two-week field trip to India. A similar course was taught at partner universities in India. Video-streaming technology permitted students on the two continents to communicate with one another. The second initiative, an eight-day Agribusiness Management Program designed for professionals, was conducted in India and Ithaca and included visits to agribusiness companies in New York State and regulatory agencies in Washington, D.C.

Starting in 2009, as we have indicated, Cornell and Tamil Nadu Agricultural University in India offered a dual degree master's program in food science and plant breeding. Requiring seven months of study in the United States and five in India, it marked the first time a degree in agricultural life science was offered by an American university to students in India. Agricultural production "has done better than the processing sector," Cornell Food Science professor Syed Rizvi claimed, "but processing is about to unleash and go through the roof, so there is tremendous demand for trained individuals" in the field. "It will also be good for American students to learn how things are done in a rapidly developing country."[20]

In 2012, IP-CALS forged new relationships with agricultural universities (and a private-sector firm, Sathguru Management Consultants) in India through a three-year grant funded by the US-India Educational Foundation under the auspices of the Obama–Singh 21st Century Knowledge Initiative. To help revamp graduate programs in seed science and nanotechnology, improve food safety, strengthen pedagogy through e-learning, and create gender studies programs at the University of Agricultural Sciences, Dharwad (UASD), and Sardar Vallabh Bhai Patel University of Agriculture and Technology (SVPUA&T), six Cornell faculty made two-week visits to Karnataka and Uttar Pradesh, the less developed Indian states where these institutions were located; fourteen professors from UASD and SVPUA&T came to Ithaca; and the Cornell faculty returned to India to present specially designed case studies.

A $50 million endowment established in 2008 by Ratan Tata '59, one of the largest gifts ever bestowed on an American university by a foreign benefactor, significantly expanded Cornell's connection with India. Tata served as chairman of Tata Sons, the holding company of the Tata Group, one of the largest, most profitable, and well-respected conglomerates in the world, employing 320,000 people in corporations in seven key business sectors, including steel and automobiles. Tata also chaired the Tata Education and Development Trust. He designated half of the endowment to a scholarship fund to help attract talented, needy students from India to Cornell. At the time, the annual appropriation for financial aid for all international undergraduate students was $1.5 million, enough to bring about a dozen new students from poor families to Cornell each year. The first four Tata Scholars graduated from Cornell in 2013. The second $25 million endowment established the Tata-Cornell Agriculture and Nutrition Initiative, TCI (formerly TACO-AN). TCI enlists universities, government agencies, and nongovernmental organizations to help increase the productivity, sustainability, and profitability of India's food industry and reduce poverty and malnutrition in rural areas. Drawing on multidisciplinary expertise throughout Cornell, TCI addressed such issues as environmental and water resource management, food safety, and child nutrition. Appointed director of TCI in 2013, Prabhu Pingali, a former World Bank economist and deputy director of agricultural development at the Gates Foundation, involved the center as well in public policy formation and advocacy.

The People's Republic of China captured even more of Cornell's attention than India. Soon after he became Cornell president, Hunter Rawlings enlisted faculty, deans, alumni, and staff to develop a "more comprehensive approach to initiatives in Asia, especially in China."[21] Cornell, they reported, was well situated in Taiwan, Hong Kong (which was undergoing a transition to control by the People's Republic), and Japan. Already in place in China, the president learned, was a memorandum of understanding between Beijing Agricultural University and Cornell's College of Agriculture and Life Sciences, signed in 1990, that facilitated visits of students and professors, and the China-Cornell Fellowship Program, which had supported the exchange of scientific knowledge since 1992. Mindful, no doubt, of Lee Teng-hui's recent visit to Cornell, Rawlings's advisers emphasized the importance of Cornell's ties to Taiwan, pointed out that Japan still accounted for 60 percent of the gross domestic product in the region, and predicted that China still had "a long way to go before it attained that kind of economic strength." All agreed, however, that there "is much at stake with China and Cornell must not lose its 'edge.' "[22]

Presidents Rawlings, Lehman, and Skorton all visited China (Lehman and Skorton also went to India). In 2004, Lehman signed an agreement with Tsinghua University to exchange students and faculty with Cornell and discussed how to assign intellectual property rights if and when joint discoveries, inventions, and patents emerged from them. The next year, Rawlings (who had made his first visit in 1998 and returned twice more as president) participated, as interim president, in an academic summit in Beijing, along with several dignitaries, including former president George H.W. Bush. Rawlings spoke as well at a Cornell-Tsinghua Computer Science Workshop, appeared on CCTV, the Chinese national television station, and visited East China Normal University in Shanghai. David Skorton made three visits (in 2007, 2009, and 2012), each time engaging in discussions with university leaders, public officials, and

Cornell alumni. In 2009, Skorton announced, much to the delight of government officials in China, including the minister of education and the minister of science and technology, that Cornell would return a collection of seventeen hundred rare fungi, fifty-seven of them "deemed irreplaceable," that had been smuggled to the university for safekeeping by a Chinese graduate student following Japan's invasion of China in 1937, and housed since then at the herbarium of the Department of Plant Pathology. The specimens "are important in themselves," Skorton said, but more so "due to their poignant history and the personal sacrifices made to save them from destruction."[23]

The most enduring Cornell–China program in these years was conceived by an alumnus. Michael Zak '75, a venture capitalist and former officer in the U.S. Marines, never forgot Professor LaFeber's claim in his course on American foreign policy that the purge of alleged communists in the State Department and other federal agencies in the 1950s had deprived the American government of experts capable of understanding the complex relationship between the United States and China during the Cold War. To remedy this public policy knowledge gap and help American businessmen respond more effectively to the rapidly expanding economy of China in the post–Cold War world, Zak proposed a Cornell Asia Pacific Studies (CAPS) program.

Designed by a group of Asian studies specialists led by professor of history Sherman Cochran, who became the first director of the program, the CAPS major, which was approved unanimously by the faculty of the College of Arts and Sciences in April 2004, attracted twelve students in its inaugural year (2005) and reached its maximum capacity of twenty in 2007. CAPS required intensive study of Mandarin Chinese, beginning, if at all possible, in high school, and continuing for four years at Cornell. Zak cited "three good reasons" for making language proficiency a foundation of the program: "in order to speak with a friend, to work with a partner, and especially when you're having disagreements."[24] During a semester at the Cornell in Washington Program, CAPS students continued their study of Chinese and enrolled in one seminar on public policy and another on U.S.-China relations, which featured presentations by Americans who devoted their careers to understanding the intersection of economics and politics in the two countries. They also worked as interns in government agencies, embassies, nonprofit organizations, and businesses. And, of course, CAPS majors were required to spend a semester in China.

Living in Beijing, on the campus of the prestigious Beida (Peking) University, which provided a "Cornell Office" for the program in the School of International Relations, they enrolled in a language course, a seminar on the politics, economy, and society of contemporary China, taught by a professor from the United States (co-taught, on one occasion, by Chen Jian, professor of history at Cornell and the second CAPS director, and Ms. Duan Hong, Cornell's local representative), and another course, taught by a Peking University professor, that presented Chinese perspectives on international affairs. In internships they tested their language skills and got hands-on experience with China's public and private sectors. "It is our hope," Rawlings declared in Beijing in November 2005, as he and Peking University president Zhihong Xu signed a formal agreement setting out the responsibilities of each institution for the program, that CAPS majors will "return to America with a deep appreciation of Chinese culture and an ability to influence American thought about China and even American policy toward China."[25] And that contact with a heretofore "strange civilization" might also stimulate the formulation of "new standards of value" through which they might reexamine and reevaluate their own culture.[26]

In the twenty-first century, the Internet was an important component of Cornell's strategy for going global (and enhancing revenue). In 1997, the university established an Office of Distance Learning to promote the delivery of online courses on and off campus. Two years later, alumni and administrators met in Jackson Hole, Wyoming, at the home of trustee Allan Tessler '58, LLB '63, the chairman of a company that provided real-time stock quotations on the Internet, and agreed that a separate, for-profit entity was needed to produce, market, and distribute the courses. In January 2000, the Cornell Board of Trustees approved further exploration of the project, which was to be called eCornell (the signature Ezra Cornell used on his correspondence).

When the board action was announced, some faculty expressed outrage at the lack of consultation and the possible impact of courses produced for profit on educational quality, academic freedom, and the university's public service mission. "The family of Ezra Cornell," declared professor of engineering Michael Todd, "is none too happy about having their name used in this way, and suggest that we change the 'e' in eCornell to a dollar sign." Johnson School professor Alan McAdams's criticism came from a different direction. He asked for a "clear business plan" that specified "that there may actually be a return to Cornell from these activities. All of the back-of-the-envelope work that I've heard of suggests that it's going to be very unlikely."[27] On March 8, the Faculty Senate voted 65–1 for a resolution asking the trustees not to take action until the impact of for-profit distance learning on Cornell's academic culture had been fully discussed.

Two days later, however, "a significant majority" of the board voted to create eCornell as a for-profit corporation. Responding to concerns that its values might "eventually collide with those of the University," several trustees noted that "every day delayed is lost to the competition." Professor of engineering and vice provost Mary Sansalone, MS '84, PhD '86, the administration's point person on distance learning, promised to protect the academic integrity of the

Cornell name, establish principles for ownership of intellectual property, and ensure that Cornell retained control over the entity and had the capacity and will to resist pressures from eCornell investors. She pledged as well to resolve tensions between the "more conservative" university governance structure and the need "to move quickly in the fast-paced world of technology."[28]

In a letter to the faculty, President Rawlings explained the board's decision as a response "in a rapidly changing environment" to "strong pressure from several directions."[29] Outside vendors, he indicated, were already trying to sign up Cornell faculty to teach distance learning courses for them. And the pressure was intensifying. Duke University offered an online MBA, and Stanford had established itself as a leader in online education. In April 2000, Columbia joined five other institutions, including the London School of Economics and the Smithsonian Institution, in an online initiative called Fathom. The University of Phoenix, a for-profit corporation, offered online undergraduate and graduate degree and certificate courses to thousands of students. And companies like Stanley Kaplan and Sylvan were developing Internet-based test preparation and remedial courses.

To address the concerns raised by faculty, Rawlings appointed an Advisory Committee on Distance Learning, chaired by William Arms, a professor of computer science. In August, Sansalone outlined a plan that was "entirely consistent," she claimed, with the recommendations that Arms's committee had submitted a few months earlier. She said that eCornell would be a legally separate, "hybrid" entity that was nonprofit in its educational mission and for-profit in its structure. To eliminate potential pressure from "outside investors," its operating budget would come entirely from unrestricted funds from the university's endowment (and, eventually, from profits). It would focus on courses that did not confer academic credit and on nondegree certificate programs. The provost would retain responsibility for academic oversight for distance learning. Profits from eCornell would be used in part to support other technology-based teaching and learning activities throughout the university. Most important, individual faculty members, academic units, and colleges would retain control over academic content and standards.[30]

In September 2000, the board of trustees transferred $12 million from the endowment to eCornell, as operating funds for the fiscal year ending on June 30, 2001. "This is a very important step for the future of the University," Rawlings declared. "The creation of eCornell presents an extraordinary opportunity to extend the high-quality educational programs of Cornell to organizations and individuals far beyond the confines of our physical campus."[31]

In October, Cornell appointed Francis Pandolfi as president and chief executive officer of eCornell. The former president and CEO of Times Mirror Magazines, Pandolfi had served as well as the first-ever chief operating officer of the United States Forest Service. Mary Sansalone became eCornell's vice president and chief academic officer. Amid great expectations, eCornell opened offices in New York City, as well as in Ithaca. Pandolfi and Sansalone estimated that over its first five years, the company would generate hundreds of millions of dollars in revenue. After paying expenses and reinvesting in personnel and equipment, they indicated, eCornell would produce $159 million for the provost's general-purpose fund.

It was not to be. As eCornell launched its first course (in human resources management) in 2001, the dot-com bubble had already burst. Hemorrhaging money, eCornell closed its New York City office and laid off many of its employees. Pandolfi and Sansalone departed, but, unlike its counterparts at many other universities, the company used additional infusions of cash from the Cornell endowment to remain in business. By 2005, with Chris Proulx '91 as CEO, eCornell began to stabilize its finances, identify a market niche, increase enrollments in several professional development certificate programs, and develop partnerships with multinational companies and nongovernmental organizations. In 2006 eCornell posted its first profit, and it has continued to grow steadily, if not spectacularly. In December 2012, the Faculty Senate voted to allow eCornell to participate in developing online for-credit courses.

On the eve of the sesquicentennial, Cornell was also offering Massive Open Online Courses (MOOCs). Often taught by "rock star" professors from the nation's leading universities, MOOCs were free online courses, distributed through consortia such as Coursera, edX, and Udacity, for which colleges rarely granted academic credit. They were hailed as having the potential to reach hundreds of thousands of students, enhance the visibility and reputation of the participating universities, and make higher education attainable and affordable to students throughout the world. According to proponents, MOOCs were also transforming pedagogy, as professors assembled massive amounts of data about classroom performance; adjusted lectures, course material, and examinations; and "flipped the paradigm," so that classroom time could be used for informed discussion, not passive absorption of the professor's presentation.

Critics at Cornell and elsewhere charged that less-well-funded colleges and universities might reduce the size of the faculty by granting academic credit for MOOCs. Dominated by courses in mathematics, computer science, and engineering, they added, MOOCs were ill-equipped to teach students to write and express themselves, supply the hands-on experience of working in a laboratory, or provide economically disadvantaged or poorly prepared students a bridge to higher-level academic work. The majority of students who signed up for a MOOC, in fact, did not finish it. The completion rate for the first MOOC, a course on artificial intelligence offered initially to more than one hundred thousand students by a Stanford professor in 2011, was 13 percent. Most important, critics claimed, MOOCs could not replicate the intellectual and developmental experiences of students who live and learn together.

Cornell tested the waters with a "mini-MOOC" on feeding infants and young children, developed jointly by its Division of Nutritional Sciences and UNICEF. Organizers expected about two hundred people to enroll. By 2012, they had registered thirty-eight hundred individuals from 150 countries, most of them employees at universities and nongovernmental organizations in the developing world. More than nine hundred of them, about 24 percent, successfully completed the course. In that year, four Cornell professors received a grant from Google to create a MOOC version of "Six Pretty Good Books," a multidisciplinary course taught by professors from Sociology, Human Development, ILR, and Communications.

In 2012, Provost Kent Fuchs also formed a committee, chaired by Eva Tardos, a professor of computer science, to advise him on MOOCs. "Online courses are in the process of transforming education," the committee report noted. "We believe that Cornell should be a leader in this transformation." Concluding that "we cannot do this alone," the committee recommended that the university join a MOOC consortium.[32] In May 2013, Cornell chose edX (a platform founded by MIT and Harvard to offer online courses to a worldwide audience at no charge; at the time, edX consisted of twenty-seven institutions in the United States and abroad and had had nine hundred thousand users). The university committed to develop four "Cornell X" courses in 2013–14. Students who completed them would not earn college credit. Cornell's goal, Fuchs declared, was for these MOOCs and those that followed them to be revenue neutral. He acknowledged, however, that neither Cornell nor any other university had developed a business plan for the initiative.

CORNELL MADE A concerted effort to enlarge its footprint in New York City during the millennial years. In its 2010 strategic plan, Edward Lawlor, professor of organizational behavior and former dean of ILR, who chaired the faculty committee, recommended that the institution "embrace a broad and inclusive definition of the land grant mission that is directed at local, state, national and global communities" and build "a stronger base" for education, research, and outreach programs in New York City.[33] As if in response, Cornell (and its partner, the Technion–Israel Institute of Technology) won a highly publicized competition on the eve of the sesquicentennial to create what Mayor Michael Bloomberg called a "game changing" applied sciences and technology campus on an eleven-acre parcel on Manhattan's Roosevelt Island.[34]

Cornell already had a substantial presence in New York City: Cornell Medical College. Founded in 1898 and affiliated since 1927 with what is now New York–Presbyterian Hospital, it had become one of the nation's top-ranked clinical and research centers. In 1998 it was renamed the Joan and Sanford I. Weill Medical College and Graduate School of Medical Sciences at Cornell

University. Offering degrees in medicine and doctoral programs in research and education and a joint MD–PhD program in partnership with the Sloan-Kettering Institute and Rockefeller University, Weill Cornell is affiliated with the Hospital for Special Surgery and the metropolitan-area institutions that make up the New York–Presbyterian Healthcare Network. In 2014, the Belfer Research Building, named in honor of Renée and Robert Belfer, opened on Sixty-Ninth Street. The building was the centerpiece of the $1.3 billion "Discoveries That Make a Difference" capital campaign, which received an extraordinary boost from a $250 million pledge by Joan and Sanford Weill in 2007 (the single largest gift ever given to a medical school) and an additional $100 million donation by the Weills in 2013. The eighteen-story, 480,000-square-foot, $650 million structure doubled and modernized the bench-to-bedside research space at Weill Cornell, enabling the college to attract the next generation of leading medical researchers. Also in 2014, the Sandra and Edward Meyer Foundation donated $75 million to expand Weill Cornell's cancer research and care programs. The college renamed its main campus building at York Avenue for the Meyers.

Research collaborations between Ithaca-based scientists and their counterparts at Weill Cornell increased during this period as well. To promote "engagement and interaction among colleagues" on both campuses, President Jeffrey Lehman '77 launched a regularly scheduled campus-to-campus bus service in 2004.[35] Equipped with twenty-one luxury seats and Internet connections, each bus traveled directly to the Cornell Club on Forty-Fourth Street and Madison Avenue and Weill Cornell and was open to faculty, staff, students, prospective students and their parents, alumni, and guests of the university. Already popular, the service became essential in 2012, when U.S. Airways ended all flights from Ithaca Tompkins Regional Airport to New York City's La Guardia Airport. Cornell was engaged in New York City in other ways as well. Working in every county in New York State, Cooperative Extension agents were active in the city's five boroughs. And several of Cornell's colleges offered semester-long or year-long programs in New York City. Early in the twenty-first century, Architecture, Art, and Planning revived an initiative started in the 1960s and '70s by Professors K. C. Parsons, MRP '53, and Stuart Stein. Located at Seventeenth Street near Union Square, in the Chelsea neighborhood of Manhattan, the AAP program offered undergraduates and graduate students courses for academic credit, often taught by distinguished practitioners (and Cornell alumni) in architecture, the fine arts, and urban planning, and internships at design firms, studios, and public, private, and nonprofit organizations.

A Human Ecology–sponsored "urban semester" in New York City, based in offices on East Sixty-Ninth Street, had a similar structure. Open to junior and senior undergraduates from every college at Cornell, the program featured courses such as "Reflexivity and Reflective Practice in Ethnography" and

"Participatory Action Research." Students also had community-service experiences in schools, day care centers, and social welfare organizations in Brooklyn and East Harlem and found internships related to careers in medicine and health services, financial services, business, government, and communications.

In 1999 the S. C. Johnson Graduate School of Management launched an off-campus Executive MBA program, with classes held at the IBM Conference Center in Palisades, New York. The program was designed for individuals who already had an undergraduate degree and a considerable amount of working experience. In 2000, ILR started a part-time master's program for working adults. Offering classes in the college's offices on Thirty-Fourth Street, the program provided an opportunity for men and women who already had experience in industrial and labor relations to add to their skills and burnish their credentials. In 2005, Operations Research and Information Engineering established a Wall Street campus at 55 Broad Street. Two years later, ORIE's three-semester Master's in Financial Engineering program required students to spend their third semester in New York City and helped arrange summer internships in industry there for them.

It was in November 2010 that Cornell got a once-in-several-generations opportunity to fundamentally and permanently transform its relationship with New York City and enhance its visibility and reputation throughout the world. Mayor Bloomberg invited research universities to compete to build an applied science campus on land donated by New York City (through a ninety-nine-year lease, with an option then to purchase it for $1), augmented by up to $100 million in infrastructure improvements. Bloomberg hoped that by providing world-class technical and entrepreneurial training, the campus would foster an economy in the city that would rival that of Silicon Valley in California. According to estimates made by the New York City Economic Development Corporation, the tech campus would generate $23 billion in economic activity, $1.4 billion in tax revenue, twenty thousand construction jobs, and eight thousand permanent positions in its first three decades.

Provost Kent Fuchs was the driving force behind the decision (which was enthusiastically endorsed by President Skorton and the board of trustees) to mobilize substantial resources to help Cornell win the competition. His academic expertise was especially well suited to the Bloomberg competition. Born in Oklahoma in 1954 and raised in Alaska, Fuchs received a bachelor of science in engineering from Duke University, a master's in divinity from Trinity Evangelical Divinity School, and a PhD in electrical engineering from the University of Illinois. A specialist in computer engineering, especially dependable computer and failure analysis, he served as a professor of electrical and computer engineering at the University of Illinois and Purdue University. He was appointed dean of the College of Engineering at Cornell in 2002 and became provost in January 2009. To lead a team of faculty and administrators tasked with drafting the proposal, Fuchs enlisted Daniel Huttenlocher, a Computer Science professor with a joint appointment in the Johnson School, who had recently been appointed dean of Computing and Information Science; Lance Collins, professor of mechanical and aerospace engineering and the first African American dean of Engineering at Cornell; and Cathy Dove, MBA '84, associate dean of Engineering. In a process Dove called "incredibly intense, fast-moving, exhilarating and challenging," this trio and their colleagues logged thousands of miles on the campus-to-campus bus to solicit advice from city officials, members of the technology industry, entrepreneurs, academics in related fields, including professors at Weill Cornell, and Cornell alumni.[36]

The Cornell proposal was submitted to the mayor's office in the fall of 2011. It described construction of a two-million-square-foot "green" and sustainable campus (with its main building harvesting as much energy as it consumed) on Roosevelt Island at a cost of about $2 billion. Projected to be fully staffed and operational by 2037, the institution they envisioned would offer a distinctive approach to graduate and professional education and foster the development of technologies rooted in the latest academic research. It would address real-world problems by creating a campus culture that attracted the brightest students and faculty in technology-related fields, immersing them in an entrepreneurial culture (already flourishing on the Ithaca campus with entrepreneurship and private enterprise programs and classes, which by 2011 enrolled over 2,000 students), establishing connections with the local business community, and stimulating the creation of start-up companies. To foster interdisciplinary research while retaining a grounding in core computing and engineering disciplines, the campus would be organized around "hubs" that were deliberately designed to be far less permanent than academic departments and to be open to interactions with tech firms. The initial three hubs were Connective Media, Healthier Life, and the Built Environment. Connective Media was concerned with the transformation in how people learn and communicate with one another associated with the advance of handheld devices, applications, and social media. The proposal emphasized that extracting useful knowledge from information often referred to as "big data" involved the behavioral and cognitive social sciences as well as technical fields. The Healthier Life hub would concern itself with the availability, reliability, and security of data, used, for example, to enable physicians to track the progress of their patients and manage complex pharmaceutical regimes. And researchers concerned with the Built Environment might design sustainable and aesthetically pleasing approaches to housing, transportation, and energy that were especially relevant "in an urban environment like New York City, where space of all kinds is at a premium, the public demands more than 'functional boxes,' and masses of people must move around efficiently."[37]

Designed to foster relationships between academia and industry and an entrepreneurial spirit, the Cornell proposal envisioned "apprenticeships" to complement classroom-based learning, with mentors from industry as well as professors supervising student projects; Fridays would be reserved for experiential learning. The proposal anticipated a highly selective graduate student body, estimated to be twenty-five hundred men and women by 2043. While the tech campus would not offer degrees for undergraduates, workshops and full-time study for a semester would eventually be available.

The faculty (expected to reach 280 individuals in thirty years) would reflect what Huttenlocher, who had worked in Silicon Valley earlier in his career, deemed "a fundamental shift" in how higher education defined computer science and engineering. "Twenty years ago," he told the *Cornell Alumni Magazine*, "there were the people who did stuff in the real world and there were the academics in those fields, and the ties weren't that strong; some people went back and forth, but that wasn't the norm. In fact, in some ways time spent out of academia damaged your career." These days, "it's the converse, especially in computer science. Getting your research ideas out in industry is a huge plus."[38] Therefore, in addition to academic excellence, the tenured and tenure-track faculty on the new campus, whose appointments would be made in departments and schools in Ithaca, would already "have distinguished themselves in the development and use of technology in the commercial sector or for the betterment of society." Some professors would commute to the tech campus from Ithaca; most would be based in New York City.[39]

On October 18, 2011, ten days before the deadline to submit proposals, Cornell revealed that the Technion–Israel Institute of Technology had agreed to enter the competition as its partner. The Technion was founded in 1912 by a group of academics, businessmen, and politicians, including Albert Einstein, to train engineers to work in the state of Israel they hoped would soon come into existence. A hundred years later, the Technion, whose campus is in Haifa, was an internationally acclaimed engineering and computer science powerhouse, largely responsible for Israel's position as home to the largest concentration of high-tech start-ups anywhere outside Silicon Valley. Companies headed by graduates of Technion employed 85 percent of the technical workforce in Israel; 59 of the 121 Israeli companies listed on the NASDAQ stock exchange were run or founded by Technion graduates.

The alliance was consummated following a series of secret meetings between leaders of the two institutions. After Mayor Bloomberg announced the competition, the Technion, which lacked the financial resources to act alone, contemplated collaborating with Columbia, but found that the views of the two institutions about the new campus did not match. In February 2011, Provost Fuchs and Paul Feigin, the Technion's senior executive vice president, discussed joining forces. According to the *New York Times*, both schools filed separate "expressions of interest" in March "so as not to tip their hand." Technion president Peretz Lavie met with Fuchs in Beijing, when both men were in

China to celebrate the centennial of Tsinghua University, and found they agreed on Roosevelt Island as an ideal site, on a multidisciplinary master's program, and on organizing around hubs rather than traditional departments. Intense conversations continued by telephone and Skype. Faculty at Cornell and the Technion, it turned out, had been cross-pollinating for years; four Cornell professors, including Michal Lipson, winner of a MacArthur "genius" Award, came from the Technion. And the two institutions shared at least one major benefactor, Irwin Jacobs '54, the cofounder and former chairman of Qualcomm. In July, more than a dozen officials conducted a three-day marathon session at the Cornell Club, rarely leaving the building for fear they might be noticed. During a tour of the Middle East, Skorton "hit it off really well" with Lavie, an expert on sleep disorders, with whom he shared a medical background and therefore "a common language." At the end of the summer, Skorton informed Robert Steel, the deputy mayor for economic development, who was overseeing the contest, that a joint bid would soon be filed. "I wasn't aware they were dating," Steel indicated, until the Cornell president said, "Good news, we're getting married."[40]

The Technion was a programmatic partner. "The physical campus is fully Cornell," Fuchs emphasized. "Cornell will own the land and the facilities. We are putting in the funding to develop the site and the buildings and therefore the campus is our responsibility."[41] On its own, Cornell would also offer degrees in such fields as electrical engineering and information science. The partnership consisted of a fifty-fifty collaboration in the Technion–Cornell Innovation Institute (TCII). Staffed by faculty (with appointments in one of the two home institutions), TCII would support basic and applied research in the interdisciplinary hubs and offer a two-year multidisciplinary dual degree master's program, which required students to demonstrate depth in computing and engineering disciplines, breadth in one of the hubs, and complete a substantive project that addressed a "domain specific problem."[42]

At the end of October 2011, Mayor Bloomberg announced that seven proposals had been submitted to New York City. Like Cornell-Technion, Stanford University proposed to build a tech campus on Roosevelt Island. Columbia University opted for West Harlem. Carnegie Mellon University (along with Steiner Studios) asked for a parcel of land in the Brooklyn Navy Yard. New York Genome Center, Mount Sinai School of Medicine, Rockefeller University, and SUNY Stony Brook designed a campus in Midtown Manhattan. Amity University wanted to build on Governor's Island. And a consortium led by New York University, which included the University of Toronto, the University of Warwick, and the Indian Institute of Technology, Bombay, identified space, not initially offered by New York City, in downtown Brooklyn. Although Bloomberg insisted that there were "no immediate front-runners," Stanford University, which had enlisted the City University of New York as its partner, was widely regarded as the favorite.[43] "Stanford is Stanford," Robert Steel acknowledged. Given its vast connections to Silicon Valley, competing with them is "a bit like lining up against the Yankees."[44]

Cornell lobbied hard to win the competition. While a poll taken by the *Stanford Daily* revealed that 50 percent of students did not want their university to build a tech campus in New York City, the undergraduate and graduate student assemblies at Cornell passed resolutions endorsing the project. And more than twenty-one thousand Cornell alumni signed an online petition of support. Deputy Mayor Steel joked that of the approximately fifty thousand Cornell graduates in the New York metropolitan area, "most of them called me directly."[45]

As New York City officials deliberated over the ten thousand pages submitted by the seven tech-campus contestants, President Skorton informed them that the Cornell Board of Trustees had authorized a $150 million allocation from the university's endowment to be used for investing in start-up companies that agreed to remain in the city for at least three years. No other bidder pledged to establish a venture fund. Cornell and the Technion promised as well to train at least two hundred New York City teachers in science education and to help teach at least ten thousand youngsters, from kindergarten through twelfth grade, each year.

Most significant, on December 3, when Cornell and the Technion made a final presentation to city officials, Skorton revealed that Atlantic Philanthropies had designated $350 million, the largest single gift in Cornell's history, to the tech campus. Initially announced as coming from an anonymous donor, the commitment became public—and was linked to Charles Feeney '56—in December. In a statement posted on his foundation's website, the soon-to-be-eighty-year-old philanthropist celebrated the tech campus as a unique opportunity "for Cornell University and Technion–Israel Institute of Technology, together with the City of New York, to create economic and educational opportunity on a transformational scale."[46] When every other institution was discussing the challenges of fund-raising, it was "pretty breathtaking," Robert Steel pointed out, to have one of the strongest competitors say about financing the entire first phase of the project: "done."[47]

On December 16, 2011, Stanford announced that it had withdrawn from the competition. "We were honored to be selected as a finalist," Stanford president John Hennessey declared. Hennessey publicly praised Bloomberg's "bold vision," but indicated that after weeks of negotiations with city officials, "the university could not be certain that it could proceed in a way that ensured the success of the campus."[48] In private, Ken Auletta reported in the *New Yorker*, Hennessey "was seething." He and his colleagues claimed that after bids were submitted, the city changed the terms of the deal, adding millions of dollars in penalties if the winner failed to stay on schedule—even if delays, such as toxicity or polluted water on Roosevelt Island, or a failure of the City Council to act, were beyond its control.[49]

"People briefed on the process," according to the *New York Times*, offered a different explanation. The scale, scope, and vision of Cornell's proposal, "its expertise and realism in taking on a huge urban project," and the partnership with the Technion "made an impression," they said. The presence of Weill Cornell Medical College in Manhattan, moreover, had given Cornell experience and expertise with building in New York City and negotiating with public officials that Stanford could not match. Behaving "as if it needed and wanted the prize more," Cornell was also more aggressive about generating enthusiasm among its alumni who lived or worked in the city and in generating financial pledges.[50]

On December 19, at a news conference held at Weill Cornell and live-streamed to jubilant supporters in Ithaca and Haifa, Bloomberg named Cornell and the Technion the winners of the competition. Flanked by David Skorton, Peretz Lavie, members of the New York City Economic Development Corporation, local politicians, and representatives from Roosevelt Island, the mayor declared that "this new land grant can help dreamers and entrepreneurs from around the world come to New York and help us become the world's leading city for technological innovation." He predicted that "today will be remembered as a defining moment" for the city and for Cornell.[51]

In his bimonthly column in the *Cornell Daily Sun*, President Skorton proclaimed that New York City's decision "is a great source of pride for our university and for the entire worldwide Cornell family." He acknowledged, however, that the announcement had also "generated questions and, at times, concerns among faculty, staff and students."[52] At Cornell, it turned out, the tech campus, which would be named "Cornell NYC Tech," had a fair share of detractors.

Among the most vocal were critics of Israel's treatment of Palestinians. They pointed to the Technion's pivotal role in Israel's military industrial complex. A partnership between Cornell and the institute, one alumnus wrote, "expresses the University's tacit approval of Israel and the security policies of the Jewish state—policies that most nations find criminal, in defiance of international law, and morally repugnant."[53] On campus, Students for Justice in Palestine demanded that Cornell sever its connection with the Technion. In 2013, "New Yorkers against the Cornell-Technion Partnership" picketed Cornell NYC Tech's temporary offices in Manhattan twice a month. The protesters held signs that read "Occupation Is Illegal" and "No to Technion in NYC"; they also sent an online petition to Cornell, signed by three hundred people. Decrying "the ways in which the Institute works against academic freedom, equal rights and the universal right to an education," a spokesperson for the organization called for "genuine discussion and debate about this issue on Cornell's campus—not a forum that is set up by the University as a propaganda tool meant to forward the present agenda."[54]

Mayor Bloomberg announces the winner of the New York City tech campus contest, December 19, 2011. (Cornell University Photography)

In response, President Skorton characterized the partnership "with one of the greatest entrepreneurial education organizations in the world" as a way for people "to interact with each other despite what their governments are doing." Pointing to Weill Cornell in Qatar, which had opened doors for women and improved the quality of medical care in the Middle East, as a case in point, he claimed that Cornell should not use government policies as a litmus test for collaborating with a country's institutions of higher education. He was more convinced than ever, Skorton added, that "we will benefit from working with colleagues who have the same goal: to improve life by discovery and innovation."[55]

The tech campus also gave a renewed sense of urgency to fears about corporate influence that, as we have seen, accompanied the emergence of the modern research university. While Stanford had been in the competition, the *Cornell Daily Sun* pointed out, Professor David Kennedy, a distinguished historian, had warned that a close relationship between business and academia "can be toxic to the mission of the university as a place of refuge, contemplation and investigation for its own sake." Skorton agreed that dealing with potential conflicts of interest and the possibility that corporations might shape the curriculum, research agendas, and the criteria for tenure and promotions were "huge concerns." Along with other Cornell administrators, however, he emphasized that firewalls were in place to ensure that decisions at Cornell NYC Tech were based on educational considerations. Work done for academic purposes, for example, could not be kept confidential. And all faculty members were required to follow university regulations involving technology transfer and intellectual property and report all external financial interests.[56]

The most pervasive concern among Cornellians, including some who supported the project, was that Cornell NYC Tech would divert energy and resources from the Ithaca campus. In April 2012, they noted, Moody's Investors Service, as it upgraded the university's overall outlook from negative to stable, warned that despite Atlantic Philanthropies' funding for Phase 1 of the project, the tech campus was a potential future funding liability. Pointing out that "the Ithaca campus has to be, in effect, the anchor," Abby Cohn '78, professor of linguistics, worried that "if we become too much out of balance, it's going to hurt all of us." Aware that at the press conference announcing the winner of the competition Mayor Bloomberg had joked that "the Ithaca campus is not closing," Skorton and Fuchs tried to reassure students, faculty, and alumni that Ithaca would remain, as the president put it, "the home of the University, the heart and soul of the university."[57] Skorton noted that the tech campus would not offer undergraduate degrees or duplicate anything offered in Ithaca; and its budget would be kept separate from the budget of the main campus. Cornell's enhanced visibility, he predicted, would attract additional financial support from alumni and gifts from non-alumni and corporations based in New York City. Fuchs promised that Cornell "would not compete with itself for resources." Emphasizing the benefits the tech campus would provide to the institution as a whole, including a two-way flow of ideas that would enrich scholarship, teaching, and public engagement, he observed: "I do think you get opportunities in life and you have to seize those. And yet, when you seize those opportunities, you can't lose track of what's important. And the Ithaca campus is what's truly important."[58]

As Cornellians debated whether "heads are going to be turned too much Downstate," work on Cornell NYC Tech began.[59] In February 2012 Huttenlocher was appointed founding dean of the new campus; Cathy Dove was named vice president for Cornell NYC Tech. In May, Greg Pass '97, the former chief technology officer at Twitter, joined Cornell NYC Tech as its founding entrepreneurial officer. That summer, Deborah Estrin, a computer scientist at UCLA, who had recently been named by CNN as one of the ten most powerful women in the tech industry, became the first professor hired by Cornell NYC Tech. The to-do list for them included acquiring academic accreditation, hiring a designer and architect for the site, planning a curriculum, hiring faculty, and recruiting students.

With the first academic building on Roosevelt Island scheduled to open in the fall of 2017, Cornell found a temporary home on the upper floor of the offices of Google Inc. at 111 Eighth Avenue. To get the new program "up and running," Google cofounders Larry Page and Sergey Brin, former Stanford graduate students, who had made a video to support their university's bid to win

Mayor Bloomberg's competition, provided Cornell NYC Tech with twenty-two thousand square feet of space, with an option to expand to thirty-six thousand, rent-free, for five years and six months, or until the first building was ready, whichever came first.[60] The market value of the space was estimated at between $10 million and $12 million. In January 2013, eight graduate students, Cornell NYC Tech's inaugural "beta class," began their course work at the Google building. "The technical and business courses, the Friday practicums, and the master's projects with industry mentors are all in place for this semester," Huttenlocher indicated.[61] In April 2013 Irwin and Joan Jacobs '54 made a $133 million gift to Cornell and the Technion to create the Joan and Irwin Jacobs Technion-Cornell Innovation Institute. "We believe strongly in the mission of this international collaboration," the Jacobses said, and share the dedication of both of "these distinguished institutions to inspire and train a next generation of entrepreneurs, forming new companies and strengthening existing ones."[62]

NYC Tech celebrated in the "Big Red Apple," an original watercolor by the Trumansburg artist Cheryl Chalmers.

BIG RED APPLE

Cornell University

477

As he expressed "humility" and "gratitude" to audiences on and off campus eager to learn the latest about Cornell NYC Tech, David Skorton cautioned against a "touchdown dance." The latest chapter in Cornell's history, he suggested, should not be "a matter of triumphalism; it's not a matter of pounding our breast and saying how great we are. The point is that we can really do something to change the world."[63] Skorton did not intend, of course, to dampen enthusiasm, either for Cornell NYC Tech or for Cornell's sesquicentennial. Indeed, the university had a lot to celebrate. For 150 years, Cornell had survived and thrived. In its second seventy-five years, throughout the industrial and postindustrial age and what Henry Luce, the publisher of *Time* magazine, called "the American Century," the "Cornell Idea" continued to animate and shape, imperfectly, to be sure, the modern research university. In the age of information, when going global was "a must," the challenges and opportunities for Cornell were, at once, different and the same. Meeting and exceeding them, face to face and virtually, in order to preserve, create, and disseminate knowledge, theoretical and practical, involved, as it always had, maintaining a dynamic and productive tension between the equally worthy ideals of freedom and responsibility.

Postscript

In the fall of 2014, to mark the beginning of the yearlong celebration of its ses-quicentennial, Cornell University dedicated the Sesquicentennial Commemo-rative Grove, designed by the New York City firm of Weiss/Manfredi, on the top of Libe Slope between Morrill and McGraw halls. A grove of trees, shrubs, stone walkways, and benches, it looks west from Cornell's original "Stone Row" buildings and is on an axis with A.D. White's seated statue, placed on the Arts Quad on the university's fiftieth birthday in 1915, and Ezra Cornell's standing statue (1919).

On the walkways appears an engraved timeline marking significant events in the university's history, with plenty of available space for future notations. On its benches the Commemorative Grove features engraved quotations from people who over Cornell's first 150 years have sought to capture its distinctive values and character. Present and future generations of students, alums, neigh-bors from "the bustling town," and visitors can see and read the tribute that follows.

THE COMMEMORATIVE GROVE TIMELINE

1862
The Morrill Land Grant Act, enacted by Congress, provides funds to states for teaching agriculture, the mechanical arts, and military tactics.

1865
State Senators A. D. White and Ezra Cornell win passage of a bill chartering Cornell as the land-grant university for New York State.

1868
Cornell University opens with classrooms and residences for students and faculty in Morrill and Cascadilla halls.

1871
The College of Architecture, the first four-year program of its kind in an American university, is created.

1880
The Cornell Sun, a daily student newspaper, is founded.

1887
Cornell Law School opens.

1888
The Department of Agriculture becomes a college (and, in 1904, the New York State College of Agriculture).

1894
Cornell's Agricultural Extension Service for New York State counties begins with the first state funding for the Cornell Experiment Station.

1894
The College of Veterinary Medicine at Cornell is established by New York State.

1898
Cornell Medical College is established in New York City, opening its first building there in 1900; a one-year program continues in Ithaca until 1938.

1921
The College of Engineering, combining mechanical and civil engineering, is founded.

1925
The Department of Home Economics in the College of Agriculture becomes the New York State College of Home Economics. Its name is changed to the College of Human Ecology in 1969.

1929
The University Christian Association changes its name to Cornell United Religious Work to include all religious communities.

1942–1945
During World War II Cornell offers training to thousands of Navy and Army servicemen and women.

1945
The New York State School of Industrial and Labor Relations opens, expanding Cornell's academic offerings.

1946
The Graduate School of Business and Public Administration, now the Johnson Graduate School of Management, opens.

1954

Hotel administration in the College of Home Economics becomes a separate School of Hotel Administration.

1958

Student protests begin the shift away from *in loco parentis* restrictions on social life and special rules for female students.

1964

President James Perkins creates a Committee on Special Educational Projects (COSEP) to attract minority students to Cornell.

1969

During the decade of the civil rights struggle, over a hundred African American students seize and occupy Willard Straight Hall for thirty-three hours, leading to the resignation of President James Perkins.

1972

Students occupy Carpenter Hall, protesting U.S. military action in Vietnam.

1980s

Students opposed to apartheid build shantytowns on campus to protest Cornell's investments in South Africa.

1995–2005

Cornell reshapes undergraduate residential life by housing all first-year students on North Campus and by constructing five residential colleges on West Campus.

2003

The Weill Cornell Medical College in Qatar is officially dedicated.

2011

Cornell, with its academic partner the Technion-Israel Institute of Technology, wins the competition to build a graduate campus focused on technologies of the digital age in the heart of New York City.

The Commemorative-Bench Quotations

"Far above Cayuga's waters . . . far above the busy humming of the bustling town."
  —(Alma Mater)

"I would found an institution where any person can find instruction in any study."
  —(Ezra Cornell)

"A place where the most highly prized instruction may be afforded to all— regardless of sex or color."
  —(President Andrew Dickson White)

"We have not invited you to see a university finished, but to see one begun."
  —(Ezra Cornell)

"To afford an asylum for science—where truth shall be sought for truth's sake."
  —(President Andrew Dickson White)

"An institution . . . which shall fit the youth of our country for the professions, the farms, the mines, the manufactories."
  —(Ezra Cornell)

"Useful things are taught here."
  —(President Charles Kendall Adams)

"A people's university, if it is true to the spirit of our age, must hold all subjects equally reputable. . . . The analysis of soils is as important as the analysis of literature."
  —(President Jacob Gould Schurman)

"It was not until I went to Cornell, where no one questioned my beliefs, that I became tolerant. . . . Cornell taught me . . . to respect the spiritual experience and religious beliefs of others."
  —(Professor Anna Botsford Comstock)

"Education is an inspiration, a taking hold of a broader life."
  —(Professor Liberty Hyde Bailey)

"The Cornell tradition . . . allows a maximum of freedom and relies so confidently upon the sense of personal responsibility for making a good use of it."
  —(Professor Carl Becker)

"I still cherish the hope that . . . freedom of choice . . . should not be exercised in a discriminatory fashion . . . distinctions drawn because of racial, religious, or other characteristics . . . have no effect on . . . worth as an individual."
  —(Trustee Mary Donlon)

"These professors of ours must have the right to profess; they must not be scourged from the public forum."
  —(President Deane W. Malott)

"It is your duty to look forward and not back, and without forgetting old wisdom to seek a wisdom ever new, to prepare an even greater Cornell."
  —(Professor Morris Bishop, Class of 1914)

"Cornell has not been content for the world to come to campus; it has also reached out to the world. Its land-grant mission has been writ large."
  —(President Frank H.T. Rhodes)

"We aim to be . . . the best research university for undergraduate education in the country."
  —(President Hunter R. Rawlings III)

Notes

Preface

1. *The Cornell Tradition: Freedom and Responsibility*, printed for the university, Ithaca, NY, 1940, p. 6.
2. Ibid.
3. Ibid., 10.
4. Ibid.
5. Ibid., 21.
6. Morris Bishop, *A History of Cornell* (Ithaca, NY: Cornell University Press, 1962), 441.
7. Ibid., 88.
8. Ibid., 245.
9. Ibid., cited on p. 177.
10. Ibid., 308.
11. *Cornell Tradition*, 17.
12. Ibid., 18, 19.

1. Building a Research University

1. *Cornell Alumni Magazine*, September 1945.
2. Cited in Morris Bishop, *A History of Cornell* (Ithaca, NY: Cornell University Press, 1962), 524.
3. *Cornell Alumni Magazine*, June 1948.
4. Bishop, *History of Cornell*, 523.
5. Ibid.
6. *Cornell Alumni Magazine*, June 1948.
7. Ibid., June 15, 1950.
8. Cornelis W. de Kiewiet Papers, Division of Rare and Manuscript Collections, Carl A. Kroch Library, Cornell University (hereafter de Kiewiet Papers), box 1, de Kiewiet to Murdock, May 11, 1949.
9. *New York Times*, January 11, 1950; de Kiewiet Papers, box 3, Dean to Meigs, January 20, 1950.
10. *Cornell Daily Sun*, September 9, 1951.
11. Ibid., November 30, 1951.
12. Ibid.; Cornell Faculty Memorial Statement, 1996.
13. *Proceedings of the Board of Trustees of Cornell University*, April 13, 1962.
14. *Cornell Daily Sun*, April 15, 1954.
15. *Cornell Alumni News*, July 1963.
16. *New York Times*, January 14, 1950.

17. Edmund Ezra Day Papers, Division of Rare and Manuscript Collections, Cornell University Library (hereafter Day Papers), box 55, Day to Becker, December 14, 1946.

18. Ibid.

19. *Cornell Daily Sun*, November 29, 1949.

20. Ibid., May 11, 1950.

21. De Kiewiet Papers, box 1, de Kiewiet to Parke, October 11, 1949.

22. *Cornell Daily Sun*, October 13, 1951.

23. Ibid., February 19, 1959.

24. Ibid., February 10, 1961; *Cornell Alumni News*, July 1960.

25. *Cornell Daily Sun*, February 10, 1961; February 27, 1961.

26. *Cornell Alumni News*, November 1945; Day Papers, box 28; *Cornell Alumni News*, November 1946; *Proceedings of the Board of Trustees*, December 31, 1961.

27. *Cornell Daily Sun*, October 15, 1948.

28. *Proceedings of the Board of Trustees*, October 11, 1945; Day Papers, box 62, L. E. Gubb to Day, October 12, 1945; Adams to Day, July 18, 1947.

29. *Cornell Daily Sun*, October 22, 1947.

30. Day Papers, box 62, "Address at Newman Lab," October 7, 1948.

31. Day Papers, box 7, Day to Biggerstaff and Sharp, November 2, 1945.

32. De Kiewiet Papers, box 5, Fahrs to de Kiewiet, August 16, 1950; Biggerstaff and Sharp to de Kiewiet, September 27, 1950.

33. *Proceedings of the Board of Trustees*, April 26, 1952; *Cornell Daily Sun*, October 4, 1952.

34. Deane Waldo Malott Papers, Division of Rare and Manuscript Collections, Cornell University Library (hereafter Malott Papers), box 13. Hill to Hollister, July 13, 1953.

35. *Cornell Daily Sun*, September 22, 1950, October 19, 1951; Malott Papers, box 13, Emerson to Ruml, November 26, 1951.

36. *Cornell Alumni News*, February 1953.

37. *Cornell Daily Sun*, November 26, 1957.

38. Malott Papers, box 25, "The Humanities Council Report of the Committee on a Humanities Center," December 9, 1957; *Cornell Daily Sun*, May 29, 1958.

39. *Cornell Daily Sun*, October 16, 1959.

40. Day Papers, box 15, Rossiter to Day, January 7, 1946.

41. *Cornell Daily Sun*, May 1, 1948.

42. Day Papers, box 32, Konvitz to Day, January 12, 1946.

43. *Cornell Daily Sun*, February 28, 1950.

44. Ibid., May 28, 1959.

45. *Proceedings of the Board of Trustees*, June 10, 1963.

46. Day Papers, box 35, Day to Patterson, April 18, 1945.

47. Cited in James W. Schmotter, *Not Just Another School of Business Administration* (Ithaca, NY: Cornell University Press, 1992), 26.

48. De Kiewiet Papers, box 6, de Kiewiet to Arthur Dean, September 7, 1949.

49. Malott Papers, box 25, Sheppard to Sloan, April 25, 1958.

50. Cited in *Cornell Alumni News*, November 1962.

51. Day Papers, box 32, Thomas Spares to Day, December 28, 1944; Teagle to Day, February 10, 1945; "Confidential Discussion of Desirability of Locating at the University a Projected New York State School of Industrial and Labor Relations," no date.

52. Ibid., Day Papers, box 57, Day to Ives, February 10, 1945.

53. Cited in *Cornell Alumni News*, April 1986; Day Papers, box 32, Gannett to Day, March 17, 1947; cited in *Cornell Alumni News*, November 1962.

54. Cited in *Cornell Alumni News*, December 1945.

55. Ibid.

56. Day Papers, box 32, Catherwood to James Milholland, March 19, 1949; Catherwood to Abraham Chetman, January 31, 1948; Catherwood to Day, May 8, 1948.

57. Cited in *Cornell Alumni News*, April 1986.

58. *Cornell Daily Sun*, January 14, 1949.

59. Day Papers, box 55, Kane to Day, December 10, 1948.

60. Day Papers, box 55, Day to Treman, February 8, 1949; Committee on Public Relations Coordination to Day, January 22, 1949.

61. *Cornell Daily Sun*, November 28, 1950; ibid., December 7, 1950.

62. De Kiewiet Papers, box 9, de Kiewiet to Donlon, December 30, 1950; box 33, de Kiewiet to Upson, December 12, 1950.

63. De Kiewiet Papers, box 9, De Kiewiet to Donlon, December 30, 1950.

64. *Proceedings of the Board of Trustees*, Executive Committee, June 13, 1954.

65. Author's personal correspondence, Jon Kohler '71 to Kramnick, June 24, 2011.

66. Malott Papers, box 51, "Cabinet Meeting," January 22, 1951.

67. Carl Becker, "The Cornell Tradition: Freedom and Responsibility," Ithaca, NY, 1940, p. 20.

68. Malott Papers, box 3, Brossman to Malott, April 10, 1953.

69. *Cornell Alumni News*, November 1958.

70. *Cornell Daily Sun*, February 19, 1949; February 28, 1952; January 13, 1958; March 4, 1957; February 24, 1958; February 10, 1958.

71. *Proceedings of the Board of Trustees*, General Committee, April 25, 1952; *Cornell Daily Sun*, February 10, 1958.

72. *Cornell Daily Sun*, March 13, 1959; *Cornell Alumni News*, May 1960.

73. *Cornell Alumni News*, May 1948.

74. *Cornell Daily Sun*, March 26, 1958.

75. Cited in Douglas Slaybaugh, *William I. Myers and the Modernization of American Agriculture* (Ames: Iowa State University Press, 1996), xii.

76. Ibid., 195.

77. Ibid., 198.

78. Ibid., 203–4; 172.

79. *Cornell Daily Sun*, April 30, 1959.

80. AAP faculty minutes, Clark to Day, November 8, 1945.

81. Report of the New York State College of Home Economics, January 1945, 19; 1946, 98–99; 1948, 16–, 1950, 211.

82. New York State College of Home Economics Council Minutes, box 1–21, Vincent to Walker, July 30, 1951; ibid., June 26, 1950.

83. Thirty-Second Report of the New York State College of Home Economics, 1957, 344.

84. Thirty-Seventh Report of the New York State College of Home Economics, 1962, 423–24.

85. Malott Papers, box 7, Nielsen to Malott, June 1, 1953.

86. Ibid., Minutes of the Council for the New York State Veterinary College, May 28, 1953.

87. De Kiewiet Papers, box 8, Babcock to Dewey, August 25, 1949.

88. Day Papers, box 56, Day to Dewey, March 9, 1948; Day to Trustees of SUNY, December 30, 1948.

89. Malott Papers, box 27, Malott to Rockefeller, August 19, 1960; ibid., box 28, Stamp to Dean, March 1, 1961.

90. Day Papers, box 27, Meigs to Day, April 26, 1948.

91. Day Papers, box 29, Daniel to Day and Knowles, May 14, 1949.

92. De Kiewiet Papers, box 11, "Resolution of East Hill Merchants," April 11, 1950.

93. *Ithaca Journal*, September 11, 1954.

94. Day Papers, box 29, Daniel to Day and Knowles, May 14, 1949.

95. *Cornell Daily Sun*, November 14, 1957.

96. Ibid., April 16, 1947; May 22, 1947; *Cornell Alumni News*, January 1948.

97. *Cornell Daily Sun*, October 13, 1951.

98. Malott Papers, box 4, Dean to Malott, June 12, 1952.

99. *Proceedings of the Board of Trustees*, April 22, 1952.

100. Malott Papers, box 4, Dean to Malott and Board of Trustees, June 12, 1952; *Proceedings of the Board of Trustees*, April 26, 1952; June 9, 1952; June 23, 1952; July 26, 1952.

101. *Cornell Daily Sun*, February 14, 1952.

102. Day Papers, box 55, Splight to Ackerman, March 23, 1945.

103. *Cornell Daily Sun*, January 15, 1953.

104. Ibid., September 20, 1954; October 28, 1954; October 21, 1958.

105. Ibid., May 7, 1958.

106. Malott Papers, box 3, Malott to H. T. Dyett, September 27, 1951.

107. *Proceedings of the Board of Trustees*, October 6, 1945.

108. Day Papers, box 45, Day to Brakely, September 18, 1946; Day to William Devane, January 14, 1947; Day to Spellman, December 10, 1948.

109. Day Papers, box 64, Kane to Day, December 5, 1944; December 20, 1944.

110. Ibid., Day to Seymour, December 30, 1944.

111. Malott Papers, box 8, Kane to Malott, February 17, 1952.

112. *Cornell Daily Sun*, February 11, 1954.

113. *Cornell Daily Sun*, February 28, 1964.

114. *Proceedings of the Board of Trustees*, January 17, 1946.

115. Day Papers, box 8, Becker to Babcock, April 9, 1945.

116. *Proceedings of the Board of Trustees*, May 4, 1946.

117. Ibid., January 24, 1948.

118. Ibid., March 16, 1948.

119. Day Papers, box 54, "Responsibilities and Duties of the Vice President for University Development," June 1948.

120. *Cornell Alumni News*, June 1, 1948.

121. *Cornell Daily Sun*, October 22, 1949.

122. *Cornell Alumni News*, March 15, 1951.

123. De Kiewiet Papers, box 5, "The Functions of the Cornell University Council," July 1950.

124. *Proceedings of the Board of Trustees*, April 13, 1962.

125. Author's personal correspondence, John W. Reps to Glenn C. Altschuler, December 9, 2012.

2. The Death of In Loco Parentis

1. *Cornell Alumni News*, September 1945.

2. Day Papers, box 41, Dewey to Day, February 15, 1946.

3. Ibid., box 30, Dewey to Day, September 30, 1946.

4. Ibid., box 27, Edward Graham to Day, January 22, 1946.

5. Cited in *Cornell Alumni News*, November 15, 1945.

6. *Cornell Alumni News*, January 1, 1946; June 7, 1947; Morris Bishop, *A History of Cornell* (Ithaca, NY: Cornell University Press, 1962), 447.

7. *Cornell Alumni News*, January 1, 1948.

8. Day Papers, box 33, Burnett to Day, July 17, 1945.

9. Ibid., Day to Burnett, July 31, 1945.

10. Ibid., Noyes to Day, October 3, 1946.

11. Day Papers, box 11, de Kiewiet to Sabine, July 30, 1945.

12. Ibid., Sabine to Day, March 3, 1945.

13. Day Papers, box 18, Speight to Day, April 2, 1946.

14. Day Papers, box 52, Anderson to Day, July 6, 1945.

15. *Cornell Daily Sun*, May 26, 1947.

16. Shelly Epstein Akabas '51 and Alice Katz Berglas '66 to the authors, June 13, 2011; Dan Meyer '83 to the authors, May 10, 2013.

17. *Cornell Daily Sun*, April 22, 1953.

18. Ibid., December 11, 1947.

19. Ibid., April 2, May 7, 15, 1952.
20. Day Papers, box 41, Day to Hoeing, October 13, 1947.
21. Ibid., Williams to Hoeing, December 8, 1948.
22. Ibid., Hoeing to Day, December 14, 1950.
23. *Cornell Daily Sun*, December 20, 1950.
24. *Cornell Alumni News*, March 15, 1950.
25. Cited in *Cornell Daily Sun*, September 22, 1952.
26. *Cornell Daily Sun*, March 10, 1949; April 11, 1949.
27. Ibid., April 10, 1949; December 8, 1947.
28. Ibid., April 7, 1952.
29. Ibid., December 10, 1955.
30. Ibid., October 30, 1956.
31. Ibid., April 26, 1961.
32. Ibid., January 10, 1962.
33. Ibid., September 19, October 18, November 5, 1949.
34. Ibid., December 17, 1959; *Cornell Alumni News*, January 1960.
35. *Cornell Daily Sun*, September 30, 1949; November 12, 1951.
36. *Cornell Alumni News*, June 1, 1951.
37. *Cornell Daily Sun*, May 15, 1951.
38. Ibid., March 6, 1952.
39. *Proceedings of the Board of Trustees*, January 26, 1952.
40. *Cornell Daily Sun*, May 22, 1952.
41. Ibid. April 8, 1954.
42. Ibid., January 20, 1948; *Widow*, May 1958.
43. Cited in *Cornell Daily Sun*, April 16, 1955
44. Ibid.
45. Ibid.
46. Malott Papers, box 23, "Sex Distribution in Enrollment," March 19, 1959.
47. *Cornell Daily Sun*, September 30, 1947.
48. Ibid., September 15, 1959.
49. Ibid., September 22, 1952; *Cornell Alumni News*, February 1951.
50. *Widow*, October 1953.
51. Ibid., October 1951, March 1952.
52. *Cornell Daily Sun*, April 30, 1947; cited in *Cornell Alumni News*, January 1960.
53. *Cornell Daily Sun*, April 16, 1955.
54. Ibid., October 18, 19, 20, 1949; October 12, 1950.
55. Ibid., September 21, 1959.
56. Ibid., May 11, 1948; December 10, 1946.
57. Ibid., May 18, 1962.
58. Malott Papers, box 12, Malott to Hathaway, November 24, 1953.
59. Ibid., Hathaway to Malott, December 5, 1953.
60. Ibid., Malott to Hathaway, December 9, 1953.
61. *Cornell Daily Sun*, December 11, 1953.
62. Ibid., December 15, 17, 1953.
63. Ibid., February 7, 1957.
64. Ibid., September 18, 1955.
65. Ibid, June 10, 1957.
66. Malott Papers, box 19, Malott to Humphrey, no date.
67. *Cornell Daily Sun*, May 13, 1957.
68. Ibid., January 2, 1958.
69. Ibid., December 16, 1957.
70. Ibid.

71. Ibid., December 18, 1957.

72. Ibid., May 21, 1958.

73. Ibid., December 17, 1957; May 14, 17, 21, 1958.

74. Ibid., November 28, 1956.

75. Ibid., May 18, 1958.

76. Richard Fariña, *Been Down So Long It Looks Like Up to Me*, (New York: Random House, 1966), 84.

77. *Cornell Daily Sun*, May 26, 1958; *Newsweek* cited in *Cornell Daily Sun*, May 5, 1978.

78. Ibid., May 26, 1958, and *Cornell Alumni News*, June 15, 1958.

79. *Cornell Alumni News*, June 15, 1958.

80. Ibid.

81. Ibid., *Cornell Daily Sun*, May 26, 28, 29, 1958; May 5, 1978.

82. Ibid., May 29, 1958.

83. Ibid., June 18, 1958.

84. *Proceedings of the Board of Trustees*, June 15, 16, 1958.

85. *Cornell Alumni News*, June 15, 1958.

86. Malott Papers, box 22, Malott to Hayford, May 30, 1958; Malott to Baker, June 2, 1958.

87. Ibid., Summerskill to Dean, June 28, 1958; box 23, Upson to Malott, October 14, 1958.

88. Malott Papers, box 53, Malott to Upson, October 23, 1958.

89. *Cornell Daily Sun*, January 21, 1959.

90. Ibid., October 6, 1958.

91. Ibid., January 21, 1959.

92. Malott Papers, box 23, "Summerskill Talk to New Students," January 1959.

3. The Cold War at Cornell

1. *New York World-Telegram*, October 19, 20, 21, 23, 1943.

2. Day Papers, box 15, Day to Horace Flanigan, August 30, 1948.

3. Morris Bishop, *A History of Cornell* (Ithaca, NY: Cornell University Press, 1962), 524.

4. Day Papers, box 15, Day to Flanigan, August 30, 1948.

5. Day Papers, box 63, de Kiewiet to Faculty, September 27, 1943.

6. Ibid., Day to Trustees, January 7, 1944.

7. *Saturday Review*, March 4, 1944.

8. Day Papers, box 11, Edward Graham to John Allen, October 17, 1944; box 63, de Kiewiet to Day, April 30, 1945.

9. *Cornell Alumni News*, May 15, 1948.

10. *Cornell Daily Sun*, May 22, 1947.

11. Ibid., April 17, 1948.

12. *Cornell Bulletin*, May 3, 1946.

13. Day Papers, box 49, Day to Gannett, January 9, 1948.

14. Day Papers, Box 9, Day to Gannett, May 25, 1948; box 8, Day to Fred Bonticou, March 11, 1947.

15. Day Papers, box 8, Speight to Day, January 30, 1946.

16. Day Papers, box 15, Day to Horace Flanigan, August 30, 1948.

17. *Cornell Daily Sun*, November 15, 1947; Day Papers, box 7, pamphlet 17, *The Enemy in Our Schools*, n.d.

18. *Cornell Daily Sun*, May 15, 1949.

19. Ibid., January 22, 1947; March 19, 1947; March 28, 1947; October 29, 1947; December 4, 1947.

20. Ibid., March 22, 1947.

21. Ibid., October 18, 1948.

22. Ibid., January 14, 1948; January 15, 1948; February 12, 1948.

23. Day Papers, box 5, Day to H. A. Stevenson, March 18, 1948.

24. Day Papers, box 15, Daniels to Day, May 27, 1948.

25. *Cornell Daily Sun*, February 24, 1949.

26. Ibid., April 11, 1949.

27. Day Papers, box 7, Noyes to Day, May 12, 1949; September 14, 1949; October 24, 1949.

28. Ibid., Adams to Trustees, September 15, 1947; October 21, 1947.

29. Day Papers, box 5, Gannett to Day, February 4, 1948.

30. Ibid., Day to Josephs, March 12, 1948.

31. Day Papers, box 7, Noyes to Day, August 30, 1946.

32. Ibid., Day to Noyes, December 3, 1946.

33. Day Papers, box 53, Day to Trustees, August 4, 1949; box 5, Day to Trustees, July 9, 1949; January 9, 1948.

34. Day Papers, box 34, Day to Wood, July 25, 1949; *Cornell Alumni News*, July 1949.

35. *Proceedings of the Board of Trustees*, April 30, 1947.

36. Day Papers, box 9, Day to Gannett, May 25, 1948.

37. Ibid., Day to Noyes, April 15, 1948.

38. Day Papers, box 62, "Mutual Radio News," April 7, 1949.

39. *Cornell Daily Sun*, October 13, 1950; April 15, 1950; May 1, 1950; May 9, 1951.

40. Malott Papers, box 9, Dean to Emmanuel, January 6, 1951.

41. De Kiewiet Papers, box 9, Donlon to de Kiewiet, December 28, 1950.

42. *Proceedings of the Board of Trustees*, January 26, 1950; *Cornell Daily Sun*, October 25, 1952.

43. De Kiewiet Papers, box 5, Senior to de Kiewiet, September 28, 1950; *Cornell Daily Sun*, September 19, 1950.

44. *Cornell Daily Sun*, October 18, 1948; November 16, 1948; March 1, 1950; April 9, 1949; December 12, 1950.

45. Cited in Ellen Schrecker, *No Ivory Tower: McCarthyism and the Universities* (New York: Oxford University Press, 1986), 151; *Cornell Daily Sun*, October 5, 1950; October 25, 1950; April 5, 1951.

46. Day Papers, box 15, Noyes to Day, October 24, 1949; de Kiewiet Papers, box 9, de Kiewiet to Emmanuel, May 25, 1948.

47. De Kiewiet Papers, box 1, de Kiewiet to E. E. Robinson, January 24, 1949.

48. *Cornell Daily Sun*, October 25, 1950.

49. Malott Papers, box 3, Wright to Morrison, April 6, 1951; April 5, 1951; box 4, April 23, 1951.

50. *Proceedings of the Board of Trustees*, April 28, 1951; Malott Papers, box 4, Wilson to Wright, April 19, 1951.

51. Malott Papers, box 4, Morrison to Wright, April 18, 1951.

52. Malott Papers, box 3, "Academic Cabinet Notes," May 4, 1951.

53. *Cornell Daily Sun*, January 5, 1953.

54. Malott Papers, box 1, Malott to Gannett, February 13, 1952; Malott to Emmanuel, October 31, 1952.

55. *Cornell Daily Sun*, March 20, 1952.

56. Ibid., April 2, 1952.

57. Malott Papers, box 3, "County Almanac," March 1, 1952; *Esquire*, March 1969, p. 141.

58. Malott Papers, box 1, Malott to Austin Story, July 1, 1954.

59. Ibid., Morrison Committee to Malott, January 31, 1953.

60. Ibid.

61. Ibid.

62. Ibid.

63. *Proceedings of the Board of Trustees*, April 23, 1953.

64. *Cornell Daily Sun*, April 11, 1953.

65. Ibid., May 8, 1953.

66. Ibid., May 9, 1953.

67. *Proceedings of the Board of Trustees*, October 16, 1953.

68. Malott Papers, box 1, Malott to Morrison, January 28, 1954.

69. Ibid., Malott to Gannett, February 13, 1952; box 4, Malott to Story, July 1, 1954.

70. Malott Papers, box 16, "Report to Alumni," June 12, 1954; *New York Herald Tribune*, June 13, 1953.

71. Keith Johnson, "Recollections of Malott: Oral History," 1974, p. 25.

72. Cornell Library, "Gould Coleman and Dale Corson: Oral History," February 2, 1992; *Proceedings of the Board of Trustees*, April 14, 1956, January 26, 1957.

73. *Cornell Daily Sun*, March 4, 1954; March 15, 1954.

74. Malott Papers, box 14, Gannett to Malott, June 3, 1953; ibid., September 28, 1953.

75. Ibid., Malott to Neal Becker, May 8, 1953.

76. Ibid., Maud Senior to Malott, September 2, 1953; September 3, 1953; September 28, 1953.

77. Ibid., Malott to Todd, May 15, 1953; Malott to Becker, May 8, 1953.

78. Malott Papers, box 16, "Report to Alumni," May 12, 1954.

79. *Cornell Alumni News*, February 1956; Malott Papers, box 22, Malott to A. Bartlett Richards, February 15, 1958.

80. *Cornell Alumni News*, July 1953; *Cornell Daily Sun*, October 18, 1954.

81. *Cornell Daily Sun*, May 27, 1953.

82. Ibid., May 3, 1954; May 5, 1954; May 24, 1954; May 27, 1954.

83. Malott Papers, box 12, O'Leary to Malott, May 3, 1954.

84. *Cornell Daily Sun*, November 23, 1954; October 18, 1954.

85. Ibid., October 24, 1955.

86. Ibid., January 4, 1956; September 24, 1956.

87. Malott Papers, box 11, Malott to O'Leary, January 17, 1955.

88. Michael Ulman, "Caught in the Crossfire," Cornell Senior Honors Thesis in History, 1980, p. 51.

89. Malott Papers, box 1, Dean to Malott, March 23, 1952; Malott to Dean, March 30, 1956.

90. *Cornell Daily Sun*, April 19, 1957; April 22, 1957.

91. Ibid., September 25, 1957.

92. Cited ibid., December 8, 1978.

93. *New York Times*, March 22, 1956.

94. Malott Papers, box 24, "Report of Subcommittee on the Finley Case," May 30, 1958.

95. Malott Papers, box 16, Malott to Stevens, December 29, 1954.

96. *Cornell Daily Sun*, April 14, 1955; January 19, 1960; May 26, 1960; Malott Papers, box 16, Malott and Dean to Gates, June 16, 1960.

97. Malott Papers, box 29, Kahn to J. D. Tuller, August 11, 1961; Malott to Kahn, August 15, 1961.

98. *Cornell Daily Sun*, December 11, 1961.

99. Malott Papers, box 29, Malott to E. K. Federov, November 13, 1962.

100. J. S. Mill, *On Liberty* (New York: Oxford University Press, 1997), 82.

101. Cited in "Memorial Statements of the Cornell University Faculty, 1996."

4. The Bureaucratic University and Its Discontents

1. *Cornell Daily Sun*, June 7, 1968.

2. Cited in George Fisher and Stephen Wallenstein, "Open Breeches: Guns at Cornell" (unpublished manuscript, 1969), 14.

3. Arthur M. Schlesinger Jr., *A Thousand Days: John F. Kennedy in the White House* (Boston: Houghton Mifflin Co., 1965), 127.

4. *New York Times*, November 7, 1965.

5. *Cornell Alumni News*, November 1963.

6. *Cornell Daily Sun*, January 7, 1963.

7. James A. Perkins Papers, Division of Rare and Manuscript Collections, Carl A. Kroch Library, Cornell University (hereafter Perkins Papers), box 23, "The Restless Decade." Convocation in New York City, March 9, 1968.

8. *New York Times*, October 29, 1968.

9. *Cornell Daily Sun*, April 28, 1968.

10. Dale R. Corson Papers, Division of Rare and Manuscript Collections, Carl A. Kroch Library, Cornell University (hereafter Corson Papers), box 132, "Perkins the Man and Perkins the President," June 9, 1969.

11. *Cornell Daily Sun*, May 3, 1966; June 9, 1968.

12. Ibid., June 9, 1968.

13. Ibid.

14. Ibid.

15. *Cornell Chronicle*, "Obituary for James Perkins," August 27, 1998.

16. Corson Papers, box 105, Corson to Perkins, November 24, 1967; Perkins Papers, box 32, "Memo to president Perkins from Dale R. Corson," March 23, 1969.

17. Corson Papers, box 105, "Memo to Messrs. Purcell, Noyes, Stewart, Kiplinger from Dale Corson," November 30, 1976.

18. *Cornell Alumni News*, June 1970.

19. Ibid.; Corson Papers, box 80, Corson to Mrs. Morris Bishop, November 21, 1973.

20. *Cornell Daily Sun*, October 16, 1969; October 3, 1969.

21. Perkins Papers, no box number, no date in 1959, "Reasons for No, Reasons for Yes"; Corson, "Oral History Interview Tapes with G. Coleman," May 4, 1992.

22. *Cornell Chronicle*, June 10, 1976.

23. Corson Papers, box 132, "Perkins the Man and Perkins the President," June 9, 1969.

24. Corson Papers, box 8, Perkins to J. Lawrence Murray, July 9, 1964; Perkins Papers, box 6, "The Division of Basic Biology at Cornell University," no date.

25. Ibid.

26. Corson Papers, box 8, Palm to Perkins, March 27, 1964; Brown to Perkins, March 20, 1964.

27. Ibid., Morrison to Corson, January 6, 1963.

28. Corson Papers, box 7, Long to Little, September 12, 1965.

29. Corson Papers, box 28, "Statement by James Perkins," February 23, 1967.

30. *Cornell Daily Sun*, February 24, 1967; March 10, 1967.

31. Perkins Papers, box 34, Rossiter to Perkins, September 25, 1967; Corson Papers, box 25, Kahin to Perkins, September 12, 1967.

32. *Cornell Daily Sun*, October 12, 1967.

33. *Proceedings of the Board of Trustees*, June 1, 1968.

34. Perkins Papers, box 1, "Priorities," June 9, 1965.

35. *Cornell Daily Sun*, December 11, 1967.

36. Ibid., December 10, 1969.

37. Perkins Papers, box 43, Corson to Parrish, no date.

38. *Cornell Alumni News*, June 1966.

39. Ibid.

40. Ibid.

41. Ibid., June 1974.

42. Corson Papers, box 104, Gurowitz to Perkins, February 16, 1973.

43. *Cornell Daily Sun*, November 17, 1972.

44. Ibid., April 21, 1972.

45. Ibid., May 4, 1973.

46. Perkins Papers, box 2, "Highlights from the Reports of Deans and Directors," no date.

47. *Cornell Alumni News*, June 1971.

48. *Cornell Daily Sun*, December 12, 1966.

49. Perkins Papers, box 15, Helen Canoyer to Perkins, no date.

50. *Proceedings of the Board of Trustees*, Executive Committee, February 11, 1975.

51. *Cornell Alumni News*, June 1971.

52. Perkins Papers, box 42, "Report of president's Commission to Study the New York State College of Agriculture," no date.

53. *Cornell Chronicle*, July 8, 1971.

54. *Cornell Daily Sun*, November 22, 1976.

55. Ibid., March 10, 1976.

56. Perkins Papers, box 23, "Development of Social Sciences at Cornell," August 26, 1968.

57. Corson Papers, box 20, Henry Landsberger to Stuart Brown, August 26, 1968.

58. Corson Papers, box 58, Justin Davidson to Mark Barlow, April 26, 1971.

59. *Cornell Chronicle*, June 5, 1975; Corson Papers, box 105, "Appointment of Senior Vice-President," January 30, 1976.

60. Corson Papers, box 35, "Program on STS," August 10, 1969.

61. *Cornell Daily Sun*, May 3, 1963.

62. Corson Papers, box 10, T. Mackesey to Deans, Directors and Administrative Officers, September 17, 1960.

63. *Cornell Newsletter*, December 16, 1966.

64. Corson Papers, box 73, "Minutes of Executive Staff Meetings," October 1970.

65. Ibid., box 91, "Memorandum for the Record," May 9, 1972.

66. *Cornell Chronicle*, October 5, 1972.

67. Ibid.

68. Ibid., April 19, 1973.

69. Corson Papers, box 118, "Corson Notes," October 14, 1975.

70. *Cornell Daily Sun*, December 16, 1974.

71. Ibid., September 21, 1975.

72. *Cornell Alumni News*, June 1966.

73. Corson Papers, box 18, Farr to Corson, December 30, 1965.

74. Ibid., Coors to Corson, no date.

75. *Proceedings of the Board of Trustees*, October 16, 1969.

76. Perkins Papers, box 3, Peterson to Perkins, January 5, 1965.

77. Perkins Papers, box 11, Corson to Perkins, March 7, 1967.

78. Corson Papers, box 86, "Report of the Ad Hoc Committee. . . ." October 2, 1972.

79. Ibid.; "Memorandum for the Record," January 7, 1972.

80. Corson Papers, box 121, Corson to Purcell at 21, September 28, 1976.

81. Corson Papers, box 123, Corson to Executive Staff and Deans, November 2, 1976.

82. *Ithaca Journal*, April 16, 1969.

83. Corson Papers, box 122, Corson to Nyquist, May 16, 1975; December 8, 1975.

84. Ibid.

85. *Ithaca Journal*, February 26, 1964.

86. Perkins Papers, box 3, Neal Stamp to Hunna Johns, May 23, 1964.

87. *Ithaca Journal*, April 16, 1969.

88. Perkins Papers, box 21, Perkins to Cornell Chapter of Students for a Democratic Study, January 15, 1969.

89. *Cornell Daily Sun*, April 10, 1969; April 15, 1969.

90. Ibid., October 18, 1967; April 23, 1969l; November 13, 1970.

91. *Cornell Daily Sun*, February 6, 1967.

92. Perkins Papers, box 22, "Minutes of the Special Meeting of the Faculty Council," January 23, 1967.

93. *Cornell Daily Sun*, February 6, 1967.

94. Ibid.

95. Ibid., October 2, 1967; March 26, 1969.

96. Ibid., May 1, 1968.

97. *Ithaca Journal*, July 24, 1972.

98. Corson Papers, box 8, Bloom et al. to Corson, November 26, 1963.

99. Allan Bloom, *Closing of the American Mind: How Higher Education Has Failed Democracy and Impoverished the Souls of Today's Students* (New York: Simon & Schuster, 1987), 339–40.

100. Ibid.; Allan Bloom, "The Democratization of the University," in *Giants and Dwarfs: Essays, 1960–1990* (New York: Simon & Schuster, 1990), 373.

101. *Cornell Daily Sun*, October 18, 1967.

102. Corson Papers, box 4, Corson to Caleb Rossiter, January 5, 1993; Frank H. T. Rhodes Papers, Division of Rare and Manuscript Collections, Carl A. Kroch Library, Cornell University (hereafter Rhodes Papers), box 200, Maud Senior to Corson, May 18, 1972.

103. *Cornell Daily Sun*, January 23, 1973.

104. Perkins Papers, box 24, "Social Analysis 377X," no date.

105. Ibid.

106. *Cornell Daily Sun*, September 24, 1969. Bloom, "Democratization of the University," 370.

107. *Cornell Daily Sun*, February 7, 1967.

108. Perkins Papers, box 27, Brown to Perkins, August 12, 1968.

109. Ibid., Barlow to Perkins, no date.

110. *Cornell Daily Sun*, April 5, 1971.

111. Bloom, "Democratization of the University," 340–41.

112. Perkins Papers, box 23, Tobias to Knapp, October 17, 1968; Corson Papers, box 29, Tobias to Corson, December 20, 1968.

113. *Proceedings of the Cornell Conference on Women*, January 22–25, 1969, ed. S. Tobias, E. Kusnera, D. Spitz.

114. Sheila Tobias, *Faces of Feminism: An Activist's Reflections on the Women's Movement* (Boulder, CO: Westview Press), xi.

115. *Cornell Daily Sun*, September 11, 1972.

116. Ibid., February 1, 1973.

117. Ibid., March 29, 1974.

118. *Proceedings of the Board of Trustees*, May 25, 1972.

119. *Cornell Chronicle*, March 21, 1974.

120. Cited in Susan Brownmiller, *In Our Time: Memoir of a Revolution* (New York: Dial Press, 1999), 281.

121. Ibid., 282.

122. *Cornell Daily Sun*, February 26, 1973; ibid., March 16, 1972.

123. Corson Papers, box 94, Knapp to Corson, February 27, 1973; box 44, Prado to Cooke, January 10, 1973.

124. Corson Papers, box 82, Kahn to COSEP Advisory Committee, March 15, 1973.

125. *Cornell Daily Sun*, May 3, 7, 1977.

126. Ibid., February 26, 1973.

127. Ibid., October 4, 1973.

128. Ibid., October 26, 1973.

129. *Cornell Alumni News*, October 1969.

130. Perkins Papers, box 5, Harp to Perkins, May 25, 1964.

131. *Cornell Daily Sun*, February 25, 1977.

132. Ibid., April 17, 1970.

133. Perkins Papers, box 26, Herz, Kiefer, Olum to Kane, November 18, 1968.

134. Robert Kane, *Good Sports: A History of Cornell Athletics* (Ithaca, NY: Cornell Magazine, 1992), 361.

135. *Cornell Daily Sun*, May 7, 1976.

136. Kane, *Good Sports*, 345.

137. Corson Papers, box 4, Corson to J. Marcham, October 28, 1991.

138. Kane, *Good Sports*, 347.

139. Corson Papers, box 4, Corson to J. Marcham, October 28, 1991.

140. *Cornell Alumni News*, June 1976.

5. Race at Cornell

1. Tom Sokol to authors, November 4, 2004.

2. Perkins Papers, box 10, Harry Wade to Nicholas Noyes, February 24, 1965.

3. *Cornell Daily Sun*, April 17, 1961.

4. Ibid., March 15, 16, 1960.

5. Ibid., March 25, 1964.

6. Cited in Donald Alexander Downs, *Cornell '69: Liberalism and the Crisis of the American University* (Ithaca, NY: Cornell University Press, 1999), 8–9.

7. Perkins Papers, box 9, Dale Rogers Marshall to Perkins, October 4, 1963.

8. Perkins Papers, box 28, "Interim Report: President's Committee on Disadvantaged Students," August 1, 1964.

9. Perkins Papers, box 18, "Committee on Special Educational Projects," January 1967.

10. Perkins Papers, box 26, Perkins to W. D. Cooke, September 19, 1968; box 22, Willers to Perkins, September 4, 1968.

11. Perkins Papers, box 2, F. A. Long to Advisory Committee on Human Rights, February 16, 1965.

12. Perkins Papers, box 31, Taubig to Perkins, November 19, 1968; *Cornell Daily Sun*, May 25, 1968.

13. *Cornell Daily Sun*, January 12, 1967; January 13, 1967.

14. Ibid., April 15, 1965; February 2, 1972; April 15, 1962.

15. Corson Papers, box 43, "Soul of Blackness Week: Berger and Munday to the Faculty," February 15, 1967; *Cornell Daily Sun*, March 1, 1967; *Esquire*, March 1969, p. 148.

16. Cited in *Cornell Daily Sun*, April 19, 1979; *Cornell Alumni News*, September 1969.

17. *Ithaca Journal*, January 17, 1968; January 29, 1968.

18. *Cornell Daily Sun*, February 16, 1968; *Ithaca Journal*, May 23, 1969.

19. *Cornell Daily Sun*, February 16, 1968.

20. Cited in Downs, *Cornell '69*, 58; and George Fisher and Stephen Wallenstein, "Open Breeches: Guns at Cornell" (unpublished manuscript, 1969), 24–25.

21. Cited in Downs, *Cornell '69*, 63.

22. *Cornell Daily Sun*, April 5, 1968.

23. Cited in C. Strout and D. Grossvogel, *Divided We Stand: Reflections on the Crisis at Cornell* (New York: Doubleday, 1970), 10.

24. *Cornell Daily Sun*, April 5, 1968.

25. Cited in Downs, *Cornell '69*, 79.

26. Cited in Strout and Grossvogel, *Divided We Stand*, 3.

27. Cited in "Summer Research Reports of Cornell Constituent Assembly 1969" (Robertson Report), Document Five.

28. Perkins Papers, box 25, Brown to Perkins, May 22, 1968.

29. Ibid., Perkins to Will, May 16, 1968.

30. Cited in "Summer Research Reports," Document One.

31. Ibid.

32. Cited in "Summer Research Reports," Document Ten.

33. Ibid., Document One.

34. Ibid., Document Eleven.

35. Ibid.

36. "Oral History, Corson to Gould Coleman," March 24, 1999, Cornell Library.

37. "Summer Research Reports," Document One.

38. *Cornell Daily Sun*, December 13, 1968.

39. Ibid., December 16, 1968.
40. Ibid., December 18, 1968.
41. Ibid., December 19, 1979.
42. Perkins Papers, box 22, Will to Corson, January 9, 1969.
43. "Summer Research Reports," Document One.
44. *Cornell Daily Sun*, June 2, 1969.
45. Perkins Papers, box 33, Purcell to Perkins, April 17, 1969.
46. *Cornell Daily Sun*, April 16, 1968; cited in Fisher and Wallenstein, "Open Breeches," 22.
47. Corson Papers, box 21, Neil Stamp to Board of Trustees, March 4, 1969.
48. *Cornell Daily Sun*, March 3, 1969.
49. Cited in Fisher and Wallenstein, "Open Breeches," 147.
50. Minutes, Faculty Meeting, March 12, 1969, pp. 3605–13.
51. *Proceedings of the Board of Trustees*, "Memo to Perkins from Barlow," p. 6131.
52. Perkins Papers, box 33, Purcell to Perkins, April 17, 1969.
53. Cited in Downs, *Cornell '69*, 151.
54. Ibid., 150.
55. *Cornell Daily Sun*, March 7, 1969.
56. Minutes, Faculty Meeting, pp. 3617–29; Downs, *Cornell '69*, 140; *Cornell Daily Sun*, March 13, 1969.
57. *Cornell Daily Sun*, March 14, 1969.
58. Ibid., March 15, 1969.
59. Ibid., March 26, 1969.
60. Ibid., April 17, 1969.
61. Ibid., April 16, 1969.
62. Ibid., March 13, 1969.
63. Ibid., April 19, 1979; *Cornell Alumni News*, June 1969.
64. Cited in Downs, *Cornell '69*, 179.
65. *Cornell Alumni News*, June 1969; *Cornell Daily Sun*, April 19, 1979.
66. Corson Papers, box 40, "Report to Trustees on Willard Straight Hall Takeover, Draft," no date.
67. Cited in Strout and Grossvogel, *Divided We Stand*, 24; *Cornell Daily Sun*, April 19, 1979.
68. Cited in Downs, *Cornell '69*, 187.
69. Cited in Strout and Grossvogel, *Divided We Stand*, 25.
70. *Ithaca Journal*, April 21, 1969.
71. Cited in Downs, *Cornell '69*, 202.
72. Cited in Fisher and Wallenstein, "Open Breeches," "Frontispiece."
73. *Cornell Daily Sun*, April 21, 1969.
74. Minutes, Faculty Meeting, April 21, 1969, pp. 3656–67.
75. *Cornell Daily Sun*, April 22, 1969; April 19, 1979.
76. Minutes, Faculty Meeting, p. 3669.
77. Ibid., pp. 3670–72.
78. *Cornell Alumni News*, June 1969.
79. Ibid.; *Cornell Daily Sun*, April 23, 1969.
80. Cited in Downs, *Cornell '69*, 239–40.
81. *Cornell Alumni News*, June 1969.
82. *Cornell Daily Sun*, April 23, 1969.
83. Ibid.
84. Corson Papers, box 61, "Minutes of the Special Meeting of the University Faculty," April 23, 1969.
85. Ibid.
86. *Cornell Alumni News*, June 1969.
87. *Cornell Daily Sun*, April 24, 1969.

88. *Cornell Alumni News*, June 1969.

89. Ibid.

90. Ibid.

91. Ibid.

92. *Cornell Daily Sun*, May 7, 1969.

93. *Cornell Alumni News*, July 1969.

94. Ibid., June 1969.

95. *Ithaca Journal*, April 28, 1969.

96. Ibid.

97. *Cornell Daily Sun*, May 2, 1969.

98. Cited in *Cornell Alumni News*, June 1969.

99. *Cornell Daily Sun*, April 25, 1969.

100. *Cornell Alumni News*, June 1969.

101. *Cornell Daily Sun*, April 24, 1969

102. Perkins Papers, box 35, Harold Bloom to Purcell, May 2, 1969.

103. *Ithaca Journal*, April 29, 1969; June 2, 1969.

104. Ibid., April 29, 1969.

105. Ibid., April 22, 1969.

106. *Texas Star Ledger*, May 1, 1969.

107. Perkins Papers, box 35, Coors to Purcell, May 5, 1969.

108. Perkins Papers, box 28, Clark to Perkins, May 4, 1969.

109. Perkins Papers, box 35, People for Racial Peace to Perkins, April 26, 1969; box 36, James Bender II to Perkins, April 24, 1969.

110. *Cornell Daily Sun*, April 28, 1969.

111. Cited in Downs, *Cornell '69*, 286.

112. *Cornell Daily Sun*, May 16, 1969.

113. Ibid., November 14, 1977.

114. "Oral History, Corson to Gould Coleman," March 18, 1992, Cornell Library.

115. Corson Papers, box 29, "Statement by Perkins to the McClennon Committee," July 28, 1969.

116. Perkins Papers, box 28, Edwards to Perkins, June 2, 1969.

117. Perkins Papers, box 34, Kahn to Perkins, June 4, 1969.

118. Ibid., Hacker to Perkins, June 4, 1969.

119. *Cornell Daily Sun*, September 11, 1969.

120. "Oral History, Corson to Gould Coleman," May 4, 1992, Cornell Library; *Cornell Chronicle*, April 20, 1989.

121. *Cornell Daily Sun*, September 23, 1969.

122. Ibid., September 30, 1969.

123. Corson Papers, box 56, Purcell to Corson, February 10, 1972; Corson to Purcell, February 15, 1972.

124. *Cornell Daily Sun*, October 2, 1969.

125. Ibid., February 13, 1973.

126. Corson Papers, box 35, Schultz to Plane, March 30, 1970; Kahn to Plane, April 8, 1970.

127. *Cornell Daily Sun*, March 9, 1970.

128. Ibid., February 12, 1970.

129. Corson Papers, box 52, "Memorandum for the Record," March 10, 1970.

130. *Cornell Daily Sun*, March 12, 1970.

131. Ibid., October 7, 1970.

132. Corson Papers, box 26, Kahn to Plane, November 19, 1969.

133. Ibid.

134. Corson Papers, box 73, "Minutes of Executive Staff Meeting," November 24, 1969.

135. *Cornell Daily Sun*, December 1, 1969.

136. Ibid., December 9, 1969.

137. Ibid., April 13, 1970.

138. *Cornell Alumni News*, May 1970.

139. *Cornell Daily Sun*, April 6, 1970.

140. *Cornell Alumni News*, May 1970.

141. Ibid.

142. *Cornell Daily Sun*, April 6, 1970.

143. *Ithaca Journal*, April 7, 1970.

144. Ibid., April 8, 1970.

145. Ibid., April 10, 1970.

146. Ibid.

147. *Ithaca Journal*, April 9, 1970.

148. Ibid., April 11, 1970.

149. *Cornell Alumni News*, May 1970.

150. *Ithaca Journal*, April 14, 1970.

151. Ibid.

152. *Cornell Daily Sun*, April 23, 1970.

153. "Oral History, Corson to Gould Coleman," December 8, 1972, Cornell Library.

154. *New York Times Magazine*, December 14, 1970.

155. *Cornell Daily Sun*, December 18, 1970.

156. Ibid., September 21, 1971.

157. Corson Papers, box 33, "Report of the University Faculty Committee to Review the COSEP Handbook," no date.

158. *Cornell Daily Sun*, October 13, 1975.

159. *Ithaca Journal*, April 16, 1975.

160. Ibid., October 15, 1975.

161. *Cornell Daily Sun*, January 23, 1976.

162. *Ithaca Journal*, March 11, 1976.

163. Ibid., January 24, 1976.

164. Ibid., March 30, 1976.

165. Ibid., April 2, 1976.

166. *Cornell Daily Sun*, April 4, 1976.

167. *Ithaca Journal*, April 19, 1976.

168. Ibid., April 20, 1976.

169. Ibid., April 29, 1976.

6. The Wars at Home

1. *Cornell Daily Sun*, January 11, 1960.

2. *Proceedings of the Board of Trustees*, April 14, 1967.

3. *Cornell Daily Sun*, April 28, 1967.

4. "Oral History, Corson to Gould Coleman," December 8, 1992, Cornell Library.

5. "Oral History, Corson to Gould Coleman," January 4, 1991, Cornell Library.

6. *Cornell Daily Sun*, February 17, 1965.

7. *Cornell Daily Sun*, April 19, 1965.

8. Ibid., April 26, 1965.

9. Cited in Irving L. Horowitz and William H. Friedland, eds., *The Knowledge Factory: Student Power and Academic Politics in America* (Chicago: Aldine, 1970), 233.

10. *Cornell Daily Sun*, May 10, 1965.

11. *Cornell Alumni News*, December 1965.

12. *Cornell Daily Sun*, May 13, 1965.

13. *Cornell Alumni News*, June 1965.

14. Ibid.

15. *Cornell Daily Sun*, May 21, 1965; *Cornell Alumni News*, June 1965.

16. Perkins Papers, box 9, "Mark Barlow Memo, Student Demonstrations," August 30, 1965.

17. Perkins Papers, box 6, Berns to Perkins, May 13, 1965.

18. *Cornell Alumni News*, July 1965.

19. Perkins Papers, box 2, Perkins to Barlow, May 24, 1965.

20. *Cornell Daily Sun*, September 13, 1968.

21. Ibid., October 4, 1968.

22. *Ithaca Journal*, November 28, 1967.

23. *Cornell Daily Sun*, May 7, 1970.

24. Perkins Papers, box 28, Perkins to Burak, January 7, 1969; "Oral History, Corson to Gould Coleman," March 24, 1992, Cornell Library.

25. *Ithaca Journal*, June 4, 1969.

26. Perkins Papers, box 30, "A Discussion of Students and University Management," June 28, 1968.

27. Perkins Papers, box 13, "Sit in Statement," May 17, 1966.

28. *Cornell Daily Sun*, May 23, 1966; May 24, 1966.

29. Perkins Papers, box 30, Corson to Perkins, March 14, 1968; Perkins Papers, box 15, S. Brown to Faculty, January 6, 1966.

30. *Cornell Daily Sun*, March 3, 1967.

31. Ibid., May 7, 1976.

32. Cited in Kirkpatrick Sale, *SDS: The Rise and Development of Students for a Democratic Society* (New York: Random House, 1974), 323.

33. *Cornell Daily Sun*, March 21, 1967; Horowitz and Friedland, *Knowledge Factory*, 249.

34. *Cornell Daily Sun*, April 18, 1967.

35. Ibid., April 15, 1967.

36. Ibid., April 17, 1967.

37. Cited in Tom Wells, *The War Within: America's Battle over Vietnam* (Berkeley: University of California Press, 1994), 132.

38. *Ithaca Journal*, February 10, 1968.

39. *Cornell Daily Sun*, October 14, 1968.

40. Ibid., February 6, 1967.

41. Ibid., October 13, 1967.

42. *Esquire*, March 1969, p. 100.

43. *Cornell Daily Sun*, November 17, 1967.

44. Ibid., December 5, 1967.

45. *Ithaca Journal*, March 21, 1967.

46. *Cornell Daily Sun*, December 15, 1967.

47. Ibid., February 20, 1968; *Ithaca Journal*, February 19, 1968.

48. Perkins Papers, box 23, Norman Tobin to Perkins, April 26, 1968.

49. Perkins Papers, box 22, Perkins to J. P. Levis, May 2, 1968; *Ithaca Journal*, June 1, 1968.

50. Perkins Papers, box 32, SDS to Perkins, no date.

51. Perkins Papers, box 32, Perkins to Cornell Chapter of SDS, May 12, 1969.

52. *Ithaca Journal*, May 5, 1969.

53. *Cornell Daily Sun*, October 1, 1969.

54. Ibid., December 12, 1969.

55. Ibid., May 14, 1970.

56. Corson Papers, box 24, "ROTC Discussions in Washington," December 10, 1969.

57. *Ithaca Journal*, August 7, 1969.

58. *Cornell Daily Sun*, October 16, 1969.

59. Cited in Wells, *War Within*, 286.

60. *Ithaca Journal*, May 5, 1970.

61. *Cornell Daily Sun*, May 9, 1970.

62. *Ithaca Journal*, June 15, 1970.

63. *Cornell Daily Sun*, September 18, 1970.

64. Ibid., May 6, 1971.

65. Ibid., April 17, 1971.

66. *Ithaca Journal*, April 27, 1972; *Cornell Daily Sun*, April 27, 1972, October 24, 1972.

67. *Cornell Daily Sun*, April 27, 1972.

68. Corson Papers, box 11, "Six Days in Spring: The Carpenter Hall Takeover," no date; "Oral History, Corson to Gould Coleman," April 4, 1996, Cornell Library; *Ithaca Journal*, May 1, 1972.

69. Corson Papers, box 11, "Six Days in Spring," no date.

70. Corson Papers, box 61, "Tom Tobin—Carpenter Hall Notes," no date.

71. *Cornell Daily Sun*, May 31, 1974.

72. Ibid., October 4, 1966.

73. Ibid., November 10, 1966.

74. *Cornell Alumni News*, January 1967.

75. Ibid., May 1971; Corson Papers, box 70, "Memo to the File: Mark Barlow, Jr.," February 23, 1970.

76. *Cornell Daily Sun*, April 24, 1967.

77. Ibid., February 19, 1965; *Cornell Alumni News*, February 1965.

78. *Cornell Daily Sun*, October 21, 1966.

79. *Ithaca Journal*, March 18, 1967.

80. *Cornell Daily Sun*, May 3, 1967.

81. *Ithaca Journal*, May 3, 1967; May 8, 1967; *Cornell Daily Sun*, May 8, 1967.

82. Corson Papers, box 70, "Statement by Cornell University President Dale R. Corson," December 6, 1972.

83. *Cornell Daily Sun*, November 19, 1966; November 30, 1966.

84. Ibid., March 23, 1967.

85. Corson Papers, box 12, "The Proctor is a Cop," no date.

86. *Cornell Daily Sun*, October 2, 1967; Corson Papers, box 43, "Memo for the Record: A Policy on Student Disturbances," January 5, 1968.

87. *Ithaca Journal*, January 1, 1974; November 12, 1973; *Cornell Daily Sun*, May 30, 1975.

88. Corson Papers, box 9, Brodeur to Corson, May 22, 1974.

89. Corson Papers, box 84, "Gurowitz Memo for the Record," November 9, 1973; *Cornell Daily Sun*, November 9, 1990.

90. *Cornell Daily Sun*, November 6, 1975; *Ithaca Journal*, November 6, 1973.

91. *Ithaca Journal*, October 27, 1971; *Cornell Daily Sun*, September 14, 1973; February 28, 1974.

92. *Ithaca Journal*, December 10, 1975.

93. Ibid.

94. Ibid.; *Cornell Daily Sun*, January 27, 1976; September 21, 1976.

95. *Ithaca Journal*, December 10, 1975.

96. *Cornell Daily Sun*, January 26, 1976.

97. *Ithaca Journal*, December 12, 1976.

98. Ibid.

99. *Cornell Daily Sun*, November 26, 1976.

100. Cited in Donald Alexander Downs, *Cornell '69: Liberalism and the Crisis of the American University* (Ithaca, NY: Cornell University Press, 1999), 278.

7. The Rhodes Years

1. Corson Papers, box 10, Les Severinghaus to Frank Rhodes, February 24, 1978.

2. *Cornell Daily Sun*, February 9, 1977.

3. Ibid., February 18, 1977.

4. Frank H. T. Rhodes Papers, Division of Rare and Manuscript Collections, Carl A. Kroch Library, Cornell University (hereafter Rhodes Papers), box 296, "Rhodes Years at Cornell—Highlights," May 2, 1995.

5. *Cornell Daily Sun*, Frank Rhodes Supplement, May 3, 1995.

6. *Cornell Chronicle*, November 17, 1977.

7. *Cornell Daily Sun*, November 11, 1977.

8. *Cornell Chronicle*, March 29, 1990.

9. *Cornell Daily Sun*, March 13, 1987.

10. *Cornell Magazine*, May 1995.

11. *Cornell Daily Sun*, March 18, 1994.

12. Rhodes Papers, box 60, Corson to Messrs. Purcell, Stewart, Noyes, Kiplinger, January 26, 1976.

13. *Cornell Alumni News*, October 1978.

14. Rhodes Papers, box 51, "Joy's Statement," March 25, 1981.

15. Rhodes Papers, box 173, J. Ballantyne to the Record, September 25, 1987.

16. Rhodes Papers, box 60, "President Rhodes' Statement on Financial Aid," February 9, 1982.

17. Rhodes Papers, box 5, Jansen Noyes Jr. to Frank H. T. Rhodes, June 23, 1978.

18. Rhodes Papers, box 153, Frank H. T. Rhodes to members of the Board of Trustees, March 25, 1985.

19. *Cornell Daily Sun*, February 13, 1985.

20. *Cornell Chronicle*, January 19, 1989.

21. Rhodes Papers, box 292, James E. Morley Jr. to Malden C. Nesheim, September 8, 1993.

22. Ibid., Alan G. Merten and Don M. Randel to Malden C. Nesheim, September 2, 1993.

23. *Cornell Chronicle*, November 29, 1990.

24. Ibid., December 20, 1990.

25. Rhodes Papers, box 256, "Sheet," no date.

26. Rhodes Papers, box 107, Joe Ballantyne to Frank Rhodes, Robert Barker, and Don Cooke, September 6, 1984.

27. Rhodes Papers, box 83, W. D. Cooke to Executive Staff, June 29, 1983.

28. Rhodes Papers, box 301, "The Importance of Centers and Institutes at Cornell University," January 1981.

29. *Cornell Chronicle*, November 15, 1990.

30. Rhodes Papers, box 107, Joe Ballantyne to Frank Rhodes, Robert Barker, and Don Cooke, September 6, 1984.

31. Rhodes Papers, box 103, Frank Rhodes to Members of the Faculty, January 20, 1986.

32. Rhodes Papers, box 202, Transcript to *The MacNeil/Lehrer NewsHour*, January 22, 1986.

33. Rhodes Papers, box 282, Frank Rhodes to Hon. Daniel Patrick Moynihan, May 12, 1993

34. *Cornell Chronicle*, May 12, 1994.

35. *Cornell Alumni News*, March 1983.

36. Rhodes Papers, box 160, "The Cornell Theory Center: Vision of Supercomputers and Science," no date.

37. *Cornell Chronicle*, August 27, 1987.

38. Ibid., February 4, 1988.

39. *Cornell Daily Sun*, September 13, 1990.

40. Ibid., April 11, 1989.

41. Ibid., September 4, 1991.

42. *Cornell Chronicle*, November 17, 1977.

43. Rhodes Papers, box 7, Harry Levin to David Knapp, February 23, 1977.

44. Rhodes Papers, box 8, Frank Rhodes to Alain Seznec, May 23, 1978.

45. *Cornell Daily Sun*, October 6, 1977.

46. Rhodes Papers, box 265, "Draft, R. Ehrenberg," October 10, 1991.

47. *Cornell Daily Sun*, September 13, 1991.

48. Ibid., May 1, 1995.

49. Ibid., March 18, 1994.

50. *Cornell Chronicle*, September 17, 1992.

51. Ibid.

52. *Cornell Daily Sun*, September 17, 1993.

53. *Cornell Chronicle*, February 17, 1994.

54. Rhodes Papers, box 97, W. K. Kennedy to President Rhodes, January 31, 1984.

55. *Cornell Daily Sun*, April 9, 1993.

56. *Cornell Chronicle*, September 3, 1992.

57. Ibid., September 10, 1992.

58. Ibid., September 17, 1992.

59. Rhodes Papers, box 17, "Cornell-SUNY Relationships: Statement of Problem," December 15, 1977.

60. Rhodes Papers, box 51, "Political Aspects of Changing Cornell's Relationship to SUNY," August 1977.

61. Rhodes Papers, box 120, W. K. Kennedy to D. L. Call, W. J. Relihan, J. W. Spencer, September 1, 1981.

62. *Cornell Alumni News*, June 1985.

63. Rhodes Papers, box 120, "Statement of Frank H. T. Rhodes before the Senate and Assembly Higher Education Committee," March 15, 1985.

64. *Proceedings of the Board of Trustees*, March 17, 1995.

65. *Cornell Daily Sun*, May 3, 1995.

66. Ibid., May 6, 1988.

67. *Ithaca Journal*, April 10, 1981.

68. Ibid., July 14, 1981.

69. *Ithaca Journal*, April 22, 1981.

70. Ibid., April 15, 1981.

71. Ibid., September 4, 1980.

72. Ibid., September 25, 1980.

73. Rhodes Papers, box 92, Randy Shew to Bill Herbster and Gil Goetz, November 12, 1983.

74. *Ithaca Journal*, October 7, 1987.

75. Rhodes Papers, box 257, "Cornell University's Response to the Report of the Mayor's Cornell-City Relations Study Commission, January 9, 1992, Draft Highlights."

76. Rhodes Papers, box 257, Frank H. T. Rhodes to Hon. Benjamin Nichols, January 30, 1992.

77. Rhodes Papers, box 313, Henrik Dullea to Hon. Benjamin Nichols, January 10, 1995.

78. Ibid., Henrik Dullea to Frank Rhodes and Malden Nesheim, May 15, 1995.

79. *Ithaca Journal*, March 3, 1980.

80. Ibid., March 10, 1980.

81. Ibid., October 29, 1980.

82. Rhodes Papers, box 90, Charles Rehmus to W. Keith Kennedy and William Herbster, August 28, 1980.

83. *Ithaca Journal*, February 18, 1981.

84. Ibid., February 25, 1981.

85. Ibid., September 23, 1981.

86. Ibid., October 5, 1981.

87. Ibid., October 6, 1981.

88. Ibid., October 5, 1981.

89. Ibid., October 6, 1981.

90. Ibid., October 12, 1981.

91. Ibid., October 7, 1981.

92. Ibid., October 12, 1981.

93. Ibid., October 19, 1981.

94. Ibid., March 10, 1983.

95. Ibid., June 3, 1983.

96. Ibid., September 21, 1987.

97. Ibid., October 7, 1987.

98. *Cornell Daily Sun*, October 12, 1987.

99. *Ithaca Journal*, May 6, 1988.

100. Ibid., May 14, 1988.

101. *Cornell Alumni Magazine*, May 1995.

102. Rhodes Papers, box 71, Frank H. T. Rhodes to Richard Ramin, November 8, 1982.

103. Quoted in Conor O'Clery, *The Billionaire Who Wasn't: How Chuck Feeney Secretly Made and Gave Away a Fortune* (New York: Public Affairs, 2007), 115.

104. *Cornell Chronicle*, October 19, 1990.

105. *Cornell Alumni Magazine*, September 1994.

106. *Cornell Chronicle*, October 17, 1991.

107. Ibid.

108. *Cornell Chronicle*, February 6, 1992.

109. Ibid., October 17, 1991.

8. *Academic Identity Politics*

1. Rhodes Papers, box 7, Harry Levin to David Knapp, June 6, 1977.

2. Quoted in Todd Gitlin, *The Twilight of Common Dreams: Why America Is Wracked by Culture Wars* (New York: Henry Holt and Co., 1995), 135.

3. Ibid., 153.

4. *Cornell Alumni News*, July 1978.

5. *Cornell Daily Sun*, August 30, 1984.

6. *Cornell Alumni News*, October 1981.

7. *Cornell Alumni Magazine*, July/August 1994.

8. Ibid.

9. Rhodes Papers, box 163, "'While You Were at Cornell, Have You Ever . . .'": An Assessment of Academic Culture at Cornell University," Spring Semester 1987.

10. *Cornell Daily Sun*, September 19, 1980.

11. Ibid., October 6, 1980.

12. *Cornell Alumni News*, June 1986.

13. *Cornell Magazine*, July/August 1994.

14. *Ithaca Journal*, September 8, 1986.

15. Ibid., March 28, 1984.

16. Ibid., September 15, 1986.

17. *Cornell Alumni News*, July 1978.

18. *Proceedings of the Board of Trustees Executive Committee*, January 26, 1978.

19. *Cornell Daily Sun*, April 17, 1978.

20. Ibid., April 12, 1978.

21. Ibid., April 26, 1978.

22. Ibid., November 28, 1983.

23. *Ithaca Journal*, January 30, 1984.

24. Ibid., March 28, 1984.

25. Ibid., January 30, 1984.

26. *Cornell Daily Sun*, March 9, 1984.

27. Ibid., March 16, 1984.

28. Rhodes Papers, box 133, "Joint Appointments," no date.

29. Rhodes Papers, box 281, "Final Report of 1992 Task Force on Freshmen Housing Assignment," no date.

30. *Cornell Daily Sun*, March 6, 1992.

31. Ibid.

32. Rhodes Papers, box 262, "Africana Center Faculty Oppose Freshman Housing Plan," no date.

33. *Cornell Daily Sun*, March 13, 1992.

34. Ibid., December 3, 1992.

35. Ibid., April 13, 1993.

36. *Cornell Chronicle*, April 6, 1995.

37. *Ithaca Journal*, March 1, 1979.

38. Rhodes Papers, box 26, Ruth W. Darling and Ann Roscoe to William Herbster, January 8, 1979.

39. Rhodes Papers, box 307, "Cornell University: Women's Athletics since Mid-70's," November 15, 1993.

40. *Ithaca Journal*, November 22, 1979.

41. Rhodes Papers, box 54, "Women of the Faculty of the College of Arts and Sciences: A Comparison of the Actual and Expected Numbers of Female Faculty at Various Professional Ranks," March 15, 1979.

42. Rhodes Papers, box 6, Don Cooke to Dave Knapp, March 21, 1977.

43. Ibid.; Rhodes Papers, box 6, Don Cooke to Dave Knapp, April 12, 1977.

44. *Ithaca Journal*, June 12, 1981.

45. Ibid., December 26, 1981.

46. Ibid., November 15, 1982.

47. Ibid., November 25, 1981.

48. Ibid., March 20, 1982.

49. Ibid., March 26, 1983.

50. Rhodes Papers, box 105, "Confidential Draft," WJR (Walter J. Relihan) August 24, 1984.

51. *Cornell Daily Sun*, February 14, 1985.

52. *Cornell Chronicle*, November 13, 1986.

53. *Cornell Alumni Magazine*, September 1995.

54. Ibid.

55. *Cornell News*, March 26, 1998.

56. *Cornell Daily Sun*, October 25, 1991.

57. Rhodes Papers, box 153, "Native American Studies Program Proposal," May 18, 1981.

58. David Call to Glenn Altschuler, November 11, 2012, in the authors' possession.

59. *Cornell Daily Sun*, September 4, 1991.

60. "The Founding of Jewish Studies at Cornell," September 17, 1997 (in the authors' possession).

61. Rhodes Papers, box 221, Isaac Kramnick to Robert Barker, December 1, 1987.

62. *Cornell Daily Sun*, October 20, 1989.

63. Ibid., January 30, 1990.

64. Ibid., October 20, 1989.

65. Rhodes Papers, box 210, Lawrence Edwards to William Gurowitz, December 1, 1989.

66. *Cornell Daily Sun*, November 8, 1985.

67. *Cornell Chronicle*, November 19, 1987.

68. *Cornell Daily Sun*, April 18, 1991.

69. Ibid., April 26, 1993.

70. Ibid., September 9, 1993.

71. Ibid., September 10, 1993.

72. Ibid.

73. Ibid., November 22, 1993.

74. *Cornell University News*, November 21, 1993.

75. *Cornell Daily Sun*, November 22, 1993.

76. Ibid., November 23, 1993.

77. Ibid., December 1, 1993.

78. Rhodes Papers, box 308, Frank Rhodes to William Sorn, February 24, 1994.

79. Rhodes Papers, box 298, "Report of the President—Full Board—Open Session," January 21 1994.

80. *Cornell Chronicle*, December 2, 1993.

81. Rhodes Papers, box 317, Eduardo Peñalver to Provost Nesheim, August 8, 1994.

82. Rhodes Papers, box 21, Roger Cramton to President Frank Rhodes, October 30, 1978.

83. *Cornell Alumni Magazine*, July 1983.

84. *Ithaca Journal*, May 15, 1983.

85. Ibid., May 17, 1982.

86. Rhodes Papers, box 112, "Position Paper on the Mariposa Collection," June 5, 1985.

87. Ibid., Robert Barker to President Rhodes, December 6, 1984.

88. *Cornell Alumni Magazine*, March/April 1997.

89. *Cornell Alumni News*, July/August 1992.

90. Rhodes Papers, box 257, Queer Nation, Ithaca, and the Cornell Lesbian, Gay, and Bisexual Coalition, to the *Cornell Daily Sun*, *Ithaca Journal*, and *Ithaca Times*, October 3, 1991.

91. Rhodes Papers, box 257, Malden Nesheim to Hon. Dick Cheney, March 25, 1992.

92. Rhodes Papers, box 279, "Resolution to Implement a Gay/Lesbian/Bisexual Living Learning Unit," no date.

93. *Cornell Alumni News*, June 1993.

94. *Cornell Chronicle*, April 29, 1993.

95. *Cornell Alumni News*, June 1993.

96. *Cornell Daily Sun*, December 1, 1993.

97. Rhodes Papers, box 317, Don Randel to Frank Rhodes, December 5, 1993.

98. Ibid., Malden Nesheim to Susan Murphy, August 26, 1994.

99. Rhodes Papers, box 296, "Rhodes Years at Cornell—Highlights," May 2, 1995.

100. Rhodes Papers, box 83, News Bureau Release on Common Learning, April 1983.

101. Rhodes Papers, box 328, "Is There a Role for Common Learning in Cornell's Undergraduate Programs?" June 17, 1981.

102. Rhodes Papers, box 113, "Presentation on Common Learning," by Urie Bronfenbrenner, September 12, 1984.

103. *Cornell Chronicle*, November 5, 1992.

104. Rhodes Papers, box 296, "Rhodes Years at Cornell—Highlights," May 2, 1995.

9. Political Engagement, Divestment, and Cornell's Two-China Policy

1. *Ithaca Journal*, April 1, 1977.

2. Ibid., November 28, 1983.

3. Rhodes Papers, box 185, "This is a note for Joy," n.d.

4. *Cornell Daily Sun*, May 3, 1995.

5. Rhodes Papers, box 7, "Cornell in Washington: Program Proposal," n.d.

6. *Cornell Chronicle*, May 15, 1980.

7. Ibid., April 18, 1985.

8. Frank H. T. Rhodes, *The Creation of the Future: The Role of the American University* (Ithaca, NY: Cornell University Press, 2001), 236–37.

9. *Cornell Chronicle*, October 10, 1985.

10. Ibid., June 28, 1990.

11. Ibid., October 10, 1985.

12. *Ithaca Journal*, December 1, 1979.

13. Ibid., April 21, 1982.

14. Ibid., March 14, 1984.

15. Ibid., November 19, 1986.

16. Ibid., November 17, 1986.

17. Ibid., April 22, 1988.
18. *Cornell Alumni News*, March 1982.
19. *Cornell Daily Sun*, March 13, 1984.
20. *Cornell Alumni News*, April 1991.
21. *Cornell Daily Sun*, February 19, 1991.
22. Ibid., April 13, 1978.
23. Ibid.
24. Rhodes Papers, box 42, Dale Corson to Frank Rhodes, April 15, 1978.
25. *Cornell Daily Sun*, April 14, 1978.
26. Rhodes Papers, box 50, W. K. Kennedy to F. H. T. Rhodes, October 2, 1978.
27. *Cornell Daily Sun*, December 8, 1978.
28. *Ithaca Journal*, April 19, 1985.
29. Rhodes Paper, box 144, Demonstration Status Report, April 25, 1985.
30. *Ithaca Journal*, April 29, 1985.
31. *Cornell Daily Sun*, April 26, 1985.
32. Minutes of a Special Meeting of the University Faculty, May 1, 1985, Cornell University Faculty Minutes Comprehensive Collection 1868–2010 (DVD).
33. *Cornell Daily Sun*, May 10, 1985.
34. *Ithaca Journal*, May 6, 1985.
35. Rhodes Papers, box 144, "Options: Positive—Negative," no date.
36. *Ithaca Journal*, May 11, 1985.
37. Ibid.
38. Rhodes Papers, box 110, "Meeting with Shantytown Representatives," May 13, 1985.
39. Ibid., "Meeting #2 with Shantytown Representatives," May 14, 1985.
40. Ibid., "Meeting #4 with Shantytown Representatives," May 17, 1985.
41. *Ithaca Journal*, May 30, 1985.
42. Rhodes Papers, box 144, "News Update," May 22, 1985.
43. *Cornell Chronicle*, June 6, 1985.
44. *Ithaca Journal*, June 4, 1985.
45. Rhodes Papers, box 111, "Summary Account of a Meeting in President Rhodes's Office", June 4, 1985.
46. Ibid., Memorandum for the Record, June 7, 1985.
47. Ibid., Robert Barker to the Shantytown Community, June 7, 1985.
48. Ibid., Cornell Coalition for Divestment to Robert Barker, June 8, 1985.
49. *Ithaca Journal*, June 11, 1985.
50. *Cornell Chronicle*, June 27, 1985.
51. *Ithaca Journal*, June 25, 1985.
52. *Cornell Chronicle*, June 27, 1985.
53. *Ithaca Journal*, June 28, 1985.
54. Ibid., July 1, 1985.
55. Rhodes Papers, box 122, "A Proposed Strategy for the Divestment Movement until October 11, 1985."
56. *Ithaca Journal*, October 3, 1985.
57. Ibid., September 25, 1985.
58. *Cornell Daily Sun*, October 14, 1985.
59. *Cornell Chronicle*, December 5, 1985.
60. Ibid., February 6, 1986.
61. Rhodes Papers, box 172, "Cornell Trustees Adopt Stronger Divestment Policy," January 31, 1986.
62. *Cornell Chronicle*, February 6, 1986.
63. *Ithaca Journal*, January 25, 1986.
64. *Cornell Daily Sun*, October 9, 1986.

65. *Ithaca Journal*, October 10, 1986.

66. *Cornell Daily Sun*, November 5, 1986.

67. Ibid., November 10, 1986.

68. *Ithaca Journal*, April 21, 1987.

69. *Cornell Daily Sun*, January 30, 1989.

70. Ibid., February 1, 1989.

71. Ibid., January 30, 1989.

72. Ibid., January 31, 1989.

73. Ibid., August 28, 1989.

74. Ibid., November 6, 1986.

75. Quoted in Glenn C. Altschuler, Isaac Kramnick, and R. Laurence Moore, *The 100 Most Notable Cornellians* (Ithaca, NY: Cornell University Press, 2001), 111.

76. Rhodes Papers, box 43, Transcript of News Conference on China Trip, August 6, 1980.

77. *Cornell Chronicle*, November 15, 1990.

78. Ibid., November 8,1990.

79. *Cornell Alumni Magazine*, June 1995.

80. Rhodes Papers, box 320, Frank Rhodes to President William J. Clinton, April 7, 1995.

81. Ibid., Bill Clinton to Dr. Frank Rhodes, May 2, 1995.

82. *New York Times*, May 11, 1995.

83. *Washington Post*, May 10, 1995.

84. *New York Times*, May 11, 1995.

85. *Ithaca Journal*, June 10, 1995.

86. *New York Times*, May 24, 1995.

87. *Cornell University News*, April 8, 1995.

88. *Cornell Alumni News*, September 1995.

89. Rhodes Papers, box 320, Ad Hoc Committee et al. to President Rhodes and the Members of the Board of Trustees of Cornell University, June 9, 1995.

90. *Cornell Chronicle*, June 15, 1995.

91. Ibid.

92. Ibid.

93. *Ithaca Journal*, June 9, 1995.

94. *Cornell Chronicle*, June 6, 1996.

10. Into the Twentieth-First Century

1. *Cornell Chronicle*, Special Supplement, May 12, 1994.

2. *Cornell Alumni Magazine*, May/June 1997.

3. *Cornell Magazine*, March 1995.

4. *Cornell Daily Sun*, September 28, 1999.

5. Ibid.

6. Ibid., August 30, 1995.

7. Ibid., May 11, 1995.

8. Hunter Ripley Rawlings Papers, Division of Rare and Manuscript Collections, Carl A. Kroch Library, Cornell University (hereafter Rawlings Papers), box 3, Memorandum of Understanding between the City of Ithaca and Cornell University, October 5, 1995.

9. Rawlings Papers, box 96, Inaugural Address, October 12, 1995.

10. Ibid.

11. *Cornell Chronicle*, October 19, 1995.

12. Rawlings Papers, box 45, Research Futures Task Force, October 16, 1997.

13. *Cornell Magazine*, January/February 2001.

14. *Cornell Daily Sun*, January, 23, 1997.

15. Ibid.

16. Rawlings Papers, box 38, "Cornell Computer Science: Vision for the Next Decade," October 1996.

17. Rawlings Papers, box 79, Don Randel to Deans, Directors, and Department Heads, August 19, 1999.

18. Charlie Van Loan, Comments to Faculty Senate, October 20, 1999, www.theuniversityfaculty.cornell.edu.

19. *Cornell Chronicle*, September 23, 1999.

20. Faculty of the School of Electrical Engineering to President Rawlings and Provost Randel, September 14, 1999, www.theuniversityfaculty.cornell.edu.

21. *Cornell Chronicle*, October 21, 1999.

22. Communiqué, Summer 2005.

23. Task Force Report, Division of Biological Sciences: Structural Review, March 12, 1998, www.theuniversityfaculty.cornell.edu.

24. Extract from Faculty Senate Discussion on Biological Sciences, November 11, 1998, www.theuniversityfaculty.cornell.edu.

25. Rawlings Papers, box 75, "Reorganization of the Division of Biological Sciences at Cornell University," November 17, 1998.

26. *Cornell Chronicle*, May 9, 2002.

27. Ibid.

28. *Cornell Daily Sun*, November 3, 2000.

29. *Cornell Chronicle*, December 6, 2001.

30. Ibid.

31. Ibid., November 5, 1998.

32. "Report on the State of the Humanities at Cornell University, 1997–1998," Society for the Humanities.

33. *Cornell Daily Sun*, November 11, 1998.

34. Ibid., September 24, 1998.

35. Ibid., November 10, 1998.

36. Rawlings Papers, box 65, Philip Lewis to James Turner, October 28, 1998.

37. *Cornell Daily Sun*, November 11, 1998.

38. Rawlings Papers, box 1, Philip Lewis to Dear Colleagues, February 16, 1999.

39. *Cornell Daily Sun*, November 11, 1998.

40. Ibid., November 17, 1999.

41. Rawlings Papers, box 71, Provost's Briefing Notes for January 20 and 21 Albany Meetings with SUNY, no date.

42. *Cornell Chronicle*, September 5, 2002.

43. Ibid., May 10, 2001.

44. *Cornell Daily Sun*, March 15, 2001.

45. *Proceedings of the Board of Trustees*, May 25/26, 2001.

46. *Cornell Chronicle*, May 10, 2001.

47. *Cornell Daily Sun*, May 8, 2002.

48. *Cornell Chronicle*, March 7, 1996.

49. Ibid., February 6, 1997.

50. Rawlings Papers, box 48, Fred Rogers to Hunter Rawlings and Don Randel, December 26, 1997.

51. Rawlings Papers, box 48, Helen Mohrmann to Don Randel and Carolyn Ainslie, May 14, 1998.

52. *Cornell Daily Sun*, September 1, 1998.

53. Ibid., August 31, 1999.

54. *Cornell Chronicle*, November 15, 2001.

55. *Cornell Magazine*, November/December 1997.

56. Ronald G. Ehrenberg, *Tuition Rising: Why College Costs So Much* (Cambridge, MA: Harvard University Press, 2000), 226–28.

57. *Cornell Magazine*, November/December 1997.

58. *Cornell Daily Sun*, March 25, 2002.

59. Rhodes Papers, box 221, "The Grad Grind," April 1989.

60. Rawlings Papers, box 15, Walter Cohen to Hunter Rawlings, March 1, 1995.

61. *Cornell Daily Sun*, October 22, 1997.

62. *Cornell Chronicle*, September 12, 2002.

63. Ibid., October 24, 2002.

64. *Cornell Daily Sun*, February 6, 2003.

65. Ibid., April 23, 1996.

66. Ibid., September 29, 2003.

67. Ibid.

68. Ibid., October 1, 2002.

69. Phil Lewis to Isaac Kramnick, April 22, 2003 (in authors' possession).

70. *Cornell Daily Sun*, September 29, 2003.

71. Ibid.

72. Ibid.

73. *Cornell Chronicle*, August 15, 2002.

74. Report from the Committee on Academic Programs and Policies (CAPP) to the Faculty Senate Concerning Architecture, Art, and Planning, September 30, 2002, Office of the Dean of the Faculty.

75. Porus Olpadwala, "Re-alignment: The Defense of the College of Architecture, Art, and Planning," March 2003, in authors' possession.

76. Minutes of the Meeting of the Faculty Senate, November 13, 2002, Office of the Dean of the Faculty.

77. *Cornell Daily Sun*, January 16, 2003.

78. *Cornell Chronicle*, January 16, 2003.

79. Porus Olpadwala to Glenn Altschuler, April 25, 2013 (in authors' possession).

80. Olpadwala, "Re-alignment."

81. *Cornell Daily Sun*, April 29, 2003.

82. *Cornell Alumni Magazine*, May/June 2003.

83. *Cornell Chronicle*, June 12, 2003.

84. *Cornell Alumni Magazine*, January/February 2003.

85. Ibid., January/February 2004.

86. Ibid.

87. *Cornell Daily Sun*, October 17, 2003.

88. Ibid., November 24, 2003.

89. *Cornell Chronicle*, January 15, 2004.

90. Ibid., January 22, 2004.

91. *Cornell Daily Sun*, October 12, 2004.

92. Ibid., November 1, 2004.

93. *Cornell Alumni Magazine*, July/August 2005.

94. Ibid., September/October 2005.

95. Ibid.

96. Ibid.

97. *Cornell Daily Sun*, September 15, 2005.

98. Hunter Rawlings, 2005 State of the University Address, October 21, 2005, http://www.cornell.edu/president/announcement_2005_1021.cfm.

99. *Cornell Alumni Magazine*, March/April 2006.

100. *Cornell Daily Sun*, January 23, 2006.

101. David Skorton, 2006 Inaugural Address, http://www.inauguration.cornell.edu/speeches/skortonAddress.cfm.

102. *Cornell Daily Sun*, September 7, 2006.

103. Ibid., October 11, 2007.

104. *Cornell Chronicle*, September 28, 2007.

105. Ibid., May 30, 2008.

106. Ibid., October 10, 2008.

107. Ibid., January 31, 2008.

108. "Cornell Awash in Debt Chases Donors in 'Pay-as-You-Go' Expansion," http://www.bloomberg.com/news/2013-07-02/cornell-awash-in-debt-chases-donors-in-pay-as-you-go-expansion.html.

109. *Cornell Alumni Magazine*, May/June 2009.

110. Ibid., January/February 2010.

111. Ibid.

112. *Cornell Chronicle*, April 17, 2009.

113. Ibid., February 27, 2009.

114. Ibid.

115. *Cornell Alumni Magazine*, January/February 2010.

116. *Cornell Chronicle*, February 27, 2009.

117. Ibid., November 25, 2009.

118. Ibid., April 2, 2009.

119. *Ezra: Cornell's Quarterly Magazine*, Fall 2012.

120. *Cornell Chronicle*, November 5, 2010.

121. *Cornell Daily Sun*, February 8, 2012.

122. *Cornell Chronicle*, February 4, 2010.

123. *Cornell Daily Sun*, March 30, 2010.

124. Ibid., September 9, 2010.

125. "Undergraduate Financial Aid Task Force: Final Report, April 27, 2012" (in authors' possession).

126. *Cornell Chronicle*, July 3, 2012.

127. *Cornell Daily Sun*, August 22, 2012.

128. Ibid., October 5, 2012.

129. Ibid., October 18, 2011.

130. David Skorton, State of the University Address, http://www.cornell.edu/president/speeches/20111021-tcam-address.cfm, October 21, 2011.

131. *Cornell Daily Sun*, October 2, 2013.

132. Ibid., October 3, 2013.

133. Ibid., May 3, 2013.

134. David Skorton, State of the University Address, http://www.cornell.edu/president/speeches/20121026-state-of-university.cfm, October 26, 2012.

135. *Cornell Daily Sun*, September 20, 2011.

136. Ibid.

137. *Cornell Chronicle*, June 8, 2010.

138. Ibid., June 14, 2007.

139. *Ezra: Cornell's Quarterly Magazine*, Winter 2012.

140. Ibid.

141. *Cornell Chronicle*, November 5, 2010.

142. *Cornell Daily Sun*, October 26, 2011.

143. *Cornell Chronicle*, October, 19, 2007.

144. *Cornell Daily Sun*, January 30, 2009.

145. *Cornell Chronicle*, August 29, 2011.

146. Ibid., April 22, 2013.

147. "Law School Breaks Ground on New Wing," http://www.lawschool.cornell.edu/spotlights/Breaking-Ground.cfm.

148. Ibid.

149. *Cornell Daily Sun*, October 21, 2011.

11. *The New Normal in Student Life*

1. *Chronicle of Higher Education*, November 5, 1999.

2. *Cornell Alumni Magazine*, November/December 2000.

3. *Cornell Chronicle*, April 27, 2006.

4. *Cornell Daily Sun*, October 21, 1997.

5. *Cornell Chronicle*, April 9, 1998.

6. *Cornell Chronicle*, November 2, 2007.

7. *Cornell Daily Sun*, September 23, 2003.

8. Ibid., March 1, 2010.

9. Ibid., February 9, 2005.

10. Ibid., September 17, 2001.

11. Ibid., September 13, 2005.

12. Ibid., March 27, 2003.

13. Rawlings Papers, box 86, Hunter R. Rawlings III to Claire Urban '00, President, Students Against Sweatshops, April 15, 1999.

14. *Cornell Chronicle*, April 13, 2006.

15. Ibid., April 19, 2001.

16. *Cornell Daily Sun*, April 15, 2013.

17. Ibid., April 5, 2013.

18. Ibid., September 29, 2009.

19. Ibid., March 3, 2013.

20. Ibid., September 10, 2007.

21. Ibid.

22. Rawlings Papers, box 53, Barbara Krause to *Cornell Review*, December 4, 1997.

23. *Cornell Chronicle*, May 9, 1997.

24. Rawlings Papers, box 54, Barbara Krause to Edward S. Newton, Editor-in-Chief, the *Cornell Review*, December 4, 1997.

25. *Cornell Daily Sun*, November 3, 2000.

26. Ibid., November 6, 2000.

27. *Cornell Chronicle*, March 9, 2006.

28. *Cornell Daily Sun*, April 12, 2010.

29. Ibid.

30. Ibid., April 15, 2012.

31. Ibid., December 2, 2010.

32. Ibid., January 20, 2011.

33. Ibid., December 2, 2010.

34. Ibid., January 20, 2011.

35. Ibid., December 2, 2010.

36. Ibid., January 20, 2011.

37. Ibid., February 8, 2011.

38. Ibid., December 6, 2013.

39. Rawlings Papers, box 81, Hunter R. Rawlings III to Members of the Cornell Community, March 25, 1996.

40. *Cornell Daily Sun*, April 12, 1996.

41. *Cornell Magazine*, June 1996.

42. *Cornell Daily Sun*, April 26, 1996.

43. *Cornell Magazine*, June 1996.

44. Rawlings Papers, box 81, "Additional Comments on the Proposed Residential Communities Policy," April 24, 1996.

45. *Cornell Daily Sun*, April 15, 1997.

46. *Cornell Chronicle*, October 9, 1997.

47. *Cornell Daily Sun*, December 3, 1997.

48. Ibid., October 20, 1997.

49. *Cornell Chronicle*, August 30, 2001.

50. Ibid., September 6, 2001.

51. *Cornell Alumni Magazine*, November/December 2001.

52. Ibid.

53. Ibid.

54. *Cornell Chronicle*, October 9, 1997.

55. "Transforming West Campus: Recommendations Submitted to Vice President Susan Murphy," September 23, 1998 (in authors' possession).

56. "Cornell University West Campus Planning Group: A Vision for Residential Life," May 9, 2000 (in authors' possession).

57. *Cornell Daily Sun*, October 13, 1999.

58. *Cornell Chronicle*, December 11, 2003.

59. *Cornell Daily Sun*, August 25, 2005.

60. *Cornell Chronicle*, July 14, 2005.

61. *Cornell Daily Sun*, April 14, 2005.

62. Ibid., April 27, 2005.

63. Ibid., April 29, 2005.

64. Ibid., May 5, 2005.

65. *Cornell Chronicle*, July 14, 2005.

66. Ibid., September 22, 2005.

67. *Cornell Daily Sun*, October 1, 2009.

68. Ibid.

69. Ibid., *Cornell Daily Sun*, February 4, 2010.

70. Ibid., August 25, 2010.

71. Ibid., November 1, 2010.

72. *New York Times*, April 12, 2012.

73. Ibid., August 23, 2011.

74. Ibid.

75. *Cornell Daily Sun*, May 7, 2012.

76. "Meeting the Challenge" (in authors' possession).

77. *Cornell Chronicle*, November 29, 2012.

78. *Cornell Daily Sun*, November 29, 2012.

79. Ibid., November 1, 2012.

80. Ibid., September 20, 2013.

81. *Cornell Chronicle*, April 14, 2013.

82. Ibid.

83. Ibid., March 13, 2013.

84. *Cornell Daily Sun*, May 2, 2013.

85. Ibid., April 14, 2013.

86. Ibid., May 2, 2013.

87. Ibid., September 15, 2009.

88. Ibid., March 12, 2010.

89. Ibid., March 29, 2010.

90. Ibid.

91. Ibid., May 7, 2010.

92. Ibid., March 30, 2010.

93. Ibid., November 23, 2010.

94. Ibid., March 30, 2010.

95. Ibid., April 6, 2010.

96. "Preventing Suicide by Jumping from Bridges Owned by the City of Ithaca and by Cornell University. Consultation to Cornell University. Extended Report," July 2010 (in authors' possession).

97. *Ithaca Journal*, May 18–19, 2013.

98. "University Health Services—Overview," presented to the Cornell Board of Trustees Student Life Committee, May 25, 2012 (in authors' possession).

99. "Project Approval Request University Health Services Facility: Project Plan and Authorization to Begin Design," March 2013 (in authors' possession).

100. Student and Academic Services Annual Report, 2013 (in authors' possession).

101. Remarks by President Skorton to Cornell Board of Trustees, March 28, 2013 (in authors' possession).

12. Going Global

1. *Cornell Chronicle*, September 20, 2001.

2. "Bringing Cornell to the World and the World to Cornell: A Presidential White Paper," January 2012 (in authors' possession).

3. Ibid.

4. Report from the Task Force on Internationalization, October 11, 2012 (in authors' possession).

5. Larry Zuidema, "Exploring the International Engagement of the New York State College of Agriculture and Life Sciences at Cornell University," July 2013 (in authors' possession).

6. Ibid.

7. *Mario Einaudi Center for International Studies 2013 Annual Report*.

8. *New York Times*, April 9, 2001.

9. Ibid.

10. Cornell University News Service, April 9, 2001.

11. *Cornell Alumni Magazine*, July/August 2001.

12. Ibid.

13. *Cornell Daily Sun*, October 18, 2002.

14. Ibid., February 25, 2008.

15. *Cornell Alumni Magazine*, September/October 2007.

16. *Cornell Daily Sun*, June 13, 2011.

17. Ibid.

18. *Cornell Chronicle*, May 16, 2007.

19. *Cornell Daily Sun*, September 24, 2010.

20. Ibid., February 11, 2009.

21. Rawlings Papers, box 25, "Minutes: Developing a Cornell Asia Strategy," June 12, 1996.

22. Rawlings Papers, box 25, Asia Strategy Meeting, January 23, 1997.

23. *Cornell Daily Sun*, April 14, 2009.

24. Ibid., November 15, 2005.

25. Ibid.

26. Ibid., November 17, 2005.

27. *Cornell Alumni Magazine*, July/August 2000.

28. *Proceedings of the Board of Trustees*, March 10, 2000.

29. *Cornell Alumni Magazine*, July/August 2000.

30. *Cornell Chronicle*, August 17, 2000.

31. *Cornell Daily Sun*, September 8, 2000.

32. "Massive Open Online Courses (MOOCs): Report by the Provost's MOOC Advisory Committee," December 14, 2012.

33. *Cornell University at Its Sesquicentennial: A Strategic Plan, 2010–2015.*

34. *Cornell Chronicle*, December 31, 2011.

35. "Campus-to-Campus Bus Service Available for Cornell Community," http://weill.cornell.edu/news/deans/2004/11_18_04/article_09-11_18.shtml, November 18, 2004.

36. *Cornell Alumni Magazine*, May/June 2012.

37. "Cornell NYC Tech: Fall 2012 Academic Update," October 18, 2012 (in authors' possession).

38. *Cornell Alumni Magazine*, May/June 2012.

39. "Cornell NYC Tech: Fall 2012 Academic Update," October 18, 2012.

40. *New York Times*, December 25, 2011.

41. *Cornell Alumni Magazine*, May/June 2012.

42. "Cornell NYC Tech: Fall 2012 Academic Update," October 18, 2012.

43. *Cornell Daily Sun*, November 1, 2011.

44. *New York Times*, December 25, 2011.

45. *Cornell Engineering News*, Spring 2012.

46. *Wall Street Journal*, December 20, 2011.

47. *New York Times*, December 25, 2011.

48. *Wall Street Journal*, December 16, 2011.

49. *New Yorker*, April 30, 2012.

50. *New York Times*, December 17, 2011.

51. *Cornell Chronicle*, December 21, 2011.

52. *Cornell Daily Sun*, February 27, 2012.

53. *Cornell Alumni Magazine*, May/June 2012.

54. *Cornell Daily Sun*, March 1, 2013.

55. *Cornell Alumni Magazine*, May/June 2012.

56. *Cornell Daily Sun*, March 1, 2013.

57. *Cornell Alumni Magazine*, May/June 2012.

58. *Cornell Daily Sun*, February 9, 2012.

59. *Cornell Alumni Magazine*, May/June 2012.

60. *New York Times*, May 21, 2012.

61. *Cornell Daily Sun*, January 22, 2013.

62. *Cornell Chronicle*, April 22, 2013.

63. *Cornell Alumni Magazine*, May/June 2012.

Index

Page numbers in *italics* indicate illustrations.